COMPARATIVE POLITICS
NOTES AND READINGS
TENTH EDITION

BERNARD E. BROWN
Professor Emeritus of Political Science
The City University of New York (Graduate School)

THOMSON

━━━━✦━━━━ ™

WADSWORTH

Australia • Canada • Mexico • Singapore • Spain
United Kingdom • United States

W9-BBD-295

THOMSON
WADSWORTH

Comparative Politics: Notes and Readings, Tenth Edition
Bernard E. Brown

Publisher: Clark Baxter
Executive Editor: David Tatom
Editorial Assistant: Eva Dickerson
Technology Project Manager: Michelle Vardeman
Senior Marketing Manager: Janise Fry
Marketing Assistant: Teresa Jessen
Senior Marketing Communications Manager: Tami Strang
Marketing Communications Manager: Kelley McAllister
Project Manager, Editorial Production: Karol Jurado
Executive Art Director: Maria Epes

Print Buyer: Doreen Suruki
Associate Permissions Editor: Stephanie Lee
Production Service: Matrix Productions Inc.
Copy Editor: Cheryl Smith
Illustrator: Brian Morris
Cover Designer: Brian Salisbury
Cover Image: Rich Iwasaki
Cover Printer: Malloy Incorporated
Compositor: Cadmus
Printer: Malloy Incorporated

© 2006 Thomson Wadsworth, a part of The Thomson Corporation. Thomson, the Star logo, and Wadsworth are trademarks used herein under license.

ALL RIGHTS RESERVED. No part of this work covered by the copyright hereon may be reproduced or used in any form or by any means—graphic, electronic, or mechanical, including photocopying, recording, taping, Web distribution, information storage and retrieval systems, or in any other manner—without the written permission of the publisher.

Printed in the United States of America
1   2   3   4   5   6   7   09   08   07   06   05

For more information about our products, contact us at:
Thomson Learning Academic Resource Center
1-800-423-0563

For permission to use material from this text or product,
submit a request online at
http://www.thomsonrights.com.

Any additional questions about permissions
can be submitted by email to
thomsonrights@thomson.com.

Library of Congress Control Number: 2005922002
ISBN: 0-534-60130-8

Thomson Higher Education
10 Davis Drive
Belmont, CA 94002-3098
USA

Asia (including India)
Thomson Learning
5 Shenton Way
#01-01 UIC Building
Singapore 068808

Australia/New Zealand
Thomson Learning Australia
102 Dodds Street
Southbank, Victoria 3006
Australia

Canada
Thomson Nelson
1120 Birchmount Road
Toronto, Ontario M1K 5G4
Canada

UK/Europe/Middle East/Africa
Thomson Learning
High Holborn House
50–51 Bedford Row
London WC1R 4LR
United Kingdom

Latin America
Thomson Learning
Seneca, 53
Colonia Polanco
11560 Mexico
D.F. Mexico

Spain (including Portugal)
Thomson Paraninfo
Calle Magallanes, 25
28015 Madrid, Spain

CONTENTS

CHAPTER SEVEN
TRANSITION TO DEMOCRACY 202

CHAPTER EIGHT
AUTHORITARIANISM: OLD AND NEW 237

CHAPTER NINE
THE CHALLENGE OF ISLAMISM 266

PART THREE   POLITICAL DYNAMICS, DECISIONS, AND EFFICACY   293

CHAPTER TEN
POLITICAL PARTIES 311

PREFACE

Over four decades ago, Roy C. Macridis and I brought out the first edition of this book. Our aim was to introduce students to major approaches in the field of comparative politics, especially those reflecting new theories and concepts. We kept successive editions up-to-date by including choice articles and essays from a wide range of professional journals and books. The extraordinary longevity of this book is a tribute to the creativity, vigor, and significance of the work being done by students of comparative politics and, I should like to think, a vindication of our original conception of the discipline.

Roy Macridis and I met regularly to argue, disagree, and then generally agree (or agree to disagree) in appraising trends within the discipline. After Roy passed away in 1991, I continued to update this volume, which has proven so useful to generations of students and teachers. As in the past I have sought to furnish selections from recent literature while retaining classic statements. The readings provide tools of analysis as well as substantive studies that illustrate their utility. I have endeavored to avoid bias in favor of any single school, theory, or concept—instead offering a balanced overview of approaches.

In seeking to understand the ongoing transformation of global society, it is important to maintain contact with the founders of the modern discipline of comparative politics. Two thinkers stand out among these founders: Max Weber and Emile Durkheim. I have added, for reasons explained later, the authors of *The Federalist Papers*. The founders offer models of comparative political analysis: a perspective on the long-term changes in state and society that have accompanied the emergence of modern science; the use of the comparative method in identifying and accounting for differences and similarities; and the need always to relate inquiry to significant issues. Hence, an extended treatment of *The Federalist Papers*, Max Weber's study of capitalism and rural society in Germany, and Emile Durkheim's *Division of Labor* is presented in the introductory essay. All methodological questions in comparative politics can be clarified by reference to these classic works.

The central concern of the founders was the nature and meaning of modernity, marked by the end of feudalism and the outbreak of political revolutions in the late eighteenth century, and its impact on all facets of political systems (legitimacy, political dynamics, decision-making, and performance). It seemed to be appropriate, then, to move to the front of this collection the analysis of political change. Theoretical issues that run through all the selections may thus be examined at the outset.

Half the readings are new to this edition. They reflect and respond to the dramatic events of the past decade: the collapse of the Soviet Union and other communist systems in Europe; the struggle of former communist nations to create democratic institutions and market economies; the explosion of ethnic conflict; and the resurgence of religious fundamentalism, culminating in terror attacks against the United States on September 11, 2001. I have therefore expanded and updated the treatment of globalization and its impact on the traditional nation-state and political processes; disaffection in the advanced democracies; growing difficulties in the process of democratization in post-communist systems and developing countries; and the challenge of Islamism. I hope this collection of writings will encourage a new generation of readers to explore and analyze the major issues of our time in a comparative perspective.

It remains difficult to do justice to all points of view within the confines of one volume, and responsibility for final choices necessarily is mine. I am grateful, of course, to authors and publishers for their kind permission to reprint.

Bernard E. Brown

ABOUT THE EDITOR

Bernard E. Brown is Professor Emeritus of Political Science at the City University of New York (Graduate School), and previously taught at Vanderbilt University and SUNY (Buffalo). A graduate of the City College of New York and Columbia University (Ph. D.), he has received numerous research awards, including several Fulbright Research Fellowships, a Rockefeller Foundation Humanities Fellowship, and a National Endowment for the Humanities Fellowship. He has served as visiting professor at the universities of Rennes (France), Dakar (Senegal), Delhi (India), and Saigon (Vietnam), and directed three National Endowment for the Humanities Summer Seminars on French politics in Paris. Among his many books are: *L'Etat et la politique aux Etats-Unis* (1994); *Socialism of a Different Kind: Reshaping the Left in France* (1982); *Intellectuals and Other Traitors* (1980); *Eurocommunism and Eurosocialism: The Left Confronts Modernity* (coauthor and editor, 1978); *Cases in Comparative Politics* (coauthor and coeditor, 3rd ed. 1976); *Protest in Paris: Anatomy of a Revolt* (1974); *The De Gaulle Republic: Quest for Unity* (coauthor with Roy C. Macridis, 1960, rev. ed. 1963); *New Directions in Comparative Politics* (also a Japanese edition, 1963); and *American Conservatives* (1951). Currently he is Transatlantic Relations Project Director at the National Committee on American Foreign Policy, and has published numerous articles on the European Union, NATO, transatlantic relations, and international politics in the NCAFP journal, *American Foreign Policy Interests*.

LIST OF AUTHORS

Joel D. Aberbach. Professor of Political Science, University of California at Los Angeles. Author, *Keeping a Watchful Eye: The Politics of Congressional Oversight* (1990). Coauthor, *Bureaucrats and Politicians in Western Democracies* (1982); *The Web of Politics: Three Decades of the US Federal Executive* (2000). Coeditor, *The Role of the State in Taiwan's Development* (1994).

Aristotle (384–322 B.C.). A good one-volume collection is the Modern Library edition, *Introduction to Aristotle* (1995), edited by Richard McKeon.

Robert H. Bates. Eaton Professor of the Science of Government, Harvard University. Author, *Markets and States in Tropical Africa* (1981); *Essays on the Political Economy of Rural Africa* (1983); *Beyond the Miracle of the Market: The Political Economy of Agrarian Development in Kenya* (1989); *Open Economy Politics: The Political Economy of the World Coffee Trade* (1997); *Prosperity and Violence: The Political Economy of Development* (2002). Coauthor, *Analytic Narratives* (1998). Editor, *Toward a Political Economy of Development: A Rational Choice Perspective* (1988). Coeditor, *Africa and the Disciplines* (1993).

Samuel H. Beer. Eaton Professor of the Science of Government Emeritus, Harvard University. Woodrow Wilson Center Senior Scholar. Author, *The City of Reason* (1949); *Treasury Control* (1956); *British Politics in the Collectivist Age* (1965, 1982); *Britain Against Itself* (1982); *To Make a Nation: The Rediscovery of American Federalism* (1993). Coeditor, *Welfare Reform: A Race to the Bottom?* (1999).

Mark Blyth. Associate Professor of Political Science, Johns Hopkins University. Author, *Great Transformations: Economic Ideas and Political Change in the Twentieth Century* (2002).

Bernard E. Brown. Professor of Political Science Emeritus, City University of New York (Graduate School). For publications, see *About the Editor*, p. ix.

Nathan J. Brown. Professor of Political Science and International Affairs, The George Washington University. Author, *Peasant Politics in Modern Egypt* (1990); *The Rule of Law in the Arab World* (1997); *Constitutions in a NonConstitutional World: Arab Basic Laws and the Prospects for Accountable Government* (2001); *Palestinian Politics After the Oslo Accords: Resuming Arab Palestine* (2003).

Bruce E. Cain. Robson Professor of Political Science, and director of the Institute of Governmental Studies, University of California at Berkeley. Author, *The Reapportionment Puzzle* (1984). Coauthor, *The Personal Vote* (1987); *Congressional Redistricting* (1991).

Thomas Carothers. Senior Associate and Director of the Democracy and Rule of Law Project at the Carnegie Endowment for International Peace (Washington, DC). Author, *Aiding Democracy Abroad: The Learning Curve* (1999); *Critical Mission: Essays on Democracy Promotion* (2004). Coeditor, *Funding Virtue: Civil Society Aid and Democracy Promotion* (2000).

Robert A. Dahl. Sterling Professor of Political Science Emeritus, Yale University. Author, *A Preface to Democratic Theory* (1956); *Who Governs?* (1961); *Polyarchy: Participaton and Opposition* (1971); *Dilemmas of Pluralist Democracy* (1982); *A Preface to Economic Democracy* (1985); *Democracy and Its Critics* (1989); *After the Revolution* (rev. ed., 1990); *On Democracy* (1997); *How Democratic Is the American Constitution?* (2002).

Russell J. Dalton. Professor of Political Science, University of California at Irvine. Author, *Germany Transformed* (1981); *The Green Rainbow* (1994); *Citizen Politics* (3rd ed., 2002); *Democratic Challenges, Democratic Choices: The Erosion of Political Support in Advanced Industrial Democracies* (2004). Coauthor, *Critical Masses* (1999). Coeditor, *Parties Without Partisans* (2001); *Democracy Transformed?* (2003).

Larry Diamond. Senior Fellow at the Hoover Institution, Coordinator of the Democracy Program at the Institute for International Studies, Stanford University. Author, *Class, Ethnicity and Democracy in Nigeria* (1988); *Promoting Democracy in the 1990s* (1999); *Developing Democracy: Toward Consolidation* (1999). Coeditor of over 20 books on aspects of democracy and development.

Samuel N. Eisenstadt. Professor of Sociology, Hebrew University of Jerusalem. Author, *The Political Systems of Empires* (1963, rev. ed. 1993); *Modernization: Protest and Change* (1966); *Tradition, Change and Modernity* (1973); *Revolution and the Transformation of Societies* (1978); *Patterns of Modernity* (1991); *Japanese Civilization: A Comparative View* (1996); *Fundamentalism, Sectarianism, and Revolution: The Jacobin Dimension of Modernity* (1999); *Paradoxes of Democracy* (1999). Coauthor, *The Early African State in Perspective* (1988). Coeditor, *Building States and Nations*, 2 vols. (1973).

François Furet (1927–1997). Late Director of the Raymond Aron Institute, Ecole des Hautes Etudes en Sciences Sociales (Paris, France), and Professor at the Committee on Social Thought, University of Chicago. Elected a member of the Académie Française shortly before his death in an accident. Author, *Interpreting the French Revolution* (1981); *In the Workshop of History* (1985); *The History of an Illusion: The Survival of the Radical Impulse in an Age of Capitalism* (1997). Also, many works in French.

Liah Greenfeld. University Professor and Professor of Sociology and Political Science, Boston University. Author, *Nationalism: Five Roads to Modernity* (1992); *The Spirit of Capitalism: Nationalism and Economic Growth* (2001).

Richard Gunther. Professor of Political Science, The Ohio State University. Coeditor, *Democracy and the Media* (2000); *Parties, Politics and Democracy in the New Southern Europe* (2001); *Political Parties and Democracy* (2002); *Political Parties: Old Concepts and New Challenges* (2002); and *Democracy in Modern Spain* (2004).

Jürgen Habermas. Professor Emeritus of Philosophy, University of Frankfurt, and Professor of Philosophy, Northwestern University. Author, *Moral Consciousness and Communicative Action* (tr. 1989); *The Postnational Constellation* (2001); *Truth and Justification* (2003). See also, *Jürgen Habermas on Society and Politics: A Reader* (1989); William Outhwaite, ed., *The Harbermas Reader* (1996). Also, many works in German.

Donald L. Horowitz. James B. Duke Professor of Law and Political Science, Duke University. Author, *Ethnic Groups in Conflict* (1985); *A Democratic South Africa? Constitutional Engineering in* *a Divided Society* (1991). *The Deadly Ethnic Riot* (2002). Coeditor, *Immigrants in Two Democracies: French and American Experience* (1992).

Piero Ignazi. Senior Lecturer in Political Science, University of Bologna (Italy). Coeditor, *The Year of the Tycoon: Italian Politics 1995* (1996); *The Organization of Political Parties in Southern Europe* (1998). Author of many works in Italian.

Ronald Inglehart. Professor of Political Science and Program Director at the Institute of Social Research, University of Michigan. Author, *The Silent Revolution: Changing Values and Political Styles Among Western Publics* (1977); *Culture Shift in Advanced Industrial Society* (1990); *Modernization and Postmodernization: Cultural, Economic and Political Change in 43 Societies* (1997). Coauthor, *Rising Tide: Gender Equality and Cultural Change* (2003); *Sacred and Secular: Religion and Politics Worldwide* (2004).

Andrew C. Janos. Professor of Political Science, University of California at Berkeley. Author, *The Politics of Backwardness in Hungary, 1825-1945* (1982); *Politics and Paradigms: Changing Theories of Change in Social Science* (1986); *Czechoslovakia and Yugoslavia: Ethnic Conflict and the Dissolution of National States* (1997); *East Central Europe in the Modern World: Political Change in the Borderlands from Pre- to Post-Communism* (2000).

Walter Laqueur. Cochair of the International Research Council at the Center for Strategic and International Studies (Washington, DC). Author: *The Age of Terrorism* (1987); *Europe in Our Time: A History, 1945–1992* (1992); *The Dream That Failed: Reflections on the Soviet Union* (1994); *Fascism: Past, Present and Future* (1996); *A History of Terrorism* (1977, rev. ed. 2002); *No End to Terrorism in the Twenty-First Century* (2003); *Voices of Terror* (2004). Also, many other works.

Arend Lijphart. Professor Emeritus of Political Science, University of California at San Diego. Author, *The Politics of Accommodation: Pluralism and Democracy in the Netherlands* (1968, rev. ed. 1975); *Democracies: Patterns of Majoritarian and Consensus Government in Twenty-One Countries* (1984); *Patterns of Democracy: Government Forms and Performance in Thirty-Six Countries* (1999). Coauthor, *Electoral Systems and Party Systems* (1994). Editor, *Parliamentary vs. Presidential Government* (1992). Coeditor, *Electoral Laws and Their Political Consequences* (1986); *Institutional Design in New Democracies* (1996).

Seymour Martin Lipset. Hazel Professor Emeritus of Public Policy, George Mason University, and Senior Fellow, Hoover Institution. Author, *Political Man: The Social Bases of Politics* (1960); *Continental Divide: Values and Institutions of the United States and Canada* (1990); *American Exceptionalism: A Double-Edged Sword* (1996); *It Didn't Happen Here: Why Socialism Failed in the United States* (2000). Also, many other works.

Roy C. Macridis (1919–1991). Late Professor of Politics, Brandeis University. Author, *The Study of Comparative Government* (1955); *French Politics in Transition* (1975); *Contemporary Political Ideologies* (5th ed., 1991). Coauthor, *The De Gaulle Republic* (1960, 1963); *France, Germany and the Western Alliance* (1967); *Modern Political Systems: Europe* (1983); *Foreign Policy in World Politics* (7th ed., 1989).

James G. March. Professor Emeritus of Political Science, Stanford University. Author, *Decisions and Organizations* (1988); *The Pursuit of Organizational Intelligence* (1999). Coauthor, *Organizations* (1958); *Ambiguity and Choice in Organizations* (1976); *Rediscovering Institutions: The Organizational Basis of Politics* (1989); *Democratic Governance* (1995); *The Dynamics of Rules* (2000).

Karl Marx (1818–1883). Useful one-volume collections include *Marx and Engels: Basic Writings on Politics and Philosophy* (1959), edited by Lewis S. Feuer; and *The Marx-Engels Reader* (rev. ed., 1972), edited by Robert C. Tucker.

Robert Michels (1876–1936). German-born Italian political sociologist. Held professorships at the universities of Turin, Basel, and Perugia. Author, *Political Parties: A Sociological Study of the Oligarchical Tendencies of Modern Democracy* (1914); *First Lectures in Political Sociology* (1949).

Andrew J. Nathan. Class of 1919 Professor of Political Science, Columbia University. Author, *Peking Politics, 1918-1923* (1976); *Chinese Democracy* (1985); *China's Crisis* (1990); *China's Transition* (1997). Coauthor, *China's New Rulers: The Secret Files* (2002). Coeditor, *The Tiananmen Papers* (2001).

Guillermo O'Donnell. Argentine political scientist, currently Helen Kellogg Professor of International Studies, University of Notre Dame. Author, *Modernization and Bureaucratic-Authoritarianism: Studies in South American Politics* (1973, rev. ed. 1995); *Bureaucratic Authoritarianism: Argentina in Comparative Perspective* (1988); *Counterpoints: Selected Essays on Authoritarianism and Democratization* (1999). Coauthor, *Transitions From Authoritarian Rule* (1986). Coeditor, *Issues in Democratic Consolidation: The New South American Democracies in Comparative Perspective* (1992); *Poverty and Inequality in Latin America* (1998)

Johan P. Olsen. Professor of Political Science, University of Oslo (Norway). Author, *Organized Democracy, The Political Institutions of a Welfare State, The Case of Norway* (1983). Coauthor, *Ambiguity and Choice in Organizations* (1976); *Rediscovering Institutions: The Organizational Basis of Politics* (1989); *The Reforming Organization* (1993); *Democratic Governance* (1995).

Susan J. Pharr. Edwin O. Reischauer Professor of Japanese Politics, Harvard University. Author, *Political Women in Japan* (1981); *Status Politics in Japan* (1990). Coeditor, *Media and Politics in Japan* (1996); *The State of Civil Society in Japan* (2003).

Marc F. Plattner. Director of the International Forum for Democratic Studies. Author, *Rousseau's State of Nature* (1979). Co-editor of the *Journal of Democracy*. Coeditor of 12 books on aspects of democracy and development.

Robert D. Putnam. Peter and Isabel Malkin Professor of Public Policy, Harvard University. Author, *Making Democracy Work: Civic Traditions in Modern Italy* (1993); *Bowling Alone: Decline and Renewal of the American Community* (2000). Coauthor, *Bureaucrats and Politicians in Western Democracies* (1981); *Hanging Together: The Seven-Power Summits* (1988); *Better Together: Restoring the American Community* (2003). Coeditor, *Double-Edged Diplomacy: International Bargaining and Domestic Politics* (1993).

Bert A. Rockman. Professor of Political Science, The Ohio State University. Author, *The Leadership Question: The Presidency in the American System* (1984). Coauthor, *Bureaucrats and Politicians in Western Democracies* (1981); *In the Web of Politics: Three Decades of the US Federal Executive* (2000). Coeditor, *Bush Presidency: First Appraisals* (1991); *The Clinton Presidency: First Appraisals* (1996); *Do Institutions Matter? Government Capabilities in the U.S. and Abroad* (1993); *Institutions and Democratic Statecraft* (1997); *The Clinton Legacy* (2000).

John Gerard Ruggie. Evron and Jeane Kirkpatrick Professor of International Affairs, Harvard University. Served as assistant secretary-general of the United Nations, 1997–2001. Author, *Winning the Peace: America and the World Order in the New Era* (1996); *Constructing the World Polity* (1998). Editor, *The Antinomies of Interdependence* (1983); *Multilateralism Matters* (1993).

H. V. Savitch. Brown and Williamson Distinguished Research Professor of Urban and Public Affairs at the University of Louisville (Kentucky). Author *Post-Industrial Cities: Politics and Planning in New York, Paris and London* (1988). Coeditor, *Big City Politics in Transition* (1991); *Urban Democracy* (2000); *Cities in the International Marketplace* (2002).

Susan E. Scarrow. Associate Professor of Political Science, University of Houston. Author, *Parties and Their Members: Organizing for Victory in Britain and Germany* (1996).

Kurt Schock. Associate Professor of Sociology, Rutgers University (Newark). Author, *Unarmed Insurrections: People Power Movements in Nondemocracies* (2004).

Lilia Shevtsova. Senior Associate, Carnegie Endowment for International Peace and the Carnegie Moscow Center. Formerly, deputy director, Moscow Institute of International, Economic and Political Studies, Russian Academy of Sciences. Author, *Yeltsin's Russia: Myths and Reality* (1998); *Putin's Russia* (2003).

Herbert A. Simon (1916–2001). Economist, Political Scientist, and Psychologist, Carnegie Mellon University. Nobel laureate in Economics, 1978. Author, *The New Science of Management Decisions* (1960); *Reason in Human Affairs* (1982); *Models of Thought*, 2, vols. (1979–1989); *Models of My Life* (1991); *Administrative Behavior* (rev. ed. 1997). See also, Mie Augier and James G. March, eds., *Models of Man: Essays in Memory of Herbert A. Simon* (2004).

Theda Skocpol. Victor S. Thomas Professor of Government and Sociology, Harvard University. Author, *States and Social Revolution* (1979); *Social Revolutions in the Modern World* (1992); *Protecting Soldiers and Mothers: The Political Origins of Social Policy in the United States* (1992); *Social Policy in the United States* (1995); *Boomerang: Health Care Reform and the Turn Against Government* (1997); *The Missing Middle: Working Families and the Future of American Social Policy* (2000). Coeditor, *Vision and Method in Historical Sociology* (1984); *Bringing the State Back In* (1985); *The New Majority: Toward a Popular Progressive Politics* (1997); *Democracy, Revolution, and History* (1998); *Civic Engagement in American Democracy* (1999).

Anne-Marie Slaughter. Bert G. Kerstetter University Professor of Politics and International Affairs, Dean of the Woodrow Wilson School of Public and International Affairs, Princeton University. Author, *International Law and International Relations Theory: Millennial Lectures* (2000); *A New World Order* (2004). Coauthor, *The European Court and National Courts: Doctrine and Jurisprudence* (1997).

Max Weber (1864–1920). German sociologist and political scientist. Held professorships at the universities of Heidelberg and Munich. Among his works in English translation are *The Protestant Ethic and the Spirit of Capitalism* (1930); *The Theory of Social and Economic Organization* (1947); *From Max Weber: Essays in Sociology* (1946), edited by H. H. Gerth and C. W. Mills; *Weber Political Writings* (1994), edited by P. Lassman and R. Speirs.

Lisa Wedeen. Associate Professor of Political Science, University of Chicago. Author, *Ambiguities of Domination: Politics, Rhetoric, and Symbols in Contemporary Syria* (1999).

Graham Wilson. Professor of Political Science and Public Affairs, University of Wisconsin-Madison. Author, *Interest Groups* (1990); *Only in America? American Politics in Comparative Perspective* (1998); *Business and Politics: A Comparative Introduction* (3rd ed., 2002). Coauthor, *The End of Whitehall: Death of a Paradigm?* (1995)

Fareed Zakaria. Editor, *Newsweek International*; columnist, *Newsweek*. Formerly, managing editor, *Foreign Affairs*. Author, *From Wealth to Power: The Unusual Origins of America's World Role* (1998); *The Future of Freedom: Illiberal Democracy at Home and Abroad* (2003). Coeditor, *The American Encounter: The United States and the Making of the Modern World* (1997).

INTRODUCTION:
ON COMPARING NATIONS

"He who knows only England," runs an old aphorism, "knows England not." Why? Surely if we immerse ourselves in the history, politics, culture, and economy of England, we will come to know England. And if we turn our attention then to France, Germany, Italy, Russia and so on, we shall know those countries. Comparative politics, as frequently taught in departments of political science, amounts to just such study of one nation after another. Why should such an endeavor, if carried out for all countries in the world, fall short of a complete knowledge of the world? To appreciate the import of the question, let us take England as our example, and John Stuart Mill as an observer of England who also pioneered the use of comparative method.

Mill hardly objected to deep study of the history and culture of England; he engaged in such study himself. There is a wealth of literature on every aspect of English life which is indispensable for anyone seeking to understand that country. The major nations of the world are so complex and multi-layered that only rare individuals can aspire to know more than one (usually their own) in depth. Yet for Mill, descriptions, no matter how complete and deep (or to use a currently popular term, "thick"), could not satisfy his curiosity. In order to get answers to questions, he found it necessary to compare England with other nations.

In his *A System of Logic*, written in 1846, two years before the appearance of Karl Marx's *Communist Manifesto*, Mill argued in a chapter on the "inverse deductive" method that historical generalizations are only possible through comparative study. For Mill, a "State of Society" is the "simultaneous state of all the greater social facts," including the degree of knowledge in the community and every social class, the state of industry, of wealth and its distribution, the occupations of the people and their division into classes, and the nature of relations among these classes, the character and degree of aesthetic development, and the form of government. All these factors—cultural, social, economic and political—are linked to one another and form a consensus. A change in one factor leads inevitably to a change in the other factors.

Here is a handle for the study of past ages and different regions of the world. What characterized the "State of Society" in England a thousand years ago as compared to Mill's time, and also as compared to other nations and continents? English life in all its aspects had been transformed in the 17th and 18th centuries. Most striking was the explosion of scientific knowledge, linked to changes in technology, and the emergence of an industrial society along with new or vastly enlarged social classes (particularly the capitalist, entrepreneurial, middle, and working classes), and greater popular participation in the state. Key trends were *not* confined to England, for science and industry were developing at a roughly similar pace in other parts of Europe and later in North America. Mill thus laid the basis for both the "system theory" and "modernization theory" that figure so largely in contemporary political science. Some features of English life in his time were unique, particularly class-conscious social relations and a special form of parliamentary government. It would be impossible to know what was general and what was unique unless England were compared to other nations.

Mill was an advocate of numerous political reforms (for example, extending suffrage, changing the electoral system, creating new institutions, legislating for the general welfare). The desirability and feasibility of these reforms could best be appraised by relating them to the "State of Society," which in turn requires comparative study. For Mill, the determining factor in the "State of Society" is the level of intellectual activity and pursuit of truth. Those engaged in the advancement of knowledge, even though only a minority of the population, are the main agents of social change. Yet people may mold as well as be shaped by circumstances, and from this reciprocal action necessarily results what for Mill is the supreme question of historical study, whether there is a "cycle or a progress." Industrialization can proceed under a Republic (as in the United States), a constitutional monarchy (as in the United Kingdom), or either a Republic or a monarchy or a Bonapartist dictatorship (as in France). The issues identified and analyzed by Mill continue to be the subject matter of comparative politics and are pursued in the contributions that follow in this volume. We are now a long way from description, no matter how dense, of England or any other individual nation. The comparative method compels us to identify similarities and differences, and then to account for them. We are led away from description, and toward explanation. We see every aspect of our subject in a new light.

THE LEVEL OF COMPARISON

Everything may be compared, but the question must always be raised, why do it? Is the comparison mechanical or dynamic, descriptive or analytic? The American Constitution, for example, may be compared to the constitution of any other nation; it may be compared with the constitutions that preceded it (Articles of Confederation, revolutionary state constitutions, colonial system); and the stages of its evolution may be compared with one another. A political party can be compared to its rival party or parties, to foreign parties, and the stages of its history to each other.

To compare by simply placing one item next to another (constitutions, legislatures, executives, political parties, interest groups, etc.) is rarely a worthwhile exercise. Suppose we note that the United States has a two-party system, the United Kingdom a two-and-a-half-party system (counting the Liberals or Social Democrats), and France a multi-party system. Our understanding of these systems is not thereby furthered. The comparison is mechanical, or formal. In order to make the comparison significant, we would have to try to account for differences and similarities. Why does France (along with most other democratic nations) have a multi-party system? What difference does it make?

To pursue those questions we have to investigate a number of factors. We might ask whether the parties in France cooperate, and in so doing take on some of the characteristics of a division between two major parties. We might ask whether parties in France resemble wings of major parties in the American and British systems. We might focus on the way in which the major social classes are linked to parties in all three systems. Why has a Communist party always been more massive in France than in the United States and Britain? At the time of the Liberation, the French Communist party received over one-fourth of the vote; it declined thereafter, particularly in the 1970s and 1980s, and is now hovering around five percent of the vote. This is a steep reduction, but is still far more than the fraction of one percent garnered by Communist parties in either the United States or Britain. Why? In answering this question we are compelled to look at all three systems in a different way. The French working class historically has been revolutionary (or alienated) to a greater degree than the American and British working classes. Again, why? We have to push the analysis still further, and in so doing we arrive at a deeper understanding of the evolution of all three political systems. Comparison leads us to question, to probe, to analyze, to interpret, to explain—and thus better to understand. Everything can be compared. But in order to be *significant*, the comparative method must have a theoretical component.

DOING COMPARATIVE POLITICS: SOME CLASSICS

One way to grasp the nature of the comparative method is to examine what students of comparative politics do. A comparative study becomes influential when it raises an issue significant for its time; it becomes a classic when the issue transcends the immediate context and becomes a continuing concern. Let us take three classic examples of the use of the comparative method in order to better understand the *why* and the *how* of comparison. The authors we choose are: three Americans, Alexander Hamilton, James Madison, and John Jay, who wrote *The Federalist Papers* under the pseudonym of PUBLIUS; one German, Max Weber; and one Frenchman, Emile Durkheim. These writers have had an immense impact on the field of comparative politics. Much of the work reproduced in this volume can be traced back to their concerns.

THE FEDERALIST PAPERS

In the very first *Federalist Paper*, Alexander Hamilton posed the crucial question confronting the people of the United States: "whether societies of men are really capable or not of establishing good government from reflection and choice, or whether they are forever destined to depend for their political constitutions on accident and force." The immediate issue was whether the citizens of New York, to whom the series of 85 essays was directed, would vote in favor of ratifying the Constitution drawn up by the Philadelphia Convention in 1787. The political constitutions of the major European nations were monarchies emerging from feudalism. A monarch ruled because he or she was the eldest child of the previous monarch ("accident and force"). Max Weber later referred to this kind of legitimacy as "traditional."

The American Revolution, followed shortly thereafter by the French Revolution, ushered in the modern era. Basic political institutions were now to be created by an act of will, and legitimacy of rulers was to be derived from the people through elections. This change was possible only in societies where large numbers of people challenged traditional authority. Max Weber coined the term "rational-legal" to describe legitimacy in the modern era. It is accepted practice today that nations may create and change their political institutions.

In drafting a constitution, framers generally seek to avoid the mistakes of the past, and to adopt practices which seem to work elsewhere. Constitution-makers review and evaluate their own past political regimes, and compare them with other regimes. Thus, the framers of the American Constitution in 1787 wished to remedy the defects of the previous constitution (the Articles of Confederation), the framers of the Basic Law of the Federal Republic of Germany in 1949 sought to correct the drawbacks of the Weimar Republic (1919–1933) and of the fascist dictatorship that followed, the framers of the Constitution of the Fifth French Republic in 1958 wanted to improve upon the previous Fourth Republic (1946–1958), and so on. They also all wanted to learn from the experience of others. Every constitutional convention is an exercise in comparative politics at the highest level. In the last decade of the twentieth century there have been two notable efforts at constitution-making reminiscent of the drama of the first efforts over two centuries ago. The collapse of communism in the Soviet Union and elsewhere in Eastern Europe offered the peoples of these countries an opportunity to create new institutions; and the nations of Western Europe are in the process of forging a new Union. Rarely have so many people in the world been engaged at the same time in so vast an exercise of comparative politics at the level of "grand" theory.

In the literature on constitution-making. *The Federalist Papers* remain a classic of political science, and of comparative politics. These papers were struck off during a heated campaign in the state of New York for ratification of the new constitution. Alexander Hamilton conceived of the project because he feared that George Clinton, the governor of New York and an opponent of the new constitution, would muster a popular majority for the Anti-Federalists. Hamilton was able to secure the cooperation of James Madison, then in New York as a delegate to the Continental Congress from Virginia, and of John Jay, the confederal secretary for foreign affairs. All 85 papers, which appeared in the New York press, were signed PUBLIUS (the public man). Despite this brilliant journalistic campaign, Hamilton's fears were fully justified; the Anti-Federalists easily won the election by a margin of almost two-to-one. It took furious political maneuvering by Hamilton and Jay, both delegates to the ratifying convention in Poughkeepsie, to secure a favorable vote.

The framers wished to create new institutions through "reflection" (in the Constitutional Convention) and "choice" (popular vote on ratification). They also sought to provide opportunities within government for reflection, and to vest that government with sufficient power to make it effective without endangering public liberties. In *Federalist Paper* Number 48, Madison compared three types of political regimes: monarchy, democracy (in which "a multitude of people exercise in person the legislative function"), and a representative republic. At that time virtually all governments were monarchies. The few historical examples of "pure" democracy had all fallen victim to internal dissension and were short-lived. There was no example of a stable, effective representative republic. The Articles of Confederation in the United States had created a republic, but it clearly was inadequate to the "exigencies of Union." Madison posed the question, what in each system (monarchy, democracy, republic) is the source of danger to liberty?

"In a government where numerous and extensive prerogatives are placed in the hands of an hereditary monarch," began Madison in Number 48, "the executive department is very justly regarded as the source of danger, and watched with all the jealousy which a zeal for liberty ought to inspire." An hereditary monarchy was ruled out by the American framers, who nonetheless saw in the British monarchy many features worth adopting in a republican perspective. The history of liberty in Britain lay in the imposition of limitations upon the power of the monarchy, first by the nobles and then by Parliament. But, for Madison, restrictions upon the power of the executive were relevant mainly in the case of the "overgrown and all-grasping prerogative of an hereditary magistrate, supported and fortified by an hereditary branch of the legislative authority." That was *not* the system created by the American framers.

The second type of political system was "pure democracy." For Madison, people, when ruling directly, are too easily swayed by orators and demagogues and are "constantly exposed by their incapacity for regular deliberation and concerted measures, to the ambitious intrigues of their executive magistrates." The historical example offered by Madison was Athenian democracy, under which a majority condemned Socrates to death. "In all very numerous assemblies, of whatever characters composed," Madison wrote in Number 55, "passion never fails to wrest the scepter from reason. Had every Athenian citizen been a Socrates, every Athenian assembly would still have been a mob."

The American political class was less interested in ancient Greece than in two contemporary instances of popular democracy. In the conclusion of Number 10 Madison identified as "improper or wicked objects" a "rage for paper money, for an abolition of debts, for an equal distribution of property." He was referring to, first, the domination of the Rhode Island legislature by a debtor-majority, which decided to issue paper money (that rapidly lost value) as legal tender. The result was runaway inflation, and the collapse of confidence in the economy. A short-term palliative had been chosen instead of a long-term solution. The second example was Shays's Rebellion; small farmers and debtors led by Daniel Shays prevented courts from foreclosing mortgages, and demanded issuance of paper money and dismantling of representative institutions. The new constitution, Madison emphasized, did not create a pure democracy, thus avoiding the instability created by factional strife and a tyranny of the majority.

Madison continued: "But, in a representative republic where the executive magistracy is carefully limited, both in the extent and the duration of its power; and where the legislative power is exercised by an assembly, which is inspired by a supposed influence over the people with an intrepid confidence in its own strength; which is sufficiently numerous to feel all the passions which actuate a multitude, yet not so numerous as to be incapable of pursuing the objects of its passions by means which reason prescribes; it is against the enterprising ambition of this department that the people ought to indulge all their jealousy and exhaust all their precautions." Madison was weighing the experience of Virginia during the Revolution, when he served on the Council of State under Governor Thomas Jefferson, and that of Congress under the Articles. He cited a key passage from Jefferson's *Notes on Virginia*, denouncing the concentration of powers in the hands of the assembly as "precisely the definition of despotic government." An elective despotism, said Jefferson, was not the government the people fought for, "but one which should not only be founded on free principles, but in which the powers of government should be so divided and balanced among several bodies of magistracy as that no one could transcend their legal limits without being effectually checked and restrained by the others."

Jefferson was infuriated by the way in which the Virginia assembly tried to tie his hands as governor and meddle in decision-making, depriving him of the autonomy and flexibility needed to deal with the invasion of Virginia by a British army (which almost succeeded in capturing him). He was incensed that on two occasions the same assembly tried, and failed by only a few votes, to install a dictator (the term used) to save the Republic. On the basis of an extensive analysis of the assemblies of the various states during the Revolution, and of Congress under the Articles, the framers concluded that government by assembly was a danger to liberty. It would lead to chaos and ultimately the call for a dictator, referred to by Hamilton in Number 85 (eerily anticipating the emergence of Bonaparte from the tumult of revolutionary French assemblies) as "perhaps the military despotism of a victorious demagogue." The Constitution was designed specifically to remedy a major defect of the Articles of Confederation, by creating an autonomous executive power that could impart an energetic impulse to government.

One reason for the continuing influence of *The Federalist Papers* is that their theory concerning legislative–executive relations has been tested constantly in democratic systems ever since, and seems to have been vindicated. In stable democracies an executive power is able to initiate policy and guide the legislature. Autonomy of the executive may be assured through party controls enabling a prime minister and cabinet, once invested by the legislature, to lead; or it may be achieved by giving the executive a measure of independence from the legislature (as in presidential systems). Legislative dominance over the executive, as in the cases of the Articles of Confederation, the revolutionary assemblies in France, the Third and Fourth French Republics, and the Weimar Republic, led to instability, collapse, and sometimes the rise of a dictator.

Another major problem faced by the authors of *The Federalist Papers* was how to create a union of states that would be effective enough to defend a common good but avoid a dangerous concentration of power in the central government. This is an inescapable issue in every society, and is especially urgent now for the peoples of the twenty-five nations (as of 2005) who make up the European Union. The great defect of the Articles, Hamilton argued in Number 15, was that the national government dealt with citizens only through the intermediary of the states. The national government could not levy taxes directly, and relied upon the states to enforce laws against individuals.

What happens in the event of disobedience? For Hamilton, penalties "can only be inflicted in two ways: by the agency of the courts and ministers of justice, or by military force; by the COERCION of the magistracy, or by the COERCION of arms. The first kind can evidently apply only to men; the last kind must of necessity be employed against bodies politic, or communities, or States. . . . In an association where the general authority is confined to the collective bodies of the communities that compose it, every breach of the laws must involve a state of war; and military execution must become the only instrument of civil obedience." The solution under the new Constitution was to create two levels of government, each able to act directly upon individuals as citizens. *The Federal Papers* are a starting point for comparison of confederations and of federal systems, and of the problem of uniting and governing diverse groups within any large society.

MAX WEBER

In 1890 a German scholarly association devoted to the study of social problems and political reform launched a major inquiry into farm labor. The *Verein für Sozialpolitik* sent out questionnaires to over 3,600 landowners in Germany; more than two-thirds of the questionnaires were completed and returned. The task of analyzing the returns from eastern Germany (mainly Prussia) was assigned to Max Weber, at the time a 26-year-old scholar trained in legal history. Weber had studied law at the University of Heidelberg, Germany, in 1882, had done a year of military service at Strasbourg, then had continued legal and historical studies at Berlin and Göttingen. After receiving a law degree in 1886, he undertook graduate work that would qualify him to teach law. His doctoral thesis on the history of medieval business organizations was published in 1889; and a second work on land tenure in ancient Rome was completed in 1891.

In accepting the assignment from the *Verein*, Weber made a leap from ancient Rome and medieval Europe to contemporary German social and political problems. His findings were published as part of the massive study put out by the *Verein* in 1892. Weber presented his work to an American audience during the World Exhibition in St. Louis in 1904, commemorating the centennial of the Louisiana Purchase. Omitting much of the detail of interest only to Germans, he brought out the importance of his study for a larger public. It is this presentation that will be examined here as a classic example of the use of comparative method by the scholar who became, arguably, the most important single figure in the field of comparative politics in the 20th century.[1]

Weber began by comparing relations among landlords, peasants, and farm laborers in America and Europe. American farmers, particularly those of the great wheat-producing states, are entrepreneurs and economic individualists producing for the market. Land tenure in Europe is completely different because of the feudal heritage. European peasants before the French Revolution produced to satisfy their own wants, and occasionally to sell surplus products. They were not trained to produce for profit. Rather, they were enmeshed in a network of controls created by landlords, who owned the land and often even had physical control of the peasant's body. The social function of the peasantry was to provide the neighboring town with food as cheaply as possible, to support the landlords by service and taxes, and to provide recruits for the army.

But the "strong blast of modern capitalistic competition," said Weber, comes into contradiction with traditional agriculture. In the old economic order the goal was to give work and sustenance to the greatest possible number of people. But for capitalism the question is rather how to produce as much as possible for the market with as few people as possible. "The thousands of years of the past struggle against the invasion of the capitalist spirit." Capitalism triumphed in the vast reaches of America, where the challenge from southern plantation owners finally was swept aside. In England, too, the peasant was transformed into an entrepreneur and a producer for the market. In western and southern Germany, where industrial capitalism developed, a similar social evolution took place. Peasants acquired title to the land, gained political rights against the landlords, and gradually became more independent economically. But in eastern Germany feudalism evolved into agricultural capitalism: A large class of propertyless farm hands confronted a landowning aristocracy. Weber thus deftly drew a contrast between American farmers on the one hand, and European peasants on the other hand; then between English farmers and continental peasants; then in Germany between farmers in the west and south and peasants in the east who lived even more precariously and were even more exploited than in the past.

In consequence of all these trends, said Weber, "European capitalism, at least on the continent, has a peculiar authoritarian stamp." Why the differences between east and west Germany, between the continent as a whole and England, between England and America? Weber described a universal trend toward greater rationality, itself a reflection of the explosion of scientific knowledge. Life in the Middle Ages was based on tradition and prerogatives. Social status was determined by ownership of land, in turn determined by birth. The scientific and political revolutions of the 18th century challenged, undermined, and eventually destroyed feudal systems. But the importance of rationality varied from one society to another, as did political solutions. Weber was asking why increasing rationality led to liberalism or constitutional democracy in some countries (some more stable or solidly based than others) and to authoritarianism (later fascism or communism) in other countries. Beginning with the returned questionnaires by landlords in east Germany, Weber thus was able to probe perhaps the single most important political question of our age.

A second issue posed by Weber loomed larger in his talks to German audiences. In the Middle Ages German power advanced from west to east, conquering Slavonic areas. These territories could be colonized, Weber explained, because of the superior technical and commercial skills of German merchants and artisans, the superior military techniques of German knights, and superior knowledge of agriculture of German peasants. But the tide of power was now flowing in the other direction. German peasants were fleeing the eastern estates and were being replaced by Slavic small farmers and laborers, with serious political consequences. In the past a sturdy German peasantry constituted a major source of manpower for the armed forces, a bulwark of the nation on its eastern borders, and a solid base for the political power of the landlord class (the Junkers). Now the Slavs were infiltrating east German society, weakening the national defense and the whole political system (within which the Junkers played a leadership role).

The phenomenon described by Weber has significance far beyond the borders of late 19th-century Germany. He was analyzing the profound reasons for the projection of power in the world, and the conditions under which the flow can be reversed. Societies with superior scientific establishments and technologies and more effective social and political structures in a first step are able to extend their influence and even physical control over weaker societies. But the peoples of dominated or colonized societies react. They may catch up by assimilating modern science and technology; they may also take the place of key players within the imperial societies, through immigration. Interaction between Germans and Slavs in the late 19th century was but one aspect of global and intricate dialectical relationships between dominating and dominated societies.

To return to Weber's central thesis: how to account for differences in the degree of democratization? The key analytic procedure for Weber is to break up a society into its major social classes, focus on the way in which each class is changed by capitalist development, and determine how relations among the major classes and their participation in the political system are affected by these changes. In short, we must see how each major social class works out its "entry into politics."

Weber identified five major social classes or groups. European societies in the feudal era consisted of two classes, the landed aristocracy and the peasantry or serfs. With capitalist development there necessarily came into existence two large groups that did not fit into the feudal structure and eventually blew it apart: the bourgeoisie (including merchants, capitalists, entrepreneurs, and various professionals) and a working class (generally former peasants driven or drifting off the land). For Weber, social class was determined by the role its members played in the productive process. But a social class was not necessarily a cohesive group. To what extent a class was indeed a self-conscious and unified community is a question for investigation. Weber added to these four classes a fifth group, which weighs heavily in the balance between democracy and authoritarianism, the intellectuals.

Throughout feudal Europe the landed aristocracy, Weber began, constituted the political class. In England, and in most of Western Europe the landed aristocracy gradually lost its dominant position, and either shared power with the rising middle classes or was eliminated through violent revolution. But the landed aristocracy in east Germany continued to play a leading political role (notably in the person of Bismarck) even as the society was being transformed. The east was essentially a Slavic land colonized by the Germans, whereas in the west peasants became landowners and small entrepreneurs. But the social base of the Junkers was eroding. German farm laborers in the east were not willing to endure the indignities inflicted upon them by their lords, said Weber; they "fled from their isolation and patriarchal dependency either across the ocean to the United States or into the smoky and dusty but socially freer air of the German factories."[2] The German bourgeoisie, however, was not able to take over political responsibility from the Junkers. It was blocked from political power by the combined hostility of aristocrats, workers, and intellectuals.

In his inaugural lecture at Freiburg, Germany, in 1895, Weber proclaimed himself a member of the bourgeois class. "I feel myself to be a bourgeois, and I have been brought up to share their views and ideals." But he went on to state that the German bourgeoisie does not have the maturity to be the leading class of the nation. The upper bourgeoisie, he said, yearns for a dictator to protect it from aristocrats above and masses below. Rich merchants and capitalists made themselves ridiculous by purchasing estates and aping the life-style of a landed aristocracy condemned by history. Nor did the workers possess the maturity to assume power themselves, though Weber believed that, properly led, they could be the social base of democratic institutions. As for the intellectual class, says Weber, it is skeptical of the advance of capitalism. The "aristocracy of education" looks distrustfully upon the abolition of traditional ethical and aesthetic values, preferring the rule of aristocrats to that of politicians. "The representatives of the highest interests of culture turn their eyes back," laments Weber, "and refuse to cooperate in rearing the structures of the future." Join together the antipathy of intellectuals, the normal hostility of workers toward their employers, the contempt displayed by aristocrats toward upstarts, and the moral bankruptcy of the bourgeois themselves, and we begin to understand what Weber terms "the downfall of German bourgeois liberalism."[3]

Virtually all of the themes in Weber's later work may be found in his early study of rural society and capitalism in Germany. The contrast between the culture of feudalism and the new conception of production introduced by capitalism is the embodiment of a more general contrast between tradition and reason, between the determination of life chances by birth or by merit, between personal rule and government by institutions and law. The contrast leads to the identification of different "types" of authority: traditional, rational-legal, and a transitional form characterized by personal or charismatic leadership.

In seeking to understand why the middle classes became more self-confident and politically mature in west Germany as opposed to east Germany, and in England and America compared to the European continent in general, Weber was led to the study of cultural factors. A Protestant revolution took place in the north, while Catholicism remained strong in the south and east. The Catholic church, Weber observed, prefers patriarchal labor relations because they are more humane and can be developed ethically while commercial relations created by capitalism are seen to be beyond human control. Protestant churches are more open to urban rationalist culture. Weber's next step was to analyze the affinity of the Protestant ethic and the spirit of capitalism, his most famous single work, and then review all world religions in terms of their retardative or accelerating effect on capitalist development.

Weber made it clear that he was trying not only to understand the world, but on the basis of that understanding to engage in political education, to help prepare the "ruling and rising classes" to assume their responsibilities. "The aim of our socio-political activity," he asserted, "is not to make everybody happy but the *social unification* of the nation." He also confided to his American audience in 1904 that he was a "resolute follower of democratic institutions."[4] His goal was to strengthen the democratic institutions through which German society could most surely achieve its unity and (in his view) realize its greatness.

EMILE DURKHEIM

In 1893 (at the same time that Max Weber began publishing the results of his research on rural society in Germany) a book appeared in France that was destined to become a classic of modern social science: *De la division du travail social*, literally "On the division of social labor," and referred to hereafter simply as *The Division of Labor*. Its author, Emile Durkheim, was a 35-year-old professor at the University of Bordeaux. Durkheim had followed the traditional path of a member of the French intellectual elite: disciplined study in a lycée; preparatory courses and coaching in order to pass the entrance exam for a *grande école*, in this case the *Ecole Normale Supérieure* (which Durkheim entered on his third try); success in the *agrégation* (a ruthlessly competitive examination required for appointment as a lycée teacher) in philosophy; and a doctorate. *The Division of Labor* was his major doctoral thesis; the minor thesis on Baron de Montesquieu and Jean-Jacques Rousseau was published long after his death. Durkheim later was named professor at the Sorbonne, where he helped found the discipline of sociology. Through the four major works published in his lifetime, his editorship of the *Année Sociologique*, and his chair at the Sorbonne, he became a major influence in French and European intellectual life.

Durkheim was born and raised in the town of Epinal, in the Lorraine, near the German border. His father was chief rabbi of the Vosges; his grandfather had been a rabbi in Alsace; and young Durkheim at first prepared to follow in their footsteps by attending a rabbinical school. He soon abandoned that goal, and eventually became totally secular. As a boy of twelve he was a witness to the humiliation of France when German troops occupied Epinal during the Franco-Prussian war. His family did not have to join in the mass migration from Alsace and Lorraine after the war, because Epinal remained French.

The subtitle of the first edition of *Division of Labor* was: "étude sur l'organisation des sociétés supérieures" (a study of the organization of advanced societies). The analytic problem (reflecting his philosophical training) was posed forcefully in the preface.

> As for the question at the origin of this work, it is that of the relations between the individual personality and social solidarity. How does it happen that, while becoming more autonomous, the individual depends ever more closely on society? How can he be at the same time more of a personality and more socially dependent ["plus solidaire"]? For it is undeniable that these two trends, however contradictory they seem, develop along parallel lines. That is the problem which we have posed. It seems to us that which resolves this apparent antinomy is a transformation of social solidarity due to the ever greater development of the division of labor. That is how we have been led to make the latter phenomenon the object of our study.[5]

Durkheim's goal was to understand the emergence and nature of the modern state, and its consequences for individualism and freedom. He tackled this philosophical issue with a passion that can only be understood in the context of the political crises of his time. France's defeat by Germany seared his consciousness. France and Germany were in a deadly competition, comparable to the struggle for existence described by Darwin. The military strength of the two countries was a reflection of and dependent upon the effectiveness of their social and political institutions and the degree to which they were able to assimilate scientific advances and apply them to technology. If the French could not remain in the forefront of scientific inquiry, technological development, and industrialization, if they could not vanquish the demons of their disunity, they would be unable to sustain their distinctive culture in a hostile world. The Second Empire of Louis Bonaparte collapsed in 1871, and was replaced in 1875 by a Republic, the third since the Revolution of 1789. But public support for a return to monarchy was still strong. The decision to create a Republic had carried in the Constituent Assembly by only one vote. At the time, monarchists probably constituted a majority in the country; only their inability to agree on a single pretender to the throne kept them from taking power again.

For Durkheim, restoration of the monarchy meant returning to a society based on birth and privilege. In that traditional society the Church played an important role in education; scientific inquiry and economic activity were downgraded. But a reversion to the Old Regime was a prescription for disaster, Durkheim believed, and in any event was impossible. Rationality and science had developed to the point where a government and social system based on heredity were simply unacceptable. The only basis for rule in a modern society is some form of popular sovereignty. With all its imperfections, the Republic for Durkheim was the only political system compatible with a culture of rationality and science.

Durkheim saw it as his mission to defend a fragile Republic from attack by both the Right and the Left. The chief enemy was on the Right, whose leaders blamed the Republic for shattering the historic unity of French society as expressed through monarchy, the Church, and the armed forces. Durkheim sought to show, through empirical analysis, that religion was destined to play a smaller and smaller role in societies as they become increasingly complex and transformed by science. Modern societies based on merit and accomplishment were also stronger because they could take advantage of the talents and abilities of all. But for advocates of monarchy, the secular Republic offered no vision, no myth that could unify the people. Modern society is atomized, they argued, producing people milling about aimlessly, without deeply held common beliefs. To meet this criticism, Durkheim wanted to show that consensus and unity could be achieved in a modern society and a Republic. Solidarity could be expressed through new structures and rituals. Religion could be replaced by a civic humanism.

Durkheim was concerned also that the extreme Left, by labelling the Republic the executive committee of the bourgeoisie and seeking to overthrow it, weakened the only system that enabled the French to defend their separate interests and yet govern themselves; it also went against the tide of history by looking backward to primitive society for its ideal of communism. Anti-capitalism was another form of anti-modernity. But Durkheim himself condemned the excesses of capitalism and the shallowness of modern values, which he considered defects to be eliminated as modern societies evolved.

Durkheim remarked in the concluding sentence of the preface to the first edition that the "object" of his study was the division of labor. Yet he viewed the growing importance of division of labor as a "problem." Why was it a problem and not simply a phenomenon? Modern society, he said, is distinguished by its "extreme" division of labor, as exemplified in factory work. Because it greatly enhances the productive capacity of a society, division of labor is "the necessary condition of the intellectual and material development of societies; it is the source of civilization." Division of labor creates a new form of social solidarity which could be (though is not necessarily) as effective as that in simpler societies. But, observed Durkheim, "morbid phenomena" such as crime and suicide seem to increase along with the progress of arts, science, and industry. People may become more productive in modern societies; they do not thereby become happier or more moral beings.

In *Division of Labor* Durkheim did not compare existing nations (France, Germany, Britain, United States, etc.) with each other. Rather he compared two "types" of societies: traditional and modern. His identification of the essential characteristics of both types was based on familiarity with modern European society, medieval European society, ancient Greece and Rome, ancient Judaic societies (which he knew through his early schooling), and ethnographic studies of primitive societies, especially at first North American Indian tribes. He did not contend that any specific society was a "pure" type, though he was drawn later to the literature on the most primitive society then still extant, the Australian aborigines, who came close to his model.

Every society, says Durkheim, has a set of core beliefs and feelings that develops a life of its own; he calls this the "collective or common conscience." In traditional societies the actions of individuals are expected to conform to this collective conscience, which is largely religious in nature. Departure from common norms calls into question the laws laid down by ancestors and by a divinity. Representation of the collective conscience through religious symbols and practices may be an illusion, says Durkheim, but it is a "necessary" illusion. Traditional societies are like simple organisms; a group of cells can split from and recreate the parent organism. The groups of cells are essentially similar to one another; they have a "mechanical" structure in that pieces can be rearranged and still fit together. Modern societies have a more developed division of labor. A common core of beliefs and feelings is still essential, but it is rooted in the realization by all individuals that they benefit from and need the contributions of others. The worship of ancestors and divinities is replaced by a "cult of the individual."

Critical in Durkheim's argument was the comparison of solidarity in the two types of society. In "mechanical" solidarity individuals are like molecules of inorganic bodies; they interact without having any action of their own. "The link which thus unites the individual with society is wholly analogous to that which attaches a thing to a person. The individual conscience, considered from this angle, is a simple dependence of the collective type and follows all its movements, as the possessed object follows those impressed upon it by its owner." The individual is "literally a thing of which society disposes."

The "organic" solidarity produced by division of labor, Durkheim continued, is quite different. It is based not on resemblance among individuals, but upon their differences. "The former [mechanical solidarity] is only possible to the degree that the individual personality is absorbed into the collective personality; the second [organic solidarity] is only possible if each one has a sphere of action of his own, consequently a personality. It is necessary, then, that the collective conscience leave open a part of the individual conscience, to permit to become established there specialized functions that it cannot regulate." The greater the realm of individual autonomy and specialized functions, the more do individuals recognize their interdependence and (contrary to the argument by advocates of a return to the Old Regime) the stronger the solidarity. "Society is more capable of moving as a collectivity at the same time that each of its elements has more of its own movements." It thus is possible for individuals to develop their own initiatives in a modern society, thereby contributing to its greater efficiency and productivity. Organic solidarity could be even more effective in creating social cohesion than mechanical solidarity.

Societies based on mechanical solidarity have simple structures in which family and clan groups are aggregated. With increases in population, development of trade and commerce, emergence of a merchant class, and creation of cities, simple structures are weakened and eventually replaced by structures reflecting a division of labor. Societies that evolve are better able to defend themselves, and even to extend their power over neighbors (much as a more productive France was able after the Revolution to dominate Germany, but fell under German domination a half-century later).

Durkheim described a general evolution from the simple to the more complex, from traditional to modern, but nothing is inevitable. Specialization, he argued, "is not the only possible solution in the struggle for life: there is also integration, colonization, being resigned to a precarious and more uncertain existence, finally the total elimination of the weakest by way of suicide or otherwise." The political implications for the French in the late 19th century were clear: they could either meet the challenges of modernization and survive; or they could be dominated if not colonized by their neighbors; or they could revert to subsistence agriculture and traditional values (which will lead to domination by others); or they could commit national suicide. It is up to individuals to choose their destiny, and the role of the social scientist is to make them aware of the implications of their choices.

There can be no turning back to traditional values, for Durkheim, unless one is willing to pay a high, even prohibitive price (such as domination by hostile forces, or withdrawal from life by suicide, abuse of drugs, or immersion in mysticism). But Durkheim does not romanticize modern society, which in his time was in crisis and turmoil, marked by cycles of economic depression, working class strikes and alienation, and high rates of crime and suicide. He believed that contemporary society was still in transition between the traditional and the modern types; rational transformation of society had still not been achieved. In this transitional phase Durkheim identified three "abnormal" forms of division of labor: anomic, forced, and a third form which was simply called "another." Each "abnormal" form represented a critique of particular social systems: capitalism, feudalism, and state-socialism or bureaucratization.

Division of labor under capitalism leads, at first, to separation of capital from labor, and of producers from consumers. In order to surmount these problems it is necessary to further develop the logic of division of labor, and to regulate labor–capital relations and the market. Durkheim called for the state to be more active in bringing the economic classes and sectors into contact, without trying to absorb the actors into its own structures.

But a satisfactory solution to the problem of anomie is impossible so long as life chances are determined by birth ("forced division of labor") rather than merit and talent. Social differences will be considered legitimate only if they result from differing abilities and talents, much as students will accept failure only if they know it is determined by a fair examination. Class differences based on traditions and family connections are inherently unjust. If division of labor is to produce solidarity, individuals must have suitable tasks. Durkheim was pleading for a meritocracy, not unlike the French educational system through which he himself had passed and of which he was an ornament. "Labor divides itself spontaneously only if society is so constituted that social inequalities express exactly natural inequalities."

A third abnormal form of division of labor occurs when functions are distributed within an enterprise in such a way that individuals are not given enough to do, which leads to waste, incoherence, and disorder. Durkheim gives as a specific example, appreciated immediately by his French readers, an administration where employees are not given enough work to occupy themselves usefully. This abnormal form of division of labor may be caused also when labor is so repetitive that individuals cannot see the consequences of their activity.

Modern society, despite its superiority over traditional society, thus is traversing a profound crisis. Durkheim's goal was to help us understand the nature and the causes of this unhealthy state, and to point the way toward adoption of policies that could preserve the advantages of modernity while putting an end to anomie, bring warring classes and groups together, and create a greater measure of social justice. *The Division of Labor* was a starting point for his subsequent analysis of democracy and dictatorship, traditionalism and modernity, and of the pressures of political transitions and social change. Every issue of concern to social scientists today can be viewed within the theoretical perspective provided by Durkheim.

CONTEMPORARY TRENDS

A major purpose of this volume is to make readily available representative selections from the contemporary literature in comparative politics. One need only peruse these selections to appreciate the diversity of approaches and schools of thought in the discipline. Two running controversies concerning methodology call for special attention. The first is whether to compare a large number of cases (ideally, the whole world) or to compare a few cases, perhaps just two, or even examine in depth only one case, but with reference to a larger problem or issue. A second, and related, controversy is whether to use the procedures of the natural sciences (formulation of hypotheses that can be falsified), or seek rather to understand a system or phenomenon through "thick" description. Those who formulate hypotheses tend to compare the largest possible number of relevant cases; those who seek better to understand one particular system tend to concentrate on that case perhaps with comparison to a few others.

Analysts who try to be rigorously scientific generally make greater use of quantitative methods and aspire to an attitude of neutrality. Those who focus on one system tend to be immersed in the culture of that nation or area, and may well reject the methods of the natural sciences as inappropriate for the study of human societies. They also consider "value-free" social science an impossibility. Inasmuch as everyone has values, they believe it the obligation of social scientists to state their underlying values as clearly as possible so that readers may make due allowances.

Each approach has serious drawbacks. It is impossible for any one person to know in depth all of the political systems of the world. The larger the number of cases, necessarily the more superficial is our knowledge of each one. Complex social and political phenomena have to be reduced to coded factors, making it impossible to comprehend the rich and unique character of individual cultures. Increasing the number of cases also means that theories must be cast in more general terms, running the risk eventually of becoming truisms. If it is asserted, for example, that all governments are similar in that they rest upon acceptance (for whatever reasons) by society, it could be concluded that tribal chiefs, medieval monarchs, and modern democrats and dictators are all alike. The statement is true, but not useful for most purposes.

More specific generalization will always be subject to exceptions. Comparison of a large number of cases may well establish a correlation, for example, between democracy and modernity (degree of development of industry, division of labor, science, and rationality). An educated citizenry is more capable of participating in elections than an uneducated, illiterate citizenry; debate about the redistribution of income is more meaningful when there is income to redistribute. The more modern and prosperous a society, the more likely it is to be a democracy. However, consider just two obvious exceptions. Germany in the 1930s was among the most advanced societies in the world, and boasted a highly educated citizenry; but far from evolving as a democracy, it fell under the rule of a virulent dictatorship. Most of the inhabitants of India, after World War II, were impoverished and illiterate, yet India created a democratic government that has functioned for half a century. Germany for over a century has been one of the dominant powers on the European continent, and India today has about one billion people. These countries bulk so large in the world, that to consider them "exceptions" to a rule borders on the absurd.

At the other extreme, studies of a single case run the risk of being parochial. Those who engage in dense description in order to understand a specific society or political system may be unable to shed light on other cases. Every system becomes unique, therefore comparison is pointless. Examination of a large number of cases (*"large n"*) and use of the scientific method may lead to superficial generalizations, while study of a small number of cases (*"small n"*) inspired by intuition may yield no general knowledge at all.

It might be useful to refer to our three "classic" examples of comparative politics before proceeding further. Let us assume that Publius (Hamilton, Madison, and Jay), Max Weber, and Emile Durkheim were indeed theorists and practitioners of comparative politics. What conclusions can be drawn from their work concerning the dispute between advocates of science as opposed to intuition and description, students of many cases as opposed to a few or even the single case?

The authors of our three classic studies used nations other than their own as points of reference for their comparisons, but did not claim to know them as well. John Jay had been ambassador to Spain and had travelled widely in Europe, but James Madison and Alexander Hamilton never visited Europe (though Hamilton was born and spent his childhood on the Caribbean island of Nevis). Max Weber was an ardent German nationalist and Emile Durkheim an equally ardent French nationalist. Weber travelled throughout Western Europe and once visited the United States; Durkheim knew Germany, and immersed himself in anthropological literature on the Australian aborigines (without ever bothering to go to Australia himself).

Jay, Madison, and Hamilton were familiar with British culture, because they came to maturity within the British Empire. Weber engaged in a massive study of the world's most important religions, and he read voraciously on universal history. Durkheim likewise had an encyclopedic knowledge of both modern and primitive societies. But all of these authors saw the outside world through the prism of their own cultures. If ethnocentrism is a disqualification for students of comparative politics, then none of these authors make the grade. It is hard to see how any work in social science can be produced by rootless people.

It is striking, also, that all of our authors were passionately involved in the politics of their own societies. Jay, Hamilton, and Madison participated actively in the Revolution; Jay served as the confederal minister of foreign affairs, and Hamilton and Madison both were members of the Constitutional Convention. *The Federalist Papers* were written for a partisan purpose, to secure a vote in favor of ratification of the new constitution. Max Weber commented extensively on political events in the popular press, was an adviser to the German delegation to the peace conference at Versailles, and considered running for office. Emile Durkheim defended the Republic against its monarchist critics, and sought to refashion the educational system as a bulwark of the Republic. He was a close friend of Socialist party leader Jean Jaurès (his fellow student at the *Ecole Normale*), and played a major role in the campaign to defend and exonerate Captain Dreyfus. Political activism may not be a requirement for social scientists, but it would appear not to be a disqualification.

All our authors also addressed "big" questions: whether societies of men can reshape their political institutions; why capitalism takes liberal and authoritarian forms; the fate of human freedom in modernizing societies. These central issues were all related to the evolution from feudal to modern society, marked by the American and French Revolutions, and the consequences of the triumph of modernity for human individuality and freedom. One lesson to be learned from the classics is that comparison should shed light on a significant issue.

Our three authors proclaimed their commitment to the scientific method, in that they sought to formulate theories or hypotheses that were then subject to rigorous scrutiny in the light of available empirical evidence. The stated goal was to help understand problems so that reasonable and effective public policies might be adopted. In Number 9, Hamilton observed that "the science of politics, like most other sciences, has received great improvement." Among its "various principles" were "the regular distribution of power into distinct departments; the introduction of legislative balances and checks; the institution of courts composed of judges holding their office during good behavior; the representation of the people in the legislature by deputies of their own election." He called them "the means, and powerful means, by which the excellencies of republican government may be retained and its imperfections lessened or avoided."

One of the most influential contemporary philosophers of science adopted a similar approach. Karl Popper contended that theories of democracy should not ask "who should rule," but rather "How can we so organize political institutions that bad or incompetent rulers can be prevented from doing much damage?" The principle of a democratic polity, he suggested, is "the proposal to create, develop, and protect, political institutions for the avoidance of tyranny." General elections and separation of powers, said Popper, may be considered well-tried and reasonably effective institutional safeguards against tyranny.[6]

Emile Durkheim likewise made it his goal to apply to the study of society and politics the methods of science, which he called in *Division of Labor* "nothing else but conscience carried to its highest point of clarity." An enlightened conscience prepares us to understand problems and how to meet them; "intelligence guided by science must play an ever greater role in our collective life."[7] Max Weber devoted his life to the pursuit of science, which he conceived as contributing "methods of thinking; the tools and the training for thought." The goal of the scientific method is to gain clarity, essentially by drawing out the full implications of one's positions. If successful, said Weber, "we can force the individual, or at least we can help him, to give himself an account of the ultimate meaning of his own conduct." What is decisive, concluded Weber toward the end of his life, "is the trained ability to look at the realities of life, to bear up under those realities and to be equal to them inwardly."[8]

For our classic authors, there is no alternative to the use of the scientific method in comparing and analyzing politics. Yet, all had a keen sense of the limits of science. The American Founders were not at all certain of carrying the day, and ratification indeed was bitterly contested in many states. In Number 1, Hamilton argued that "wise and good men" may be found "in the wrong as well as the right side of questions of the first magnitude to society." He knew that some people were beyond persuasion, perhaps because of perceived "jealousies and fears" or "ambition, avarice, personal animosity, party opposition. . . ."

Similarly, Durkheim was not at all confident that the buffeted Third Republic would survive. He feared the possibility of a return to Rightist authoritarianism or the advent of Leftist revolution, even though both were in his view "irrational." In the preface to the first edition of his *Rules of the Sociological Method* (1895) he asserted his belief in "scientific rationalism" and in "the future of reason"; but he viewed his age as one of "renascent mysticism." He did not know whether reason would emerge victorious over unreason. During the height of the Dreyfus Affair, in 1898, Durkheim spoke of the failure of the Republic to resolve social problems. "It was from this moment that one felt the growth in the country of this current of gloom and despondency, which became stronger with each day that passed, the ultimate result of which must inevitably be to break the spirit of those least able to resist."[9]

The same pessimism over the limits of reason periodically overcame Weber. "No science is absolutely free from presuppositions," he declared in his speech on "science as a vocation," and no science can prove its fundamental value to those who reject its presuppositions. Social scientists have no alternative other than to theorize, clarify, test those theories by reference to reality, try to probe and understand the consequences that flow from certain policies or acceptance of certain values. But, ultimately, it is up to individuals to choose, and forces other than reason will have their say. "I do not know how one might wish to decide 'scientifically' the value of French and German culture; for here, too, different gods struggle with one another, now and for all times to come. . . . Fate, and certainly not 'science,' holds sway over these gods and their struggles." And at the end of a life devoted to the relentless pursuit of truth, after living through Germany's defeat and then personally witnessing the creation of soviets in Heidelberg and Munich, he virtually abandoned hope. He feared the rise of dictatorship on both the Left and the Right, and of unreason. "Not summer's bloom lies ahead of us," he said, anticipating a fascist reaction to turmoil, "but rather a polar night of darkness and hardness."[10]

COMPARATIVE POLITICS TODAY

Most work in the field of comparative politics today, as represented in the selections that follow, falls somewhere between the two methodological models described above: testing hypotheses with reference to large numbers of cases, using statistics as a convenient way of managing complex factors; and describing single cases. Rarely do students of comparative politics use quantitative methods without first posing a political or analytic problem and examining some cases in depth. Rarely do they engage in description of a single case without reference to larger issues. In practice, most work in comparative politics partakes of both methods. There has to be a reason why researchers wish to examine a large number of political systems, and the reason usually is related to political problems in their own nations or cultures. For example, Max Weber undertook a vast study of the five world religions not because he wished to produce an encyclopedia, but rather to test his theory concerning the importance of Protestant sects in setting off or facilitating capitalist development. He could not rest until he examined other religious currents to see how and why they hindered or favored economic activity. This global analysis grew out of his original problem: why capitalism had a more authoritarian stamp in Germany, or to put it another way, why social forces supporting liberal democracy were weaker in Germany than in Northern Europe, Britain, and the United States. The unique cannot be explained without analysis of the universal.

To take another example, the search for correlations between economic development and democracy worldwide is usually a reflection of the concerns of scholars in the West over the fate of democracy in developing countries. Frequently, they undertake their studies in order to see what policies might be adopted by Western nations to foster democracy, in the belief that such a development benefits all peoples.

At the other end of the scale, study of single cases usually is undertaken by political scientists because of problems that are revealed through comparison. This is almost always the case when scholars examine a country other than their own; comparison is then at the very least implicit. Scholars try to understand how and why their own country and the one under study are either similar or different, and in so doing deepen knowledge of both. If I may be permitted a personal note, let me refer to some of my own work on French politics. In rough chronological order I have undertaken studies of the role of interest groups, major instances of decision making, the May Revolt of 1968, the transformation of the ideology of the Left in the 1970s, and the introduction of a measure of workers control in the 1980s. In each case empirical study was intended to clarify larger theoretical issues, for example, whether the strengthening of the executive under the Fifth Republic diminished the role of interest groups; whether the bureaucracy is the real and abiding power in the French policy-making process; why a revolt took place during a period of relative prosperity in an advanced society; how changes in ideology are indicators of underlying social trends; and whether masses of people are able to govern directly. Interaction between theory and practice is typical of work done on single cases by students of comparative politics.

Rigid adherence to either of the ideal-types (statistical analysis of a large number of cases or single case studies) is unproductive. To make our overriding goal the elaboration of formal theory (such as rational choice, culture, and structuralism) could lead to sterile scholasticism, just as "thick" description might lead to barefoot empiricism. All of the work in this volume falls between these two extremes. Comparison of large numbers of cases should be inspired by a theoretical problem that determines the method of selecting and analyzing data, and also leads to anomalies that require further explanation. Description of an individual case likewise should be inspired by theoretical problems. Both approaches are ways of identifying significant similarities and differences, and seeking to explain them. Diversity of approaches is a sign of creativity within the discipline, always provided that the generalizations and analyses shed light, directly or ultimately, on major issues and crises of our time.

ENDNOTES

1. Weber's talk was published in the proceedings of the *Congress of Arts and Sciences, Universal Exposition, St. Louis,* Boston and New York: Houghton Mifflin, 1905, vol. VII, pp. 725–745, and is reprinted in H. H. Gerth and C. Wright Mills, editors, *From Max Weber,* New York: Oxford University Press, 1946, pp. 363–385. Weber dealt with the political implications of this research in his inaugural address, "The Nation State and Economic Policy," when he assumed a chair of political economy at the University of Freiburg, Germany, in May 1895. It is reprinted in Peter Lassman and Ronald Speirs, editors, *Weber, Political Writings,* Cambridge University Press, 1994, pp. 1–28. For a convenient summary of the early studies, see Reinhard Bendix, *Max Weber: An Intellectual Portrait,* Garden City, NY: Anchor Books, 1962, pp. 13–48. Weber's early studies, observes Bendix, "contain in rudimentary form the basic concepts and central problems which occupied him for the rest of his life" (p. xxiii).
2. *From Max Weber, op. cit.,* p. 382.
3. *Ibid.,* p. 372.
4. *Weber, Political Writings, op. cit.,* p. 16; *From Max Weber, op. cit.,* p. 370.
5. Emile Durkheim, *De la Division du travail social,* Paris: Presses Universitaires de France, 1967, 8th edition, pp. xliii, xliv. All translations from this book are mine.

6. Cf. David Miller, editor, *Popper Selections,* Princeton, NJ: Princeton University Press, 1985, pp. 319–325 (excepts from the 1945 edition of *The Open Society and Its Enemies*).

7. *De la Division du travail social, op. cit.,* pp. 14–15.

8. Max Weber, "Science as a Vocation," *From Max Weber, op. cit.,* pp. 150–152; and "Politics as a Vocation," reprinted below. Full speech is reprinted (note differences in translation) in *From Max Weber, ibid.,* pp. 77–128, and *Weber, Political Writings, op. cit.,* pp. 309–369.

9. Anthony Giddens, editor, *Emile Durkheim, Selected Writings,* New York: Cambridge University Press, 1972, p. 150.

10. *From Max Weber, op. cit.,* pp. 128, 148.

HOW AND WHY COMPARE?

Roy C. Macridis played a (perhaps even *the*) leading role in the post-World War II rebirth of comparative politics as a discipline. In the essay written especially for an earlier edition of this book, the evolution of the discipline since World War II is encapsulated. His ringing critique of the traditional country-by-country approach (denounced as Eurocentric, parochial, and descriptive) resonated throughout the profession. But the great expectations of the new crusaders were not realized. The quest for testable hypotheses too often led to a sterile caricature of science, and results that frequently were trivial. The study of government seemed to be more of an art than a science. But there could be no return to mere description of individual political systems.

The next stage was to keep the comparative method focused on the state and politically relevant forces and attitudes. The goal was now "middle range theory," avoiding the pitfalls of rudderless empiricism and unexamined ideology. At the end of the day, Macridis returned to the classic Greek political theory he knew so well, urging that the comparative method be enlisted in the study, in Aristotelian terms, of the good life and justice. But the question remained: How can general concern over the human condition translate into researchable problems?

The comparative method was built into Roy Macridis's very being. As a child he, along with his Greek family, was compelled to leave Turkey as part of an enforced population transfer. He then immersed himself in Greek culture and politics even as he attended an American school. He began university studies in law and political science at the Sorbonne, which ended prematurely with the German occupation in 1940. Somehow he managed to join the exodus, pass through German lines, secure an American visa, and reach the United States. After serving in the American army during the war, he received his doctorate from Harvard, specializing in French politics, and made his career in the United States. As a citizen of three worlds, he was personally and passionately involved in his youth in a clash of cultures, ethnicities, and nationalisms; and in maturity in the clash of 20th century values (democracy, fascism, and communism).

The changing interests of students of comparative politics in the last half-century reflected Macridis's own personal and political odyssey. Traditional comparative politics was a country-by-country approach focused on Western Europe. The rise of both the United States and the Soviet Union as superpowers, and the subsequent emergence of dozens of new states in Africa and Asia, shifted interest away from Western Europe. Yet, Macridis could not be satisfied with testing of hypotheses and empirical studies that did not help him better understand the great conflicts of his time, and the countries that were part of his own makeup.

Macridis called for relevance and focus. But what is "relevant" and should be the "focus"? Should we concentrate on one system or area sharing a common heritage and values, or should we rather see particular systems as instances of larger political processes? Robert H. Bates calls for explanation of cross-cultural differences within the framework of general theories. Mark Blyth examines rational choice theory in relation to the role of ideas and political preferences. Robert D. Putnam stresses the importance of using the comparative method to "shed light" on the "big issues" of our time, which he then identifies. Do his issues differ from those in the "classics" of comparative politics dealt with earlier (*The Federalist,* John Stuart Mill's *A System of Logic,* Max Weber's study of rural capitalism in Germany, Emile Durkheim's *Division of Labor*)? Does Professor Putnam leave out any important issues? Are you willing to accept and work with his list? Deciding on the issues we wish to clarify and explore is the indispensable first step in using the comparative method. Otherwise, our study may be condemned to irrelevance. At the same time, the debate over methodology inevitably reflects larger philosophical and political concerns and orientations.

We are led back to the central question raised by Macridis at the outset: What can we learn through comparison that would not emerge from the study of political systems one-by-one? *How* compare, and *why*?

ROY C. MACRIDIS

1   The Search for Focus

The road to the development of a solid base of theoretical conceptualization continues to be long and uncertain. I shall trace the history of and trends in comparative politics, identify some of the major achievements, and indicate some of the continuing sources of discontent.

GENERAL OBSERVATION OF TRENDS

After the Second World War, dissatisfaction with the state of comparative politics was widespread.

Among the major shortcomings of the traditional approach:

1. It dealt primarily with a single-culture configuration, i.e., the Western world.

2. Within this cultural configuration, comparative study dealt mainly with representative democracies, until recently treating nondemocratic systems as aberrations from the democratic "norms."

SOURCE: This is an edited version of an essay written by Roy C. Macridis specifically for an earlier edition of this volume.

3. This approach prevented the student from dealing systematically not only with nondemocratic Western political systems, but also with colonial systems, and culturally distinct societies that superficially exhibit the characteristics of the representative process (e.g., India, Japan).

4. Research was founded on the study of isolated aspects of the governmental process within specific countries; hence it was comparative in name only.

The comparative study of politics was excessively formalistic in approach to political institutions.

1. It focused analysis on the formal institutions of government, to the detriment of a sophisticated awareness of the informal arrangements of society and of their role in the formation of decisions and the exercise of power.

2. In neglecting such informal arrangements, it proved to be relatively insensitive to the non-political determinants of political behavior and hence to the nonpolitical bases of governmental institutions.

3. Comparison was made in terms of the formal constitutional aspects of Western systems—that is, parliaments, chief executives, civil services, administrative law, and so on—which are not necessarily the most fruitful concepts for a truly comparative study.

The comparative study of politics was preponderantly descriptive rather than problem-solving, explanatory, or analytic in its method. Except for some studies of proportional representation, emergency legislation, and electoral systems, the field was insensitive to hypotheses and their verification. Even in the purely descriptive approach to political systems it was relatively insensitive to the methods of cultural anthropology, in which descriptions are fruitfully made in terms of general concepts or integrating hypotheses. Thus, description in comparative government did not readily lend itself to the testing of hypotheses, to the compilation of significant data regarding a single political phenomenon—or a class

of such phenomena—in a large number of societies. Description without systematic orientation obstructed the discovery of hypotheses regarding uniformities in political behavior and prevented the formulation, on a comparative basis, of a theory of political dynamics (i.e., change, revolution, conditions of stability.)

How was one to counter these trends and develop a more sophisticated approach to comparative study? The prescription appeared simple at the time.

1. Comparison involves abstraction, and concrete situations or processes can never be compared as such. Every phenomenon is unique; every manifestation is unique; every process, every nation, like every individual, is in a sense unique. To compare them means to select certain types or concepts, and in so doing we have to "distort" the unique and the concrete.

2. Prior to any comparison it is necessary not only to establish categories and concepts but also to determine criteria of relevance of the particular components of a social and political situation to the problem under analysis (i.e., relevance of social stratification to the family system, or of sunspots to political instability).

3. It is necessary to establish criteria for the adequate representation of the particular components that enter into a general analysis or into the analysis of a problem.

4. It is necessary in attempting to develop a theory of politics to formulate hypotheses emerging either from the context of a conceptual scheme or from the formulation of a problem.

5. The formulation of hypothetical relations and their investigation against tested data can never lead to proof. A hypothesis or a series of hypothetical relations would be considered proven (i.e., verified) only as long as it withstands falsification.

6. Hypothetical series rather than single hypotheses should be formulated. In each case the connecting link between general hypothetical series

and the particular social relations should be provided by the specification of conditions under which any or all the possibilities enumerated in this series are expected to take place.

7. Comparative study, even if it falls short of providing a general theory of politics, can pave the way to the gradual and cumulative development of theory by (1) enriching our imaginative ability to formulate hypotheses, in the same sense that any "outsidedness" enhances our ability to understand a social system; (2) providing a means for the testing of hypotheses; and (3) making us aware that something we have taken for granted requires explanation.

8. Finally, one of the greatest dangers in hypothesizing in connection with comparative study is the projection of possible relationships ad infinitum. This can be avoided by the orderly collection of data prior to hypothesizing. Such collection may in itself lead us to the recognition of irrelevant relations (climate and the electoral system, language and industrial technology, etc.). Such a recognition in itself makes for a more manageable study of data. *Hence importance is attached to the development of some rough classificatory scheme prior to the formulation of hypotheses*

In summary, then, the major criticism of the traditional approach to the study of comparative politics was that it is centered upon the description of the formally established institutions of government—that it was in general singularly insensitive both to informal factors and processes (such as the various interest groups, the wielders of social and economic power, and at times even of political power operating outside of the formal governmental institutions) and to the more complex contextual forces that can be found in the ideological patterns and the social organization of the system. It lacked a systematic approach.

The very word "system" causes a number of people to raise their eyebrows. It has connotations of group research that suggest the suppression of the imagination and sensitivity of the observer for the sake of conceptually determined and rigidly adhered to categories. This is far from being the case, however. A systematic approach simply involves the development of categories for the compilation of data and the identification of interrelationships within the data so compiled in the form of theories—that is, the suggestion of variable relationships.

The development of common categories establishes criteria of relevance. Once such categories are suggested, their relevance for the compilation of data should be determined through the study of problems in as many political systems as possible. For instance, if it is shown that the composition or recruitment of the elite in certain political systems accounts for the degree to which the system is susceptible to change, which in turn may lead us to certain general suppositions about political stability, then a systematic approach would require the examination of the same phenomenon in a number of political systems in the light of the same general categories. Although the traditional approach did not claim to be explanatory, a systematic approach claimed to be precisely this, for explanation simply means verification of hypothetical propositions. In the field of politics, given the lack of experimentation, only the testing of a hypothesis in as many systems as possible will provide us a moderate degree of assurance that we have an explanation.[1]

These general observations on the state of comparative politics appear in retrospect both modest and wistful: To develop a framework for comparison and to abandon the "country-by-country" approach in favor of either comparisons of problems, processes, and institutions or the comparative testing of hypotheses was not too much to ask. Nor was it too demanding to ask for a theory—virtually any theory—that spells out significant interrelationships in terms of crucial political phenomena that could be studied, compared, and evaluated. Nor was it extravagant to ask that the horizon of comparison in effect be broadened to include non-European countries. Finally, the hope that institutions—political institutions—would be studied in the context of the socioeconomic and ideological forces within which they operated was more than legitimate.

In general, the field of comparative politics has shown remarkable progress in at least two ways: We look upon politics in one or more countries with far greater sophistication than in the past, and we approach it with a set of general concepts, even if they are not always agreed upon. We are no longer satisfied with institutional studies—either descriptive or legalistic—or with the study of constitutional provisions and the formal distribution of power they set up. We probe deeper into the political elite, the socioeconomic and ideological contextual forces within which they operate, political parties and interest groups, communication mechanisms between leaders and led, and the impact of economic and social change upon political participation and behavior. We search for the fundamentals, so to speak, of a political system: stability, legitimacy, authority (or, conversely, for the reasons for instability), nonperformance, and revolutions. This is no mean accomplishment.

But there is no common theory, no generally accepted or acceptable proposition for further research, and no cumulative effort in the form of data collection, data sorting, and hypothesizing. There is no common body of theory and knowledge to which the student of comparative politics can be directed.

For a theory to be useful, a number of requirements must be fulfilled. The theory should be both comprehensive and parsimonious; it should be geared to the proper level of generality and abstraction to include the essentials for political analysis; it should be capable of generating hypotheses (fundamental "if-then" propositions that can be investigated empirically); it should allow the investigators enough freedom to choose from among the empirical data the particular phenomena and structures that relate to the general concepts embedded in the theory; and it should not prescribe one and only one research procedure but rather make it possible to use the procedure that is most likely to be feasible under the existing field situations. If, for instance, survey research is the *only procedure* prescribed, then it is obvious that only those countries where surveys are possible can be included; all others will have to be excluded.

To view the science of politics as the discovery of fixed laws may be a contradiction in terms. There can be no such laws where the element of human will and purpose predominates. Even if laws could be discovered, our discipline would be primarily concerned with an effort to explain why they are not obeyed—why the laws are really nonlaws. The study of nature began by investigating empirical phenomena in order to understand, explain, and control them. The ultimate goal of the natural sciences has been to control nature. The higher the level of generalization that subsumes a number of measurable relationships, the higher the potentiality for control. It is the other way around with politics. The study of politics explicitly divorces knowledge from action and understanding from control. The laws that some constantly seek will tell us little about our political problems and what to do about them. Our concern becomes scholastic. The ultimate irony is that not even in the natural sciences are theories considered laws; they are rather trials, tentative hypotheses tried out to see whether they work.[7]

We therefore suggest that we reconcile ourselves to the fact that although we can have an understanding of some political phenomena—a history of politics and political movements, an understanding of the functioning of governmental forms and structures, a concern and indeed a focus on such major concepts as power, decision making, interest, organization, control, political norms and beliefs, obedience, equality, development, consensus, performance, and the like—we do not and cannot discover laws. We may manage to arrive at some inductive generalizations based upon fragmentary empirical evidence. An inductive generalization is at best a statement about behavior. It can be derived from identical action and interaction under generally similar conditions over a long period of time in as many different contexts as possible. The behavior is not explained, but the weight of evidence allows us to anticipate and often predict it. A series of solidly supported inductive generalizations may in the last analysis be the most fruitful way to move gradually to a scientific approach, as it provides us with a rudimentary form of behavioral patterns.

Our knowledge of politics is then at most an understanding of our accumulated experience. It is in this area that comparative politics has an important role to play: By carefully identifying a given behavior or structure or movement and by attempting to study it in as many settings as possible and over as long a period of time as possible, we can provide generalizations backed by evidence.

If we limit the goals of our discipline to inductive generalizations about politics (that is, a well-ordered and catalogued table or listing of accumulated experience), then three imperatives for research emerge, providing focus and satisfying the need for pastimony. First, we must study the practitioners, the political leaders who hold office and, more generally, the governing elite that aspire to or possess political power. Second, we must study the structures and organizations and mechanisms through which the elite gain political power and exercise it (that is, the parties and other political associations). Third, we must be concerned with governmental institutions through which demands are channeled or, just as often, by which they are generated. These imperatives do not exhaust our immediate task, but rather give us a starting point.

In studying the governmental elite and the institutions through which they gain and exercise power, we ought to consider the art of government as a problem-solving and goal-oriented activity. This kind of activity characterizes any art. The task of government is to identify problems (or to anticipate them) and provide solutions. Our study then is to ask ourselves constantly: How well is the art performed? Who within the government listens, who foresees, who advises and suggests policy? What are the skills of the practitioners, and what are their objective capabilities? Finally, what is the impact of a decision upon the problem or the predicament it was designed to alleviate or to remove? The practitioner is not strictly bound by determinants. Communal life suggests and often sets goals of performance and achievement that become more than normative goals. They become in a way the "operative goals" that give direction to political action. The governing elite play an independent role in seeking out the goals and in implementing them. In his book on planning Andrew Shonfield refers to the French planning as the result of an

"elitist conspiracy."[3] More often than not decision making is an elitist conspiracy, the study and assessment of which would be far more rewarding than the survey and elaboration of all the input factors or the nonpolitical determinants involved.

But in the last analysis government is an act of will that can shuffle and reshuffle many of the determinants. Government involves choice, and the parameters are often wider than we are inclined to think. Any government will begin by surveying the conditions that appear to indicate the limits of freedom and choice; a government must always ask "what it has." But any government must also be in a position to assess what it wills. To say this is not to return to metaphysical speculation about the "will" of the state or the government; it is simply to reintroduce as integral parts of our discipline the state's performance and choices and the institutions through which they are implemented.

RELEVANCE AND FOCUS: A SET OF PRIORITIES

First and above all, it is our obligation to study all those organized manifestations, attitudes, and movements that press directly for state action or oppose state action. No matter what terms we use—decision making, authoritative allocation of values, regulation, adjudication, enforcement—we are concerned with the same old thing: the state. What is it asked to do? And what is it that people in a community do not want to see it do? The demand for state action or the demand that a given action cease is the very guts of politics. No science of politics—or for that matter, no science—can be built upon concepts and theories that disregard or avoid empirical phenomena. Why do French farmers throw their peaches in the river and their beets on the highway? Why did American students leave their comfortable homes to demonstrate in the streets? Why have American workers patterned their political demands in one way, but French workers in another? Obviously, to control, to influence, or to oppose state action.

Thus, our second priority also relates to what we have called the state, resurrecting what may appear to many graduate students to be an ancient term.

We mean by it, of course, what we have always understood the term to mean, stripped of all its metaphysical trimmings. It means all the structures and organizations that make decisions and resolve conflicts with the expectation that their decisions will be obeyed—the civil service, the legislature, the executive, the judiciary, the host of public or semi-public corporations and organizations that are called upon to resolve differences and to make decisions. We include also the agencies whose function is to study facts, to deliberate about them, to identify areas of conflict, and to suggest policy decisions. What is important is to study the preparedness of the state to discern predicaments or problems. Potential problems can be theorized about. The actual political phenomenon, however, is the existing machinery through which problems are perceived—the agencies, the research, the flow of information, the manner in which individual values and constituency considerations enter into the minds of the men and women who work for the state—and it ultimately includes that happy or fatal moment when the state copes with, ignores, or is simply unable to perceive the problem. The state can also, while perceiving the problem, either alleviate the predicament or suggest solutions utterly unrelated to it.

It is this second priority—the study of the state and all state agencies; of their organizations and performance; of the scope of their decision making; of the attitudes of the men and women who perform within their structures the roles of informing, studying, consulting, and deciding; and of the major constituencies they serve—that has been so sadly neglected until very recently. Few are the studies that focus on the state as an agency of deliberation, problem identification, and problem solving. Few are the studies of the institutions of the state in the modern, developed systems. This is no accident at all. After the state was ostracized from the vocabulary of politics, we found it far more fashionable to study the systems in which there was no state—that is, the so-called developing, emerging, or new systems. The result was to eschew the urgent and nagging empirical situations in the modern and highly industrialized societies in which our fate is to be decided, in order to study political phenomena and especially political development in the societies in which there

was no state. No wonder Huntington began to despair of studying the process of development in any terms other than "institutionalization"—that is, the building of institutions with authority and legitimacy, such as the state and the party.[4]

The third priority is the study of political attitudes—the "civic culture," as Almond puts it, or what Beer calls "the structure of norms and beliefs"[5] and what others have very loosely called ideology. But whatever name we give to them, the phenomena to be studied must point directly to peoples' beliefs, norms, and orientations about the state (its authority, scope of action, legitimacy, sense of participation, and involvement). If we are to remain strictly within the confines of relevance we must narrow our scope to those manifestations and attitudes that directly link the personal, economic, or psychological phenomena with the political. The linkage between "micro" and "macro" so well developed by Almond in his *Civic Culture* in order to identify meaningful political orientations needs to be carried a step forward. This can be done only when we reintroduce the state and its agencies and link them directly to political orientations. Unless we take this step, we shall remain at the "micro" level. We shall not link attitudes to structures and forms, to decisions and policies. The substance of governmental decisions and performance will elude us.

Finally, the fourth priority—which in a real sense is no priority at all—relates to the study of what may be called the infrastructure of the political world: attitudes and ideas; social, economic, and cultural institutions; norms and values that are prevalent in any given society, national or international. There is no reason why we shouldn't study child rearing, the patterns of socialization, the degree of concentration of economic power, the identification of personality types and traits, family life patterns, small groups and private associations, religious attitudes, and so on. All of these, as we indicated, *may* have a relevance to politics. In a number of cases—and they are the ones that count—the relevance is only too clear. It suggests itself by the very nature of the empirical phenomenon we are studying. It links a given organized political manifestation with a contextual factor that may explain it. It would be difficult to understand the role of the French military prior to the *Dreyfus case* without knowing something about the education its members received in Jesuit schools.[6] But in this case we study education because we begin with the army as a political force operating within the government and the state. We go deeper into contextual factors in order to find an explanation for a manifest political phenomenon.

What we are trying to suggest by these priorities, then, is primarily a change of focus. Our concern is simply to pinpoint what is political. We begin with the political; we catch it, so to speak, in its most visible, open, and raw manifestation; we begin with the top of the iceberg before we go deep to search for its submerged base. We focus on the state and its agencies, on its types of action or inaction, and on all those organized manifestations that call for action or inaction on its part. We study the forms of decision making and analyze and evaluate its substance. We explore the reaction of groups, interests, and power elites within the system; we study in turn their reactions to state actions and their counterdemands as they are manifested through various media from political parties down to voting.

Therefore, the central focuses of politics, and of the study of comparative politics, are the governmental institutions and the political elite, their role, and their levels of performance and non-performance. Stating this in such blunt terms appears to be utterly naive. Should we return then to the descriptive study of governmental institutions? Far from it. What we are suggesting is a starting point and a focus of investigation. Any such investigation, we know today, will inevitably lead us, as it should, far and wide in search of the contextual factors (rather than determinants) within the framework of which a government operates and to which its action, its performance, and its policies may often be attributed. We shall have to probe the infrastructure, but without losing sight of either our focus or the relevant question with which we began our investigation.

What accounts for a well-organized civil service? What is the impact of large-scale organizations—parties, bureaucracy, and so on—upon the citizen? Under what conditions does public opinion exercise its influence on the government? What accounts for

political instability? Is an executive who is responsible to the people more restrained than one responsible to the legislature? How and under what conditions does representation degenerate into an expression of particular interests? Under what conditions do young people maintain political attitudes different from those of their parents, and at what point do they revolt? Under what conditions do ruling groups become responsive to popular demands?

We can multiply these questions, but they illustrate the point. None of them can lead to hard hypotheses and proof (or disproof). Some cannot be easily answered. But this is not too important unless we are to accept that only those questions that can lead to testing in the rigorous—and therefore impossible—meaning of the term have the freedom of the market. In fact, the questions we suggest lead to a comparative survey, both historical and contemporaneous, of some of the most crucial political phenomena: responsiveness, performance, change, development, and a host of others. Such a survey will inevitably produce inductive generalizations, perhaps in the manner of Machiavelli, but with far more sophisticated tools and greater access to data than was ever the case before. It will inevitably help us to qualify our questions and to reformulate them as hypotheses that will suggest other qualifications—new variables, if you wish—and lead to further investigation—testing, if you wish—and to the reformulation of the questions—the gradual development of theory, if you like.

RECENT CONTRIBUTIONS— "CLUSTERING"

The vitality of a discipline lies, let us repeat, in its capacity to project theories and concepts that help us familiarize ourselves with the outside world. Comparative politics is emerging as the most comprehensive and theoretical branch of political science. We do not use the term *familiarize* pejoratively. To familiarize means to identify and engage the facts in a dialogue that seeks explanations. To do so intelligently, however, one must know what questions to ask. Any dialogue must lead to intellectual processes whereby certain facts are discarded because they provide no answers while others are taken into account. In order to discard and to accept facts, one must have established certain "linkages" that make facts cluster together into patterns, so that sentences in the dialogue are meaningful. Like words, facts take on coherence and give at least a tentative answer to questions.

Nobody will deny that students of politics today are far more familiar with the empirical processes of politics than were students in the past. Familiarization has taken place in both horizontal and vertical teams. Horizontally, the world has indeed become our oyster. A mere perusal of articles on individual countries listed in the International Political Science Abstracts will show that the Eurocentric approach no longer prevails. We do not imply that with the world as our oyster, new pearls of wisdom have been found. We are simply pointing out that our laboratory for comparative study has been expanded as never before, so much so as to lead to some confusion and a pause.

Comparative politics has also been greatly enriched vertically: It has gained in depth. No other branch of political science has made so much effort to relate the state to society and to seek determinants of political phenomena in the larger socioeconomic matrix.

We mentioned some of the factors that led to the expansion of the vertical dimension of comparative politics. They include the general behavioral revolution (the development of general system theories and borrowing from sociological and psychological theory) and a broadening of comparative political analysis (relating institutions to social factors such as class, status, personality, groups, culture, socialization). Especially important has been the interest in modernization and its socioeconomic determinants or correlates. The dialogue has been refined. Institutions and their performance (or "outputs") are related to a multiplicity of inputs (perceptions, aspirations, outlooks, interests, claims). The enrichment of comparative politics literature has accounted, as noted, for an embarrassment of choices and perhaps a confusion of priorities.

At the scholarly level, the literature in comparative politics has led even the aficionados to distraction. There is a burgeoning subdivision of specializations—we call it clustering—not only by area or country as in the past, but by such subfields as developmentalism, public policy, neocorporatism, culturalism, institutionalism, and political economy. Most recent publications (1) compare political processes and a variety of political phenomena across a limited number of countries; (2) do so with regard to a coherent categorical concept—culture, interests, the elite, electoral processes, policy outputs, modernization, and so on; and (3) propose to given an explanation—that is, seek to identify the factors that account for a given political process or manifestation.

Clustering reflects a search for the development of middle-range theory capable of handling a limited number of variables applicable to a limited number of empirical situations. Typical topics include: the role of the military; the role of the military in modernization; the study of structures, including bureaucracy, in the formulation of social and public policy; the pervasive trend toward authoritarianism in developing nations; the impact of modernization on political stability and institution formation; the relationship between interests and the state in the making of public policy; electoral processes; the impact of international economic factors on public policy; and comparative assessment of policy outputs or performance of individual states.

In the last decade or so a number of clusters (often also referred to as "foci" or "islands") for comparative study have emerged. They have in common the development of middle-range theories that apply to limited phenomena or countries. One cluster is corporatism or, properly speaking, neocorporatism. It comprises the study of linkages between the state and its agencies with interest groups, including labor. The theories underlying it explore patterns of accommodation and decision making, regime stability or instability, and redistributive policies and outputs. A second cluster is comparative history, either the study within one country or among many countries at different periods of time (dyachronic) or the study of specific events (like revolutions or democratization) in the same period in many countries (synchronic).

A third cluster is the focus on international economy, which posits that domestic behavior is constrained by international economic considerations. Fourth, there has been a growing interest in regime transitions—from authoritarian to democratic and from military to civilian. Most of these studies focus on the relationship between the state (and various forms of statism) and the civil society, seeking in society both the obstacles to authoritarianism and the seeds of its own ultimate demise. Finally, there is a wholesale return to what may be called "cultural history," which seeks in the interstices of tradition and crystallized forms of behavior, whether in law or in parliamentary practices and constitutional arrangements, the explanation of differing patterns of behavior. This approach links up to a tradition expressed in the works of British political philosophers such as A. V. Dicey or Walter Bagehot.

In the last few years the state has returned to prominence as a critically important variable. Viewed in traditional literature in legalistic and at times transcendental terms, it was downgraded by behavioral political scientists, especially in the United States. The state was considered by behaviorists and by orthodox Marxists alike as an entity that is dependent upon the sum total of societal interests—whether groups or the dominant class—and that lacks autonomy and independence. Today both neomarxists and many political scientists see in the state an agency that enjoys autonomy and independence, that weight heavily in the initiation and making of policies, and that is capable of reacting against and even transforming the social forces that press upon it.

Although comparative politics in its various approaches purports to describe and explain differences and similarities in political behavior, the student should not lose sight of the fact that the study of politics is and must be the study, in Aristotelian terms, of the "good life," of justice. "Kingdoms without justice how like they are robber bands," exclaimed St. Augustine. Such "kingdoms" without justice continue to be so, and their number is not getting smaller! How do regimes stack up qualitatively in terms of the basic ingredients of justice–equality and freedom? Students of comparative politics should always be prepared to move from the instrumental and the behavioral to the normative.

ENDNOTES

1. For a fuller development, see Roy C. Macridis, *The Study of Comparative Government* (New York: Random House, 1955).
2. See: David Miller, editor, *Popper Selections* (Princeton University Press, 1985), p. 314.
3. Andrew Shonfield, *Modern Capitalism* (London: Oxford University Press, 1965).
4. Samuel P. Huntington, "Political Development and Political Decay," *World Politics* (April 1965) pp. 383–430. See also his *Political Order in Changing Societies* (New Haven: Yale University Press, 1968).
5. Gabriel Almond and Sidney Verba, *The Civic Culture* (Princeton: Princeton University Press, 1963), and Samuel H. Beer, ed., *Patterns of Government,* 3rd ed.
6. Note by the Editor: In 1894 Captain Alfred Dreyfus, a Jewish officer on the French general staff, accused of passing information to Germany, was convicted and imprisoned. Despite evidence that another officer was the traitor, Dreyfus was found guilty again in a retrial in 1899. He was subsequently pardoned and reinstated in the army. The "Affair" divided the country, pitting monarchists against supporters of the Republic, the Right against the Left. It revealed also the depth of anti-semitism in France, especially in the officer corps.

ROBERT H. BATES

2   Area Studies and the Discipline

When arguments become polarized, it often signals that divisions are falsely drawn. Such appears to be the case with this controversy. Why must one choose between area studies and the discipline? There are strong reasons for endorsing both. In this essay, I sketch the current debate and explore the ways in which local knowledge can and is being incorporated into general analytic frameworks. I conclude by stressing the work that lies ahead. In doing so, it should be stressed, I deal only with the political science. The dynamics in other disciplines, I have found, differ greatly from those within our own (Bates et al. 1993).

CARICATURING THE PRESENT DIVIDE

Within political science, area specialists are multidisciplinary by inclination and training. In addition to knowing the politics of a region or nation, they seek also to master its history, literature, and languages. They not only absorb the work of humanists but also that of other social scientists. Area specialists invoke the standard employed by the ethnographer: serious scholarship, they believe, must be based upon field research. The professional audience of area specialists consists of researchers from many disciplines, who have devoted their scholarly life to work on the region or nation.

Those who consider themselves "social scientists" seek to identify lawful regularities, which, by implication, must not be context-bound. Rather than seeking a deeper understanding of a particular area, social scientists strive to develop general theories and to identify, and test, hypotheses derived from them. Social scientists will attack with confidence

SOURCE: Robert H. Bates, "Area Studies and the Discipline: A Useful Controversy?," *PS, Political Science and Politics*, vol. 30, no. 2 (June 1997), pp. 166–169. © American Political Science Association. Reprinted with the permission of the Cambridge University Press, and the author. Article abridged by the Editor.

political data extracted from any region of the world. They will approach electoral data from South Africa in the same manner as that from the United States and eagerly address cross-national data sets, thereby manifesting their rejection of the presumption that political regularities are area-bound. Social scientists do not seek to master the literature on a region but rather to master the literature of a discipline. The professional audience of social scientists consists of other scholars from their discipline who share similar theoretical concerns—and who draw their data from a variety of regions of the world.

Like all caricatures, these depictions distort in order to highlight important elements of reality. The implications of this reality have profoundly unsettled our discipline.

Most immediately, the shift from area studies to "social scientific" approaches has influenced graduate training. Graduate students, whose resources of time and money are necessarily limited, increasingly shift from the study of a region to instruction in theory and methods. When confronted by a choice between a course in African history or one in econometrics, given their constraints, many now choose the latter. . . .

The result of these changes in heightened tension within the field, as the controversy resonates with divisions between scholars of different generations, locations within the university, and stages in their careers. . . .

REACTING TO THE NEW REALITIES

Many departments [of political science] were once characterized by a core of technocrats, many of whom specialized in the study of American politics, and a congery of others, many of whom studied foreign political systems. Students of American politics viewed themselves as social scientists; but the political system on which they concentrated, they came to realize, was singularly devoid of variation. Even comparisons across states within the greater federation failed to provide insight into differences, say, between presidential and parliamentary systems, much less between polities in market as opposed to centrally planned economies. A vocal minority within American politics had long dismissed students of comparative politics as "mere area specialists"; but the more sophisticated increasingly realized that their hard won, cumulative, scientific knowledge about politics in the United States was itself area-bound. There therefore arose *among Americanists* a demand for *comparative* political research, and some of the most theoretically ambitious among them sought to escape the confines imposed by the American political system.

On the one hand, this trend creates allies for comparativists who seek to resist retrenchment; their knowledge of political variation has acquired greater significance. On the other, this trend will promote a transformation in the comparative study of politics; it will force those who have a command of local knowledge to enter into dialogue with those who seek to understand how institutional variation affects political outcomes or who see particular political systems as specific realizations of broader political processes.

Pressures from outside the discipline amplify these changes; they emerge from trends that have affected political systems throughout the world. Following the recession of the 1980s, authoritarian governments fell, and the collapse of communism in Eastern Europe further contributed to the spread of democracy. This change underscored the broader relevance of the Americanists' research into elections, legislatures and political parties. The spread of market forces and the liberalization of economic systems highlighted the broader significance of research conducted on the advanced industrial democracies as well. The impact of economic conditions upon voting, the politics of central banking, the effect of openness upon partisan cleavages and political institutions: long studied in the Western democracies, these subjects have recently become important, and researchable, in the formerly socialist systems in the North and in the developing nations of the South. As students of comparative politics have addressed them, they have come increasingly to share intellectual orientations, and a sense of necessary skills and training, with their more "social scientific" colleagues in the discipline.

The attention given to King, Keohane, and Verba's *Designing Social Inquiry* (1994) provides a measure of the impact of these trends. It suggests the urgency with which students of comparative politics feel a need for guidance, as they have sought ways to move from the in-depth study of cases, typical of area studies, to sophisticated research designs, required for scientific inference.

....

DEEPER FUSION

The field is thus undergoing significant changes, and the increased stringency of funding strengthens these trends. Less visible, but highly significant, forces run just below the surface and these too will shape the final outcome. Insofar as they do so, they may well define a new synthesis. I refer to a synthesis not only between area studies and the discipline but also between context-specific knowledge and formal theory, as developed in the study of choice.

Area studies emphasizes the importance of cultural distinctions. Cultures are distinguished by their institutions. Game theoretic techniques, established for the study of economic and political organizations, provide a source of formal tools for investigating such institutions. They show how institutions shape individual choices and collective outcomes, and therefore provide a framework for exploring the origins of political difference.

Cultures are also distinguished by their histories and beliefs. The theory of decisions with imperfect information, newly prominent in political science, can be used to explore the manner in which such differences arise and matter. Individuals with similar expectations, it shows, come to diverge in their beliefs if exposed to different data; persons can be shaped by their histories. Even if exposed to the same data, decision theory suggests, persons will revise their beliefs in different ways, if they bring different likelihood functions to bear upon observations. The theory of decisions thus yields insight into the way in which history and world views shape individual choices and therefore collective outcomes. The theory thus provides a framework for exploring cross-cultural differences.

The relationship between "local knowledge" and rational choice theory can be illustrated by Elizabeth Colson's well-known research into the Plateau Tonga of Zambia (1974). The lives of the Tonga, she reports, resemble the Rousseauian myth, with people residing in peaceful communities, sharing their belongings, and legislating wisely in village assemblies. But, Colson reports, the surface harmony disguises deep fears: of the greed and envy of neighbors, of their wrath, and of their desire and capacity to harm. While the lives of the Plateau Tonga may resemble the accounts of Rousseau, their beliefs, she finds, are better captured in the writings of Hobbes. Colson resolves the paradoxical contrast between beliefs and behavior by arguing that it is the beliefs that support peaceful conduct: people scrupulously choose to act in ways that preserve the peace, she argues, for fear of the violence they would unleash should they impinge upon the interests of others.

Viewed in terms of game theory, Colson's argument represents a claim that behaving courteously constitutes an equilibrium strategy. The strategy is supported in equilibrium by beliefs as to the costs that would be incurred were people to stray from the equilibrium path. It would be easy to use the theory of games to specify the conditions under which the argument follows. More significantly, doing so would suggest additional insights into what must also necessarily be true for the argument to hold. Given that this is so, transforming the narrative into a rational choice account would generate additional testable implications (Freejohn 1991). Some of these implications might be non-obvious; when this is the case formalization inspires new insights as well. Others might be crashingly obvious. But even jejune propositions, if deduced from a theory, are significant; for when they are tested, it is the theory from which they derive that is put at risk. Embedding narrative accounts in theories thus increases the opportunities for testing; it therefore increases our ability to judge the adequacy of an explanation.

By the same token, theory must be complemented by contextual knowledge. Consider the problem faced by an observer who encounters a person who is inflicting damage upon another. If a family head, he may be refusing a request for bride wealth; if a faction leader, he may be withholding patronage; if a mayor, she may be bringing the forces of the law to bear upon a rival political. Such actions inflict harm. But, in interpreting their political importance, the observer will need to know: Do they represent initial defections? Or do they represent punishments for an earlier defection? Without knowledge of the history, the investigator cannot determine the *significance* of these behaviors. The first history suggests that they should be analyzed as a political rupture; the second, that they should be treated as a punishment phase of a game—a phase that may in fact constitute a prelude to reconciliation. In the absence of local knowledge, the actions remain observationally equivalent; nothing in the theory alone suggests their strategic significance and thus their implications for subsequent interactions. Just as in the parable related by Geertz, a "wink" differs from a "twitch," so too does strategic behavior thus require interpretation. To be analyzed correctly, such behavior needs to be addressed by theory that is informed by empirical observation (1973).

To the degree that rational choice theory comes to occupy a central position within the discipline, then, the conflict between area studies and the "social scientific" core of political science will be misplaced. The approach provides explanations for difference; it requires knowledge of the difference for the construction and testing of its accounts. It provides a framework which transforms ethnography and narratives into theory-driven claims, amenable to refutation, and it requires precisely targeted observations to establish the force of its arguments (Bares et al. forthcoming).

It is important to realize that the present debate has been energized by adjacent controversies. It echoes recent ideological struggles. The debate over area studies is often exacerbated by debates over the merits of the market, the state, or the impact of the West, with those who endorse area studies viewing those who use rational choice theory as being pro-market, anti-state, and given to applying historically contingent categories in a universalistic manner. And it resonates with earlier battles over the qualitative and quantitative, between numeracy and literacy, and between the humanities and the sciences. In other cultures, well educated people are expected to excel at both; strength in the one need not imply weakness in the other. But the division remains powerful within our own culture, particularly among academics, where it limits and impedes. It reinforces the foundations for the present debate between area studies and the discipline.

Not being hard-wired, the division between "the scientific" and "the humanistic" can be transcended. The issue is not whether to use the left side of the brain rather than the right. It is, rather, how to employ both. The combination of local knowledge and general modes of reasoning, of area studies and formal theory, represents a highly promising margin of our field. The blend will help to account for the power of forces that we know shape human behavior, in ways that we have hitherto been able to describe but not to explain. It is time to insist upon the pursuit of both rather than upon the necessity of choosing sides.

CONCLUSION

To pursue this agenda, departments will have to accommodate the special needs of graduate training in comparative politics. For not only will our students need to possess area skills, such as languages; they will also need training in the skills long expected of students in the American subfield: formal theory, statistics, and the mathematics to do both. Others will need to train in economics as well. . . .

How will we know when reconciliation has been achieved? One test will be the capacity of someone who has invested heavily in the knowledge of an area to respond to a dean, provost, or departmental chair who inquires: "What has the study of your area contributed to the broader discipline?" Each of us who specializes in the study of an area should be able to respond to this question. We will, I am afraid, increasingly have to do so.

ENDNOTE

This article draws heavily on Robert H. Bates, "Area Studies and Political Science: Rupture and Possible Synthesis," *Africa Today*, Volume 44, No. 2 (1997), special issue on "The Future of Regional Studies."

REFERENCES

Bates, Robert H., Jean O'Barr, and V. S. Mudimbe, 1993 *Africa and the Disciplines.* Chicago: University of Chicago Press.

Bates, Robert H., Avner Grief, Margaret Levi, Jean-Laurent Rosenthal, and Barry Weingast, Forthcoming. *Analytic Narratives.*

Colson, Elizabeth. 1974. *Tradition and Contract.* Chicago: Aldine.

Ferejohn, John. 1991. "Rationality and Interpretation," in *The Economic Approach to Politics,* ed. Kristen Renwick Monroe. New York: Harper Collins.

Geertz, Clifford. 1973. *Interpretation of Cultures.* New York: Basic Books.

King, Gary, Robert Keohane, and Sydney Verba, 1994. *Designing Social Inquiry.* Princeton: Princeton University Press.

MARK BLYTH

3   Interests and Ideas

During the 1990s, political science seemed to embrace one paradigm more than any other: rational choice theory. Indeed, by the end of the decade, some leading rational choice theorists argued that their perspective had effectively replaced most other theories. One scholar asserted that very few of the old nonrationalist perspectives would "have lasting influence," since "if the arguments turn out to be true, it will be because of their author's intuitions and luck" rather than good theory. Another argued that "area studies" could best serve as empirical data for the work of formal theorists.[1]

The point of this article is not to rebut expansive rational choice claims with equally expansive nonrationalist ones. To do so would merely add to the cacophony of opinions surrounding rational choice theory rather than tell us anything substantively interesting. Instead, I analyze the recent turn to ideas in comparative politics and international relations as a reaction to some inherent limits within rational choice scholarship, particularly its conception of change and its theory of interests.

The reasons for this ideational turn are multifarious, but two factors stand out. The first is a facilitating condition: *internal* changes in the social sciences are often precipitated by *external,* real-world events. Much of this may be "guilt by association" rather than direct linkage; but either way, a connection exists. For example, the actual failure of modernization *projects* in the 1960s certainly contributed to the perceived crisis of modernization *theory* during the 1970s.[2] Similarly, the failure of Keynesian *institutions* in the 1970s helped delegitimate Keynesian *ideas* in the 1980s. It is hardly surprising, then, that unexpected changes of the 1990s—a

peaceful end of the Cold War, resurgent interethnic conflict, the rise of international terrorism—called into question the hegemonic frameworks of the day.[3]

These frameworks—neorealism and neoliberal institutionalism in international relations, and rational choice institutionalism in comparative politics—were rightly or wrongly seen by some as having been overtaken by events.[4] Of course, other approaches were no better at predicting such changes. But being "actively hegemonic" during moments of change opened windows of opportunity for emergent challengers emphasizing the ideational rather than the rational or the material.[5]

A second and more theoretically consequential set of reasons for this shift to ideas has to do with the "biases" inherent in any theory: what a theory focuses upon and what it misses. In this case, rational choice's core concepts—equilibrium, transaction costs, path-dependence—focused on statics (why things did not change all that much). By the mid-1990s, this static bias had become more apparent, and its limits more contested. In response to these internal and external challenges, both rationalist and nonrationalist research began to focus more explicitly on explaining political change.

Reorienting research from the analysis of stasis to that of change required a search for new causal factors. Concepts such as ideas, identity, culture, and norms were rediscovered by both rationalist and nonrationalist scholars. However, this ideational turn proved to have very different consequences for the two camps. For rationalists, it was both brief and limiting, but it rescued and resuscitated nonrationalist research.

Given the foregoing, my objectives in this article are threefold. First, I analyze the theoretical problems that rational choice research encountered during the 1990s and discuss why some rationalist scholars began to seek solutions in ideas. Through this new lens, the notion of structurally determined self-interest—a major explanatory concept for all political scientists, but

SOURCE: Mark Blyth, "Structures Do Not Come with an Instruction Sheet: Interests, Ideas, and Progress in Political Science," *Perspectives on Politics*, vol. 1, no. 4 (December 2003), pp. 695–696, 699, 701–702. © American Political Science Association. Reprinted with permission of the Cambridge University Press. Article abridged by the Editor.

particularly for rationalists—became problematic. The shift in perspective thus undermined many of the features that made rational choice theory distinctive and powerful in the first place. Being more accustomed to rethinking how interests are formulated, nonrationalists were better able to develop a new, albeit diverse, body of theory. Second, I survey this variegated research in light of the analytic problems that gave rise to it, and discuss its advantages and disadvantages vis-à-vis rationalist and structuralist formulations. Third, I argue that this new wave of ideationalist scholarship not only marks an important contribution to theory in its own right, but also tells us something important about how the discipline of political science evolves. Genuine theoretical advances are achieved neither through declarations of hegemony nor through the blanket rejection of alternatives. They are made when the limits of one theory engender something new.

THE UNEXPECTED LIMITS OF RATIONALISM

MAKING STABILITY A PROBLEM

By the early 1990s, two of the main currents in comparative politics—historical and rational choice institutionalism—each ran into theoretical problems. While historical institutionalists had made great strides in understanding the sources of policy stasis and institutional stability, their theories had difficulty in accounting for change. So these scholars began turning to ideas.[6] Rationalists had a different challenge: they needed to more adequately explain stasis, for reasons internal to their models.

In line with their methodological individualist foundations, rationalists make agents' interests the basis of their theories. In short, what people want drives politics. To elevate such a claim beyond truism, rationalists add to their model assumptions about agents' preferences (the ordering of what people want) and behavior (some postulated function that agents maximize, such as "utility"). So far, so good. But as Mancur Olson informed us, left alone, self-interested maximizing agents will suffer endemic collective-action problems. And when one adds into

the mix uncertainty over the possible outcomes of actions (multiple equilibria), then the set of possible choices facing agents becomes too complex for stability to occur naturally. Indeterminacy, defection, and a lack of successful collective action seem to be the unavoidable outcomes of a rationalist world. Such a conclusion pointed to a complex problem for rational choice. Its theory derived from a model that focused on stasis but predicted indeterminacy; and while the real world was always changing, it did not appear to be nearly as much "in flux" as the theory would predict. Therefore, because of this internal theoretical problem, rational choice theorists invoked *institutions* to explain *stability*. Institutions were invoked as instruments that help agents realize their structurally given interests. They were the glue that made the social world stick.

It quickly became apparent, however, that this approach created a second-order difficulty. For if supplying institutions was itself a collective action problem, then it made little sense to appeal to institutions to provide stability, since institutions, like other public goods, would be undersupplied. Given this problem, rational choice theorists needed to search for another source of stability; hence, the turn to ideas. But rationalism's individualist ontology and its understanding of interest meant that the adoption of ideas threatened to open a Pandora's box of complications. . . . [The author's discussion of the work of Douglass North, Sheri Berman, Hilary Appel and Kathleen McMamara has been omitted.—ED.]

BEYOND NEOREALISM AND NEOLIBERALISM

Similar to what was under way in comparative politics at this time, real-world changes—specifically, the unexpected and peaceful end to the Cold War—opened the door to internal theoretical challenges already issued against the two dominant theories of IR in the late 1980s: neorealism and neoliberal institutionalism. While the end of the Cold War seemed to cast doubt upon the predictive capacity of neorealism, for neoliberal institutionalists the problem was different. Because their body of theory had the same conceptual framework as did the rational institutionalist school in comparative politics, it was argued that many of the issues that IR had to grapple with in the post–Cold War era (the growth of transnational actors and advocacy networks, the importance of international organizations, et cetera) only had so much to do with increasing transparency and information flows.

As a result, while rationalist scholarship still flourished, especially in the international political economy, it began to do so with new competitors, particularly those who grouped themselves under the rather heterogeneous rubric of constructivism. Norms, dentity, and culture—instead of ideas or ideologies—are the weapons of choice for constructivist theorists.[7] What unites them all is a desire to problematize interests as a basic category and move beyond rationalist explanations.

IDEAS AND (NATIONAL) INTERESTS

Peter Katzenstein's edited volume *The Culture of National Security* constitutes a major statement in this new tradition of scholarship. Rather than use ideas or ideologies as explanatory concepts, the authors in this book "adhere to the sociological use of such concepts as norms, identity, and culture . . . to characterize the social factors they are analyzing." The authors argue that the international environment's cultural specificity engenders different identities among states. Power becomes as much about culture as it is about structure. Therefore, since "material power and coercion often derive their causal power from culture," it makes little sense to take state interests as given. Instead, interests develop from states' identities, with materialism playing second fiddle to meaning. In such a world, norms are endowed with causal properties and are viewed as "collective expectations about the proper behavior for a given identity." Norms can have either constitutive effects that define who a state is—holder of the balance, lender of last resort—or regulative effects that define appropriate behavior given a specific identity. Putting it plainly, if all states are not the same, then who you are will say a lot about how you will probably act, irrespective of material capabilities. . . .

In international relations, constructivist scholars who use identity, norms, and culture as explanatory variables have similarly challenged many of the basic assumptions of rationalist theory. However, given their disparate conceptual arsenal, a question remains as to how these new concepts fit together. Do they add explanatory value, or do they simply label the same concepts with different words? I argue that these concepts—norms, identities, and culture—do in fact fit rather well together, but are nonetheless different in kind from the concepts deployed by comparativists.

In the work of such theorists, one can view culture, norms, and identities as operating on different levels of analysis. However, whereas traditional international relations theory tends to prioritize one level at the expense of others, in a constructivist framework the interaction across levels becomes all important. For example, if norms operate on the meso level of analysis, culture can be seen as its macro correlate. Culture can be conceptualized as being composed of multiple competing norms and identities that set the evaluative and cognitive standards of world politics as a whole. Evaluative standards of behavior are governed by the norms of the system, while cognitive standards are the rules by which actors are recognized as such. Thus, specific norms are a function of, and embedded in, particular cultures. Following this logic, state identity refers to the micro level of theory to the socially constructed interests of states defined by this wider normative (meso) and cultural (macro) context. Within this framework, scholars have developed a research agenda that offers a fundamentally different way of viewing world politics from that offered by rationalist accounts.[8]

These concepts are, however, not simply the international relations analogues of those developed by ideationalists in comparative politics, since the two sets of concepts refer to different worlds, both theoretically and empirically. But what they do share is striking: a focus on how agents' interests are specified and how nonmaterial factors constitute those interests. That these two bodies of scholarship appeared at the same time and voiced essentially similar concerns tells us something about how the discipline evolves—a point I now turn to in conclusion.

INTERESTS, IDEAS, AND PROGRESS IN POLITICAL SCIENCE

PLUS ÇA CHANGE, OR EVOLUTION, IN POLITICAL SCIENCE?

In this article, I have argued that, like the world around it, political science is undergoing another round of change. The dominant theory of our discipline, rational choice, built its justified reputation on being able to explain statics with concepts such as equilibrium, information, veto points, and path-dependence. Yet it did so with a theory that predicted a world where stability was hard to maintain. Indeed, some of the most successful applications of rational choice theory in political science were so impressive *because* they made the discipline think about how achieving stability was a problem. Olson explained why collective action does not happen easily, Robert Bates explained why Africa failed to develop, and Douglass North and Robert Thomas explained why growth is so difficult to achieve. All of these analyses, milestones though they are, focus on statics rather than dynamics. Change is not explained easily within such frameworks.

Yet events inside and outside the discipline in the past decade have made the search for adequate models of change all the more pressing; and in an effort to be responsive—while paradoxically addressing internal theoretical problems concerning stability—some rationalists turned to ideas. But the cost of doing this was to threaten the hard core of rational choice theory itself, given interests, thin rationality, prediction, and generalizability. In turning toward ideas to explain stability, rational choice began to encounter its own limits. That this is the case should not be a surprise, for something similar has occurred in political science before.

At the moment victory was declared in the behavioral revolution, real-world changes and internal theoretical developments together signaled the limits of the behavioralist framework. Its central concepts of positivism, pluralism, and modernization were called into question. Consequently, the field splintered into a variety of approaches, one of which was rational choice theory.[9] Analogous to what we saw at the end of the behavioral revolution, some of the most innovative works in contemporary political science are not being developed within what is arguably the mainstream disciplinary approach. They are instead constructed because of it and in opposition to it.

One area of growth lies in the turn to ideas by nonrationalist scholars. The fact that these works have appeared at a time when rational choice's claims are so hotly contested, and that they have done so in direct opposition to its basic tenets, is significant. It suggests that progress in political science is perhaps dialectic rather than paradigmatic. Without the very real and important advances that rational choice theory made, and therefore the problems it left unattended, new scholarship that seeks to advance beyond it could not have come into being. Whether or not such scholarship on ideas does in fact constitute an advance beyond rational choice theory is obviously contentious, but I have made a case here for why it does.

THE LIMITS OF IDEATIONAL EXPLANATIONS

Legitimate methodological concerns remain in this nonrationalist turn to ideas. Such scholarship does not come with the elegant tool kit that rational choice offers, and some scholars may be justifiably wary about trading in what they have for an uncertain future. Indeed, while the scholarship reviewed in this article is interesting precisely because it is willing to tackle the issues with which rational choice has problems, there is a price to be paid in generalizability, conceptual clarity, and rigor. However, stark opposition and all-or-nothing alternatives need not be the choice facing the discipline.

As the scholarship reviewed here demonstrates, ideas give content to preferences and thus make action explicable, but they need not be conceptualized in this way. Ideas can also be seen as power resources used by self-interested actors or as weapons in political struggles that help agents achieve their ends. Such an approach obviously is compatible with rational choice and is of great theoretical importance.[10] It would be a mistake, though, to limit ideas to such a role and to assign analytical priority to structurally given interests as a matter of course. The work of comparativists shows what would be lost to us in terms of explanatory power if we did limit ideas in this way, while IR constructivists demonstrate that the price paid for ignoring such factors may be to foreclose entire research agendas.

Nonetheless, rationalists may object that my analysis of the evolution of political science draws all-too-dark distinctions. After all, some rationalist scholars have attempted to apply "thick" notions of rationality to political problems that get at exactly the same issues as the approaches used by ideational theorists. But such a response is fundamentally unconvincing. Regarding thick rationalist approaches: the point of rational choice theory was to do away with the need to posit unobservables as causes, so bringing them back in merely expands the theory beyond its own epistemological limits and robs it of its distinctiveness. As Wendt points out, "[A] key assumption of the traditional rationalist model is that beliefs have no motivational force on their own; they merely describe the world."[11] While one can indeed treat ideas as instruments, they are also much more than that. Ideas are not simply surrogates for information, nor are they shortcuts to structures that are somehow lodged between the ears. Ideas are powerful because they are intersubjective. They constitute our interests. They do not simply alter our strategies, and they do not come with an instruction sheet.[12]

Critics of my approach may note that thick versions of rationality need not posit egoism as an assumption; altruism would do just as well, and rationality can be bounded as well as instrumental.[13] Yet such responses run into their own problems. Just as people are never always selfish, they are never always altruistic. The point, then, is to understand how and why different behaviors pertain, which unavoidably assumes that interests are something to be explained and not something with which to do the explaining. Positing alternative motivations a priori keeps the concept of a given self-interest intact by simply substituting one preference function for another, thereby making anything and everything consistent with a rationality assumption. But the works under

discussion here show both how productive it can be to do away with such an assumption and how limiting it is to maintain strict methodological individualist foundations.

Some may also argue that I overstate what rationalists in fact claim. In practice, no rationalists assert that models of strategic calculation based upon preexisting preferences *always* provide useful explanations of politics. Rather, most would argue that such models *sometimes* provide useful explanations of politics. This more moderate stance runs into the problem that Donald Green and Ian Shapiro, and Gerardo Munck, have called "segmented universalism," in which the restriction of a theory to particular domains "where it is sometimes useful" weakens its distinctive claims to superior generalizability and scope.[14] Moreover, if the point of a theory is to abstract from context, then such abstractions can offer no guide as to where the appropriate context for such a theory is.

This is not to say that models of strategic calculation based upon preexisting preferences never provide useful explanations of politics; they do. But surely it costs the discipline as a whole to specify one approach as intrinsically better than another before even asking what the research question is, especially when a priori domain specification is such a difficult task. Taking ideas seriously does not mean abandoning social science; it means accepting that the limits of one set of theories open up space for others to move forward and enrich the discipline.

I am not suggesting that we embrace a naive, "the best theory eventually wins out" notion of progress.[15] However, the field evolves when we discover the limits of what has gone before. Exploring those absences is path-dependent and uneven, not linear and progressive. All theories have their biases, and political science as a field may well swing from one theoretical support to another. It may not be linear progress, but I would suggest that progress is still being made.

Rational choice theory is far from finished. Reports of its death are surely both premature and exaggerated. However, its very success has created a situation where it again has to share the field with other approaches. That this is the case should not be a cause for concern. For if what happened after the behavioral revolution is anything to go by, running into intrinsic theoretical limits is nothing to fear, since this is exactly how political science moves forward. The literature on ideas, norms, identity, and culture has given theoretical voice to the limits of existing theories. Such a development should not be rejected, for it is only through a dialectic process that the field evolves.

REFERENCES

Appel, Hilary. 2000. The ideological determinants of liberal economic reform: The case of privatization. *World Politics* 52:4, 520–49.

Ashley, Richard K. 1986. The poverty of neorealism. In *Neorealism and Its Critics,* ed. Robert O. Keohane New York: Columbia University Press, 255–300.

Bates, Robert H. 1981. *Markets and States in Tropical Africa The Political Basis of Agricultural Policies.* Berkeley: University of California Press.

———. 1997. Area studies and the discipline: A useful controversy? *PS: Political Science and Politics* 30:2, 166–69.

Bates, Robert H., Rui J. de Figueiredo, Jr., and Barry R. Weingast. 1998. The politics of interpretation: Rationality, culture, and transition. *Politics and Society* 26:2, 221–56.

Berger, Thomas U. 1998. *Cultures of Antimilitarism: National Security in Germany and Japan.* Baltimore: Johns Hopkins University Press.

Berman, Sheri. 1998. *The Social Democratic Moment: Ideas and Politics in the Making of Interwar Europe.* Cambridge: Harvard University Press.

Blyth, Mark M. 1997. "Any more bright ideas?" The ideational turn of comparative political economy. *Comparative Politics* 29:2, 229–50.

———. 2002. *Great Transformations: Economic Ideas and Institutional Change in the Twentieth Century.* Cambridge: Cambridge University Press.

Blyth, Mark M., and Robin Varghese. 1999. The state of the discipline in American political science: Be careful what you wish for? *British Journal of Politics and International Relations* 1:3, 345–65.

Dahl, Robert A. 1961. The behavioral approach in political science: Epitaph for a monument to a successful protest. *American Political Science Review* 55:4, 763–72.

Davidson, Donald. 1980. *Essays on Actions and Events.* Oxford: Clarendon Press.

Denzau, Arthur T., and Douglass C. North. 1994. Shared mental models: Ideologies and institutions. *Kyklos* 47:1, 3–31.

Elster, Jon, ed. 1986. *Rational Choice.* New York: NYU Press.

Finnemore, Martha. 1996. *National Interests in International Society.* Ithaca: Cornell University Press.

Friedman, Jeffrey, ed. 1996, *The Rational Choice Controversy.* New Haven: Yale University Press.

Goldstein, Judith, and Robert O. Keohane, eds. 1993. *Ideas and Foreign Policy: Beliefs, Institutions, and Political Change.* Ithaca: Cornell University Press.

Green, Donald P., and Ian Shapiro. 1994. *Pathologies of Rational Choice Theory: A Critique of Applications in Political Science.* New Haven: Yale University Press.

Hall, Peter A. 1986. *Governing the Economy: The Politics of State Intervention in Britain and France.* Oxford: Oxford University Press.

———, ed. 1989. *The Political Power of Economic Ideas: Keynesianism Across Nations.* Princeton: Princeton University Press.

Hardin, Russell. 1982. *Collective Action.* Baltimore: Johns Hopkins University Press.

———. 1995. *One for All: The Logic of Group Conflict.* Princeton: Princeton University Press.

Katzenstein, Peter J. 1996. Introduction: Alternative perspectives on national security. In *The Culture of National Security: Norms and Identity in World Politics,* ed. Peter J. Katzenstein. New York: Columbia University Press, 1–32.

Kesselman, Mark. 1973. Order or movement? The literature of political development as ideology. *World Politics* 26:1, 139–54.

Knight, Jack, and Douglass C. North. 1997. Explaining economic change: The interplay between cognition and institutions. *Legal Theory* 3, 211–26.

Kratochwil, Friedrich V. 1989. *Rules, Norms, and Decisions: On the Conditions of Practical and Legal Reasoning in International Relations and Domestic Affairs.* Cambridge: Cambridge University Press.

———. 1993. The embarrassment of changes: Neo-realism as the science of Realpolitik without politics. *Review of International Studies* 19:1, 63–81.

Laffey, Mark, and Jutta Weldes. 1997. Beyond belief: Ideas and symbolic technologies in the study of international relations. *European Journal of International Relations* 3:2, 193–237.

Lieberman, Robert C. 2002. Ideas, institutions, and political order: Explaining political change. *American Political Science Review* 96:4, 697–712.

McNamara, Kathleen R. 1998. *The Currency of Ideas: Monetary Politics in the European Union.* Ithaca: Cornell University Press.

Mitchell, Timothy. 1991. The limits of the state: Beyond statist approaches and their critics. *American Political Science Review* 85:1, 77–96.

Munck, Gerardo L. 2001. Game theory and comparative politics: New perspectives and old concerns. *World Politics* 53:2, 173–204.

North, Douglass C. 1990. *Institutions, Institutional Change, and Economic Performance.* New York: Cambridge University Press.

North, Douglass C., and Robert Paul Thomas. 1973. *The Rise of the Western World: A New Economic History.* Cambridge: Cambridge University Press.

Olson, Mancur. 1971. *The Logic of Collective Action: Public Goods and the Theory of Groups.* Cambridge: Harvard University Press.

Oren, Ido. 2003. *Our Enemies and US: America's Rivalries and the Making of Political Science.* Ithaca: Cornell University Press.

Orren, Karen, and Stephen Skowronek. 1994. Beyond the iconography of order: Notes for a "new institutionalism." In *The Dynamics of American Politics: Approaches and Interpretations*, eds. Lawrence C. Dodd and Calvin Jillson. Boulder, Colo.: Westview Press, 311–330.

Ostrom, Elinor. 1990. *Governing the Commons: The Evolution of Institutions for Collective Action.* Cambridge: Cambridge University Press.

Wade, Robert. 1996. Japan, the World Bank, and the art of paradigm maintenance: The East Asian miracle in political perspective. *New Left Review* 217, 3–36.

Wendt, Alexander. 1999. *Social Theory of International Politics.* Cambridge: Cambridge University Press.

Wohlforth, William C. 1995. Realism and the end of the Cold War. *International Security* 19:3, 91–129.

NOTES

1. Bates 1997.
2. See Blyth and Varghese 1999; Kesselman 1973.
3. This is not to posit a "hubris of the present"—a belief that the world in the 1990s was more "in flux" than it was, for example, in the 1970s. Rather, dominant social scientific theories are always being buffeted by real-world changes, and the 1990s was no exception. See Oren 2003.
4. For one such criticism, see Kratochwil 1993. For a defense of these frameworks, see Wohlforth 1995.
5. As Robert Lieberman put it, "[W]ithout reference to the ideological nature of these transformations, the new world of the twenty-first century seems unfathomable and the pathways by which it arrived incomprehensible." Lieberman 2002, 697.
6. See North 1990. I focus primarily on North since his work is arguably the most theoretically advanced attempt to incorporate ideas into a rationalist framework. For other such attempts, see Goldstein and Keohane 1993; Denzau and North 1994; Knight and North 1997; Bates et al. 1998.
7. Constructivism is a broad church. There are at least three schools: a heterogeneous poststructuralist wing, a linguistic-structuralist wing that is Wittgensteinian or Habermasian in orientation, and a sociological wing that has a diverse lineage ranging from Giddens to Meade. For statements of each position, see Ashley 1986; Kratochwil 1989; Wendt 1999.
8. See, for example, Berger 1998; Finnemore 1996a.
9. See Dahl 1961.
10. See Wade 1996.
11. Wendt 1999, 117.
12. See Laffey and Weldes 1997.
13. The work of Russell Hardin has been particularly influential in this regard. See Hardin 1982; Hardin 1995.
14. Green and Shapiro 1994; Munck 2001, 181.
15. Nor should we ignore how, in the last decade, ideas external to the discipline—the supposed utility of unfettered markets, individual liberty, the "inevitability" of capitalism and democracy as social forms—fed back into disciplinary understandings of good and bad theory.

ROBERT D. PUTNAM

4 The Public Role of Political Science

What is the job of political science? In part, it is the pursuit of knowledge for its own sake. As is true of all intellectual endeavors, an important part of what draws us into the discipline is the sheer aesthetic pleasure of it—a novel insight into a familiar passage of Machiavelli, an elegant proof of a theorem about public choice, the dawning recognition of an unexpected pattern in survey data, the subtle appreciation of politics in a foreign culture. Every one of us has felt the excitement of successfully pursuing deep scholarship. As Picasso and Einstein and Elvis agreed in their imaginary encounter as Steve Martin's guests at the Lapin Agile, art and science share a fundamental reverence for elegance. Any intellectual field develops, at least in part, according to its own autonomous rhythms, untrammeled by utilitarian concerns, as each new (inevitably partial) truth opens unexpected vistas.

However, I wish to make a different point here, a more utilitarian argument about the purposes of political science. My argument is that an important and underappreciated part of our professional responsibility is to engage with our fellow citizens in deliberation about their political concerns, broadly defined. Political science must have a greater public presence.

This facet of our professional responsibilities—our contributions to public understanding and to the vitality of democracy—is not the only goal of political science, but it has been an important one since the founding of the discipline and the profession. . . .

To be sure, eloquent voices have frequently been raised in recent years in defense of the public responsibilities of the profession—Rogers Smith, Larry Diamond, Raymond Seidelman, and many

others.[1] However, in recent debates the strongest advocates of public purpose for our profession have also been the most severe critics of our scientific aspirations. They have argued passionately that a mistaken pursuit of rigor has undermined the relevance of our scholarship.

Conversely, the most powerful advocates of our scientific mission have been largely silent on our public purposes. I do not mean that our statisticians and behaviorists and formal theorists have entirely ignored public issues in their own work, but rather that they have not articulated the argument that attending to these issues is part of our professional duty. On the contrary, some of the smartest and most systematic of our colleagues have expressed deep skepticism that contribution to the public weal is a feasible or desirable aspiration for political science. . . .

Let me offer an example of how this attitude has stunted our contribution to public life. As is well known, for most of the last four decades more and more of our fellow citizens have expressed distrust in the fidelity and operations of government in America.[2] Since government is our business, one might have thought that this public alienation would have occasioned a great debate within the profession about how to respond. But if you had thought that, you would have been wrong.

As a profession, we traced the trend but largely dismissed it as a mere curiosity. We explained, first, that our fellow citizens were simply wrong—that malfeasance in high places had declined, not increased. We added that since trust in government seemed uncorrelated with any of the other variables that we typically survey it was essentially statistical noise. And even when we admitted that this public unease might be a settled judgment, we dismissed, the idea that we had any professional ability—much less any professional obligation—to respond. None of the reforms proposed by non–political scientists would work, we condescendingly explained. Finally and most devastatingly, we took it as our job

SOURCE: Robert D. Putnam, "The Public Role of Political Science," *Perspectives on Politics*, vol. 1, no. 2 (June 2003), pp. 249–255. © American Political Science Association. Reprinted with permission of the Cambridge University Press. This essay is a slightly expanded version of Professor Putnam's presidential address at the 2002 APSA annual meeting. Article abridged by the Editor.

to show why any really promising reform could never be enacted and implemented. We warned of unanticipated consequences ("It could be worse," we said). Our advice to our fellow citizens who expressed growing unease about politics and government: "Cool it."

As Thomas Mann notes in an article on campaign finance reform, we "fancied ourselves an intellectual truth squad, endowed by our training and research to cut through the cant in the public debate, exposing specious claims and ill-advised reform proposals."[3] We became the profession of the three *nos*: no problem no solution, no reform.

I do not deny for a moment that "intellectual truth squad" is a valuable role. Cant needs exposing. I genuinely admire the work of our distinguished colleagues who have performed that role. However, we also have other obligations as a profession. If the role of debunker is the only one we play on issues of concern to wide swaths of our fellow citizens, then we are in the position of a cancer researcher who counsels a worried patient that nothing can be done. The advice might be clinically accurate, but it is in a deeper sense unresponsive. Finding better answers is the whole point of medical research—and although the analogy is imperfect, finding better answers should be a more important part of what political scientists do.

In short, I believe that attending to the concerns of our fellow citizens is not just an optional add-on for the profession of political science, but an obligation as fundamental as our pursuit of scientific truth. And yet unlike others who have recently argued a similar point of view, I do not believe that ignoring and even ridiculing quantitative and mathematical rigor is the right path forward.

It matters, both ethically and practically, whether democratic regimes are more peaceable than are nondemocratic ones, but it is impossible to adjudicate that claim without counting. It matters whether (and how) congressional oversight restrains bureaucratic misbehavior, but it is impossible to parse that issue fully without careful logic and systematic evidence. Trends in social and political inequality are of the highest moral and practical urgency, but quantitative methods are essential to measuring inequality. Rigorous formal analysis is

essential to designing institutional frameworks for resolving ethnic conflict.

If you listened to the debate in the discipline over the last several years, you might reasonably conclude that political scientists need to choose between scientific rigor and public relevance. Note the title of Rogers Smith's essay that I have already cited approvingly: "Should We Make Political Science More of a Science or More about Politics?" I believe that the *or* in that question presumes a false dichotomy. Advocacy of relevance cannot be left to the critics of rigor, just as advocacy of rigor should not be the monopoly of skeptics of relevance.

The idea that political science can be either rigorous or relevant, but not both, is analogous (though not identical) to the fallacy that Donald E. Stokes explored in his book *Pasteur's Quadrant*—namely, the mistaken idea that research must be either "basic" (that is, aimed at fundamental understanding) or "applied" (that is, aimed at practical utility). Stokes showed that, in fact, much research (including the biochemical research of the eponymous French scientist) aims simultaneously at basic understanding and practical utility. Research on global warming has produced advances in basic understanding of atmospheric chemistry, and John Maynard Keynes's contributions to economic theory arose in response to the Great Depression.[4] Often the best science is done while pursuing the most urgent public problems. . . .

It would, I fear, sidetrack us to pause here for an extended discussion of what "science" means in political science. My use is both catholic and conventional: theoretically framed, empirically rigorous (replicable) generalizations—in short, "portable, testable knowledge." . . .

What contributions do we have to make? Now as in the past, political scientists contribute to public life in varied ways:

First, we influence public policy by personal involvement. That involvement may be in elective office (as illustrated by the career of our colleague Congressman David Price) or senior positions in the executive branch, either locally (as our colleague Doug Rae did in his service as city manager of New Haven, Connecticut) or nationally (as our colleague Condoleezza Rice is now doing as national security adviser). Many of us, I conjecture, are active in various social movements—locally, nationally, and internationally. More often, we offer expertise on issues as diverse as electoral redistricting, welfare reform, and democratization, although in this domain our efforts are dwarfed by those of our colleagues in other social sciences, especially economics.

Second, we train undergraduate, graduate, and mid-career students who then participate in public life in the United States or, abroad. . . .

Third, we produce scholarship that is relevant to public issues (in recent years, this has been the most underexploited avenue). In some cases the implications of our scholarship may be immediately relevant to ongoing debates within the polity—campaign finance is one recent example, as Thomas Mann has shown, but other colleagues have undertaken similar work on topics as diverse as health care, military strategy, and the pursuit of human rights. Nor is this sort of contribution limited to "policy analysis" in a narrow sense. For example, as America grapples with the continuing risks or facts of war in the Middle East and South Asia, political scientists with expertise on the history and politics of the region—able to provide careful, insightful "thick description"—can make a crucial contribution to enlightened public debate, quite apart from whatever policy recommendations they themselves offer.

However, the most important contribution that political scientists might make to public life consists not in answering questions currently being asked, but in framing new questions. Our role here is to highlight ignored values, to identify important but underappreciated factors that affect those values, and to explicate the underlying logic that links facts and values. As Carol Weiss has observed,

> The social sciences. . . bring fresh perspectives into the policy arena, new understandings of cause and effect; they challenge assumptions that had been taken for granted and give credibility to options that were viewed as beyond the pale. They provide enlightenment. . . . Although good data are useful and build credibility,

equally important is the [social science] perspective on entities, processes, and events. Participants in the policy process can profit from an understanding of the forces and currents that shape events, and from the structures of meaning that [social scientists] derive from their theories and research.[5]

Because our discipline, more than any other social science, gives a place of honor to explicit, reasoned debate about normative issues, we have an unusual potential to frame issues that inevitably straddle the fact–value boundary. To do publicly engaged political science, we have to be prepared to be boundary-crossers in this sense. Our values powerfully influence what we choose to study, as well as our policy recommendations, and in that sense our work is intrinsically value-laden. On the other hand, our investigation of the facts can and should be governed by objective rules. In that sense, I agree with Max Weber's view, as synthesized in a fine recent essay by Steve Hoenisch: "Science and politics are, for Weber, not mutually exclusive; rather, they are mutually inclusive."

In order to foster the kind of political science I am advocating, we need to make a special effort, both in the research we publish and in the courses we teach, to combine careful attention to facts and careful attention to values, while recognizing the difference between the two. I am skeptical about a value-free social science and about a fact-free philosophical critique. Investigation of the facts is not sufficient to resolve social issues, but it is necessary. Those of us who seek to frame major public issues need to be equally respectful of demands for normative and empirical rigor. To my more scientific colleagues, I urge (paraphrasing, I believe, the statistician John Tukey), "Better an approximate answer to an important question than an exact answer to a trivial question," while to my less scientific colleagues, I urge, "More precise is better." . . .

A more difficult boundary-crossing is between theory and practice, between the congenial ivy-covered tower and the hurly-burly of the public square. An engaged political science must talk with our fellow citizens, not just at them. Rather than the European intellectual, a "gadfly" (in the language of Rogers Smith) standing apart from current politics and viewing with a critical, philosophical eye the gap between what is and what ought to be, my hero is the midwestern progressive of a century ago, seeking to learn from the experience of nonacademic reformers. My image of a more engaged political science is neither a wise counselor whispering truth to power nor a distanced gadfly. It is a political scientist engaged in genuine dialogue with our fellow citizens, learning as well as teaching. . . .

And we should be modest about what we have to offer in public life. My claim is not that as philosopher-kings we have indispensable knowledge, but that we can be helpful in framing problems, elucidating values, and adducing facts. I prefer Charles Beard's metaphor: political science doesn't really solve public problems, but we can "shed light" on them. And we have a professional obligation to do so.

So far I've made a case in theoretical terms, but not in terms of examples. Political science can contribute professional insights and evidence to many public discussions. Indeed, many were illustrated at the 2002 APSA convention.

- The role of religion in politics; the rise of Islamic fundamentalism and its implications for world order.

- The challenges that ethnic cleavages, which are clearly not fading with modernization, pose to democratization.

- The growing role of wealth in American politics, the implications for political equality, and what might be done to address that issue.

- The normative and historical complexities of reconciling civil liberties and national security.

Beyond these illustrations, I want briefly to cite three specific cases that seem to me especially ripe for our professional attention.

First, what is the role of political science in helping to frame a sensible debate about globalization and perhaps in helping to craft new institutions for a globalizing world? The United States has a degree of power in the world today that is probably historically unprecedented, a dominion that exceeds that of Great Britain at its peak and perhaps Rome at its peak. How should we use this moment? Political scientists should be even more present in that debate. . . .

Second, what should be the role of political science in helping to frame and diagnose issues of social justice? The most important contemporary example in this domain, I believe, comes from the simultaneous increase in the United States (and some other advanced nations) of ethnic diversity and social and economic inequality. Recent research suggests as stylized facts that equality, homogeneity, and community (social capital) are strongly correlated, both across space and across time. American society has witnessed rapid declines in all three domains during the last several decades.

The most certain prediction about all advanced societies, from New Zealand to Finland, is that ethnic diversity will grow in the years ahead. In itself, that is basically a healthy trend. Yet social justice demands that we reverse the decline in equality, and social health demands that we reverse the decline in social capital. Perhaps the most fundamental problem facing America, and most other advanced democracies, over the next several decades will be to reconcile the demands of diversity, equality, and community. This is a quintessential *big issue*, needing contributions from many disciplines, from theoreticians and empiricists and practitioners. If my argument here is correct, then political scientists have a professional responsibility to contribute to the nascent debate.

Third, what is the role of political science in helping to frame and remedy civic disengagement? Five years ago, there was still a lively and necessary debate about the facts. (Has there been disengagement or not?) As a party to that debate, I am not entirely objective, but I believe that it has been largely settled both in the academy and beyond. We now widely agree that involvement by Americans in political life has declined over the last three decades, that much of that decline is concentrated among youth, and that this development is unhealthy both individually and collectively. The same trend, at least in broad outline, appears in other advanced democracies, and we can learn from their attempts to grapple with the problem, but for American political scientists, our first obligation is to attend to the problem here at home.

If that is so, we need to work simultaneously at both the institutional and the individual level—that is, we must consider political and social reforms that invite and facilitate greater citizen engagement, and we must consider how to enhance the civic skills and interests of young people. . . .

While the balance between activism and scientism within our profession has varied over the last century, the right image for this, as for our intellectual development more generally, is not a pendulum but a spiral, which never returns to exactly the same point. In the middle years of the last century, formal institutional analysis was succeeded by the so-called behavioral revolution, which was then succeeded by a *new* institutionalism, far from identical to the older institutionalism and incorporating many advances of the intervening years. So too I hope that as we return to a phase of more active engagement with the public world, we will do so informed by the contributions of our more recent, scientific phase. I seek a more problem-driven political science—not instead of our more recent method-driven political science, but alongside it, relying on, not rejecting, the valuable analytic tools that we have fashioned. . . .

On American empire, diversity and inequality, civic engagement, and many more issues, we have a professional obligation to engage in dialogue with our fellow citizens. Within the profession, we need a vigorous dialogue in which advocates of a critical, reformist political science take seriously the work of our self-consciously scientific colleagues, not merely as the activities of a foreign tribe contending for the same disciplinary turf. And similarly, those of us who are more comfortable with counting and modeling should take more seriously our public obligations. None of this will be easy. As Max Weber said when contemplating precisely the same issue in an equally confusing, epoch-making period more than eight decades ago, "[P]olitics is a strong and slow boring of hard boards."[6] It is our highest calling.

REFERENCES

Beard, Charles A. 1993. Politics. In *Discipline and History: Political Science in the United States,* eds. James Farr and Raymond Seidelman. Ann Arbor: University of Michigan Press, 113–127.

Diamond, Larry. 2002. What political science owes the world. *PS: Online.* Available at 209.235.241.4/PS/post911/diamond.cfm.

Hoenisch, Steve. n.d. Max Weber's view of objectivity in social science. Available at www.criticism.com/md/weber1.html.

Mann, Thomas. 2003. Linking knowledge and action: Political science and campaign finance reform. *Perspectives on Politics* 1:1, 69–83.

Pharr, Susan J., and Robert D. Putnam, eds. 2000. *Disaffected Democracies: What's Troubling the Trilateral Countries?* Princeton: Princeton University Press.

Putnam, Robert D. 2000. *Bowling Alone: The Collapse and Revival of American Community.* New York: Simon and Schuster.

Ross, Dorothy. 1993. The development of the social sciences. In *Discipline and History: Political Science in the United States,* eds. James Farr and Raymond Seidelman. Ann Arbor: University of Michigan Press, 81–104.

Seidelman, Raymond, with Edward J. Harpham. 1985. *Disenchanted Realists: Political Science and the American Crisis, 1884–1984.* Albany: SUNY Press.

Smith, Rogers M. 2002. Should we make political science more of a science or more about politics? *PS: Political Science and Politics* 35:2, 199–201.

Stokes, Donald E. 1997. *Pasteur's Quadrant: Basic Science and Technological Innovation.* Washington, D.C.: Brookings Institution Press.

Weber, Max. 1946. Politics as a vocation. In *From Max Weber: Essays in Sociology,* eds. Hans H. Gerth and C. Wright Mills. New York: Oxford University Press, 77–128.

Weiss, Carol H. 1993. The interaction of the sociological agenda and public policy. In *Sociology and the Public Agenda,* ed. William Julius Wilson. Newbury Park, Calif.: Sage Publications, 23–39.

Wilson, William Julius, 2002. Expanding the domain of policy-relevant scholarship in the social sciences. Lecture at the Institute for the Study of Social Change, University College, Dublin, Ireland, 7 October.

ENDNOTES

1. Smith 2002; Diamond 2002; Seidelman 1985.
2. This growing political alienation is not limited to the United States. See Pharr and Putnam 2000.
3. Mann 2003, 72–3.
4. Stokes 1997.
5. Weiss 1993, 28, 37, as cited in Wilson 2002. Weiss refers specifically to sociology; but her point applies to the other social sciences as well.
6. Weber 1946, 128.

PART ONE

Political Change and the State

The classic theorists of comparative politics (notably, Emile Durkheim and Max Weber, discussed in the Introduction) sought to understand how political systems have changed, particularly before and after industrialization, and the causes and consequences of these transformations. A theory of political change, more specifically the evolution of societies from the simple to the complex (as Durkheim viewed it) or from traditional to rational-legal rule (in Weber's terms) has been and remains the single most important framework for the analysis and comparison of nations.

TRADITIONAL AND MODERN SOCIETIES

Drawing upon the work of Durkheim and Weber, it is useful for analytic purposes to distinguish between two "ideal types" or models of societies: the *traditional* and the *modern*. These terms do not imply any value judgment. A traditional society may include a large number of highly educated people whose level of culture and social grace is higher than that of the mass of inhabitants of any modern society. Furthermore, these terms refer only to abstract "constructs"; they do not describe any existing societies. For example, the nations of Western Europe and North America are predominantly modern societies, but contain many traditionally oriented groups in their population. Weber suggested that claims to legitimacy may be based on

1. Rational grounds—resting on a belief in the "legality" of patterns of normative rules and the right of those elevated to authority under such rules to issue commands (legal authority);

2. Traditional grounds—resting on an established belief in the sanctity of immemorial traditions and the legitimacy of the status of those exercising authority under them (traditional authority); or finally,

3. Charismatic grounds—resting on devotion to the specific and exceptional sanctity, heroism, or exemplary character of an individual person, and of the normative patterns or order revealed or ordained by him (charismatic authority).[1]

One implication which may be drawn from Weber's scheme is that the three types correspond to historical development from simple to more complex societies. In the former, obedience is to the person of the chief, and the values of the family permeate the whole social system. A society breaks out of this stage usually under the leadership of a charismatic chief, who is obeyed because of his personal or heroic qualities. In modern societies obedience is to the legal order; it is associated with the office more than with the person who occupies it.

In both traditional and modern societies the individual participates in the political process through groups or associations, but there are fundamental differences as regards their nature and importance. Traditional societies are characterized by the predominance of the family and family-type groups (that is, primary organizations) in which the members are in a face-to-face relationship. An individual's status in the society is determined by his or her family's status. He or she is nurtured, cared for, educated, and protected by the family, which tends to be a self-sufficient economic as well as social unit. The dominant economic activity is agriculture, which requires the participation of the family as a cohesive group. Virtually the entire population (and not 1 in 10 to 20, as in modern societies) is engaged in agriculture, the hunt, or fishing in order to provide sustenance. There is little knowledge of science or technology, no opportunity to accumulate reserves of food, and no leisure class able to devote itself to the arts and culture. The people live close to nature, even as part of nature. They are almost completely at the mercy of the seasons, storms, droughts, and rains. Superstition and magic permeate the society. People seek to relate events in their own lives to external occurrences, the stars, or the seasons.

Family values—personal loyalty, authority, reverence—pervade the whole social structure. The state tends to resemble the family, with the king or chief of state in the role of father, whose paternal authority derives from a superhuman source. The various families gathered together in clans or tribes are his children, bound to obey for the same reason that each elder in the tribe is obeyed by the younger leaders. Insofar as a bureaucracy comes into existence to administer the will of the chief, it is like a huge household—with nepotism an expected practice.

There have been, historically, a wide range of types *within* the general category of "traditional societies," from the subsistence agricultural and pastoral societies of primitive tribes in Africa, to the military structure of Egypt, the land empires of Asia Minor and China, the island civilization of the Aegean, Ancient Greece, and Rome, and the feudal age. All of these societies, however, preceded the technological and industrial breakthrough of the eighteenth century.

Technical and scientific progress brought in their wake far-reaching change in social and political organization. The old agricultural subsistence economy was replaced by an industrial marketplace economy. In the model modern society, individuals gain their livelihood not within the family, but in a factory, commercial enterprise, or office. Population concentrates in the great urban centers, creating a host of administrative problems (sanitation, transportation, education, etc.). Modern societies are characterized by the predominance of *secondary organizations*—large specialized and impersonal associations like labor unions, corporations, farm cooperatives, political parties, universities, and churches. Unlike the family, the secondary organizations have large numbers of members who need not be in a face-to-face relationship, are joined by a voluntary action of the prospective members, and carry on highly specialized activities. Most of the former functions of the family are assumed by the new associations (education by the schools, charity by the state, religious instruction by the church, and exchange of produce by the banks and marketplace). The state itself tends to take on the character of these secondary organizations: It becomes large, complex, impersonal, and increasingly rational. Old ideas of divine right fall into disrepute, and more rational themes of legitimacy (for example, popular sovereignty) come into vogue. The family itself is grievously weakened and is based more and more on consent and mutual interest.

After a period of evolution, the state expands to meet the needs of an industrialized economy. The civil service, for example, cannot fulfill its obligations as the closed preserve of a single family or clan, but must recruit able people from all layers of society. As Max Weber has pointed out, a modern bureaucracy is "rational"; that is, it recruits universally and boasts a system of tenure, grade classifications, and fixed salaries. Political conflict resembles the marketplace itself: Each specialized group puts forth its offers and demands, with the state acting as a broker. Individuals express their interests primarily through the secondary organizations to which they belong.

Let us briefly summarize the differences between the two ideal types. *Traditional* societies are characterized by subsistence economies; face-to-face social structures in which the family predominates; cultural systems that emphasize heredity, devotion, and mystery; and a highly personalized political system that is virtually an extension of the joint family. *Modern* societies are the exact opposite in all these respects. They are characterized by industrial economies; complex and impersonal social structures; a culture that emphasizes the values of science, knowledge, and achievement; and a highly bureaucratized political system that is legitimized through rational processes, such as elections.

Typological analysis is only a first step in the study of modernization. In effect, it constitutes a checklist for the observer, pointing to relationships among social, economic, cultural, and political factors that might otherwise escape attention. It also makes possible an assessment of the pace and extent of modernization in any given society. But the explanatory power of typologies is limited. The complexities of world history, the rise and decline of great powers and of civilizations, and the shifting balance of international power cannot be reduced to a handful of sociological concepts. Modernization provokes crises to which there are any number of possible reactions or solutions within a political system. It is perhaps most fruitful to consider modernization as a complex process that produces a series of challenges to both modern and traditional societies. How these challenges are met is the major concern of the student of political change.

....

COMPARATIVE ANALYSIS OF MODERN POLITICAL SYSTEMS

All nations on the modern side of the scale may be compared in terms of their distinctive experience of modernization. Each of these nations at one time was traditional; in each case the traditional society was undermined and eventually displaced by new forms of organization. The process of modernization inevitably causes a series of political crises. Whatever the nature of the traditional society and whatever the nature of the modern political institutions (whether one-, two-, or multiparty, presidential or cabinet, democratic or authoritarian), at least three political crises must be surmounted in the course of modernization: the crises of legitimacy, participation, and conflict management. The way in which these crises occur and are dealt with is of great consequence for the functioning of modern political systems.

The crisis of legitimacy is inevitable because of the close link between political values and the systems they serve to justify. The kinds of values that permeate a traditional society, such as divine right or rule by a hereditary aristocracy, must undergo modification as that society is transformed. Throughout Western Europe, for example, the breakup of feudalism was accompanied by a shift in the basis of political legitimacy. Everywhere the rights of monarchs were circumscribed and the power of parliaments increased. Whether monarchy continued to exist with reduced prerogatives or was replaced by a republic, the political systems of Europe sought to justify themselves in some way as the expression of popular will and national sovereignty. The crisis of legitimacy also involved the status of the church, which was generally a bulwark of the traditional ruling classes.

A new but related crisis comes into being with the rapid growth of industry. Power continues to be wielded by a landed aristocracy, the church, and the wealthier strata. But new social groups, above all the industrial middle classes and the working class, enter upon the political scene.

These classes are officially excluded from power in the traditional society; they demand entry into the political system, and they gain this entry by organizing themselves behind and through political parties. How this is accomplished—whether through slow and successful integration or with violence and grudging acceptance—makes a deep mark upon the political life of the country. In some cases the working class is never fully incorporated into the political system, and in countries like France and Italy large Communist parties constituted a permanent opposition of principle. In Communist systems integration was achieved by eliminating the aristocracy, small peasantry, and middle classes as autonomous political forces.

Whether in stable parliamentary democracies, unstable parliamentary democracies, or authoritarian regimes, mature industrial societies pose grave problems for the political system. Specialized groups proliferate within both the middle and working classes; the scientists, managers, bureaucrats, military, and intellectuals compete with party leaders for a share of decision-making power. The state must organize itself so as to cope with these strong interest groups, integrate them into the political system, and satisfy their demands. As the technology becomes more complex, the task of the political leaders requires more and more technical knowledge and competence, as well as the ability to manage the distinctive political tensions of highly industrialized societies.

Comparative analysis of modern political systems requires broad knowledge of their historical evolution. The student should compare the way in which each of the crises of modernization was handled in individual systems, and the extent of "carry-over" from one crisis to another. Many observers have suggested that the *timing* of the crises of modernization is of critical importance. Did these crises occur one by one, with a considerable period elapsing between crises? In these cases the political system has a greater opportunity to resolve them singly and thus acquire stability. Or were the crises "telescoped"? Did the political system have to confront the crises of participation and conflict management while the controversy over its basic institutions and values continued? In such cases a much greater load is placed upon the system, and an immense collective effort is required to create dynamic, effective, and stable government. Special attention should be paid to the problems of mature industrial societies. Are similar techniques being used in all modern political systems in dealing with rapid technological development, the information revolution, urbanization, and the maintenance of individual creativity in mass societies? Or are there significant differences between democratic and authoritarian systems? Are there differences among such parliamentary democracies as the United States and the countries of Western Europe? Between the West on the one hand and Japan and other rapidly industrializing Asian countries on the other? Modernization theory provides us with a framework for inquiry; it is the starting point for the formulation of hypotheses concerning political life in all industrialized societies.

COMPARATIVE ANALYSIS OF DEVELOPING NATIONS

Modernization theory can also be used for a study of contemporary trends in developing nations. There is a clear tendency for these societies to move from the traditional category into a *transitional period* during which they acquire many of the characteristics of modern society while retaining some traditional features. But it is impossible to foretell the exact development of any of these societies. Most Third World nations are doubtless on the way to modernization. But there are two chief prototypes of advanced industrial states in the world: the Western countries (especially the United States) and the Communist nations (China and the former Soviet Union). Developing countries could pattern themselves after either model of modernity. Authoritarianism and the command economy, despite the collapse of the Soviet Union, continue to have wide appeal to Asian, African, and Latin American elites.

Comparative study could usefully be focused on the decision-making or political elite: their social origin, position with respect to the masses, technical or educational qualifications for governing, relationship with the important social groups within the nation (for example, landowners, army, church, civil service, and intellectuals), and characteristic ideologies. At least four different leadership types can be distinguished in the developing nations: traditional, liberal, authoritarian, and radical.

The *traditional* leaders derive their authority from historical status and prestige and from one predominant form of property—land. They constitute a self-perpetuating group in that recruitment comes from a small circle (either royalty or landowning nobility) by virtue of birth. Their values vary from one system to another but generally reflect a family structure—the emphasis is on kinship, loyalty, devotion, duty, and courage. They are averse to changes that will endanger their economic and social position. They are apt to react unfavorably to any economic or technological innovations that might weaken the political system. They insist upon the preservation of prevailing modes of political recruitment and hence are hostile to popular participation in politics.

The *liberal* leaders are in favor of "reforming out of existence" the traditionalist-oriented economy, society, and political system. They welcome industrialization and mass participation in political affairs. They accept both the goals and the methods of the Western constitutional democracies. Thus, the liberals desire political reforms, establishment of a constitutional government with guarantees of individual rights, the articulation of interests within an accepted legal order, and the gradual displacement of the traditionalist groups from positions of power. They wish to create the proper conditions within which meaningful political choices can be made by the whole people. Recruitment of the liberal elite is usually from the professional and middle classes, particularly among those who have attended European and American universities. The traditionalists and liberals tend to be allied in their respect for property rights but split over the question of democratic reforms and modernization.

Authoritarian leaders, like the liberals, tend to accept democracy as an ideal or goal, but they do not believe it can be achieved by indiscriminate adoption of all features of Western systems. They distinguish between "formal" or "procedural" democracy (elections, parliaments, organized opposition, etc.) and "real" or "substantive" democracy (equal opportunity, economic development, moral regeneration). An active opposition only obstructs the efforts of the government to bring about "real" democracy and hence must be suppressed. The emphasis is therefore on national unity and the direction of the efforts of the masses by an educated, informed, morally responsible elite. Frequently the hope is held out that the people, one day in the future, after rapid economic progress has been accomplished, will be ready for representative government of the Western type. Authoritarian leaders, like the liberals, come mainly from the professional and middle classes and occasionally from the landed aristocracy.

The fourth type of leadership is *radical.* Inspired by a revolutionary ideology, the radicals are committed to drastic and rapid change of the economic and social structure. They organize their followers in a manner that will enable them to take the system by assault. The classic pattern is the single mass party led by professional revolutionaries, along lines laid down by Lenin. Radical leadership comes from the "alienated" groups, particularly the intelligentsia, and it appeals to the disaffected elements of the population—the peasants, the students, and the city workers. It is in favor of industrialization, but at the expense of the liberal values—individual rights, political freedoms, and private property. Above all it imposes collective goals upon the total society and disciplines the masses in order to achieve those goals. The main differences between the authoritarians and radicals are of degree and social origin: Radicals want more change more rapidly, with greater social control and discipline, and they tend to be drawn from less favored social classes. The radicals are also much more suspicious of the Western powers and in the past tended to seek aid as well as ideological inspiration from the Communist camp.

One of the striking developments of the past several decades is the rise of religious fundamentalism as a synthesis of both authoritarian and radical ideology. Within religious movements a conflict rages between those (for example, the Taliban of Afghanistan) who repudiate modern science and technology as the essence of a pernicious Western civilization, and those who see science and technology as achievements of humanity that can be made to serve religious ends, and even be used in the battle against Western influence.

The "benefits" of modernization have been felt throughout the world in the form of manufactured goods, films, radio and television, and so on. All native populations have had their expectations aroused or modified as a consequence: The economic structure of traditional systems has been undermined; land ownership is no longer a secure base for a political elite; new economic activities have created new social groups and stimulated others who view the traditional elite as a stumbling block on the road to further economic development.

Industrialization, however, is viewed frequently as a means for the attainment of economic goals and the satisfaction of wants. Its prerequisites—the development of skills; the training of the masses; and the establishment of an orderly pattern of social intercourse, particularly discipline and regular work in the factory—are less well understood. Industrialization is often equated with a vision of plenty in the foreseeable future, and as such it becomes a potent political force. The discipline required for industrialization, however, is perhaps best appreciated by the "radicals."

As the conflict develops over demands for industrialization, the political position of the traditional elite becomes precarious. Their legitimacy is brought into question. There follows a period of instability, overt defiance of authority, and sporadic uprisings. The new political leaders—liberal, authoritarian, and radical—vie for control. A limited number of alternatives for future political development present themselves.

One alternative is the maintenance of traditional social organization and leadership. This alternative, though always possible, is becoming anachronistic. Most of the traditional forces are fighting a losing battle for survival. The independence movement is associated with an ideology calling for social and economic reforms that are inconsistent with the interests of the traditional forces. Mobilization of the masses in the struggle for independence brings with it profound modifications in the economic and social structure. Change may be held off by a temporary alliance between the traditional and new leaderships and groups for the realization of independence, or by the inability of one particular group to impose its ideology, or by foreign intervention. But the will for change in a society generally indicates that the emerging political elite will use every means available to eliminate the traditional leaders who are still desperately clinging to the last vestiges of their rule.

At a certain stage, the liberal elements come into sharp conflict with the authoritarian and radical elements. The liberals advocate a relatively slow pace of structural modifications and industrialization, technological improvements, a rising standard of living, the gradual training of managerial and labor groups, progressive land reforms, and involvement of the masses in politics through the extension of literacy and education. But these demands are made with little urgency, and the envisaged manner of their implementation is permissive rather than coercive. The liberal elite attempts to create the conditions within which the individual can become capable of choice, which is always considered in the best tradition of liberalism to be an individual act. The system should provide opportunities for the individual and only "hinder the hindrances."

The authoritarians and radicals, on the other hand, urge coercive and authoritarian practices in order to bring about quickly the same overall goals. Suspicious of the continuing strength of the traditionalist elements (particularly among the peasants), they insist on rapid mobilization of the masses in a manner that will wrench them from their former way of life. Distrustful of the colonial powers, they seek to industrialize rapidly by using their own human resources and, in the past, by accepting aid from the Communist countries. This political leadership, therefore, uses force and not persuasion, seeks the outright organization of the masses rather than a gradual process of political education, and stresses social discipline rather than general rules, norms, and guarantees of individual freedom.

Religious fundamentalists have been highly successful in arousing popular enthusiasm and imposing divinely sanctioned discipline. In the contest for power, the liberal leaders are at a disadvantage. In relatively simple economies, the application of liberal economic doctrine does not result in rapid industrialization or structural change. Development of a market economy favors the merchant class and production of consumer goods, but it fails to satisfy the pent-up demand of large social groups. Subordination of social goals to individual choice only increases the feeling of social injustice among the masses. Politically, liberalism has no slogan that can activate and mobilize the masses. Most important, liberalism as a social force fails to inculcate new social incentives for the purpose of industrialization. On the other hand, the great advantage enjoyed by the authoritarian and especially the radical leaders is that they create a system of controls.

Industrialization may follow the Western historical experience and lead to the establishment of a legal order within which individual freedoms are guaranteed. The technician and the manager may win out over the party boss, the commissar, and the religious prophet. The demise of communism in the former Soviet Union and Eastern Europe has tarnished the image of collectivism, giving new luster to the Western model. Some formerly radical groups, abandoning their faith in command economies, see no alternative to market principles. But market economics may produce great social disparities; and the political systems of developing countries lack the power to redistribute national income. Authoritarianism, both secular and religious, continues to be an attractive model for many groups in developing countries. Analysis of political change in both industrial and traditional societies is perhaps the most compelling and challenging task of contemporary political science.

NOTE

1. Max Weber, *The Theory of Social and Economic Organization* (New York: Oxford University Press, 1947), p. 328. See also comments on types of legitimacy in Weber's speech on "Politics as a Vocation," excerpted in Chapter 3.

CHAPTER TWO

MODERNIZATION/GLOBALIZATION

European societies today are strikingly different from those same societies during the period of feudalism, which in turn differed from the ways of the primitive people who inhabited those lands, say, five thousand years ago. How can these differences be conceptualized? One of the keenest historians of the 19th century characterized life in traditional village society in India as "undignified, stagnatory, and vegetative," enslaving the human mind. (See the comments in the essay by Karl Marx on "British Rule in India".) For Emile Durkheim the individual in primitive societies is merely an extension of the group; only with the creation of a more complex division of labor could individuals be free to develop their full intellectual powers. Can we identify factors that caused primitive and then feudal societies to evolve as they did?

Drawing largely upon the classic work of Emile Durkheim, these issues are explored by Samuel H. Beer in the second essay. The basic orientations of modernity are identified as increasing differentiation and scale. Those communities most successful at developing a complex division of labor were able to become more productive, and hence tended to become more powerful than their neighbors. The process accelerated with the explosion of science and technology beginning in the 18th century, and changed the nature of political systems as well. An example of the analysis of a contemporary state within the framework of modernization theory is Professor Beer's *To Make a Nation: The Rediscovery of American Federalism* (Harvard University Press, 1993), where American federalism is interpreted as "a rejection of and escape from the Middle Ages."

For Ronald Inglehart, carrying forward the argument of both Durkheim and Max Weber, there is a core syndrome of modernization, involving urbanization, industrialization, economic development, occupational specialization, and the spread of mass literacy. He also contends that in the past twenty-five years there has been a "post-modern shift" emphasizing self-expression and quality of life issues. The exponential increase in communications ushered in by the computer age has led to the intensification and worldwide diffusion of trends described by Durkheim, to the point where the term "globalization" is now current. Division of labor has enabled the complex societies (to continue to use

Durkheim's term) not only to gain an advantage over close neighbors, but to extend their sway over the entire world. As H. V. Savitch shows, trends previously evident have intensified, deepened, and spread in an altogether new way, with unpredicted consequences.

The previous diversity of reactions to modernization within nations is repeated today on the global level. Workers, capitalists, managers, professionals, farmers, and intellectuals react in different ways to the process. They disagree on how to control it, for whose benefit, and for what final goal. The controversies among anarchists, communists (orthodox, Trotskyist, Maoist), other revolutionaries, liberals, reformers, conservatives, fascists, etc. (to run the gamut from Left to Right) have erupted on a global scale. Protest and riots that used to take place in national capitals now are organized wherever in the world leaders of international financial and trade institutions hold meetings. A basic divide remains between those who welcome and those who revolt against the increasing division of labor, complexity, and rationality (as described by Durkheim and Weber).

All aspects of the political system have been affected by and even transformed in the ongoing process of modernization, as is evident throughout this volume.

....

KARL MARX

5 British Rule in India

. . . There cannot . . . remain any doubt but that the misery inflicted by the British on Hindostan is of an essentially different and infinitely more intensive kind than all of Hindostan had to suffer before. . . .

All the civil wars, invasions, revolutions, conquests, famines, strangely complex, rapid and destructive as the successive action in Hindostan may appear, did not go deeper than its surface. England has broken down the entire framework of Indian society, without any symptoms of reconstruction yet appearing. This loss of his old world, with no gain of a new one, imparts a particular kind of melancholy to the present misery of the Hindoo, and separates Hindostan, ruled by Britain, from all its ancient traditions, and from the whole of its past history.

There have been in Asia, generally, from immemorial times, but three departments of Government: that of Finance, or the plunder of the interior; that of War, or the plunder of the exterior; and, finally, the department of Public Works. Climate and territorial conditions, especially the

vast tracts of desert, extending from the Sahara, through Arabia, Persia, India and Tartary, to the most elevated Asiatic highlands, constituted artificial irrigation by canals and waterworks the basis of Oriental agriculture. As in Egypt and India, inundations are used for fertilizing the soil of Mesopotamia, Persia, etc.: advantage is taken of a high level for feeding irrigative canals. This prime necessity of an economical and common use of water, which, in the Occident, drove private enterprise to voluntary association, as in Flanders and Italy, necessitated, in the Orient where civilization was too low and the territorial extent too vast to call into life voluntary association, the interference of the centralizing power of Government. Hence an economical function devolved upon all Asiatic Governments the function of providing public works. This artificial fertilization of the soil, dependent on a Central Government, and immediately decaying with the neglect of irrigation and drainage, explains the otherwise strange fact that we now find whole territories barren and desert that were once brilliantly cultivated, as Palmyra, Petra, the ruins in Yemen, and large provinces of Egypt,

SOURCE: Published in the New York *Daily Tribune*, 25 June 1853.

Persia and Hindostan: it also explains how a single war of devastation has been able to depopulate a country for centuries, and to strip it of all its civilization. . . .

. . . However changing the political aspect of India's past must appear, its social condition has remained unaltered since its remotest antiquity, until the first decennium of the 19th century. The hand-loom and the spinning-wheel, producing their regular myriads of spinners and weavers, were the pivots of the structure of that society. From immemorial times, Europe received the admirable textures of Indian labor, sending in return for them her precious metals, and furnishing thereby his material to the goldsmith, that indispensable member of Indian society, whose love of finery is so great that even the lowest class, those who go about nearly naked, have commonly a pair of golden earrings and a gold ornament of some kind hung round their necks. Rings on the fingers and toes have also been common. Women as well as children frequently wore massive bracelets and anklets of gold or silver, and statuettes of divinities in gold and silver were met with in the households. It was the British intruder who broke up the Indian hand-loom and destroyed the spinning-wheel. England began, with driving the Indian cottons from the European market; it then introduced twist into Hindostan and in the end inundated the very mother country of cotton with cottons. . . .

These two circumstances—the Hindoo, on the one hand, leaving, like all Oriental peoples, to the central government the care of the great public works, the prime condition of his agriculture and commerce, dispersed, on the other hand over the surface of the country, and agglomerated in small centres by the domestic union of agricultural and manufacturing pursuits—these two circumstances had brought about, since the remotest times, a social system of particular features—the so-called *village system,* which gave to each of these small unions their independent organization and distinct life. . . .

These small stereotype forms of social organism have been to the greater part dissolved, and are disappearing, not so much through the brutal interference of the British tax gatherer and the British

soldier, as to the working of English steam and English free trade. Those family-communities were based on domestic industry, in that peculiar combination of hand-weaving, hand-spinning and hand-tilling agriculture which gave them self-supporting power. English interference having placed the spinner in Lancashire and the weaver in Bengal, or sweeping away both Hindoo spinner and weaver, dissolved these small semi-barbarian, semi-civilised communities, by blowing up their economical basis, and thus produced the greatest, and to speak the truth, the only *social* revolution ever heard of in Asia.

Now, sickening as it must be to human feeling to witness those myriads of industrious patriarchal and inoffensive social organizations disorganized and dissolved into their units, thrown into a sea of woes, and their individual members losing at the same time their ancient form of civilization, and their hereditary means of subsistence, we must not forget that these idyllic village communities, inoffensive though they may appear, had always been the solid foundation of Oriental despotism, that they restrained the human mind within the smallest possible compass, making it the unresisting tool of superstition, enslaving it beneath traditional rules, depriving it of all grandeur and historical energies. We must not forget the barbarian egotism which, concentrating on some miserable patch of land, had quietly witnessed the ruin of empires, the perpetration of unspeakable cruelties, the massacre of the population of large towns, with no other consideration bestowed upon them than on natural events, itself the helpless prey of any aggressor who deigned to notice it at all. We must not forget that this undignified, stagnatory, and vegetative life, that this passive sort of existence evoked on the other part, in contradistinction, wild, aimless, unbounded forces of destruction and rendered murder itself a religious rite in Hindostan. We must not forget that these little communities were contaminated by distinctions of caste and by slavery, that they subjugated man to external circumstances instead of elevating man to be the sovereign of circumstances, that they transformed a self-developing social state into never changing natural destiny, and thus brought about a brutalizing worship of nature, exhibiting its degradation in the fact that man, the sovereign of nature, fell down on his knees in adoration of *Hanuman,* the monkey, and *Sabbala,* the cow.

England, it is true, in causing a social revolution in Hindostan, was actuated only by the vilest interests, and was stupid in her manner of enforcing them. But that is not the question. The question is, can mankind fulfill its destiny without a fundamental revolution in the social state of Asia? If not, whatever may have been the crimes of England she was the unconscious tool of history in bringing about that revolution. . . .

SAMUEL H. BEER

6 The Dynamics of Modernization

ECONOMIC MODERNIZATION

. . . [I have] . . . sought to characterize the attitudes that distinguish modern Western society from the Western societies that preceded it. I have not argued that there was a complete break. Clearly, on the contrary, there were major continuities. Indeed, I would accept Arnold J. Toynbee's argument that one of the major "intelligible fields of historical study" for the social scientist is Western Christian civilization.[1] What this means is that the continuities in European history for the past 1500 years are so fundamental as greatly to transcend the differences between the medieval and modern periods. The new attitudes, however, which with increasing prominence spread throughout Europe from the seventeenth century onward, did involve matters of very great, if not ultimate, importance.

Moreover, these ideas had consequences. The chain of effects descending from them transformed behavior and social structure, bringing into existence the distinctive traits of modern society. I wish in particular to focus attention upon two distinguishable, but interrelated, processes—increasing differentiation and increasing scale. Operationally, these embody the two basic orientations of modernity and by their interaction create the ever larger networks of social,

SOURCE: Samuel H. Beer, "Modern Political Development", in Samuel H. Beer, ed., *Patterns of Government: The Major Political System of Europe,* New York: McGraw-Hill, 1973, pp. 54–70. By permission of the author. Essay abridged by the Editor.

economic, and political interdependence that characterize modern society. The general image of this evolution is familiar. Communities were at first small, relatively self-subsistent and similar in economy, polity, and culture—as was still the case with the village and manorial society of late medieval times. Gradually these communities were drawn together by ties of political and governmental activity, trade and industry, education and communication. This increasing interdependence introduced outside influences into the original communities, disrupting their solidarities and at the same time reshaping the fragments and binding them into vast, impersonal, highly differentiated, highly interdependent social, economic, and political wholes. Such, in brief and impressionistic terms, is the manner of creation of what Emile Durkheim called "the great society."[2]

The general formula exhibited in this process characterizes development in many different modes and different ages. Indeed, the Middle Ages displayed a process of development—we may call it "medievalization"—that also followed this general formula in the creation of its own special sort of highly developed society. My concern here is to elucidate the mechanisms of that special form of development that we call modernization—to say more precisely how the basic orientations of modernity were expressed in increasing differentiation and increasing scale and how these two processes interacted to create the large, complex networks of interdependence constituting the great society. The concepts of differentiation and scale can be used in the analysis of social, economic, or political processes. Their meaning and their manner of interaction, however, can be most readily illustrated from economic analysis, from which they originally derived. While my interest is primarily political, it will best serve the purposes of clarity to consider first the economic significance of the terms.

....

THE DIVISION OF LABOR

In economic analysis differentiation is more commonly referred to as the *division of labor.* The eighteenth-century economist Adam Smith, who invented the term, was also the first to explore systematically its influence on productivity. On the very first page of his great work *An Inquiry into the Nature and the Causes of the Wealth of Nations* he introduces the topic, going on to illustrate it with his famous description of the pin factory in which specialization—the division of the business of making a pin into about eighteen distinct operations—increases the productive powers of labor hundreds of times over what it would be if each man worked separately, making the whole pin by himself. Smith argues that the tendency to division of labor arises from exchange, holding that it is the prospect of getting a larger return from marketing what he produces that incites the individual to raise his productivity by specialization. From this relationship it follows that "the division of labor is limited by the extent of the market." As the market is widened—for instance, by improvements in transportation—a higher degree of specialization becomes feasible, since its greater production can now be absorbed. In short, as the scale of the economy increases, so also does the division of labor within it. And as scale and differentiation increase, productivity rises.

Writing in 1776 Smith reflected—and analyzed—the experience of the first phase of economic modernization in Britain. This was the era of the "commercial revolution" when, as his analysis suggests, extension of the market (that is, increase in the scale of the economy) within Britain and abroad greatly stimulated agriculture and industry. The discovery of America, he observed,

> by opening a new and inexhaustible market to all the commodities of Europe . . . gave occasion to new divisions of labor and improvements of

art, which, in the narrow circle of the ancient commerce, could never have taken place for want of a market to take off the greater part of their produce.

Smith was not unaware of the importance of machines and made their invention one of the principal reasons for the increase in productivity resulting from specialization. Yet he wrote before the second great phase of economic modernization in Britain, when the industrial revolution made new machinery the principal means of a vast economic advance. Writing after a hundred years of industrialization in Britain, Alfred Marshall in his *Principles of Economics* (1890) still made the division of labor central to his analysis of economic development. Like Smith he was acutely aware of the importance of scale, laying great stress on how "man's power of productive work increases with the volume of work that he does." Naturally, he was far more aware of the importance of the organization of the individual firm. But although he wrote at a time when the modern corporation was coming to be widely used and British managers were making their first large-scale experiments with industrial combinations, he still assumed that the free market controlled the firm, not vice versa.

After another long interval, which has seen "the organizational revolution" and the rise of collectivism in economics as in politics, John Kenneth Galbraith takes a very different view of the role of the market. In his *New Industrial State* (1967) he argues that the classical relation has been reversed, the great oligopolistic firms now tending to control the market rather than the market the firms. In spite of these many differences, he still finds that the division of labor is central to economic development. Writing when science has come even more prominently to the fore as the principal motor of advance, he stresses the role of technology, "the systematic application of scientific or other organized knowledge to practical tasks." Still the "most important consequence" of technology is "in forcing the division and subdivision of any such task into its component parts." The division of labor is very largely derived from specialized branches of scientific knowledge and is carried on by machines.

As in the Smithian example, however, it depends upon an expansion in the scale of the economy. Only thus can its increases in productivity be used. Economies of scale resulting from such specialization are a main reason for the creation of huge business organizations and the effort to create larger trading areas such as the Common Market.

One reason these three discussions of the mechanism of economic development are interesting is that they correspond to three main periods in European economic modernization, the commercial revolution, the industrial revolution, and the organizational revolution. . . .

INTERACTION OF SPECIALIZATION AND SCALE

The two processes of the mechanism of economic development are *division of labor* (or specialization) and *increase in scale*. Smith stressed the division of labor itself as the source of improvement in "the productive powers of labor." The present analysis, which finds the dynamic of economic growth in the advance of science and technology, puts the emphasis upon some step forward in scientific knowledge that, in turn, when applied to economic processes, involves their division and subdivision. Such an improvement in productivity can take place prior to an expansion of the market, as we see in the present phase of scientific advance, when a leaping technology continually presents us with goods and services we never dreamed of, let alone demanded in the marketplace. Hence, the constant need to keep the market adjusted by the cultivation of appropriate new tastes among potential buyers.

Yet the factor of scale can also vary independently. As Smith saw it, a widening of the market stimulates further division of labor. Such an expansion of scale could be brought about by more efficient modes of transportation, as when canals and then railways opened up markets in eighteenth- and nineteenth-century Europe. It could also be brought about by political means, as when the French Revolution through an act of governmental centralization struck down local imposts and other burdens on free trade within the country. Similarly, a change in cultural standards, by producing new tastes for more consumption goods and services, could sharply stimulate economic activity.

The first proposition to derive from this analysis is that the two processes, increase in differentiation and increase in scale, can vary independently. Either type of process—for instance, a new stage of productivity resulting from greater specialization, or a new level of demand resulting from a widening of the market—can be the primary process of change. Neither theoretically nor empirically is there reason for saying that one is more important than the other. While science and technology have driven forward the productive power of the economy through new stages of specialization, so also has the growing scale of modern economies initiated new thrusts forward. The fact that each can be and has often been an independent variable should be kept in mind when we come to consider the political embodiment of these two types of social process.

The point is obvious in the case of economic development, which, depending on the situation, may be driven forward by initial changes in either specialization or scale. When these concepts are applied to other spheres, however, this dual possibility is sometimes lost sight of. In Durkheim's classic discussion, The *Division of Labor in Society,* from which I have borrowed a great deal, he makes specialization derivative. Defining "density" essentially as I have defined "scale"—that is, as the "number of social relations"—he insists that the division of labor follows from an increase in density, not vice versa. . . . In applying the concepts of scale and specialization to political development, it seems clear to me that we should return to the lesson of economic analysis and approach any concrete situation with an open mind, ready to find the initiation of change on either side.

The second proposition is that the two processes interact, mutually reinforcing one another. An increase in scale promotes economic specialization; an advance in specialization encourages the search for markets where the added product can be disposed of. From time to time, each has taken the lead in stimulating economic development, as when the voracious markets developed by the commercial revolution conditioned the great leaps forward in technology of the industrial revolution, and the rise in productivity in the later nineteenth century promoted the search for markets in the later stages of European imperialism. While each may vary independently, if an advance in one sphere is to be maintained, it must meet with an appropriate and concomitant response in the other. This "functional" relationship does not in itself constitute a causal connection. It is, however, readily translated into activities that do bring about effects with regard to technological advance or market expansion, as the case may be. Such a mechanism of interaction, it may also be observed, is properly called a mechanism. It is not an instance of the influence of ideas. On the contrary, it is a type of process in which "pressures," "opportunities," and "structures" are the basis for explaining the generation of change. The cultural orientations of modernity motivate distinctively new types of behavior. But once these floods of consequence have been sent forth into the world, they interact with profound effect on one another in ways that may be only dimly understood or barely perceived and not at all intended by contemporaries. The industrial revolution, the rise of the factory system, the creation of the great manufacturing city were only in part—in small part—the intentional creations of their time.

The third proposition concerns the overall result of development. Together the increase in specialization and the increase in scale constitute a growth in interdependence. As Alfred Marshall said, drawing an analogy between economic development and organic evolution, the development of the organism, whether social or physical, involves, on the one hand, an increasing subdivision of functions between its separate parts and, on the other hand, more intimate connections between the parts, each becoming less and less self-sufficient and so more and more dependent upon the others. Economic development involves such a growth in interdependent complexity as more and more complex networks of exchange join together the increasingly differentiated parts of the growing economy.

In the conventional image of such development, the expansion of the economy is seen as involving a spread of exchange from a limited to a wider area, bringing more and more people into the system of relationships. That did often happen, as, for instance, in the expansion of the European economy to include trade with America in the seventeenth century. Yet it is crucially important to understand that economic development—and development generally—can take place and often has taken place quite apart from any increase in the number of individual units included in the expanding system. An increase in scale consists in an increase in the number of exchange relations. This can occur within an economic system and does not require physical expansion to include more people or more territory. The same number of individual units can be arranged in a simple, segmented economy or in a complex, developed economy. . . .

POLITICAL MODERNIZATION

The general ideas expressed in these familiar terms of economic analysis have an equally important, though less familiar, application to the study of political development. Increases in differentiation and scale have also characterized political modernization, the upshot being the great networks of interdependent complexity and centralized power that we call modern states.

In the course of political modernization, the dual orientation of modernity has been expressed in the pattern of interests and the pattern of power, respectively, of the modern polity. Scientific and technical advance has made its impact on the mobilization of power, while the thrust toward equality and democracy has been expressed in the mobilization of interests. . . . Most studies of the modern state have shown an overwhelming concern with the latter topic. It has long been an interest of historians and political scientists to trace the course by which political demand has broadened and deepened, involved more and more people, and been made effective in the political arena. This is the story of the rise of constitutionalism and popular government; of how over time civil, political, and social rights were made effective. Even where major defeats have taken place, as in the modern dictatorships, there has been an immense growth in political scale in the sense that the spectrum of interests imposing demands and extracting satisfactions from the state has vastly increased. The populations of the various modern polities have grown, but even more important have been the unremitting increase and variegation of demands for new and more activities and services by the state. Like the modern economy, the modern state depends upon this vast and mounting demand to maintain its activity.

Along with the mobilization of interests has gone the mobilization of power, surely no less important, although much neglected by scholars. In part driven by the demands of the groups, classes, and leaders who have constituted the effective citizenry at various times, the modern state has continually developed its potential for acting on man and nature. This story has not been told in the detail it deserves. There are histories of the "output" of the modern state—from mercantilism, through laissez-faire, to the welfare state and socialism. But the mobilization of power—like the growth of productivity in the economy—consists in the increase of the capacity to produce outputs. Its history is the history of the development of the "extractive" and "repressive" functions: not only the rise of bureaucracy, but also the expansion of the tax system, the police, and especially the armed forces. It has often been remarked that the huge productive capacity developed by the modern economy is totally unprecedented when seen in a long historical perspective. The power of the modern state is no less a historical wonder, reflecting a capacity for policy outputs as vast and unprecedented as the productivity of its remarkable economic system. The centerpiece in this mobilization of power has been the growing capacity of the civilian and military bureaucracy, fed by knowledge in law, economics, engineering, and the proliferating specialties of modern science and technology. . . .

ENDNOTES

1. Arnold J. Toynbee, *A Study of History,* abr. ed. (New York and London: Oxford University Press, 1947), "Introduction."
2. Emile Durkheim, *The Division of Labor in Society,* George Simpson (tr.) (New York: Macmillan, 1933), p. 222. The original version in. French was published in 1893.

RONALD INGLEHART

7 Modernization and Postmodernization

INTRODUCTION

Modernization theory has long been divided into two main schools: (1) a Marxist version, which claims that economics, politics and culture are closely linked because economic development determines the political and cultural characteristics

SOURCE: Ronald Inglehart, "Changing Values, Economic Development and Political Change," *International Social Science Journal,* no. 145 (September 1995), pp. 379–388, 400–403. © 1995 by United Nations Educational, Scientific, and Cultural Organization (UNESCO). Reprinted by permission of Blackwell Publishing Ltd. Abridged by the Editor.

of a society; and (2) a Weberian version, which claims that culture shapes economic and political life. Despite an enduring debate between the two schools, they agree on one crucial point: that socioeconomic change follows coherent and relatively predictable patterns. Thus they imply that key social, political and economic characteristics are not randomly related; they tend to be closely linked, so that from a knowledge of one such trait, one can predict the presence of other key traits with far better than random success.

From the perspective of cultural relativism, on the other hand, it would be ethnocentric not to believe that all cultures are equally conducive to economic development and democracy. And dependency theorists tended to view a given society's culture as largely irrelevant to economic development and democracy: in all but the core capitalist societies, these are determined by external forces linked with global capitalism. Both of the latter views suggest that culture, economics and politics are randomly related.

This paper analyses an unprecedented body of data on the values and beliefs of the publics of 43 societies representing 70 per cent of the world's population.[1] It demonstrates that, far from being randomly related, cultural, economic and political variables are closely correlated. Although we do not attempt to demonstrate in this article whether causality flows in the Marxist or the Weberian direction, the linkages we find are so strong that they suggest that at least one school of modernization theory was right.

Though we find strong support for one central claim of modernization theory, we disagree with it on several narrower points—above all, the notion that socioeconomic change is linear. Instead, we find evidence that a major change of direction occurs when societies reach an advanced level of industrial development. The modernization phase involves the familiar syndrome of industrialization, occupational specialization, bureaucratization, centralization, rising educational levels and a configuration of beliefs and values closely linked with high rates of economic growth; but among advanced industrial societies, a second syndrome of changes seems to emerge in which economic growth becomes less central, but a syndrome of cultural and institutional changes occurs that is linked with emphasis on the quality of life in general, and on democratic political institutions in particular. . . .

MODERNIZATION AND POSTMODERNIZATION IN CROSS-SECTIONAL PERSPECTIVE

The concepts of both modernization and postmodernization are based on two key assumptions.

1. That various cultural elements tend to go together in coherent patterns. For example, do societies that place relatively strong emphasis on religion, also tend to favour large families (or respect for authority or national pride, or other distinctive attitudes)? If each culture goes its own way, elements such as these would be uncorrelated, and one would find no consistent patterns of constraint.

2. Coherent cultural patterns exist, *and* they are linked with economic and technological development. For example, industrialization was accompanied by secularization in Western history. But some observers point to the fact that part of the Islamic world has grown rich (though not industrialized) without showing any clear signs of secularization, as evidence that there is no linkage between economic development and secularization. We suggest that modernization (which is not just the possession of large oil reserves) does tend to be linked with secularization. Still more broadly, we suggest that economic modernization and cultural modernization tend to go together in coherent syndromes.

Together these two postulates imply that some patterns are more probable than others and hence that development is to some extent predictable. *Is economic development linked with coherent cultural patterns, distinct from those found in less developed societies?* If so, then (regardless of which is causing which) cross-national surveys should reveal clear configurations, with one syndrome of orientations being found in economically developed societies and another syndrome being found in less developed societies. If such patterns are present, then the evidence supports modernization theory. Even more important, it implies that sociopolitical change has an element of predictability.

In this article, we will examine whether coherent cultural patterns exist, and whether they are linked with levels of economic development. To do so, we will analyse the 1990–1991 World Values Survey, which measured key values and beliefs among representative national samples of the publics of 43 societies. This survey was designed to test the hypothesis that economic development leads to certain changes in mass values and belief systems—which in turn produce feedback, leading to changes in the economic and political systems of these societies. This does not imply that all elements of culture will necessarily change, leading to a uniform global culture: we see no reason to expect that the Chinese will stop using chopsticks, or that Brazilians will learn to polka, in the foreseeable future. But certain cultural and political changes do seem to be logically linked with the dynamics of a core syndrome of modernization, involving urbanization, industrialization, economic development, occupational specialization and the spread of mass literacy.

Change is not linear in any system subject to feedback. This is unfortunate analytically, because if the process of economic-cultural-political change moved smoothly in one continuous direction, a cross-section of the world's societies would show a simple developmental progression of cultural changes, as one moved from the least developed to the most developed societies. Analogously, a cross-section of the earth's surface sometimes reveals neatly ordered geological layers, with the oldest stratum of rock being lowest and the newer strata located above the older ones. But reality is not this simple: social change produces feedback, which eventually changes the direction of change. Thus, we are likely to find a pattern like those produced by tectonic upheavals, in which identifiable geological layers are shifted and juxtaposed with other strata. The result is not chaos, but it is also not a simple layering from oldest to newest strata.

We suggest that we will find the residue of two major waves of change (along with many lesser ones) mirrored in the World Values Survey's cross-section of the world's cultures: we will refer to them as the modern shift and the postmodern shift, respectively.

The literature on modernization focuses on the first of these movements. It argues (correctly, we believe) that a broad syndrome of changes has been linked with modern economic development. These changes include urbanization, industrialization, occupational specialization, mass formal education, development of mass media, secularization, the rise of entrepreneurs and entrepreneurial motivations, bureaucratization, the mass production assembly line and the emergence of the modern state. Although there are arguments about what is the

"real" driving force behind this syndrome, there is widespread agreement that these changes include technological, economic, cultural and political components. In our view, these changes are mutually supporting, in much the same way as the skeletal system, the muscular system, the circulatory system, the respiratory system and the gastrointestinal system of the human body: it is pointless to try to determine which one of them is crucial, and which are epiphenomena (although when a given factor such as food or oxygen is in short supply, it may seem to be the one crucial factor).

RELIGION AND ECONOMIC GROWTH

We propose a modified interpretation of Weber's thesis concerning the role of the Protestant ethic in economic development. Weber was correct in arguing that the rise of Protestantism was a crucial event in modernizing Europe. But this was not due to factors unique to Protestantism—it has been argued that everything Weber ascribed to Puritanism might with equal justice be ascribed to Judaism (Sombart, 1913). European Judaism had taken on a largely urban, and in some ways modem, outlook; but it could not transform Europe, because it held a marginal position there. The crucial impact of Protestantism was due to the fact that it replaced a set of religious norms that are common to most pre-industrial societies, and which inhibit economic achievement; and it replaced them with norms favourable to economic achievement.

Because they experience little or no economic growth, pre-industrial economies are zero-sum systems: upward social mobility can only come at someone else's expense. In any pre-industrial society that has lasted for some time, the cultural system is adapted accordingly: social status is hereditary rather than achieved, and the culture encourages one to accept one's social position in this life by emphasizing that meek acceptance, and denial of worldly aspirations will be rewarded in the next life. Aspirations toward social mobility are sternly repressed. Such value systems help to maintain social solidarity and discourage economic accumulation in a variety of ways, ranging from norms of sharing and charity to the norms of *noblesse oblige,* to the potlatch and similar institutions in which one attains prestige by recklessly giving away one's worldly goods.

For Weber, the central element in the rise of modernity was the movement away from traditional religious authority to secular rational–legal authority: a shift from ascriptive status to impersonal, achievement-based roles; and a shift of power from society to state. Traditional value systems must be shattered in order for modern economic development to take place. In a society undergoing rapid economic expansion, social mobility is acceptable—even a virtue. But in hunting and gathering or agrarian societies, the main basis of production—land—is a fixed quantity, and social mobility can occur only if an individual or group seizes the lands of another. To preserve social peace, virtually all traditional cultures discourage upward social mobility and the accumulation of wealth. They help to integrate society by providing a rationale that legitimates the established social order, in which social status is hereditary, but these cultures also inculcate norms of sharing, charity and other obligations that help to mitigate the harshness of a subsistence economy.

The Confucian system was a partial exception. Although, like virtually all traditional cultural systems, it inculcated the duty to be satisfied with one's station in life and to respect authority, it did permit some social mobility based on individual achievement, through the narrowly controlled channels of the Confucian examination system. Moreover, it did not justify meek acceptance of one's lot in this world by stressing the infinitely greater rewards that this would bring in the next world. It was based on a secular worldview: if one were to rise, one would do so in this world or not at all.

On the whole, however, the traditional value systems of agrarian society (China included) are adapted to maintaining a stable balance in unchanging societies. Accordingly, they tend to discourage social change in general and accumulative entrepreneurial motivation in particular, which is likely to be stigmatized and relegated to pariah groups, if tolerated at all. Economic accumulation is characterized as ignoble greed. To facilitate the economic accumulation needed to launch industrialization, these cultural inhibitions must be relaxed.

In Western society, the Protestant Reformation helped break the grip of the medieval Christian worldview on a significant part of Europe. It did not do this by itself. The emergence of scientific inquiry had already begun to undermine this worldview. But Weber's emphasis on the role of Protestantism seems to capture an important part of reality. Prior to the Reformation, Southern Europe was economically more advanced than Northern Europe. During the three centuries after the Reformation, capitalism emerged, mainly among the Protestant regions of Europe and among the Protestant minorities in Catholic countries. Within this cultural context, economic accumulation was no longer despised. Quite the contrary, it was highly respected because it was taken as evidence of divine favour: those whom God had chosen, he made rich.

Protestant Europe manifested a subsequent economic dynamism that was extraordinary, moving it far ahead of Catholic Europe. Shifting trade patterns, declining food production in Southern Europe and other factors also contributed to this shift, but the evidence suggests that cultural factors played a major role. Throughout the first 150 years of the Industrial Revolution, industrial development took place almost entirely within the Protestant regions of Europe and the Protestant portions of the New World. This began to change only during the second half of the twentieth century, when precisely those regions that had been most strongly influenced by the Protestant ethic— and had become economically secure—began to de-emphasize economic growth. At the same time, an entrepreneurial outlook had emerged in Catholic Europe and, even more strikingly, in East Asia, both of which are now showing higher rates of economic growth than Protestant Europe. The concept of the Protestant ethic is outdated if we take it to mean something that can exist only in Protestant countries. But Weber's more general concept that culture influences economic growth is an important insight.

MODERNIZATION: THE SHIFT FROM RELIGIOUS AUTHORITY TO STATE AUTHORITY

Secularization is one of the pervasive tendencies linked with modernization. This holds true although it is often asserted today that there is a rapid growth of fundamentalist religion throughout the world. Although the fundamentalist backlash is an important phenomenon, this generalization reflects a misconception of what is happening, generalizing from two very different phenomena. The fundamentalist phenomenon reflects two disparate elements.

1. In advanced industrial societies such as the US, Western Europe and East Asia, traditional forms of religion have been, and still are, experiencing a steep decline. During the past 40 years, church attendance rates have been gradually eroding and public adherence to traditional norms concerning divorce, abortion, suicide, single parenthood and homosexuality has been eroding—and continues to erode. Resurgent fundamentalist activism has indeed been a dramatic phenomenon: such events as gay-bashing and bombing of abortion centres have received widespread coverage in the mass media, encouraging the perception that it has a rapidly growing constituency. It does not. Instead, precisely because fundamentalists perceive that many of their central norms are being rapidly eroded, they have been galvanized into unprecedented activism. But this reflects the rear-guard action of a dwindling segment of the population, not the wave of the future.

2. Islamic fundamentalism, on the other hand, does have a growing mass constituency. But it is most intense in societies that have not modernized. Although some of these societies, such as Libya and Iran, are rich, they have not become rich through the modernization trajectory of industrialization, occupational specialization, rising educational levels, and so on, but by virtue of the fact that they possess large oil revenues.

I do not claim that all societies have modernized; some, clearly, have not. Some societies that have not modernized, have nevertheless become rich simply by possessing large petroleum reserves which can now be sold to industrialized countries, enabling their elites to buy the external trappings of modernization. The possession of large oil deposits offers an alternative path to becoming rich, without moving on the main trajectory of industrialization, occupational specialization, higher education, etc. But this is not modernization. Modernization consists in a specific syndrome of economic and cultural changes, not in the fact of having large currency reserves.

The presence of this wealth is by no means irrelevant: it has enabled oil-rich fundamentalist regimes to obtain such things as modern medical treatment for elites, automobiles, air conditioning and modern weapons; without them, the fundamentalist regimes have been able to purchase the equipment of modernity. Without it, they would be militarily weak and technologically backward—and their viability and mass appeal would be far weaker.

Modernization involved more than the shift away from cultural traditions (usually based on religious norms) that emphasize ascribed status and sharing, towards placing a positive value on achievement and accumulation. For Weber, the key to modernization was the shift from a religion-oriented worldview to a state-oriented worldview. Key components of modernization were

1. Secularization—Weber emphasized the *cognitive* roots of secularization: the rise of the scientific worldview, to replace the sacred/mystical pre-rational elements of religious faith; and

2. Bureaucratization—the rise of "rational" organizations, based on rules designed to advance efficiently towards explicit goals; and with recruitment based on impersonal goal-oriented achievement standards.

A key element paving the way for modernization was the erosion of the belief systems supporting ascriptive traditional authority, linked with zero-sum economies, and their replacement by achievement-oriented, rational and scientifically oriented belief systems that supported the authority of large, centralized bureaucratic states geared to facilitating economic growth. In large part, cultural modernization was the shift from traditional (usually religious) authority, to rational–legal authority.

Along with this went a shift of prestige and socioeconomic functions away from the key institutions of traditional society—the family and the church—to the state, and a shift in economic activity from the small family enterprise to mass production that was state-regulated or even state-owned. Globally, it was a shift of prestige and power from society to state.

During the modernizing phase of history, it seemed to Marxists and non-Marxists alike that the direction of social evolution was towards the increasing subordination of the individual to a Leviathan-state having superhuman powers. The state would become an omnipotent and benevolent entity, replacing God in a secular world. And for most of the nineteenth and twentieth centuries, the dominant trend—the wave of the future, as it was sometimes called—was a shift from societal authority towards state authority, manifested in the apparently inexorable growth of the economic, political and social role of government. Even non-Marxist thinkers such as Schumpeter (1947) reluctantly considered the triumph of socialism to be inevitable. And until quite recently, such mainstream figures as Lindblom (1977) pondered whether socialism would triumph over capitalism, or whether capitalism and socialism would continue to co-exist. The possibility that socialism might give way to capitalism was not even entertained.

....

THE POSTMODERN SHIFT

The socialist Leviathan-state *was* the logical culmination of the modernization process, but it did not turn out to be the wave of the future. Instead, the expansion of the bureaucratic state eventually approached a set of natural limits, and change

began to move in a new direction. Figure 1 illustrates what happened. From the Industrial Revolution until well into the second half of the twentieth century, industrial society followed the process of modernization. This transformed political and cultural systems from traditional regimes legitimated by religious belief systems to rational–legal states legitimated by their claim to maximize the welfare of their people through scientific expertise. It was a transfer of authority from family and religious institutions to political institutions.

Within the last 25 years, a major change in the direction of change has occurred, which might be called the postmodern shift. Its origins are rooted in the economic miracles that occurred first in Western Europe and North America and then, increasingly, in East Asia and (incipiently) in Southeast Asia. Coupled with the safety net of the modern welfare state, this has produced unprecedentedly high levels of economic security. It has given rise to a cultural feedback that is having a major impact on both the economic and political systems of advanced industrial societies. It shifts authority away from *both* religion and the state to the individual, with an increasing focus on individual concerns such as friends and leisure. The postmodern shift differs from the process of modernization in five crucial ways.

I. A SHIFT FROM SCARCITY VALUES TO POSTMODERN OR SECURITY VALUES

The root cause of the postmodern shift has been the gradual withering away of value systems that emerged under conditions of scarcity, and the spread of security values among a growing segment of the publics of these societies. This, in turn, grows out of the unprecedentedly high levels of subjective well-being that characterize the publics of advanced industrial society, as compared with those of earlier societies. In advanced industrial societies, most people take survival for granted. Precisely *because* they take it for granted, they are not aware of how profoundly this supposition shapes their worldview.

• **FIGURE 1** •

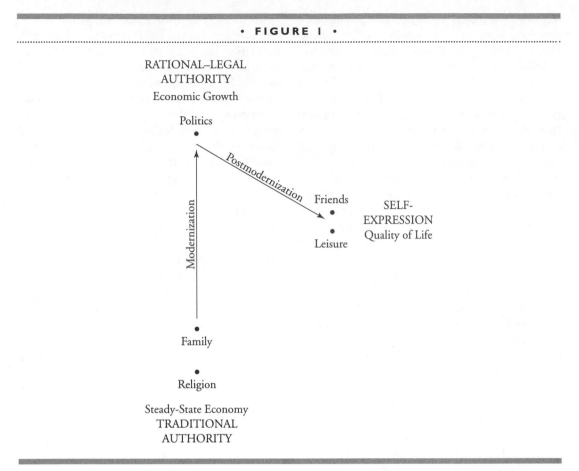

The shift from modernization to postmodernization: Changing emphasis on key aspects of life

Both traditional and modern societies were crucially shaped by scarcity, though industrial society developed the belief that scarcity could be alleviated by individual achievement and economic growth. Scarcity has prevailed throughout most of history: it follows from the ecological principle that population increases to meet the available food supply and is then held in check by starvation, disease and war. The result has been chronic scarcity, with the possibility of starvation shaping the daily awareness and life strategies of most people.

Starvation is no longer a real concern for most people living in high-technology societies where production has been increasing much faster than the rate of population growth. These societies have attained unprecedentedly high life expectancies

and unprecedentedly high levels of subjective well-being. One consequence of this fact has already been explored extensively: the rise of postmaterialist values throughout advanced industrial society. But this is only one component of a much broader cultural shift. Inglehart (1990) hypothesized that a wide range of related orientations are also undergoing change. The evidence presented below supports this claim: the emergence and spread of postmaterialist values is only the tip of the iceberg—one component of a much broader syndrome of cultural changes that we term postmodernization.

Within this new value system, values that played a key role in the emergence of industrial society—economic achievement, economic growth, economic rationality—have faded in salience.

At the societal level, there is a radical shift from the priorities of early industrialization—a growing tendency for emphasis on economic growth to become subordinate to concern for its impact on the environment. At the individual level, maximizing economic gains is gradually fading from top priority: self-expression and the desire for meaningful work are becoming even more crucial for a growing segment of population. Prevailing motivations for work are changing, from an emphasis on maximizing income as the top priority towards increasing emphasis on the quality of the work experience. There is even some willingness to accept ascriptive criteria rather than achievement criteria for recruitment, if it is justified by social goals.

During the modernization era, there was a consensus throughout industrial society that economic growth was not only a good thing, but virtually the *summum bonum;* although Marxists and capitalists disagreed about how the fruits of production should be distributed, both sides shared an unspoken consensus that economic growth was a good thing. This consensus was unspoken because it seemed self-evident. Economic growth and scientific discoveries constituted Progress: they were good by definition.

During the Cold War, there was a similar shared sentiment that the question of whether East or West was the better society would be decided by which one attained the greatest economic growth. And for most of the first three decades of the Cold War, the Eastern bloc seemed to be winning by the test that really counted: high growth rates. In 1972, *The Limits to Growth* called this consensus into question, arguing that economic growth was *not* desirable and that it should be brought to a stop before it was too late. Shortly afterwards, Schumacher's (1973) *Small is Beautiful* questioned another key principle of the modernization era: the tendency to equate Biggest with Best, which was widely accepted, especially among the socialist bloc where bigness and centralization were elevated almost to the rank of moral virtues. Both of these critiques reflected the emergence of security values, a core component of postmodernism. But there are several other components, among them the following.

2. DIMINISHING EFFECTIVENESS AND ACCEPTABILITY OF BUREAUCRATIC AUTHORITY

Hierarchical authority, centralization, bigness are all under growing suspicion. There are two reasons for this: (a) they have reached a point of diminishing effectiveness; and (b) they have reached a point of diminishing acceptability.

Every stable culture is linked with a congruent authority system. But the postmodern shift is a move away from *both* traditional authority and state authority. It reflects a declining emphasis on authority in general—regardless of whether it is legitimated by societal or state formulae. This is producing a declining confidence in hierarchical institutions in general, throughout advanced industrial society. From 1981 to 1990, confidence in established hierarchical institutions declined in virtually all of the 21 societies surveyed at both time points in the World Values Surveys. By no coincidence, political leaders throughout the industrialized world were experiencing some of the lowest levels of support ever recorded. This was not because they were less competent than previous leaders; it reflects a systematic decline in mass support for established political institutions, and a shift of focus towards individual concerns.

3. REJECTION OF THE WEST AS A MODEL, AND THE COLLAPSE OF THE SOCIALIST ALTERNATIVE

Initially, postmodernism focused on discontent with the dehumanizing aspects of bureaucratic, impersonal modernity as manifested in the West, its place of origin. Many of the most visible Western postmodernists even considered themselves Marxists. But it was inevitable that these discontents would eventually turn to the rejection of hierarchical, bureaucratic, centralized big government in the socialist world as well, where it was most extreme. This contributed to a major and unexpected shift in the direction of the wave of the future: the collapse of socialism. State socialism failed because (a) it no longer functioned well in advanced industrial society—although it *had* functioned reasonably well during the modernization era; and (b) because it was no longer acceptable (which reinforced its tendency to no longer function well). The declining effectiveness and acceptability of massive, centralized bureaucratic authority is one reason for the collapse of state socialism; the other is the fact that postmodernism contains an inherent tendency towards democratization, which grows out of the following points.

4. GROWING EMPHASIS ON INDIVIDUAL FREEDOM AND EMOTIONAL EXPERIENCE, AND REJECTION OF ALL FORMS OF AUTHORITY

Because postmaterialists place heightened emphasis on self-expression and political participation as things that are valuable in themselves, the postmodern phase of development is inherently conducive to democratization. There is nothing easy or automatic about this tendency. Determined authoritarian elites can repress it almost indefinitely, although at growing cost to the morale and co-operativeness of their subjects. Similarly, the institutional structure and cultural heritage of a given society can facilitate or retard this tendency, as can external pressures and other macropolitical factors. But as economic development takes place, mass input to the political process becomes increasingly widespread and effective. Economic development leads mass publics to place growing emphasis on participatory values.

5. DIMINISHING PRESTIGE OF SCIENCE, TECHNOLOGY AND RATIONALITY

One of the core components of modernization was a growing faith in the power of science and rational analysis to solve virtually all problems. And one of the most striking ways in which the postmodern shift differs from modernization, is that postmodernization is linked with a diminishing faith in rationality and a diminishing confidence that science and technology will help solve humanity's problems. This change in worldview has advanced furthest in those societies which are economically

and technologically most advanced; and where there has been severe erosion in the belief that science contributes to progress.

....

ELEMENTS OF CONTINUITY BETWEEN MODERNIZATION AND POSTMODERNIZATION

In some ways, postmodernization continues trends that were launched by modernization. In particular, the processes of specialization, secularization and individuation continue to develop. The growing complexity of advanced industrial society results in increasing specialization of functions in all areas of life. But the process of secularization and individuation have taken on a new character.

Secularization

Weber attributed the decline of religious belief largely to the rise of the scientific worldview, which increasingly replaced the sacred/mystical pre-rational elements of religious faith. Although the scientific worldview has lost its glamour, secularization continues, but for a new reason: the emergence of security values among the economically more advanced societies makes their people psychologically less in need of the reassurance that has traditionally been provided by absolute belief systems, which purport to provide certainty and the assurance of salvation, if not in this world, at least in the next. Although postmodernism goes with a continuing decline in traditional religious beliefs, it is linked with a growing concern for the meaning and purpose of life.

Individuation

The erosion of religious social controls opened up a certain amount of room for individual autonomy, but it was largely taken up by growing obligations to the state. The postmodern shift away from *both* religious and state authority continues this long-standing shift towards individuation, but in a stronger form. Increasingly, individual rights and entitlements take priority over any other obligation ... [The author's analysis of empirical data from the World Values Survey has been omitted—ED.]

MODERNIZATION, POSTMODERNIZATION AND DEMOCRATIZATION

Finally, the postmodernization process has important political implications. Inkeles and Diamond (1980), Inglehart (1990) and others have argued that economic development is linked with cultural changes that are conducive to democracy, an argument that has been hotly disputed by dependency theorists, neo-Marxists and some rational-choice theorists. [T]here is no correlation whatever between the modernization axis and the number of years for which a given society has been democratic. Industrialization, urbanization and the other elements of modernization can give rise to either democratic or authoritarian regimes. . . .

WHY DOES CHANGE FOLLOW PREDICTABLE PATTERNS?

Coherent trajectories of cultural change exist, with some cultural patterns being far more probable than others. Why?

The evidence suggests that in the long run, cultural change behaves as if it were a process of rational choice, subject to substantial cultural lags, and to the fact that the goals being maximized vary from one culture to another and can only be understood through empirical knowledge of the specific culture. In this loosely rational process, peoples are maximizing a variety of goods, the most basic of which is survival, and their cultures are survival strategies for a given people. Cultural variation tends to follow predictable patterns because some ways of running a society work better than others. If one is willing to concede that most people prefer survival to non-survival, then both modernization and postmodernization are linked with outcomes that almost anyone would consider 'better'. . . . [T]here is a 0.54 correlation between a society's mean life expectancy and its degree of modernization, and a 0.62 correlation between life expectancy and postmodernization. Neither process bestows

moral superiority, but both modernization and postmodernization markedly diminish the likelihood of dying prematurely from disease or malnutrition. Life expectancy today ranges from as low as 39 years in the poorest countries, to almost 80 years in developed ones. This is a difference few people would fail to appreciate, regardless of cultural background. It is one reason (along with such attributes as superior military technology) why the modernization syndrome had such pervasive appeal. Successful industrialization required an impersonal, bureaucratic, competitive, achievement-oriented form of social relations that tends to be dehumanizing; but in societies of scarcity around the globe, it came to be viewed as a worthwhile tradeoff. Islamic fundamentalism remains an alternative model in so far as oil revenues make it possible to obtain many of the advantages of modernization, from modem medical care to advanced military technology, *without* industrializing; but this model's credibility may not outlast the oil reserves.

The modernization process brought substantial gains in life expectancy by maximizing economic growth, making it possible to sharply reduce the two leading causes of death in pre-industrial societies—malnutrition and disease. But the linkage between economic development and rising life expectancy eventually reached a point of diminishing returns.

Postmodernization can be seen as a shift in survival strategies, from maximizing economic growth to maximizing survival and well-being through lifestyle changes. Modernization focused on rapid economic growth, which was also a means to the broader goal of maximizing survival and well-being under the conditions which emerged when rationalization and industrialization first became possible. But no one strategy is optimal for all times. Modernization was dramatically successful in raising life expectancies, but it has now begun to produce diminishing returns in advanced industrial societies. Emphasizing competition, it reduced the risk of starvation, but may have increased psychological stress. Postmodernization, on the other hand, has a mildly negative linkage with economic growth, but a strong positive linkage with subjective well-being. With the transition from modernization to postmodernization, the trajectory of change seems to have shifted from maximizing economic growth to maximizing the quality of life.

CROSS-SECTIONAL EVIDENCE OF SOCIAL CHANGE

Cross-sectional data can be a useful supplement to time series data in understanding processes of socioeconomic change. Although time series data provide the only reliable measurements of changes over time, appropriate cross-sectional data can greatly extend the scope of one's perspective in time and space: its configuration may reflect processes that occurred over many decades or even centuries.

Interpreted in connection with the available time series data, the cultural configurations found in the 43-nation World Values Survey suggest that coherent, and even to some extent predictable, trajectories of political and cultural change are linked with given socioeconomic developments. These trajectories are not deterministic: the leaders and the cultural heritage of a given society also help shape its course. And development does not move in a simple, linear fashion; all trends eventually change direction.

But neither is socioeconomic change random and unpredictable, with each society following an idiosyncratic course. On the contrary, change tends to follow clear configurations, in which specific clusters of cultural characteristics go together with specific types of political and economic change. The familiar modernization syndrome of urbanization, industrialization and mass literacy, tends to have foreseeable consequences such as increasing mass mobilization. And, as we have seen, modernization is linked with specific cultural changes, such as the shift from traditional to rational–legal authority.

Similarly, the emergence of advanced industrial society, with an increasing share of the public having higher education, being employed in the service sector, and feeling assured that their survival needs will be met, gives rise to a process in which high levels of subjective well-being and postmodern values emerge, and in which a variety of attributes, from equal rights for women to democratic political institutions, become increasingly likely.

BEYOND POSTMODERNISM?

Every stable culture is linked with a congruent authority system. But the postmodern shift is a move away from both traditional authority and state authority. It reflects a declining emphasis on authority in general, regardless of whether it is legitimated by societal or state formulae. This leads to declining confidence in hierarchical institutions, throughout advanced industrial society. From 1981 to 1990 confidence in governmental institutions fell in virtually all industrial societies, and by the early 1990s political leaders were experiencing some of the lowest levels of support ever recorded. This was not just because they were less competent than their predecessors; it reflects a systematic decline in the basis of mass support for established political institutions.

Such trends cannot continue forever. Political systems either adapt in ways that generate some measure of internalized support, or they collapse and are replaced by new political systems. Ultimately, the systems that emerge and survive will be systems that have found some effective legitimating formula. This formula, whatever it is, may mark the emergence of post-post-modern politics.

ENDNOTE

1. The World Values Surveys were carried out from March 1990 to January 1991 in 43 societies. Representative national samples were used in all cases except East Germany, Northern Ireland and the greater Moscow region (surveyed in *addition* to the entire Russian Republic). The quality of the samples varies from country to country. Surveys in Western countries were carried out by professional survey organizations with a great deal of experience, most of them members of the Gallup chain. In Eastern Europe they were carried out by the respective national academies of sciences or university-based

institutes, some of which had carried out few surveys previously. The surveys from low income countries generally have larger error margins than those from other countries. The samples from India, Nigeria and China overrepresent the urban areas and the more educated strata. Since these groups tend to have orientations relatively similar to those found in industrial societies, our data probably underestimate the size of cross-national differences involving these countries. Nevertheless, these three countries frequently show very distinctive orientations. The data from the 1990–1991 surveys were released through the ICPSR survey data archive in July 1994; for details concerning fieldwork, see the ICPSR codebook.

REFERENCES

Basáñez, M., 1993. 'Protestant and Catholic Ethics: An Empirical Comparison.' Paper presented at conference on 'Changing Social and Political Values: A Global Perspective', Complutense University. Madrid. 27 September–1 October.

Bell, D., 1973. *The Coming of Postindustrial Society.* New York: Basic Books.

Deutsch, K. W., 1961. 'Social Mobilization and Political Development'. *American Political Science Review,* 55, pp. 493–514.

Inglehart, R., 1990. *Culture Shift in Advanced Industrial Society.* Princeton: Princeton University Press.

Inglehart, R.; Abramson, P., 1994. 'Economic Security and Value Change'. *American Political Science Review,* 88:2, pp. 1–18. June, 336–354.

Inglehart, R.; et al., 1996. *The North American Trajectory.* New York: Aldine de Gruyter.

Inglehart, R., 1997. *Modernization and Postmodernization: Cultural, Economic and Political Change in 43 Societies.* Princeton: Princeton University Press.

Inkeles, A; Diamond, L., 1980. "Personal Qualities as a Reflection of National Development." In F. Andrews and A. Szalai (eds.). *Comparative Studies in Quality of Life.* London: Sage.

Inkeles, A.; Smith, D., 1974. *Becoming Modern: Individual Change in Six Developing Countries.* Cambridge, MA: Harvard University Press.

Lerner, D., 1958. *The Passing of Traditional Society: Modernizing the Middle East.* New York: The Free Press.

Lindblom, C, 1977. *Politics and Markets: The World's Political–Economic Systems.* New York: Basic Books.

Lipset, S. M., 1960. *Political Man.* New York: Doubleday.

Meadows, D. H.; et al., 1972. *The Limits to Growth.* New York: Universe.

Putnam, R. D. (with R. Leonardi and R. Nanetti), 1993. *Making Democracy Work: Civic Traditions in Modern Italy.* Princeton: Princeton University Press.

Rostow, W. W., 1961. *The Stages of Economic Growth.* Cambridge: Cambridge University Press.

Schumacher, E. F, 1973. *Small is Beautiful: Economics as if People Mattered.* New York: Harper and Row.

Schumpeter, J., 1947. *Capitalism, Socialism and Democracy.* 2nd edn. New York: Harper and Brothers.

Sombart, W., 1913. *The Jews and Modern Capitalism.* London; Fisher, Unwin.

Weber, M. (1904–1905), 1958. *The Protestant Ethic and the Spirit of Capitalism.* New York: Scribner's.

Wilson, R. W., 1992. *Compliance Ideology: Rethinking Political Culture.* Cambridge, England: Cambridge University Press.

H. V. SAVITCH

8   What Is New About Globalization?

QUESTIONING GLOBALISATION

Some years ago at the Hebrew University of Jerusalem I presented a paper on globalisation, attempting to define it as something of unparalleled and intense change. One of the university's many distinguished professors remained unconvinced, and responded to me by saying, "I see nothing new here. All of this existed a century ago." The session ended with an unresolved debate about whether globalisation was new or not. Since then most scholars have taken global change for granted, but a significant and influential number continue to question the arrival of a new global era. Hirst and Thompson (1996) contend that globalisation has yet to rear its head. Limiting their analysis to economic matters, they contend that what we are seeing is not so much globalisation as the continuation of an "internationalised economy". The world is in the midst of greater "internationalisation", and that has continued from the previous century. These writers go on to elaborate models of a "globalised" versus an "internationalised" economy, and purport that global criteria have not been met. Among other things they claim that if "economic globalisation" did exist it would not be dominated by a single nation-state; in fact the world is led by an American superpower. If it existed globalisation would not be subject to political control; in fact it is regulated by international organisations like the International Monetary Fund, the World Bank, and the G-8. If it existed globalisation would be characterised by footloose transnational firms with no national identity; in fact it is characterised by more constrained multinational firms with numerous national locations.

Scepticism about globalisation also has some resonance in the popular press. A recent feature in the *New York Times* (11 August, 2001) looks backward and draws a picture of globalisation just prior to the First World War. The article goes on to say:

> The inhabitant of London could order by telephone, sipping his morning tea in bed the variation of products of the whole earth . . . He could at the same moment and by the same means adventure his wealth in the natural resources and new enterprises of any quarter of the world, and share, without exertion or even trouble in their prospective fruits and advantages . . . He could secure . . . cheap and comfortable means of transit to any county or climate without passport or other formality.

We could add to this version of early globalisation some pertinent data. This includes the fact that before the First World War half of British savings were actually invested overseas and levels of international investment in Germany, France, Belgium, and the Netherlands were quite similar. Some of the largest spurts in world trade took place in the late nineteenth century. Despite all the hoopla about mass migration, the greatest era for immigration was not the twentieth but the early nineteenth century, when approximately 60 million people left Europe for the Americas, Oceania, and South Africa. During this era Chinese and Japanese populated continents outside of Asia, and whole nations were created out of immigrant waves.

We have then claims that globalisation represents nothing new in foreign trade, little that is new in worldwide communication, and was preceded by massive migrations a century earlier. Yet globalisation is on everyone's lips, and its currents are thought to dominate the next century. The question is compelling—what is truly new about

SOURCE: H. V. Savitch, "What Is New About Globalization and What Does It Portend for Cities?," *International Social Science Journal*, no. 172 (June 2002), pp. 179–189. © 2002 by United Nations Educational, Scientific, and Cultural Organization (UNESCO). Reprinted by permission of Blackwell Publishing Ltd. Abridged by the Editor.

globalisation? Before we can begin to answer this question we should clarify how the term is commonly understood.

EXAMINING GLOBALISATION ANEW

First and foremost, just as the feudal and industrial eras are best seen as totalities, so too should globalisation. Epochal change is a complex bundle of economic, technological, political, social, and cultural forces. These forces interact in a myriad ways, and that interaction is larger than the sum of its parts. Examining a single phase of globalisation is at best problematic and at worst a truncated distortion of the phenomenon.

Second, epochal change does not usually come about through a "big bang". Globalisation is not a thing that suddenly appears. It is a dynamic process that is gradual and always in motion. Different parts of that process may be forerunners or lag behind other parts. Sediments of an older order may endure even as total change is manifest. Thus, even when industrialisation was in full swing and there was a shift in the use of energy from animal to mechanical, horse drawn carriages were still prevalent. In much the same way, one could imagine multinational firms existing side-by-side with transnational corporations—gradually blending their operations. The critical factor is not the abruptness or completeness of change, but its tangible momentum, its contextual impact and its effect on peoples' behaviour and beliefs.

Third, these points turn on the issue of what is change, what does it look like, and how can we determine its presence? Generally change means a significant transformation in the established character of something, and it entails substantial modifications in the nature of life. But it does not obliterate everything. Rarely is change a reversal or negation of everything, and more frequently it contains an element of continuity. The functionalist school of social science sees change as a retention of basic tasks (or functions) coupled to a different way of carrying them out. Indeed a basic theorem of functionalism is that all societies must carry out certain essential tasks like socialising individuals into the mores of the community. As Merton (1968: 135) puts it, any attempt to "eliminate an existing social structure without . . . fulfilling (those) functions . . . is doomed to failure".

Bringing this point back to globalisation, to claim that the volume of international trade in the nineteenth century took a similar proportion of GDP as twentieth century trade misses the point. One might equally claim that medieval trade took an even greater proportion of gross domestic product, yet this would not reveal the radical change in the nature of that trade during the last 500 years. . . . To put this in functionalist terms what counts here is not the amount of international trade, but the radically changed way in which it is now carried out and the impact of that transformation on peoples' lives. Trade may always be a necessary commercial function, but globalisation has brought it to new depths, in an altogether new way, with unprecedented consequences.

DEFINING GLOBALISATION

We begin with the notion that globalisation contains five basic elements: (1) new technology, (2) the centrality of information made possible by instant communication, (3) an increasing trend toward the standardisation of economic and social products, (4) growing cross-national integration, and (5) mutual vulnerability stemming from greater interdependence.

Globalisation is driven by a technological revolution that has shrunk time and distance. By now advanced technology moves $1.5 trillion in capital around the world each day. In the United States international flows of bonds and equities are 54 times higher today than in 1970. The comparable figures for Germany and Japan are 60 and 50 times higher. Other research has shown that international trade sustains the global patterning, and has brought about changes in economic relationships, social structure, and the significance of geographical place. Technology also moves people in unprecedented time, frequency, and numbers. Between 1991 and 2000 average airline traffic passengers jumped by 51% while cargo increased by 131%.

The current era is propelled by the transmission of information. The last quarter of this century is appropriately called "the information age," and it portends revolutionary technological achievements. The new world of cyberspace is just one technology that allows this. At the dawn of the post-industrial age, during the mid 1970s, just 50,000 computers existed in the world. That number has now rocketed to 556 million, giving individuals access to each other across the globe. More than half of Americans and more than a quarter of West Europeans own computers. In North America and West Europe big and small cities are hard-wired for instant communication. Carriers, like BBC or CNN, have established global news networks, allowing the world to witness the same events at the same time. Impressions are created instantly, and reactions occur swiftly. The decreasing cost of telephone service and the spread of fibre-optic cables (simultaneously transmitting 1.5 million conversations within the diameter of a human hair) catapulted personal information to new levels. By the year 2000 international telephone calls reached an all-time high of 100 billion minutes.

Another characteristic of globalisation is standardisation. Once goods and information are alike, they become recognisable and interchangeable. Common standards of measurement, universal criteria, interchangeable parts and identical symbols are essential for globalisation. Just as the grid system of streets helped land development so too does standardisation facilitate globalisation. This includes a common currency, established procedures for registering and enforcing patents, and compatible mechanical or electronic equipment. Licences and professional certification have also become standardised in order to allow human resources to flow across boundaries. Even sports have become standardised. The Olympic Games and Olympic committees legitimate certain sports and sanction rules through which athletic contests are held. Traditionally, American baseball has been capped by the misnomer of a "World Series". Up until recently this was entirely an American affair, but increasingly players and even some teams have been drawn from other nations. The progressive universality of sports today is incontrovertible.

Cross-national integration is vital to a global world. Globalisation has magnified the intercourse between states, localities and social movements across the world. Signs of this are visible in the rise of multilateral organisations, regional pacts, and talk of a borderless world. States, localities, non-governmental organisations, and labour increasingly ignore old boundaries, and are driven more than before by the seemingly contradictory stimuli of cooperation and competition. Integration also has a socio-cultural component. This involves diffusion of a more open, multipolar, and multicultural society in which migration is a major by-product. What distinguishes current migration from preceding movements is its truncated and temporary patterns of settlement. Commonly, single men live abroad for lengthy periods, while sending remittances to the homeland. When whole families do migrate, they often are treated as long-term aliens, rarely assimilating, and even children born in the host country may not acquire citizenship. Indeed, the telecommunications revolution has given permanency to this temporary status. Cheap, efficient technology compresses space and time, enabling groups to retain homeland ties and preserve indigenous culture. Overseas, ethnic cultures are now said to thrive in "transnational space" in which language, habit and tradition continue regardless of geography.

The integrative features of globalisation lead to greater interdependence. This in turn fosters a mutual vulnerability between nations, regions, and continents. Free trade may have made societies more efficient, but they have also made them more fragile and susceptible to crisis. In a matter of minutes, turmoil in a single great bank can upset finance at the other end of the world. Currency fluctuations can overturn decades of progress, hitting those at the bottom of the economic scale hardest. The exuberance and then depression of stock markets began in the United States and was quickly telegraphed across the world. Disease travels as swiftly as airline flights and has acquired an international character. West Nile Virus and even more tragically the Aids epidemic are unfortunate examples of this exposure. Still another dark side of globalisation is the spread of terrorism. The ease of travel, instantaneous communication, and easy transfer of money make it possible for terrorists to do their work and attack fragile international linkages.[1]

....

PORTENTS FOR CITIES: THE GOOD NEWS

How do cities fit into this picture? One might suppose that globalisation makes cities less important, as they are swept into a common world of economic competition and social interchange. Presumably, people could be located anywhere, and conduct business via the internet from a mountaintop retreat. In fact the opposite is true—at least for some cities. A knowledge-based economy has accelerated face to face and informal contact. It has increased an appetite for conferences, seminars, and annual meetings. Additionally, business searches for that extra edge that comes from personal contact.

Globalisation also has generated a need for central direction in which financial, legal and professional services are concentrated within a common locale. Cities have made free trade much easier to accomplish, they have facilitated a new international division of labour, and they have absorbed waves of migration. While not all cities have been blessed with these advantages, many are still efficient and enormously productive work stations for the post-industrial era. Whether one selects a handful of global cities, a larger number of primate cities or a sampling of regional cities, urban centres lead national productivity, and their total output in goods and services has quickened during the last few decades. Rising urbanisation has occurred concomitantly with globalisation, and is associated with rising GDP. Metropolitan areas of Europe and North America grew rich during transformation, though clearly as the process matures the rate of urbanisation flattens....

We can better formulate ... positive aspects by listing them.

1. Partly through open competition, prosperity is rising, it is contagious and it is associated with growing urbanisation. Most nations and most localities are better off today than they were 30 years ago. As cities grow into great metropolises, so too does the economic well-being of most inhabitants. The relationship is not invariable. As economies mature, prosperity appears to gradually plateau and eventually flatten. Moreover, many parts of Sub-Saharan Africa have experienced urbanisation without development, and this part of the world remains an exception. But the overall pattern between urbanisation and economic well-being is positive, and even nations in Sub-Saharan Africa have begun to take off.

Reaching back to 1970 up to the end of this decade, we know that increased urbanisation is positively correlated with rises in Gross Domestic Product (GDP). This is true for the most-developed as well as the least-developed regions of the world. In the United States and Canada urban populations have risen by 20% and per capita income by a third. West Europe shows a similar trend. In most of South America urbanisation and economic gain are incremental and steady, growing by 20% or more. The most notable progress has been made in Argentina, Brazil, and Chile. South-East Asia, East Asia, and Oceania bear out similar lessons. Despite recent downslides, younger industrial economies in South Korea, Indonesia, and Thailand have just about doubled their urbanisation and GDP.

The causal relationships between increased urbanisation and GDP are complex. But the association is unmistakable and the underlying logic is strong. Once agricultural, mining, or timber production reaches a certain level and surpluses can be brought to market, new opportunities arise for the new conversion of raw products into new goods. The conversion takes place in urbanised areas, whose technological and trading capacity are fed back into rural economies, enabling still greater efficiencies and freeing more individuals for work elsewhere. New technology and investment provide still more opportunities and a seamless synergy between all sectors of production. This is why urbanised populations are far more prosperous than rural ones as well as why giant megalopolises continue to attract populations from the countryside.

2. Global and regional cities have played a vital and disproportionate role in contributing to this prosperity. Global cities (New York, London, Tokyo) have made free trade much easier to accomplish. Contrary to the impressions of central city decline, great cities have proven themselves to be efficient and enormously productive work stations for the post-industrial era. . . .

3. We are beset by an explosion of information, and this not only promotes democracy, but also encourages pluralism and greater accountability. Overall advances contribute to the strength of the middle class and ultimately to institutional stability. While the internet cannot guarantee democracy, it can assure the dissemination of information; facilitate free exchange between groups; and, allow increasing communication between rulers and the ruled. While there may be setbacks and there will always be exceptions, the democratic future is promising. Sooner or later and in most places, technology will stimulate pluralism, diversity, and accountability.

It is no sheer coincidence that prosperity and free information have been accompanied by rising waves of democratisation. Since the early 1970s democratic states have been replacing authoritarian ones. During this period, those states classified as "democratic" rose from 30 to 59, while nations classified as "authoritarian systems" decreased from 92 to 71. In Western Europe, Spain and Portugal joined the other democratic states. In Latin America, the transition to democracy was especially marked. Brazil, Ecuador, Chile, Argentina, Guatemala, and Bolivia have now joined the democratic ranks. In East Europe, the collapse of communism brought a swarm of nations into the democratic fold. In the Middle East only Israel can be counted within the world's liberal democracies, though a handful of other nations (Jordan and smaller states on the Arabian Peninsula) have begun to loosen the reins of authoritarianism. Independent Arab news stations transmit around the region and have attracted a following. In Iran more moderate followers have begun to challenge the theocratic regime, and while the struggle may be long, it is increasingly difficult to monopolise information or control public opinion. Again Africa constitutes a mixed and more complex picture, with only a minority of states classified as democratic while a majority are thought to be in various stages of transition.

PORTENTS FOR CITIES: THE BAD NEWS

The positives also have their downside. Every new age creates disruption. The transition from feudal to industrial eras divorced peasants from open land and fresh air, throwing them into wretched urban hovels. For all their travail feudal peasants once enjoyed frequent festivals, days off from work, and a deep sense of community. Under industrialisation they were trapped in stench-filled, poorly lit factories, labouring 15 hours a day, 7 days a week. Extended families were destroyed, and capitalism was especially merciless to women and children who laboured at dangerous factory machines. This transition was all part of what Joseph Schumpeter (1950) called "creative destruction." The process allows market forces to act with impersonal ruthlessness in crushing old, inert practices and initiating a new, dynamic way of doing things. The immediate welfare of people mattered little when set against the prospect of new machines, more goods, and higher profits. Change always comes with a cost, and the cost for some generations can be exorbitant.

It is these very costs that have engendered strong opposition to globalisation. Logically, the strongest reaction to globalisation has come from the more extreme fringes of the right and left. As in most epochal change, groups at the ends of the social spectrum are often the most threatened. Pensioners, union workers, small business people and unemployed youth are the first to incur the penalties of economic revolution. Not surprisingly these groups turn to marginal political parties to voice their opposition. Right-wing political antagonism is readily apparent in America's Reform Party, France's National Front, Italy's National Movement, Austria's Freedom Party, and throughout other parts of Europe. Patrick Buchanan, Jean Marie Le Pen, Gianfranco Fini, and George Haider are their most visible proponents. Their rhetoric is often prone to flourishes of xenophobia, attacks upon immigration policy, and hostility to international engagement. Fears over global change lay at the heart of Ross Perot and Patrick Buchanan's campaign against Mexican immigration and their complaints about rampant illegal immigration. Rather than an opportunity, both of these candidates saw free trade via NAFTA as a "giant sucking sound" vacuuming away American jobs.

Globalisation has encouraged the internationalisation of complaints, and the political left has used these opportunities to put pressure on decision makers. The left-wing coalition against globalisation has been more ambiguous in its demands, in part because it is a broader coalition. This coalition ranges from anarchists and neo-Marxists to Green Party activists and environmentalists and finally encompassing more conventional union leaders and politicians. In frustration, demonstrators turned to very aggressive tactics. Protests in Seattle, Quebec, Göteborg and Genoa, tried to confront political elites, and activists filled the streets with parades and placards. "People's tribunals" held mock trials for alleged wrongdoers, and some of their activities erupted into violent confrontations with the police. Representatives from less developed nations have also joined the fray, and are using an international forum to air past grievances against colonialism. "The World Conference Against Racism, Racial Discrimination, Xenophobia and Related Intolerance" (Durban, South Africa) is just one in a line of international meetings. These sessions are designed to redress grievances (or exact concessions) stemming from global economic imbalances, and they are likely to continue.

The list of grievances held by the anti global right and left is quite extensive. The negative aspects are real, with far reaching consequences; a few are cited below.

1. The force of transformation is connected to sharpened economic polarities, disparate geographical conditions and highly uneven investment. These polarities are multi-sided and can be seen between different areas of the world as well as within localities of many nations. The paradox of contemporary economic development is that while most localities have become wealthier, they also contain rising numbers of the poor. The explanation for this incongruity lies in differences of income generation and distribution of wealth within nations as well as between them. Taking urbanised areas, 40% of the population in sub-Saharan Africa (e.g., Gambia, Mozambique) is below the poverty line. In North Africa (e.g., Egypt, Morocco) the poor account for roughly 30% of the population. While these numbers diminish in Asia and South America, the poor still make up between 25 and 30% of the urbanised population (Indonesia, Pakistan, Brazil, Venezuela). The numbers descend as we reach the United States (21% in central cities and 9% in suburbs, and West Europe (15% urban poor). In the most advanced nations differences are accentuated between areas, and the most distressed can match those in less developed nations. In the American Midwest and in the north of England the poor account for close to 40% of the population.

These polarities ramify into patterns of investment, so that the potential for economic growth or recovery is profoundly affected. Wealthier areas gain an increased capacity to reinforce their market position, and this can be seen through disparities in infrastructure investment. Taking 34 metropolitan centres around the world, we find those with the greatest wealth (Tokyo, Vienna, Paris, and Amsterdam) received over 700 times more per capita expenditures in infrastructure than did those in less developed economies (Dar es Salaam, Delhi, Cairo, and Quito). This pattern has continued over the past decade. Should it persist, we can expect to see wealthy areas enhancing their economic capacity, while those already marginalised within the global system will become even less attractive for investment.

2. Economic transformation and polarisation have contributed to higher social disorder. The last 25 years have seen greater migration, more severe family dislocation, sharper social segregation and ruptures in the social fabric. While migration is not new to the world, it was never so closely associated with family separation and temporary living status. The shift has not just occurred in the West, but in less developed nations that host millions of migrants. In most cases migrants flock to inner cities, and today a quarter of the populations in New York, London and Toronto are foreign born. Even homogeneous Tokyo holds 250,000 foreign residents and a large number of ethnic Koreans.

What distinguishes post-industrial migration is its enduring character and its translation into what Smith (2001) calls transnational communities. These communities are likely to retain their national socio-cultural identities and even their political citizenship, while residing in foreign locations. Communication and travel continue unabated with an immigrant's native country. Commonly, single men live abroad for lengthy periods while sending remittances to the homeland. When whole families do migrate, they are treated as long-term aliens, rarely assimilating or acquiring citizenship. The situation is particularly acute in Germany which today hosts 6.5 million foreigners or 10% of the population. More than 70% of Germany's "guest workers" have lived in the country for more than 10 years. Germany is not alone. Mexico and Thailand received hundreds of thousands of migrants in the last 5 years. Today, São Paulo hosts nearly a million foreign residents, while Bangkok holds 500,000.

3. The cumulative impacts of these changes have washed onto the steps of government and are creating inordinate pressures. At both policy and administrative levels, localities are faced with heightened expectations and a surfeit of demands. . . .

Meanwhile citizens are expecting and asking for more. The rise of cable television, narrowcasting, and the internet has created an aware citizenry who demand that problems be resolved and services be provided. This is especially true for affluent and sophisticated "yuppie" populations. These constituencies expect that streets be safe and clean; that open spaces be preserved and that fairness ordinances be adopted and implemented. Ironically, as citizens expect and often receive more, favourable attitudes toward government at all levels have declined. In the United States confidence in national institutions peaked during the 1970s and plummeted by the 1990s. In 1995 only 9% of the population had confidence in the executive branch. Confidence ratings for state and local government are higher, but they too have fallen.

It is not coincidental that so many of us are interested in "reinventing government" and promoting "privatisations," "public–private partnerships" or "matrix organisations." In Europe and America these innovations are subsumed under a larger concept of local "governance." The idea of governance is to seek flexible ways through which public power can be leveraged with private entrepreneurship and market capital. Public officials, journalists and researchers spend enormous amounts of time searching for new ways of doing old things. Innovation in government has become the watchword, buttressed by calls for greater accountability and transparency. All this can only be a response to cumulative pressures and popular awareness that government can do more with less.

....

CONCLUSIONS: A CHANGING, MORE COMPETITIVE AND UNCERTAIN FUTURE

Though producing both positive and negative effects, the complex of global forces is inextricably linked, they have a reciprocating influence, and they are bound to a common future. We can expect that efforts to enhance GDP will stimulate investment, but also create greater disparities within and between localities. Struggles over regional primacy will lead to greater affluence, but also beget family disruption, social polarisation, and a more pervasive informal economy. The explosive tendencies of information both on site and across cyberspace, makes government more accountable and more transparent, but also heightens public expectations and increases popular demands, putting inordinate pressures upon local institutions. The uncertainty of change and doubts about who is actually "in charge" also leads to a perilous instability and a thunderous reaction from the extremes of the left and the right.

Still early in their life cycle, these forces are bound to accelerate and create still more uncertainties. Mounting and accumulating pressures have already begun to fashion a new world. As decentralisation and free trade proceed, more localities are fragmenting and behaving as solitary, proactive, competitors in a global marketplace. The melting away of older restraints gives rise to a new international division of labour, and a search by localities for their own, distinct, competitive advantage. A gradual but inexorable process of self-examination obliges local decision makers to ask, how can we find our niche in the world, national, or regional national market?

One way to establish a competitive advantage is to offer goods and services more cheaply, and sometimes to establish supply lines for contraband items. High growth regions create an increased demand for inexpensive household labour, customised services and hard to find goods. Some of this demand has been transformed into an informal economy, heavily staffed by migrants. The army of prosperous white collar commuters who pack financial districts each weekday is passed by another army of blue collar "reverse commuters" who work "off the books" as housekeepers, gardeners, or day labourers. Other participants in the informal economy work in tiny garment factories or as unlicensed street vendors and artisans. A smaller number may be involved in gambling or illicit activities.

Another way of dealing with global competition is to lower the costs of doing business. Any number of methods can be employed, but the most popular fall into "supply side" techniques. These include lowering taxes, supplying cheap labour, training labour forces, building new infrastructure,

relaxing or abolishing environmental regulations, and forming government–business partnerships, which reduce investment risks. Once localities try to lower taxes or attract business through supply-side incentives, they may find themselves either reducing social services or on the road to fiscal stress.

Fiscal stress can become a long-term issue on the local agenda. Chronic economic distress is not new for national and sub-national governments in less developed economies. It is, however, a more recent occurrence in advanced economies that is both long term and transnational. Over the years fiscal stress has created a climate where localities take risks to stay afloat. When those risks do not turn out well, the results can reverberate well beyond local boundaries. New York's default of 1975, Liverpool's receivership of 1984, Orange County's bankruptcy of 1995 forced major changes in how government operates. Fiscal austerity in South Korea, Malaysia, Indonesia, Argentina, and Brazil have led to major crises, and these are likely to continue in other parts of the globe.

There are too socio-cultural elements in this new world that are integral to the information explosion and middle-class growth. Post-industrial societies are thought to possess modern life styles that emphasise environmental protection, consumer interests, and identity politics (feminism, gay rights). Some scholars have found evidence of a new political culture based on individual motivation (rather than class consciousness), a respect for markets (instead of hierarchy) and greater attention to local government (in contrast to national authority). Other scholars see post-industrial societies as the hothouse for a post-materialist society with its emphasis on citizen activism and social issues. The more likely scenario is that new cultures will develop and either overlay, mix with or function alongside more traditional attitudes.

While global markets, technology and society are in a period of rapid transformation, governmental institutions have lagged. The intensely decentralised composition and flexibility of global forces stand in marked contrast to hierarchical and fixed behaviour of government institutions. Particularly acute are the contrasting modes of operation between markets and governmental institutions.

Markets are flexible, prolific, and immensely responsive to mass demands, while government institutions are steeped in formalism and routine.

While we cannot be sure about all that the next decades will bring, they will have to bring new markets and new governments into alignment. Contrary to how some writers describe globalisation, it need not be out of control. Indeed we have already seen a spate of regional and international organisations regulating parts of the global economy. Cities have begun to form transnational confederations that foster information sharing, economic cooperation and technological assistance. Supra-national and regional governments will have to play a greater role, working incrementally though steadily in making adjustments. Not the least, localities will have to be more accountable if they are to satisfy citizens, maintain popular legitimacy, and cope with daily pressures.

ENDNOTE

1. Every action has its reaction and globalisation is no different. Vulnerability also has a more fortunate side that can be found in cross-national cooperation and synergy. This kind of complementary interdependence has brought about cooperation in regulating currencies, controlling Aids, and combating terrorism.

REFERENCES

A.T. Kearney, Inc. April. 2001. "The Globalisation index," *Global Outlook: International Urban Research Monitor.*

Hirst, Paul & Thompson, Grahame 1996. *Globalisation in Question.* Cambridge: Polity Press.

Knight, R. & Gappert, G. (EDS.) 1989. *Cities in a Global Society.* Newbury Park, California: Sage Publications.

Merton, Robbrt K. 1968. *Social Theory and Social Structure.* New York: Free Press.

Sassen, S. 1991. *The Global City: New York, London, Tokyo.* Princeton, New Jersey: Princeton University Press.

Schumpeter, Joseph 1950. *Capitalism, Socialism and Democracy.* New York: Harper and Row.

Smith, Michael 2001. *Transnational Urbanism.* Oxford: Blackwell Publishers.

Williamson, J. G. 1995. "The evolution of the global labour market since 1830: Background evidence and hypotheses" *Explorations in Economic History 32,* pp. 141–196.

CHAPTER THREE

STATE AND IDENTITY

The traditional subject of comparative politics is the state. In order to understand the state we must also examine the social and economic forces that impinge upon it, and the culture within which it functions. Max Weber's celebrated definition of the state distinguishes those "human communities" or groups that enjoy a legitimate monopoly on the use of violence from those (like parties, trade unions, corporations, churches, sports associations, etc.) that do not. For Weber, violence entails unforeseen consequences; the use of violent means makes it more difficult if not impossible to achieve even the noblest of ends. Does his argument hold up? Does coercion, necessarily bound up with state action, always lead to negative consequences? His distinction between the ethic of principled conviction and the ethic of responsibility should be tested with reference to real political systems and historical episodes. What are the institutional forms taken by these two ethics? What examples are given by Weber? It is important also to relate each ethic to Weber's classification of the types of legitimacy. What combination of traditional, charismatic, and rational-legal legitimacy would best promote an ethic of responsibility? Can examples be given?

Weber's social and political theory is a powerful tool of comparative analysis. The reader will find Weberian theory incorporated into many of the selections in this volume. Theda Skocpol centers her analysis on the "differing abilities of states" to realize policy goals. How can this kind of comparison be carried out? Does Professor Skocpol establish valid distinctions concerning the capacities of the state in the United States and Britain on the one hand, and continental Europe on the other?

Before people can create a state, they must first agree that they form a political community. Ethnic groups with local loyalties could be brought together under common rule only when technological and economic development enabled political elites to unify extended territories, usually through conquest. The most serious threat to consensus is at the level of the community itself. One challenge confronting students of comparative politics is to identify the conditions under which national sentiment either coheres or dissipates. The tension between ethnicity and nationalism exists everywhere; it became an especially urgent problem in the aftermath of the dissolution of communist systems in Yugoslavia and in the former Soviet Union. Modernization makes creation of nation-states possible in a first step; but later phases of modernization encourage flexibility and decentralization. Ethnic groups may become more viable and better able to resist domination from the center. Liah Greenfeld calls attention to the varieties of ethnicity and nationalisms, reflecting different principles of popular sovereignty. Donald Horowitz also explores the complex relationship between ethnicity and nation, and the degree of consensus among ethnic groups needed to sustain a state. Students should ask whether approaches to the state by Weber, Skocpol, Greenfield, and Horowitz reflect larger political orientations and concerns.

....

MAX WEBER

9   What Is a State?

What do we understand by politics [*Politik*]? The notion is extraordinarily broad and includes every kind of independent leadership [*leitende*] activity. We speak about the foreign exchange policy of banks, the interest rate policy of the Reichsbank, the policy of a labor union during a strike; we can speak of the educational policy of a city or village, of the policies of a club's management, and, finally of the policies of a clever wife trying to guide her husband. Of course, our reflections today are not based on so broad a notion. Today we wish to understand by that notion only the leadership, or the exercise of influence on the leadership, of a *political* association [*Verband*], hence today, of a state.

But what from sociological viewpoint is a "political" association? What is a "state"? Sociologically,

this too cannot be defined in terms of the content of its actions. There is hardly any task which some political association has not undertaken, and there is no task that could be said is always, much less exclusively, the domain of those associations defined as political (today, called states), or which were the predecessors of the modern state. Ultimately, the modern state came to be defined sociologically only in terms of a specific means [*mittel*] peculiar to it, as to all political association, namely, physical violence [*Gewaltsamkeit*].

"Every state is founded on force [*Gewalt*]," as Trotsky said at Brest-Litovsk. That is indeed correct. If there existed only social structures in which violence as a means was unknown, then the notion of the "state" would be eliminated, then the condition would arise that we can call "anarchy" in the strict sense of the word. Naturally, violence is not the normal or the only means employed by the state. Nobody says that. But it is the means specific to the state. At the present time the relation between the state and violence is particularly close. In the past, the most varied associations—beginning with the clan—have viewed physical violence as quite normal means. Today, however, we have to say that a state is that human community which (successfully) claims the *monopoly of legitimate physical violence* within a given territory; this territory is another of the defining characteristics of the state. At the present time,

SOURCE: Weber was invited by the student organization at the University of Munich to participate in a lecture series on intellectual work as a vocation (or calling, *Beruf*). His talk, "Politik als Beruf" (Politics as a Profession and Vocation, or Calling), was given in January 1919, and published as a pamphlet in October 1919 by the student organization. A synthesis of his social and political theory, it was reprinted subsequently in several collections of Weber's writings, including the *Gesammelten politischen Schriften*. The full text is also available (note differing translations) in: H. H. Gerth and C. W. Mills, editors, *From Max Weber* (Oxford University Press, 1946), pp. 77–128; and P. Lassman and R. Speirs, editors, *Weber, Political Writings* (Cambridge University Press, 1994), pp. 309–369. Translation below, and words or phrases in brackets supplied by Bernard E. Brown.

the specific right to use physical violence is delegated to other associations or individuals only to the extent that the state for its part permits it. The state is considered to be the sole source of the "right" to use violence. "Politics," then, would mean for us a striving for a share of power or for influence on the distribution of power, either among states or among groups within a single state.

Essentially, this corresponds to ordinary usage. If a question is said to be a "political" question, or that a minister or official is a "political" official, or that a decision is "politically" determined, what is always meant is that interests in the distribution, preservation, or transfer of power are decisive in answering that question, determining the decisions or the sphere of activity of the official. Anyone active in politics is striving for power, either as a means to achieve other goals (either ideal or selfish), or as power "for its own sake," that is, in order to enjoy the feeling of prestige afforded by power.

Like the political associations preceding it historically, the state is a relationship of *rule* or domination [*Herrschaft*] by men over men, one that rests on the use of legitimate (that is, considered to be legitimate) violence. For the state to continue to exist, those who are ruled must obey the authority claimed by those who rule at any given time. When and why do people do this? Upon what inner justifications and external means does this rule rest?

To begin with the inner justifications: there are in principle three grounds legitimating any rule.

First, the authority of the "eternal past" of custom, sanctified by being in effect from time immemorial and by a habitual tendency to conform. This is "traditional" rule, as exercised by the patriarch and the patrimonial princes of old.

Then there is the authority of the exceptional and personal *"gift of grace"* (charisma), the entirely personal devotion to and confidence in revelations, heroism, or other qualities of leadership in an individual. This is "charismatic" rule as exercised by the prophet or, in the domain of politics, by the chosen war lord, the plebiscitarian ruler, the great demagogue, or the leader of a political party.

Finally, there is rule by virtue of "legality," by virtue of belief in the validity of legal statute and appropriate competence based on rationally devised rules. This type of rule rests on willingness to fulfill statutory obligations. This is the kind of rule exercised by the modern "servant of the state" and by all those bearers of power who in this respect resemble him.

It goes without saying that obedience by the ruled is determined in reality not only by motives of fear and hope (fear of vengeance from magical powers or power-holders, hope for reward in this world or in the hereafter), but also by interests of the most varied sort. We shall return to this point presently. However, in asking for the reasons "legitimating" this obedience, we indeed encounter these three "pure" types.

These notions of legitimacy and their inner justifications are of great significance for the structure of rule. To be sure, the pure types are rarely found in reality. But today we cannot go into the extremely complex variants, transitional forms, and combinations of these pure types, which problems belong to "political science" [*allgemeine staatslehre*]. Here we are interested above all in the second of the three types: rule by virtue of the devotion to the purely personal "charisma" of the "leader" by those who obey. For this is the root of the idea of a *calling* or vocation [*Beruf*] in its highest form.

Devotion to the charisma of the prophet or wartime leader or the great demagogue in the ecclesia [assemblies of citizens in Ancient Greek city-states] or in parliament means that the leader is personally seen as inwardly "called" to be a leader of people. Those who are led submit to him, not because of tradition or statute, but because they believe in him. If he is something more than a narrow and vain upstart of the moment, then he lives for his cause [*Sache*], and "aspires after his work." The devotion of his disciples or followers, his personal party supporters, is focused on his person and its qualities.

Leadership has emerged in all spheres and in all historical periods. In the past its most important embodiments were the magician and the prophet on the one hand, and the chosen warlord, gang leader, and condotierre on the other. In the West, however, we find something characteristic which is of greater concern to us, namely political leadership, first in the form of the free "demagogue" who grew from the soil of the city-state, a unique creation of the West and especially of Mediterranean culture.

Political leadership in the person of the party leader then also grew in the soil of the constitutional state, an institution indigenous only to the West. . . .

* * *

We have to make it clear that all ethically oriented activity can be guided by two fundamentally different, irreconcilably opposed maxims. It can guided by the "ethic of principled conviction" or ultimate ends [*Gesinnungs*], or by the "ethic of responsibility. This is not to say that an ethic of conviction is identical with irresponsibility, or that an ethic of responsibility is identical with the absence of conviction. Naturally no one says that. But there is a deep opposition between activity that follows the maxim of the ethic of conviction (to put it in religious terms, "The Christian does what is right and leaves the outcome in the hands of God"), and authority that follows the maxim of the ethic of responsibility, in which case one must answer for the (foreseeable) consequences of one's action.

You may show to a syndicalist who believes in an ethic of conviction that the probable consequences of his action will be, say, increased opportunities for reactionary forces, increased oppression of his own class, blocking the rise of his class. But you will not make the slightest impression on him. If bad consequences result from an action flowing from pure conviction, then, this kind of person blames not himself, but the world, or the stupidity of others, or the will of God who made them thus. A man who believes in an ethic of responsibility makes allowances for precisely these shortcomings of ordinary people. As Fichte correctly observed, he has no right to presuppose goodness and perfection in people. He does not feel that he can evade the consequences of his own actions, as far as he could foresee them, and places the burden on others. He will say: these consequences may be attributed to my actions. The believer in an ethic of conviction feels "responsible" only for making sure that the flame of pure conviction (for example, the flame of protest against the injustice of the social order) is never put out. To rekindle this flame again and again is the purpose of his actions, which are utterly irrational when judged in terms of their possible success. These acts can and will have only exemplary value.

But we have still not come to the end of the problem. No ethics in the world can get around the fact that in many instances the attainment of "good" ends is linked to the need to use morally dubious or at least morally dangerous means, and that one must face the possibility or even the probability of evil side effects. Nor can any ethics in the world tell us when and to what extent the ethically good end "justifies" the ethically dangerous means and side effects. . . .

* * *

Whoever makes a pact with these means of violence for whatever purpose—and every politician does—is exposed to its specific consequences. This holds especially for the person battling for a belief, whether religious or revolutionary. Let us simply take the present as an example. Whoever wishes to establish absolute justice on earth by force needs a following, a human "apparatus." He must offer these people the necessary internal and external prizes—heavenly or worldly rewards—otherwise the apparatus will not function. Under conditions of modern class struggle, the internal prizes are the satisfaction of hatred and revenge above all, of resentment and the need for pseudo-ethical self-righteousness; the desire to slander opponents and make them heretics. The external rewards are adventure, booty, power and payoffs. The success of the leader is completely dependent on the functioning of his apparatus. He is, however, dependent on its motives, not his own. He is dependent also on the possibility of granting those prizes *permanently* to his following, the Red Guard, the informers, the agitators he needs. What he actually achieves under the conditions of his activity is therefore not in his own hands but is, rather, prescribed for him by the motives of his following, which, in ethical terms, are predominantly base. He can maintain control of his following only so long as an honest belief in his person and in his cause inspires at least some of the following, probably never on this earth even the majority. This faith, even when held with subjective sincerity, in a great many cases is merely an ethical "legitimation" of cravings for revenge, power, booty and payoffs. Let no one try to tell us differently; the materialist interpretation of history is not a cab which can be taken at will, and there are no exceptions for the supporters of revolution! The emotionalism of revolution is succeeded by a return to traditional everyday existence; the hero of the faith disappears, and so, above all does the faith itself, or, even more effectively, the faith becomes part of the conventional rhetoric of political philistines and technicians. This development is especially rapid in wars of faith, because these are generally led or inspired by genuine leaders, prophets of revolution. For here, as with every apparatus under a leader, one of the conditions of success is that everything is made empty and routine, and the following must become psychically proletarianized, in order to create "discipline." The following of a battler for a faith, when it comes to power, tends to degenerate very easily into a quite common structure of spoils seekers.

Whoever wishes to engage in politics of any kind, and especially in politics as a calling [*Beruf*] has to be conscious of these ethical paradoxes and of his responsibility for what may become of himself under the pressure of these paradoxes. He leaves himself open to the diabolical powers that lurk in all violence. The great virtuosi of otherworldly goodness and love of humanity, whether they came from Nazareth or Assisi or from Indian royal palaces, did not use the means of politics, force [*Gewalt*]. Their kingdom was "not of this world," and yet they worked and still work in this world. The figures of Platon Karatajev [a character in Tolstoy's writings] and Dostoyevsky's saints still are what most closely resembles them. Whoever seeks to save his soul and the souls of others, should not seek that goal through the path of politics, for the quite different tasks of politics can be achieved only through force. The genius or demon of politics lives in inner tension with the god of love, and even with the Christian God as expressed in the institution of the Church. This tension can erupt at any time into unresolvable conflict. People knew that even in the times of church rule. Again and again the interdict—which at the time meant a far greater power over men and for the salvation of their souls than (what Fichte called) the "cold approbation" of Kant's ethical judgment—was imposed on Florence, and yet the citizens fought against the Church-state. And it is regarding such situations that Machiavelli in a beautiful passage of his *Florentine Histories,* if I am not mistaken, has one of his heroes praise those citizens who accorded the greatness of their native city a higher place than the salvation of their souls.

If instead of native city or "fatherland" (which at present may not be an unambiguous value to some), you say "the future of socialism" or "planning for international peace," then you have the problem in its current incarnation. Everything people strive to attain through political action, using the means of violence and based on an ethic of responsibility endangers the "salvation of the soul." But if the salvation of the soul is pursued in a war between faiths, following a pure ethic of conviction, then the goal might be damaged and discredited for generations, because responsibility for the consequences is lacking. In such circumstances, those engaged in action remain unaware of the diabolic forces in play. These are inexorable, and bring about consequences for actions and even for the inner self, to which one will fall a helpless victim if one is blind to them. "The devil is old," and the saying does not refer to one's age measured in years, "so grow old to understand him." I have never permitted myself to lose a debate simply by referring to a date on a birth certificate; but the mere fact that someone is twenty and I am over fifty is no reason for me to think that this in itself is an achievement before which I must expire in awe. It is not age that matters, but rather the trained ability to look at the realities of life unsparingly, to bear up under those realities and to be equal to them inwardly.

THEDA SKOCPOL

10 Bringing the State Back In

The explanatory importance of "the state" has been highlighted during the last decade in a variety of comparative and historical studies by social scientists from several disciplines and geographical area specialties. The topics of these studies have ranged from the roles of Latin American states in instituting comprehensive reforms from above to the activities of states in the advanced industrial democracies of Europe, the United States, and Japan in developing social programs and managing economic problems. No explicitly shared research agenda or general theory has tied such diverse studies together, yet they have arrived at complementary arguments and strategies of analysis.

States, or parts of states, have been identified in these studies as taking weighty, autonomous initiatives—going beyond the demands or interests of social groups—to promote social change, manage economic crises, or develop innovative public policies. The administrative and coercive organizations that form the core of any modern state have been identified as the likely generators of autonomous state initiatives and varying organizational structures and resources of states have been probed in order to explain why and when states pursue their own strategies and goals. Finally, much interest has centered on the differing abilities of states to realize policy goals and a number of concepts and research strategies have been developed to address this issue through case studies and cross-national comparisons focused on state efforts to implement goals in particular policy areas.

The value of recent studies converging on common concerns about states as both actors and organizational structures can best be demonstrated by concrete illustrations from the literature. But, first, it makes sense to underline the paradigmatic reorientation embodied in the phrase "bringing the state back in."

SOURCE: Reprinted from *Items*, vol. 36, nos. 1/2 (June 1982), pp. 1–8. By permission of the Social Science Research Council.

SOCIETY-CENTERED THEORIES OF POLITICS AND GOVERNMENT

Not long ago, the dominant theories and research agendas of the social sciences spoke of anything and everything but "the state." This was true even—indeed especially—when politics was at issue. Cultural values, socialized personalities, clashing interest groups, conflicting or allying classes, and differentiating social systems—these were supposed to provide sufficient keys both to the political process and to political conflicts. "The state" was an old-fashioned concept, associated with dry and dusty legal-formalist studies of nationally particular constitutional principles. The real dynamics of political life could only be discerned by social scientists willing to look at societies and economies, sites of the processes or structures believed to be universally basic to politics and social change. In place of the state, social scientists conceived of "government" as simply the *arena* in which social classes, or economic interest groups, or normative social movements contended or allied with one another to influence the making of public policy decisions. Interest centered on the societal "inputs" to government, and on the socioeconomic effects of governmental "outputs." Government itself was not considered to be an independent actor, and variations in governmental structures were deemed less significant than general functions shared by the political systems of all societies.

Society-centered ways of explaining politics and governmental activities were especially characteristic of the pluralist and structural-functional theories predominant in political science and sociology in the United States during the 1950s and 1960s.[1] Yet even when rebellious "neo-Marxists" began to theorize about "the capitalist state," they too emphasized the social functions of the state as an arena for class struggles and as an instrument of class rule.[2] Indeed, the reluctance of pluralists and structural-functionalists to speak of states, and the near-unwillingness of even most neo-Marxists to grant autonomous substance to states, resonates with proclivities present from the start in the modern social sciences. These sciences emerged along with the industrial and democratic revolutions of Western Europe in the 18th and 19th centuries. Their founding theorists quite understandably perceived the locus of societal dynamics to be located not in outmoded monarchical and aristocratic states but in civil society, variously understood as "the market," "the industrial division of labor," or "class relations." Founding theorists as politically opposed as Herbert Spencer and Karl Marx (who now, not entirely inappropriately, lie just across a lane from one another in Highgate Cemetery, London) agreed that industrial capitalism was triumphing over the military and territorial rivalries of states. For both of these theorists, 19th century British socioeconomic developments presaged the future for all countries—and for the world as a whole.

···

FOCUSING ON BRITAIN AND THE UNITED STATES

As world history moved—via colonial conquests, two world wars, and various state-building revolutions and anticolonial movements—from the Pax Britannica of the 19th century to the Pax Americana of the period after World War II, the Western social sciences managed to keep their eyes averted from the explanatory centrality of states as potent and autonomous organizational actors. It was not that such phenomena as political authoritarianism or totalitarianism were ignored—just that the preferred theoretical explanations were always in terms of economic backwardness or the unfortunate persistence of non-Western "traditional" values. As long as capitalist and liberal Britain, and then capitalist and liberal America, could plausibly be seen as the unchallengeable "lead societies," the Western social sciences could manage the feat of downplaying the explanatory centrality of states in their major theo-

retical paradigms. For the dominant social science paradigms were riveted on understanding modernization—its causes and direction. And in Britain and America—the "most modern" societies—industrialization seemed to be spontaneous, socioeconomic and cultural processes appeared to be the primary loci of change, and the decisions of governmental legislative bodies were apparently the basic stuff of politics.

But by the 1970s, both Britain and the United States were unmistakably becoming beleaguered industrial economies in a world of competitive national states. It is probably not surprising that, at this juncture, it became theoretically fashionable to begin to speak of "the state" as an actor and as a society-shaping institutional structure. Indeed, social scientists are now willing to offer state-centered arguments about Britain and the United States themselves. Fittingly, many of these new arguments stress ways in which state actions and structures have distinctively shaped British and American national economic development and international economic policies. And some of them also ponder how the British and American states might fetter or facilitate current efforts at industrial regeneration in these countries.[3] In short, especially now that Britain and the United States seem much more like particular state-societies in an uncertain, competitive, and interdependent world of many such entities, a paradigmatic shift seems to be under way in the social sciences, a shift that involves a fundamental rethinking of the role of states in relation to societies and economies.

···

REVIVAL OF A CONTINENTAL EUROPEAN PERSPECTIVE

In the 19th century, social theorists oriented to the realities of social change on the European Continent refused to accept the de-emphasis of the state characteristic of those founders of the modern social sciences who centered their thinking on Britain. German scholars, especially, insisted upon the institutional reality of the state and its continuing impact upon and within civil society. Now that comparative social scientists are similarly reemphasizing the importance of states, it is perhaps not surprising that there is renewed reliance upon the basic understanding of "the state" passed down to contemporary scholarship through the widely known writings of such major German scholars as Max Weber and Otto Hintze.[4]

Max Weber argued that states are compulsory associations claiming control over territories and the people within them. Administrative, legal, and coercive organizations are the core of any state. These organizations are variably structured in different countries, and they may be embedded in one sort or another of a constitutional-representative system of parliamentary decision making and electoral contests for key executive and legislative posts. Nevertheless, as Alfred Stepan nicely puts it in a formulation that captures the biting edge of the Weberian perspective: "The state must be considered as more than the 'government.' It is the continuous administrative, legal, bureaucratic and coercive systems that attempt not only to structure relationships *between* civil society and public authority in a polity but also to structure many crucial relationships within civil society as well."[5] Moreover, as Otto Hintze demonstrated, thinking of states as organizations controlling territories leads us away from positing basic features common to all polities and leads us toward consideration of the varying ways in which state structures and actions are conditioned by historically changing transnational environments. These environments impinge upon individual states through geopolitical patterns of interstate domination and competition, through the communication of ideas and models of public policy, and through world-economic patterns of trade, division of productive activities, investment flows, and international finance. States necessarily stand at the intersections between domestic sociopolitical orders and the transnational structures within which they must maneuver for survival or advantage in relation to other states. The modern state as we know it, and as Weber and Hintze conceptualized it, has always been, since its birth in European history, part of a system of competing states.

STATES AS AUTONOMOUS ACTORS

States conceived as organizations controlling territories and people may formulate and pursue goals that are not simply reflective of the demands or interests of social groups, classes, or society. This is what is usually meant by "state autonomy." Unless such independent goal formulation can be demonstrated and explained, there is little need to talk about states as important actors. In recent comparative-historical scholarship on different kinds of topics in separate parts of the world, collectivities of state officials are shown formulating and pursuing their own goals. Their efforts, moreover, are related to the order-keeping concerns of states, and to the linkages of states into international systems of communication and competition.

REFORMIST MILITARY COUPS IN LATIN AMERICA

An unusually comprehensive kind of autonomous state action is analyzed in Alfred Stepan's book, *The State and Society: Peru in Comparative Perspective,* which offers a causal explanation of attempts by state elites in Latin America to install "inclusionary" or "exclusionary" corporatist regimes.[6] A key element in Stepan's explanation is the formation of a strategically located cadre of officials holding great power inside and through existing state organizations, and also enjoying a unified sense of ideological purpose about the desirability of using state intervention to ensure political order and promote national economic development. To account for Brazil's "exclusionary" corporatist coup in 1964 and for Peru's "inclusionary" corporatist coup in 1968, Stepan stresses the prior socialization of what he calls "new military professionals." These were career military officers who, together, passed through training schools that taught techniques and ideas of national economic planning and counterinsurgency, along with "traditional" military skills. Such new military professionals then installed corporatist regimes in response to perceived crises of political order and of national economic development. The military professionals used state power to stave off or deflect threats to national order from subordinant classes and groups. They also used state power to implement socioeconomic reforms or plans for further national industrialization—something they saw as a basic requisite for their country's improved international standing.

CIVIL BUREAUCRATS AND EUROPEAN SOCIAL POLICIES

If Stepan deals with extraordinary instances of state autonomy, in which nonconstitutionally-ruling strategic elites have used the state as a whole to redirect and restructure society and politics, other scholars have teased out more circumscribed instances of state autonomy in the histories of public policy making in liberal-democratic, constitutionalist polities. For example, Hugh Heclo's *Modern Social Politics in Britain and Sweden* provides an intricate comparative-historical account of the long-term development of unemployment insurance and policies of old-age assistance in these two nations.[7] Without being explicitly presented as such, Heclo's book is about autonomous state contributions to social policy making. The autonomous state actions Heclo highlights are not all acts of coercion or domination; they are, instead, the intellectual activities of civil service administrators engaged in diagnosing societal problems and framing policy alternatives to deal with them. According to Heclo, civil service administrators in both Britain and Sweden have consistently and substantively made more important contributions to social policy development than have political parties or interest groups. Socioeconomic conditions, especially crises, have stimulated only sporadic demands from parties and interest groups, he argues. It has been civil servants, drawing upon "administrative resources of information, analysis, and expertise," who have framed the terms of new policy elaborations as "corrective(s) less to social conditions as such and more to the perceived failings of previous policy" in terms of "the government bureaucracy's own conception of what it has been doing."[8] Heclo's evidence also reveals that the autonomous bureaucratic shaping of social policy has been greater in Sweden than in Britain. Sweden's premodern, centralized bureaucratic state was, from the start of industrialization and prior to the full liberalization and democratization of national politics, in a position to take the initiative in diagnosing social problems and proposing universalistic solutions.

Heclo says much less than he might about the influences shaping the timing and content of distinctive state initiatives. But he does present evidence of the sensitivity of civil administrators to the requisites for maintaining social and political order in the face of cycles of industrial unemployment. And he also points to the constant awareness of administrators of foreign precedents and models of social policy. Heclo demonstrates, above all, that well-institutionalized collectivities of administrative officials can have pervasive direct and indirect effects on the content and development of major government policies. He shows how to locate and analyze autonomous state contributions to "normal" politics.

CAN STATES ACHIEVE THEIR GOALS?

Some comparative-historical scholars have not only investigated the underpinnings of autonomous state actions but have also tackled the still more challenging task of explaining the varying *capacities* of states to implement their policies. Of course, the explanation of such capacities is not entirely separable from the explanation of autonomous goal formulation by states, because state officials are most likely to try to do things that plausibly seem feasible. Nevertheless, not infrequently states pursue goals (whether their own, or those pressed upon them by powerful social groups) that are beyond their reach. Thus, the capacities of states to implement strategies and policies deserve close analysis.

A stable administrative-military control of a given territory is a precondition for any state's ability to implement policies. Beyond this, loyal and skilled officials and plentiful financial resources are basic factors relevant to state effectiveness in attaining all sorts of goals. Not surprisingly, histories of state building zero in on exactly these universal sinews of state power.[9] It is clear that certain of these resources come to be rooted in institutional relationships that are slow to change and relatively impervious to short-term manipulations. For example: Do state offices attract and retain career-oriented incumbents with a wide array of skills and keen motivation? The answer may well depend upon historically evolved relationships among elite educational institutions, state organizations, and private enterprises that compete with the state for educated personnel. The best situation for the state may be a regular flow of elite university graduates—including many with sophisticated technical training—into official careers that are of such high status as to keep the most ambitious and successful from moving on to posts outside the state. But if this situation has not been historically established by the start of the industrial era, it is difficult indeed to undo alternative patterns that are less favorable to the state.

FINANCES AS "THE NERVES OF THE STATE"

Factors determining a state's financial resources may sometimes be more manipulable over time. The amounts and forms of revenues and credit available to a state grow out of institutionally conditioned, yet historically shifting, political balances and bargains among states and between a state and social classes. Basic sets of facts to sort out in any study of state capacities involve the sources and amounts of state revenues and the degree of flexibility possible in their collection and deployment. Domestic institutional arrangements and international situations set difficult-to-change limits within which state elites must maneuver to extract taxes and obtain credit. Does a state depend on export taxes (e.g., from a scarce national resource, or from products vulnerable to sudden world-market fluctuations)? Does a nonhegemonic state's geopolitical position allow it to reap the state-building benefits of military aid, or must it rely on international bankers or aid agencies which insist upon favoring private investments and restrict the domestic political options of the borrower state? What established authority does a state have to collect taxes, borrow, and invest in potentially profitable public enterprises; and how much "room" is there in the existing constitutional-political system to change patterns of revenue collection unfavorable to the state? Finally, what authority and organizational means does a state have to deploy whatever financial resources it does enjoy? Are particular kinds of revenues rigidly "earmarked" for special uses that cannot easily be altered by official decision makers?[10] Can the state channel (and manipulate) flows of credit to particular enterprises and industrial sectors, or do established constitutional-political practices favor only aggregate categorical expenditures? All of these *sorts* of questions need to be asked in any study of state capacities; the answers to them, taken together, provide the best possible general insight into the direct or indirect leverage a state is likely to have for realizing any sort of goal it may pursue. For a state's means of raising and deploying financial resources tell us more than could any other single factor about its existing (and immediately potential) capacities to create or strengthen state organizations, to employ personnel, to coopt political support, to subsidize economic enterprises, and to fund social programs. "Financial means," are indeed, as the 16th century French jurist Jean Bodin said, "the nerves of the state."

POLICY INSTRUMENTS FOR SPECIFIC KINDS OF STATE EFFORTS

Basic questions about a state's territorial integrity, financial means, and staffing may be the place to start in any investigation of its capacities to realize goals, yet the most fruitful studies of state capacities tend to focus on particular policy areas. As Stephen Krasner puts it: "There is no reason to assume a priori that the pattern of strengths and weaknesses will be the same for all policies. One state may be [able] to alter the structure of its medical system but be [unable] to construct an efficient transportation network, while another can deal relatively easily with getting its citizens around but cannot get their illnesses cured."[11] Many studies of the abilities of states to realize particular kinds of goals use the concept of "policy instrument" to refer to the relevant means that a state may have at its disposal. The nature and range of institutional mechanisms that state officials may conceivably be able to bring to bear on a given kind of problem must be specified through cross-national comparative research.

For example, Susan and Norman Fainstein compare the urban policies of northwest European nations to those of the United States. Accordingly, they are able to conclude that the U.S. national state lacks certain policy instruments for dealing with urban crises that are available to European states—instruments such as central planning agencies, state-controlled pools of investment capital, and directly administered national social welfare programs.[12] Analogously, Peter Katzenstein brings together a set of related studies of how six advanced-industrial capitalist countries manage the international trade, investment, and monetary involvements of their economies.[13] Katzenstein is able to draw fairly clear distinctions between the strategies open to states such as the Japanese and the French, which have policy instruments that enable them to intervene at the level of particular industrial sectors, and other states, such as Britain and the United States, which must rely upon aggregate macroeconomic manipulations. Once again, as in the Fainstein study, it is the juxtaposition of different nations' approaches to a given policy area that allows relevant policy instruments to be highlighted. Neither study, however, treats such "instruments" as the deliberate short-term creations of state officials. Both studies move out toward macrohistorical explorations of the broad institutional patterns of divergent national developments that determine why various countries now have—or do not have—policy instruments for dealing with particular problems or crises.

STATES IN RELATION TO SOCIETAL ACTORS

Fully specified studies of state capacities not only entail examinations of the resources and instruments states may have for dealing with particular sorts of problems; they also necessarily look at more than states as such. They examine states *in relation* to particular kinds of socioeconomic and political environments, populated by actors with given interests and resources. One obvious use of a relational perspective is to investigate the power of states over domestic or transnational nonstate actors and structures, especially economically dominant ones. What capacities do states have to change the behavior or oppose the demands of such actors, or to transform recalcitrant structures? Answers lie not only in features of states themselves, but also in the balances of states' resources and situational advantages compared to those of nonstate actors.

This sort of relational approach is used by Stephen Krasner in his exploration of the efforts of U.S. officials to implement foreign raw-materials policy in interactions with large corporations, whose preferences and established practices frequently ran counter to the state's definition of the "national interest."[14] This is also the sort of approach used by Alfred Stepan to analyze Peruvian military leaders' relative successes and failures in using state power to change the patterns of foreign capital investments in their dependent country.[15] Stepan does a brilliant job of developing a consistent set of causal hypotheses to explain the diverse outcomes across industrial sectors—i.e., sugar, oil, and manufacturing. For each sector, he examines regime characteristics—degree of commitment to clear policy goals, technical capacities, monitoring abilities, state-controlled investment resources, and the state's international position. He also examines the characteristics of existing investments and markets as they impinge upon the advantages to Peru and to foreign multinationals of any given further investments. The entire argument is too complex to reproduce here, but its significance extends well beyond the foreign investment issue area and the Peruvian case. By taking a self-consciously relational approach to the balances of resources that states and multinational corporations may bring to bear in their partially symbiotic and partially conflictual dealings with one another, Stepan has provided an important model for further studies of state capacities in many policy areas.

Another relational approach to the study of state capacities appears in Peter Katzenstein's *Between Power and Plenty*, where (as was indicated above) the object of explanation is ultimately not state power over nonstate actors, but nations' strategies for managing "interdependence" within the world capitalist economy. One notion centrally invoked in the Katzenstein collection is that of a "policy network" embodying a patterned interrelationship between state and society within each domestic national structure. The idea is that the definition and implementation of foreign economic policies grows out of the nexus of state and society. Both state goals and the interests of powerful classes may influence policy orientations. And the implementation of policies is shaped not only by the policy instruments available to the state but also by the organized support it receives from key societal groups. Thus, national policies—for example, industrial reorganization—may be efficaciously implemented because a strong central state controls credit and can intervene within industrial sectors. Yet it may be of equal importance that industries are organized into disciplined associations willing to cooperate with the state. In short, a complete analysis requires examinations of the organization and interests of the state, of the organization and interests of socioeconomic groups, and of the complementary as well as the conflicting relationships of state and societal actors. This is the sort of approach consistently used by the contributors to *Power and Plenty* to explain the foreign economic objectives of Britain, France, Germany, Italy, Japan, and the United States, as well as to explain the capacities of their domestic political systems to implement existing or conceivable alternative policies.

AGENDAS FOR FUTURE COMPARATIVE RESEARCH

Now that states are back at the center of attention in macroscopic studies of societal change and public policy making, there are new needs and possibilities for comparative research and theory. Since it is clear from existing studies that the organizational structures of states underpin the initiatives they take and their capacities to achieve policy goals, we need to know much more about the long-term development of states themselves. How are states built and reconstructed? What roles have been played by wars or major economic and political crises; and how do state agencies and activities develop in more normal times? What social, economic, and political factors influence patterns of official recruitment, the acquisition and deployment of state financial resources, and the establishment and use of specific policy instruments to address given kinds of problems faced by states and societies? We also need to know much more about the changing patterns of state-society relationships. How do states and socioeconomic groups affect one another's organization and goals? And how do conflicts and alliances between organized social or economic actors and state agencies affect the formulation and implementation of various kinds of public policies?

Answers to questions such as these will necessarily develop through analytically sharply-focused comparative and historical studies. And it seems very likely that some of the most strategic findings will arise from the juxtaposition of research findings about very different geographical areas and historical time periods. On issues of state building or the states role in industrial development, for example, scholars looking at the contemporary Third World might have much to learn from, and say to, students of earlier eras in European and U.S. history. On other issues, such as the state's management of relationships to the world economy, contemporary comparisons of, say, very small or very large countries the world over may yield refreshing insights. And on matters such as the rise and development (and demise?) of Keynesian economic strategies, comparisons of European nations with the United States might be most appropriate. Exact comparative strategies are bound to depend upon the specific issues addressed. But it is clear that further scholarly dialogue will need to transcend parochial specialties based on time and geography in order to explain the processes by which states develop, formulate policies, and seek to implement them in domestic and international contexts.

Comparative, state-centered research along the above-suggested lines will have policy implications—but not of the short-term, how-to-do-it sort. Other sorts of social scientific research are better tailored to helping public officials decide what to do on a month-to-month basis. Yet given the fact that states are so obviously and inextricably involved in the economic development, social change, and politics of all contemporary nations, social scientists also need to address the broader and longer-term determinants of the state's role. The limits and the possibilities of public policy are profoundly influenced by historically developed state organizations and their structured relationships to domestic and international environments. Citizens, public officials, and social scientists alike therefore share an interest in better understanding states themselves both as actors and as organizational structures.

ENDNOTES

1. See, for example, David B. Truman, *The Governmental Process,* 2nd ed. (New York: Knopf, 1971; originally 1951); and the series of books on political development written under the auspices of the Council's Committee on Comparative Politics (1954–1972), published by the Princeton University Press.
2. For some examples of recent neo-Marxist theorizing on the capitalist state, see Nicos Poulantzas, *Political Power and Social Classes,* translated by Timothy O'Hagen (London: New Left Books, 1973); Claus Offe, "Structural Problems of the Capitalist State," *German Political Studies,* volume 1 (1974); Göran Therborn, *What Does the Ruling Class Do When It Rules?* (London: New Left Books, 1978); and Erik Olin Wright, *Class, Crisis, and the State* (London: New Left Books, 1978).
3. For some suggestive brief treatments, see the articles by Stephen Krasner and Stephen Blank in Peter Katzenstein (editor), *Between Power and Plenty: Foreign Economic Policies of Advanced Industrial States*

(Madison: University of Wisconsin Press, 1978); Andrew Martin, "Political Constraints on Economic Strategies in Advanced Industrial Societies," *Comparative Political Studies* 10:3 (October 1977), pp. 323–354; and Paul M. Sacks, "State Structure and the Asymmetrical Society: An Approach to Public Policy in Britain," *Comparative Politics* 12:3 (April 1980), pp. 349–376.
4. See Max Weber, *Economy and Society,* edited by Guenther Roth and Claus Wittich (New York: Bedminister Press, 1968, originally 1922), Volume 2, Chapter 9, and Volume 3, Chapters 10–13; and *The Historical Essays of Otto Hintze,* edited by Felix Gilbert (New York: Oxford University Press, 1975, originally 1897–1932).
5. Alfred Stepan, *The State and Society: Peru in Comparative Perspective* (Princeton, N.J.: Princeton University Press, 1978), p. xii.
6. Ibid., Chapters 3–4. See also Alfred Stepan, "The New Professionalism of Internal Warfare and Military Role Expansion," pp. 47–65 in Alfred Stepan (editor), *Authoritarian Brazil* (New Haven: Yale University Press, 1973).
7. Hugh Heclo, *Modern Social Politics in Britain and Sweden* (New Haven: Yale University Press, 1974).
8. Ibid., pp. 303, 305–306.
9. See, for examples: Charles Tilly (editor), *The Formation of National States in Western Europe* (Princeton, N.J.: Princeton University Press, 1975); Michael Mann, "State and Society, 1130–1815: An Analysis of English State Finances" in Maurice Zeitlin (editor), *Political Power and Social Theory* (A Research Annual), Volume 1 (Greenwich, Conn.: JAI Press, 1980), pp. 165–208; and Stephen Skowronek, *Building a New American State: The Expansion of National Administrative Capacities, 1877–1920* (Cambridge and New York: Cambridge University Press, 1982).
10. See John A. Dunn, Jr., "The Importance of Being Earmarked: Transport Policy and Highway Finance in Great Britain and the United States," *Comparative Studies in Society and History* 20:1 (January 1978), pp. 29–53.
11. Stephen D. Krasner, *Defending the National Interest: Raw Materials Investments and U.S. Foreign Policy* (Princeton, N.J.: Princeton University Press, 1978), p. 58.
12. Susan S. and Norman I. Fainstein, "National Policy and Urban Development," *Social Problems* 26:2 (December 1978), pp. 125–146. See especially pp. 140–141.

13. Peter J. Katzenstein (editor), *Between Power and Plenty: Foreign Economic Policies of Advanced Industrial States* (Madison: University of Wisconsin Press, 1978).

14. Krasner, *National Interest,* especially Parts Two and Three.

15. Stepan, *State and Society,* Chapter 7.

....

LIAH GREENFELD

11 Varieties of Nationalism

[The author's discussion of culture has been omitted–ED.] . . . We use the term "ethnicity" to refer to various ascriptive characteristics—that is, characteristics which are not of one's own choosing, but with which one is associated due to the accident of birth—believed today to be the sources of our essential political identity which defines our place as political actors in the widest possible context. Some of these ascriptive characteristics, such as language and religious or secular traditions and customs, are obviously cultural, but others, such as physical type or territorial roots, are not. Yet, the term "ethnicity" applies equally to all of them, and all of them, equally, are considered capable of generating ethnic identity. More important, however, than the fact that only some of these presumably identity-generating qualities are cultural, is the circumstance that ascriptive, or ethnic, characteristics as such cannot generate identity at all. All of us have ascriptive qualities which distinguish us from others, including members of our very families, and [we] are born into certain sub-communities which are distinguished from others in the larger communities to which we belong in numerous potentially noticeable ways. Every society, in other words, is ethnically diverse, ethnic homogeneity being utterly impossible and hardly imaginable. The reason why we do not think of it this way is that, in the vast majority of cases, we do not notice ethnic, or ascriptive, differences among people, and attach to them no importance whatsoever. For instance, in Europe and North America today we do not class people by the color of their eyes. It would seem preposterous to see eye color as the basis for one's ethnic identity, but, in itself, eye color is not less noticeable or real than the tint of one's skin. In Russia, one does not attach too much importance to the differences in pronunciation and phraseology that distinguish residents of Moscow from those of St. Petersburg, and one certainly does not see these as an indication of ethnic differences. But this linguistic disparity, however slight, is nevertheless more pronounced than the one presumed to exist between the languages of Serbians, Croatians, and now Bosnians, all of whom not long ago would have been recognized as the speakers of one and the same Serbo-Croatian language.

The fact is that ethnic, ascriptive differences are noticed and form elements of an identity only when the culture invests them with special significance and assigns them a place in its symbolic model for the social order. It is clear from the above examples that such investment and assignment does not at all depend on the actual magnitude of the difference or on the salience of any particular ascriptive characteristic: the attribution of the cultural significance is quite independent of the so-called "objective" situation, for, as I have already said, we perceive only such elements of that situation which are made culturally significant. Our social world is culturally constructed, and none of our qualities as social actors exist outside of the magic circle drawn by our collective imagination. Now, the political significance of ethnicity is, in the first place, a function of its cultural significance. Though the investment of any set of ascriptive characteristics with cultural significance does not automatically lead to ethnic politics, it forms the necessary first condition for such politics.

SOURCE: Liah Greenfeld, "The Political Significance of Culture," *The Brown Journal of World Affairs,* vol. IV, issue 1 (Winter/Spring 1997), pp. 187–195. Reprinted by permission of the editor, *The Brown Journal of World Affairs.* Article abridged by Bernard E. Brown.

Until quite recently, ethnicity had been of little importance in politics. Politically significant identities were not ethnic but rather estate (that is, reflective of social stratification) and religious in a sense very different from the one attached to religion when it is defined as an ethnic characteristic. The identity of Christians, Muslims, and Jews was constituted essentially by the bond between the individual soul and the Deity and inconceivable outside of the Christian, Muslim, or Jewish faith. This faith was not carried in one's blood—as it is presumed to be, for instance, in the case or the secular descendants of South Slav Muslims—and even in Ireland one could not care less whether an atheist came from a Protestant or a Catholic family (as one does in the telling joke, bandied around among students of ethnicity). Religious identity was a matter of personal belief, commitment, and responsibility; as an element of ethnicity it became a matter of biology, a quality of a group, entirely independent of individual choice. It became possible to speak of "the religion of origin"—a meaningless notion for a believer; at the same time, one's socio-economic position was increasingly recognized as a matter of achievement, and in most societies the importance of "class of origin" declined dramatically.

These changes in the nature of identity, in general, and the increased political significance of ethnic identities, specifically, reflected the emergence and quick ascendancy of a new cultural model for social order which was to transform the social—and political—reality, making our world what it is today. This cultural model, the symbolic and very real foundation of modern society, was nationalism, A discussion of the emergence of nationalism will take us too far afield; in the present context, it will be sufficient to define it and relate national identity to ethnic identity.

Nationalism is best approached as a type of socio-political ideology, similar to a type of religion—for instance, monotheism—and representing a set of basic principles which, within certain limits, lend themselves to various interpretations and, as such, may serve as the foundations of different and, from certain points of view, even contradictory cultural systems. Christianity is vastly different from Islam which, nevertheless, shares with it the fundamental principle of one omnipotent God. Similarly, one may distinguish between several dramatically different types of nationalism, easily recognizable as types of nationalism despite pronounced differences among them, because they share the basic principles of the nationalist form of consciousness. The core political principle of nationalism is the principle of popular sovereignty. Its core social principle is the principle of the fundamental equality of membership in the national community. Finally, it is important to mention the essentially secular focus of nationalism, which sharply distinguishes this modern form of culture from the great transcendental religions that provided models for civilizations of the past, and which has profound implications for almost every area of social and political experience in modern society.

Different types of nationalism are based on different interpretations of the first two principles: the principle of popular sovereignty and the principle of equality of membership. Specifically, nationalisms are distinguished in accordance with the definition of the nation they adopt (the bearer of popular sovereignty) and the criteria of membership in the nation (who is to be included in the community of equals). The nation can be defined as a composite entity, an association of free and equal individuals, or in unitary terms, as a collective individual. The first definition gives rise to individualistic nationalisms and favors the development of liberal political arrangements. The interests of the nation, as well as its sovereignty or will, in this case, are but reflections of the interests of the majority of its members and their wills. The rights of individuals—human rights—are supreme among the nation's values, and very few circumstances justify the sacrifice of the human life. The definition of the nation as a collective individual, by contrast, results in collectivistic nationalisms which tend to spawn authoritarian political arrangements. In this case, the nation is believed to possess a will and interests of its own, to which the wills and interests of its individual members are subservient and may at any moment be sacrificed. It is the rights of the nation, rather than human rights, that have the pride of place among social values, and human life is held in far lesser esteem. Collectivistic nationalisms tend to be authoritarian, because the will of the nation, which cannot be gauged from the wills of the majority of its members, has to be deciphered and interpreted by an elite claiming special qualifications to do so. This elite (which can assume the character of intellectuals, as is very often the case, or of a political party, of which we also know some examples) then acquires the right to dictate this will to the masses of the population, who must obey.

The criteria of membership in the nation, which represent the second set of characteristics that distinguishes between types of nationalism, can be either civic or ethnic. In the case of civic criteria of membership, nationality is coterminous with citizenship and in principle is believed to be a matter of individual choice and commitment. As such, it can be acquired or lost. In distinction, ethnic criteria of membership presume that nationality is inherent and, as such, unchangeable: one can neither acquire a particular national identity if one is not born with it, nor abandon it if one is.

Theoretically, the superimposition of these two sets of features creates four types of nationalism, but an individualistic and ethnic nationalism is logically impossible; thus, nationalism exists in three basic varieties: individualistic and civic, collectivistic and civic, and collectivistic and ethnic. Whenever we speak of ethnic identity, we in fact refer to this last type of nationalism. It is nationalism which invests ethnicity with cultural significance. In this sense, ethnic identity, which is so often seen as the primordial raw material of nationalism, is a product of this modern form of consciousness.

. . . The different types of nationalism have dramatically different propensities in the sphere of internal politics as well as international relations. Specifically, ethnic nationalisms differ markedly in their characteristic tendencies from individualistic and civic nationalisms. Among other things, ethnically defined nations are more likely to engage in aggressive warfare than individualistic nations. This is so for several reasons. Individualistic nationalisms are not, in principle, particularistic, for they are based on the universalistic principle of the moral primacy of the individual. This goes for any individual, whether or not he or she belongs to the national community; as a result, the borderline

between "us" and "them" is frequently blurred. One's nation is not perceived as an animate being which can nurture grievances, nor are other nations regarded as individuals harboring malicious intentions and capable of inflicting insults. The culprits and the victims in every conflict are specified, and sympathies and antipathies change with the issues and points of view. Moreover, individualistic nationalisms are by definition pluralisms, which implies that at any point in time there exists a plurality of opinions in regard to what constitutes the good of the nation. For this reason, it is relatively difficult to achieve a consensus necessary for the mobilization of the population for war in individualistic nations; it is especially difficult in the case of aggressive war, when no direct threat from the prospective enemy is perceived by the national population. Ethnic nationalisms, by contrast, are necessarily forms of particularism. The borderline between "us" and "them," as regards memberships, is relatively clear. The nations are seen as individuals capable of suffering and inflicting insults, and the national collectivity is essentially a consensual, rather than conflictual, pluralistic society. All these qualities facilitate mobilization.

In addition, during war, ethnic nationalisms are more conducive to brutality in relation to the enemy population than civic nationalisms. This is so because civic nationalism, even when particularistic, treats humanity as one fundamentally homogeneous entity. Foreigners are not fellow nationals, but they are still fellow men, and with some effort on their part, it is assumed they may become fellow nationals. In ethnic nationalisms, by contrast, the borderline between "us" and "them" is in principle impermeable. Nationality is defined as an inherent trait, and nations are seen, in effect, as separate species. Foreigners are no longer fellow men in the same sense, and there is no moral imperative to treat them as one would treat one's fellow nationals, just the same way as there is no imperative to treat our fellow mammals, or even fellow great apes as fellow men. The very definitions of ethnic nations presuppose a double-standard of moral or humane conduct. The tendency to "demonize" the enemy population, considered to be a necessary condition for "crimes against humanity," is built into ethnic nationalisms, for enemy populations within them are not necessarily defined as humanity to begin with.

According to the characteristic psychologic of ethnic nationalisms in which both one's own nation and other nations are defined in terms of inherent traits, the evil other (whoever that may be) is always harboring malicious intentions, and is ready to strike against the innocent nation at an opportune moment. For this reason, ethnic nations tend to feel threatened and to become aggressive—both to pre-empt perceived threats of aggression against them and because the evil nature of the adversary justifies aggression, even if no immediate threats are perceived, at the same time as it justifies brutality in relation to the enemy population. All these tendencies of ethnic nationalisms have been clearly reflected in the conduct of the Serbian and Croatian parties throughout the course of the devastating conflict in former Yugoslavia. But they are just as characteristic of other ethnic nationalisms, even though under certain circumstances they may be hidden from view.

The greater salience of nationalist sentiments, especially ethnic nationalist sentiments, and the re-activation of national conflicts in Eastern Europe following the conclusion of the Cold War—which made the end of the twentieth century so visibly unstable and, understandably, heightened security concerns in Europe—can be attributed neither to the change of modern political identities nor to the introduction of culture into politics, but solely to the disintegration of imperial systems which held these sentiments and hostilities in check without modifying them in the least. It must be emphasized that the resurgence of nationalism and the so-called "politics of culture" are related to the end of the Cold War only as simultaneous but independent effects of the same cause—the collapse of the Soviet Union. The Cold War itself was not, as was thought, a confrontation between the embodiments of two universalistic ideologies, Communism and Liberalism, but of two nations whose identities are to this day defined by two contradictory types of nationalism. The ease with which former Communist bosses transform into right-wing nationalists attests to the deep affinity between communism and ethnic nationalism. The former . . . is in fact a metamorphosed variety of the latter. Ostensibly an internationalist and a universalistic doctrine, Communism only thinly camouflaged the nationalist character of the regimes in the Soviet bloc, and in particular of the regime in the Soviet Union itself. The abandonment of the camouflage was unlikely to change the nature of our formidable adversary of the past decades, and only at peril to our security can be interpreted as victory over it.

With concepts of national self-definition remaining unchanged, one cannot expect changes in the dispositions of major players on the political stage. However, this very absence of change in the character of nationalism in the changed international circumstances which allow for a more open expression of nationalist ambitions creates both an opportunity and a necessity to rethink the theoretical vision of international relations which has informed our security concerns thus far. We need a new paradigm, so to speak. The end of the Cold War may not have changed the nature of our security concerns so much as revealed their source. It has made the influence of cultural values, especially values reflecting the national identities and consciousness of different societies, on politics undeniable, and we must come to grips with the notion that such values represent an essential ingredient of the political process. We must understand that nationalism, like culture in general, is not a uniform phenomenon, and that the political implications of various types of nationalism, and thus of culture, differ dramatically. One type of nationalism, ethnic nationalism, contributes disproportionately to the volatility of politics and constitutes, in the absence of restraints, a permanent threat to international stability. It is a dangerous, potentially violent form of culture. Security alliances of liberal democracies (and here I speak as a concerned citizen rather than as a social scientist) must deem subscription to the principles of ethnic nationalism unacceptable among their members. It must be closely watched and contained, and the first step toward containing it is the ability to distinguish clearly between it and alternative forms of identity.

DONALD L. HOROWITZ

12   A Right to Secede?

Many things changed with the end of the Cold War. One of the main changes is the new enthusiasm for public international law. In a world freed of an overwhelming rivalry of two great power blocs, but by no means freed of conflict, it became possible to think of a qualitatively enhanced role for the rule of law in the regulation of international relations. Nowhere has this thinking been more evident than in the regulation of conflict and warfare between ethnic groups. Two main prongs of international legal activity are the establishment of tribunals to punish genocide and crimes against humanity and the elaboration of various doctrines of human rights, including a possible right of ethnic groups to secede from states in which they are located. This asserted right, which would be a reversal of existing international law, is, in my view, ill considered.

The newly asserted right to secede is to be held by ethnic groups and is derived from a reinterpretation of the principle of the self-determination of nations. Theorists display varying degrees of enthusiasm in their advocacy of such a right, but all of them, whether they would permit secession generously or only reluctantly after certain conditions have been fulfilled, see secession as an answer to problems of ethnic conflict and violence. The position I shall take here is that secession is almost never an answer to such problems and that it is likely to make them worse. The proposals, in short, are not informed by any serious understanding of patterns of ethnic conflict or ethnic-group political behavior.

Secession, I shall argue, does not create the homogeneous successor states its proponents often assume will be created. Nor does secession reduce conflict, violence, or minority oppression once successor states are established. Guarantees of minority

protection in secessionist regions are likely to be illusory; indeed, many secessionist movements have as one of their aims the expulsion or subordination of minorities in the secessionist regions. The very existence of a right to secede, moreover, is likely to dampen efforts at coexistence in the undivided state, including the adoption of federalism or regional autonomy, which might alleviate some of the grievances of putatively secessionist minorities. Since most secessionist movements will be resisted by central governments and most secessionists receive insufficient foreign military assistance to succeed, propounding a right to secede, without the means to success, is likely to increase ultimately fruitless secessionist warfare, at the expense of internal efforts at political accommodation and at the cost of increased human suffering. Efforts to improve the condition of minorities ought to be directed at devising institutions to increase their satisfaction in existing states, rather than encouraging them to think in terms of exit options. In those rare cases in which separation of antagonists is, at the end of the day, the best course, partition can be accomplished reluctantly, as a matter of prudence, without recognizing a right to secede. But neither partition nor secession should be viewed as generally desirable solutions to the problems of ethnic conflict.

SECESSION AND SELF-DETERMINATION: A BRIEF SKETCH

The so-called right to secede has its origins in the principle of national self-determination. As is well known, that principle formed an integral part of Woodrow Wilson's plans for post-World War I Europe. The establishment of, for example, Rumania as a state for Rumanians certainly exemplified application of the self-determination principle, but, even apart from the presence of minorities in such new states, the Wilsonian policy fell far short of according

SOURCE: Donald L. Horowitz, "The Cracked Foundations of the Right to Secede," *Journal of Democracy*, vol. 14, no. 2 (2003), pp. 5–17. © National Endowment for Democracy and The Johns Hopkins University Press. Reprinted with permission of The Johns Hopkins University Press. Abridged by the Editor.

national or ethnic groups their own states. Indeed, Wilson may well have envisioned autonomy rather than independence, and he did not necessarily think in terms of an ethnic fulfillment for the right to self-determination. Yugoslavia and Czechoslovakia, for example, were multinational states, and Wilson's proposal that a right of self-determination be incorporated in the Covenant of the League of Nations was rejected. By the time of the Atlantic Charter in 1941, self-determination was to be limited to peoples living under foreign domination. Decolonization was thus an exercise of self-determination, and it was soon made clear by the United Nations (in 1960) and the Organization of African Unity (in 1964), among others, that secessionist threats to the territorial integrity of states would not be regarded as further exercises of self-determination.

With the exception of decolonization and the extraordinary emergence of Bangladesh, territorial boundaries proved to be remarkably stable for a half century: from just after World War II to the end of the Cold War.[1] And then a concatenation of events—the reunification of Germany, the dissolution of the Soviet Union (and various sub-secessions in Georgia. Moldova, and Azerbaijan), Yugoslavia, and Czechoslovakia, the secession of Eritrea from Ethiopia and of the former Somaliland from Somalia, and finally the de facto detachment of Kosovo from Serbia—combined in the course of a decade to render boundaries much less stable and to encourage territorially separate groups to consider the possibility of secession.

As all this was happening, international lawyers and philosophers had been rethinking the meaning of self-determination and proceeding to unsettle the former understandings that had discouraged secession and international support for it. One practical exercise along these lines was the ill-considered decision of the Badinter Commission that, asked to pronounce on the validity of secessions from Yugoslavia, declared Yugoslavia to be a federation in process of dissolution—a state of affairs that entitled its constituent republics to secede intact, taking with them their minority areas. After this decision, many fewer states than should consider adopting a federal form of government will do so.

Most of the work of international lawyers has been, however, theoretical. It proceeds along several lines.

For some, self-determination forms an integral part of the right of people to choose their own political regime and to be free of authoritarian oppression. (For Wilson, too, self-determination was connected to ideas of popular sovereignty.) It is a building block of what was emerging in the thinking of a few international lawyers as a right to live under a democratic regime. That such a legal right is at best aspirational might be suggested by the fact that more than half of all regimes in the world are still not democratic, but the early aftermath of the Cold War was a time of great optimism.

Equally expansive are justifications of secession that rest on the right of people in general or people with common group characteristics to choose those with whom they wish to associate politically. Among philosophers who have endorsed the right of ethnic groups to secede, most have begun from the premise that self-determination is to ethnic groups what moral autonomy is to individuals. As individuals have rights to political self expression, so, too, do groups: and for groups, self-expression means self-government, which, in the era of the territorial state, implies control of territory.

The analogy of collective self-determination to individual autonomy is entirely specious. For one thing, collective identity fluctuates, as individual identity does not. New groups come into being, and old ones merge or divide. No new political entity can solve the problem of collective self-expression, as Pakistanis, divided in 1947, redivided in 1971, and still dividing further, have long since discovered. Moreover, even at the outset, the minorities problem is not a trivial detail in recognizing secessions; it is, instead, the central reason why the idea of a clean break is a chimera.

A more cautious version of the right to secede is espoused by those who view secession principally as a "remedial right," a last-ditch response to discrimination or oppression by a central government. If interethnic accommodation fails and one portion of a population is "unalterably hostile" to a group of its fellow citizens, then, it is said, "republican theories may support political divorce on the ground that separation would produce two states in which republican democracy is viable instead of one that lacks essential preconditions to its successful practice."[2]

Despite important differences in scope and reasoning among these justifications for secession, there is a substratum of assumptions in all of them. Secession, it is assumed, can produce homogeneous successor states. In those cases in which heterogeneity remains, it is asserted, minority rights can nevertheless be guaranteed. Like the Badinter Commission, most writers advocating a right to secede make no provision for further secessions, except, of course, insofar as infinite regress of secessionist rights may be implied in their formulations. Secession will also, it is assumed, result in a diminution of conflict that produced the secessionist movement. Rarely are these assumptions discussed or even rendered explicit, but they are essential to the analysis.

"If you can think about something which is attached to something else without thinking about what it is attached to, then you have what is called a legal mind."[3] So pronounced the late constitutional lawyer, Thomas Reed Powell, three-quarters of a century ago. Most theorists of a right to secession have, in this caricatured sense, legal minds. They have generally not concerned themselves with the ethnic politics that produces secessionist claims and that will be affected by new rights to secede. It is no accident that most people who do study ethnic politics are decidedly less enthusiastic about secession than are the international lawyers and philosophers who are the main proponents of a right to secede.

HETEROGENEITY BEFORE, HETEROGENEITY AFTER

There are always ethnic minorities in secessionist regions. There were Efik and Ijaw, among others, in Biafra; there are Hindus in Kashmir, Muslims in Tamil areas of Sri Lanka, Javanese in Aceh and Irian Jaya, Serbs and Roma in Kosovo; and there are minorities in all the rump states as well. As a matter of fact, it is often the desire of regional majorities to deal with minorities—and not to deal with them in a democratic way—that motivates or contributes to the secessionist movement in the first instance. Proponents of rights to secession assure us that minority rights must be guaranteed in secessionist states and that secession should be less favored if minority rights are unlikely to be respected, but the verbal facility of this formulation masks the difficulty of achieving any such results. If, after all, conditions on the exercise of an international law right to secede can be enforced, why not enforce those conditions in the undivided state so as to forestall the need to secede? International law has been notoriously ineffective in assuring longstanding, internationally recognized minority rights, and proponents of secession have no new ideas to offer on this matter. If the failure to respect minority rights in the undivided state induced a regional group to consider secession, why should anyone assume that the situation will be different when that group, a minority in the undivided state, comprises a majority in the secessionist state? If anything, the treatment of minorities in smaller states is less visible to outsiders.

The more circumscribed the asserted right to secede, ironically enough, the more dangerous conditions may become for minorities in the secessionist region. By the time it is concluded that the majority in the undivided state is unalterably hostile to minority interests, thus in some formulations permitting the minority to secede, that group may have accumulated so many grudges that, in their turn, minorities in the secessionist region may be particularly vulnerable to the expression of violent hostility or the settlement of old scores. There are many examples: the fate of Serbs and Roma in Kosovo, of Biharis in Bangladesh, of Sikhs and Hindus in Pakistan at the time of partition, and of Muslims in India at the same time. If the problem of minorities is that they do not enjoy "meaningful political participation" in the undivided state, there is no reason to think that minorities will enjoy it in the secessionist state either. Secession merely proliferates the arenas in which the problem of intergroup political accommodation must be faced—and often more starkly. Contrast Yugoslavia, with six or seven groups and the complex alignments they created with Bosnia, in which three groups confront each other. Secession can hardly be said to solve the problem of intergroup accommodation, except, of course, insofar as it enables the former minority, now a new majority, to cleanse the secessionist state of its minorities—which it could not do previously—and induces the rump state to do the same with members of the secessionist group who find themselves left on the wrong side of a new international boundary.

THE EFFECT OF NEW INTERNATIONAL BOUNDARIES

Recognition of a right to secede is thus not likely to be the end of an old bitterness but the beginning of new bitterness. It is, of course, easy to question whether a slavish devotion to territorial integrity is still appropriate. There has been a great deal of loose talk about the allegedly artificial character of many international boundaries and the part played by colonial convenience in settling them. In point of fact, even in Africa, where this charge is most frequently encountered, boundaries were not settled as disrespectfully of ethnic patterns as is frequently asserted.[4] In any event, patterns of settlement are such that virtually any boundaries would have a large element of arbitrariness to them. Secession would not be a way of rectifying boundaries, because there are no truly natural boundaries.

If it does not solve boundary problems, secession does do something else. A secession or partition converts a domestic ethnic dispute into a more dangerous international one. And since states are able to procure arms with few of the restraints that periodically bedevil insurgents, the international dispute often involves escalating weapons and the prospect of international warfare. Consider the nuclear armaments possessed by India and Pakistan and the recurrent warfare between those states.

One reason for the greater danger that often follows secession is the activation of irredentist claims. For reasons I have explicated elsewhere,[5] the serious pursuit of irredentas—movements to retrieve kindred people and their territory across international boundaries—has been relatively rare in the post-World War II world. But successful secession or partition is likely to change this benign state of affairs. Either the rump state or the secessionist state will desire to retrieve minorities stranded on the wrong side of the border. There are examples readily at hand: Kashmir, Serb claims in Bosnia and in the Krajina region of Croatia, warfare between Ethiopia and Eritrea. And when irredentism gets going, it usually involves ethnic cleansing, so as to eliminate troublesome minorities in the region to be retrieved. A recent quantitative study of the effects of partition finds that partition does not prevent further warfare between ethnic antagonists, and it has only a negligible (and easily reversed) positive effect on low-grade violence short of war.[6]

The recurrent temptation to create a multitude of homogeneous mini-states, even if it could be realized, might well increase the sum total of warfare, rather than reduce it. The right direction for international boundaries is upward, not downward, so that states are so heterogeneous that no one group can plausibly dominate others. Although this degree of benign ethnic complexity is exceedingly difficult to achieve, it is still true that India, with its many groups, is a better model than Kosovo or Rwanda, with just two or three.

SECESSION RIGHTS AND INTERNAL ACCOMMODATION

Articulating a right to secede will undermine attempts to achieve interethnic accommodation within states. As things now stand, the principal reason that states are reluctant to devolve power to territorially concentrated minorities, either by means of regional autonomy or federalism, is their fear that it will lead to secession. That fear is usually unfounded, unless the conflict has already dragged on for a long time and the central government has been utterly ungenerous. Nevertheless, central governments are risk averse about devolution. The best way to dry up devolution as a tool of interethnic accommodation—and a promising tool it is—is to establish a right, recognized in international law, for territorially concentrated minorities to secede. If there is a well-recognized right to secede, the first stirrings of territorially based ethnic discontent will be likely to be met with repression. The possibility that federalism or regional autonomy can lawfully ripen into secession will make any such experiment too costly to entertain. It has been difficult to persuade central decision makers in Indonesia and Sri Lanka to devolve power to regions. A right to secession would easily dissuade them.

One reason central governments are so reluctant to countenance the possibility of secession, even for troublesome regions that some central decision makers might wish to be free of, is that the secession of one region upsets ethnic balances and forces groups in other regions to think afresh about whether they wish to remain in the truncated state with its new ethnic balances. This was clearly visible in Yugoslavia after the Slovene and Croat decisions to secede, when others had to decide in turn whether the relative expansion in Serb power in the rump state was in their interest. Yoruba narrowly decided to stay in Nigeria, despite the relative increase in Hausa power when Ibo decided to leave the state in 1967, and the departure of East Bengal (Bangladesh) from Pakistan destabilized relations among the groups that remained in the rump state. Quite often the fears of central authorities about secession are derided as unsubstantiated apprehensions of domino effects. But domino effects are usually conceived as action based merely on a successful example in another location, whereas what is involved in the first secession is action that affects directly, rather than just by example, the relative positions of other groups remaining in the state.

The creation of a right to secede could not be more untimely. More and more states have been designing internal political arrangements, including devolution, to reduce the incidence of ethnic conflict. That is where the emphasis needs to be, not on making exit strategies more plausible. More about this shortly.

A right to secede effectively advantages militant members of ethnic groups at the expense of conciliators. Since most central governments will not recognize the right to secede, those who wish to pursue such a course will need to resort to arms. Those who are willing to resort to arms are by no means simply latter-day versions of the politicians of their own group whom they seek to displace. Contrast Hashim Thaci of the Kosovo Liberation Army with the Kosovar political leader Ibrahim Rugova; Prabhakaran of the Tamil Tigers with Amirthalingham of the Tamil United Liberation Front, whom he had assassinated; the Southern People's Liberation Army in the Sudan with the old Liberal Party that preceded it. Violence disproportionately attracts people with an interest in aggression. The people willing to take up arms for secession are those who are willing to be brutal with their ethnic enemies and with their own rivals as well. As their advantage grows, new bouts of ethnic cleansing can be expected.

In some formulations, secession is said to be an "exceptional" right that "comes into play if" it "is the only way that a defined population can exercise its right of internal self-determination." But the facts do not support the assumption that secession is ever "the only way." Are the Kurds in Iraq secessionist or autonomist? They have gone back and forth. Are Philippine Muslims? They, too, have gone back and forth. Ibo tried unsuccessfully to secede and then reintegrated into Nigerian politics. In such cases, it looks to outsiders at any given moment as if secession is "the only way" minorities can participate in determining their own future, but there is more fluidity to ethnic politics than those who write about populations that are "unalterably hostile" to each other have sensed.

Moreover, the seemingly moderate position of some proponents of a right to secession that secession is justified only if others are unalterably opposed or minorities have been victimized is not likely to work out moderately in practice, for it is an incentive to ethnic polarization. If independence can only be won legitimately after matters have been carried to extremes, then, by all means, there are people willing to carry them to extremes. In the 1980s and early 1990s, Sikh separatists in the Indian Punjab were willing to attack Hindus in order to precipitate attacks on Sikhs elsewhere in India. There is no shortage of methods to satisfy tough standards of victimization or oppression. A right to secede could indeed contribute to the sense that secession is the only way.

There may be times when it is felt best to part peoples. The British believed such a time had come in India in 1947, and the United Nations believed such a time had come a year later in Palestine. When it is prudent, parting can be done by consent, as in the former Soviet Union and in Czechoslovakia, or occasionally by international action. To do this requires the creation of no rights.

Consider the pernicious effect on the balance of intragroup opinion of a right to secede in a concrete case: Sri Lanka. Will the Sri Lankan Tamils return as readily as they would otherwise to a thoroughly reconstructed but undivided Sri Lanka if they discover that the secession to which they turned so reluctantly was merely an exercise of their rights under international law? It is always hard for antagonistic groups to accommodate each other in a single state. A right to secede will make it harder.

THE CASE FOR HUMILITY IN PUBLIC INTERNATIONAL LAW

. . . Why the connection of international law to democratic governance is thin should be very clear. However much we may favor the worldwide spread of democracy—and I have done my time trying to spread democratic institutions to reduce ethnic conflict—valorizing a right to democratic governance would imperil the universality of international law. Despite the developments of the post–Cold War period, there are almost as many authoritarian as democratic states. If international law is to enhance its influence on state behavior, which it needs to do in order to reduce and regulate interstate conflict and to facilitate interstate transactions, it cannot simultaneously undercut the governing arrangements of nearly half the states that are to be subjected to the rules laid down.

There is, of course, an even more obvious reason why international law ought to be exceedingly restrained in its enthusiasm for secession. Secession is an anti-state movement, and an international law that forgets that states are its main subjects risks its own survival. . . .

LIVING WITH HETEROGENEITY

I said earlier that emphasis needs to be on fostering interethnic accommodation within states. The choice between secession or partition, on the one hand, or murderous conflict, on the other, is a false choice. Institutions can mitigate conflict. This is much too large a topic to discuss at length here, but, since I have been so critical of those who have readily endorsed the right of ethnic groups to leave states, it is incumbent on me at least to sketch briefly what some alternatives might look like.

Most states are ethnically heterogeneous, and many are severely divided. Many groups seek to treat the state as an ethnic patrimony, as if it were homogeneous or as if they had a prior claim to legitimacy and others were there merely on sufferance. Why this is so is a complicated story. Despite these depressing tendencies—which are highly variable rather than universal—it is long past the time when ethnic kinship could form the foundation for homogeneous communities. Territorial proximity is now an inescapable basis for political community.

In general terms, there are two competing prescriptions for solving the problem of ethnic conflict in a democratic framework. Each has its proponents and detractors, its strong and weak points.

The first prescription goes by the name of consociational democracy: a formula for government by grand coalition of all groups, for minority vetoes on important policy issues, for ethnic proportionality in cabinet positions, civil-service posts, and financial allocations, and for cultural autonomy for all groups as well.[7] Many criticisms have been made of consociational theory, for its neglect of democratic opposition (if everyone is in a grand coalition, where will opposition come from?) and its alleged propensity for excessively limited government and immobilism. My own criticism is that grand coalitions are impossible where divisions are severe, because the very formation of such a coalition produces opposition based on the accusation that group interests have been sold out. Moreover, consociation is essentially a system of guarantees, and so is attractive to minorities, but not to majorities, who prefer majority rule. As a result, there are consociational features adopted occasionally by states, but few full-blown consociational regimes. Grand coalitions and minority vetoes are particularly scarce.

My own preferred course involves the use of political incentives to encourage interethnic moderation. There are various institutions, particularly electoral systems, that are capable of inducing moderate behavior on the part of politicians. If election depends, at the margin, on the ability to gain some votes from members of groups other than one's own, then political leaders will behave in an ethnically conciliatory fashion for that purpose. One thing we know is that politicians like being elected and reelected. If consociational theory provides no motive for compromise behavior, incentive theory, by definition, does not share that defect.

Yet there are obstacles to the adoption of incentives schemes as well. Although one can find incentive-based devices adopted by states, a full ensemble of institutions containing incentives to foster conciliation is not easy to find. There is evidence that these devices work, but what are the incentives to adopt the incentives?

Often, processes of bargaining over institutions produce compromises that dilute the effect that could have been expected, had there been a more thoroughgoing and consistent set of institutional changes. Still, partial adoptions can have some positive effect on conciliation.

The upshot of the problem of adoption is that most severely divided societies will not soon become dramatically more harmonious. Over time, some have, and others will, but not necessarily wholly as a result of political engineering. Political engineering will play its part, a greater part at certain unusually propitious times (and such moments should be seized), but the difficulty of wholesale adoption means that many societies will muddle along, sometimes severely conflicted, sometimes better able to achieve compromise if their partial adoption of conciliatory devices is well considered. But, for present purposes, what needs to be emphasized is that efforts at conciliation will not be helped by providing either a liberal or a constrained right to secede. There is an inevitable tradeoff between encouraging participation in the undivided state and legitimating exit from it. The former will inevitably produce imperfect results, but the latter is downright dangerous.

ENDNOTES

1. The so-called secession of Singapore was actually an expulsion of the city-state from Malaysia and was portrayed in legal instruments as occurring by mutual consent.
2. Diane F. Orentlicher, "International Responses to Separatist Claims," pp. 17–18.
3. Quoted by Thurman Arnold, "Criminal Attempts— The Rise and Fall of an Abstraction," *Yale Law Journal* vol. 40 (1930–31), p. 58.
4. See Saadia Touval, *The Boundary Politics of Independent Africa* (Cambridge: Harvard University Press, 1972).
5. See Donald L Horowitz, *Ethnic Groups in Conflict* (Berkeley: University of California Press, 2000), pp. 281–88; and Donald L. Horowitz, "Irredentas and Secessions: Adjacent Phenomena, Neglected Connections," in Naomi Chazan, ed., *Irredentism and International Politics (Studies in International Politics)* (Boulder, Colo.: Lynne Rienner, 1991), pp. 9–22.
6. Nicholas Sambanis, "Partition as a Solution to Ethnic War: An Empirical Critique of the Theoretical Literature," *World Politics*, vol. 52 (July 2000), pp. 437–83.
7. See Arend Lijphart, *Democracy in Plural Societies: A Comparative Exploration,* (New Haven: Yale University Press, 1977).

CHAPTER FOUR

GOVERNING GLOBALIZATION

The state, said Max Weber, is the only association within society that enjoys a legal monopoly on the use of violence. Put another way, the state makes the "authoritative allocation of values." But how can any one state control today's massive movement of capital and goods, or regulate the multi-national corporations that now are astride the globe? We have seen that in this age of globalization $1.5 trillion in capital is transferred across state boundaries every day. The transatlantic economy as a result of mergers and acquisitions now is about one fourth the size of either the American or the European Union economics. Can the state continue to perform essential functions, such as regulation of commerce and provision of security, when so much activity is beyond its borders? Whether international or regional organizations can step into the breach is problematic. These institutions are essentially intergovernmental, requiring the consent of each state participant. Although the United Nations Security Council is empowered to make decisions concerning threats to the peace, including authorization of the use of force, the five permanent members (the United States, United Kingdom, France, Russia, and China) each have a veto. International institutions also lack popular or democratic legitimacy. A majority of the members of the United Nations, for example, may have authoritarian regimes.

Of special interest is the European Union, the most important regional organization in the world. It was created as the European Economic Community by the original six members in 1957 (the Treaty of Rome, signed by France, the Federal Republic of Germany, Italy, Belgium, Netherlands, and Luxembourg), and renamed the European Union (EU) in 1994. As of 2005 it included 25 member states, with a total population fifty percent greater than that of the United States. Through a series of treaties, decision-making power has been vested increasingly in central institutions, particularly relating to the movement of goods, capital and people among member states. Does the EU represent a new political form, transcending the traditional nation-state by pooling national sovereignty? Unlike the United Nations, the EU reposes on a consensus of member states concerning basic values of democracy and the rule of law. But the popularly elected European Parliament has mainly advisory power. Proposals made by the administration (the European Commission) are subject to the approval of the political heads of the member states, meeting as the Council. The evolution of the EU raises profound questions. Is the nation-state still capable of exercising sovereignty? Are the people adequately represented in the decision-making structure? Is the bureaucracy in Brussels democratically accountable? Is the EU itself basically a federation of nation-states, or the harbinger of a new type of political system based on transnational agreements and permanent dialogue rather than diplomatic negotiations backed ultimately by the threat and use of force?

In the selections in this chapter, John G. Ruggie suggests that sovereignty is being separated from territoriality under the pressure of modernization/globalization. Jürgen Habermas argues that globalization is compelling a redefinition of the state, assesses the significance of the European Union as a new political form, but wonders whether it is possible to master globalization without a global state. Anne-Marie Slaughter points to the emergence of global networks of regulators that enable states to cope with problems originating beyond their borders. Transgovernmental cooperation enables us to solve pressing problems without waiting for a global state that may never come. Marc Plattner, on the other hand, believes that democracy is expressed through states, and is skeptical of claims that the European Union can transcend the state as a political form.

The nature of the state is changing under pressures generated by globalization. Does this development endanger democracy? Can regional and global institutions take up the slack, and resolve problems now beyond the reach of states? Or are all international institutions, including the European Union and the United Nations, still basically intergovernmental and fated to remain so?

....

JOHN GERARD RUGGIE

13 Territoriality and Beyond

The year 1989 has already become a convenient historical marker: It has been invoked by commentators to indicate the end of the postwar era. An era is characterized by the passage not merely of time but also of the distinguishing attributes *of a time,* attributes that structure expectations and imbue daily events with meaning for the members of any given social collectivity. In that sense, what the journalist Theordore H. White observed in 1945 is

SOURCE: John Gerard Ruggie, "Territoriality and Beyond: Problematizing Modernity in International Relations," *International Organization,* 47:1 (Winter 1993), pp. 139–144, 171–174. © 1993 by the World Peace Foundation and the Massachusetts Institute of Technology. Reprinted with permission of MIT Press Journals. Abridged by the Editor.

true once again: the world, he wrote, is "fluid and about to be remade."[1] Arguments will continue for many years to come about the determinants of the collapse of the old postwar order and the contours of the new post-postwar order. But even among diverse theoretical traditions there exists a shared vocabulary describing "the world" that has become fluid and is being remade: In its simplest, irreducible terms, it is the world of strategic bipolarity.

The same cannot be said of another "world" that also may be fluid and in the process of being remade: the modern system of states. This world exists on a deeper and more extended temporal plane, and its remaking involves a shift not in the play of power politics but of the stage on which that play is performed.[2] Here, no shared vocabulary exists in the literature to depict change and continuity. Indeed, little vocabulary for it exists at all.

Take efforts to express the emerging architecture of the European Community (EC) as a case in point.* "It is a negative characteristic which first imposes itself," the Marxist theorist Etienne Balibar concedes. "The state today in Europe is *neither national nor supranational,* and this ambiguity does not slacken but only grows deeper over time."[3] From the other side of the political spectrum, *The Economist* agrees and gropes for metaphor: In place of older federative visions, it sees "a Europe of many spires," a European "Mont Saint Michel."[4] For their part, Eurocrats speak of overlapping layers of European economic and political "spaces," tied together, in the words of EC Commission President Jacques Delors, by the community's "spiderlike strategy to organize the architecture of a Greater Europe."[5]

These formulations are not terribly precise or definitive. Still, they are improvements over the treatment Europe typically receives in the standard academic literatures. In Kenneth Waltz's classic neorealist treatise, the EC earned only a few fleeting references, and then only to argue that it would never amount to much in the "international structure" unless it took on the form of a unified state.[6] In the instrumental rationality of game theory and transactions cost analysis, macrostructures are either taken for granted or treated as relatively unproblematic consequences of the interplay of micromotives, and hence generate little interest as independent social facts. And, regional integration theory long ago acknowledged its own obsolescence in the face of the new European reality.[7] In none of these theoretical perspectives is there so much as a hint that the institutional, juridical, and spatial complexes associated with the community may constitute nothing less than the emergence of the first truly postmodern international political form.

Prevailing perspectives may have difficulty describing and explaining the process of European transformation, but none suggests that it is not occurring. At the level of the global economy, in contrast, the phenomenon of transformation not only strains the available vocabulary but on some accounts, its very occurrence remains in doubt.

There has been a remarkable growth in transnational microeconomic links over the past thirty years or so, comprising markets and production facilities that are designated by the awkward term "offshore"—as though they existed in some ethereal space waiting to be reconceived by an economic equivalent of relativity theory. In this offshore area, sourcing, production, and marketing are organized within "global factories," in some instances "global offices,"[8] and most recently the "global lab"[9]—real-time transnational information flows being the raw material of all three. Financial transactions take place in various "Euro" facilities, which may be *housed* in Tokyo, New York, and European financial centers but which are considered to *exist* in an extranational realm. Cross-investment among the leading firms or other means of forging transnationalized intercorporate alliances increasingly are the norm. Trade is made up disproportionately of intrafirm transactions as opposed to the conventional arms-length exchange that is the staple of economic models and policy.[10] And, the financial sector, which historically (and in theory) is assumed to follow and service the "real" sector, now dwarfs it completely.[11]

Furthermore, the largest share of the "goods" that are "traded" in this offshore world actually are "services."[12] *The Economist* magazine, with tongue only half-in-cheek, has proposed defining services as "things which can be bought and sold but which you cannot drop on your foot,"—acknowledging the difficulty of devising a more rigorous definition.[13] Nor is it entirely clear what it means to say that services are traded. In merchandise trade, factors of production stand still and goods move across borders; in traded services, typically the factors of production do the moving while the good (service) stands still: It is produced for the consumer on the spot. What is called trade, therefore, is really "investment," or at the least "right of establishment," baffling trade theorists and negotiators alike.

The orthodox liberal position that these developments somehow imply the growing irrelevance of

*The EC became the European Union (EU) in 1994. Three new members were added in 1995, and ten nations joined in 2004, for a total membership of twenty-five.–ED.

states is, as Janice Thomson and Stephen Krasner suggest, "fundamentally misplaced."[14] Indeed, states are anything but irrelevant even in the ever more integrated EC. Nevertheless, the standard realist ground for rejecting the transformational potential of these developments is equally misplaced. A leading realist journal of opinion recently offered a particularly egregious illustration in response to Robert Reich's probing question about the new world of transnationalized production networks, "Who is 'Us'?"[15] Reich sought to voice the conceptual complexities entailed in determining whether something is an American product any longer and whether the legal designation, "an American corporation," still describes the same economic entity, with the same consequences for domestic employment and economic growth, that it did in the 1950s and 1960s. The response to Reich was a baffling and bizarre— but not atypical—string of non sequiturs, for example: "Only the state can defend corporate interests in international negotiations over trade, investment, and market access. . . . If the existence of the state is in doubt, just ask the depositors of BCCI in some fifty countries who woke up one morning in July to find their accounts frozen. . . . If the United States wanted to prevent the gathering or transmission of information by satellite, it could easily do so by shooting the satellite down." And thus the conclusion, in the title of the essay, that "*We* are US."

There is an extraordinarily impoverished mindset at work here, one that is able to visualize long-term challenges to the system of states only in terms of entities that are institutionally substitutable for the state. Since global markets and transnationalized corporate structures (not to mention communications satellites) are not in the business of replacing states, they are assumed to entail no potential for fundamental international change, Q.E.D. The theoretical or historical warrant for that premise has never been mooted, let alone defended.

Illustrations of analytical problems of this sort can be multiplied many times over in other issue-areas. The global ecological implosion inherently invites epochal thinking, yet analytically informed empirical studies of "ozone diplomacy" or of attempts to save the Mediterranean invariably focus on negotiation processes and the dynamics of regime con-struction, as opposed to exploring the possibility of fundamental institutional discontinuity in the system of states. They do so because, among other reasons, prevailing modes of analytical discourse simply lack the requisite vocabulary.

The worst offender by far is the American field of security studies. Notwithstanding its alleged renaissance, no epochal thought has been expressed by any serious specialist in that field since 1957, when John Herz published his essay, "Rise and Demise of the Territorial State"—and this despite the fact that changes in military technology and in the relations of force are widely acknowledged to have been driving factors of political transformation throughout human history.[16]

The long and the short of it is, then, that we are not very good as a discipline at studying the possibility of fundamental discontinuity in the international system; that is, at addressing the question of whether the modern system of states may be yielding in some instances to postmodern forms of configuring political space.[17] We lack even an adequate vocabulary; and what we cannot describe, we cannot explain. It is the purpose of this article, in Clifford Geertz's apt phrase, to help us "find our feet" in this terrain, which is the necessary first step of any scientific endeavor, no matter how hard or soft the science.[18] . . . .

The bulk of this article . . . is devoted to a relatively modest and pretheoretical task: to search for a vocabulary and for the dimensions of a research agenda by means of which we can start to ask systematic questions about the possibility of fundamental international transformation today. The central attribute of modernity in international politics has been a peculiar and historically unique configuration of territorial space. Hence, I shall proceed by re-examining the transformation whereby this configuration of territorial space first came to be. . . .

Our examination of the emergence of modern territoriality . . . has substantive implications for the study of potential transformation in the international system today. . . . I close with an overall analytical lead, as well as some working hypotheses. . . .

The preceding analysis suggests that the unbundling of territoriality is a productive venue for the exploration of contemporary international transformation. Historically, as we have seen, this is the institutional means through which the collectivity of sovereigns has sought to compensate for the "social defects" that inhere in the modern construct of territoriality.[19] This negation of the exclusive territorial form has been the locale in which international sociality throughout the modern era has been embedded. The terrain of unbundled territoriality, therefore, is the place wherein a rearticulation of international political space would be occurring today.

Take first the EC, in which the process of unbundling territoriality has gone further than anywhere else. Neorealism ascribes its origins to strategic bipolarity; microeconomic institutionalism examines how the national interests and policy preferences of the major European states are reflected in patterns of EC collaboration; and neofunctionalism anticipated the emergence of a supranational statism. Each contains a partial truth. From the vantage of the present analysis, however, a very different attribute of the EC comes into view: It may constitute the first "multiperspectival polity" to emerge since the advent of the modern era. That is to say, it is increasingly difficult to visualize the conduct of international politics among community members, and to a considerable measure even domestic politics, as though it took place from a starting point of twelve separate, single, fixed viewpoints. Nor can models of strategic interaction do justice to this particular feature of the EC, since the collectivity of members as a singularity, in addition to the central institutional apparatus of the EC, has become party to the strategic interaction game. To put it differently, the constitutive processes whereby each of the twelve defines its own identity—and identities are logically prior to preferences—increasingly endogenize the existence of the other eleven. Within this framework, European leaders may be thought of as entrepreneurs of alternative political identities—EC Commission President Delors, for example, is at this very moment exploiting the tension between community widening and community deepening so as to catalyze the further reimagining of European collective existence. There is no indication, however, that this reimagining will result in a federal state of Europe—which would merely replicate on a larger scale the typical modern political form.

The concept of multiperspectival institutional forms offers a lens through which to view other possible instances of international transformation today. Consider the global system of transnationalized microeconomic links. Perhaps the best way to describe it, when seen from our vantage point, is that these links have created a nonterritorial "region" in the world economy—a decentered yet integrated space-of-flows, operating in real time, which exists alongside the spaces-of-places that we call national economies. These conventional spaces-of-places continue to engage in external economic relations with one another, which we continue to call trade, foreign investment, and the like, and which are more or less effectively mediated by the state. In the nonterritorial global economic region, however, the conventional distinctions between internal and external once again are exceedingly problematic, and any given state is but one constraint in corporate global strategic calculations. This is the world in which IBM is Japan's largest computer exporter, and Sony is the largest exporter of television sets from the United States. It is the world in which Brothers Industries, a Japanese concern assembling typewriters in Bartlett, Tennessee, brings an antidumping case before the U.S. International Trade Commission against Smith Corona, an American firm that imports typewriters into the United States from its offshore facilities in Singapore and Indonesia. It is the world in which even the U.S. Pentagon is baffled by the problem of how to maintain the national identity of "its" defense-industrial base. This nonterritorial global economic region is a world, in short, that is premised on what Lattimore described as the "sovereign importance of movement," not of place. The long-term significance of this region, much like that of the medieval trade fairs, may reside in its novel behavioral and institutional forms and in the novel space-time constructs that these forms embody, not in any direct challenge that it poses as a potential substitute for the existing system of rule.

Consider also the transformative potential of global ecology. The human environment is of central importance for future planetary politics from many perspectives. Central among them is its potential to comprise a new and very different social episteme— a new set of spatial, metaphysical, and doctrinal constructs through which the visualization of collective existence on the planet is shaped. This episteme would differ in form from modern territoriality and its accoutrements insofar as the underlying structural premise of ecology is holism and mutual dependence of parts. The difficulty is in tapping this social epistemological dimension empirically. Nonetheless, it may be possible to infer from state behavior whether and to what extent it is coming to express new and different principles of international legitimacy, for example. The concept of international custodianship is an obvious candidate for closer scrutiny. Under it, no other agency competes with or attempts to substitute for the state, but the state itself acts in a manner that expresses not merely its own interests and preferences but also its role as the embodiment and enforcer of community norms—a multiperspectival role, in short, somewhat in the manner of medieval rulers vis-à-vis cosmopolitan bodies of religion and law. Another possible approach is to examine the impact of real or simulated environmental catastrophes on the thinking of policymakers and on the popular imagination at large: Chernobyl, the Antarctic ozone hole, and global warming scenarios come to mind.

Finally, this analysis also potentially enriches the field of international security studies. To cite but one example, despite the severe dislocations that have accompanied the collapse of the Soviet Union's East European empire and then of the Soviet Union itself, no one in any position of authority anywhere in Europe to date has advocated, or is quietly preparing for, a return to a system of competitive bilateral alliances. Thus far, all of the options on the table concerning the external mechanisms for achieving security in Europe, East and West, have been multilateral in form. These mechanisms include NATO reaching out institutionally to the EC via the West European Union*

on one side; and, on the other side, to the East European states via the newly created North Atlantic Cooperation Council, comprising the membership of the two formerly adversarial alliances, as well as to the Conference on Security and Cooperation in Europe. This development suggests a hypothesis for further exploration. Within the industrialized world, and partially beyond, we may be witnessing emerging fragments of international security communities—alongside the traditional war system that continues elsewhere. These security communities are not integrated in the sense that the ill-fated European Defense Community would have been, but they are more extensively institutionalized than the "pluralistic security communities" of integration studies in the 1950s.[20] Once more the term "multiperspectival" seems appropriate. Within the scope of these security communities the imbalances of advantage that animated positional wars throughout the modern era now are resolved by more communitarian mechanisms instead. Such mechanisms do not imply the abolition of the use of force; they do imply, however, that the use of force is subject to greater collective legitimation.

It is truly astonishing that the concept of territoriality has been so little studied by students of international politics; its neglect is akin to never looking at the ground that one is walking on. I have argued that disjoint, mutually exclusive, and fixed territoriality most distinctively defines modernity in international politics and that changes in few other factors can so powerfully transform the modern international polity. What is more, I have tried to show that unbundled territoriality is a useful terrain for exploring the condition of postmodernity in international politics, and I have suggested some ways in which that might be done. The emergence of multiperspectival institutional forms was identified as a key dimension in understanding the possibility of postmodernity.

On reflection, though, the reason territoriality is taken for granted is not hard to guess. Samuel Becket put it well in *Endgame*: "You're on earth, there's no cure for that." Unbundled territoriality is not located some place else; but it is becoming another place.

---

*The West European Union was the defense arm of the EC. It was subsequently absorbed by the European Union–ED.

ENDNOTES

1. Theodore H. White, *In Search of History: A Personal Adventure,* New York: Harper & Row, 1978, p. 224.

2. For a specification of the ontological and epistemological differences among incremental, conjunctural, and secular or epochal time frames, see John Gerard Ruggie, "Social Time and International Policy," in Margaret P. Karns, ed., *Persistent Patterns and Emergent Structures in a Waning Century,* New York: Praeger, 1986, pp. 211–36. Within that typology, the "normal politics" studied by much of the international relations field falls into the incremental category, the cold war exemplifies the conjunctural, and the modern system of states the epochal time frames.

3. Etienne Balibar, "*Es Gibt Keinen Staat in Europa:* Racism and Politics in Europe Today," *New Left Review,* vol. 186 (March/April 1991), p. 16, emphasis original.

4. "Many-spired Europe," *The Economist,* 18 May 1991, p. 16. Some twenty years ago, I suggested that integration theory move from the model of a "tree" (in graph-theoretic terms) to depict the institutional end-point of the integration process to one of a semi-lattice—the definition of which sounds very much like a formal representation of *The Economist's* European Mont Saint Michel. See John Gerard Ruggie, "The Structure of International Organization: Contingency, Complexity, and Postmodern Form," Peace Research Society (International) *Papers,* no. 18, 1972.

5. "Inner Space," *The Economist,* 18 May 1991. Delors is cited in Alan Riding, "Europeans in Accord to Create Vastly Extended Trading Bloc," *New York Times,* 23 October 1991, p. A1.

6. See Kenneth Waltz, *Theory of International Politics,* Reading, Mass.: Addison-Wesley, 1979.

7. See Ernst B. Haas, *The Obsolescence of Regional Integration Theory,* Research Mongraph no. 25 (Berkeley: Institute of International Studies, University of California, 1976).

8. Steve Lohr, "The Growth of the 'Global Office'." *New York Times,* 18 October 1988. For example, Citibank does some of its financial data processing in Jamaica; American Airlines processes ticket stubs in Barbados and the Dominican Republic; and New York Life processes claims and McGraw-Hill, magazine subscription renewals, in Ireland.

9. The term is drawn from Pollack: "Just as they once moved manufacturing plants overseas, American companies are now spreading their research and product development around the world, helping to turn the creation of technology into an activity that transcends national borders." See Andrew Pollack, "Technology Without Borders Raises Big Questions for U.S.," *New York Times,* 1 January 1992, p. A1.

10. Some 40 percent of U.S. trade is of the intrafirm variety, a ratio that increases to close to two-thirds if more relaxed definitions of "related party" are used. Moreover, intrafirm trade has been growing more rapidly than the standard stuff, and it is less sensitive to such macroeconomic factors as exchange rates. . . .

11. International trade amounts to some $2.5 to $3 trillion per year; international capital markets turn over at least $75 trillion, and foreign exchange transactions now amount to approximately $1 trillion per day.

12. Definitions are so bad that the balance of world services imports and exports routinely is off by as much as $100 billion per annum—a margin of error equivalent to fully one-fifth of all traded services; see Ronald K. Shelp, "Trade in Services," *Foreign Policy,* vol. 65 (Winter 1986–87). Bhagwati suggests several creative definitional distinctions but ends up recommending that the term "trade in services" be abandoned in favor of "international service transactions"; see Jagdish Bhagwati, "Trade in Services and the Multilateral Trade Negotiations," *The World Bank Economic Review,* vol. 1, no. 1 (1987). . . .

13. "A Gatt for Services," *The Economist,* 12 October 1985, p. 20. . . .

14. Janice E. Thomson and Stephen D. Krasner, "Global Transactions and the Consolidation of Sovereignty," in Ernst-Otto Czempiel and James N. Rosenau, eds., *Global Changes and Theoretical Challenges,* Lexington, Mass.: Lexington Books, 1989, p. 198. . . .

15. See Ethan B. Kapstein, "*We* are US: The Myth of the Multinational," *The National Interest,* vol. 26 (Winter 1991/92), pp. 55–62. The full exposition of Reich's argument is in *The Work of Nations,* the final chapter of which is entitled "Who is 'US'?"

16. On the field's alleged "renaissance," see Stephen M. Walt, "The Renaissance of Security Studies." *International Studies Quarterly,* vol. 35 (June 1991), pp. 211–39. For John Herz's view, see his articles "Rise and Demise of the Territorial States," *World Politics,* vol. 9 (July 1957), pp. 473–93, and "The Territorial State Revisited—Reflections on the Future of the Nation-State," *Polity,* vol. 1 (Fall 1968), pp. 11–34, in which he elaborated and modified some of his earlier ideas. . . . A partial exception to my characterization of the security studies literature is Robert Jarvis. *The Meaning of the Nuclear Revolution,* Ithaca, N.Y.: Cornell University Press, 1989. On the historical relation between military changes and

political transformation, see William H. McNeill. *The Pursuit of Power,* Chicago: University of Chicago Press, 1982; and Charles Tilly, *Coercion, Capital, and European States AD 990–1990,* Cambridge, Mass.: Basil Blackwell, 1990.

17. One recent attempt to correct this shortcoming . . . is James N. Rosenau, *Turbulence in World Politics,* Princeton, N.J.: Princeton University Press, 1990.

18. Clifford Geertz, *The Interpretation of Cultures,* New York: Basic Books, 1973, p. 13.

19. . . . I have in mind a Lockean understanding, namely those "Inconveniences which disorder Mens properties in the state of Nature," the avoidance of which is said to drive "Men [to] unite into Societies." See Locke, *Two Treatises of Government,* sec. 2.136. These "social defects" thus may be thought of as the generic form of international "collective action problems," of which various types of externalities, public goods, and dilemmas of strategic interaction are but specific manifestations.

20. The classic study is Karl W. Deutsch et al., *Political Community and the North Atlantic Area,* Princeton, N.J.: Princeton University Press, 1957.

JÜRGEN HABERMAS

14   Nation-State or Global State?

"The dominant question at present," we read in the introduction to a new collection on *Global Dynamics and Local Life World,* "is whether the ecological, social and cultural dynamics of global capitalism can be re-mastered beyond the nation-state, at a supranational and a global level."[1] No one disputes the power of markets for innovation and coordination. But markets react only to messages written in the code of price. They remain deaf to the externalities that they generate in other areas. The liberal sociologist Richard Münch fears that the exhaustion of nonrenewable natural resources, massive levels of cultural alienation, and social crises will make it impossible to place political controls on markets that have already overflowed the boundaries of weakened and overburdened nation-states. Münch observes an "inflationary overdraft" of economic modernization, touching off a "deflationary downward spiral" toward aggressive forms of group particularism, even within the prosperous societies of the global North.

Of course, the call for an "ecological, social, and cultural *re*-embedding of global capitalism" is something of a euphemism. Over the course of the postwar period, the states in advanced capitalist societies have sharpened, not reduced ecological threats. And the social-security systems these states developed through social-welfare bureaucracies did not exactly demand personal autonomy from their clients. Yet over the course of the third quarter of the twentieth century in Europe, as in OECD countries elsewhere, the social state was still capable of offering broad compensations for the undesired consequences of highly productive economies. It was capitalism that first made possible the fulfillment of the republican promise of the inclusion of all citizens with equal rights. The democratic constitutional state guarantees equal treatment in the sense of citizens' equal opportunity to make use of their rights as well; John Rawls, the most influential theorist of political liberalism, spoke in this context of the "fair value" of equally distributed rights. But in view of the homeless population swelling silently before our eyes, one is reminded of Anatole France's remark: People should not merely have the equal right "to sleep under bridges."

If we understand the texts of our national constitutions in this material sense, that of the realization of social justice, then the idea of self-*legislation*—the idea that the addressees of law should understand themselves as the authors of law as well—acquires a *political dimension,* that of a *self-effectuating* or

SOURCE: Jürgen Habermas, "Toward a Cosmopolitan Europe," *Journal of Democracy,* vol. 14, no. 4 (2003), pp. 86–100. © National Endowment for Democracy and The Johns Hopkins University Press. Reprinted with permission of The Johns Hopkins University Press. Footnotes abridged by the Editor.

self-directing society. Politicians of every stripe have been guided by this dynamic understanding of the democratic process in the construction of the social state in Europe during the postwar period. The success of this project confirmed, in turn, the concept of self-direction—of a society directing itself through political means. We know that this concept has so far been realized only within the framework of the nation-state. But insofar as nation-states are running up against the limits of their own capacities in the transformed circumstances of a global economy and world society, the entire project of placing political controls on a globally unleashed capitalism—along with the only form of state that even halfway measures up to the ideals of democracy—comes into question. Can this form of democratic self-direction of modern societies extend beyond national borders?

I will explore this question in three stages. First, we must clarify the relation between the nation-state and democracy, and the ways in which the unique symbiosis between them has come under increased pressure. Guided by this diagnosis, I will then briefly describe four political responses to the challenges of the postnational constellation, responses that also define the terms for current discussions of a "third way." Finally, this debate points toward a clear position on the future of the European Union. If the generally privileged citizens of Europe want to take the perspectives of other countries and continents into account, then they will have to work toward deepening the federative aspect of the European Union, with the cosmopolitan goal of creating the conditions necessary for a global domestic policy.

....

CHALLENGES FOR THE NATION-STATE AND DEMOCRACY

Developmental trends collected under the catchphrase "globalization" have transformed a historical constellation that had defined state, society, and economy as more or less coextensive within national boundaries. In the wake of market globalization, the *international* economic system—in which states establish the boundary between their domestic economies and foreign trade relations—has been transformed into a *transnational* economy. The controversy surrounding the increased volume and intensity of cross-border trade (especially in industrial goods and services), like discussions over the significance of the sharp rise in direct investment, has focused on degrees of magnitude within a single medium, but not very much on the crucial changes in the relation between the medium of the market and that of political power itself. Most significant is the acceleration of the movement of global capital and the competitive valuation of national economies via globally networked financial markets. These facts explain why national-state actors are no longer the nodal points that give global economic exchange the form of interstate or international relations. States are now embedded in markets, rather than national economies being embedded within state borders.

Naturally, the trend toward the disestablishment of borders characterizes more than just the economy. A recently published study by David Held and colleagues on *Global Transformations* includes—in addition to chapters on global trade, financial markets, and multinational corporations with global production links—chapters on global domestic policy; peacekeeping and organized force; the rising tide of migration; the new media and communication networks; hybrid forms of mixed cultures; and identity conflicts in the wake of the diffusion, superimposition, and interpenetration of forms of cultural life.[2] This broad "de-bordering" of economy, society, and culture thus touches on the very existential presuppositions of a state system that had been constructed according to a territorial principle, and still comprises the most important collective actors on the political stage. As the limits placed on national governments' spheres of action endanger the social state, they also endanger the project whose success until now has been possible only within the nation-state framework: compensating for the socially undesirable effects of capitalism. The democratic self-direction of society toward this goal has been institutionalized only within the framework of the nation-state. How do we explain this affinity between the nation-state and democracy?

Four conditions must be met in order for freely associating citizens to govern their lives democratically and influence their own social conditions through political means:

- There must be an effective political apparatus for the execution of collectively binding decisions.

- There must be a clearly defined "self" for political self-determination and self-direction, to which collectively binding decisions can be ascribed.

- There must be a citizenry that can be mobilized for participation in political opinion-formation and will-formation, with an orientation toward the common good.

- There must be an economic and social milieu in which a democratically programmed administration can successfully provide legitimate steering and organization.

The instrumental requirement for effective political action is fulfilled by the *administrative state,* which since the seventeenth century has been based on the functional separation of public administrative power from civil society, initially as a tax-levying state and subsequently as a legal state. The identity requirement for the determination of a collective subject capable of self-determination and self-direction is fulfilled by the *sovereign territorial state* of classical international law, which establishes the state population and political rule by reference to the borders of a sovereign territory defended by military force. The requirement of active participation is fulfilled by the *national state,* which since the beginning of the nineteenth century has manufactured an abstract form of solidarity among strangers from a combination of the cultural symbolism of "the people" and the republican status of citizens. Finally, the requirement for a mode of politics capable of shaping social conditions was fulfilled by the *social state* over the course of the second half of the twentieth century, when conditions of rapid economic growth made it nearly possible to secure the fair value of equal rights.

This model of a territorial, national, and social state equipped with effective administrative power

accommodates democracy insofar as a political-cultural collective has to be (1) adequately integrated; and (2) adequately autonomous in geographic, social, economic, and military respects—that is, independent of external influences. Only in this way can unified citizens regulate themselves through the familiar forms of the democratic constitutional state and politically shape their society. Within nation-state democracies, both of these conditions were more or less assured through the congruence of state, society, and economy. But the postnational constellation effectively disconnects this constructive assemblage of political and legal systems, economic cycles, and national traditions within the borders of a territorial state. The trends referred to by the term "globalization" do not merely threaten the idea of a more or less homogenously composed population, and therefore the prepolitical basis for integrating citizens, through immigration and cultural segmentation. More decisive still is the fact that states, increasingly *ensnared* in the interdependencies of a global economy and society, forfeit their own capacities for autonomous action as well as their democratic substance.

I will not examine the factual harms to the formal sovereignty of states, and will limit my discussion to three aspects in which nation-states have been effectively disempowered: (a) the loss of state capacities for control; (b) the growing legitimation deficits in decision-making processes; and (c) the increasing inability to provide legitimate and effective steering and organizational services.

a. Among other things, the reduction of state autonomy reveals that individual states can no longer adequately protect their citizens from the external effects of decisions made by *other* actors, or from causal chain of decision-making processes originating beyond the national borders. We see this in "spontaneous border crossings" such as environmental degradation; organized crime; security risks produced by advanced technology, the arms trade, epidemics, and so forth; as well as in the calculated and cumulative consequences of the policies of other states, policies whose formation and legitimation do not involve everyone affected by them.

b. Regarding the demand for democratic legitimacy, deficits will always result when the circle of all those involved in democratic decision making does not extend to cover the circle of all those affected by those decisions. Democratic legitimacy is more subtly but more durably harmed when the need for coordination, which rises with increasing interdependency, is increasingly met through intergovernmental agreements. In some political areas, the institutional embedding of the nation-state in a network of transnational treaties and regimes does produce equivalents for competencies that have been lost at the national level. But the more numerous and important the matters that are regulated via inter-state decisions, the more the decision-making process is withdrawn from democratic opinion formation and will formation, which remain anchored in national arenas. In the European Union, the sweeping bureaucratic decision-making processes of the experts in Brussels offer an example of the kind of democracy deficit that emerges as the competencies of national decision-making bodies are transferred to intergovernmental commissions staffed by governmental representatives.

c. At the heart of the discussion, however, is the reduction in the capacity for intervention that nation-states had previously employed in drafting and implementing social policies. As the (territorially limited) sphere of action of nation-state actors gradually falls behind globalized markets and accelerated capital mobility, what Wolfgang Streek calls the "functional completeness of national economies" vanishes: "Functional completeness cannot be equated with autarky . . . [I]t requires not so much a 'complete' range of products but rather the dependable, national presence of those complementary factors—above all capital and organization—that socially generated labor offers are based on, in order to be productive."[3] Once the search for investment opportunities and speculative profits has released capital from its national duty, so to speak, it becomes a free agent and can use its exit option as a threatened sanction as soon as governments—in consideration of consumer capacities, social standards, or job security—begin overburdening the national economy in the international competition for the most favorable commercial conditions.

Under the terms of global competition for economic advantage for one's own national location, high wages and benefits act as an incentive for economic rationalization. Mass layoffs underline the growing leverage that highly mobile corporations maintain against the weakened position of labor unions, which remain tied to particular locations. At the same time, national governments are losing their capacity to exploit the tax resources of their domestic economies, to stimulate growth, and therefore to secure the basis of their own legitimacy. Policies of demand management generate external effects that are counterproductive for national economic cycles (as the experience of the first Mitterand administration showed in the early 1980s) insofar as international equities markets have taken responsibility for the valorization of national economic policies. In many European countries, the displacement of politics by markets manifests itself as a vicious circle of rising unemployment, overburdened social-security systems, and shrinking taxpayer contributions. The nation-state is confronting the dilemma that the more necessary economic stimulus packages and higher tax rates on moveable property become for its exhausted public budget, the harder it becomes to carry out these measures within the state's own national borders.

COORDINATION OF A DISCUSSION

There are two simple responses to this challenge, and two more nuanced ones. The polarization between two positions that react flatly either a) for or b) against deterritorialization and globalization have motivated the search for a "third way," which in turn can take the form of either c) a reactive or d) a proactive variant.

a. Supporters of globalization appeal to a neoliberal orthodoxy that has overseen the transition to supply-side economic policies over recent decades. There has never been a more influential "epistemic community" than the Chicago School. It urges the subordination of states to the imperatives of a process of worldwide social integration via markets, and advocates an *entrepreneurial state* that bids farewell both to the project of de-commodifying labor power and, more generally, to the state's role as protector of the resources of the life world. A state *engaged* in the transnational economic system consigns its citizens to the legally secured negative freedoms of global competition, and essentially confines itself to the businesslike construction and maintenance of the infrastructures that make the state's position more attractive from the point of view of profitability, and thus promote entrepreneurial activity. This is not the place for me to go into the various assumptions of the neoliberal model and the time-honored dogmatic battles over the relation between market efficiency and social justice.[4] But two considerations do become pressing, even according to the premises of neoliberal theory itself.

Let us assume that a thoroughly liberalized global economy with unlimited mobility of all productive forces (including labor power) were to come about, at some future point, together with an (anticipated) global equilibrium of national positions and a symmetrical division of labor. Even under those premises, we would still have to reckon not only with a drastic increase in social inequities and social fragmentation, but also with the decay of moral standards and cultural infrastructures during a transition period, both nationally and worldwide. The questions are how long it would take to travel this "trail of tears," and who would be the victims offered up during this period: How many marginalized lives would be cast by the wayside, how many precious achievements of civilization would fall victim to "creative destruction"?

Just as unsettling is the question regarding the future of democracy. The democratic procedures and arrangements that grant united citizens the chance for collective self-determination and political control over the conditions of their own social existence can only diminish as the nation-state loses its functions and capabilities, unless some equivalent for them emerges at the supra-state level. Wolfgang Streek calls this the "falling purchasing power of the ballot" and sees "the danger that democratic governance will decay into the ability to come to power on the basis of illusionary expectations, while at the same time taking precautions to ensure that one cannot be held responsible if those expectations are not fulfilled."[5]

b. On the other hand, the reaction to the devaluation of the nation-state and democracy has produced a coalition of those fighting for the actual or potential losers of these structural transformations, and against the disempowerment of the democratic state and its citizens. But in the end the powerful desire to draw up the national gates also leads what Charles Maier calls the "territoriality party" into a battle against the egalitarian and universalistic foundations of democracy itself. The protectionist reaction against various border transgressions—whether directed against drug and arms merchants or mafiosi who endanger national security, or against the flood of information or American movies that endanger indigenous cultures, or against labor immigrants and refugees who endanger national living standards—ends up lending grist to the mill of ethnocentric reactions against diversity, xenophobic reactions against others, and antimodern reactions against the complexity of contemporary living conditions.

Even if we take the rational kernel of these defensive reactions into account, it is easy to see why the nation-state cannot win back its old strengths through a politics of national self-reliance. The liberalization of the global economy that was established on the basis of a system of fixed exchange rates at the end of the Second World War, and that assumed the (temporary) form of an *embedded liberalism,* has only accelerated since the end of the Bretton Woods system. This was not an inevitable outcome. The systemic pressures that have since emerged from the imperatives of a free-trade regime strongly anchored within the WTO are the results of political voluntarism. While the United States also had dominated the GATT, the WTO's predecessor organization, here too it was a question not of a one-sided imposition but rather of heavily negotiated, undirected decisions that ended up coordinating the actions and omissions of many different governments. And because global markets have emerged in the wake of such negative integrations among many independent actors, there is little prospect for the restorative project of *unilaterally* withdrawing from the systematic results of decisions that have been made in concert, without expecting inevitable sanctions.

The stalemate between the pro- and antiglobalization parties has motivated the search for a "third way." This path is forked. The defensive variant c) proceeds on the assumption that globalized capitalism can no longer be reined in but can be nationally *cushioned;* the offensive variant d) is based on the formative power of a politics capable of expanding to *catch up* with markets that have already become supranational.

c. According to the defensive variant, the subordination of politics to the imperatives of a market-integrated global society is now irrevocable. But the nation-state ought not to play a merely reactive role in shaping the commercial conditions for investment capital; it should act proactively to render its own citizens qualified and competitive. This new social politics is no less universally applied than the old one. But now its job is less to protect citizens from the standard risks of working conditions than to equip them with the entrepreneurial qualities of "players" who know how to take care of themselves. The familiar maxim "helping people to help themselves" still preserves the economistic sense of a fitness program designed to whip everyone into shape for assuming personal responsibility and developing the initiative for competent self-assertion in the market. "Failures" can no longer count on help from the government: "Social democrats have to shift the relationship between *risk* and *security* involved in the welfare state, to develop a society of 'responsible risk takers' in the spheres of government, business enterprise and labor markets.... Equality must contribute to diversity, not stand in its way."[6]

What the "old" socialists find irritating in the outlook of this "new middle" or "New Labour" is not just its normative chutzpah but also the dubious empirical assumption that wage labor, even outside the form of normal labor relations, still counts as "the key scale of social integration." Both the strong trend toward rising productivity and labor-saving technologies, and the increased demand on the labor market—especially by women—make the opposite assumption, what the German economist Georg Voruba refers to as the "end of the full employment society," seem more plausible. But once the goal of full-employment is given up, either public standards of distributive justice will have to be scaled back, or alternatives will have to be found that place considerable burdens on the competitive position of the national economy: projects such as redistributing the reduced volume of jobs, or granting shares of capital goods to broad strata of the population, or decoupling a basic guaranteed income above the poverty line from wage income— all hardly cost-neutral options under existing global economic conditions.

From a normative point of view, the advocates of this "third way" have fallen in line with a form of liberalism that sees social equality only from the input side and therefore reduces it to the equality of opportunity. Alongside this *moral* similarity, the distinction between Margaret Thatcher and Tony Blair has become blurred in the public's eye due to the *ethical* resemblance of New Labour to the worldview of neoliberalism. What I mean is the willingness to rely on the ethos of a "global market-oriented way of life" that expects all citizens to develop themselves into "employers of their own human capital."

d. For all those still unwilling to change their spots, an offensive variant of the third way is attractive: the priority of politics to the logic of the market. "In a modern society, how far the systematic logic of the markets should be 'unleashed,' where and in which contexts markets should 'rule' is to be determined in the final instance through political deliberation."[7] This sounds like voluntarism, nothing more than a normative postulate that, given our previous reflections, can no longer be realized within the framework of the nation-state. Nevertheless, in the search for a solution to the dilemma between the disarmament of social-state democracy and the rearmament of the nation-state, this demand draws our attention to larger political entities and transnational regimes that might be able to compensate for the functional loss of the nation-state without breaking the chain of democratic legitimacy. The European Union, of course, offers itself as an initial example for a form of democracy beyond the nation-state. The creation of larger-scale political entities certainly does not in itself change the mode of economic competition between states—that is, the priority of market integration as such. Politics will succeed in "catching up" with globalized markets only if there is a broader prospect for creating a stable infrastructure for a global domestic policy, one that is nevertheless not completely decoupled from processes of democratic legitimation.

Reference to a politics that "catches up" with markets should certainly not be taken as suggesting a power struggle between political and economic players. The problematic consequences of a form of politics that seeks to assimilate society as such into market structures can be explained by the fact that money cannot simply substitute for political power in every circumstance. The successful exercise of legitimate power is measured by criteria other than economic ones; markets, unlike political entities, cannot be democratized. It is more appropriate to imagine a competition between different media. Market-creating policies are self-referential insofar as each step toward market deregulation means a disempowerment or self-limitation of political power as the medium for realizing collectively binding decisions. A political attempt to catch up with markets, by contrast, reverses this process: It is a reflexive politics under reversed conditions. And since the democratic construction of political power relies on communicative processes which alone authorize the application of power, political communication too must be directed toward the goal of a self-reflexive appropriation of a politics of this sort—even at the cost of displacing other mechanisms for regulation.

....

EUROPE AND THE WORLD

If we see the development of the European Union from this perspective, the paradoxical result is that the creation of new political institutions—the Brussels bureaucracy, the European Court of Justice, and the European Central Bank—does not at all imply a strengthening of the political per se. Notwithstanding its original, programmatic significance for Robert Schuman, Alcide de Gasperi, and Konrad Adenauer, currency union was the final step along a path best described, with the humility of hindsight, as "intergovernmental market construction." Today the European Union is a regime of continental magnitude that is very thickly networked horizontally via markets while maintaining relatively weak political regulation vertically through indirectly legitimated authorities. Because its member states have lost the steering capacities of exchange-rate adaptation as they have transferred their monetary sovereignty to the central bank, problems of a new magnitude have arisen with the predictable intensification of competition within the unified currency zone.

Formerly national economies find themselves at different development levels and shaped by different economic styles. Until an integrated economy emerges from this heterogeneous situation, the congeries of interactions between individual economic spheres, still linked to different political systems, will inevitably lead to frictions. Initially weaker economies must counteract their competitive disadvantages with caps on wages, while stronger economies fear wage dumping. This suggests an unfavorable scenario for all those social security systems that remain within national competences, which are very differently structured from one another and are already pregnant with conflicts. While some fear being robbed of their cost advantages, others fear equalization downward. Europe will face the alternative either of disposing of this problem through markets—in the end, as a competition between sociopolitical regimes and national economies—or of handling the pressure politically by attempting a "harmonization" and a gradual adaptation on a range of important social, labor, and taxation policies. In essence, the question is whether the institutional status quo, an international balancing of national interests, will be defended with a race to the bottom, or whether the European Union should be developed further into a true federation beyond its current status as a league of states. Only this second option would grant it the political power to make *market-correcting* decisions and enforce regulations with *redistributive* effects.

Given their positions in the current discussion of globalization, neither the neoliberals nor the nationalists have much difficulty in choosing between these two alternatives. *Euroskeptics,* desperate in the face of the completed process of currency union, call for protection and exclusion; *market Europeans,* on the other hand, regard currency union with satisfaction as the completion of a European domestic economy. Distinct from both of these positions, *Eurofederalists* push for a process that will transform existing international treaties into a political constitution for Europe, as a way of achieving a broad basis of legitimacy for the decisions of the European Commission, the Council of Ministers, and the European Court of Justice. Finally, the *cosmopolitan* position is distinct from all three of these. Cosmopolitans see a federal European state as a point of departure for the development of a transnational network of regimes that together could pursue a world domestic policy, even in the absence of a world government. The basic distinction between Eurofederalists and market Europeans is complicated by the fact that the latter have now entered into a silent coalition with ex-Euroskeptics, whose search for a third way is based on the *fait accompli* of the currency union. Tony Blair and Gerhard Schröder, it appears, are not so far from Hans Tietmeyer (the former president of the Deutsche Bundesbank).

Market Europeans want to preserve the European status quo insofar as it seals the subordination of fragmented national-state actors to market integration. A spokesman for the Deutsche Bundesbank can therefore view distinctions between a unified state, a United States of Europe, or a European Federal Republic, as merely "academic": "Given the integration of economic spheres, in the end the difference between civic and economic activity is disappearing. Indeed this is what processes of integration pursue as their central goal."[8] From this point of view, European competition is supposed to "lift the taboo" on reducing national living standards—as maintained by such institutions as the public-legal credit branch or social security—for the ultimate purpose of dissolving these standards altogether. The position of market Europeans rests on a premise also shared by social-democratic loyalists to the nation-state pursuing a third way: "Remedying the limitations of state power in the age of globalization is not possible; [globalization] demands above all the strengthening of the free forces of civil society," namely, "the individual initiative and responsibility of citizens."[9] This shared premise explains the reversed alliances. Former Euroskeptics, even if inspired by other motives and pursuing other goals, now support market Europeans in their defense of the European

status quo. Thus while they do not seek to dismantle the state's social policies, or to let the range of social "shock absorbers" fall entirely into private hands, they do want to redirect social aid toward investments in human capital.

Thus the controversy between neoliberals and Eurofederalists has become blurred with a controversy between the defensive and the proactive variants of the third way, which smolders within the social-democratic camp (between Gerhard Schröder and Oskar Lafontaine). This conflict does not involve just the question of whether the European Union—through a harmonization of different national taxation, social, and economic policies—can regain the room for action that the individual nation-states have lost. In any event, the European economic realm at present still enjoys a relatively large degree of independence from global competition, due to its thickly interwoven commercial relationships and direct investments. The controversy between Euroskeptics and Eurofederalists is primarily focused on the question of whether the European Union—in light of the diversity of its member states and their populations, cultures, and languages—can ever achieve the quality of an authentic state, or whether it will remain caught within the boundaries of a neocorporatist bargaining system. Eurofederalists want to strengthen the governing capacities of the Union in order to make possible the pan-European enforcement of policies and regulations that will compel member states to hew to a coordinated process if they want redistribution as a result. From this viewpoint, expanding the capacities for political action must go hand in hand with expanding the bases of legitimacy.

It is undisputed that there can be no Europe-wide democratic will-formation capable of enacting and legitimating positively coordinated and effective redistributive policies without an expanded basis of solidarity. Civic solidarity, long limited to nation-states, will have to be appropriated by citizens of the Union such that Swedes and Portuguese, for example, are prepared to stand up *for each other*. Only then could they be expected to support a roughly equivalent minimum wage, or the general equality of conditions for pursuing individual life projects, even as they remain shaped by national belonging. Skeptics doubt whether this can happen, arguing that there is no such thing as a European "people" who could constitute a European state. On the other hand, peoples emerge only with the constitutions of their states. Democracy itself is a legally mediated form of political integration. It is a form that depends, to be sure, on a political culture shared by all citizens. But if we consider the process by which European states of the nineteenth century gradually *created* national consciousness and civic solidarity—the earliest modern form of collective identity—with the help of national historiography, mass communications, and military duty, there is no cause for defeatism. If this artificial form of "solidarity among strangers" owes its existence to a historically influential abstraction from local and dynastic to national and democratic forms of consciousness, why should this learning process not continue on, beyond national borders?

The hurdles are high, of course. A constitution will not be enough. It can only set democratic processes in motion, processes into which it will then have to put down roots. Insofar as the element of *agreement* between member states does not vanish within a politically *constituted* union, a European federal state will have to assume a different form than other federal states and will not be able simply to copy their paths toward legitimation. A European party system will take shape only to the extent that existing parties initially fight it out within their own national arenas over the future of Europe and, in the course of such fights, come to discover interests that cross national borders. These discussions have to be synchronized within national public spheres that are networked across Europe—that is, conducted at the same time and on the same topics—so that a European civil society with interest groups, non-governmental organizations, citizens' initiatives, and so on, can emerge. Transnational mass media, in turn, can construct a multivocal, communicative context only if national educational systems provide for a common linguistic basis. Only then can the legacies of a shared European history, disseminated from their scattered national centers, increasingly rediscover themselves in a common political culture.

Let me conclude with a few words about the cosmopolitan perspective on this development.

Given its expanded economic basis, a European Federal Republic would at the very least aim at economies of scale, and therefore advantages in global competition. But if the federalist project only pursues the goal of bringing a new global player of the magnitude of the United States onto the field, it will remain particularistic and only add a further, economic dimension to the "Fortress Europe" attitude now evident in asylum policies.

Accordingly, neoliberals could even insist on the "morality of the market," on the global market's nonpartisan judgments, which are already offering countries at the point of economic take-off the chance to exploit their relative cost advantages and to make up for lost time on their own—a chance that well-intentioned economic development policies have not been able to offer them. I need not go any further into the social costs of this developmental dynamic. But it is hard to deny that supranational decisions to create powerful global political entities can only be above normative suspicion provided that a second step follows the first.

This raises the question of whether the small set of globally influential political actors can construct a reformed world organization from a loosely connected network of transnational regimes—and, if so, in such a manner that a change of course, toward a global domestic policy without a global state, is possible. A political project of this kind would have to be carried out from a perspective that aims at harmonization instead of synchronization, without granting a false, long-term legitimacy to the temporary multiplicity of ecological and social standards. The long-term goal must be the steady overcoming of social division and stratification within a global society, but without damaging cultural distinctiveness.

ENDNOTES

1. Richard Münch, *Globale Dynamik, locale Lebenswelt: Der schwierige Weg in die Weltgesellschaft,* Frankfurt am Main: Suhrkamp Verlag, 1998.
2. David Held, Anthony McGrew, David Goldblatt, and Jonathan Perraton, *Global Transformations: Politics, Economics and Culture,* London: Polity, 1999. See also David Held and Anthony McGrew, eds., *The Global Transformations Reader,* London: Polity, 2000.

3. Wolfgang Streek, "Introduction," in Wolfgang Streek, ed., *Internationale Wirtschaft, nationale Democratie: Herausforderungen für die Demokratietheorie,* Frankfurt am Main: Suhrkamp Verlag, 1998, pp. 19f.

4. See Jürgen Habermas, *The Postnational Constellation: Political Essays,* Cambridge: MIT Press, 2001, pp. 58ff.

5. Wolfgang Streek, *Internationale Wirtschaft, nationale Democratie,* p. 38.

6. Anthony Giddens, *The Third Way: The Renewal of Social Democracy,* London: Polity, 1988 100; see also Joshua Cohen and Joel Rogers, "Can Egalitarianism Survive Internationalism?" Wolfgang Streek, ed., *Internationale Wirtschaft, nationale Democratie,* pp. 175–94.

7. Peter Ulrich, *Integrative Wirtschaftsethik: Grundlagen einer lebensdienlichen Ökonomie,* Bern: Paul Haupt, 1997, p. 334.

8. Rolf E. Breuer, "Offene Bürgergesellschaft in der globalisierten Weltwirtschaft," *Frankfurter Allgemeine Zeitung,* vol. 4 (January 1999), p. 9.

9. Rolf E. Breuer, "Offene Bürgergesellschaft in der globalisierten Weltwirtschaft."

ANNE-MARIE SLAUGHTER

15 Everyday Global Governance

With the creation of a new International Criminal Court and the sudden proliferation of international, regional, and hybrid criminal tribunals for Rwanda, the former Yugoslavia, Kosovo, East Timor, and—potentially—Cambodia and Sierra Leone, it is possible to discern the outlines of a new global system of criminal justice. However flawed, these are real achievements—almost unimaginable even a decade ago. But the tribunals and courts are only a part—and arguably only a small part—of the institutions of global governance that already exist, laying an inconspicuous foundation for future progress and reform.

I define global governance here as the collective capacity to identify and solve problems on a global scale. We must develop this capacity without risking what Immanuel Kant called the "soulless despotism" of world government. And we must develop it in a way that is genuinely global. That does not necessarily mean including all states in the world, but rather all the government institutions that regulate the lives of the world's peoples.

In this essay I will describe the quiet emergence of an informal global system of governance comprising networks of regulators around the world—regulators responsible for everything from environmental protection to competition policy to securities regulation. Similar networks are beginning to link judges and even legislators in different countries.

Transgovernmental networks are not one-shot deals. While the activities of a given network may focus on a particular issue, such as environmental enforcement, they occur within a broader framework of sometimes formal, sometimes informal, interaction. And as they come together over time, the parties develop relationships that allow them in turn to understand the context in which their counterparts operate.

It is hardly surprising that such relationships help defuse major conflicts. They enable regulators to keep an issue from becoming the source of conflict in another issue-area. Indeed, cooperation on one issue can be a means of keeping the lines of communication open when states are unable to agree on anything else, as with China and the United States's cooperation on environmental protection. Equally important is the transgovernmental network's role as a transmitter or 'bearer' of reputation—as a forum in which behavior has consequences, for good or ill. In other words, members of a government network are likely to try to meet agreed standards of professional behavior and substantive commitments to one another because they know everyone else is watching.

SOURCE: Anne-Marie Slaughter, "Everyday Global Governance," *Daedalus,* 132:1 (Winter 2003), pp. 83–87. © 2003 by the American Academy of Arts and Sciences. Reprinted with permission of MIT Press Journals. Abridged by the Editor.

In the context of the larger drama of global justice—capturing terrorists, trying war criminals, creating new international courts—the activities I will describe may seem humdrum indeed. But justice requires order, and order requires at least a measure of regulation—or, in the global sphere, some form of governance, short of the Leviathan that Kant feared creating. The emergent global system of government networks performs precisely this function. Within this system, national and supranational officials must cooperate, coordinate, and regulate, but without coercive power.

Each member of a transgovernmental network—a national securities regulator, say, or a utilities commissioner—may exercise a measure of coercive power at home. But within the network, regulators cannot compel one another to take certain measure, either by vote or the binding force of international law. They do not have the power to conclude treaties or to establish by themselves new international rules. In effect, the new transgovernmental networks exercise a kind of "soft power" (as Joseph Nye calls it); what power they have flows from an ability to convince others that they want what you want, rather than from an ability to compel them to forego what they want by using threats or rewards.[1]

The new networks thus coexist along-side a much more traditional world order, structured by both the threat and use of "hard" power. In that old world order, states still jealously guard their sovereignty and undertake commitments to one another with considerable caution. Still, it is possible to glimpse the outlines of a very different kind of world order in the growing system of government networks. In this system, political power will remain primarily in the hands of national government officials, but will be supplemented by a select group of supranational institutions far more effective than those we know today. And in it, global justice could become more than a dream.

The logs of embassies around the world are perhaps the best evidence for the growing importance of the networks of national regulators. U.S. embassies, for instance, host far more officials from various regulatory agencies than from the State Department, and foreign affairs budgets for regulatory agencies across the board have increased dramatically, even as the State Department's budget has shrunk. Regulators, at both the ministerial and bureaucratic level, are becoming a new generation of diplomats.

Where are these networks of national regulators? In some familiar places, and in some surprising ones. Briefly I will outline the genesis of several such networks.

Transgovernmental regulatory networks have long existed within the traditional framework of international organizations. Robert Keohane and Joseph Nye have described these networks of government ministers as emblematic of the "'club model' of international institutions. (C)abinet ministers or the equivalent, working in the same issue-area, initially from a relatively small number of relatively rich countries, got together to make rules. Trade ministers dominated GATT; finance ministers ran the IMF; defense and foreign ministers met at NATO; central bankers at the Bank for International Settlements (BIS)."[2]

More recently, transgovernmental networks have arisen through executive agreement. Between 1990 and 2000, the U.S. president and the president of the European Union (EU) Commission concluded a series of agreements to foster increased cooperation, including the Transatlantic Declaration of 1990, the New Transatlantic Agenda of 1995 (with a joint U.S.–EU action plan attached), and the Transatlantic Economic Partnership agreement of 1998. Each of these agreements spurred ad hoc meetings between lower-level officials, as well as among business enterprises and environmental and consumer activist groups, on issues of common concern. Many of these networks of lower-level officials were emerging anyway, for functional reasons, but they undoubtedly received a boost from agreements at the top. . . .

The most highly developed and innovative transgovernmental regulatory system is of course the EU. Legal scholar Renaud Dehousse describes a basic paradox in EU governance: "increased uniformity is certainly needed; [but] greater centralization is politically inconceivable, and probably undesirable."[3] The response is "regulation by networks"— networks of national officials. The question now confronting a growing number of legal scholars and political theorists is how decision making by these networks fits with varying national models of European democracy.

The EU itself sits within a broader network of regulatory networks among Organization for Economic Cooperation and Development (OECD) countries. The primary function of the OECD has been to convene government officials in specific issue-areas for the purpose of addressing a common problem and making recommendations or promulgating a model code for its solution. But more broadly, OECD officials see all OECD member states—including all EU members, the United States, Japan, South Korea, and Mexico—as participating in a "multilayered regulatory system"[4] whose infrastructure is government networks. . . .

I have just described a world of concentric circles of government networks, most dense among the world's most highly developed countries. The relative density of these circles reflects the relative willingness of national governments to delegate government functions beyond their borders to networks of national officials rather than to a supranational bureaucracy. Thus the EU is pioneering a way for states to govern themselves collectively without giving up their identity as separate and still largely sovereign states. The challenge, however, is to make such networks truly global.

So what exactly do the new transgovernmental networks do?

Above all, their members talk a lot. So much, in fact, that it is easy and common to write them off as mere talking shops. But talk is the first prerequisite of information exchange; in the process, trust is fostered, along with an awareness of a common enterprise. This experience reinforces norms of professionalism that in turn strengthen the socializing functions of these networks, through which regulatory agencies reproduce themselves in other countries.

Indeed, what sometimes starts as haphazard communication may lead officials to recognize the need and opportunity for coordination, across the range of domestic governmental concerns—from enforcement efforts to codes of best practices. For example, U.S., Canadian, and Mexican environmental officials now coordinate the release of information

to the public as one means of enhancing effective environmental enforcement. Similarly, U.S. and Mexican environmental officials now coordinate training sessions for the private sector.

As transnational corporations have become genuinely global in scope, international cooperation has become crucial for the effective enforcement of domestic laws. In the case of drug enforcement efforts at the U.S.–Mexican border, cooperation allows the U.S. Drug Enforcement Agency, with its large budget, many agents, sophisticated equipment, and extensive files, to compensate for Mexico's limited resources to battle drug production and trafficking. Such cooperation involves more than coordination, but something less than policy harmonization. Cooperation to combat international crime takes place both through formal organized bodies, such as Interpol (International Criminal Police Organization) and Europol, and on a more regional and bilateral level through national agencies. For instance, Interpol has a general secretariat that provides information exchange through an automated search facility operating twenty-four hours a day in four languages; issues international wanted notices; distributes international publications and updates; convenes international conferences and symposia on policing matters; offers forensic services; and makes specialists available for support of local police efforts. With a membership of 179 police agencies from different countries, making it the second largest international organization after the UN, it is striking that Interpol was not founded by a treaty and does not belong within any other international political body. . . .

In addition to providing part of the critical infrastructure for any hope of global justice, transgovernmental networks teach us several lessons that are vital for future efforts to achieve anything on a global scale.

First is the value of soft power, not as a substitute but as a complement, for hard power. Second is the value and strength of pluralism, based on a concept of legitimate difference. Third is the need for active cooperation and collaboration, an ethos of positive engagement rather than of respectful noninterference. Finally, governance networks are a direct outgrowth of the disaggregation of the state—that is, of the ability of different political institutions to interact with their national and supranational counterparts on a quasi-autonomous basis. That disaggregation permits the creation of a wide range of new forms of governance, including relationships between national and international courts, that will be the backbone of a genuinely global justice system.

Overall, the most important lesson that transgovernmental networks can teach is the appreciation of the simple fact of their existence and the preconditions for it. Networks of national regulators can only exist as a form of global governance if the purported architects of world order—whether scholars, policy-makers, pundits, or the members of innumerable task forces and commissions—think of the state not as a unitary entity but as an aggregate of its component official parts.

Individuals in domestic and transnational society do not interact with states; they interact with specific branches of government. Thus, in imagining the projection of domestic institutions onto a global screen, we should be thinking less of replicating domestic institutions—courts, regulatory agencies, even legislatures—at the global level, than of connecting the national institutions we already have in global networks. These government institutions exercise an indispensable measure of coercive power, combined with an as yet unmatched measure of public legitimacy.

Further, once we have gotten used to thinking about domestic government institutions linking up with their foreign counterparts, it is also easier to start thinking about how they might link up with supranational equivalents.

Here the judicial possibilities are by far the richest. As has been demonstrated in the EU, it is possible for a supranational court such as the European Court of Justice to forge a dynamic and highly effective relationship with different national courts for the interpretation and application of EU law. The International Criminal Tribunals for Rwanda and the former Yugoslavia also have structured relationships with national courts built into their charters; they can ask a national court to cede jurisdiction over a particular defendant. In the

International Criminal Court (ICC) the relationship will work the other way: National courts will be primarily responsible for trying perpetrators of war crimes, genocide, and crimes against humanity, while the ICC will serve as a backup if a national court proved unable or unwilling to do the job.

At the same time, national courts are networking with one another in a variety of interesting ways. National constitutional judges are exchanging ideas and decisions on thorny issues that they all must face, such as the constitutionality of the death penalty, the balance between privacy and liberty, the limits of free speech, and the enforceability and scope of economic, social, and cultural rights. Ordinary courts involved in transnational litigation are openly communicating with one another to try to figure out where and how a particular case should be tried. And bankruptcy judges are negotiating mini-treaties to ensure the orderly management of defunct multinational corporations' finances. All of these developments open new "institutional horizons for the possibility of global justice."

The new world order has thus far promoted a healthy amount of transgovernmental comity. "Neither a matter of obligation on the one hand, nor of mere courtesy and good will on the other . . . comity," in the words of the U.S. Supreme Court in 1895, "is the recognition which one nation allows within its territory to the legislative, executive, or judicial acts of another nation. . . ."[5] "Recognition" is generally a passive affair, signaling deference to another nation's action, as regulators participating in government networks must often choose between passive recognition and active application of their national law extraterritorially.

The EU competition authorities and the U.S. antitrust regulators, however, have developed a more robust notion of "positive comity," a principle of affirmative cooperation between government agencies of different nations. As a principle of governance for transgovernmental regulatory cooperation, positive comity requires regulatory agencies to substitute consultation and active assistance for the seesaw of noninterference and unilateral action. More generally, as a principle of global governance, positive comity mandates a move from deference to dialogue, from "I-thinking" to "we-thinking."

This shift hardly means the end of conflict—far from it. Regulators in regular interaction with each other will bump heads just as they would in a domestic system, as demonstrated by the regulators of the different states of the United States. And just because action is requested does not mean it is achieved. But the point of departure in a world of positive comity is a presumption of assistance rather than distance, of transgovernmental cooperation based on coordinated national action. In a world in which crime depends on global networks as much as corporations do, that is a positive step. Global justice is a noble but sadly distant ideal. Global disorder is more evident than order. But in the everyday rhythms of regulators around the world, new forms of global governance are being born.

ENDNOTES

1. Robert O. Keohane and Joseph S. Nye, Jr., "Power and Interdependence in the Information Age," *Foreign Affairs* vol. 77, no. 5 (September/October 1998), pp. 81, 86.
2. Robert O. Keohane and Joseph S. Nye, Jr., "The Club Model of Multilateral Cooperation and Problems of Democratic Legitimacy," paper prepared for the American Political Science Convention, Washington, D.C., 31 August–3 September 2000.
3. Renaud Dehousse, "Regulation by networks in the European Community: The role of European agencies," *Journal of European Public Policy* vol. 4, no. 2 (June 1997), p. 259.
4. Scott H. Jacobs, "Regulatory Co-Operation for an Interdependent World: Issues for Government," in *Organisation for Economic Co-operation and Development, Regulatory Co-operation for an Interdependent World* (Paris: OECD, 1994), p. 18.
5. *Hilton v Guyot*, 159 US 113, 163–164 (1895).

············

MARC F. PLATTNER

16   Sovereignty and Democracy

A "European Convention" chaired by former French President Valéry Giscard d'Estaing recently finished drafting a new constitution for the European Union, but the parallels with the Philadelphia Convention of 1787 that this inevitably conjures up for American observers are extremely misleading. Anyone who expects the current debate over European unification to mirror the historic contest in the United States between Federalists and Anti-Federalists is quickly disabused. That was an argument about the proper locus of sovereignty and the appropriate scale of the state. Politicians can sometimes be heard voicing such concerns in Europe today, but in scholarly and intellectual circles the predominant tendency is not

SOURCE: Marc F. Plattner, "Sovereignty and Democracy," *Policy Review*, no. 122 (December 2003–January 2004), pp. 3–17. Published by the Hoover Institution, Stanford University. Reprinted by permission of the Hoover Institution. Abridged by the Editor.

to argue about where sovereignty should be lodged, but to call into question the concept of sovereignty; not to argue about how big the state should be, but to wonder about whether the era of the modern state is coming to an end.

This may seem odd at a time when the modern state seems to be enjoying the hour of its greatest triumph. Virtually the entire world now consists of independent states, their numbers greater than ever before. And the most important global institutions, beginning with the United Nations itself, are intergovernmental organizations whose members are states, represented by the delegates of their governments. Yet there is no denying the fact that in many quarters, especially in some of the advanced democracies, there is a widespread feeling that the modern state is becoming obsolete, that it is increasingly incapable of responding to the problems of the contemporary world, and above all to the challenges posed by globalization. It is this feeling that shapes the moral and political context in which European unification is unfolding. In one sense, of course, the EU is merely a regional organization, but the debate over its future is intimately bound up with the issue of globalization.

Globalization is a subject on everyone's lips today, not just in Europe but around the world. I am inclined to believe that recent advances in telecommunications technology and in the internationalization of markets have created a greater degree of mutual interpenetration among societies worldwide than ever existed before. But the trends that are summed up by the term "globalization" are not new. Following the rise of multinational corporations and the oil price shocks of the 1970s, many observers called attention to the idea of international "interdependence." And some scholars have plausibly argued that there was greater international openness and mobility during the period prior to World War I than there is today. In my view, what is distinctive about the current discourse on globalization is the jaundiced view that it takes of the modern state. After having long been regarded as the culmination of political evolution and the indispensable framework for freedom and democracy, the state is now often seen as a historically contingent institution built on shaky moral foundations.

....

DECONSTRUCTING THE STATE

One of the scholars who appears to have been especially influential in shaping current thinking about the modern state is John Ruggie. Fittingly enough, Ruggie not only is a distinguished professor of international relations, but has recently served as assistant secretary-general of the United Nations. His writings, and especially his *International Organization* article "Territoriality and Beyond: Problematizing Modernity in International Relations" (Winter 1993), are widely cited not only in the academic literature but also in more policy-oriented discussions regarding the future of the European Union. What Ruggie "problematizes" in his essay is not just modernity, but the modern state and the concept of sovereignty.

The discipline of international relations tends to take for granted the "modern system of states,"

Ruggie argues. Thus, while it is adept at understanding changes in the balance of power among states, it is poorly equipped to understand the more momentous kind of transformation that may result in "fundamental institutional discontinuity in the system of states." Yet there are signs that such a period of "epochal" change may now be upon us. This is seen both in the transformation of the global economy due to ever more extensive transnational links and in the rise of the European Union, which "may constitute nothing less than the emergence of the first postmodern international political form."

Ruggie's essay includes a brief account of the debate about postmodernism in the humanities, but for the purposes of international relations he distinguishes the modern from the postmodern in terms of their different "forms of configuring political space." The modern system of rule is based upon "territorially defined, fixed and mutually exclusive enclaves of legitimate domination. As such, it appears to be unique in human history." How else has political space been configured in the past? Ruggie refers briefly to primitive kin-based systems and to the conception of property rights held by nomadic peoples, but by far the greatest part of his analysis is devoted to the "nonexclusive territorial rule" that characterized medieval Europe, with its complex patterns of multiple allegiances and overlapping jurisdictions.

It is by analyzing the earlier transformation of the feudal order into the modern world of states claiming absolute and exclusive sovereignty over their territories that we can gain insight into the new transformation that may now be under way. The modern state has been invented or "socially constructed," and thus its persistence cannot be taken for granted. In fact, the European Union, where "the process of unbundling of territoriality has gone further than anywhere else," may point the way toward a postmodern future that will in important respects resemble the medieval past.

The general orientation of Ruggie's analysis is reflected in a great deal of contemporary writing about sovereignty, the nation-state, and the European Union. (To be sure, Ruggie draws upon a body of prior academic studies, most notably the work on the formation of the modern state prominently associated with Charles Tilly.[1]) One encounters in this literature surprisingly frequent references to the fleeting and historically contingent character of the modern nation-state. And the European Union is most often described not as the germ of some larger form of the nation-state (often disparagingly referred to as a "superstate") but as a new kind of postmodern or "neomedieval" structure that transcends the "Westphalian" framework.

Yet while Ruggie's argument incorporates a number of useful insights, I believe that it is misguided in several crucial respects. The first is an overemphasis on the wholesale uniqueness of the modern state. It is true that the modern state differs in some ways from all previous political orders, and its persistence, despite its current worldwide predominance, should not simply be taken for granted. Yet the fact that the modern state is new is sometimes elided into the view that the division of the world into separate political orders is also something new. Ruggie's assertion that an order based upon "territorially defined, fixed and mutually exclusive enclaves of legitimate domination . . . appears to be unique in human history" is, I believe, simply wrong.

Analyses like Ruggie's that hold that the modern state was invented or constructed tend to take the feudal Europe that preceded it as a more gradually evolved and thus somehow more natural and less arbitrary form of political order. They do not consider the possibility that the feudal order, shaped by the universalist claims of pope and emperor, was itself a radical departure in human history, occasioned by the rise of Christian revelation. But this is surely how feudalism was viewed by the theoretical founders of modern politics.

The notion that the earlier transition from feudalism to modernity somehow supplies the key to understanding the coming transformation to a new system that will transcend modernity recalls the doctrine of Karl Marx. And as is also true of the Marxist schema, Ruggie's perspective has very great difficulty fitting the ancient world into its analytical framework. Most such contemporary approaches, including Ruggie's, do not even try to account for classical Greece and Rome; they simply ignore them. Willful neglect of the ancient city is, in fact, a striking feature of this entire literature. One can read histories of the state or of international state systems that deal with primitive tribes, nomadic

peoples, the Chinese Empire, ancient India, and the Islamic world but do not even have an entry in the index for ancient Greece. This is especially odd, first, because the cities of ancient Greece certainly constituted a system of political units based on "territorially defined, fixed and mutually exclusive enclaves of legitimate domination" and, second, because part of the inspiration for the creation of the modern European state unmistakably came from the rediscovery of ancient political thought and practice. . . .

The focus on the medieval world and neglect of the ancient in the literature to which Ruggie's essay belongs tend to be paralleled by a lack of concern with the issue of self-government or democracy. Those who write approvingly of the Holy Roman Empire as a model for Europe or praise the diversity and permeability of borders in the "pre-Westphalian" era do not appear to reflect on the human consequences of those arrangements. It is not mere happenstance that the feudal period was a time not only of disorder but of oppression and severe inequality. An absence of firm borders and of clear lines of jurisdiction may not be a problem in empires or other political forms where governments are not accountable to their citizens. But if the citizens are to govern, or at least to hold their governors accountable, it must be clear who is and who is not included in the polity. And it is hard to see how this can be accomplished without clear lines of demarcation indicating whose voices have the right to be counted.

There is more than a merely verbal connection between the modern concept of sovereignty and the contemporary idea of the sovereignty of the people. Notwithstanding the fact that Bodin and Hobbes were champions of monarchy, it is their doctrine of sovereignty that prepared the way for the notion that all political power ultimately derives from the consent of naturally free and equal individuals. It is the modern nation-state that provided the indispensable framework for building a political order that protects the rights and heeds the voices of all the people who belong to it.

Two of the leading contemporary scholars of democracy, Juan Linz and Alfred Stepan, affirm the necessity of this link with particular forcefulness: "[W]ithout a state," they argue, "no modern democracy is possible. . . . Modern democratic government is inevitably linked to stateness. Without a state, there can be no citizenship; without citizenship, there can be no democracy."[2]

....

DEMOCRACY WITHOUT SOVEREIGNTY?

What, then, is the attitude toward democracy of those who proclaim the obsolescence of the nation-state and welcome the erosion of the "Westphalian" notion of sovereignty? While there are some who ignore or are indifferent to this question, it would be inaccurate and unfair to claim that this is the general view of the champions of transnationalism. There is, for example, a lively and intense debate about the EU's "democracy deficit" or "legitimacy deficit" and how to repair it. This concern even appears prominently in the EU's Laeken Declaration, the official document that initiated the process leading to the new draft constitution. A cynic might say that this is the defensive response of European elites, worried that disillusionment among European publics with the remote and opaque decision making of the EU may derail the entire project of "ever closer union." But I believe that it also reflects the fact that the global prestige of the democratic principle is perhaps higher than it has ever been—notwithstanding the growing tendency to question the legitimacy of the modern state.

As a result, many students and proponents of the EU seem to be groping toward the view that the EU can become a democratic *non*-state. They refuse to accept the dichotomy according to which the EU must be *either* (1) an essentially intergovernmental organization that derives its democratic legitimacy through the national parliaments of its member states *or* (2) a genuine federal state that derives its democratic legitmacy through governing institutions directly responsible to the European electorate. They say, with more than a little justification, that the EU already has gone well beyond being a merely intergovernmental institution yet falls far short of being a federal state. At the same time, their argument is not that the EU has found some "middle way" between intergovernmentalism and traditional

federalism but rather that its organizing principles must be understood as existing on a different plane from the continuum that runs from intergovernmentalism to federalism. Thus, they define the EU as a non-state, non-nation polity (or entity).[3]

It may be true that so far this is largely the language of academics rather than politicians or publics, but the argument has a considerable attraction for the latter as well. First, this non-state conception appeals to a strong antipolitical disposition that is seen today in many parts of the world but is especially powerful in Europe. This disposition is reflected in the enormous prestige enjoyed by "civil society" and by "nongovernmental organizations," as compared to political parties or to governments. One way of viewing the non-state vision of the EU is that it promises to provide governance *without* the need for government. Indeed, some Europeans, far from wishing to build a new kind of polity, seem to aspire to the creation of a new *non*governmental organization—the EU as the world's largest and most influential NGO. Second, the non-state conception seems to offer a means of what is frequently referred to as "squaring the circle"—that is, building an ever closer European Union without taking away the sovereignty of member states that many Europeans continue to hold dear.

According to the classic modern doctrine of sovereignty, of course, it was regarded as impossible to maintain sovereignty in both a political union and its constituent parts. In contemporary language, one might say that the lodging of sovereignty was regarded as a kind of "zero-sum game." Here is how Alexander Hamilton, in *Federalist* 15, characterizes the opponents of the Constitution drafted by the Philadelphia convention: They aim, he charges, "at things repugnant and irreconcilable; at an augmentation of federal authority without a diminution of State authority; at sovereignty in the Union and complete independence in the members. They still, in fine, seem to cherish with blind devotion the political monster of an *imperium in imperio.*"

A bit further on, Hamilton elaborates on what he calls "the characteristic difference between a league and a government"—namely, that only the latter can extend its authority to individuals, while the authority of the former reaches no further than to member governments. Government, according to Hamilton, involves the power not only of making laws, but of enforcing them. For if they are without sanctions, "resolutions or commands which pretend to be laws will, in fact, amount to nothing more than advice or recommendation." While governments may deal with recalcitrant individuals through the "courts and ministers of justice," there is no way a league can enforce its decisions against one of the sovereign entities that compose it without resorting to military force. Thus, in a league "every breach of the laws must involve a state of war; and military execution must become the only instrument of civil obedience."

The *Federalist* goes on to support this reasoning by appeals both to the nature of man and to the experience of previous confederations. Because men love power, those who exercise sovereignty are likely to resist attempts to constrain or direct them. Thus, in confederations that attempt to unite sovereign bodies, there is inevitably a centrifugal tendency for the parts to free themselves from the center. The subsequent numbers of the *Federalist* then explore the experience of confederations both ancient and modern. The conclusion drawn from this examination of the historical record is emphatically stated at the end of *Federalist* 20 (a paper sometimes attributed jointly to Hamilton and James Madison)—namely, "that a sovereignty over sovereigns, a government over governments, a legislation for communities, as contradistinguished from individuals, as it is a solecism in theory, so in practice it is subversive of the order and ends of civil polity, by substituting *violence* in place of the mild and salutary coercion of the magistracy."

Hamilton justifies this sweeping conclusion by appealing to "experience [which] is the oracle of truth." Yet proponents of the new views put forward by theorists of the European Union would point precisely to the experience of European integration to contradict Hamilton's conclusions. First of all, though in many respects it seems closer to a league than to a government in Hamilton's terms, the EU, thanks to various rulings of the European Court and their acceptance by national courts, does have authority that in important respects reaches to individuals as well as collectivities. Second, in spite of the lack of a

mechanism to enforce compliance, the decisions of the EU are largely accepted by member states—and this without resort to the sword.

In fact, the EU seems to present the spectacle of constituent units obeying the dictates of the center not only without violence but even without visible coercion. In trying to understand this unprecedented phenomenon, I have found particularly helpful a formulation offered by J.H.H. Weiler, one of the most distinguished scholars of European law. Weiler argues that the EU has evolved a federal constitutional or *legal* structure alongside a largely "confederal" or intergovernmental *political* structure.[4] In other words, Europe has accepted the "constitutional discipline" characteristic of federalism without becoming a federal state. In effect, it has become a federal non-state whose decisions are accepted voluntarily by its constituent units rather than backed up by the modes of hierarchical coercion classically employed by the modern state. In fact, the EU combines a "top-to-bottom hierarchy of norms" with "a bottom-to-top hierarchy of . . . real power." It achieves what Hamilton would have regarded as either disastrous or impossible—the separation of law from the power to enforce it.

However accurate Weiler's analysis may be in describing the current state of the EU, it surely raises a couple of larger questions: First, what conditions have enabled this structure to work so far, and can it continue to do so? Second, presuming that the federal non-state can continue to maintain itself, what would be the ultimate consequences for democracy? The first of these questions concerns the viability or practicability of the federal non-state, while the second concerns its ultimate desirability. . . .

WAR AND THE POSTMODERN STATE

In seeking to understand what has enabled the EU to function effectively as a federal non-state, I would emphasize the fact that its member states are all liberal democracies. This means not only that they are "open societies" but that they are averse to using force against other open societies. Here I think that what has been dubbed the "democratic peace" thesis is directly relevant. That thesis, based on an imposing record of historical evidence, holds that liberal democracies rarely if ever fight wars against each other (though they are quite prone to fight wars against countries that are not liberal democracies). The web of ties that bind member states of the EU has undoubtedly contributed to the sense that war among them is unthinkable, but one might argue that the nature of the member states is more important in this regard than the framework that connects them. After all, war is equally unthinkable between an EU member state and a nonmember like Norway or Switzerland, just as it is unthinkable between the United States and Canada or between Australia and New Zealand.

The fact that contemporary liberal democracies do not fear that force will be used against them by their fellow liberal democracies makes possible a previously unprecedented degree of integration among them. In Europe, a region where most regimes—and certainly the most powerful ones—are liberal democracies, it has made possible the success of the European Union in achieving an extraordinary degree of cooperation without erecting a "superstate." In understanding this achievement I have found very useful the analysis offered by the British diplomat Robert Cooper (a former foreign policy advisor to Prime Minister Tony Blair who is now working as director-general for external and politico-military affairs for the Council of the European Union). In his remarkably concise essay *The Postmodern State and the World Order* (London: DEMOS and the Foreign Policy Center, 1996), Cooper provides what, to my mind, is a much more persuasive case than does John Ruggie for the novelty of the EU and for the willingness of its member states to surrender some of their sovereignty.

Cooper convincingly demonstrates that there has been a fundamental change in the international aims and behavior of many of the advanced democracies, but he also emphasizes that the postmodern order most clearly represented by the EU constitutes only one portion of today's world. For it coexists with two other orders: the modern order of robust national states still jealous of their sovereignty (among his examples are India, China, and Saddam Hussein's Iraq) and the premodern order of "failed states" (Afghanistan, Somalia, Sierra Leone)

incapable of exercising real control over their territories. This means that the postmodern states, while they may eschew the use of force among themselves, cannot wholly escape the need of employing it in their dealings with modern and premodern states. It also means that the ability to preserve and enhance the postmodern achievements of the EU depends on a willingness to depart from the norms of postmodern behavior and to employ the "rougher methods of an earlier era" when the situation demands. As Cooper puts it, "Among ourselves, we keep the law but when we are operating in the jungle, we must also use the laws of the jungle."

As we have recently witnessed, however, the perceived need to resort to "rougher methods," especially those involving the use of military force, tends to create political disputes among postmodern states that are not easily resolved consensually. Some would no doubt argue that the current contentions within the EU are largely provoked by the policies of the United States and that the fault lines dividing Europeans have their origins in Washington. Others would surely respond that the U.S. security umbrella provides the indispensable shelter that allows the EU to function as a wholly civilian non-state polity.

Be that as it may, the difficulty underlined by Cooper remains. Even if the European Union succeeds in taming national sovereignty and in subordinating force to law within its own postmodern sphere, can it continue to resist the pressures and dangers that arise from the still untamed parts of the world? As Cooper notes, "States reared on *raison d'état* and power politics make uncomfortable neighbors for the postmodern democratic conscience. Supposing the world develops . . . into an intercontinental struggle. Would Europe be equipped for that?" To put it somewhat differently, will a non-state be able to defend and preserve itself in a world that still contains powerful modern states? Or would such external pressure drive Europeans to try to recover their "stateness," whether by the formation of a real European "superstate" or by a reassertion of sovereignty at the level of the nation-state?

So even if Europe is undergoing a far-reaching transformation such that the old notions of sovereignty no longer apply within the intra-European sphere, the question remains whether "postmodernism in one region" can really work. Can Europe renounce the use of force if other parts of the world refuse to do so? And can Europe continue to govern itself within a non-state framework if its member states must continually wrestle with life-and-death issues of war and peace that intrude upon it from other regions? The EU's perennial difficulties in fashioning a common foreign policy underline the seriousness of this dilemma.

TRANSCENDING THE STATE?

But let us for argument's sake presume that the rest of the world can be postmodernized and, thus, that this problem can be resolved. There would still remain the question of what might be lost in leaving behind or transcending the nation-state. Here I have in mind precisely the issue of democracy. This problem is also briefly noted by Cooper, who formulates it in the following terms: "A difficulty for the postmodern state . . . is that democracy and democratic institutions are firmly wedded to the territorial state. . . . Economy, law-making, and defense may be increasingly embedded in international frameworks, and the borders of territory may be less important, but identity and democratic institutions remain primarily national."

Cooper's reference here to identity being "primarily national" raises an important ambiguity inherent in the word "national," so let me make clear that I am not suggesting that political identity must be tied to some form of ethnicity. As the case of the United States proves, such identity can be established among citizens of very diverse ethnic origins. Though it would not be easy, I do not think it is out of the question that a European political identity could be nurtured that would come to supersede the attachment of Europeans to their existing national states. So I am not arguing that European unification as such is hostile to democracy, or that the only way to preserve democracy in Europe is to reaffirm the sovereignty of the EU's member states. I am not a "euroskeptic."

My argument is that for democracy to work, there must be an overarching political order to which people feel they owe their primary political loyalty—in short, a state, with clear boundaries and clear distinctions as to who does and does not enjoy the rights and obligations of citizenship. In principle, such an order could equally well be constituted at the level of the European Union or remain at the level of its member states. What I doubt is that it is possible to square the circle of competing sovereignties over the long run or that democracy can work outside or across the framework of a sovereign state. So my plea is that those who are seriously devoted to democracy reconsider their devaluation of the state, or at least think harder about how it can be left behind without also undermining democracy.

The strong tendency today for many proponents of liberal democracy to turn against the state, despite the long and intimate relationship between liberal democracy and the modern state, is striking. I think the reason behind it lies not only in certain historical developments but in a tension that has always existed at the heart of liberal democracy. Elsewhere I have explored the tension between the liberal and the democratic elements that form the cohesive but unstable compound known as liberal democracy.[5] The liberal or cosmopolitan element, which emphasizes the universal human rights of the individual, fits uneasily with the particularistic demands of self-government and citizenship that constitute its specifically democratic element. In my view, the European Union, especially as understood by the approach that I have been discussing, represents the exaltation of liberal democracy's liberal aspect at the expense of its democratic aspect. The real issue is whether liberalism can flourish—or even survive—if it is not anchored in the framework of a democratic state. . . .

CITIZENS AND THE OTHER

The most revealing account that I have found of the principled and moral refusal to "put things in common" in a political fashion is provided by J.H.H. Weiler in the essay cited above. Not coincidentally, that essay concludes by explicitly casting doubt on the value of democracy. For Weiler, Europe's non-state constitutional federalism "represents . . . its deepest set of values," rooted in what he calls the Principle of Constitutional Tolerance. This principle rejects not just nationalism but even the idea of "constitutional patriotism," of an ethos that "implicitly celebrates a supposed unique moral identity, the wisdom, and yes, the superiority of the authors of the constitution, the people, the constitutional *demos.*" Weiler denies that democracy should be regarded as a goal of the EU. The goal, instead, "is to try, and try again, to live a life of decency, to honour our creation in the image of God, or the secular equivalent." And "in the realm of the social, in the public square, the relationship to the alien is at the core of such decency." Nothing is "normatively more important to the human condition and to our multicultural societies."

How, then, should we deal with the alien? Weiler describes two strategies. The first, which involves inviting the alien to become one of us, e.g., by making him a fellow citizen, is rejected because "it risks robbing him of his identity." It is thus "a form of dangerous internal and external intolerance." Instead, Weiler argues in favor of a strategy that maintains boundaries and respects difference, but in which "one is commanded to reach over the boundary and accept [the alien], in his alienship, as oneself." This points to the "deeper spiritual meaning" of Europe's non-statist constitutional architecture. It calls upon Europeans to bond not with fellow citizens but precisely with *others.* It asks them to "compromise" their "self-determination" in the name of tolerance. It calls for voluntary subordination to the decisions of others, "which constitutes an act of true liberty and emancipation from collective self-arrogance and constitutional fetishism." In sum, Weiler attacks the moral basis of the constitutional democratic state, in which people become fellow citizens by "putting things in common," in favor of the allegedly more elevated principle of respecting what is alien.

Weiler's essay is one of the most brilliant things I have read about the European Union, but, as is no doubt apparent, I believe it is profoundly misguided, both morally and practically. Central to Weiler's discussion is his invocation of the fact that "Europe was built on the ashes of World War II, which witnessed the most horrific alienation of those thought of as aliens; an alienation which became annihilation." But what is the proper lesson to be drawn from the Holocaust? Is it that the constitutional democratic state is inadequate, or is it that the worst evils come from the failure to establish and consolidate constitutional democratic states? To me, it seems obvious that the correct lesson is the latter. Certainly, I know that if neo-Nazis or other alien-haters were to target me, I would vastly prefer to entrust my rights and my fate to the protections offered by a constitutional democratic state that combines law with force than to a transnational architecture of any sort.

ENDNOTES

1. See Charles Tilly, "Reflections on the History of European State-Making," in Charles Tilly, ed., *The Formation of National States in Western Europe,* Princeton University Press, 1975.

2. Juan J. Linz and Alfred Stepan, *Problems of Democratic Transition and Consolidation: Southern Europe, South America, and Post-Communist Europe,* Johns Hopkins University Press, 1996, p. 17, 28.

3. One of the clearest statements of this point of view may be found in Philippe C. Schmitter, *How to Democratize the European Union . . . and Why Bother?* Rowman & Littlefield, 2000. See especially Chapter I.

4. J.H.H. Weiler, Epilogue, "Fischer: The Dark Side," in Christian Joerges, Yves Mény, and J.H.H. Weiler, eds., *What Kind of Constitution for What Kind of Polity? Responses to Joschka Fischer,* San Domenico di Fiesole, Italy: Robert Schuman Centre for Advanced Studies, 2000.

5. Marc F. Plattner, "Globalization and Self-Government," *Journal of Democracy* (July 2002); "From Liberalism to Liberal Democracy," *Journal of Democracy* (July 1999); "Liberalism and Democracy," *Foreign Affairs* (March–April 1998).

CHAPTER FIVE

REVOLUTION AND PROTEST

The emergence of modern society was punctuated by four "classic" revolutions: the English Civil War of the seventeenth century, the American and French Revolutions of the late eighteenth century, and the Russian Revolution of the twentieth century. Revolutions have taken place in many other countries as well, notably Turkey, China, Cuba, and Vietnam. What do these revolutions have in common, and in what ways are they distinctive? Were these upsurges a necessary condition for shattering traditional society and ushering in new forms of legitimacy and political rule? Under what conditions has it been possible to reshape societies without violence? The functioning of modern political systems is greatly affected by the extent to which the transition to modernity was marked by revolution.

Political scientists have generally viewed the classic revolutions as progressive stages, from the mainly political (English Civil War and American Revolution), to the bourgeois (French Revolution), to the proletarian (the Russian Revolution), or from partial to total revolution. With the crisis and then collapse of the Soviet Union, the Russian Revolution no longer appears as a culminating event. S. N. Eisenstadt and François Furet provide frameworks for a re-evaluation of revolutionary change. Sweeping change can also take place in the absence of revolution, through legal channels offered in democracies.

Historic turning points have also resulted from passive resistance or nonviolent action; both terms require clarification, as suggested by Kurt Schock. The campaign led by Mohandas Gandhi against British rule in India, the civil rights movement in the United States in the 1960s, and more recently the struggle led by Nelson Mandela against apartheid in South Africa have called attention to the effectiveness of nonviolent action in achieving major political change. However, in these and similar cases other factors may also have been important, such as the pressure exerted on the UK to promise independence to India as a way of countering the very real violence of invading Japanese armed forces; decisions by the American federal government in response to political demands from a national majority (within which African-Americans played a large role); and a combination of domestic and international pressures in South Africa. As regards revolutionary ferment and protest in democracies, are we now in the presence of a permanent resistance to modernizing processes, particularly within a portion of the intellectual class? Emile Durkheim's concept of anomie may be tested with reference to revolutionary groups (such as Trotskyists, Maoists, and anarcho-surrealists) in any advanced democracy.

S. N. EISENSTADT

17   Frameworks of the Great Revolutions

.... [I]

In the following discussion, we shall take up . . . problems as related to historical and comparative analysis by a reexamination of the characteristics and conditions of the "great," "classical" revolutions: the English Civil War, the American and French Revolutions, and later, the Chinese and Russian ones, also others such as the Turkish or the Vietnamese Revolutions. These were closely connected with the emergence of the modern world, of modern civilization; since revolutionary ideologies, the revolutionary image and movements have become a basic component of the modern perspective.

Revolutions, or revolutionary change, have become the epitome of "real" social change and the revolutionary phenomenon has become a central topic and a focus of great interest and fascination in modern intellectual, ideological and scholarly discourse.

Large portions of the literature on revolutions and social change have assumed that revolutions are true, pristine, "real" social change, other processes being judged or scaled according to their proximity to some ideal type of revolution. In this way the specificity of both these "great" revolutions and of other processes and types of change was often lost.

SOURCE: S. N. Eisenstadt, "Frameworks of the Great Revolutions: Culture, Social Structure, History and Human Agency," *International Social Science Journal*, no. 133 (August 1992), pp. 385–401. Reprinted by permission of the Editor, *International Social Science Journal*. Article and footnotes abridged.

Accordingly, we shall first attempt to indicate the specific characteristics of these revolutions as distinct from other processes of change, especially of drastic changes of political regimes. Second, we shall turn to the perennial question of the causes of revolutions and reexamine the wide-ranging literature on this subject. Throughout our analysis we shall attempt to understand the specificity of revolutions by comparison with other, somewhat similar cases of political and social change.

[II]

Revolutions, of course, denote first of all radical change in the political regime far beyond the deposition of rulers or even the replacement of ruling groups. They denote a situation in which such deposition and change—usually very violent—results in a radical transformation of the rules of the political game and the symbols and bases of legitimation, a change closely connected with novel visions of political and social order. It is this combination that is distinctive of revolutions. In other words, such revolutions tend to spawn (to use Said Arjomand's term) certain distinct cosmologies, certain very marked cultural and political programs.[1]

The combination of violent changes of regime with a very strong ontological and political vision happened not only in "great" revolutions. The crystallization of the Abbasid caliphate, often called the Abbasid revolution, is a very important—even if possibly only partial—illustration of such a combination in an earlier historical period. What is characteristic of modern revolutions is the nature of their ontologies or cosmologies: certain central aspects of the revolutionary process that developed within them and the relations between the changes and regimes and in major institutional arenas of the affected societies.

The cosmologies promulgated in these revolutions were characterized first of all by an emphasis on themes of equality, justice, freedom and the participation of the community in the political center. These were combined with "modern" themes such as the belief in progress, and, with demands for full access to the central political arenas and participation in them. Second, what was new was the combination of all these themes with an overall utopian vision of the reconstruction of society and of political order, not just with millenarian visions of protest.

Third, in all these revolutions, society was seen as an entity to be remolded through political action according to the visions. These also entailed the reconstruction of society, including far-reaching institutional change, radical restructuring of class and status relations, doing away with traditional ascriptive criteria of stratification, unseating or destroying old and upper classes and shifting the relative hegemony to new ones, be it the bourgeoisie or the proletariat.

Fourth, these visions emphasized dissociation from the preceding historical background of societies, a denial of the past, and emphasis on a new beginning, and the combination of such discontinuity with violence.

The fifth major characteristic of these revolutions was their universalistic and missionary vision. Although each set up a new regime in a certain country, a regime which, especially in its later stages, proclaimed strong patriotic themes, and although such regimes always bore an ineradicably national stamp yet the revolutionary visions were projected in different degrees, as universal, extendable in principle to all of humanity. This universal message became most strongly connected with a missionary zeal reminiscent, as Maxine Rodinson has shown, of the expansion of Islam. As in the case of Islam, the spread of this vision was supported by revolutionary armies ready to carry it abroad. As in the case of Islam, again, such missionary zeal did not necessarily make for greater tolerance or "liberalism" but certainly bore an unmistakably universalistic stamp.[2]

The specifically "national," primordial or patriotic revolutionary themes were usually secondary to the more general, universalistic ones which constituted the core of the revolutionary vision and of nations as bearers of their universalistic relevance.

....

[III]

The central institutional change was, as Michael Walzer has pointed out, that in the first revolutions (the English and the French and, in a different, less personal way, in the American one) the rulers were not just driven out, exiled or killed, but deposed through a legal procedure.[3] Even if the rulers themselves did not accept its legality or legitimacy, the fact that such a legal procedure was undertaken at all is of immense significance: It indicated very serious attempts to find a new institutional grounding for the accountability of rulers.

This idea itself was not new. It was part and parcel of the basic premises of the Axial civilizations within whose frameworks these revolutions occurred, though it became transformed in very far-reaching ways.

Closely related were the distinct characteristics of the political process that arose out of these revolutions, first, as Eric Hobsbawm[4] has shown, the direct impact on the central political struggle of popular uprisings through their movement into the center.

Second was the continuous interweaving of several types of political action (such as rebellions, movements of protest and struggles at the center) previously to be found in many, sometimes in all societies, within certain common frameworks of political action and a common ideology, however fragile and intermittent. Such currents were contingent on a new type of leadership, one which appealed to various sectors of the population.

Third, and possibly the most distinctive feature of the political processes was the role of autonomous cultural, religious or intellectual groups: heterodox religious or secular groups like the English (and to an even greater extent American) Puritans, the French intellectual clubs analyzed by A. Cochin and later by F. Furet, the Russian intelligentsia and the like.[5]

They constituted the crucial element which, to no small degree, shaped the whole revolutionary political process. It is impossible to understand these revolutions without taking account of the ideological, propagandist and organizational skills of such intellectuals or cultural elites. Without them the entire revolutionary movement as it crystallized would probably not have occurred.

Yet another aspect of this revolutionary process was the transformation of the liminal aspects and symbols, especially of peripheral movements of protest. In most cases, the central political arena became, for relatively long periods, shaped in a liminal mode. The center itself became, perhaps temporarily, a quasi-liminal situation or arena, a series of such situations, or the arena in which liminality was played out. These dimensions were closely connected to the centrality of violence, to its very sanctification, as can be seen in the rise and sanctification of terror.

....

[IV]

Thus these revolutions were characterized not only by three distinct characteristics—their cosmologies and political programs, novel overall cultural agendas, and the political processes that developed within them—but perhaps above all by their combination, not to be found, even incipiently, in all social transformations.

This can perhaps best be illustrated by a brief consideration of one radical change which has often been compared with "great" revolutions, the so-called Meiji restoration of 1868 in Japan. It has often been compared with the "great" revolutions because, like them, it gave rise to far-reaching processes of social, economic and political transformation and because it spawned a new cultural and political agenda which, for all its "traditionalist" components, constituted a radical break with the preceding Tokugawa shogunate.

And yet, with respect to certain crucial features, especially revolutionary ideology and the nature of the political process generated by it, the Meiji restoration differed greatly from "great" revolutions.

As before the revolutions, three types of political movements—rebellions (especially of peasants), movements of protest and political struggle at the center—abounded in the pre-Restoration setting and in the process leading to Restoration as well as in the first two decades of the new regime.

Many *ad hoc* contacts were forged naturally between these groups and between them and certain urban groups and rebellious peasants: They all constituted a very important background to the toppling of the Tokugawa regime but were not a basic component of the political aspect of the Restoration.

Significantly enough, however, in the process which toppled the Tokugawa regime no new patterns of political organization crystallized in which such groups would combine for common political action. Nor was there any political leadership which attempted to mobilize disparate social forces for the more central political struggle.

The Meiji Restoration, unlike the "great" revolutions, was characterized by an almost total absence of autonomous, distinct religious or secular intellectual groups as politically active elements.

It was above all samurai, some of them learned in Confucian lore and the shishi who were most active in the Restoration, but they did not act as autonomous intellectuals bearing a new Confucian vision. They acted as members of their respective social and political groups bearing a distinct political vision.

But this vision differed greatly from that of the "great" revolutions: They were in a way the mirror images of those of the latter. The Restoration was presented as a renovation of a previous archaic system, which in fact never existed, not as a revolution aimed at directing the social and political order in an entirely fresh direction. There were almost no utopian elements in the vision. The whole reversion to the Emperor could be seen, as Hershel Webb has pointed out, as an "inverted utopia." The message of the Meiji Restoration was addressed to the renovation of the Japanese nation; it had no basic universalistic or missionary dimensions.[6]

Similar processes of radical change in modern times arose in such countries as India, Thailand and the Philippines. Most Latin American countries evolved in ways markedly different from the classical revolutions, with but certain of the distinctive characteristics of the "great" revolutions.

[V]

How can we then explain this specific combination of such characteristics in the classical "great" revolutions? Here we come to the analysis of the causes of revolution, a problem of central importance for historical and comparative sociology.

Several broad types of cause have been analyzed in the literature. The first concerns structural conditions, the second, the socio-psychological preconditions of revolutions and the third, special historical causes.

Several structural conditions have been singled out. One concerns aspects of internal struggles, such as those between the major classes predominant in pre-revolutionary societies, or inter-elite struggles between components of the ruling or upper class as leading to revolution.

A special subtype of such analyses is the emphasis (to be found in the work of Theda Skocpol and other scholars, building on the earlier work of Barrington Moore) on the more general relations between the state and the major social strata, especially the aristocracy and the peasantry.

Second and closely related to such explanations are those which emphasize the weakening or decay of the pre-revolutionary political regimes from internal causes such as economic or demographic trends or through the impact of international forces such as economic trends, through wars or some combination thereof.

Earlier studies were also devoted to the contribution to revolutionary situations of broad economic factors or trends like economic fluctuations and rising inflation with the resulting impoverishment of large sectors of society, not only of the lower strata but also of wide sectors of the middle and even upper classes.

In some of the Marxist literature such economic explanations, together with those of class struggle, were elevated into ineluctable contradictions between old and newly emerging forces of production.

Such studies have often been connected with the third type of explanation, the socio-psychological one. Often, following Tocqueville's brilliant analysis, these have emphasized the importance of relative deprivation and frustration arising in bad times following good ones when the aspirations of large sectors of the population were raised, in generating widespread dissatisfaction which could give rise to rebellions or revolutionary predispositions.

Thus it was inter-class and inter-elite struggles, demographic expansion, the domestic (above all fiscal) and international weaknesses of the state, economic imbalances and socio-psychological frustrations attendant on worsening economic conditions, that constituted the most important items in the causes of revolutions.

The exploration of how these "causes" coalesce, their relative importance and the actual constellations in different revolutions should and will continue. But in themselves such analyses, important as they are, will not provide an adequate answer to the search for "the causes" of revolution.

It is not that the answers to the questions posed in this literature are sometimes unsatisfactory or controversial, which, of course, is inherent in any scholarly enterprise. What is more important is that the questions asked are not sufficient for the analysis of some of the most important aspects of the problem. For a very simple reason: these causes are not specific to revolutions. The same causes, in different constellations, have been singled out in the vast literature on the decline of Empires.

The fact that these causes can be found in all pre-revolutionary societies, but not only in them, should not be surprising. Revolutions are, after all, first and foremost synonymous with decline or breakdown of regimes and with the results thereof.

Jack Goldstone has recently summarized very accurately the combination of these processes leading to the breakdown of regimes.

The four related critical trends were as follows. (1) Pressures increased on state finances as inflation eroded state income and population growth raised real expenses. States attempted to maintain themselves by raising revenues in a variety of ways, but such attempts alienated elites, peasants, and urban consumers, while failing to prevent increasing debt and eventual bankruptcy. (2) Intra-elite conflicts became more prevalent, as larger families and inflation made it more difficult for some families to maintain their status, while expanding population and rising prices lifted other families, creating new aspirants to elite positions. With the state's fiscal weakness limiting its ability to provide for all who sought elite positions, considerable turnover and displacement occurred throughout the elite hierarchy, giving rise to factionalization as different elite groups sought to defend or improve their position. When central authority collapsed as a result of bankruptcy or war, elite divisions came to the fore in struggles for power. (3) Popular unrest grew, as competition for land, urban migration, flooded labor markets, declining real wages, and increased youthfulness raised the mass mobilization potential of the populace. Unrest occurred in urban and rural areas and took the various forms of food riots, attacks on landlords and state agents, and land and grain seizures, depending on the autonomy of popular groups and the resources of elites. A heightened mobilization potential made it easy for contending elites to marshal popular action in their conflicts, although in many cases popular actions, having their own motivation and momentum, proved easier to encourage than to control. (4) The ideologies of rectification and transformation became increasingly salient.[7]

These causes of decline and breakdown of regimes, especially of Imperial or Imperial-feudal ones, are also necessarily causes or preconditions of revolutions. But they do not explain the specific revolutionary outcome of the breakdown of regimes. Certainly, they constitute necessary conditions of revolutions, but by themselves are not sufficient. For the sufficient causes we must look beyond the breakdown of regimes.

[VI]

One possible direction in the search for such sufficient conditions is the specific historic "timing" or historical contexts of revolutions. All have taken place in the early modern (though chronologically varying) phases of societies, within the framework of modernizing autocracies, of modern absolutist regimes which created the early modern territorial, often bureaucratic states, and provided the strong impetus toward economic modernization, the development of early mercantile and even the beginnings of industrial capitalist economies, and of the rise of a market-based political economy.

It was the internal contradictions in the political systems of early absolutism, situated between traditional monarchical, semi-aristocratic legitimation and new economic cultural and ideological currents challenging such legitimation as well as between these groups and the more traditional ones that provided the motor forces for the breakdown of such regimes. The ideological or symbolic components of revolutions were to no small degree fed by contradictions in the ideological legitimation of absolutist monarchies, especially between traditional or semi-traditional legitimation and components of enlightenment bearing the seeds of a new cultural agenda.

And yet, even this combination is not yet the end of our exploration of the causes of revolutions. Not all such combinations causing the decline of regimes within the historical framework of early modernity have generated revolution and revolutionary outcomes. India, or in a somewhat different mode Thailand, and many provinces of the Ottoman Empire—with the possible exception of Turkey itself where the establishment of the Kemalist regime was sometimes called a revolution (even if one from above) and possibly of Algeria— are among cases of non-revolutionary outcomes in situations of early modernity. Another such "negative" illustration is provided by the Latin American countries, where the wars of independence were not revolutionary in the sense of promulgating an entirely new socio-political order, and where many of the crucial aspects of the revolutionary process were very weak, especially the continuous interweaving between political actors and the liminal characteristics of the central revolutionary struggle.

But perhaps the most important case is once again Japan—the downfall of the Tokugawa regime, and the Meiji-Ishin.

The Tokugawa regime was characterized by some of the major structural features of early modernity and of its contradictions; by the rise of vibrant new economic (merchant and peasant) forces, by the undermining of older aristocratic "traditional" forces; by the breakdown of the regulatory economic policies of the older regime. It was also characterized by a very wide spread of education apparently making Japan the most literate pre-industrial society in the world, and by the emergence of a very intensive political discourse.

The Tokugawa regime was weakened by these internal processes as well as by the impact of external forces. It also faced a crisis of legitimization, but one not couched in the ideological terms characteristic of the pre-revolutionary *"ancien régimes"* of Europe and China.

....

[VII]

Note that the explanations referred to above do not address themselves to what is probably the most important distinctive element in the revolutionary process: new ontological visions or cosmologies and bearers of such visions, the autonomous cultural or intellectual groups which, as we have seen, constitute one of the most important reservoirs of new political leadership and organizations most characteristic of revolutions. Indeed, in large parts of the literature the ideological factors (new ideologies, religious beliefs, ideologies and the like) are rarely analyzed as causes of revolution. Usually, even among non-Marxist historians, with the exception of Albert Cochin and François Furet, they are seen more as epiphenomena of the "deeper" social processes or as a general background to revolutionary processes.

It may therefore be worth enquiring under what conditions, or in what societies, such ideologies or cosmologies and the groups which bear them and which unlike rebellions, movements of protest, class and inter-elite struggle are not to be found in all societies, become so central. They tend to develop in very specific civilizations, the so-called Axial civilizations.[8] By this term, we mean those civilizations that crystallized during the period from 500 B.C. to the first centuries of the Christian era, within which new ontological visions, including

conceptions of basic tension between the transcendental and mundane orders emerged and were institutionalized in many parts of the world—in ancient Israel, later in Second-Commonwealth Judaism and Christianity, in ancient Greece, very partially in Zoroastrian Iran, in early Imperial China under Hinduism and Buddhism, and, beyond the Axial Age proper, under Islam.

These conceptions were developed and articulated by a relatively new social element: elites that carried models of a cultural order, particularly intellectual elites, ranging from the Jewish prophets and priests, Greek philosophers, Chinese literati, Hindu brahmins, to Buddhist sangha or Islamic ulema. Their activities were centered on belief in the creation of the world according to some transcendental vision or command.

The successful institutionalization of such conceptions and visions resulted in the internal restructuring of these societies and of the interrelations between them.

Thus, there developed first a high level of distinctiveness of societal centers and their perception as symbolic and organizational entities, and a continuous interaction between center and periphery. Further, there was the rise of distinct collectivities, especially cultural or religious ones with a very high symbolic component as well as the somewhat ideological structuring of social hierarchies.

Third, and most important for our analysis, there took place a far-reaching restructuring of the relationship between the political and transcendental orders. The political order, as the central locus or framework of the mundane order, was usually conceived of as being subordinated to the transcendental order and so had to be restructured according to the precepts of the latter, above all according to the perception of the right way of overcoming the tension between the transcendental and the mundane orders of "salvation." The rulers were usually responsible for structuring the political order.

At the same time, the nature of the rulers was greatly transformed. The king-god—the embodiment of both the cosmic and the earthly orders—disappeared and a secular ruler emerged in principle accountable to some higher order; hence the possibility of calling a ruler to account before a higher authority, be it God or divine law. The first and most dramatic appearance of this conception occurred in ancient Israel, in priestly, especially prophetic, pronouncements. A different conception of such accountability to the community and its laws occurred on the northern shores of the eastern Mediterranean in ancient Greece. The notion of accountability occurred in all these civilizations in different ways.

Fourth is the development of relatively autonomous primary and secondary elites, especially of cultural, intellectual and religious ones which continuously struggled with each other and with political elites.

It was such elites in general—the religious or intellectual ones in particular, many of which were also carriers of strong utopian visions with universalistic orientations—that constituted the most crucial elements in different heterodoxies and in political struggles and movements of protest.

....

[VIII]

These distinctive ideological and structural components of the political process characteristic of the Axial civilizations gave rise, within their regimes, to very specific political dynamics, in which many kernels of the "great" revolutions could be found, but not to such revolutions themselves.

The basic cultural orientations and civilizational premises prevalent in them inspired visions of new social orders with very strong utopian and universalistic orientations, while the organization and structural characteristics provided the frameworks within which certain aspects of these visions could be institutionalized. The two became combined through the activities of the different elites analyzed above.

The combination of all these characteristics gave rise in these usually Imperial or Imperial-feudal regimes to a relatively higher degree of coalescence than in other Axial Age civilizations between movements of protest, institution-building, articulation and ideological levels of political struggle and changes in the political system. . . .

But only when these ideological and structural components coincided in periods of early modernity did they generate revolutionary processes in the sense used here. It was only in these historical contexts that the elective affinities between the political process which developed in the Axial civilizations and the core ideological and organizational characteristics of revolution were achieved that the major components of change in general and of the political process in particular became transformed in the revolutionary direction.

Such transformation of ideological components and cultural or symbolic themes did not, especially in the first revolutions—the English, American and French ones—usually emerge at the very beginning of the rebellion and upheavals destined to topple various "ancient" regimes. It was only with the intensification of the revolutionary dynamic that such transformation evolved. But this does not mean, as proposed by Goldstone, that ideology became important only in the outcome of revolutions. The comparison between revolutionary dynamics in Axial and non-Axial civilizations as well as between Japan on the one hand and China and the revolutions in the realm of Christianity on the other, indicates that ideological elements, in combination with their institutional settings, were of crucial importance, from relatively early stages, in the transformation of both the ideological and the political process in a revolutionary direction. . . .

....

[IX]

Not all revolutionary attempts under conditions similar to those of the accomplished revolutions have succeeded. Spain, Italy, and Germany are probably the most important locations of failed revolutions, along with those of Central Eastern Europe in 1848. How can we explain such failures?

Some scholars attribute these failures to the predominance within the *"ancien régimes"* of Spain, Italy and the Eastern European countries of many patrimonial components explaining the relatively low levels of free resources and weak autonomous elites.

But this is not the whole story, for it certainly does not apply to Germany. At least two additional sets of factors must be taken into account when discussing "failed" revolutions. The first is the simple fact that all revolutions result from civil war with many contestants and participants and that their success depends on both coherent and efficient behavior of the revolutionary groups, as well as on the relative weakness of the rulers, on a failure of their nerve or their will. Neither of these conditions is naturally given in a revolutionary situation. In some cases, as in Eastern Europe in 1848, where the autocratic rulers showed a marked strength of will which was reinforced by international circumstances—a sort of "autocratic international"—revolutionary attempts failed.

Failure was reinforced by divisions within would-be revolutionary forces, above all, in the case of Germany, between the rising bourgeoisie and the lower class, the former being afraid, after the experience of the French revolution, of the latter. Further divisions arose between sectors of the intelligentsia or cultural elites bearing different visions, especially between "liberals" and constitutionalists, different groups of "patriots" and nationalists and incipient socialists.

Another factor to be taken into account was the absence of a unified German (or Italian) state and very strong aspirations to the creation of such a state by national movements among many sectors of German and Italian society. Unlike in England, France or Russia, such national entities had yet to be constructed, which competed with the revolutionary agendas. Above all, such agendas could be subsumed, as in Germany and to a lesser extent in Italy, by certain groups and leaders (like Bismarck) closely allied with the *ancien régime*.

....

[X]

We have thus come full circle in our analysis of the causes or conditions of revolutions. As revolutions are, by definition, equivalent to the breakdown of regimes, it is the causes of such breakdowns, the constellations of inter-elite and inter-class struggles,

the rise of new social groups and economic forces which are blocked from access to power; the weakening of regimes through such struggles, through economic turbulence and the impact of international forces that constitute the necessary conditions for the outbreak of revolutions.

But it is only insofar as such processes take place under specific historical circumstances, and within the frameworks of specific civilizational premises and political regimes, as well as of specific political economies that they may trigger revolutionary conditions and outcomes.

The specific historical circumstances are those of early modernity when the autocratic modernizing regimes faced the contradictions inherent in their own legitimation and policies and confronted the rise of new economic strata and "modern" ideologies.

The civilizational frameworks are those of "this-worldly" or combined this-and other-worldly Axial civilizations and Imperial or feudal-Imperial regimes. If, for various historical reasons, such regimes are not thrown up in these civilizational frameworks the processes of change tend to be deflected from the revolutionary path.

The concrete outcome of these processes further depends greatly on the balance of power between revolutionary and counter-revolutionary forces and their cohesion.

....

[XI]

The combination of civilizational and structural conditions and historical contingencies that generated the "great" revolutions has been rather rare in the history of mankind. With all their dramatic importance, these revolutions certainly do not constitute the only, or even the major or most far-reaching types of change, whether in pre-modern or modern times. Where other combinations of structural and institutional factors exist, for instance, in Japan, India, South Asia or Latin America, they give rise to other processes of change and novel political regimes. These are not just "failed" would-be revolutions. They should not be measured by the criteria of the "great" revolutions; rather they represent different patterns of social transformation, just as "legitimate" and meaningful, and should be analyzed in their own terms.

Accordingly, this analysis also indicates the relations between culture and social structure, history and structure, human agency and structure, as well as between order-maintaining versus order-transforming dimensions of culture.

Beliefs and cultural visions are basic elements of the social orders, of crucial importance in shaping their institutional dynamics. Beliefs or visions become such elements by the assimilation of their content into the basic premises of patterns of social interaction, that is, into clusters of regulative principles governing the major dimensions of social roles. These were classified by the "founding fathers of Sociology" as the social division of labor, the building of trust (or solidarity), the regulation of power, and the construction of meaning.

One of the most important processes through which beliefs or visions are transformed into such regulative principles is the crystallization of models of cultural and social order and of codes. This closely resembles Weber's concept of "economic ethics" which specify how to regulate the frameworks of concrete social organizations and institutional settings, the patterns of behavior and the range of major strategies of action appropriate to different arenas.[9]

Such transformations of religious and cultural beliefs into "codes" or "ethics" for a social order is effected through the activities of visionaries, themselves transformed into elites and who then form coalitions and counter-coalitions with other elites. Such dynamics are not limited to the exercise of power in the narrow political or coercive sense. As even the more sophisticated Marxists, especially Gramsci,[10] have stressed, they are pervasive and include many relatively autonomous symbolic aspects; they represent different combinations of "ideal" and "material" interests. Such measures of control, as well as the challenges to them among elites and broader strata, shaped class relations and modes of production.

The institutionalization of such cultural visions, through the social processes and mechanisms of control, as well as their "reproduction" in space and time, necessarily generates tensions and conflicts, movements of protest and processes of change which offer certain opportunities to reconstruct the premises themselves.

Thus, in principle, the order-maintaining and order-transforming aspects of culture are but two sides of the same coin. Not only is there no basic contradiction between the two: They are part and parcel of the symbolic dimensions in the construction of social order.

The potential of change and transformation is not accidental or external to the realm of culture. It is inherent in the basic interleaving of culture and social structure as twin elements of the construction of social order. Precisely because the symbolic components are inherent in the construction and maintenance of social order they also bear the seeds of social transformation.

Such seeds are indeed common to all societies. Yet the actual ways in which they work out, the configurations of liminal situations, of different orientations and movements of protest, of modes of collective behavior and their impact on societies within which they develop, vary greatly between societies giving rise to contrasting social and cultural dynamics.

But new civilizational settings and social organizations, whether the Axial civilizations, those that ushered in capitalism in the West, or the great revolutions, are not "naturally" brought about by the basic tenets of a religion. Rather, they arise out of a variety of economic and political trends, as well as ecological conditions, all interrelated with the basic civilizational premises and with specific institutions.

Many general historical changes, especially the constructions of novel institutional orders, were probably the outcome of factors listed by J. G. March and John Olsen (1984).[11] These are the combination of basic institutional and normative forms; processes of learning and accommodation and types of decision making by individuals in appropriate arenas of action in response to a great variety of historical events.

As Said Arjomand has pointed out, the crystallization of any pattern of change is the result of history, structure and culture, with human agency bringing them together.[12] It is also human agency, manifested in the activities of institutional and cultural entrepreneurs and their influences on different sectors of society, that shapes actual institutional formations. The potential for the crystallization of such formations is rooted in certain general societal conditions, such as degrees of structural differentiation or types of political economy. But these are only potentials, the concretization of which is effected through human agency.

It is the real constellations or configurations of these factors that are the major objects of comparative historico-sociological analysis and discourse.

ENDNOTES

1. S. Arjomand, "History, Structure and Revolution in the Shi'ite Tradition in Contemporary Iran." *International Political Science Review,* vol. 10, no. 2. (April, 1989), pp. 111–21.

2. M. Rodinson, *Marxism and the Muslim World,* London: Lend Press, 1979; *Europe and the Mystique of Islam* (London: I. B. Tauris, 1989).

3. M. Walzer, *Regicide and Revolution* (Cambridge: Cambridge University Press, 1974).

4. E. Hobsbawm, *The Age of Revolution* (London: Weidenfeld & Nicholson, 1964).

5. A. Cochin, *La Révolution et la libre pensée* (Paris: Plon-Nourrit, 1924). A. Cochin, *L'esprit du Jacobinisme* (Paris: Presses Universitaires de France, 1979). F. Furet, *French Revolution,* New York: Macmillan, 1970. F. Furet, *Interpreting the French Revolution* (Cambridge: Cambridge University Press, 1981). A. Cochin, 1979, op. cit.; F. Furet, 1981, op. cit.; V. C. Nahirny, *The Russian Intelligentsia: From Torment to Silence* (Rutgers N.J.: Transaction Publications).

6. H. Webb (1968). *The Japanese Imperial Institution in the Tokugawa Period* (New York: Columbia University Press).

7. J. A. Goldstone (1991). *Revolution and Rebellion in the Early Modern World* (Berkeley, Los Angeles: University of California Press).

8. S. N. Eisenstadt, ed. (1986). *The Origins and Diversity of Axial Age Civilizations* (Albany, N.Y.: State University of New York Press).

9. M. Weber (1951). *Religion of China* (Glencoe, Ill.: Free Press). idem. (1958). *Religion of India* (Glencoe, Ill., Free Press).

10. A. Gramsci (1957). *The Modern Prince* (London: Lawrence & Wishart).

11. J. G. March and J. Olsen, "The New Institutionalism: Organizational Factors in Political Life." *American Political Science Review,* vol. 78, no. 3 (1984), pp. 734–49.

12. S. Arjomand, op. cit.

....

FRANÇOIS FURET

18 On Revolutions: French, American, and Russian

The subject of democracy and utopia may be approached in a philosophical fashion. Since the eighteenth century, democracy has presented itself to the modern individual as a promise of liberty, or more precisely, of *autonomy.* This is in contrast to earlier times when men were viewed as subjects, and consequently were deprived of the right of self-determination, which is the basis of the legitimacy

SOURCE: François Furet, "Democracy and Utopia," *Journal of Democracy,* vol. 9, no. 1 (January 1998), pp. 65–79. © National Endowment for Democracy and The Johns Hopkins University Press. Reprinted with permission of The Johns Hopkins University Press.

of modern societies. Ever since the democratic idea penetrated the minds and peoples of Europe, it has not ceased to make inroads nearly everywhere through a single question, inherent in its very nature, that crops up continuously and is never truly resolved. That question, which was posed very early on by all the great Western thinkers from Hobbes to Rousseau and from Hegel to Tocqueville, was as follows: "What kind of society should we form if we think of ourselves as autonomous individuals? What type of social bond can be established among free and equal men, since liberty and equality are the conditions of our autonomy? How can we conceive a society in which each member is sovereign over himself, and which thus must harmonize the sovereignty of each over himself and of all over all?"

In the course of these probings into the central question of modern democracy, one is necessarily struck by the gap between the expectations that democracy arouses and the solutions that it creates for fulfilling them. In the abstract, there is a point in political space where the most complete liberty and the most complete equality meet, thus bringing together the ideal conditions of autonomy. But our societies never reach this point. Democratic society is never democratic enough, and its supporters are more numerous and more dangerous critics of democracy than its adversaries. Democracy's promises of liberty and equality are, in fact, unlimited. In a society of individuals, it is impossible to make liberty and equality reign together or even to reconcile the two in a lasting way. These promises expose all democratic political regimes not only to demagogic appeals, but also to the constant accusation of being unfaithful to their own founding values. In premodern systems, legitimacy, like obedience, found its guarantee in *la durée* [longevity]. In the democratic world, neither legitimacy nor obedience is ever lastingly secured.

A century and a half ago, one of the best minds of French liberalism, Charles de Rémusat, explained how the congenital instability of liberal democracy is a consequence of the limitless vistas that it makes available to the human imagination.

The speculations of social philosophy, particularly when everyone gets involved in them, have an inconvenient way of making people disgusted with real things, of blocking all contentment while the dream of the absolute remains unrealized, and of casting discredit upon all the opportunities for improvement and progress that fortune offers to nations. All that is not yet ideal is misery. If the principle of authority is not established without restriction, all is anarchy. If pure democracy is still to come, all is oppression. There is never anything to do in the present except start a new revolution, and it is necessary to agitate incessantly, to roll again and again the

dice of politics in an attempt to turn up some abstract number that may not even exist.

Thus the modern world is a place that is particularly sensitive to the claims of utopia. It is necessary, in this context, to give the word "utopia" a slightly different meaning than it had in earlier centuries. Before the modern era, the word referred either to a literary genre or to an eschatology tied to Christianity. In the first case, it attached to that type of work in which the author imagines a perfect social universe, exempt from human vice and wickedness, outside of space and time. In the second, it designated the messianic emotions that animated a number of popular insurrections in Christian Europe, notably at the end of the Middle Ages, through the passion for obtaining eternal salvation by means of action here below. The utopia of democratic times, however, belongs to a third category, one that was unheard of until the French Revolution. While it also can be bookish, as so many political works from the nineteenth and twentieth centuries attest, it is never outside of time and space; on the contrary, it tends to be based upon time—in the guise of "history"—and to incarnate itself within a specific territory. It has severed all ties with religious hopes, and seeks only earthly human happiness. It is charged with emotions of a political kind. These emotions are nourished by the frustrations engendered by the promises of democracy, and seek to fulfill these promises by making liberty and equality finally *real*. The commitment is merely terrestrial, but it is so total that the legitimacy of the social contract depends upon the fulfillment of these promises.

We might thus undertake a philosophical analysis of the psychological inevitability of utopianism in modern politics, by listing the traits that characterize it during the contemporary age, in contrast to the past. But I prefer to follow a mode of exposition that is more historical than philosophical. Let us trace the course of democratic utopias from their first appearance during the French Revolution up to our own day, the end of the twentieth century, in the hope that in studying their history, we might clarify their nature and profundity.

THE FRENCH REVOLUTION AND THE AMERICAN REVOLUTION

Let us begin, then, with the French Revolution, that laboratory of modern democracy. And let us consider its first objective: to make a *tabula rasa* of the past. This was a goal that was shared by the American Revolution, but which in France carried a particular utopian charge.

In both cases, the notion of erasing the past bespeaks modern artificialism, the obsession with *constructing* society rather than considering it as given by the natural or divine order of things, with founding it upon nothing but the free consent of its members. Thus the original founding is clothed in a particular reverence and solemnity. "Original" does not necessarily mean "definitive," since, as Jefferson once said, society must be refounded every 20 years so that each generation may have the opportunity to correct or remake the constitution according to its own will. Yet this attempt to institutionalize revolution at periodic intervals merely emphasizes the extraordinary character of a society whose members must never be bound by a contract that they would not have freely subscribed to themselves.

United by this common ambition to invent a society that would be the product of free wills, the American Revolution and the French Revolution nonetheless display a capital difference in this regard. The former did not need to overturn an aristocratic social order to institute a society of free and equal individuals. The American colonists had left the aristocratic social order behind them when they left England or Europe to live in freedom and equality in a new land: It was the trans-Atlantic voyage that effected a revolutionary rupture, which emancipation from the British Crown would later merely reinforce. The difference from the French case is so great that Tocqueville, drawing a contrast with what happened in France in 1789, saw in the American case an example of the *nonrevolutionary* establishment of democracy. "The Americans' great advantage," he wrote, "is to have arrived at democracy without having suffered democratic revolutions, and

to have been born equal instead of becoming equal." For Americans, the conventional founding of society by the will of its members accords with the reality of their history.

Lacking the option of moving to a new territory, the French at the end of the eighteenth century had to deny their nation's feudal and aristocratic past in order to invent themselves as a new, or, to use the vocabulary of the time, *regenerated,* people. It was on this condition only that they could act out the grand drama of the *social contract,* which so many philosophers of the age had identified as the basis of legitimacy. That is no doubt why they tended to go too far in the vein of democratic philosophy and the universality of natural rights. The Americans had no need to make a great effort of abstraction in order to proclaim themselves free and equal, since their social condition was not too far from these ideals.

The French, by contrast, had to insist all the harder on the normative character of their "Declaration of the Rights of Man and Citizen," for which their history offered neither precedent nor support. On the contrary, it was precisely under the *ancien régime* that these rights were trampled underfoot. In its French setting, then, the idea of "revolution" was inseparable from the condemnation of the past, which sharpened the will to exclude or eliminate those corrupt beneficiaries of the old order, the aristocrats. The American revolutionaries, it is true, also had to fight a certain number of their compatriots who rallied to the English cause. But the American republic, once it became independent, possessed only a single history, which served as a source of pride and unity. The French, on the other hand, quickly became—and long remained—that strange people incapable of loving their whole national history: For loving the Revolution meant detesting the *ancien régime,* and loving the *ancien régime* meant detesting the Revolution.

This tendency penetrated more and more deeply into the national consciousness, extending the revolutionary *tabula rasa* into the future and renewing the emotion surrounding it for the generations of the nineteenth and twentieth centuries. Yet this tendency also perpetuated a fiction by hiding the Revolution's relationship to the past from which it sprang—namely, absolutism. While the Anglo-Americans formed a new people by means of their exodus from the Old World, the French of the late eighteenth century became obsessed with a passionate desire to cut themselves off from their past, and thus were condemned to overlook that this passion for separation was itself a legacy of this past: The ancient constitution of the kingdom already had been destroyed by a series of absolute monarchs before the men of 1789 made their solemn proclamation of a new starting point and principle of regeneration. Revolutions, wrote Guizot, "are far less the symptom of something beginning than the declaration of something that has already occurred." Viewed from this angle, the two revolutions of the late eighteenth century, the American and the French, are the offspring of two preceding revolutions. The American reinforced what had begun when people left England in the name of individual liberty. The French was heir to the subversion of the traditional order by the administrative monarchy. This was a subversion that the Revolution appropriated and completed, through the proclamation of the *tabula rasa,* before weighing its consequences for the reconstitution of a body politic. Yet the failures that the Revolution met in this very enterprise would constantly give new life to the idea of an absolutely fresh start: If this enterprise failed in 1789 or 1791, it had only to be resumed in 1792 or 1793. In France, revolutionary consciousness combined the view of the times as a curse with the view of the times as a new dawn.

This consciousness was thus free of any reference to a restoration, to say nothing of a return to a golden age. Like its opposite, the idea of the *ancien régime,* this consciousness constituted itself very quickly, taking the form of a universal promise opening out onto an unlimited future. In this sense, as Michelet wrote when trying to characterize the spirit of 1789, "time no longer existed; time had perished." Yet this fictitious exorcism of an accursed past did not exempt the French Revolution from also being, in its turn, a history, constantly judged against its promise, and therefore constantly obliged to begin anew its efforts to fulfill it. The American idea of revolution found its fulfillment in the founding of an independent republic through the federal Constitution of 1787 and the constitutions of the several states. The French idea of revolution passed from one phase to the next of revolutionary history, searching for a fulfillment that it could never attain.

....

RESTARTING THE REVOLUTION

The French Revolution was utopian in the sense that it had nothing but abstract objectives, and thus no foreseeable end. It left in its wake an initial, failed Revolution (that of 1789) in order to begin its course anew, this time solemnly decked out with a new calendar dating time from the beginning of the Republic on 21 September 1792. Its goal was no longer to embody itself in constitutional law, but rather to ensure that liberty and equality would triumph over their enemies—an indispensable first step in the making of a new man, delivered from his age-old subordination to his fellows. This is why the Revolution stressed its character as an annunciation, which gave a unique value to its course. It was the extraordinary contrasted with the ordinary, the exceptional contrasted with the quotidian, to the point where the adjective that appeared to define it could only be tautological: the Revolution was "revolutionary," just as the circumstances were "revolutionary" and the government was "revolutionary." It was no longer solely a question of the health of the fatherland, as in the great perils of the monarchy, or of a Roman-style temporary dictatorship, as described in Rousseau's *Social Contract.* It was a regime new to history, as Robespierre underlined in his famous speech of 5 Nivôse, Year II (25 December 1793), where he drew the contrast between "revolutionary" and "constitutional" government. His goal was not to preserve the Republic, but to *found* it, getting rid of its enemies by means of the Terror.

Hence his superiority to the law and consequent independence from it: Thus what authorizes the provisional suspension of law goes beyond the public safety; it is the higher imperative to found society upon the virtue of its citizens. The

Revolution inherited corrupt and denatured human beings from the *ancien régime;* before the Revolution could be ruled by means of the law, it would have to regenerate each actor in the new social contract. What for Rousseau constitutes the difficult, even almost impossible passage from man to citizen became for Robespierre the meaning of the Revolution, to be realized through the radical actions of the revolutionary government.

Thus the Revolution of 1789 found itself pregnant with a second Revolution, that of 1792. The latter aimed at being both a correction and an expansion of the former: more radical, more universal, more faithful to its emancipatory goal than its predecessor had been. By means of this intensification, it unfolded in a movement of negation and self-transcending that had no limit. Its horizon—the regeneration of humanity—was so abstract that it fostered political passions that tended toward the quasi-religious, although invested in the world of here and now. It is this which imparts to revolutionary politics its character of ideological intolerance and, at the same time, leaves it open to a constant upping of the ante. Yet this is also what protects the revolutionary idea against its own eventual failure: Those who take it up again find its seductive power intact, for the revolutionary idea contains all that modern politics can offer in the way of messianic charm. It is thus that the French Revolution overflows its chronological definition and escapes being trapped amid the prosaic shoals of Thermidoreanism. To those who came after, the Revolution bequeathed the memory of its ambition, which the nineteenth century would not cease to refashion.

The political impasse had been grasped at the end of the Terror by the actors in or witnesses of the Revolution themselves. To understand this, one need only think back to the period that followed Robespierre's fall, after the month of Thermidor, Year II (July 1794). Circumstances demanded the rehabilitation of the "legal" at the expense of the "revolutionary" by writing the Revolution into the law—hence the Constitution of the Year III. Those who had toppled Robespierre found themselves caught between two contradictory imperatives. They neither wished nor were able to renounce the Revolution,

since it alone had made them what they were. Yet they could not totally endorse it, since the Terror had been part of it. It was the young Benjamin Constant, a newcomer to Paris in 1795, who furnished the solution to this dilemma by distinguishing two types of revolutions. The first results from a gap between the institutions and the ideas of a people, and consists in the violent adjustment of the former to the latter; it is the manifestation of a historical necessity. The second, on the contrary, comes about when the revolution, lost within utopia, has passed beyond the progress of the human spirit. The revolution loses itself in the unreal, the impossible, and the arbitrary, eventually provoking the threat of an about-face. Yet this young Swiss thinker's historicist philosophy was too biased to avoid appearing as a rationalization of power, or to erase the messianic dimension of revolutionary hope.

Moreover, at the very moment when Benjamin Constant was seeking to "fix" the Revolution within the movement of history, Gracchus Babeuf was working to start the Revolution up again, since it had produced merely the bourgeois world, such a far cry from its revolutionary promises. Constant invoked the laws of history, Babeuf the Jacobin cult of will. For the former, the Revolution was the achievement of a necessity; for the latter, it was the invention of a future. The European left would thenceforth ceaselessly explore these two alternatives, contradictory yet born of the same event. Marx would spend his intellectual life trying to reconcile them, but he would remain too deterministic for his voluntarist side, and too voluntaristic for his determinist side. The principal charm that Bolshevism held for some imaginations, 120 years after the French Jacobins, was that it reprised the revolutionary enterprise within this combination of necessity and will.

....

THE ROLE OF RELIGION

Yet before we turn to that, we must highlight a final aspect of the revolutionary idea, one that has furnished a foundation for democracy in Europe—namely, the notion that the promise of a good society is no longer inscribed in sacred texts (as in the English case), or in political and religious harmony (as in the American example), but must be fulfilled solely by the unfolding of history. This story is too long and too complex to go into here, but we may at least attempt to sketch its consequences by continuing my comparison, following many historians of the last century. The English Revolution of the seventeenth century offers an example of the mutation of a religious revolution into a political revolution, with the former laying down the spiritual and moral basis of the latter. The American republic, founded at the end of the following century, was born out of an insurrectionist movement that was never cut off from its Christian roots. In France, on the contrary, the men of 1789 were forced to break with the Catholic Church, one of the pillars of the hated *ancien régime,* without ever succeeding in substituting another Christian or post-Christian cult in its place. At that time, Protestantism's hour had passed, and deist rationalism, whatever form it took, left people indifferent. The upshot was that the spirit of the Revolution revealed merely politics pure and simple, even though, by virtue of the universal character of its promise, this politics shared something with the message of the gospels. The paradox of modern French history lies in recovering the spirit of Christianity only through revolutionary democracy. Or to put it another way: The French Revolution renewed universalism without ceasing to limit itself to the level of the political. The French divinized modern liberty and equality without giving the new principles any support other than the historic adventure of a people still otherwise faithful to the Catholic tradition. For a republican historian like Edgar Quinet, this contradiction spelled out the inherent failure of the French Revolution. It is also by means of this contradiction that we can best come to understand the utopian dimension of the Revolution, and of the tradition that it inaugurated.

The problem, moreover, is older than the Revolution. It was already present within the philosophy of the Enlightenment, which in its French version was, not more antireligious, but surely more anticlerical than any other in Europe. The Catholic Church and its priests in France were the quintessential targets (think of Voltaire) of that great movement

toward the reappropriation of man by man that formed the basic tendency of the age. But eighteenth-century philosophy, unlike that of the sixteenth, showed itself powerless to fashion any religious renewal or even any new spiritual principle from the critique of tradition. Voltairean deism, parliamentary Jansenism, the doctrine of Rousseau's Savoyard vicar, the natural religion of the physiocrats, and Masonic esotericism were all alike in this regard: They served more to embellish political expectations than to shape collective beliefs. The France of the Enlightenment lived under the empire of the political even before it became the France of the Revolution. And those elements of religion it retained, as Tocqueville perceived, were reinscribed within the core of the political: the universalism of "civilization," faith in progress, and the emancipation of the human race. Marx also keenly sensed this; he defined the French Revolution, at the time when he was seeking to decode its mystery, as "the illusion of the political."

The boundless investment in historical action, a flame that burned brightest during the years of the Jacobin dictatorship, led the French revolutionaries toward such utopian objectives as the regeneration of humanity. Condemned to waste away under the weight of actual history, as can be seen after Thermidor and under Napoleon, this messianic hope nonetheless survived the event that formed it, as a universal promise of earthly salvation, oriented simply toward the future. There may be found its link with Bolshevism, to which I now turn.

....

THE OCTOBER REVOLUTION

If you will allow me, I would like to take a giant step across the nineteenth century to examine our own, which is richer still in the utopian idea. Indeed, if we take the nineteenth and twentieth centuries together we can consider them as belonging to the same category, for between them, they constitute the European experience of democracy. Yet they may be viewed as two separate *epochs,* each of which possesses (both by itself and in relation to the other) enough distinctive traits to have its own *esprit du temps.* Nineteenth-century Europe, which followed upon the French Revolution, mastered the storm that preceded it. Despite the revolutionary upsurge of 1848, the nineteenth century offers the spectacle of a relatively stable ensemble of nations and regimes sharing a single vision of moral and political civilization. (It is true that it combined many aristocratic elements with what it had already acquired in the way of democracy.) The twentieth century, however—if we accept the idea that it began with the First World War in 1914—has known two world wars and several radically contradictory types of social and political organization. If it is finally ending up before our eyes in a sort of universalization of humanity thanks to the dual impact of the market and the democratic idea, this is only after having passed through tragedies without precedent. From the utopian standpoint, it should also be readily apparent that our own century is the one in which the idea of a collective salvation by history has exerted its full fascination over the masses—a thought sometimes expressed by saying that it has been, in the words of Raymond Aron, the age of "secular religions." Ours has been the first fully democratic century in human history (given that the nineteenth remained partially aristocratic), and it is not by chance that it has also been the one in which the utopian vision of politics has played an essential role.

Hence I come to the question that I sought to understand in my book, *Le passé d'une illusion* (The History of an Illusion). This question was not the history of communism. It was rather the very different one of the sway that the communist idea held over so many minds during the twentieth century: a sway so deep and so vast that it gave rise to a universal belief whose geographic reach exceeded that of Christianity. Born in Europe during the nineteenth century, the idea of communism spread throughout the whole world during the twentieth. I mean by this not that it dominated everyone's imagination, but simply that it was endowed with an exceptional ubiquity; not that it failed to arouse adversaries, but simply that it was more universal than any known religion. Whether in its soft or hard versions, whether reassuring or demanding of sacrifices, it spanned nations and civilizations as a prospect inseparable from the political order of every society in the modern epoch.

Yet this prospect presented the paradoxical character of being linked to a historical event and a historical reality: the October Revolution of 1917 and the regime to which it gave birth. Without the October Revolution, without the USSR, the communist idea would have remained what it had been in the nineteenth century: a vague promise, a far horizon, a post-bourgeois-alienation world that each could imagine according to his own inclination. It was October 1917 and the USSR that gave this vision its unity, its substance, and its force. Its voyage through the century would never stop depending on discussion of the regime that was supposed to illustrate it. The communist idea was no longer free, as it had been in the preceding century, but subordinated to the constraint of a constant affirmation of the veracity of its Soviet incarnation. This was its strength—that the idea had taken root in history—but also its weakness, for the idea was dependent upon its manifestation in reality. The interesting thing is that its strength triumphed over its weakness. Until its end, the Soviet Union managed to embody for millions of people the promise of a new society. The mere fact of its existence and its expansion justified its claims. No amount of massive, organized violence committed by its government and no failure in the economic realm could ever snuff out the dogma of its superiority to capitalism. The mystery of the communist idea in this century is thus that of a hope grafted onto a tragedy.

Another way to make the same observation is to consider the recent end of the USSR. This end came about in a nonrevolutionary fashion, through the self-dissolution of the metropolitan regime—which had itself set the stage for the fall of the satellite regimes—without a purge of old personnel from the new system. Yet what was a gentle transition for the system's personnel (so different in this respect from the liquidation of fascism in 1945) stood in stark contrast to the radical abandonment of communist ideas: The ex-communist countries all tried to base their rebirth on the very "bourgeois" principles that they once had claimed to have abolished and surpassed. As a result, the presence or return to power of former members of communist parties did nothing to change the fact that communism had come to an end along with the regime that had taken it as its banner; communism died with the Soviet Union. The proof is that the European of the present *fin de siècle* [end of century] finds himself bereft of a vision of the future. If bourgeois democracy is no longer what comes before socialism, but rather what comes after it, then those living in bourgeois democracy can no longer imagine anything beyond the horizon within which they now dwell.

Thus nothing less than the disappearance of the USSR was required to break the spell that had linked the regime born in October 1917 to the idea of a better society. The hour of general disillusionment came not from the spectacle of Soviet history, but only from its end. This permits us to attach precise dates to the lifespan of the illusion, from Lenin to Gorbachev, and also to gauge the extent to which, powerful though it was, it possessed a very ephemeral character: The illusion did not survive beyond its object, that is, it was to last less than three-quarters of a century. Hence the word *illusion,* in the title of my book, does not designate the same type of belief that Freud had in view in his *The Future of an Illusion.* He was writing about religion, whereas I attempted to analyze the brief trajectory of a political idea tied to the history of a government and a regime. If I have used this same term, illusion, it has been to indicate that while the object may be earthly rather than divine, a comparable psychological investment is at stake. Moreover, the idea of the universality of men forms a minimal common ground between Christianity and communism. Finally, this particular illusion, unlike religious belief, has the advantage (for the observer, at least) of no longer having anything but a past. Today, the history of communism is closed, and thus can be documented. This is not to say that modern democracies shall henceforth live without political utopia; I believe the contrary. But in the form through which it exerted such power over men's minds during our century, the communist idea has died before our eyes and will not be reborn. The mystery of its strength and its short lifespan forms the subject of my book.

THE POLITICAL IMAGINATION OF TWENTIETH-CENTURY MAN

I had no intention particularly to focus on the case of intellectuals. If I accorded them a large role, it is because they write things down and thus leave testimony behind—and God knows that, in our time, they have written a great deal on politics! But what is interesting about them is less their case in itself than what it reveals about opinion in general. Contrary to what is usually written, the communist illusion was not peculiar to those who write and think for a living. It was far more widespread, and the intellectuals drew it from the atmosphere of their times, where they found it in all its forms, from a militant faith to a vague notion about the meaning of history. But in every case it endows the political universe with much vaster stakes. It superbly illustrates the character of an epoch when politics was the great dividing line between good and evil. In the illusion of communism, in the imaginary and fraught journey of the communist idea, I have tried to recover one of the starting points, perhaps the principal one, from which twentieth-century man has imagined his situation in the world. My book is a contribution to the history of the political imagination of twentieth-century man.

At the heart of this political imagination, stands the figure of revolution, established since the end of the eighteenth century in the minds of Europeans—even those who hate it—as the quintessential means of historical change. The revolution took place in order to inaugurate the reign of the bourgeoisie over the feudal world. It must recommence in order to inaugurate the reign of the proletariat—precursor to the emancipation of humanity—over the bourgeois world.

The idea is first of all nourished by hatred of that which it seeks to destroy. Its mainspring is the rejection and even the hatred of the bourgeois, the central personage of modern society and the scapegoat for all the troubles that this society is constantly fostering. The bourgeois is the symbol of man's division within himself, first diagnosed by

Rousseau, and this existential difficulty has weighed ceaselessly upon his destiny. All his inventions turn against him. He rises by means of money, which has allowed him to dissolve aristocratic gradations of "rank" from within, but this instrument of equality transforms him into an aristocrat of a new type, even more the prisoner of his wealth than the noble was the prisoner of his birth. He inaugurated the Rights of Man, but in fact prefers the right of property. Liberty frightens him, and equality scares him even more. He was the father of democracy, in which every man is the equal of every other, associated with all in the construction of the social order, and in which each one, by obeying the law, obeys only himself. Yet democracy has exposed the fragility of bourgeois governments along with the threat posed by the masses, that is to say, by the poor. Thus the bourgeois is more reticent than ever about the principles of 1789, even though they facilitated his spectacular entrance into history.

If the bourgeois is the man of denial, it is because he is the man of falsehood. Far from incarnating the universal, he has but one obsession, his interests, and one passion, money. It is money that arouses the worst hatred against him, that unites in opposition to him the prejudices of the aristocrats, the jealousy of the poor, and the contempt of the intellectuals, past and present, who expel him from the future. The source of his power over society also accounts for his weak hold over the imagination. A king is infinitely more vast than his person, an aristocrat derives his prestige from a past far older than he is, a socialist preaches struggle to bring forth a better world where he will no longer exist. But the rich man is only what he is: rich, that is all. Money is not a sign of his virtue, or even of his labor, as in the Puritan understanding; instead, it is a sign of his luck or his greed. Money, moreover, divides the bourgeois from his fellows without bringing him the respect that allows the aristocrat to govern his inferiors; it reduces the bourgeois to a private condition by closing him up within the economic realm. The bourgeois has no appeal against this political deficiency, since it arises from a handicap of birth. It is at the very moment when the consent of the governed becomes explicitly necessary for the government of men that it is the most difficult to unite them.

The revolution represents the inversion of the bourgeois world as well as the principal sign of its having been transcended. As its inversion, the revolution is the revenge of the public on the private, the triumph of politics over economics, the victory of will over the everyday order of things. As the transcending of the bourgeois world, the revolution tears society away from its past and its traditions in order to undertake anew the construction of a social world. The revolution carries modern artificialism to its absolute form by rejecting all traditions. If bourgeois interests foiled the French Revolution's drive to wipe the slate clean, the only thing to do is to direct the struggle against them.

NECESSITY, WILL, AND THE REVOLUTIONARY IDEA

I am well aware that there is another version of the revolutionary idea, one that does not attribute such a Promethean role to the human will. Far from it, since this version consists not in making, but in waiting for, the revolution, as one waits for fruit to ripen, from the maturation of mentalities and things. The analogy with a natural cycle indicates that a more or less deterministic vision of the evolution of societies has taken the place of the creative virtues of human initiative. In both versions, the revolution constitutes the privileged mode of history's unfolding; but the second leaves nothing or almost nothing to the poetry of action, while the first exalts political invention without stripping from it the dignity of a necessary accomplishment. Marx never ceased oscillating between the two conceptions, and his heirs have done so still more. One of the Bolsheviks' great charms, perhaps their main one, was their extreme voluntarism, drawn from the example set by the Jacobins: What could be more extraordinary than to make a proletarian revolution in the land of czars and *muzhiks* [peasants]? Yet Lenin managed to drape even this extraordinary event in the authority of science: The revolutionary party had grasped the laws of history. He thus recovered the necessity of the revolution, yet did so by putting it at the service of political decision. It matters little that the two ideas are contradictory. Their peculiar marriage beguiles the imagination as the union of liberty and science. There, modern subjectivity finds both its plenitude and its guarantee.

As a rupture in the temporal order, although it fulfills history's promises, the revolution is invested with almost infinite social expectations. It must free the world from the bourgeois curse: from the reign of money, from the alienation brought by the market, from the division of classes, and even from the division within man himself. For it emancipates not only the proletarian, or the poor, but also the bourgeois, or his son. It makes everything depend upon history, which henceforth becomes the arena of human salvation, and upon politics, through which people choose their destiny: Everything can be achieved by a good society, if one can be established. Modern society disrupts the social bond by imprisoning individuals within the obsessive urge for money. Burdened from the start with a political deficit, it ignores the idea of the common good, since all those who compose it, plunged in relativism, each have their own good. Such a society is incapable of forming a community of members freely associated around a collective project. The revolutionary idea is the exorcism of this unhappiness. It divinizes the political so as to avoid having to be contemptuous of it. In these traits we can recognize the hopes invested in the foundation of socialism by the revolution of October 1917.

Now one of the features—and one of the novelties—of the twentieth century is fascism's appropriation, to the profit of the right, of the revolutionary idea. One can easily understand this by looking back through the thought of the nineteenth century. During that epoch, revolution formed part of a conception of history that was monopolized by the left. It was a conception so powerful that even the right depended on it to a large degree, under the inverted form of its negation: the right was counterrevolutionary. But the idea of counterrevolution was compromised by this very dependence, for it evokes a return to a bygone past, out of which was born the revolution that the counterrevolutionary idea wanted to erase. This return, moreover, could only be achieved by means of revolutionary violence, which the counterrevolutionary idea claimed to detest. Whether seen as an end or a means, the counterrevolution was caught in a contradiction. It offered neither a policy nor a strategy. It was from this impasse that fascism delivered the European right that opposed the principles of 1789. Fascism gave the right a future.

Fascism fought the modern individualism and bourgeois egotism for which the French Revolution had paved the way, but it did not do so in the name of a return to aristocratic society. Fascism had no more esteem for the old aristocracy than it did for the new bourgeoisie. It aimed to destroy both in the name of the people, assembled without distinction of rank or class under the authority of a leader who incarnated that people. To serve this end it stopped at nothing, no matter how violent or illegal it might be, for the national or racial community of tomorrow could be brought into being only at the price of overthrowing the classes in power.

To fascism, then, were annexed all the seductions of the revolutionary idea, so essential to the modern absolutization of history. Fascism presented itself as an uprooting of the past, a violent and radical triumph over the corruption of the world of yesterday, an instance of political will revenging itself upon the alienating forces of the economy. It also fulfilled the conditions for a refoundation of the social, but in the name of the nation. One cannot recover a sense of the popularity that fascism enjoyed during the period between the two world wars unless one considers the promises of which it claimed to be the bearer. One can grasp nothing of our century's tragedies, moreover, unless one sees that the revolutionary idea took not one, but two paths into people's minds.

....

THE END OF UTOPIA?

I shall not recount these tragedies here, contenting myself with having underlined what they owed, from the outset, to the divinization of political action that is one of the characteristics of the utopian thought of the democratic age. I would instead like to offer some observations on our situation today, when this type of thought has been discredited by history.

Communism never conceived of any tribunal other than history's, and it has now been condemned by history to disappear, lock, stock, and barrel. Its defeat, therefore, is beyond appeal.

But must we conclude from this that it is necessary categorically to banish utopia from the public life of our societies? That might perhaps be going too far, because it would also mean destroying one of the great props of civic activity. For if the social order cannot be other than what it is, why should we trouble ourselves about it? The end of the communist idea has closed before our eyes the greatest path offered to the imagination of modern man in the matter of collective happiness. But it has by the same token deepened the political deficit that has always characterized modern liberalism.

In reality, this collapse affects not just communists, nor even just the left. It forces us to rethink convictions that are as old as democracy, especially that famous notion of a clear direction of history that was supposed to have anchored democracy in time. If capitalism has become the future of socialism, and the bourgeois world has succeeded that of the "proletarian revolution," what becomes of this conviction about time? The inversion of the canonical ordering obscures the articulation of epochs along the road of progress. History again becomes a tunnel where man enters as in the darkness, without knowing where his actions will lead, uncertain of his destination, dispossessed of the illusory sense of security about what he is doing. Most often bereft of belief in God, the democratic individual of our *fin de siècle* sees that the divinity called history is trembling on its foundations. From this comes an anguish that must be dispelled.

The democratic individual finds himself poised before a closed future, incapable of defining even vaguely the horizon of a *different society* from the one in which we live, since this horizon has become almost impossible to conceive. We need only to look at the crisis into which political language has been plunged in today's democracies in order to understand this. The right and the left still remain, but they are stripped of their reference points, and almost of their substance: The left no longer knows what socialism is; the right, deprived of its best argument (namely, anticommunism), is also searching for something which can distinguish it. The political scene in both France and Italy offers good examples of this situation.

Can such a situation last? Will the end of communism deprive democratic politics of a revolutionary horizon for long? With this question, I take my leave.

KURT SCHOCK

19   Nonviolent Action

INTRODUCTION

Prior to the wave of people power movements that erupted across the globe in the late twentieth century, scholars of social movements and revolution rarely addressed nonviolent action as a strategy for political change in non-democratic contexts. By the beginning of the twenty-first century this changed, as increasingly more social scientists began turning their attention to a topic once addressed primarily by peace studies scholars. The analysis of nonviolent action by social scientists other than peace studies scholars should be welcomed. Yet, since popular and scholarly misconceptions about nonviolence abound, it would be useful to examine some of these in the hope that biases in the social scientific analysis of nonviolent action can be attenuated.

SOURCE: Kurt Schock, "Nonviolent Action and Its Misconceptions: Insights for Social Scientists," *PS: Political Science and Politics*, vol. 36, no. 4 (October 2003), pp. 705–706, 709–711. © American Political Science Association. Reprinted with permission of the Cambridge University Press. Article abridged by the Editor.

NONVIOLENT ACTION AND ITS MISCONCEPTIONS

What is nonviolent action? As the name implies, nonviolent action is *active*—it involves activity in the collective pursuit of social or political objectives—and it is *non-violent*—it does not involve physical force or the threat of physical force against human beings. More specifically, nonviolent action involves an active process of bringing political, economic, social, emotional, or moral pressure to bear in the wielding of power in contentious interactions between collective actors. Nonviolent action is non-institutional, i.e., it operates outside the bounds of institutionalized political channels, and it is indeterminate, i.e., the procedures for determining the outcome of the conflict are not specified in advance. Nonviolent action occurs through: (1) acts of omission, whereby people refuse to perform acts expected by norms, custom, law, or decree; (2) acts of commission, whereby people perform acts which they do not usually perform, are not expected by norms or customs to perform, or are forbidden by law, regulation, or decree to perform; or (3) a combination of acts of omission and commission. Rather than viewing nonviolent action as one-half of a rigid violent-nonviolent dichotomy, nonviolent action may be better understood as a set of methods with special features that are different from both violent resistance and institutional politics. That said, let us look at some common misconceptions about nonviolent action.

1. Nonviolent action is *not* inaction (although it may involve the refusal to carry out an action that is expected, i.e., an act of omission), it is *not* submissiveness, it is *not* the avoidance of conflict, and it is *not* passive resistance. In fact, nonviolent action is a direct means for prosecuting conflicts with opponents and an explicit rejection of inaction, submission, and passivity.

2. Anything that is not violent is not considered to be nonviolent action. Nonviolent action refers to specific actions that involve risk and that invoke non-physical pressure or nonviolent coercion in contentious interactions between opposing groups.

3. Nonviolent action is not limited to state sanctioned political activities. Nonviolent action may be legal or illegal. Civil disobedience, i.e., the open and deliberate violation of the law for a collective social or political purpose, is a fundamental type of nonviolent action.

4. Nonviolent action is not composed of regular or institutionalized techniques of political action such as litigation, letter writing, lobbying, voting, or the passage of laws. Although institutional methods of political action often accompany nonviolent struggles, nonviolent action occurs outside the bounds of institutional political channels. Contrary to regular and institutionalized political activity, there is always an element of risk involved for those implementing nonviolent action since it presents a direct challenge to authorities. Thus, nonviolent action is context-specific. Displaying anti-regime posters in democracies would be considered a low risk and regular form of political action, whereas the same activity in non-democracies would be considered irregular and would involve a substantial amount of risk. It would therefore be considered a method of nonviolent action in a non-democratic context. Similarly, strikes in democracies that occur within the bounds of institutionalized labor relations cannot be considered nonviolent action, since they are not non-institutional or indeterminate. However, a wildcat strike in a democracy and most strikes in non-democracies would be instances of nonviolent action given their non-institutionalized, indeterminate, and high-risk features.

5. Nonviolent action is not a form of negotiation or compromise. Negotiation and compromise may or may not accompany conflicts prosecuted through nonviolent action, just as they may or may not accompany conflicts prosecuted through violent action. In other words, nonviolent action is a means for prosecuting a conflict and it should be distinguished from means of conflict resolution.

6. Participation in nonviolent action does not require that activists hold any sort of ideological, religious, or metaphysical beliefs. Contrary

to popular and scholarly assumptions, those who engage in nonviolent action are rarely pacifists. Those who engage in nonviolent action hold a variety of different beliefs, one of which may be pacifism, but pacifism is not prevalent among those engaged in nonviolent action. As noted by George Lakey, "most pacifists do not practice nonviolent resistance, and most people who do practice nonviolent resistance are not pacifists" (Lakey 1973, 57).

7. There are also significant misconceptions concerning the role of activists' perceptions about the methods used in struggles. Those who implement methods of nonviolent action may not recognize them as "methods of nonviolent action," and they certainly do not have to adhere to a theory of nonviolence or a moral code to successfully implement them.

8. Nonviolent action does not depend on moral authority, the "mobilization of shame," or the conversion of the views of opponents in order to succeed. Conversion of the oppressor's views, whereby the challenge effectively alters the view of the oppressors thereby resulting in the acceptance of the challenger's aims and an alteration in the oppressor's policies, is commonly assumed to be the only mechanism by which nonviolent action promotes political change.[1] In fact, conversion is only one of four mechanisms through which nonviolent action can promote change and it is the least likely of the four to promote change. The other more common mechanisms are accommodation, nonviolent coercion, and disintegration. Through accommodation, the challenge effectively produces changes in the oppressor's policies even though the oppressor's views have not changed. Through nonviolent coercion, change is achieved against the oppressor's will as a result of successfully undermining its resources, legitimacy, and ability to control the situation. Through disintegration, the oppressor's ruling apparatus falls apart in the face of mass nonviolent action. Thus, while conversion of the opponent's views may occur, more often than not, nonviolent action succeeds through nonviolent coercion, i.e., it forces the opponent to make changes by undermining its power. Of course, moral pressure may be mobilized, but in the absence of political and economic pressure, it is unlikely to produce change.

9. Those who implement nonviolent action do not assume that the state will not react with violence. Violence is to be expected from governments, especially non-democratic governments. The violent reaction of governments is not an indication of the failure of nonviolent action. In fact, governments respond with violence precisely because nonviolent action presents a serious threat to their power. To dismiss the use of nonviolent action because people are killed is no more logical than dismissing armed resistance for the same reasons.

10. That said, suffering is not an essential part of nonviolent resistance. The view that suffering is central to nonviolent resistance is based on misguided assumptions that nonviolent action is "passive resistance" and that nonviolent action produces change through the conversion of the oppressor's views. While nonviolent challenges should expect a violent response by the government, they should also prepare to mute the impact of the opponent's violence. That is, they should, as stated by Peter Ackerman and Christopher Kruegler, "get out of harms way, take the sting out of the agents of violence, disable the weapons, prepare people for the worst effects of violence, and reduce the strategic importance of what may be lost to violence" (Ackerman and Kruegler 1994, 38). Nonviolent resistance is much more sophisticated than the widespread conception of activists meekly accepting physical attacks.

11. Nonviolent action is not a method of contention that is used only as a last resort, when the means of violence are unavailable. Although nonviolent action may be used when no weapons are available, it may also be used *instead* of violence.

12. Nonviolent action is not a method of the "middle class" or a "bourgeois" approach to political contention. Nonviolent action can and has been implemented by groups from all

classes and castes, from slaves to members of the upper-class. For obvious reasons, it is used more frequently by the less-powerful, i.e., those without regular access to power-holders, than by the powerful.

13. The use of nonviolent action is not limited to the pursuit of "moderate" or "reformist" goals. It is just as appropriate for the pursuit of "radical" goals. Anders Corr, for example, has documented the extensive use of nonviolent action in land and housing struggles across the developed and less-developed worlds (Corr 1999). Challenges to private property relations can hardly be considered "reformist," "moderate," or "bourgeois." Similarly, the feminist movement has radically challenged patriarchal gender relations—almost entirely through methods that do not involve violence. Challenging groups can be militant, radical, *and* nonviolent.

14. The mass mobilization of people into campaigns of nonviolent action in non-democracies does not depend on coercion. While some campaigns of nonviolent action in non-democracies have involved coercion to promote mass mobilization, it is not a necessary feature.

15. While nonviolent action by its very nature requires patience, it is not inherently slow compared to violent action in producing political change. Armed insurgencies that served as models for a generation of revolutionaries took decades to succeed: The Communists in China were engaged in armed combat for over 20 years before they assumed power in 1949, and the Vietnamese were engaged in armed combat against French, Japanese, and American imperialists for over three decades before national liberation. Similarly, numerous campaigns of terror, such as the Basque ETA in Spain and the IRA in Northern Ireland, have been operating for decades without meeting their objectives. By contrast, the nonviolent Solidarity movement in Poland took office about a decade after its emergence, and it took a mere 30 months, following the assassination of Benigno Aquino in August, 1983, for the people power movement in the Philippines to topple Ferdinand Marcos—something the Filipino Communists had been trying to do through armed methods since 1969.

16. The occurrence of nonviolent action is not structurally determined. While there are empirical relationships in geographically and temporally bound places and time periods between political contexts and the use of a given strategy for responding to grievances, the method used to challenge unjust or oppressive political relations is not determined by political context. Processes of learning, diffusion, and social change may result in the implementation of nonviolent action in contexts or situations historically characterized by violent contention. Conflicts involving land, separatism, autonomy, or self-determination, for example, are generally assumed to be—and have historically been—violent. However, nonviolent strategies are increasingly being used in such conflicts (e.g., see Cooper 1999). Certainly the context of the struggle and the issues at stake influence the strategies used by challengers, but not in a deterministic manner.

17. The effectiveness of nonviolent action is not a function of the ideology of the oppressors. It is often claimed that nonviolent action can only succeed in democracies or when it is used against benign or "universalist" oppressors. Certainly the beliefs of the oppressors influences the dynamics of nonviolent struggles, but they are not the sole determinant of their outcomes.

18. The effectiveness of nonviolent action is not a function of the repressiveness of the oppressors. In fact, nonviolent action has been effective in brutally repressive contexts, and it has been ineffective in open democratic polities. Repression, of course, constrains the ability of challengers to organize, communicate, mobilize, and engage in collective action, and magnifies the risk of participation in collective action. Nevertheless, repression is only one of many factors that influence the trajectories of campaigns of nonviolent action, not the sole determinant of their trajectories.

BLURRED LINES?

To illustrate how some of these misconceptions may influence the work of social scientists, I will briefly examine Gay Seidman's essay "Blurred Lines: Nonviolence in South Africa" (*PS: Political Science and Politics*, June 2000). This is not meant to be a personal attack on the work of Seidman. She is a respected scholar who has published path-breaking work on social movement unionism in Brazil and South Africa (Seidman 1994). Moreover, we agree on many points in her essay. We agree that the anti-apartheid struggle in South Africa stands as a monument to the power of nonviolent action in challenging systems of injustice, exploitation, and oppression. We agree that social scientists must not glorify the use of nonviolent action in the anti-apartheid movement, or in any other predominantly nonviolent struggle. We agree that social scientists should develop historically nuanced and empirically accurate analyses of predominantly nonviolent struggles. Nevertheless, since more and more social scientists are beginning to study nonviolence, and since Seidman's essay may be representative of some of the general biases that social scientists bring to the table when turning their attention to the study of nonviolence, it is hoped that by offering a constructive criticism of these misconceptions, biases in the social scientific analysis of nonviolence can be attenuated.

PASSIVE RESISTANCE

Seidman uses the term "passive resistance" to describe nonviolent action (Seidman 2000, 161). This is a misnomer. There is nothing passive or evasive about nonviolent resistance, as it is an active and overt means for prosecuting conflicts with opponents. While Mohandas Gandhi at first used the term "passive resistance," he subsequently rejected the term due to its inaccurate connotations. Similarly, Martin Luther King rejected the term "passive resistance" and used words such as "aggressive," "militant," "confrontational," and "coercive" to describe his campaigns of nonviolent action. The

term "passive resistance" has not been used by activists or scholars of nonviolent action for decades, yet social scientists continue to use the term when addressing nonviolent action. Like Gandhi and King, social scientists should abandon the term "passive resistance" and use the more accurate and precise term "nonviolent action." This is not a mere semantic distinction, but rather is critical to the understanding of nonviolent resistance. . . .

Seidman also refers to the struggle for national liberation in India as a case where nonviolent action succeeded because of the views of the oppressors (Seidman 2000, 161). In the case of the Indian independence struggle, the attribution of "universalist" views to the British is questionable. British rulers hardly believed that Indians were their equal. They viewed non-whites in a racist and exclusionary, rather than in an universalist, manner. Seidman also suggests that Britain's commitment to the Atlantic Charter contributed to the success of the national liberation movement in India.[2] But, if Britain was committed to the Atlantic Charter, then why weren't they compelled to grant independence to their other colonies in the 1940s as well?

A closer examination of the Indian struggle for national liberation suggests that it worked because it made India ungovernable for the British and it rendered Britain's military might useless. The Indian struggle for national liberation succeeded, not because of the humanitarian views of the British, but because the force of nonviolent action undermined the power of British rule, showed that Great Britain's rule in India was based on force rather than legitimacy, reduced the justification for violent repression, influenced reference publics in Great Britain, and illuminated the futility of trying to violently repress a nationwide movement of nonviolent action with military force. Claims that the nonviolent struggle in India contributed to political change because the British were soft, humanitarian, or universalist are simply inaccurate.

Even if the British were less brutal or more universalist than the "typical" oppressor, there are a number of historical cases where nonviolent challenges worked against ruthless oppressors. Moreover, nonviolent action worked not because the oppressor's views were converted as a result of extreme suffering, but because it undermined the oppressor's ability to rule and rendered their repressive capacities ineffective. Nonviolent action, for example, worked when it was implemented against the Nazis, undoubtedly one of the most brutal regimes in recent history. Nonviolent protest demonstrations by German wives against the imprisonment of their Jewish husbands in Berlin led to their release. Nonviolent resistance to Nazis in Norway, Finland, Denmark, the Netherlands, Bulgaria, and Romania saved the lives of countless Jews. Nonviolent resistance to Nazi occupation in Norway prevented the implementation of a corporatist system. Non-cooperation in Denmark through tactics such as work slowdowns and strikes severely hindered the German effort to extract resources and exert control over the country. Generally, the Nazi military machine was dumbfounded in the face of widespread nonviolent resistance. B. H. Liddell Hart, a British military strategist who interrogated Nazi generals after the war, found that "they were experts in violence, and had been trained to deal with opponents who used that method. But other forms of resistance baffled them . . . It was a relief to them when resistance became violent, and when non-violent forms were mixed with guerrilla action, thus making it easier to combine drastic suppressive action against both at the same time" (Liddell Hart 1968, 205).

More recently, of course, nonviolent action worked with unprecedented effectiveness against communist regimes—regimes that although they were no longer Stalinist, could not be characterized as soft or embracing of universalist principles. The nonviolent Solidarity movement in Poland seriously challenged the communist regime well before Gorbachev implemented reforms. In fact, the Solidarity movement made it clear to the more enlightened segments of the Soviet political elite, like Gorbachev, that reforms had to be implemented. The success of the Solidarity movement subsequently set the stage for successful nonviolent challenges throughout the Soviet sphere, from East Germany to Mongolia. The Soviet Union itself disintegrated in the face of predominantly nonviolent secessionist movements from the Baltic states to Central Asia.[3]

Moreover, in instances where *violent action* failed against brutal oppressors lacking universalist views, *nonviolent action* succeeded. The Shah of Iran did not hold "universalist" beliefs and his regime was supported by a ruthless military and internal security apparatus, SAVAK. Iran's two underground armed guerrilla movements, the *Fedayeen* and the *Mujahhadin*, were small and ineffective in challenging the state. Their membership did not surpass 300 at their peak, and they were infiltrated by the SAVAK. While there were armed battles between military forces loyal to the Shah and soldiers who deserted the regime immediately prior to the transfer of power, the Shah was not toppled by an armed insurgency, but rather by an unarmed insurrection whereby ordinary citizens engaged in nonviolent action, such as protests demonstrations, strikes, boycotts, and civil disobedience.[4]

MORAL LOGIC

No assumptions that "nonviolent activists hold a higher moral ground" or have the "sole proprietorship of the moral high ground" (Seidman 2000, 164) are necessary for nonviolent action to work. The operation of nonviolent action does not have to be based on any moral logic, hidden or otherwise. While some major proponents of nonviolent action have been morally committed to nonviolence, nonviolent action *per se* does not require proponents or activists to be morally committed to nonviolence, or hold any sort of ideological, religious, or metaphysical beliefs.

Morality aside, there may be *pragmatic* reasons for proponents of nonviolent action to encourage nonviolent discipline, i.e., the strict adherence to nonviolent methods. While responding to state violence with violence seems appropriate and justified to most people, it permits the state, not the challenging group, to choose the means by which the conflict will be prosecuted. This takes the comparative advantage away from the challengers and gives it to the state, as the ability of governments to use violence almost always exceeds the ability of challengers. In fact, violent rebellion by challengers often strengthens regimes since it justifies the government's use of violence in the name of "law and order," "political stability," or a "stable business climate."

Thus, nonviolent discipline is useful for very pragmatic reasons, such as keeping the movement and reference publics focused on the issues rather than on acts of violence, and attenuating fears that reference publics may have about the challengers. The exposure of state violence in contrast to the unarmed methods of the challengers reveals that the state's rule is based on force, not legitimacy, and this may lead to shifts in public and international opinion that ultimately reshape the balance of power. What is the likelihood that the United States Congress, during the Cold War, would have passed sanctions against South Africa if the challenge to apartheid occurred primarily through an armed insurgency? What is the likelihood that American churches and universities would have imposed sanctions and divested if the challenge to apartheid was primarily armed and violent?

Sustained nonviolent resistance in the face of violent repression may invoke a dynamic whereby the suppression of unarmed protesters merely fuels the determination of the activists, catalyzes the support of reference publics, and reduces the effectiveness of further violent repression. This dynamic has been variously referred to as "political jiu-jitsu," the "paradox of repression," and the "critical dynamic."[5] In South Africa, the sustained campaign of nonviolent action in the face of repression had the effect of "eroding the state's capacity and will to govern through repression. . . . In the meantime, the capacity and will of black South Africans to reject their continued domination grew more quickly" (Marx 1992, 162). Significantly, this dynamic has absolutely nothing to do with what assumptions the proponents of nonviolent action hold about the "moral purity" of nonviolence. The dynamic may operate even when the proponents of nonviolent action are as Machiavellian as the targets of their dissent.

In South Africa, for example, numerous UDF-affiliated street and area committees attempted to make a clear distinction between the nonviolence and accountability of "people power" and the undisciplined violent action of "ultra-militant" youth, and promoted highly organized forms of contention that would not lead to unnecessary violence. "People's courts" were organized to maintain order and justice within the townships and to promote nonviolent discipline, as violence threatened the support that

had been cultivated among South Africa's churches, whites, and the international community. The calls for nonviolent discipline were not based on principled nonviolent action; i.e., those calling for nonviolent action were not concerned that violence would "sully" their struggle. The calls were based on pragmatic nonviolent action; i.e., the realization that they could generate greater pressure against the state through methods of nonviolent action than through methods of violence.

I suspect that some of the misconceptions that social scientists have about nonviolent action are that nonviolent action is principled nonviolence, or that those promoting nonviolent struggle adhere to principled nonviolence. Scholars of nonviolent action, however, have traditionally made clear distinctions between principled and pragmatic nonviolent action. Those who practice principled nonviolent action view nonviolence as a way of life and assume that violence is inherently wrong. Those who practice pragmatic nonviolent action view nonviolent action as efficacious or convenient for attaining their goal in a given context, and do not reject the possibility that violent action may be a practical means for alleviating oppression under some conditions. Thus, methods of nonviolent action are used without any objection to violence in principle. Most campaigns of nonviolent action (including the struggle in South Africa) are pragmatic rather than principled. Yet when mainstream social scientists turn their attention to nonviolent action they fail to distinguish between principled and pragmatic nonviolence, or make (hidden?) assumptions that it is principled nonviolent action. A more nuanced understanding of struggles implementing nonviolent action must recognize the difference between pragmatic and principled nonviolent action. . . .

CONCLUSION

. . . Empirically, political contention is transgressive and there are rarely cases of purely nonviolent struggle, especially in non-democratic contexts. Yet, this should not prevent social scientists from attempting to disentangle and understand the impact of different strategies and tactics of contention. Social scientists do not have to idealize nonviolence or make the (faulty) assumption that the anti-apartheid movement in South Africa followed a similar logic to the America civil rights movement in order to analyze the crucial role of nonviolent action in the toppling of apartheid. But they do have to understand what nonviolent action is and how it operates. . . .

ENDNOTES

1. Part of the confusion results from the fact that Gandhi believed that conversion was the mechanism through which nonviolent action worked. See Shepard 2001.

2. Since Gandhi's campaign of nonviolent action in India emerged in the 1920s and 1930s and the Atlantic Charter was declared in 1941, it could be argued that the national liberation movement in India was one of the factors contributing to the declaration of the Atlantic Charter, which contained a statement on the right of people to choose their own form of government. By assuming that the Atlantic Charter provided the opportunity for the Indian struggle to succeed, without considering that the struggle in India and in other colonies may have contributed to the formulation of the Charter reflects a structural bias in the social movement literature. That is, the study of how social movements *alter* the political context and create opportunities is woefully under-examined compared to the study of how social movements *respond* to the political context. See Goodwin and Jasper 1999.

3. Violent exceptions, of course, include the revolution in Romania and the separatist movement in Chechnya.

4. See Shivers 1980; 1997. Also see Zunes 1994. Nonviolent action contributed to a *revolutionary outcome* in Iran, which is defined as a "transfer of state power from those who held it before the start of multiple sovereignty to a new ruling coalition" (Tilly 1993: 14). Of course, the *consolidation* of the rule of the Ayatollahs involved substantial violence and coercion.

5. According to Sharp (1973), *political jiu-jitsu* refers to the dynamic by which a sustained nonviolent challenge in the face of repression highlights the stark brutality of the regime, produces dissension within the government, and mobilizes support for the challengers among the general population, the regime's usual supporters, and third parties that would not have occurred during the course of a violent challenge. In effect, the use of violent repression against persistent nonviolent

challenges rebounds against the states' sources of strength. This dynamic has been observed in a variety of empirical contexts. According to Smithey and Kurtz (1999), the *paradox of repression* refers to the dynamic by which efforts to violently repress nonviolent challenges backfires and leads to increased support for the challengers, as occurred in the Soviet Bloc between 1988 and 1991. According to McAdam (1999), the *critical dynamic* of the civil rights movement in the American South in the 1950s and 1960s was that the challengers broadened the conflict by inducing local and state authorities to disrupt public order by violently repressing the nonviolent challenge. The result was third party intervention by the federal government, the sustaining of activist commitment, the generation of public sympathy, and the mobilization of financial support.

REFERENCES

Ackerman, Peter, and Jack DuVall. 2000. A *Force More Powerful: A Century of Nonviolent Conflict.* New York: St. Martin's Press.

Ackerman, Peter, and Christopher Kruegler. 1994. *Strategic Nonviolent Conflict: The Dynamics of People Power in the Twentieth Century.* Westport, CT: Praeger.

Bond, Doug. 1994. "Nonviolent Action and the Diffusion of Power." In *Justice Without Violence,* ed. Paul Wehr, Heidi Burgess, and Guy Burgess. Boulder, CO: Lynne Rienner Publishing, pp. 59–79.

Cooper, Joshua. 1999. "The Ogoni Struggle for Human Rights and a Civil Society in Nigeria." In *Nonviolent Social Movements: A Geographical Perspective,* ed. Stephen Zunes, Lester Kurtz, and Sarah Beth Asher. Malden, MA: Blackwell Publishers, pp. 189–202.

Corr, Anders. 1999. *No Trespassing: Squatting, Rent Strikes, and Land Struggle Worldwide.* Cambridge, MA: South End Press.

Galtung, Johan. 1989. *Nonviolence and Israel/Palestine.* Honolulu: University of Hawai'i Press.

Goodwin, Jeff, and James M. Jasper. 1999. "Caught in a Winding, Snarling Vine: The Structural Bias of Political Process Theory." *Sociological Forum* 14(1) pp. 27–54.

Lakey, George. 1973. *Strategy for a Living Revolution.* New York: Grossman.

Liddell Hart, B. H. 1968. "Lessons from Resistance Movements- Guerrilla and Non-violent." In *Civilian Resistance as a National Defense: Non-violent Action against Aggression,* ed. Adam Roberts. Harrisburg, PA: Stackpole Books, pp. 195–211.

Martin, Brian. 1997. Critique of Violent Rationales." *Pacifica Review* 9(1) pp. 83–91.

Marx, Anthony W. 1992. *Lessons of Struggle: South African Internal Opposition, 1960–1990*. New York: Oxford University Press.

McAdam, Doug. 1999. *Political Process and the Development of Black Insurgency, 1930–1970*. 2nd ed. Chicago: University of Chicago Press.

McCarthy, Ronald M. 1990. "The Techniques of Nonviolent Action: Some Principles of Its Nature, Use, and Effects." In *Arab Nonviolent Struggle in the Middle East*, ed. Ralph E. Crow, Philip Grant, and Saad E. Ibrahim. Boulder, CO: Lynne Rienner Publishing, pp. 107–120.

McCarthy, Ronald M. 1998. "Introduction: The Possibilities of Research on Nonviolent Action." In *Nonviolent Action: A Research Guide*, ed. Ronald M. McCarthy and Gene Sharp. New York: Garland Publishing, pp. xv–xxxiii.

Seidman, Gay W. 1994. *Manufacturing Militancy: Workers' Movements in Brazil and South Africa, 1970–85*. Berkeley: University of California Press.

Seidman, Gay W. 2000. "Blurred Lines: Nonviolence in South Africa." *PS: Political Science and Politics* (June), pp. 161–167.

Seidman, Gay W. 2001. "Guerrillas in Their Midst." *Mobilization* 6(2): pp. 111–127.

Sharp, Gene. 1973. *The Politics of Nonviolent Action*. 3 volumes. Boston: Porter Sargent Publishers.

Shepard, Mark. 2001. *Mahatma Gandhi and His Myths*. Los Angeles: Simple Productions.

Shivers, Lynne. 1980. "Inside the Iranian Revolution." In *Tell the American People: Perspectives on the Iranian Revolution*, ed. David H. Albert. Philadelphia: Movement for a New Society, pp. 58–80.

Shivers, Lynne. 1997. "Iranian Revolution, 1963–1979." In *Protest, Power, and Change: An Encyclopedia of Nonviolent Action from ACT-UP to Women's Suffrage*, ed. Roger S. Powers and William B. Vogele. New York: Garland Publishing, pp. 263–266.

Smithey, Lee, and Lester Kurtz. 1999. " 'We Have Bare Hands': Nonviolent Social Movements in the Soviet Bloc." In *Nonviolent Social Movements: A Geographical Perspective*, ed. Stephen Zunes, Lester R. Kurtz, and Sarah Beth Asher. Malden, MA: Blackwell Publishers, pp. 96–124.

Tilly, Charles. 1993. *European Revolutions, 1492–1992*. Cambridge, MA: Blackwell Publishers.

Zunes, Stephen. 1999a. "The Role of Non-Violent Action in the Downfall of Apartheid." *Journal of Modern African Studies* 37(1): pp. 137–169.

Zunes, Stephen. 1999b. "The Origins of People Power in the Philippines." In *Nonviolent Social Movements: A Geographical Perspective*, ed. Stephen Zunes, Lester R. Kurtz, and Sarah Beth Asher. Malden, MA: Blackwell Publishers. pp. 129–157.

Zunes, Stephen, Lester R. Kurtz, and Sarah Beth Asher. 1999. *Nonviolent Social Movements: A Geographical Perspective*. Malden, MA: Blackwell Publishers.

BERNARD E. BROWN

20   *Revolution and Anomie*

THE CRISES OF MODERNIZATION

One fruitful way of studying the complex process of modernization is to view it as a series of crises or challenges, to which a number of different responses are possible. A distinction can be made

SOURCE: Bernard E. Brown, *Protest in Paris: Anatomy of a Revolt* (Morristown, NJ: General Learning Press, 1974), pp. 212–222. By permission.

among the crises of legitimacy, participation, and tension-management (occurring roughly in that chronological order). As European societies went through the experience of modernization they necessarily had to cope with each of these crises. Feudal societies could not survive the Enlightenment, and the concept of divine right gave way to more rational theories of political legitimacy. With industrialization new groups emerged (an energetic entrepreneurial class, a managerial and clerical class, and a massive working class), and the existing political elites somehow had to deal with the demands of these new groups and integrate them into the political system. As the European economy became more complex each national society had to devise a system of controls, enabling it to coordinate the activities of increasingly-specialized associations.

Nothing is fated to work out in favor of modernization in any of these crises. Revolt against the monarchy may be crushed; reactionary forces may overthrow a republic and reestablish monarchy; new or greatly expanded social groups, in particular the working class, may not be effectively integrated into the political system; and a society may be unable to cope with the problems of coordination. But punishment for failure is severe. A country that falls behind is likely to come under the influence or even the rule of those who have been more successful in meeting these challenges.

Each of the crises of modernization has posed serious problems for the French. Take, for example, the crisis of legitimacy. One of the basic assumptions of modernization theory is that as a society becomes more complex, the values serving to legitimize political authority become more rational. Or, rather than imply any causal relationship, rationalization of authority proceeds along with industrialization and increasing complexity of social structure. This assumption is borne out in a striking manner by the French experience, because of the great divide of the Revolution of 1789. The Tennis Court Oath, the August decrees abolishing feudalism, and the Declaration of the Rights of Man and Citizen marked an irrevocable break with absolutism and feudalism, and signaled the emergence of more rational principles of political legitimacy. Although France was converted almost overnight into a modern state as regards its official pattern of legitimacy, it did not thereby achieve a large popular consensus on its basic institutions. The revolution was repudiated by conservatives, and the revolutionaries were themselves divided. The result was a long period of constitutional instability. The transformation of French society continued. But the way in which the French tackled the successive crises of modernization was drastically affected by inability to agree on political structures. In the first great crisis of modernization in France, bursting forth in the Revolution of 1789 but continuing to this day, intransigence rather than compromise became characteristic of the political process.

Dissensus carried over from one historical phase to another. When the French turned to the problem of integrating the working class into the political system a pattern of rejection, opposition, and violence had already taken hold and made it more difficult (though not impossible) to formulate policy. The French working and business classes, from the outset, have been reluctant to bargain with each other—although compelled to do so by circumstances. The heritage of class distrust and conflict continues to interfere with the smooth functioning of the political system. That 20 to 25 percent of the electorate votes fairly consistently for the Communist Party, and that the Communist-led CGT is the most powerful of the French trade unions, are indications of profound dissatisfaction within the French working class. In turn, exclusion of the Communist Party from governing coalitions drives the political balance to the right, placing the working class at a disadvantage in the political process and further intensifying feelings of class consciousness and alienation from the political system. Without having completely resolved the crises of legitimacy and participation, the French have plunged into the later phase of modernization, for the alternative is national decline. But the carry-over of dissensus creates friction and grievances throughout the society. Much of the May Revolt—in particular the readiness of masses of students, workers, and even professionals to defect—can be explained by the relative failure of the French, compared with other industrial nations, to cope with successive crises of modernization.

However, revolutionary dissent combined with an intensive destructive urge is a general trend among students and middle class intellectuals in all liberal-industrial societies today. The May Revolt never could have begun in a stagnant or traditional society. It came about in the first place only because, despite all the difficulties in their way, the French managed to create an advanced industrial nation by 1968. We are led to the paradoxical conclusion that not only the failures, but also the very *success* of a society in meeting the challenges of modernization may lead to its own downfall.

ANOMIE

Accompanying modernization in France, and every-where else, is the phenomenon of *anomie*—a term popularized almost a century ago by Emile Durkheim. We have already encountered explanations of the May Revolt along the lines of Durkheim's theory, for example in Raymond Aron's *La révolution introuvable,* and the remarks of Georges Pompidou (before the National Assembly on May 14, 1968) and of General de Gaulle (during the television interview with Michel Droit on June 7, 1968). Durkheim asserted that the appetites and desires of men are infinite and that every society must impose a discipline or "regulator" in order to survive. In traditional society the family and religion constitute the regulator. Every person knows his role in family and religious activities; his desires are limited by his own perception of social status. But when a traditional society breaks up, the family structure and the church are brought into question. New values and new social structures arise (science, the republic, the corporation, the university, and so on); but frequently the individual in transition cannot accept them. Caught between the traditional and modern forms, his reactions may be those of resignation (ranging from apathy to suicide) or of rage against established authority. It is Durkheim's great insight that every modern society carries within itself the seeds of its own destruction. The more the individual is encouraged by society to realize his individuality, the greater is the risk that he will reject discipline and become perpetually discontent.[1]

The "anomic" reaction to social change in France has taken the form of violent opposition to the modern state and to urban industrial life. Hostility to industrial life has been especially vigorous in France among artists and writers, who have drawn a sharp contrast between bucolic nature and the polluted inhumanity of cities. As we have seen, under the influence of Proudhon and Bakunin, French anarchists have traditionally celebrated the glories of village and farm society. Such literary movements as Dada and surrealism have questioned science, rationality, and modern society, exulting instead in the gesture of the child, the unpredictable happening, and the immediate gratification of desires. The anarchist, dadaist, and surrealist traditions resurfaced in the May Revolt with astonishing force.

The anomic opposition to modernization is only one form of protest against poverty and exploitation. The dominant wing of the global revolutionary movement fully accepts modernization, though not through capitalism. The goal is to eliminate the capitalist, not science and technology—to base socialism on a modern, not a primitive economy. The question of whether to fight against exploitation by recapturing the spirit of traditional societies, or by transcending that spirit altogether has been a running controversy among revolutionaries ever since the Industrial Revolution started, and was especially pressing in May 1968.

Anomie is an unexpected consequence of the ability of modern societies to triumph over obstacles that seemed insurmountable a century ago. The development of science and technology has resulted in extraordinary increases in economic production and national wealth, in France and elsewhere; and though income differentials persist, it would require an excessive devotion to 19th-century Marxist texts to believe that workers in France, Britain, the United States, or any other industrial society have become increasingly miserable and impoverished in the past hundred years. There are always enough grave instances of social injustice, no matter how productive an economy, to inspire any number of protest movements—but this cannot account for the astonishing spurt of revolutionary activity in all modern societies today.

It is not only poverty that causes protest and revolt in a modern society, but also prosperity—a fatal defect in societies whose very rationale is to create more wealth. Poverty, however lamentable may be its consequences for individuals, is a school for discipline. A man fearful of losing his job because he will cease to eat is remarkably receptive to commands from his superiors. He may rebel from time to time but even in revolt he continues to carry out orders. In contrast, prosperity gives people the illusion that they are totally independent of others, that any obstacles can be overcome by an effort of individual will. When life is easy there is no reason to obey commands and no penalty for insubordination or indiscipline. When an individual successfully defies one authority he is tempted to defy another, and another, until finally the very notion of authority becomes unbearable. Prosperity unaccompanied by a strong sense of social responsibility undermines collective effort and may undo a society.[2]

The possibility of the dissolution of social discipline is especially great when wealth increases suddenly or when opportunities open up for a previously depressed class of people. It was precisely this kind of change in the condition of life that fascinated Durkheim from the time he first noticed that suicide rates increase sharply along with the progress of civilization. It is the dream of the poor that sudden wealth (winning first prize in the national lottery, an unexpected inheritance, a fabulous marriage) will open wide the gates of paradise—and in some cases it may. But the struggle to be successful may be more satisfying than success itself, in all walks of life. It is classic that the writer or artist who finally gains recognition after many years of effort goes through a crisis of confidence, fearing that he cannot repeat his success or, worse, so disappointed with the fruits of success that going on seems pointless. Similarly, the active businessman thrives on his work, telling himself that his goal is to retire young and enjoy life, only to discover later that he is incapable of savoring an existence without the challenge of work.

When the moorings of a society give way, everything goes—social discipline, political authority, the incentive to produce, and sometimes the incentive to live. As Durkheim perceptively remarked, "one cannot remain in contemplation before a vacuum without being progressively drawn into it."[3] He had in mind primarily suicide; lesser variations on the same theme are to "drop out" of normal society or to escape the real world through the use of drugs. This form of anomic behavior is especially noticeable among the children of parents who themselves had to work hard to succeed. The corroding effect of prosperity is most evident at one remove.

Once in a condition of anomie, the individual may react in altogether unforeseeable ways. One tendency, we have noted, is toward renunciation, withdrawal, loss of zest for life, or suicide. But, as is stressed by Durkheim in a less well-known part of his analysis, anomie gives birth to a state of exasperation and irritated lassitude, "which can, depending upon circumstances, turn the individual against himself or against other."[4] He was referring not only to the extreme cases of suicide and homicide, but also to alternating political attitudes of apathy and violent attacks upon authority, the attempt either to escape from reality or to destroy it. Apathy and terrorism are related aspects of the same continuing reaction to modernization.

The May Revolt displayed many of the characteristics of the instability characterized by Durkheim as anomie. It took place in a society that had just experienced 20 years of unprecedented economic growth and that was more prosperous than at any other time of its history. Poverty and injustice had hardly been eliminated, but the workers scraping along on the minimum wage, and other unfavored groups, took no initiatives and even throughout the general strike remained primarily concerned with improvement of material conditions rather than with revolution. Those who were in the forefront of the revolutionary movement were precisely those labeled by Durkheim as prime candidates for anomie—the children of the newly prosperous middle classes. It is significant that the most raucous and undisciplined campus in the entire French university system was Nanterre, whose students are drawn from the comfortable sections of the west of Paris. It was striking that students from modest backgrounds were more interested in their own social mobility than in abstract revolution in May.[5] Also noteworthy was the interaction and in many cases interchangeability between the two related anomic tendencies of apathy and rage. Once they had lost their ties to French society, many students and others glided back and forth between a diffuse counter-culture of dropouts and organized revolutionary groups. Extreme individualism blossomed into extreme collectivism only to disintegrate again upon meeting the slightest resistance. Those who wanted to escape all authority and those who wanted to impose iron discipline upon everyone else were the two marching wings of the revolutionary coalition; the ease with which many people switched from one to the other called attention to anomie as the common element of the diverse revolutionary groups.[6]

The May Revolt highlights in dramatic fashion the existence of a new dimension in the continuing crisis of participation or "entry into politics" of important social groups. Anomie was Durkheim's formulation of the problem of integrating the middle and working classes into political systems that had previously been dominated by a landed aristocracy. He saw that the working class was becoming increasingly isolated from the owning class. The life style of the capitalists was more and more remote from the reality of workday experience. A point is reached where it is beyond the capacity of workers and capitalists even to understand each other. He later broadened the meaning of anomie to include the lack of purpose in life under capitalism where individuals are engaged in the single-minded pursuit of wealth.[7]

In later stages of industrialization the social force undergoing the greatest rate of expansion is the intellectual class—the scientists, engineers, technicians, administrators, and so on—who receive their training in scientific institutes and universities. This newly massive intellectual class follows in the tradition of its predecessors by making demands upon the political system. Just as hereditary monarchy was repudiated by the bourgeoisie, and parliamentary democracy questioned by the revolutionary wing of the working class, so many intellectuals find the dominant liberal synthesis inadequate. Liberalism seems to many to be a cover for the supremacy of money or numbers. Intellectuals are uncomfortable with political values that give an advantage to the wealthy and to demagogues. The life style of the intellectuals is also distinctive. In Durkheims's sense, many intellectuals are in a condition of anomie because they are increasingly isolated from the rest of society.

In addition, a certain amount of alienation is generated simply because there is a confrontation between an existing elite and a rising social group. At every stage of the modernizing process there is an anomic reaction due to the weakening of traditional values and the failure of the new values to replace them. The conflict between old and new norms must affect the intellectuals in the scientific civilization, as it affected workers in the industrial civilization. Just as the assembly line provoked irritation and revolt among workers, so the organization of social activity on the basis of scientific and rational criteria creates a feeling of "dehumanization" in many intellectuals. It is to be expected that a certain number of individuals will be left, at least during a transitional period, in a state of normlessness, or "deregulation." Those who repudiate the old and fear or disdain to accept the new display the symptoms of anomie.

That there should be an anomic reaction to modernization among intellectuals is not unusual; but the depth and intensity of this reaction—expressing itself in withdrawal and rage, political apathy and political terrorism—is startling. Why should the mass of anomie increase so sharply? At least three reasons may be suggested.

First, a large number of people break under the greater strain. In a scientific civilization there necessarily are rigorous standards of education and performance. There is no short cut to acquisition of scientific knowledge. Those who are not capable of acquiring this knowledge, or are not sufficiently motivated, fall by the wayside. Furthermore, the amount of knowledge to be mastered is increasing at an enormous rate, and with it the pressure on students. While examinations and student anxiety have always existed, in the past there have also been many ways of getting ahead on the basis of a modest education. When the major avenue to success is the university, those who cannot meet its demands are at a greater disadvantage than ever before.

Secondly, the productivity of the scientific civilization makes it possible to carry a marginal element within the society. Technically, it is feasible for any advanced industrial society to support a large class of dropouts and drones—provided that this class remains within manageable bounds and does not deprive the productive classes of their motivation to work. Many young people are able to enjoy—or endure—a life of anomie with the bemused support of their parents. Poverty is a highly effective social technique for imposing limits on anomie; prosperity, however, creates the conditions for the existence of a large alienated group.

Freedom itself may be a major cause of anomie in the intellectual class. Modernization makes possible a great expansion of individual freedom. As Durkheim points out, primitive man is merely an extension of the group, hemmed in by custom and taboo. He has no mind of his own. Modern man enjoys greater autonomy and is free to think as he pleases.[8] But the heavy responsibility of making a free choice can be utterly demoralizing, leading either to a desire to escape or to revolt. In authoritarian regimes the masses and the intellectuals can be conditioned, mobilized, and commanded. Problems may not actually be solved, but the individual is relieved of the burden of choice. The disorder inherent in liberalism and the scientific civilization is eliminated. Anomic groups serve as pile drivers, splitting the foundations of the liberal state. Authoritarian elites pick up the pieces and impose the discipline that so many desperately crave.

In the scientific civilization what Durkheim called the "regulator" is more essential than ever. The intellectual must be imaginative, creative, and even enthusiastic if the collective scientific enterprise is to flourish. Doubts, hesitation, and withdrawal will block the system. The political integration of the intellectual class may well prove to be inherently more difficult than was the case for the capitalist and working classes. The landed aristocrats and capitalists were numerically weak in relation to the rest of the society and could be outmaneuvered in politics. But while the working class had the advantage of numbers, its function within the economy was to carry out orders rather than to give them, to obey rather than to innovate. As a class the workers were unable to direct themselves, let alone the rest of society. The intellectual class is not subject to the same handicaps. Unlike the old aristocrats or the capitalists, intellectuals are a large social force. Unlike the workers, they have ability, inculcated by their social function, to direct and command.

The question may be raised whether parliamentary democracies like France can cope with the entry of the intellectuals as a massive social force into the political system. Wherever freedom of criticism is permitted, opportunities for exploiting tensions are almost unlimited. In a climate of freedom the intellectuals are even more likely to rebel than the old working class, and more likely to withdraw their cooperation from the establishment. The parliamentary democracies that experienced great difficulty in securing the integration of the working class probably will continue to be unstable as they move into the scientific civilization and deal with the intellectual class. Even relatively consensual parliamentary democracies may have difficulty in adjusting to these new circumstances. It may well be that integration of the intellectuals into the political system can be accomplished only by an authoritarian elite (whether of the left or right) in order to eliminate that anarchy which is incompatible with the continued functioning and further development of a scientific civilization.

We are living through an era of reversal of values and of social relationship perhaps best comprehended through Hegel's parable of the master and the servant in which the servant, compelled to live by his work, becomes self-reliant, while the master comes to depend completely on the servant. Thus, capitalists may be overturned proletarians, any dominant group may be subverted by any dominated group, the most contradictory and unforeseen developments may occur in the unfolding of history.

Most social scientists postulate that science is sweeping all before it, thrusting aside magic, superstition, and religion, bringing about the rationalization of social behavior, laying the basis for modern industry, unprecedented prosperity, and the full flowering of human freedom. In the model modern society it is assumed that the ideological conflict of early industrialization will be transcended and replaced by pragmatic negotiation among claimant groups for larger shares of ever increasing national revenues. The long-term trend would thus be toward stability, prosperity, and freedom. But, through an irony of history, mastery can be converted into dependence, political trends can be reversed. A complex economy can be paralyzed by the determined opposition of relatively few people in key positions. An abundance of material wealth can lead to dissipation of individual motivation and disintegration of social ties. The privilege of exercising a free choice can turn into an agony. From stability may come instability, from prosperity may come misery, and out of freedom may come a new and fearful discipline.

ENDNOTES

1. For Durkheim's views on anomie: *De la division du travail social*, Paris: Presses Universitaires de France, 1967, 8th ed., pp. 343–365; and *Le suicide*, Paris: Presses Universitaires de France, 1960, pp. 264–311. An excellent contemporary interpretation is in Robert M. MacIver, *The Ramparts We Guard*, New York: Macmillan, 1950.

2. On the connection between poverty-wealth and discipline-anomie, see the suggestive comments of Durkheim in *Le suicide*, p. 282. Note also Raoul Vaneigem's call for a revolt against prosperity, in *Traité de savoir-vivre à l'usage des jeunes générations*, Paris: Gallimard, 1967, pp. 73, 88–91.

3. E. Durkheim, *Le suicide*, p. 316.

4. Durkheim quote on the link between suicide and homicide, *Le suicide*, p. 322. See also, ibid., p. 408, and on the correspondence between suicide-homicide and apathy-terrorism, ibid., p. 424.

5. That revolutionary students came in large proportion from "comfortable" situations is remarked by R. Boudon, "Quelques causes de la révolte estudiantine," *La Table Ronde* (Dec. 1968–Jan. 1969), no. 252, p. 180. Also generously represented are Jews—corresponding to Durkheim's category of previously depressed groups suddenly enjoying new opportunities for advancement. Alain Krivine has publicly charged that the French police are now using Vichy records because so many Jews are in the New Left.

6. We have previously commented on the way in which surrealists suddenly became Communists or Trotskyists, and just as suddenly returned to anarchism. Note the recent overnight conversion of a leading American activist to an Eastern religion. In a press conference reported by the *New York Times* (May 6, 1973) one of the "Chicago 7" defendants, Rennie Davis, relates that during a flight to Paris on his way to meet Vietcong negotiators in January 1973 he heard about a 15-year-old guru in India called Maharaj Ji. His immediate reaction was skepticism and even hostility. But he went to India and after eight days "received knowledge" from a disciple of the guru, whom he now calls "the one perfect master" on earth at this time. Although at first uncomfortable with the boy (who was about 10 years old at the time of the Chicago riots), Mr. Davis told the press conference that he now loved him. "I would cross the planet on my hands and knees," he said, "to touch his toe." The guru has been under investigation by the government of India on the charge of smuggling money, jewels and watches (all gifts from devoted followers) into the country.

7. For general treatments of the "entry into politics" problem, see T. H. Marshall, *Citizenship and Social Class*, Cambridge: Cambridge University Press, 1950; S. M. Lipset, *Political Man*, Garden City, N.Y.: Doubleday Publishing, 1960; Reinhard Bendix, *Nation-Building and Citizenship*, New York: John Wiley, 1964; Barrington Moore, Jr., *Social Origins of Dictatorship and Democracy*, Boston: Beacon Press, 1967; and J. G. LaPalombara and M. Weiner, ed., *Political Parties and Political Development*, Princeton: Princeton University Press, 1966.

8. For Durkheim's views on freedom in primitive and modern societies, Cf. *De la division du travail social*, pp. 35–102. See also Alvin Toffler, *Future Shock*, New York: Bantam Books, 1971, pp. 98, 319–322.

PART TWO

Patterns of Legitimacy

An indispensable condition for the efficient functioning of political systems is widespread acceptance of the decision-making process—which we shall call "consensus." Wherever this kind of consensus exists, the state itself becomes legitimized. Legitimacy and consensus are key indicators of the effectiveness and performance of the system and conversely of the existence of basic instabilities that may undermine it. Ultimately, the phenomenon of government—what Mosca calls "the political fact"—is a matter of will as well as force; that is, political relations are willed relations.

POLITICAL AUTHORITY

One aspect of legitimacy is the use of the power of the state by officials in accordance with prearranged and agreed-upon rules. A legitimate act is also legal, but a lawful command is not always legitimate. For example, the commands issued by the Nazi government in Germany were legal, and presumably subordinate officials down to the private soldier or individual citizen had to obey them. But at the same time, these orders violated a code of civilized behavior and morality that brought into question their legitimacy. Legality refers to the letter of the law as decreed by a state organ, whereas legitimacy involves the very character of the state and the substance and purpose of a legal enactment. But who will decide when there is a difference between legality and legitimacy? No clear answer can be given. On the one hand, the state always claims legitimacy for its legal commands: "What is pleasing to the prince has the force of law," according to an old axiom of the Romans. On the other hand, many individuals see a higher law beyond the formal law of the state. Ultimately, they obey their own conscience and consider some acts of the state to be illegitimate; this is the justification of civil disobedience as advocated by Thoreau, Tolstoy, and Gandhi.

But these extreme formulations are hypothetical. In actual political life, legality, legitimacy, and consent *tend* to converge. Consensus is more than agreement; it denotes acceptance of a given political system. Acceptance may be due to individual consent stemming from recognition of the beneficent purposes of the state; acceptance is also the product of tradition and habit. Consensus is generally addressed to the basic rules that establish, define, limit, and channel political power—that is, to the constitution. It is not limited to specific laws or specific acts of the government, or even to governmental forms. Consensus transforms power into authority, and the legal enactments emanating from the government into legitimate orders.

Democratic theory postulates canons of legitimacy that clarify the distinctions we are trying to make. Force can be used only in accordance with certain previously agreed-upon procedures. There is an elaborate setting of limitations upon the exercise of power, which can be used only by persons elevated to office through elections. Individuals agree to the basic rules so long as they are not violated. The government derives its authority from these basic rules; whenever disagreements about the government and its policies erupt, they are resolved through popular choice. The substance of political life, therefore, is the consensus—or "agreement on fundamentals"—that binds the citizens into an organized common political life.

The contract theory as developed by John Locke is a classic formulation of this consensual model. According to it, the formation of a political community is an act of will embodying the cardinal rule that the majority of the people, acting through their legislature, govern. However, property rights and individual freedoms may not be infringed upon by the majority, and there must be periodic free elections of the legislative body. In such a political community, a minority can be coerced only in order to implement the basic agreement entered into by the whole community. But such coercion cannot be used to destroy or silence the minority. The consensus on a free and open society gives the majority the right to act while allowing the minority the right to protest peacefully and ultimately to appeal to the community at large in favor of its positions—in other words, the right to become the majority. This model, then, incorporates the obligation to obey and the right to protest, criticize, and oppose. It allows the force of the state to be transformed into authority, deriving its legitimacy from the basic agreement. Individual dissent is expressed not in disobedience, but through organized opposition seeking to present alternative policies. Thus, opposition in the democratic scheme is harnessed to the total political system, which is strengthened, not weakened, by dissent.

The model helps us to see more clearly the distinctions between force and authority, consensus and legitimacy. It also has analytic value in calling our attention to the conditions under which consensus is likely to emerge or be disrupted. But many political systems at present are not based on the Lockean model. Force rather than authority is frequently the rule, and this is an indication of a lack of consensus binding the citizens together. More important, values other than free elections, including national or ethnic identity, may serve to legitimize the state. Political decisions may be accepted by a population for a variety of reasons. Freely given consent is only one basis of legitimacy, and in the modern world is not universal.

CONSENSUS BUILDING

The contract theory that Locke used to illustrate the formation of a political community—all citizens agree to form it through a solemn compact—is a fiction or simply an illustration with no historical foundation. It holds that, under certain conditions, a state of mind develops among a given people to establish a set of fundamental rules about the manner in which they would cooperate and live peacefully together. But what accounts for such a state of mind? And why was it reached in some societies and not in others? When and under what conditions does a community become a political one accepting a common agreement?

There are no simple answers to these questions, but some general indications may be given. First, there must be a fairly extensive acceptance of common norms of social conduct. Customs must begin to develop—even become everyday habits—before we can begin to talk of a community. Second, social behavior must be predictable, at least to the extent that makes human intercourse possible. Third, a political community requires common expectations of material benefits for all members. The utilitarian argument was put forward by Thomas Hobbes and, later, more persuasively by

James Mill and John Stuart Mill. Put simply, this means that the chances for achieving consensus are greater in political communities that enjoy economic prosperity.

Finally, the role of the elite is crucial in the formation of consensus. It is axiomatic that leadership is always lodged in the hands of a few. In all countries that have experienced the Industrial Revolution, rule by a relatively small traditional elite was challenged by new groups, in particular the bourgeoisie and the working class. This was a momentous period in the evolution of political systems, because claims to political leadership had to be subordinated to the requirements of popular participation and support. Two developments can be discerned. In some cases, the ruling groups became restrictive and negative, attempting to thwart participation and to maintain themselves in a position of control and leadership through the use of repressive measures. In other cases they became permissive and supportive, allowing their claims to leadership to be qualified and indeed ultimately subverted by new symbols, forms, and practices deriving from popular participation. The greater the degree of permissiveness on the part of the traditional elite, the smoother was the transition to a consensual and participant society; the greater their tendency to reject newcomers, the more difficult and the less likely was the emergence of consensus.

In Britain, for example, ever increasing participation and influence was offered to the citizenry at large throughout the nineteenth century. But in Russia, despite some half-hearted reforms, autocratic rule was maintained. The result was that in Britain the people began to value and accept their system as an instrument for the satisfaction of their wants, whereas the rising groups in Russia either rejected their government or remained apathetic to it. In the one case, consensus was built; in the other, its very preconditions were denied. Thus, we may postulate that the congruence between mass demands for participation and influence and a positive elite response to these demands is a fundamental condition for the development of consensus.

This hypothesis is equally relevant for developing societies today. Throughout Asia, Latin America, and Africa, many of the preconditions of consensus—the sense of national identity, compatibility of values, and predictability of behavior—are lacking. In all these societies demands for material progress have been stimulated. The role of the elite then becomes critical for the development of political consensus. Rejection of new groups may lead to sharp conflict between the few and the many, and to a state of virtual civil war. Complete permissiveness, on the other hand, may thrust unprepared and unqualified groups into power prematurely. Inability to advance industrialization produces popular disenchantment and apathy.

We have emphasized the relationship between mass and elite under conditions of economic modernization in order to illustrate the complexity of the phenomenon rather than to identify it as a single causal factor. For the very attitude of the elite—whether it is permissive and open or restrictive and negative—in turn depends upon many other historical and social factors. Common linguistic or religious bonds, prolonged community life behind natural barriers that deter attack or invasion, feelings of ethnic or racial identity, continuing economic progress, and the impact of technology and science upon the society are all factors that we subsumed earlier under the general terms of common values, predictability of behavior, and perception of common material benefits. It is only when these factors materialize at the proper time that the conditions for consensus also emerge and that the Lockean model is relevant.

Consensus is always under stress, even in systems with a long tradition of legitimacy. Efforts to create an independent Quebec, the conflict between the Flemish and Walloons in Belgium, the appearance of a black power movement in the United States, Irish and Scottish nationalism in the United Kingdom, and Corsican and Basque separatism in France and Spain are all threats to the basic consensus in previously stable systems. In these cases, dissidence stems from the conditions we have discussed—repressive or rejective measures by the elite and a relative inability to fulfill the demands for economic well-being aroused by the elite themselves and the ideology prevalent in the whole system. A theory of consensus therefore can be used to assess and to measure degrees of alienation, including the emergence of revolutionary situations.

The processes of socialization and politicization—whereby individuals are conditioned to accept their society and government—are of special importance in consensus building. Through ceremony, ritual, and outright indoctrination, the young learn to cherish their national community and their political system. The manner in which national history is taught and the emphasis upon the unique and superior traits of the national culture are calculated to create an emotional acceptance of the political system.

In many societies there is a tradition of unrest and political alienation among university students, though radical students of middle-class backgrounds frequently tend to be absorbed readily into the system once they complete their studies and enter the job market. But revolutions can rarely, if ever, be traced to intergenerational strife. Disagreement about norms and symbols of authority is sharp, and the young are inducted into a system that is embroiled in conflict. The agencies of socialization, including the family, school, and church, cultivate contradictory ideas involving the very nature and character of the system itself. Revolutions stem from discontinuities in historical development and basic divisions within the society that split the generations internally. In revolutionary situations, consensus is already undermined.

Analysis of any aspect of a given political system—such as interest groups, parties, ideologies, decision making, and administration—always leads back to the critical question of consensus.

CHAPTER SIX

DEMOCRACIES

As the scientific revolution progressed in the 18th and 19th centuries the intellectual basis for hereditary rule eroded. The legitimacy of the state had to be placed on a more rational basis involving directly or ultimately the principle of popular sovereignty. Weber conceptualized this development as a contrast between traditional and rational-legal rule. But modernization does not lead inexorably to the creation of stable, consensual, effective democracies. Representative governments may be paralyzed by internal strife and incapable of meeting social needs. A majority may support policies that deprive minorities of their rights. The people may vest their power in or support an authoritarian leader, as happened, for example, in England (Oliver Cromwell), France (Napoleon Bonaparte, Louis Napoleon, Philippe Pétain), Italy (Benito Mussolini), Germany (Adolf Hitler), and Russia (Lenin and Stalin).

The fall of the Berlin Wall in 1989, leading to the overthrow of communist rule in East Germany and its subsequent integration into the Federal Republic, has been called the triumph of Max Weber over Karl Marx. With the collapse of the Soviet Union and communist regimes throughout Eastern Europe, the trend away from authoritarianism and toward democracy seemed to be a vindication of the Western model of democracy, rule of law, and mixed economy. But François Furet (see his essay in the preceding chapter) points out that democratic promises are difficult if not impossible to fulfill. Many people will always be disappointed or dissatisfied under any regime. Advanced democracies are real societies, not utopias in which all problems dissolve. Economic growth is always uneven; social disparities can increase; unemployment may be stubbornly resistant; the role of money in politics distorts the electoral process; and corruption and scandals are always in the news. Pharr, Putnam, and Dalton report that public confidence in democratic institutions has declined in most advanced democracies in the past two or three decades. Are the democracies themselves at risk? Dalton, Scarrow, and Cain take the analysis to another level, asking what can be done to strengthen democracy. Should we search for new institutional forms of representation and public participation? Would democracies be less governable if they become more participative? Do citizens have the capacity and the civic virtue to participate directly in making political decisions? One of the most important experiments in recent times to institute "worker democracy" was carried out under the Socialist government in France in 1982. No one case study is sufficient to prove or disprove general theories; nonetheless, the case of the Auroux laws is a large slice of empirical reality, and offers an interesting test of the theory of participatory democracy. Did workers seize the opportunity offered them to express grievances and share actively in management decisions? If not, why not? May any conclusions be drawn from this episode concerning the capacity of masses of people to displace elites and take charge of their own destinies?

....

SUSAN J. PHARR, ROBERT D. PUTNAM, and RUSSELL J. DALTON

21   Trouble in the Advanced Democracies?

A quarter-century ago, Michel J. Crozier, Samuel P. Huntington, and Joji Watanuki argued that the nations of Europe, North America, and Japan confronted a "crisis of democracy."[1] Their starting point was a vision, widespread during the 1960s and 1970s, of "a bleak future for democratic government," an image of "the disintegration of civil order, the breakdown of social discipline, the debility of leaders, and the alienation of citizens."

The central thesis of the subtle, nuanced, and wide-ranging analysis by Crozier, Huntington, and Watanuki (hereafter CH&W) was that the Trilateral democracies were becoming overloaded by increasingly insistent demands from an ever-expanding array of participants, raising fundamental issues of governability. Within that common framework, the three authors offered somewhat distinct diagnoses of the problems facing their respective regions. In Europe, Crozier emphasized the upwelling of social mobilization, the collapse of traditional institutions and values, the resulting loss of social control, and governments' limited room for maneuver. Huntington asserted that

America was swamped by a "democratic surge" that had produced political polarization, demands for more equality and participation, and less effective political parties and government. His provocative therapy was to "restore the balance" between democracy and governability. By contrast, Watanuki argued that Japan did not (yet?) face problems of "excessive" democracy, thanks in part to rapid economic growth and in part to its larger reservoir of traditional values. Whatever the regional and national nuances, however, the authors sketched a grim outlook for democracy in the Trilateral countries: delegitimated leadership, expanded demands, overloaded government, political competition that was both intensified and fragmented, and public pressures leading to nationalistic parochialism.

In historical perspective, the sense of crisis that permeated *The Crisis of Democracy* may have reflected the confluence of two factors: first, the surge of radical political activism that swept the advanced industrial democracies in the 1960s, which began with the civil rights and antiwar movements in United States and was then echoed in the events of May 1968 in France, Italy's "Hot Autumn" later that year, and student upheavals in Japan; and second, the economic upheavals triggered by the oil crisis of 1973–74 that were to result in more than a decade of higher inflation, slower growth, and, in many countries, worsening unemployment. The Trilateral

SOURCE: Susan J. Pharr, Robert D. Putnam, and Russell J. Dalton, "A Quarter-Century of Declining Confidence," *Journal of Democracy*, vol. 11, no 2 (April 2000), pp. 5–25. © National Endowment for Democracy and The John Hopkins University Press. Reprinted with permission of The Johns Hopkins University Press. Statistical tables and footnotes abridged by the Editor.

governments were thus trapped between rising demands from citizens and declining resources to meet those demands. Moreover, the legitimacy of governments was suspect in the eyes of a generation whose motto was: "Question Authority." CH&W warned that these ominous developments posed a threat to democracy itself.

A quarter-century is an opportune interval after which to revisit the issue of the performance of our democratic institutions. The intervening years have witnessed many important developments in our domestic societies, economies, and polities, as well as in the international setting.

Most dramatic of all, of course, was the end of the Cold War, symbolized by the fall of the Berlin Wall in 1989. If it did not signal the end of history, the removal of the communist threat surely did mark the end of a historical epoch. It transformed the fundamental underpinnings of security alliances and eliminated the principal philosophical and geopolitical challenge to liberal democracy and the market economy. In some of the Trilateral countries it also coincided with, and to some extent triggered, an intellectual and ideological revolution. In each country it transformed domestic political calculations and alignments in ways that are still being played out.

Economically, the decades that followed the appearance of the CH&W volume were distinctly less happy than those that preceded it. The oil shocks of 1973–74 and 1979–80 drew the curtain on that fortunate early-postwar combination of high growth, low inflation, and low unemployment. Although economists differ on the origins of the pervasive slowdown, virtually all econometric analyses confirm the view of the man and woman in the street: Western economies took a turn for the worse around 1973–74, and recovery was a slow and uncertain process. The immediate inflationary effects of the oil crises were overcome by means of stringent monetary policies, but the economic malaise continued. In subsequent years, Europe had unprecedentedly high structural unemployment, the United States endured sharply reduced rates of real wage growth, and after 1992 Japan experienced the longest recession in the country's postwar history.

"Interdependence" was already widely discussed in the early 1970s, and integration of the world economy has continued at a rapid pace in the years since then. International trade has grown faster than gross domestic products, and foreign investment more rapidly than either of them. Western economies are even more porous internationally now than when CH&W wrote, and our economic fates are even more intertwined. Nowhere is this more true, of course, than in Europe: The European Union has taken shape and extended its reach to an increasing number of policy domains with stunning speed. Moreover, the rise of newly industrializing economies challenges the competitiveness of all the Trilateral countries. Finally, immigration from the less-developed to the more-developed nations of the world has accelerated, creating new difficulties and social tensions.

Socially and culturally, these decades have witnessed significant change. Increased mobility and growing individuation have eroded traditional family and community ties. Some observers believe that the decline in respect for authority that CH&W underscored has continued apace in all sectors of society; others see evidence of increased tolerance of diversity. The role of women in economic life (and to some extent in public life more generally) has grown. The expansion of higher education during the 1950s and 1960s continues to boost the university-educated share of the electorate. The electronic media have transformed how we spend our leisure time as well as how we follow public affairs. In many of our cities, the problems of drugs, crime, homelessness, and blight are even more visible now than a quarter-century ago. Finally, older people occupy a growing share of the population in all Trilateral countries, which is certain to have major consequences for both social and economic policy in the decades to come.

THE TRILATERAL DEMOCRACIES TODAY

When *The Crisis of Democracy* appeared, citizens in the Trilateral world were still primarily concerned about market failure in sectors as diverse as social services, culture, and the environment. Demands for government intervention to redress those failures were ascendant. This ideological climate fed the preoccupation of CH&W with governability. As symbolized by the advent of Thatcher, Reagan, Nakasone, Kohl, and similar figures elsewhere, however, public concern had shifted by the early 1980s from *market* failure to *government* failure. Responding to and in part encouraging this sea change in public opinion, conservative leaders proposed a reduced role for government, and this ideological shift to the right was accelerated everywhere by the discrediting of state socialism after 1989. Facing an altered electoral marketplace, political leaders everywhere now call for less government—less bureaucracy, less regulation, less public spending—although policy has yet to catch up with rhetoric. Even a relatively liberal Democratic president in the United States has proclaimed that "the era of big government is over." In one sense, the problem of "overload" identified by CH&W appears to have solved itself: Many people seem to have concluded that government action is not the answer to all their problems.[2] Yet citizens still hold government responsible for their social and economic well-being, and cutting "entitlement" programs remains difficult everywhere.

Against this backdrop of geopolitical, economic, social, and ideological change, how should we assess the current status of the advanced industrial democracies of North America, Western Europe, and Japan? At the outset we want to emphasize a distinction that CH&W felt less need to stress: the distinction between the effectiveness of specific democratic governments and the durability of democratic institutions per se. On the one hand, we see no evidence in any of these countries that democracy itself is at risk of being supplanted by an undemocratic political regime or by social or political anarchy. On the other hand, we do see substantial evidence throughout the Trilateral world of mounting public unhappiness with government and the institutions of representative democracy.

Earlier alarm about the stability of democracy itself—which CH&W were in part responding to and in part amplifying—now seems exaggerated. The happy contrast between political developments in the advanced industrial democracies after World Wars I and II is indeed dramatic. Within two decades after the end of World War I, fledgling democracies had collapsed in Italy, Germany, Spain, and Japan, and more established democracies elsewhere were under siege. Now, more than half a century after the end of World War II, democratic regimes are deeply rooted throughout the Trilateral world and have multiplied in other parts of the world as well. Bearing in mind the tragic failures of democracy in the interwar period, it was entirely natural in the first decades after World War II for observers of Western politics to ask whether the same thing could happen again. Political science has a poor record of prognostication, especially with respect to radical change, and we should not be too presumptuous in writing about such fundamental issues, but with half a century of democratic stability under our collective belts, the answer is almost certainly no.

The case for this optimism does not simply rest on the passage of time. Decades of surveys in North America, Western Europe, and Japan yield little evidence of diminished support for liberal democracy among either mass publics or elites. If anything, the opposite is true: Commitment to democratic values is higher than ever. In sharp contrast to the period after World War I, no serious intellectual or ideological challenge to democracy has emerged. Whether tracked over the more than five decades since the end of World War II or over the decade since the fall of the Berlin Wall, opponents of democracy have lost support. Even where public discontent with the performance of particular democratic governments has become so acute as to overturn the party system (as in Japan and Italy in 1993–95), these changes have not included any serious threat to fundamental democratic principles and institutions. In this sense we see no significant evidence of a crisis of democracy.

Nevertheless, to say that democracy per se is not at risk is far from saying that all is well with the Trilateral democracies. In fact, public confidence in the performance of representative institutions in Western Europe, North America; and Japan has declined since the original Trilateral Commission report was issued, and in that sense most of these democracies are troubled.

SYMPTOMS OF DISTRESS

Public attitudes toward democracy can be assessed at various levels of abstraction. We find no evidence of declining commitment to the principles of democratic government or to the democratic regimes in our countries. On the contrary, if anything, public commitment to democracy per se has risen in the last half century. At the other extreme, we are not concerned with day-to-day evaluations of specific leaders, policies, and governments (in the European sense of the word); we assume that evaluations of this kind of governmental performance will rise and fall in any well-functioning democracy. Rather, our concern is with popular confidence in the performance of representative institutions. Among the specific indicators we focus on are trends in (1) attachment to, and judgments of, political parties; (2) approval of parliaments and other political institutions; and (3) assessment of the "political class" (politicians and political leaders) and evaluations of political trust. Whatever the "normal" background level of public cynicism and censure of politics, citizens in most of the Trilateral democracies are less satisfied—often much less satisfied—with the performance of their representative political institutions than they were a quarter-century ago.

North America The onset and depth of this disillusionment vary from country to country, but the downtrend is longest and clearest in the United States, where polling has produced the most abundant and systematic evidence.[3] (The evidence from Canada, if less abundant and dramatic, conforms to this general picture.) When Americans were asked in the late 1950s and early 1960s, "How much of the time can you trust the government in Washington to do what is right?" three-quarters of them said "most of the time" or "just about always." Such a response would sound unbelievably quaint to most people today. This decline in confidence followed a decade or more of exceptionally turbulent political conflict—the civil rights movement, Vietnam, and Watergate and its successor scandals—that transformed American politics. Third-party challengers for the presidency, divided government, a term-limits

movement, and other political developments signaled the public's increasing disenchantment with the political status quo. Public confidence in the ability and benevolence of government has fallen steadily over this period. The decline was briefly interrupted by the "It's Morning in America" prosperity of the Reagan administration, and even more briefly by victory in the Gulf War, but confidence in government ended up lower after 12 years of Republican rule. Indeed, of the total decline, roughly half occurred under Republican administrations and half under Democratic ones. The economic prosperity of the late 1990s has seen an uptick in confidence in government, but the figures still remain well below those of the 1970s, not to mention those of the halcyon days of the late 1950s and early 1960s.

Public-opinion data tell the story of this decline. For example, whereas three-quarters of the American public once trusted the government to do what is right, only 39 percent felt this way in 1998. In 1964, only 29 percent of the American electorate agreed that "the government is pretty much run by a few big interests looking out for themselves." By 1984, that figure had risen to 55 percent, and by 1998, fully 63 percent of voters concurred. In the 1960s, two-thirds of Americans rejected the statement "Most elected officials don't care what people like me think"; in 1998, nearly two-thirds of Americans agreed with it. This negative assessment applies to virtually all parts of government. Those people expressing "a great deal" of confidence in the executive branch fell from 42 percent in 1966 to only 12 percent in 1997, and equivalent trust in Congress fell from 42 percent in 1966 to 11 percent in 1997.[4]

Almost every year since 1966, the Harris Poll has presented a set of five statements to national samples of Americans to measure their political alienation. (1) "The people running the country don't really care what happens to you." (2) "Most people with power try to take advantage of people like yourself." (3) "You're left out of things going on around you." (4) "The rich get richer and the poor get poorer." (5) "What you think doesn't count very much anymore." Every item on this list has won increasing assent from Americans since the opinion series began. In the late 1960s—at the very height of the Vietnam protests—barely one-third of Americans endorsed these cynical views; by the early 1990s fully two-thirds of all Americans concurred. By almost any measure, political alienation has soared over the last three decades. A single comparison captures the transformation: In April 1966, with the Vietnam War raging and race riots in Cleveland, Chicago, and Atlanta, 66 percent of Americans *rejected* the view that "the people running the country don't really care what happens to you." In December 1997, in the midst of the longest period of peace and prosperity in more than two generations, 57 percent of Americans *endorsed* that same view.

Europe Comparable public-opinion trends in Europe are more variegated, but there, too, the basic picture is one of spreading disillusionment with established political leaders and institutions. Trust in politicians and major political institutions has fallen over the last quarter-century in countries as diverse as Britain, Italy, France, and Sweden.

Britons' traditional deference to elites has been replaced by growing skepticism. In 1987, for example, fewer than half of Britons believed that either civil servants, the national government, or local councils could be trusted to serve the public interest. And while 48 percent of the British public expressed quite a lot of confidence in the House of Commons in 1985, that figure had been halved by 1995. Public protests over government decisions had become a common feature of politics in a nation once known for popular deference to political elites. As a symbol of this spreading skepticism, a series of high-profile Parliamentary committees in the 1990s studied issues of government corruption, ethical standards in politics, and campaign-finance abuses. Sweden, which invented the consummate welfare state and was once widely considered to have found a happy "middle way" between the free-for-all of market capitalism and the oppression of state socialism, is emblematic of Europe's troubled mood. The proportion of Swedes who rejected the statement that "parties are only interested in people's votes, not in their opinions" decreased from 51 percent in 1968 to 28 percent in 1994. In 1986,

even after the onset of the trend of decreasing political trust, a majority (51 percent) of Swedes still expressed confidence in the Riksdag; by 1996, however, only 19 percent did.

Especially striking are the patterns for the postwar democracies of Germany and Italy. Political support grew in these nations during the postwar decades, but the trends reversed at some point, and support has now eroded significantly from postwar highs. For instance, the percentage of Germans who said they trusted their Bundestag deputy to represent their interests rose from 25 percent in 1951 to 55 percent in 1978; by 1992, it had declined to 34 percent. Other survey responses point to a general erosion of Germans' trust in government since the early 1980s. Similarly, student unrest and extremist violence in the 1970s strained Italians' postwar democratic agreement, and public skepticism broadened and deepened with the political scandals of the past decade. This was signaled most dramatically by the radical restructuring of the party system in the mid-1990s. The percentage of Italians who say that politicians "don't care what people like me think" increased from 68 percent in 1968 to 84 percent in 1997.

At least until recently, such trends have been less visible in some of the smaller European democracies. Still, patterns of growing political cynicism have become more common in Austria, Norway, Finland, and other small states during the past decade. Almost everywhere, it seems, people are less deferential to political leaders and more skeptical of their motives. Across Europe the pattern of declining political support has apparently accelerated in the past decade. A recent evaluation of all the relevant long-term evidence found "clear evidence of a general erosion in support for politicians in most advanced industrial countries."[5]

Japan Public evaluations of politics and government in Japan reveal similarly disturbing trends. While *The Crisis of Democracy* portrayed Japan as an outlier, buffered from travails the authors saw looming elsewhere by a deferential political culture in which state authority was accepted, Japanese citizens' disillusionment with government and political institutions has, if anything, proven to be more persistent than elsewhere in the Trilateral world. Japan began the postwar era with confidence levels at a low point. With a generation of leaders discredited by wartime defeat and with the new democratic institutions imposed by the Occupation as yet untested, it is little wonder that political uncertainty prevailed, as attested to by extremely high proportions of Japanese responding "Don't know" to survey questions. By the 1960s, confidence in democracy per se was well established, and people's evaluations of government and politics had improved somewhat from these abysmal beginnings, but they nevertheless remained low relative to those in most other advanced industrial democracies. Although the mid-1980s witnessed a brief upturn, confidence levels declined noticeably in the politically turbulent and economically distressed 1990s. The long-term trends toward less deference to political leaders, diminished loyalty to established political parties (including the long-dominant Liberal Democratic Party, or LDP), and increased political dissatisfaction all predate the scandals that finally brought down the LDP in 1993 after 38 years of uninterrupted rule.

The proportion of Japanese voters who agree with the deferential view that "in order to make Japan better, it is best to rely on talented politicians, rather than to let the citizens argue among themselves" has fallen steadily for 40 years. Although this is probably a good indicator of the *strengthening* of the cultural and sociological foundations of Japanese democracy, the proportion of voters who feel that they exert at least "some influence" on national politics through elections, demonstrations, or expressions of public opinion also fell steadily between 1973 and 1993. In other words, Japanese voters have become less and less satisfied over the last 20 years with their limited role in politics, and less content to leave public affairs in the hands of political leaders. This is the backdrop against which a series of political corruption scandals broke prior to 1993, discrediting the LDP and causing public esteem for political leadership to decline still further. In yet another sign of a downturn in confidence, trust in the country's once-esteemed elite civil servants has also plummeted over the past decade.

TRENDS IN POLITICAL CONFIDENCE

When we step back from surveying the Trilateral landscape region by region, the overall picture that emerges is disturbing. Long series of national-election studies and reputable commercial public-opinion surveys provide extensive evidence of how public sentiments have changed over time. Evidence of the decline in political support has been especially apparent in three areas: disillusionment with politicians, with political parties, and with political institutions.

Politicians If public doubts about the polity surfaced only in evaluations of politicians or the government in power at any particular point in time, there would be little cause for worry. After all, citizens' dissatisfaction with an incumbent government routinely spurs voters to seek a change in administration at the next election and then extend support to the new incumbents. In that case, disaffection is a healthy part of the democratic process. Because citizens have the power to "throw the rascals out," democracy has a potential for renewal and responsiveness that is its ultimate strength. If dissatisfaction is generalized to the point where citizens lose faith in the entire political class, however, then the chances for democratic renewal are seriously diminished.

The patterns we have described separately, region by region, appear to be common to most Trilateral democracies. When the date for recent decades are assembled, the picture that emerges is stark. . . . Overall, *there is evidence of some decline in confidence in politicians in 12 out of 13 countries for which systematic data are available.* The convergence of results across Trilateral democracies is striking, because each has experienced its own unique political events over the past quarter-century. Although the decline is not universal, there is a general pattern of spreading public distrust of politicians and government among the citizens of Trilateral democracies. The political process undoubtedly faces strains when an increasing number of people distrust those individuals who are running the institutions of democratic governance.

Political Parties For more than a century, political parties have played a central role in the theory and practice of democratic government. To be sure, classical philosophers conceived of democracy as a kind of unmediated popular sovereignty in which "the people" rule directly, but they had in mind the context of a small city-state and never imagined that democratic government could function in societies as large and complex as today's Trilateral nations. This hurdle of scale was overcome by the greatest modern political innovation—representative democracy—which required intermediary institutions to link citizens to their government, to aggregate the increasingly diverse universe of conflicting social and economic interests into coherent public policies, and to ensure the accountability of rulers to the ruled. With the advent of universal suffrage, these functions came to be performed by political parties throughout the democratic world.

Although parties have long been the target of vociferous criticism, without them, the eminent scholar E.E. Schattschneider once asserted,[6] democracy would be unthinkable. One need not be blind to the deficiencies of partisanship nor romanticize the internal workings of party organizations to recognize the importance of parties to representative government. Joseph Schumpeter once defined democracy as "that institutional arrangement for arriving at political decisions in which individuals acquire the power to decide by means of a competitive struggle for the people's votes."[7] Although Schumpeter did not specifically emphasize the role of parties in this competition, his theory did clarify how parties contribute to democracy. Just as firms in a free market are led to innovate and to satisfy consumers by a combination of self-interest and the rules of open competition, party competition provides the linchpin between voters and public policy and the mechanism for turning disparate "special interests" into some version of "the public interest." Just as brand names allow consumers to choose on the basis of past experience and to penalize shoddy performance, party labels ensure that voters can reward the successful stewardship of public affairs and punish incompetence or dishonesty. Partisan "brand loyalty" gives political leaders the right incentives: They are free to innovate and make difficult decisions that may be painful in the short run, while they remain accountable to their constituents in the long run. Parties, in short, make the political marketplace orderly. Parties offer other advantages as well. They allow the voters to rise above their feelings about individual politicians; party supporters can be dissatisfied with a set of candidates, yet remain committed to the party's goals and the principle of representative democracy.

Because of the centrality of parties to democracy, people's feelings of attachment to or identification with political parties are one of the most widely studied of political attitudes. Fine-tuned efforts have been made to measure both affinities toward specific parties and acceptance of the general system of party-based democracy.

Signs of waning public attachment to political parties first emerged in several Trilateral democracies during the 1970s. The collapse in citizen engagement with political parties over the subsequent decades is as close to a universal generalization as one can find in political science. Card-carrying membership has always been less important for American than for European parties, but the proportion of Americans who reported that they engaged in party work at least once during the previous year fell by 56 percent between 1973 and 1993, and the proportion who reported attending a campaign rally or speech fell by 36 percent over the same period. Comparably massive declines in party membership have been registered in most Trilateral countries over the last 25 years. As attachments to political parties have eroded, electorates have become more volatile and skeptical. A comprehensive look at this pattern of weakening party ties, or "dealignment," reveals that popular identification with political parties has fallen in almost all the advanced industrial democracies. *The percent of the public expressing a partisan attachment has declined in 17 of the 19 Trilateral nations for which time-series data are available.* The strength of party attachments was separately measured in 18 nations: All show a downward trend.

Seldom does such a diverse group of nations reveal so consistent a trend. The only major variation is in the timing of the decline. Dealignment in the United States, Great Britain, and Sweden has been a long-term and relatively steady process that moved partisanship to a lower baseline level. For example, 65 percent of the Swedish public claimed party ties in 1968, compared to only 48 percent in 1994. In other countries, the change has been more recent. French and Irish partisanship has eroded over the past two decades. German partisanship, which had grown during the early postwar decades, began to weaken in the late 1980s and dropped off markedly in the 1990s. In Canada, the collapse of the Progressive Conservative and New Democratic Parties in the 1993 elections accentuated a similar trend toward dealignment. In Japan and Austria, too, detachment from parties accelerated in the 1990s, in response to a breakdown of political consensus in both nations. Specific variations aside, the overall pattern is consistent and striking. If party attachments represent the most fundamental type of citizen support for representative democracy, as many scholars assert, then their decline in nearly all advanced industrial democracies offers strong and disturbing evidence of the public's disengagement from political life.

Beyond reflecting dissatisfaction with politicians and current party leaders, weakening partisan ties also signal a growing disenchantment with partisan politics in general. For example, responses to several questions from the American National Election Study indicate a trend of declining faith that parties and elections are responsive to the public's interests.[8] A variety of other evidence points to Americans' growing disillusionment with political parties as agents of democratic representation. Along with other factors, disenchantment with political parties fueled public demand for major electoral reforms in Japan, Italy, and New Zealand. Across most of the Trilateral democracies, more citizens are now maintaining their independence from political parties and the institutions of representative democracy that they represent.

Political Institutions   In the Trilateral democracies, citizens' skepticism about politicians and political parties extends to the formal institutions of democratic government. It is one thing for citizens to be skeptical of the president or the prime minister (or even the group of politicians in parliament); it is

quite different if this cynicism broadens to include the institutions of the presidency and the legislature.

Because of its abundance of long-running, high-quality public-opinion surveys, the best evidence once again comes from the United States. One question gauges confidence in the officials running the three branches of American government. In the mid-1960s, a large proportion of Americans expressed a great deal of confidence in the Supreme Court, the executive branch, and Congress, but that confidence dropped dramatically by the early 1970s, and slid even further for the executive and Congress over the following two decades. Significantly, it is the Supreme Court, the least partisan and political institution, that has best retained the public's confidence. By the mid-1990s, barely a tenth of the American public had a great deal of confidence in the people running the executive branch or Congress—dramatic evidence of Americans' dissatisfaction with government. . . .

The time coverage and the extensiveness of the evidence varies considerably across nations, but the overall pattern is quite apparent. *In 11 out of 14 countries, confidence in parliament has declined.* Although in a number of cases the evidence does not rise to the level of statistical significance (largely because of the limited number of time points), in the five countries (Britain, Canada, Germany, Sweden, and the United States) for which the most extensive data are available, the drop in confidence in the national legislature is both pronounced and statistically significant.

Citizens' declining confidence in the institutions of democratic government extends beyond parliament. A separate analysis, using the 1981 and 1990 World Values Surveys, evaluated confidence in the armed services, judiciary, police, and civil service, as well as parliament. Although some institutions have scored gains in public trust over time, the general downward trajectory is clear. On average, confidence in these five institutions decreased by 6 percent over this single decade. In fact, only Denmark and Iceland displayed absolute increases in institutional confidence during the 1980s, and those increases were small.

The trends described here are not homogeneous across all the Trilateral countries. The degree and timing of growing distrust of political leaders, dissatisfaction with government performance, and estrangement from established parties vary greatly, depending on national traditions, specific political events, the effectiveness of individual leaders, and so on. Generally speaking, the trends are clearer in the larger countries (and clearest of all in the largest of all) and less visible (or, in a few cases, almost wholly absent) in some of the smallest countries.

Quite apart from any temporary disenchantment with the present government or dissatisfaction with particular leaders, most citizens in the Trilateral world have become more distrustful of politicians, more skeptical about political parties, and significantly less confident in their parliament and other political institutions. Compared to the state of public opinion at the time that CH&W wrote, the political mood in most of our countries today is not just grumpy, but much grumpier.

....

WHY WORRY?

Although public concern over these trends is widespread, it is nevertheless reasonable to step back and ask whether we should be worried about the many signs of erosion in popular confidence in government and the institutions of representative democracy. Some observers would reply with a resounding "No," offering three main arguments. The first holds that a critical citizenry signals not illness in the body politic but rather the health of democracy, and that the real challenge is to explain not the long-term decline in confidence, but why it was as high as it was in the 1950s and early 1960s, especially in the United States. A variation on that same view sees changes in values, driven by prosperity, technology, and other factors, as having created a more critical citizenry that rejects the political status quo and is also forcing new issues such as environmentalism and women's rights onto the political agenda, thus reforming and revitalizing democracy.

A second objection holds that new forms of political participation (such as referenda and "town-hall"–style fora) and an upsurge in certain types of grassroots activism (including social movements that are more broad-based than in the past) have supplanted previous forms of political engagement. A third objection proceeds from a particular perspective on the appropriate relation between government and citizens. The task of government, this view holds, is to give citizens not necessarily what they want, but what they need. Thus sound and appropriate policies are the best measure of governmental performance. Confidence levels are immaterial as long as the public supports the government enough to comply with its laws, pay taxes, and accept conscription.

Although each of these arguments has merit, we see reason to worry in the fact that voters' "report cards" on their representative institutions in the Trilateral democracies have generally become more critical—and often much more critical—in recent decades. Although we do not believe that this sour mood is a precursor of the collapse of Western democracy, a decent respect for our fellow citizens' views compels us to consider why they are increasingly distrustful of, and discontented with, their political institutions. If the decline in public confidence is justified (because of growing corruption, for example), then we might applaud citizens' ire but not its cause, just as we would be glad to have discovered a child's fever without being glad that her temperature was high.

If citizens are less satisfied with their representative institutions, this is a politically relevant and important fact. Yet few would argue that popularity is the sole measure of democratic performance, and most of us would admit that governments often must (or should) take actions that might reduce their popularity in the short run. Opinions differ on whether public satisfaction per se is a relevant measure of democratic performance. Some believe that democracy is not (just) about making citizens happy, and that it is also supposed to facilitate "good government," whether or not citizens are pleased with government actions. Others endorse the more populist view that what is distinctive about democracy is that the ultimate criterion of performance is citizens' collective judgment, so if public confidence declines over the long run, that is prima facie (though not irrefutable) evidence that the performance of representative institutions has declined.

A MODEL FOR EXPLAINING THE DECLINE

For disaffection in particular countries, explanations have been offered that are studded with proper nouns: Vietnam, Nixon, Craxi, Mulroney, Thatcher, Recruit, and so on. Such interpretations offer important insights into the national catalysts for democratic distress, but it seems surprising that so many independent democracies just happened to encounter rough water or careless captains simultaneously. Although we do not discount the importance of specific national factors, we seek more generalizable explanations.

Unraveling the question of why confidence in government has declined to varying degrees across the Trilateral world is a complex task. In our view, public satisfaction with representative institutions is a function of the information to which citizens are exposed, the criteria by which the public evaluates government and politics, and the actual performance of those institutions (see Figure 1). Thus, a decline in satisfaction might be due to a change in any of these variables.

First, the accuracy and comprehensiveness of publicly available *information* about democratic performance might have changed. Logically, this might be due to either deterioration (worse information about good performance) or improvement (better information about bad performance), but the most common interpretation is that voters have over time become better informed about their governments' performance, particularly about leaders' conduct in office (for example, corruption), even though malfeasance per se might not have worsened. Here, the role of the media is clearly central.

Second, the public's *criteria for evaluation* of politics and government might have changed in ways that make it harder for representative institutions to meet those standards. This in turn might be due to either rising or diverging expectations (or both). If public demands on government spiral insatiably upward, satisfaction could fall even if performance remains unchanged. In part, this was the interpretation offered by CH&W. If the heterogencity of

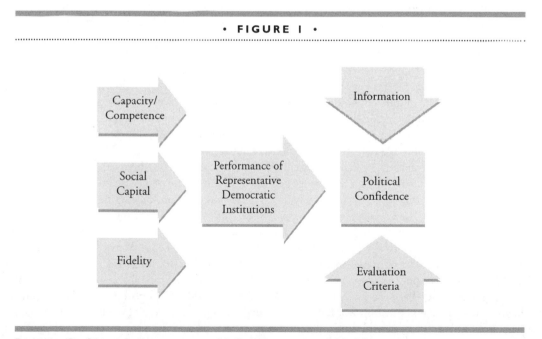

• FIGURE 1 •

Explaining Confidence in Government and Political Institutions: A Model public desires increases, either by polarization along a single dimension or by divergence across multiple dimensions, then it becomes more difficult for government to identify any feasible set of policies that would satisfy its constituents.

Third, the *performance of representative institutions* might have deteriorated. Measuring performance objectively is a challenging task, of course. Because it is reasonably well established in most of the Trilateral countries that cyclical fluctuations in citizens' evaluations of incumbents correlate with macroeconomic indicators, one obvious approach is to measure macroeconomic outcomes (inflation, unemployment, growth, and the like). A growing body of work, however, generally discounts this as the primary explanation for the decline in public confidence in political institutions. As Nye and his colleagues[9] note with regard to the United States, for example, the largest decline in confidence occurred over the high-growth decade between 1964 and 1974; confidence actually increased during the recession of the early 1980s.

Once these economic measures are set aside, there is little agreement over which dimensions of performance are relevant across countries, time, and individual citizens. One obvious measure might be gains or losses in social welfare. One might argue that levels of confidence have remained high in countries in which social-welfare guarantees are secure while they have dropped elsewhere as a result of rollbacks of the welfare state. Yet testing such a hypothesis runs into the problem of how to measure governmental performance on social welfare. If we use government outlays, we run up against the fact that, despite the rhetoric hailing "small government," governmental transfers (which are heavily skewed toward social programs) as a percentage of GNP have increased strikingly in the Trilateral countries precisely over those decades in which confidence has decreased. Alternatively, to measure results like increased longevity and improved health would fail to take into account the many factors other than government policies (diet and economic prosperity, for example) that produce them. Another problem is choosing a point in time at which policy success or failure can be judged. For example, some people believe that the American war in Vietnam or

the process of German reunification constituted massive policy failures that contributed powerfully to declining political confidence; other observers might argue that, in the long run, these policy "failures" represent historic successes.

Thus objective measures of policy performance have obvious limits. When searching for why citizens feel the way they do about their government, their subjective appraisal of governmental performance is what ultimately matters. The fact that public confidence has declined can be taken to mean that governmental performance is less satisfactory than it once was. We consider citizens' falling confidence in government to be focused specifically on political institutions and to have principally political roots and therefore seek to identify broad explanations for the deterioration of governmental performance. These can be collected under two rubrics.

The first of these is declines in the *capacity* of political agents to act on behalf of citizens' interests and desires (see Figure 1). Thus we seek to identify forces that may have undermined the ability of national governments to implement their chosen policies and to respond to citizen demands in a satisfactory way. The principal such force is internationalization, which creates a growing incongruence between the scope of territorial units and the issues raised by interdependence, reducing the output effectiveness of democratic nation-states.

The second broad explanation concerns declines in the *fidelity* with which political agents act on citizens' interests and desires. Within this category fall arguments about failures of political leadership, failures of political judgment on the part of voters, and deterioration of the civic infrastructure (or social capital) by means of which interests are articulated and aggregated.

A final problem relating to the issue of fidelity arises from the complex relationship among three sets of variables: confidence in government; governmental performance; and civic engagement, social capital,[10] and social trust. A key issue is precisely how an erosion of social capital and social trust may affect citizens' confidence in government. Much evidence to date suggests low levels overall of social capital and social trust in any given society do indeed contribute to poor governmental performance, which, in turn, adversely affects all citizens to varying degrees; as a consequence, they will give the government low marks. Metaphorically speaking, no citizen (no matter how high his or her *own* social trust or civic engagement) can escape the rain precipitated by poor governmental performance, perhaps produced in part by the social disaffection or civic disengagement of his or her neighbors.

Over the quarter-century since CH&W issued their report, citizens' confidence in governments, political parties, and political leaders has declined significantly in most of the Trilateral democracies, even though the depth and timing of this decline have varied considerably from country to country. Some commentators may tell their fellow citizens that the problem is "just in your head"—a function of unrealistic expectations rather than deteriorating performance—but we are inclined to think that our political systems are not, in fact, performing well, although perhaps for reasons beyond their immediate control. These criticisms of governments and leaders do not necessarily translate into a "crisis of democracy" that threatens constitutional and representative government.

Nevertheless, the fact that representative democracy per se is not at risk does not imply that all is well with our political systems. Indeed, most of our fellow citizens believe that all is *not* well. Due regard for their views, as well as a prudent concern for the future, suggests that we should explore the sources of this democratic discontent.

ENDNOTES

1. Michel Crozier, Samuel P. Huntington, and Joji Watanuki, *The Crisis of Democracy,* New York: New York University Press, 1975, p. 2.
2. Polls do not, in fact, generally confirm the thesis that ordinary citizens' views about the proper role of government have shifted nearly as much as has the climate of elite opinion. Equally important, however, there is little survey evidence that citizens have become more insistent on government action in recent decades.
3. The most comprehensive assessment of the evidence for declining confidence in government in the United States, as well as initial evaluations of alternative explanations, is Joseph S. Nye, Philip D. Zelikow, and David C. King, eds., *Why People Don't Trust Government,* Cambridge, Mass.: Harvard University Press, 1997.
4. Seymour Martin Lipset, "American Democracy in Comparative Perspective," in Robert S. Leiken, ed., *A New Moment in the Americas,* (New Brunswick, N.J.: Transaction Publishers, 1994); Seymour Martin Lipset and William Schneider, *The Confidence Gap,* New York: Free Press, 1983.
5. Russell J. Dalton, "Political Support in Advanced Industrial Democracies," in Pippa Norris, ed., *Critical Citizens: Global Support for Democratic Government,* p. 63.
6. Elmer Eric Schattschneider, *The Semi-Sovereign People,* New York: Holt, Rinehart and Winston, 1960.
7. Joseph A. Schumpeter, *Capitalism, Socialism, and Democracy,* 4th ed., London: Allen and Unwin, 1952, p. 269.
8. Russell J. Dalton, *Citizen Politics: Public Opinion and Political Parties in Advanced Industrial Democracies,* Chatham, N.J.: Chatham House, 1996, p. 271.
9. Joseph S. Nye, Philip D. Zelikow, and David C. King, eds., *Why People Don't Trust Government,* pp. 10–11.
10. By analogy to physical and human capital, some scholars have introduced the term "social capital" to refer to the norms and networks of civil society that enable citizens and their institutions to perform more productively. Without adequate supplies of social capital—that is, without civic engagement, healthy community institutions, norms of mutual reciprocity, and trust—democracies and market economies may begin to falter.

**RUSSELL J. DALTON, SUSAN E. SCARROW,
BRUCE E. CAIN**

22 The New Politics in Advanced Democracies

Over the past quarter-century in advanced industrial democracies, citizens, public interest groups, and political elites have shown decreasing confidence in the institutions and processes of representative government. In most of these nations, electoral turnout and party membership have declined, and citizens are increasingly skeptical of politicians and political institutions.[1]

Along with these trends often go louder demands to expand citizen and interest-group access to politics, and to restructure democratic decision-making processes. Fewer people may be voting, but more are signing petitions, joining lobby groups, and engaging in unconventional forms of political action. Referenda and ballot initiatives are growing in popularity; there is growing interest in processes of deliberative or consultative democracy,[2] and there are regular calls for more reliance on citizen advisory committees for policy formation and administration—especially at the local level, where direct involvement is most feasible. Contemporary democracies are facing popular pressures to grant more access, increase the transparency of governance, and make government more accountable.

Amplifying these trends, a chorus of political experts has been calling for democracies to reform and adapt. Mark Warren writes, "Democracy, once again in favor, is in need of conceptual renewal. While the traditional concerns of democratic theory with state-centered institutions remain importantly crucial and ethically central, they are increasingly subject to the limitations we should expect when nineteenth-century concepts meet twenty-first century realities."[3] U.S. political analyst Dick Morris similarly observes, "The fundamental paradigm that dominates our politics is the shift from representative to direct democracy. Voters want to run the show directly and are impatient with all forms of intermediaries between their opinions and public policy."[4] As Ralf Dahrendorf recently summarized the mood of the times, "Representative government is no longer as compelling a proposition as it once was. Instead, a search for new institutional forms to express conflicts of interest has begun."[5]

Many government officials have echoed these sentiments, and the OECD has examined how its member states could reform their governments to create new connections to their publics. Its report testifies:

> New forms of representation and public participation are emerging in all of our countries. These developments have expanded the avenues for citizens to participate more fully in public policy making, within the overall framework of representative democracy in which parliaments continue to play a central role. Citizens are increasingly demanding more transparency and accountability from their governments, and want greater public participation in shaping policies that affect their lives. Educated and well-informed citizens expect governments to take their views and knowledge into account when making decisions on their behalf. Engaging citizens in policy making allows governments to respond to these expectations and, at the same time, design better policies and improve their implementation.[6]

If the pressures for political reform are having real effects, these should show up in changes to the institutional structures of democratic politics. The most avid proponents of such reforms conclude

SOURCE: Russell J. Dalton, Susan E. Scarrow, and Bruce E. Cain, "Advanced Democracies and the New Politics," *Journal of Democracy*, vol. 15, no. 1 (January 2004), pp. 124–138. © National Endowment for Democracy and The Johns Hopkins University Press. Reprinted with permission of The Johns Hopkins University Press. Statistical tables and footnotes abridged by the Editor.

that we may be experiencing the most fundamental democratic transformation since the beginnings of mass democracy in the early twentieth century. Yet cycles of reform are a recurring theme in democratic history, and pressures for change in one direction often wane as new problems and possibilities come to the fore. What is the general track record for democratic institutional reforms in the advanced industrial democracies over the latter half of the twentieth century? And what are the implications of this record for the future of democracy?

THREE MODES OF DEMOCRACY

In a sense, there is nothing new about the call to inject "more democracy" into the institutions of representative government. The history of modern democracies is punctuated by repeated waves of debate about the nature of the democratic process, some of which have produced major institutional reforms. In the early twentieth century, for example, the populist movement in the United States prompted extensive electoral and governing-process reforms, as well as the introduction of new forms of direct democracy. Parallel institutional changes occurred in Europe. By the end of this democratic-reform period in the late 1920s, most Western democracies had become much more "democratic" in the sense of providing citizens with access to the political process and making governments more accountable.

A new wave of democratic rhetoric and debate emerged in the last third of the twentieth century. The stimulus for this first appeared mainly among university students and young professionals contesting the boundaries of conventional representative democracy. Although their dramatic protests subsequently waned, they stimulated new challenges that affect advanced industrial democracies to this day. Citizen interest groups and other public lobbying organizations, which have proliferated since the 1960s, press for more access to government; expanding mass media delve more deeply into the workings of government; and people demand more from government while trusting it less.

The institutional impact of the reform wave of the late twentieth century can be understood in terms of three different modes of democratic politics. One aims at improving the process of *representative democracy* in which citizens elect elites. Much like the populism of the early twentieth century, reforms of this mode seek to improve electoral processes. Second, there are calls for new types of *direct democracy* that bypass (or complement) the processes of representative democracy. A third mode seeks to expand the means of political participation through a new style of *advocacy democracy,* in which citizens participate in policy deliberation and formation—either directly or through surrogates, such as public interest groups—although the final decisions are still made by elites.

1. Representative democracy A major example of reform in representative democracy can be seen in changes to processes of electing the U.S. president. In a 30-year span, these elections underwent a dramatic transformation, in which citizen influence grew via the spread of state-level primary elections as a means of nominating candidates. In 1968, the Democratic Party had just 17 presidential primaries while the Republicans had only 16; in 2000 there were Democratic primaries in 40 states and Republican primaries in 43. As well, both parties—first the Democrats, then the Republicans—instituted reforms intended to ensure that convention delegates are more representative of the public at large, such as rules on the representation of women. Meanwhile, legislators introduced and expanded public funding for presidential elections in an effort to limit the influence of money and so promote citizen equality. If the 1948 Republican and Democratic candidates, Thomas E. Dewey and Harry S Truman, were brought back to observe the modern presidential election process, they would hardly recognize the system as the same that nominated them. More recently, reformers have championed such causes as term limits and campaign-finance reform as remedies for restricting the influence of special interests. In Europe, populist electoral reform has been relatively restrained by institutionalized systems of party government, but even so, there are parallels to what has occurred in the United States in many European countries. On a limited basis, for example, some European political parties have experimented with, or even adopted, closed primaries to select parliamentary candidates.

Generally, the mechanisms of representative democracy have maintained, and in places slightly increased, citizen access and influence. It is true that, compared with four decades ago, electoral turnout is generally down by about 10 percent in the established democracies. This partially signifies a decrease in political access (or in citizens' use of elections as a means of political access). But at the same time, the "amount of electing" is up to an equal or greater extent. There has been a pattern of reform increasing the number of electoral choices available to voters by changing appointed positions into elected ones. In Europe, citizens now elect members of Parliament for the European Union; regionalization has increased the number of elected subnational governments; directly elected mayors and directly elected local officials are becoming more common; and suffrage now includes younger voters, aged 18 to 20. Moreover, the number of political parties has increased, while parties have largely become more accountable—and the decisions of party elites more transparent—to their supporters. With the general expansion in electoral choices, citizens are traveling to the polls more often and making more electoral decisions.

2. Direct democracy Initiatives and referenda are the most common means of direct democracy. These allow citizens to decide government policy without relying on the mediating influence of representation. Ballot initiatives in particular allow nongovernmental actors to control the framing of issues and even the timing of policy debates, further empowering the citizens and groups that take up this mode of action. In recent decades, changes in both attitudes and formal rules have brought about a greater general reliance on mechanisms of direct democracy within the advanced industrial democracies. The Initiative and Referendum Institute calculates, for example, that there were 118 statewide referenda in the United States during the 1950s but 378 such referenda during the 1990s. And a number of other nations have amended laws

and constitutions to provide greater opportunities for direct democracy at the national and local levels. Britain had its first national referendum in 1975; Sweden introduced the referendum in a constitutional reform of 1980; and Finland adopted the referendum in 1987. In these and other cases, the referendum won new legitimacy as a basis for national decision making, a norm that runs strongly counter to the ethos of representative democracy. There has also been mounting interest in expanding direct democracy through the innovation of new institutional forms, such as methods of deliberative democracy and citizen juries to advise policy makers.[7]

How fundamental are these changes? On the one hand, the political impact of a given referendum is limited, since only a single policy is being decided, so the channels of direct democracy normally provide less access than do the traditional channels of representative democracy. On the other hand, the increasing use of referenda has influenced political discourse—and the principles of political legitimacy in particular—beyond the policy at stake in any single referendum. With Britain's first referendum on European Community membership in 1975, for instance, parliamentary sovereignty was now no longer absolute, and the concept of popular sovereignty was concomitantly legitimized. Accordingly, the legitimacy of subsequent decisions on devolution required additional referenda, and today contentious issues, such as acceptance of the euro, are pervasively considered as matters that "the public should decide." So even though recourse to direct democracy remains relatively limited in Britain, the expansion of this mode of access represents a significant institutional change—and one that we see occurring across most advanced industrial democracies.

3. Advocacy democracy In this third mode, citizens or public interest groups interact directly with governments and even participate directly in the policy-formation process, although actual decisions remain in official hands. One might consider this as a form of traditional lobbying, but it is not. Advocacy democracy involves neither traditional interest groups nor standard channels of informal interest-group persuasion. Rather, it empowers individual citizens, citizen groups, or nongovernmental organizations to participate in advisory hearings; attend open government meetings ("government in the sunshine"); consult ombudsmen to redress grievances; demand information from government agencies; and challenge government actions through the courts.

Evidence for the growth of advocacy democracy is less direct and more difficult to quantify than is evidence for other kinds of institutional change. But the overall expansion of advocacy democracy is undeniable. Administrative reforms, decentralization, the growing political influence of courts, and other factors have created new opportunities for access and influence. During the latter 1960s in the United States, "maximum feasible participation" became a watchword for the social-service reforms of President Lyndon Johnson's "Great Society" programs. Following this model, citizen consultations and public hearings have since been embedded in an extensive range of legislation, giving citizens new points of access to policy formation and administration. Congressional hearings and state-government meetings have become public events, and legislation such as the 1972 Federal Advisory Committee Act even extended open-meeting requirements to advisory committees. While only a handful of nations had freedom-of-information laws in 1970, such laws are now almost universal in OECD countries. And there has been a general diffusion of the ombudsman model across advanced industrial democracies. "Sunshine" provisions reflect a fundamental shift in understanding as to the role that elected representatives should play—one which would make Edmund Burke turn in his grave, and which we might characterize as a move away from the *trustee* toward the *delegate* model.

Reforms in this category also include new legal rights augmenting the influence of individuals and citizen groups. A pattern of judicialization in the policy process throughout most Western democracies, for instance, has enabled citizen groups to launch class-action suits on behalf of the environment, women's rights, or other public interests. Now virtually every public interest can be translated into a rights-based appeal, which provides new avenues for action through the courts. Moreover, especially

in European democracies, where direct citizen action was initially quite rare, the expansion of public interest groups, *Bürgerinitiativen,* and other kinds of citizen groups has substantially enlarged the public's repertoire for political action. It is worth noting that "unconventional" forms of political action, such as protests and demonstrations, have also grown substantially over this time span.

CITIZENS AND THE DEMOCRATIC STATE

If the institutional structure of democracy is changing, how does this affect the democratic process? The answer is far from simple and not always positive, for democratic gains in some areas can be offset by losses in others, as when increased access produces new problems of democratic governability. In the following pages, we limit our attention to how these institutional changes affect the relationship between citizens and the state.

Robert A. Dahl's writings are a touchstone in this matter.[8] Like many democratic theorists, Dahl tends to equate democracy with the institutions and processes of representative democracy, paying much less attention to other forms of citizen participation that may actually represent more important means of citizen influence over political elites. Thus, while we draw from Dahl's *On Democracy* to define the essential criteria for a democratic process, we broaden the framework to include not only representative democracy but direct democracy and advocacy democracy also. Dahl suggests five criteria for a genuinely democratic system.[9]

1. Inclusion: With minimal exceptions, all permanent adult residents must have full rights of citizenship.

2. Political equality: When decisions about policy are made, every citizen must have an equal and effective opportunity to participate.

3. Enlightened understanding: Within reasonable limits, citizens must have equal and effective opportunities to learn about relevant policy alternatives and their likely consequences.

4. Control of the agenda: Citizens must have the opportunity to decide which matters are placed on the public agenda, and how.

5. Effective participation: Before a policy is adopted, all the citizens must have equal and effective opportunities for making their views known to other citizens.

The first column of the Table lists Dahl's five democratic criteria. The second column summarizes the prevailing view on how well representative democracy fulfills these criteria. For example, advanced industrial democracies have met the *inclusion* criterion by expanding the franchise to all adult citizens (by way of a long and at times painful series of reforms). General success in this regard is illustrated by the bold highlighting of "universal suffrage" in the first cell of this column.

Nearly all advanced industrial democracies now meet the *political equality* criterion by having enacted the principle of "one person, one vote" for elections, which we have highlighted in the second cell. In most nations today, a majority of citizens participate in voting, while labor unions, political parties, and other organizations mobilize participation to achieve high levels of engagement. Indeed, that noted democrat, the late Mayor Richard Daley of Chicago, used to say that electoral politics was the only instrument through which a working-class citizen could ever exercise equal influence with the socially advantaged. At the same time, certain problems of equality remain, as contemporary debates about campaign financing and voter registration illustrate, and full equality in political practice is probably unattainable. We note these problems in the shaded area of the second cell. Nevertheless, overall the principle of equality is now a consensual value for the electoral processes of representative democracy.

At first glance, it may seem that expanding the number of elections amounts to extending these principles. But increasing the number of times that voters go to the polls and the number of items on ballots actually tends to depress turnout. And when voter turnout is less than 50 percent, as it tends to be in, say, EU parliamentary elections—or less than 25 percent, as it tends to be in local mayoral or school-board elections in the United States—then one must question whether the gap between "equality of access" and "equality of usage" has become so wide that it undermines the basic principle of *political equality*. Moreover, second-order elections tend to mobilize a smaller and more ideological electorate than the public at large, and so more second-order elections tend to mean more distortions in the representativeness of the electoral process.

The tension between Dahl's democratic criteria and democratic practice becomes even more obvious when we turn to the criterion of *enlightened understanding*. Although we are fairly sanguine about voters' abilities to make informed choices when it comes to high-visibility (for instance, presidential or parliamentary) elections, we are less so when it comes to lower-visibility elections. How does a typical resident of Houston, Texas, make enlightened choices regarding the dozens of judgeship candidates whose names appeared on the November 2002 ballot, to say nothing of other local officeseekers and referenda? In such second- and third-order elections, the means of information that voters can use in first-order elections may be insufficient or even altogether lacking. So the expansion of the electoral marketplace may empower the public in a sense, but in another sense may make it hard for voters to exercise meaningful political judgment.

Another criterion is citizen *control of the political agenda*. Recent reforms in representative democracy have gone some way toward broadening access to the political agenda. Increasing the number of elected offices gives citizens more input and presumably more avenues for raising issues, while reforming political finance to equalize campaign access and party support has made for greater openness in political deliberations. More problematic, though, is performance on the *effectiveness of participation* criterion. Do citizens get what they vote for? Often, this principal-agent problem is solved through the mechanism of party government: Voters select a party, and the party ensures the compliance of individual members of parliament and the translation of electoral mandates into policy outcomes. But the impact of recent reforms on the *effectiveness of participation* is complex. On the one hand, more openness and choice in elections should

· TABLE ·

Robert A. Dahl's Democratic Criteria

DEMOCRATIC CRITERIA	REPRESENTATIVE DEMOCRACY	DIRECT DEMOCRACY	ADVOCACY DEMOCRACY
Inclusion	**Universal suffrage provides inclusion**	**Universal suffrage provides inclusion**	Equal citizen access
			(Problems of access to nonelectoral arenas)
Political Equality	**One person, one vote with high turnout maximizes equality**	**On person, one vote with high turnout maximizes equality**	Equal opportunity
	(Problems of low turnout, inequality due to campaign finance issues, etc.)	*(Problems of equality with low turnout)*	*(Problems of very unequal use)*
Enlightened Understanding	*(Problems of information access, voter decision processes)*	*(Problems of greater information and higher decision-making costs)*	**Increased public access to information**
			(Problems of even greater information and decision-making demands on citizens)
Control of the Agenda		**Citizen initiation provides control of agenda**	**Citizens and groups control the locus and focus of activity**
	(Problems of control of campaign debate, selecting candidates, etc.)	*(Problems of influence by interest groups)*	
Effective Participation	**Control through responsible parties**	**Direct policy impact ensures effective participation**	**Direct access avoids mediated participation**
	(Principal-agent problems: fair elections, responsible party government, etc.)		

Note: Criteria that are well addressed are presented in **bold,** criteria that are at issue are presented in *italics* in the shaded cells.

enable people to express their political preferences more extensively and in more policy areas. On the other hand, as the number of officeholders proliferates, it may become more difficult for voters to assign responsibility for policy outcomes. Fragmented decision making, divided government, and the sheer profusion of elected officials may diminish the political responsiveness of each actor.

How much better do the mechanisms of direct democracy fare when measured against Dahl's five criteria (see column 3 of the Table)? Because referenda and initiatives are effectively mass elections, they seek to ensure inclusion and political equality in much the same way as representative elections do. Most referenda and initiatives use universal suffrage to ensure inclusion and the "one person, one vote" rule to ensure political equality. However, whereas turnout in direct-democracy elections is often lower than in comparable elections for public officials, the question of democratic inclusion becomes more complicated than a simple assessment of equal access. For instance, when Proposition 98—which favored altering the California state constitution to mandate that a specific part of the state budget be directed to primary and secondary education—appeared on the 1996 general election ballot, barely half of all voting-age Californians turned out, and only 51 percent voted for the proposition. But as a consequence, the state's constitution was altered, reshaping state spending and public financing in California. Such votes raise questions about the fairness of elections in which a minority of registered voters can make crucial decisions affecting the public welfare. Equality of opportunity clearly does not mean equality of participation.

Moreover, referenda and initiatives place even greater demands for information and understanding on voters. Many of the heuristics that they can use in party elections or candidate elections are less effective in referenda, and the issues themselves are often more complex than what citizens are typically called upon to consider in electing office-holders. For instance, did the average voter have enough information to make enlightened choices in Italy's multi-referendum ballot of 1997? This ballot asked voters to make choices concerning television-ownership rules, television-broadcasting policy, the hours during which stores could remain open, the commercial activities which municipalities could pursue, labor-union reform proposals, regulations for administrative elections, and residency rules for mafia members. In referenda, voters can still rely on group heuristics and other cues that they use in electing public officials, but obviously the proliferation of policy choices and especially the introduction of less-salient local issues raise questions about the overall effectiveness of such cue-taking.

The real strengths of direct democracy are highlighted by Dahl's fourth and fifth criteria. Referenda and initiatives shift the locus of agenda-setting from elites toward the public, or at least toward public interest groups. Indeed, processes of direct democracy can bring into the political arena

issues that elites tend not to want to address: for example, tax reform or term limits in the United States, abortion-law reform in Italy, or the terms of EU membership in Europe generally. Even when referenda fail to reach the ballot or fail to win a majority, they can nevertheless prompt elites to be more sensitive to public interests. By definition, moreover, direct democracy should solve the problem of effective participation that exists with all methods of representative democracy. Direct democracy is unmediated, and so it ensures that participation is effective. Voters make policy choices with their ballot—to enact a new law, to repeal an existing law, or to reform a constitution. Even in instances where the mechanisms of direct democracy require an elite response in passing a law or a revoting in a later election, the link to policy action is more direct than is the case with the channels of representative democracy. Accordingly, direct democracy seems to fulfill Dahl's democratic criteria of agenda control and effective participation.

But direct democracy raises questions in these areas as well. Interest groups may find it easier to manipulate processes of direct democracy than those of representative democracy. The discretion to place a policy initiative on the ballot can be appealing to interest groups, which then have unmediated access to voters during the subsequent referendum campaign. In addition, decisions made by way of direct democracy are less susceptible to bargaining or the checks and balances that occur within the normal legislative process. Some recent referenda in California may illustrate this style of direct democracy: Wealthy backers pay a consulting firm to collect signatures so as to get a proposal on the ballot, and then bankroll a campaign to support their desired legislation. This is not grassroots democracy at work; it is the representation of wealthy interests by other means.

The expansion of direct democracy has the potential to complement traditional forms of representative democracy. It can expand the democratic process by allowing citizens and public interest groups new access to politics, and new control over political agendas and policy outcomes. But direct democracy also raises new questions about equality of actual influence, if not formal access, and the ability of the public to make fair and reasoned judgments about issues. Perhaps the most important question about direct democracy is not whether it is expanding, but *how* it is expanding: Are there ways to increase access and influence without sacrificing inclusion and equality? We return to this question below.

....

FORMAL ACCESS AND ACTUAL USE

The final column in our Table considers how new forms of advocacy democracy fulfill Dahl's democratic criteria. These new forms of action provide citizens with significant access to politics, but it is also clear that this access is very unevenly used. Nearly everyone can vote, and most do. But very few citizens file lawsuits, file papers under a freedom-of-information act, attend environmental-impact review hearings, or attend local planning meetings. There is no clear equivalent to "one person, one vote" for advocacy democracy. Accordingly, it raises the question of how to address Dahl's criteria of inclusion, political equality, and enlightened understanding.

"Equality of access" is not adequate if "equality of usage" is grossly uneven. For instance, when Europeans were asked in the 1989 European Election Survey whether they voted in the election immediately preceding the survey, differences in participation according to levels of education were very slight. . . . A full 73 percent of those in the "low education" category said they had voted in the previous EU parliamentary election (even though it is a second-order election), and an identical percentage of those in the "high education" category claimed to have voted. Differences in campaign activity according to educational levels are somewhat greater, but still modest in overall terms.

A distinctly larger inequality gap emerges when it comes to participation through forms of direct or advocacy democracy. For instance, only 13 percent of those in the "low education" category had participated in a citizen action group, while nearly three times [that] percentage . . . in the "high education" category had participated. Similarly, there are large inequalities when it comes to such activities as signing a petition or participating in a lawful demonstration.

With respect to the criterion of *enlightened understanding*, advocacy democracy has mixed results. On the one hand, it can enhance citizen understanding and make for greater inclusion. Citizens and public interest groups can increase the amount of information that they have about government activities, especially by taking advantage of freedom-of-information laws, attending administrative hearings, and participating in government policy making. And with the assistance of the press in disseminating this information, citizens and public interest groups can better influence political outcomes. By ensuring that the public receives information in a timely fashion, advocacy democracy allows citizens to make informed judgments and hold governments more accountable. And by eliminating the filtering that governments would otherwise apply, advocacy democracy can help citizens to get more accurate pictures of the influences affecting policy decisions, with fewer cover-ups and self-serving distortions. On the other hand, advocacy democracy makes greater cognitive and resource demands on citizens, and thus may generate some of the same inequalities in participation noted above. It requires much more of the citizen to participate in a public hearing or to petition an official than it does simply to cast a vote. The most insightful evidence on this point comes from Jane Mansbridge's study of collective decision making in New England town meetings.[10] She finds that many participants were unprepared or overwhelmed by the deliberative decision-making processes.

Advocacy democracy fares better when it comes to the remaining two criteria. It gives citizens greater control of the political agenda, in part by increasing their opportunity to press their interests outside of the institutionalized time and format constraints of fixed election cycles. By means of advocacy democracy, citizens can often choose when and where to challenge a government directive or pressure policy makers. Similarly, even though advocacy democracy typically leaves final political decisions in the hands of elites, it nevertheless provides direct access to government. Property owners can participate in a local planning hearing; a public interest group can petition government for information on past policies; and dissatisfied citizens can attend a school board session. Such unmediated participation brings citizens into the decision-making process—which ultimately might not be as effective as the efforts of a skilled representative, but greater direct involvement in the democratic process should improve its accountability and transparency (see the bold entries in these last two cells of the Table).

All in all, advocacy democracy increases the potential for citizen access in important ways. It can give citizens and public interest groups new influence over the agenda-setting process, and it can give them unmediated involvement in the policy-formation process. These are significant extensions of democratic participation. At the same time, advocacy democracy may exacerbate political inequality on account of inequalities in usage. New access points created through advisory panels, consultative hearings, and other institutional reforms empower some citizens to become more involved. But other citizens, relatively lacking in the skills or resources to compete in these new domains, may be left behind. In other words, advocacy democracy may in some ways respond to the strength of the claimants, rather than to the strength of their claims. It can even alter the locus of political expertise. While advocacy democracy values know-how and expertise in the citizenry, it devalues those same characteristics among policy makers.

Environmental policy provides a good illustration of this problem. Here, citizens and public interest groups have gained new rights and new access to the policy process. But these are disproportionately used by relatively affluent and skilled citizens, who are already participating in conventional forms of representative democracy, while the poor, the unskilled, and the otherwise disadvantaged tend to get left behind. So while environmentalism is an example of citizen empowerment, it is also a source of increasing inequality.

No form of democratic action is ideal, each having its advantages and limitations. As democratic practice shifts from a predominant reliance on representation toward a mixed repertoire—including greater use of direct and advocacy democracy—a new balance must be struck among democratic goals. It is possible that new institutional arrangements will maximize the benefits of these new modes while limiting their disadvantages—as, for example, the institutions of representative democracy depend on parties and interest groups. But thus far, the advanced industrialized democracies have not fully recognized the problems generated by the new mixed repertoire of democratic action, and so have yet to find institutional or structural means of addressing them. Democratic reforms create opportunities, but they also create challenges. Our goal should be to ensure that progress on some democratic criteria is not unduly sacrificed for progress on others.

ENDNOTES

1. Martin P. Wattenberg, *Where Have All the Voters Gone?*, Cambridge: Harvard University Press, 2002; Susan E. Scarrow, "From Social Integration to Electoral Contestation," in Russell J. Dalton and Martin P. Wattenberg, eds., *Parties Without Partisans: Political Change in Advanced Industrial Democracies*, New York: Oxford University Press, 2000; Russell J. Dalton, *Democratic Challenges, Democratic Choices: The Decline in Political Support in Advanced Industrial Democracies*, Oxford: Oxford University Press, 2004; Susan J. Pharr and Robert D. Putnam, eds., *Disaffected Democracies: What's Troubling the Trilateral Countries?*, Princeton: Princeton University Press, 2000.

2. James S. Fishkin, *The Voice of the People: Public Opinion and Democracy*, New Haven: Yale University Press, 1995; John Elster, *Deliberative Democracy*, New York: Cambridge University Press, 1998.

3. Mark Warren, *Democracy and Association*, Princeton: Princeton University Press, 2001, p. 226.

4. Dick Morris, *The New Prince: Machiavelli Updated for the Twenty-First Century*, New York: Renaissance Books, 2000.

5. Ralf Dahrendorf, "Afterword," in Susan J. Pharr and Robert D. Putnam, eds., *Disaffected Democracies: What's Troubling the Trilateral Countries?*, p. 311.

6. OECD, *Citizens as Partners: OECD Handbook on Information, Consultation and Public Participation in Policy-Making*, Paris: Organization of Economic Co-operation and Development, 2001, p. 9.

7. James S. Fishkin, *The Voice of the People: Public Opinion and Democracy;* Forest David Matthews, *Politics for People: Finding a Responsive Voice,* 2nd ed., Urbana: University of Illinois Press, 1999.

8. Robert A. Dahl, *Polyarchy: Participation and Oppostition* (New Haven: Yale University Press, 1971); *Democracy and Its Critics,* New Haven: Yale University Press, 1991; *On Democracy,* New Haven: Yale University Press, 1998.

9. Robert A. Dahl, *On Democracy,* pp. 37–38.

10. Jane Mansbridge, *Beyond Adversary Democracy,* New York: Basic Books, 1980.

BERNARD E. BROWN

23   *Worker Democracy: A Test Case*

It was the intention of the Left government in 1981 to transform authority relations within enterprise. The stated goal was eventually to achieve economic democracy, summed up in the slogan, "autogestion" (literally, self-management). Roundly condemning both capitalism (Socialists agreed with Communists on the need to "break" with this evil system) and Russian-style communism (Communists agreed with Socialists that the Soviet Union represented a form of "authoritarian socialism" that had to be transcended), the united Left pledged to enable workers to become masters and shapers of their own destinies.[1]

In the summer and fall of 1982 a series of four laws was enacted by the National Assembly creating "new rights for workers," known popularly thereafter by the name of the Socialist Minister of Labor, Jean Auroux. The lois Auroux mandated the creation in all enterprises employing over 200 people of "groupes d'expression directe" (expression groups), in which workers would be able to speak up directly and collectively on any aspect of their workday life. Important new powers were also devolved upon the enterprise committees, whose members are elected only by workers. Management was required to inform enterprise committees ahead of time concerning any important decisions—including production and pricing strategy, introduction of new technology, and investment policies. And enterprises were also required to bargain collectively with unions every year. What happened? Did the French Left find a "third way" between grasping capitalism and authoritarian socialism? . . .

The purpose of this article is to call attention to new developments in industrial relations in France since the adoption of the lois Auroux, and to show that the failure to achieve the stated goal of the French Left sheds precious light on the theory of economic democracy.[2]

SOURCE: Bernard E. Brown, "Worker Democracy in Socialist France," Occasional Paper no. 7 of the CUNY Center for Labor-Management Policy Studies (1989). Article and footnotes abridged. Reprinted also in Stephen R. Sleigh, editor, *Economic Restructuring and Emerging Patterns of Industrial Relations,* Kalamazoo, MI: W. E. Upjohn Institute, 1993. For a fuller statement, see B. E. Brown, "The Rise and Fall of Autogestion in France," in M. Donald Hancock, John Logue, and Brent Schiller, editors, *Managing Modern Capitalism,* Westport, CT: Greenwood-Praeger, 1991.

MANAGERIAL SUPREMACY— BUT WHY?

One key point must be made at the outset: The participative structures created by the lois Auroux have come under the domination of management. To understand why, let us take a closer look at these structures. Between 1983 and 1985, when the lois Auroux were reviewed, amended, and reenacted by the National Assembly, some 6000 agreements were reached between management and the representatives of workers (either unions or enterprise committees), leading to the creation of about 100,000 expression groups. Typically, an expression group consists of 15 to 20 people, who meet two or three times a year, and have the right to "express" themselves on any aspect of their working conditions.

Some major trends were immediately evident. Better educated workers tended to speak up and monopolize the time of most groups; only skilled leadership was able to prevent this from happening. After the initial period of enthusiasm, as predicted by the skeptics, apathy set in. Workers generally lost interest in attending meetings, even though they were on company time. Within two years about one-third of the expression groups had ceased to meet altogether, and another one-third met only intermittently.

Expression groups that meet regularly share a crucial characteristic: Their worker-members are mobilized and actively supported by management. As one French sociologist put it, successful expression groups have been a creation of "the Prince."[3] This development resulted from a turnaround of business policy on workforce participation. Immediately after the adoption of the lois Auroux, the Conseil National du Patronat Français (CNPF)—which had fought their adoption tooth and nail—encouraged its members to play the game according to the changed rules in order to prevent the Communist-led Confédération Générale du Travail (CGT) from taking over. An Estates-General of the CNPF in 1983 urged managers to train foremen and supervisory employees (cadres) as discussion leaders and to throw their resources and energies into the struggle to control the new groups.

Managers were advised through the business press to take the following steps: set up training courses for cadres; reward cadres for taking the lead in groups; make sure that questions and criticism receive the attention of the hierarchy; rapidly resolve problems thus called to the attention of superiors; and communicate this information to the groups. When managers were reluctant to take these measures (either because they were unconvinced of the need, had too much difficulty with cadres who wished to preserve their traditional prerogatives, or were harassed by a strong union leadership), expression groups faded away or were easily contained.

It was virtually impossible for the CGT or the more moderate Confédération Française Démocratique du Travail (CFDT) to displace management in giving a firm lead to the groups. Most militants were formed in the school of class conflict, and were not ready for instant conversion into apostles of class cooperation. Nor did their training prepare them to be adept at two-way communication between rank-and-file at one end and management at the other. In rare cases where unions were able to mobilize and guide workers, management was able to contain unruly expression groups by ignoring them. After a while, discouraged workers simply give up.

An unforeseen development after 1982 was the phenomenal expansion not of expression groups but, of all things, quality circles. A handful of French businessmen, inspired by Japanese production methods during an Asian tour, founded the Association Française des Cercles de Qualité (AFCERQ) a year before the passage of the lois Auroux. The attempt to introduce Japanese-style quality circles was a failure—considered by workers to be the latest of many business-sponsored schemes to intensify class exploitation. It was only after the passage of the lois Auroux that the quality circle movement took off. As of 1988, AFCERQ had presided over the creation of some 40,000 quality circles, and the principle was extended by the Chirac government to the civil service.

How did it happen? Managers were advised to consider the expression group as a useful technique for involving workers in their enterprise and identifying problems. In a second step, workers were to be encouraged to help resolve problems—through quality circles. AFCERQ consultants warn that quality circles will wither unless substantial resources, time, and energy are invested in them. Successful quality circles, according to AFCERQ, require a commitment from top management; organization of study groups that travel to the U.S. or Japan; weekend seminars for all managers and cadres in order to consider the recommendations of the consultants; discussion by all employees of the new procedures; and, finally and only then, creation and constant care of the quality circles.

The pressure on workers to enter and participate in the quality movement was irresistible. The unions, including even the CGT, gave up their boycott. Alas (for management), quality circles are subject to the same trends of apathy that wreaked such havoc with expression groups. The most recent development is to make emphasis on quality part of the productive process through work teams, suggestion boxes, and collective participation in definition of goals for the enterprise, along with expression groups and quality circles.[4]

Equally disappointing to advocates of worker control has been the performance of enterprise committees. In the original conception, delegates elected by workers are to give an opinion on all important decisions by management before they are taken. Management is also required to submit annual reports to enterprise committees, which are permitted to hire specialists (accountants, lawyers, engineers, etc.)—at company expense—to help them understand these reports. Great hopes were placed in enterprise committees, suitably aided by outside experts, union headquarters, and political parties, to counter management proposals with their own. Enterprise committees were to constitute a rival power within the structure of enterprise, and perhaps prepare the way for the assumption of managerial prerogatives by workers. The Communist party planned to use enterprise committees to impose its celebrated "new criteria of management"—production for use rather than for profit—throughout the economy.

Enterprise committees suffered the same sad fate as expression groups, and for much the same reasons. Management with relative ease could ignore recommendations from hostile enterprise committees. More positively, it made the agreeable discovery that it could communicate more effectively with workers through their elected delegates, and with delegates through their hired experts. Instead of challenging capitalism, enterprise committees and expression groups for the most part were enrolled in a vast campaign to strengthen it—in order to protect jobs and raise salaries.

The fate of participative structures thus points up the inherent difficulty of maintaining worker autonomy against the formidable pressure that can be brought to bear by the concentrated power of management. Only one effective counterforce can

be envisaged: the unions. But worker autonomy has meant in France independence of workers from all external constraints, including that of unions—which are bureaucratized and linked to potentially domineering political parties and the State. Worker control is not the same as control by unions and parties in the name of workers.[5]

The failure of enterprise committees to offer a feasible alternative to management policies is highly instructive. Almost immediately after the passage of the lois Auroux, the Confédération Française Démocratique du Travail (CFDT) found that its resources were stretched too thin to be able to take on managerial functions as well, and it stopped submitting counterproposals. The CGT, on the other hand, drew up a number of counterproposals, particularly in industries threatened by layoffs or plant closings.

Invariably, the CGT counterproposals consisted of a detailed inventory of customer needs, and of functions performed by each work post, all leading to the triumphant conclusion that the enterprise is viable and not a single job need be lost. What if there is no longer a market? That is because management is thinking in terms of short-term profit instead of social use. Plenty of customers are out there, in the third world and in Eastern Europe. How those customers would be able to pay for goods without subsidies from French taxpayers is never explained. Part of the standard counterproposal was also elimination of bothersome imports, while foreigners presumably would be happy to go on buying French goods without any thought of retaliation. CGT proposals were considered unconnected to reality not only by management of private enterprises, but also (perhaps even more forcefully) by the Socialist state responsible for the nationalized industries.[6]

Why has it been impossible to maintain worker autonomy against bureaucratic pressure? For Edmond Maire, perhaps the most important advocate of autogestion in the 1970s, the reasons go beyond contingent factors (such as unemployment, austerity, lack of political will). It is the very notion of worker autonomy that he calls into question. For a long time, Maire concedes, the labor movement contrasted monarchical enterprise (where the boss wields absolute power) with models reflecting the belief that workers can decide everything. But now we must go further, declares the former general secretary of the CFDT, and recognize the specificity and legitimacy of the managerial function, which cannot be the result of collective deliberation. Autogestion, he concludes, remains a valid ideal, but is not a model for enterprise. The need today is not for a "break with capitalism" (termed by Maire "a dangerous illusion and non-operative") but vigorous defense of workers' interests and "logic" within enterprise. In effect, virtually every plank of the CFDT's radical program of the 1970s has been discarded since the adoption of the lois Auroux.[7]

"LE CAPITALISME N'EST PLUS CE QU'IL ÉTAIT"

A new model of enterprise has emerged in France, and has become dominant within the large, professionally managed sector of the economy (both public and private). Before 1981 it was taken for granted that management made all decisions, which were then transmitted downward to employees. Negotiations with unions took place mainly at the branch or industry level (not within individual enterprises), following guidelines set by the State. In turn, business was expected to follow the lead of the State, whose top functionaries were presumed to have a sense of national interest. This patriarchal model reflected the prevailing belief within the French political class after the Liberation that French capitalism was backward, and that only a dynamic State, served by specially trained civil servants, could accomplish the task of rapid modernization.

"Capitalism is no longer what it was" recently exclaimed Edmond Maire, who can hardly be accused of special sympathy for the profit motive. Capitalism has undergone a "cultural revolution" observes Pierre Rosanvallon, not an admirer of capitalism in the past. And Henri Weber, former Trotskyist and now close collaborator of Laurent Fabius, speaks of a "mutation" of French capitalism.[8] What they all refer to is the new model of the dynamic sector, based on a freer flow of information throughout enterprises oriented to the market rather

than to the State. A significant portion of the budget of a modern French enterprise (about five percent of the total payroll) is now devoted to securing information from the base, circulating it through the hierarchy, and ensuring collaboration of employees, cadres, and managers in the achievement of agreed-upon goals. This emphasis on permanent dialogue, two-way communication, and service to customers rather than carrying out the commands of the State, is a break with past practice.

However, management's very success in creating participative structures opens the way for a possible counterattack by unions and workers from within the citadel. The process of dialogue changes attitudes and affects power relationships. In an enterprise fully committed to participation, managers must eventually recognize the legitimacy of a "workers' logic," to use Edmond Marie's term, and the importance of workers' contributions to production. Absolute monarchy is converted into at least a *rechtsstaat* (rule of law), with democracy perhaps in the offing. But industrial democracy in this sense means interaction between managers (who retain their prerogatives) and workers, not the absorption of elites into a self-governing community.

The new model enterprise poses a formidable problem for unions, which lost half of their members between 1976 and 1988. Pierre Rosanvallon estimates union membership as of 1988 as follows: 600,000 for the CGT; 400,000 each for the CFDT and the Force Ouvrière (FO); and 200,000 for the teachers' union.[9] The virtual collapse of unions, says Rosanvallon, is due to their inability so far to cope with the cultural revolution that has taken place in enterprise. Unions traditionally represent workers in negotiations with business and the State, and also in social security and welfare councils. They have not been oriented towards participation in an "informational" enterprise in which workers, cadres, and managers are in direct communication with each other and collectively regulate daily life. To meet this immense challenge unions must recast their structures and create a new culture based on communication rather than either confrontation or meek submission. Only CFDT leaders have thought through the problem, but so far they have not been able to gain the support of their own militants in bringing about the necessary reforms.

PRIMACY OF THE POLITICAL

Political factors have been and remain crucial determinants of the nature of labor-management relations in France. Paradoxically, it was the victory of the Left that led to an expansion of managerial power. Before 1981 all attempts by business and parties of the Right to integrate workers into enterprise were rejected by unions and the parties of the Left. But when the Left in power vowed to "break with capitalism," workers and unions were carried into new structures of participation on a wave of enthusiasm. Radicalization of the Socialist party was a deliberate tactic by François Mitterrand to outflank the Communist party on its left, and to demonstrate to workers that they could have socialism of a democratic rather than an authoritarian variety. Autogestion was an integral part of a Socialist program designed to reduce the Communist party's appeal; it was a useful fiction. But, as it turned out, once workers entered into the structures created by the lois Auroux they could not resist domination by cadres and managers.

When the Socialists returned to power after the legislative elections of 1988, they did not revive the ideological battle cries of 1981. On the contrary, Prime Minister Michel Rocard fully accepted the principle of worker participation and free flow of information within enterprise. He embraced quality circles, instructed every ministry to draw up plans for improving quality, and called for constant dialogue between workers and managers as a top *Socialist* priority—thus trying to appropriate the quality movement for the Left. The Socialists are seeking ways to push the balance of power back in the direction of workers and unions—an extraordinarily difficult task. The experience of the lois Auroux so far demonstrates that management enjoys an inherent advantage in the contest for control of decision-making within enterprise. . . .

Nonetheless, the social base of French politics is no longer what it was before the passage of the lois Auroux. The major actors within the system—business and labor—have in the past decade undergone at least the beginning of a mutation. Labor-management relations in France have not reverted to their pre-1981 status; nor have they become a copy of foreign models. Traditions of Jacobinism, business paternalism, revolutionary syndicalism, and mass communism have produced unique conditions for the ongoing experiment in workforce participation. Industrial relations surely will continue to evolve and to reflect a distinctively French political culture somewhere this side of utopia.

ENDNOTES

1. I have dealt with the conversion of the PS and the PCF into parties of "autogestion" in *Socialism of a Different Kind: The Reshaping of the French Left* (Westport, CT: Greenwood Press, 1982), chs. 4 and 5.

2. The literature on the implementation of the lois Auroux is a treasure trove for students of workforce participation. See in particular: Annie Borzeix, Danièle Linhart, and Denis Segrestin, *Sur les traces du droit d'expression*, 2 vols. Paris: CNAM, 1985; Philippe Bernoux et al., *De l'expression à la négotiation*, Minstère de la Recherche et de l'Industrie, 1985; Jean Bunel, *Le triangle de l'entreprise*, Ministère de la Recherche et de l'Industrie, 1985; and Daniel Mothé-Gautrat, *Pour une nouvelle culture de l'entreprise*, Editions de la Découverte, 1986.

3. Daniel Mothé-Gautrat, op. cit., p. 145.

4. AFCERQ, apparently in need of expert advice itself, declared bankruptcy in August 1989. But support for the quality circle movement is continuing through management, government, and other consulting firms.

5. A point well made by Jacques Julliard, *Autonomie ouvrière: études sur le syndicalisme d'action directe* (Gallimard, 1988), pp. 30, 32.

6. See Elie Cohen, "Le 'moment lois Auroux' ou la désublimation de l'économie," *Sociologie du Travail*, vol. 28, no. 3 (1986), especially pp. 277–279.

7. Edmond Maire, *Nouvelles frontières pour le syndicalisme* (Syros, 1987), pp. 131–149. See also Jean-Paul Jacquier, *Les cowboys ne meurent jamais, l'aventure syndicale continue*, Syros, 1986.

8. See Edmond Marie, *Nouvelles frontières*, op. cit., p. 138; Pierre Rosanvallon, "Participation et syndicats," *Management et Qualité*, no. 25 (mars 1988), pp. 14–16; and *La question syndicale*, Calmann-Lévy, 1988; and Henri Weber, *Le parti des patrons*, Seuil, 1986, p. 420.

9. Rosanvallon, *La question syndicale*, op. cit., p. 15.

CHAPTER SEVEN

TRANSITION TO DEMOCRACY

Samuel P. Huntington popularized the term "third wave" to denote the trend to democracy since 1974, when a military dictatorship was overthrown in Portugal. The first long wave of democratization began in the early 19th century, he argues, leading to democracy in about 30 nations by the end of World War I. However, the rise of fascist and other regimes reduced the democracies to about a dozen by 1942. A second wave began after World War II, increasing the number of democracies to about 30, but many of these democracies also foundered. The third wave began in Portugal, and now has spread from roughly one-third of the countries in the world to almost two-thirds, at least in terms of fairly free and competitive elections. But is democracy the model toward which developing countries aspire? Under what conditions may democracy be transplanted from the West to "the rest"?

Guillermo O'Donnell calls attention to the complexity of the problem. Free elections are a key element of democracy, or, to use Robert A. Dahl's term, "polyarchies." But, going back to the concerns expressed by the authors of *The Federalist Papers,* O'Donnell stresses the importance also of "liberal" and "republican" components that must coexist with free elections if democracy is to survive. For Thomas Carothers, the "transition to democracy" paradigm is no longer an appropriate model as an explanation of trends in developing countries. On the other hand, Larry Diamond remains "cautiously optimistic" about the chances for the expansion of democracy in the world. Are these two analyses compatible? What can explain the differences between these two keen observers of the same phenomenon? The debate is of critical importance to policymakers responsible for economic and other assistance to developing countries.

In assessing the prospects of democracy in the world, two groups of countries constitute special cases: Russia and China; and Islamic societies, particularly in the Middle East. These cases will receive more detailed treatment in separate chapters.

GUILLERMO O'DONNELL

24 *Horizontal Accountability in New Democracies*

My interest in horizontal accountability stems from its absence. Many countries, in Latin America and elsewhere, have recently become political democracies, or to borrow Robert A. Dahl's term, "polyarchies," satisfying the criteria of fair and free political competition that Dahl stipulates.[1] This is no mean feat; even some countries that regularly hold elections fail to meet these criteria. My focus here, however, is on countries that do qualify as polyarchies, but have weak or intermittent horizontal accountability. This description fits almost every Latin American case except Costa Rica, Uruguay, and (perhaps) Chile, and includes such long-established polyarchies as Colombia and Venezuela. It also describes such new Asian polyarchies as the Philippines, South Korea, and Taiwan, as well as the older Asian polyarchy of India. Finally, the description applies to a number of postcommunist countries that might qualify as polyarchies, such as Croatia, Russia, Slovakia, and Ukraine; and perhaps also to countries, such as the Czech Republic, Poland, and Hungary, which clearly are polyarchies.

Reasonably free and fair elections provide a means of vertical accountability in these countries, along with freedoms of speech, the press, and association, which permit citizens to voice social demands to public officials (elected or not) and to denounce these same officials for wrongful acts that they may commit. Elections, however, occur only periodically, and their effectiveness at securing vertical accountability is unclear, especially given the inchoate party systems, high voter and party volatility, poorly defined issues, and sudden policy reversals that prevail in most new polyarchies. As for social demands and media coverage, in the absence of duly authorized state agencies of investigation and oversight capable of parceling out responsibility and sanctions, they are extremely important, but sometimes they risk merely creating a climate of public disaffection with the government or even the regime itself.

Just as vertical accountability implies the presence of *democracy,* the weakness of horizontal accountability implies a corresponding weakness in the *liberal* and also the *republican* components of many new polyarchies. Polyarchies are complex and at times uneasy syntheses of these three components—not two, as the more common analyses of liberalism versus republicanism or democracy versus liberalism would suggest. Each of the three components is the product of a distinct historical and intellectual current. The democratic tradition springs from ancient Athens; republicanism's roots lie in preimperial Rome and certain medieval Italian cities; and the liberal tradition has beginnings traceable to the feudal societies of medieval Europe, and later and more pointedly, to the England of John Locke and the France of the Baron de Montesquieu. The three traditions are partly contradictory, for each has basic principles that are inconsistent with the basic principle of at least one of the other currents. The tensions thus generated give polyarchies much of their uniquely dynamic and open-ended character.

Stated simply, the liberal component embodies the idea that there are rights which no power, prominently including the state, should violate. The republican component embodies the idea that the discharge of public duties is an ennobling activity that demands exacting subjection to the law and selfless service to the public interest. Both the liberal and the republican traditions distinguish between a public and a private sphere, but to different ends. For liberalism, the private sphere is the proper arena in which to pursue the fullness of human development. Hence liberalism's inherent ambivalence toward the public sphere and more particularly the state: the latter must be strong

SOURCE: Guillermo O'Donnell, "Horizontal Accountability in New Democracies," *Journal of Democracy,* vol. 9, no. 3 (July 1998), pp. 112–128. © National Endowment for Democracy and The Johns Hopkins University Press. Reprinted with permission of The Johns Hopkins University Press. Footnotes abridged by the editor.

enough to guarantee the freedoms enjoyed in private life, yet limited enough to prevent it from encroaching on those same freedoms.[2] Republicanism, by contrast, holds that wholehearted dedication to the public good—not the lesser undertakings of the private sphere—is what demands and nurtures the highest virtues. Meanwhile, the democratic tradition ignores these distinctions. Those who participate in the collective decisions are not a virtuous elite and do not renounce an active private life.[3] Moreover, as Socrates and others discovered, the *dēmos* has an unencumbered right to decide any matter it deems fit.

The differing values attached to the public and private spheres by liberalism and republicanism lead to diverging conclusions about political rights and obligations, political participation, the character of citizenship and of civil society, and other issues that are the very stuff of political debate; nonetheless, both currents posit the duality of public versus private life.[4] By contrast, the purely democratic current is monistic, rejecting both the liberal and the republican versions of the public–private distinction. Democracy in this strict sense does not share republicanism's insistence that those who discharge public responsibilities be particularly virtuous and singlemindedly dedicated to public life; rather, the most characteristically democratic procedures, rotation or selection by lot, presuppose that all citizens are roughly equally qualified for those roles. Nor does democracy share liberalism's conviction that there are private or individual rights that raise decisive barriers to what the *dēmos* may decide.

In contrast, liberalism and republicanism both seek—each in its own way and for its own reasons—to establish sharp limits, or boundaries, between the public and the private spheres. Consequently, representative government is a republican and liberal, but not a democratic notion. As for rights and obligations, liberalism is basically concerned with the private rights of individuals; republicanism with the public duties of individuals placed in the public sphere; and democracy with the positive right to take part in the decisions of the *dēmos*.

But there is an important convergence. Democracy's concern with equality, liberalism's commitment to freedoms in society, and republicanism's

severe view of the obligations of rulers all support another fundamental aspect of polyarchy and of the constitutional state that is supposed to coexist with it: the rule of law. All citizens are equally entitled to participate in collective decisions under the existing institutional framework, a democratic rule to which is added the republican injunction that no one, including those who govern, is above the law and the liberal caution that certain freedoms must not be infringed. We shall see, however, that the actual effectiveness of the rule of law varies significantly across different kinds of polyarchies.

THREE CONVERGING CURRENTS

Democracy and republicanism embody two common-sense views of political authority. Democracy asks, why should those who are in charge of the common good accept restraints on what they decide? Republicanism asks, why should the best not govern on behalf of the common good? Liberalism, by contrast, is profoundly counterintuitive. It arose in a small corner of the world influenced by the traditions of feudalism, conciliarism, and natural rights, and shocked by the horrors of religious warfare. Only there—in Western Europe, beginning about the sixteenth century—was it successfully argued that there are rights that no public or private agent should violate. Liberalism cannot justify the exercise of political authority over a territory (which always involves coercion or its threat) except by recurring to the artificial device of a foundational social contract. Republicanism does not go beyond an assertion that is typical of nearly all kinds of authority—namely, that it is for the good of its subjects. But republicanism contributed a historically counterintuitive idea of its own, the notion that virtuous rulers should subject themselves to the law no less and even more than ordinary citizens. Earlier, democracy had introduced another counterintuitive novelty: rule not only *for,* but also *from* and *by* those who are members of a given polity.

Over the last several centuries, these three currents have combined in complex and changing ways. Any one of them carried to an extreme would become a threat to polyarchy, and no single one can be said to be more basic than the other two. This is fortunate, for while polyarchy is a complicated and at times exasperating mixture, it is vastly preferable to a regime based exclusively on only one of its component traditions. Democracy without liberalism and republicanism would become majority tyranny; liberalism without democracy and republicanism would become plutocracy; and republicanism without liberalism and democracy would degenerate into the paternalistic rule of a self-righteous elite.

The various historical currents that have come together to form polyarchy are not mere abstractions, but rather form lively traditions. They have been memorably formulated, discussed, and revised by brilliant authors; have inspired innumerable discussions and tracts; have been invoked in the most varying circumstances and rituals; have imbued numerous pieces of legislation and whole constitutions; and through all this have profoundly influenced political thought, debate, and policy.

In particular, these currents converged in the constitutions and a good part of the legislation of a peculiar entity, one that came into full existence more or less simultaneously with liberalism and capitalism, but after democracy and republicanism were initially formulated—the territorially based state. Each of these currents has its own logic, articulating reasonably consistent basic principles and their corollaries, but the state also has its logic, one that is partially inconsistent with these three currents. States exhibit great variations across time and space. These variations, like the differing strains of capitalism that have been found in various times and places, have significant consequences for the kind of polyarchy that any given country has, and for the ways in which it is likely to change.[5]

POLYARCHY'S LATECOMERS

Thus polyarchies are complex and unstable mixtures of four elements—the three political traditions and the state. Many, if not all, political struggles can be understood as arguments about what is the best mix at a given time in a given country. Each element brings diverging values, reflecting different views of human nature, into play. After Britain began to develop what we now recognize as foreshadowings of polyarchy, it drew much admiring attention from intellectual and political leaders in other countries. Diffusion, first from Britain, and later on from the United States and France, has done much to shape subsequent polyarchies—outside of the North Atlantic world, polyarchy has never been a truly homegrown product. Around the globe, countries seeking to establish polyarchies of their own have looked to the foundings of the original modern polyarchies, their "classic" thinkers, and the power and prestige of their political traditions. The founders of the original polyarchies looked to Greece and Rome for concepts and examples, whether edifying or cautionary. Later, the French Revolution served as a cautionary example, not only in Britain and the United States but even in France itself, as observers appalled by the Jacobin link between democracy and republicanism reinforced or reformulated their ideas about how to maintain liberal safeguards against such risks.

Polyarchy's latecomers—including the Latin American republics that to this day feature some of the world's oldest (and least effective) constitutions—often adopted without much variation the institutional ensembles already familiar to them from the formal or informal empire to which they belonged. The newer polyarchies of the global east and south have looked to transplanted laws and constitutions to serve as engines of political and economic modernity, sparking persistent and often heated debates over the gap thus created between the *pays légal* and the *pays réel*. This gap—long discussed by politicians, historians, novelists, and social scientists—between formal rules and what most people most of the time actually do, has raised never-ending debates as to whether it would be better firmly to establish the *pays légal* or organize political life around the *pays réel*. One way or the other, successful social navigation requires keen awareness of both the formal and the informal codes, as well as their interlacings. This is true everywhere, but nowhere more pointedly so than in those countries that are furthest removed from the geographical and historical core areas of polyarchy.

For a long time and with only few exceptions, none of the counterintuitive principles of democracy, liberalism, and republicanism fared well outside these core areas. Many kinds of regimes persisted or emerged east and south, but few were polyarchies, even though some paid homage to the power of the democratic tradition by seeking a mantle of legitimacy through elections. These various kinds of authoritarian rule denied the boundaries advocated by liberalism, even if expediency or impotence caused them to tolerate a varying range of autonomous activities in society. Although republicanism, as we saw, can be conceived in an authoritarian way, most authoritarian rulers were not at all republican. Rather, they behaved in ways that, following Max Weber and Juan Linz, can be called neopatrimonialist, if not sultanistic.[6] They claimed to rule *for* the common good, but held themselves above the law, and often ignored for their personal advantage the ethical injunctions of republicanism. Yet elections were sometimes held, even if they were not free and fair. Moreover, in some countries where elections were suppressed (such as in Latin military dictatorships) people could remember "democratic" times of reasonably competitive balloting, even if little in the way of liberalism or republicanism had ever obtained.

While rotation and lot are the most primally democratic procedures, it is voting that has become identified with democracy according to both scholarly and common-sense notions. The pervasive modern tendency to identify "democracy" (i.e., polyarchy) with elections has obscured the no less constitutive roles played by liberalism and republicanism. A simple-minded failure to appreciate these latter (mixed with a dash of cynicism) helps to explain why so many Western governments are willing to grant democratic bona fides to countries that hold plausible elections, even when, like Russia's Boris Yeltsin and Peru's Alberto Fujimori, the victorious chief executive runs roughshod over the legislature and the judiciary. Nor is this the end of it, for as we shall see, the underappreciation of liberalism and republicanism creates serious problems when we want to discuss horizontal accountability.

MAKING ACCOUNTABILITY EFFECTIVE

This hasty *tour d'horizon* of several important and complicated issues, each of which merits a huge bibliography, provides a necessary context for my discussion of horizontal accountability. This kind of accountability depends on the existence of state agencies that are legally empowered—and factually willing and able—to take actions ranging from routine oversight to criminal sanctions or impeachment in relation to possibly unlawful actions or omissions by other agents or agencies of the state.

Such actions or omissions can be seen as harmful from the democratic, the liberal, and the republican points of view. Democracy is impinged upon, for example, by decisions that cancel the freedom of association or introduce fraud into elections. These are obviously important decisions, but I will not consider them here because they entail the abolition of polyarchy and, consequently, the exclusion of the given case from the set that I am discussing here. The liberal dimension of polyarchy suffers if state agents violate or fail to enforce guarantees against invasions of the domicile, domestic violence, torture, or punishment without a fair trial. In polyarchies most of these actions are perpetrated at the frontiers between the state apparatus and the weaker and poorer segments of society, by officials of relatively low rank who are not directly accountable to voters. (When these phenomena become widespread and systematic, however, they usually include the participation or connivance of higher-placed officials.) Republicanism is damaged if public officials, elected or not, refuse to subject themselves to the law, or prefer private interest to public duty. . . .

The main issue here is about boundaries, or limits, in two related senses. One is the already noted public–private distinction as propounded by liberalism and republicanism. The other, which is derived from these two currents, is entailed by the notion of horizontal accountability that I have proposed. For this kind of accountability to be effective, there must exist state agencies that are authorized and willing to oversee, control, redress, and if need be sanction unlawful actions by other state agencies. The former agencies must have not only legal authority but also sufficient de facto autonomy vis-à-vis the latter. What I am talking about, of course, is nothing new and goes under the familiar headings of separation of powers and checks and balances. It includes the executive, legislative, and judicial branches, but in contemporary polyarchies also extends to various oversight agencies, ombudsmen, accounting offices, *fiscalías* (public prosecutors), and the like. An important but seldom noticed point is that these agencies can only rarely be effective in isolation. Their proceedings can move public opinion, but normally their ultimate effectiveness depends on decisions by courts (or eventually by legislatures willing to consider impeachment), especially in major cases. Effective horizontal accountability is not the product of isolated agencies, but of networks of agencies (up to and including high courts) committed to upholding the rule of law. We shall return to this topic, because it gives us a glimpse into some of the peculiar difficulties, as well as possibilities, that come with the task of enhancing horizontal accountability.

The basic idea is to prevent, or at any rate sanction, the improper actions to which officials of the sort whom I characterized above are prone. To be autonomous, institutions must have boundaries, these boundaries must be acknowledged and respected by other relevant actors, and still other actors must be available to defend and eventually redress those boundaries if they are transgressed. At the level of the three major institutions of polyarchy, as Bernard Manin has shown, the wisdom of the American Federalists provided not for the rather mechanical division of powers proposed by their opponents, but for institutions that partially overlap in their authority.[7] This produced an arrangement that, by building several strong powers that partially intrude into each other, enhanced the autonomy of each of them with respect to what would have resulted from a simple separation of such powers.

LIMITING EXECUTIVE POWER

I have noted problems that stem from what I suspect are widespread and deep-seated views about the exercise of political authority in many countries, polyarchic or not. An additional problem results from the monistic bent of democracy, particularly as interpreted in many new polyarchies. Plebiscitarianism, caesarism, populism, and other such tendencies are deeply rooted in many countries. Seen through the lens they provide, democracy takes on a delegative cast: Reasonably free and fair elections are held to decide who is to govern for a certain time; governing is what is done by the executive, who has the right and duty to look after the good of the country as he or she sees fit; if the electorate grows unhappy, it can vote out the government in the next election—no less and not much more. In this view, apparently shared by significant numbers of political leaders and citizens in many new polyarchies, the existence of powers that are autonomous with respect to the executive, especially when or if they are supposed to exercise controls over the latter, is an utter nuisance. In the short term, delegative executives tend to ignore such agencies, while elimination, co-operation, or neutralization are the preferred longer-term strategies. As long as the executive's policies succeed, its freedom of action remains broad, all the more so when officials in other branches and substantial portions of the public at large agree with a delegative conception of authority. With the good conscience resulting from its felt obligation to pursue the public good, a scarcely liberal and republican executive will attempt to maximize its power by eliminating or denying the validity of other, potentially controlling state powers. The monistic logic of the *dēmos,* transplanted to the logic of delegation, is in evidence here.

None of this means that the executive is all-powerful. This kind of executive comes up against limits, even among its political allies, in the course of power plays that often involve the invocation of legal rules. But the crucial difference remains that these rules are instruments in such power plays, not independent norms that set the legal parameters of stabilized institutional interactions. Other limitations spring from the sheer size of some countries and from federal arrangements: The existence of local powers, themselves often delegative, unaccountable, and adept at the instrumental use of legal rules, can represent a check on the central executive.

It may be that in the long run the executive branch would maximize its power by subjecting itself to horizontal controls, but undermining horizontal accountability remains the dominant strategy. As for other state agencies, their incentives to resist or sanction unlawful actions by the executive (or, as sometimes happens, by the legislature) are not obvious. To complicate the problem further, we should remember that the effectiveness of horizontal accountability depends on networks of properly committed agencies (including courts)—networks that delegative leaders such as Fujimori, Yeltsin, and Argentina's Carlos Menem are skilled at disrupting through divide-and-conquer tactics.

Why, after all, should we expect something like horizontal accountability to exist? Authoritarian rulers face no obligation to obey the existing law or to accept a careful separation between the public good and private interests. In polyarchy, the mainstay of horizontal accountability is the high value that both liberalism and republicanism place on the rule of law. Of course, the force of either current's injunction to honor the rule of law depends on the relative strength of that current in defining the prevailing conception of political authority.

There are two distinct (though sometimes coinciding) ways in which horizontal accountability can be violated. The first, which I call "encroachment," occurs when one state agency trespasses upon the lawful authority of another. The second, which I loosely term "corruption," occurs when a public official obtains illegal advantages, whether for personal use or for the benefit of associates. Liberalism fears encroachment as a threat to freedom, but has little to say about corruption. Republicanism, in its turn, prohibits encroachment and strongly condemns corruption *(corruptio optimi est pessima)*. Indeed, the more classical versions of republicanism tend to view the very neglect of public affairs upon which liberalism looks so benevolently as itself a form of corruption.

Democracy's monistic view, finally, ignores the very idea of encroachment, even though there is another aspect of democracy that makes an important contribution to horizontal accountability. Holding that political authority comes *from* each and every member of the *dēmos,* democracy demands that those who—by rotation, lot, or election—are in charge of public affairs must act on behalf of the good of all. Furthermore, if power is from all and if every citizen is at least potentially a participant in the making of collective decisions, then—as in Athens—all decisions must be public both in their content and in the process that is used to reach them. Even though these democratic expectations do not bear directly on horizontal accountability, they have the consequence of demanding a high degree of transparency in political decision making, and transparency creates a climate in which corruption does not thrive. Liberalism as such is indifferent to transparency, and in some cases may gladly waive it if it seems conducive to better protection. Presumably virtuous republican rulers, meanwhile, have a way of finding excellent reasons for the nontransparency of their decisions. Somewhat curiously, then, the monistic principle of democracy interposes no obstacles to encroachment but fosters hostility to corruption. Perhaps, then, it is not surprising that in new polyarchies, where the democratic element predominates, we see relative indifference to executive encroachments but much less tolerance for corruption.

I suspect, however, that in the long run polyarchy has more to fear from encroachment than from corruption. The former intrinsically threatens to eliminate polyarchy, while the latter does not (though it will surely weaken it). Furthermore, encroachment raises a stronger obstacle to the emergence of relatively autonomous state agencies acting according to properly defined authority that characterizes formally institutionalized polyarchies. In such polyarchies it is probably no accident that, in my admittedly impressionistic opinion, there is much more corruption than encroachment. Where the liberal and republican components are weak, however, as in many of the new polyarchies, the democratic current per se is little help against encroachment.

....

ENHANCING ACCOUNTABILITY

But not all the news is bad. Survey after survey has shown that in many new polyarchies official corruption is a major concern, and one notes an unprecedentedly strong and widespread mood of condemnation of it. Despite some differences, most if not all societies seem to agree in damning certain behaviors, including direct embezzlement of public funds and the solicitation and acceptance of major bribes. Although corruption is not my primary topic here (even though this plague is both an expression and a consequence of feeble horizontal accountability), it is worth asking whether the widespread condemnation aroused by some of the more highly visible forms of corruption might provide a handle for thinking more positively than I have done so far about the prospects for improving horizontal accountability.

Nor is that all the good news. On the liberal front, many new polyarchies can boast various organizations (some of them human rights groups that have broadened their mission) that first arose to oppose or rectify authoritarian abuses, and now vigorously demand that postauthoritarian officials respect basic rights and freedoms, especially of the weak and poor. Other organizations enhance democracy by monitoring elections or teaching people their political rights and how to exercise them. Still others act as republican watchdogs, guarding against both illegal encroachments by one state agency on another and against unethical conduct by public officials. Although watchdog groups often lack bite if their efforts are not followed up by properly authorized state agencies, such groups can, in conjunction with conscientious journalists, highlight wrongful doings that otherwise would go unnoticed, and provide potential allies for state agencies that might want to undertake appropriate action. Such tactics can be particularly effective when a case involves high-ranking officials, large amounts of money, or both.

What more can be done to enhance horizontal as well as vertical accountability? All I can offer at this point are some modest and scarcely original suggestions.

1. Give opposition parties that have reached some reasonable level of electoral support an important role in directing the agencies (such as Latin America's *fiscalías*) charged with preventing and investigating corruption.

2. Ensure that preventive agencies like general accounting offices or *contralorías* are highly professionalized, adequately and independently endowed with resources, and insulated from political interference.

3. Take similar steps regarding the judiciary, with this caveat: "Judicial autonomy" is tricky; it could mean that the courts will become dominated by a political party or coalition of not very commendable interests, or that judges will adopt a notion of their powers and mission that leaves no room for accountability to other powers in the state and society.[8]

4. Despite the risks and potential drawbacks of these and similar institutional devices, their implementation in a Madisonian spirit of sober mistrust of everyone's republican inclinations is preferable to the situation presently existing in many new polyarchies, where such institutions do not exist or have been rendered ineffective by delegative presidents and compliant legislatures.

5. For the sake especially of the weak and poor in the many new polyarchies marked by poverty and profound inequalities, do the utmost to shore up the liberal side of horizontal accountability. There is a world of work to be done in this most difficult area to help ensure that the weak and poor are at least decently treated in their manifold encounters with the state and its agents.[9]

6. Encourage domestic actors—especially the media and the various social organizations working on behalf of vertical accountability—to

remain active and persistent. Transnational organizations and networks can be helpful too, but their ideas and actions risk being stamped as "meddling" unless domestic agents take them up. Public opinion can be crucial to the pursuit of horizontal accountability, a conclusion that is tantamount to saying—as I must emphasize—that the effectiveness of horizontal accountability depends to a significant degree on the mechanisms of vertical accountability (including but not limited to elections) that only polyarchy provides.

7. Because of the vital role of information in making possible both kinds of accountability, new polyarchies need not only independent media, research, and dissemination institutions, but also agencies independent of the government that gather and publicly circulate data on a broad range of indicators, economic and otherwise. The list of indicators to be studied, the methodology to be used, and the schedule for the gathering and publication of data should be agreed on by a pluralist and not a purely governmental set of decision makers.

Finally, there is another factor that is important but hard to pin down. I speak of the importance of individuals, especially political and other institutional leaders. Even in countries where corruption and encroachment are widespread, the good example of highly placed individuals who act—deliberately and publicly—according to liberal and republican injunctions can be highly valuable in shaping public opinion. No less importantly, such leadership can encourage other strategically located individuals or agencies to risk taking similar positions. Why and how such leaders emerge is a mystery to me. The melancholy truth is that they do not seem to be too abundant or successful in most new polyarchies, and that, when and if they reach the top, they too often fail to live up to expectations.

These reflections and their not very optimistic mood reflect a problem to which I alluded above: the incentives for many powerfully positioned individuals and their affiliates to continue with their scarcely liberal and republican practices are extremely strong, and the prevailing democratic component, especially when read delegatively, is little help. In contrast, the incentives for pursuing horizontal accountability are weak, especially since, as I have insisted, achieving a significant degree of such accountability requires the coordinated efforts of several agencies. The problem, in the last analysis, is the one that Madison and his allies tried to solve: how to build powers that in a liberal and a republican mood counter the trespassing temptations of other powers, yet honor the democratic demand that governments never forget that they owe their authority to the governed.

ENDNOTES

1. See esp. Robert A. Dahl, *Democracy and Its Critics,* New Haven: Yale University Press, 1989, p. 221. The attributes that Dahl lists are: (1) elected officials; (2) free and fair elections; (3) inclusive suffrage; (4) the right to run for office; (5) freedom of expression; (6) alternative information; and (7) associational autonomy. In my essay "Illusions About Consolidation." *Journal of Democracy* 7 (April 1996), pp. 35–36, following several authors cited there, I proposed adding: (8) elected officials—and some appointed ones, such as high-court judges—who cannot be arbitrarily terminated before the end of their constitutionally mandated terms; (9) the freedom of elected officials from severe constraints, vetoes, or exclusions imposed by nonelected actors, especially the armed forces; and (10) an uncontested territory that clearly defines the voting population.

2. I believe that this ambiguity is an important reason for liberalism's primarily defensive character—which endures despite recent efforts to cast it in a more positive, close to republican, light, See, for example, Stephen Macedo, *Liberal Virtues: Citizenship, Virtue, and Community in Liberal Constitutionalism,* New York: Oxford University Press, 1991. I hasten to add that this does not preclude that some of the "negative liberties" and constitutional constraints typical of liberalism can have empowering consequences for their individual or institutional carriers, as argued especially by Stephen Holmes in "Precommitment and the Paradox of Democracy," in Jon Elster and Rune Slagstad, eds., *Constitutionalism and Democracy,* Cambridge: Cambridge University Press, 1988, pp. 195–240; and *Passions and Constraint: On the Theory of Liberal*

Democracy, Chicago: University of Chicago Press, 1995.

3. Pericles, as rendered by Thucydides, told the people of Athens, "Our public men have, besides politics, their private affairs to attend to, and our ordinary citizens, though occupied with the pursuits of industry, are still fair judges of public matters." *The Peloponnesian War,* New York: Random House, 1951. Before Pericles, Athens had adopted the radical innovation of paying the equivalent of a day's wage for taking part in its various decision-making institutions, thus making possible the participation of its poor citizens; see Mogens H. Hansen, *The Athenian Democracy in the Age of Demosthenes: Structures, Principles, and Ideology,* London: Basil Blackwell, 1991.

4. In this respect, although they present the issue as between two terms, not three as I am doing here, I have found the following extremely useful: Michael Walzer, "Citizenship," in Terence and Hanson Bell Russel, eds., *Political Innovation and Cultural Change,* Cambridge: Cambridge University Press, 1989, pp. 211–19; Charles Taylor, "Modes of Civil Society," *Public Culture* 3 (Fall 1990), pp. 95–118; and Claus Offe and Ulrich K. Preuss, "Democratic Institutions and Moral Resources," in David Held, ed., *Political Theory Today,* Stanford: Stanford University Press, 1991, pp. 143–71.

5. To illustrate, one may say that in the United States the democratic component has been relatively weak, while the republican and particularly the liberal element has been strong. In France, the democratic and republican components have been strong and the liberal weak. In contemporary Germany, probably as a

reaction to the democratic emphasis of the ill-fated Weimar Republic, the republican and liberal elements predominate. In many new polyarchies, meanwhile, the democratic component, while shaky in itself, is still much stronger than the exceedingly frail republican and liberal elements. Even though the differences that I have noted are highly simplified, they suggest that there are important historically rooted variations in the kinds of presently existing polyarchies, just as there are in the kinds of states and capitalist economies that one finds in today's world.

6. Max Weber, *Economy and Society: An Outline of Interpretive Sociology,* 2 vols., Berkeley: University of California Press, 1979, 1:226–37, and 2:1006–69; and Juan J. Linz, "Totalitarian and Authoritarian Regimes," in Fred Greenstein and Nelson Polsby, eds., *Handbook of Political Science,* Reading, Mass.: Addison-Wesley, 1984, pp. 175–411.

7. See Bernard Manin, "Checks, Balances, and Boundaries: The Separation of Powers in the Constitutional Debate of 1787," in Biancamaria Fontana, ed., *The Invention of the Modern Republic,* Cambridge: Cambridge University Press, 1994, pp. 27–62.

8. Brazil is an example of this. The judiciary there has obtained great autonomy in relation to the executive and Congress, but there has been no visible improvement in its performance, which remains mostly poor. But judges and other court personnel collect extremely high salaries, and senior judges enjoy enormous privileges.

9. I allude here to Avishai Margalit, *The Decent Society,* Cambridge: Harvard University Press, 1996. Margalit argues that a decent society is one whose institutions do not humiliate its members.

··

THOMAS CAROTHERS

25   *The End of the Transition Paradigm*

In the last quarter of the twentieth century, trends in seven different regions converged to change the political landscape of the world: (1) the fall of right-wing

SOURCE: Thomas Carothers, "The End of the Transition Paradigm," *Journal of Democracy,* vol. 19, no. 1 (January 2002), pp. 5–21. © National Endowment for Democracy and The Johns Hopkins University Press. Reprinted with permission of The Johns Hopkins University Press. Footnotes abridged by the editor.

authoritarian regimes in Southern Europe in the mid-1970s; (2) the replacement of military dictatorships by elected civilian governments across Latin America from the late 1970s through the late 1980s; (3) the decline of authoritarian rule in parts of East and South Asia starting in the mid-1980s; (4) the collapse of communist regimes in Eastern Europe at the end of the 1980s; (5) the breakup of the Soviet Union and the establishment of 15 post-Soviet republics in 1991; (6) the decline of one-party regimes in many parts of sub-Saharan Africa in the first half of the 1990s; and (7) a weak but recognizable liberalizing trend in some Middle Eastern countries in the 1990s.

The causes, shape, and pace of these different trends varied considerably. But they shared a dominant characteristic—simultaneous movement in at least several countries in each region away from dictatorial rule toward more liberal and often more democratic governance. And though differing in many ways, these trends influenced and to some extent built on one another. As a result, they were considered by many observers, especially in the West, as component parts of a larger whole, a global democratic trend that thanks to Samuel Huntington has widely come to be known as the "third wave" of democracy.[1]

This striking tide of political change was seized upon with enthusiasm by the U.S. government and the broader U.S. foreign policy community. As early as the mid-1980s, President Ronald Reagan, Secretary of State George Shultz, and other high-level U.S. officials were referring regularly to "the worldwide democratic revolution." During the 1980s, an active array of governmental, quasi-governmental, and nongovernmental organizations devoted to promoting democracy abroad sprang into being. This new democracy-promotion community had a pressing need for an analytic framework to conceptualize and respond to the ongoing political events. Confronted with the initial parts of the third wave—democratization in Southern Europe, Latin America, and a few countries in Asia (especially the Philippines)—the U.S. democracy community rapidly embraced an analytic model of democratic transition. It was derived principally from their own interpretation of the patterns of democratic change taking place, but also to a lesser extent from the early works of the emergent academic field of "transitology," above all the seminal work of Guillermo O'Donnell and Philippe Schmitter.[2]

As the third wave spread to Eastern Europe, the Soviet Union, sub-Saharan Africa, and elsewhere in the 1990s, democracy promoters extended this model as a universal paradigm for understanding democratization. It became ubiquitous in U.S. policy

circles as a way of talking about, thinking about, and designing interventions in processes of political change around the world. And it stayed remarkably constant despite many variations in those patterns of political change and a stream of increasingly diverse scholarly views about the course and nature of democratic transitions.

The transition paradigm has been somewhat useful during a time of momentous and often surprising political upheaval in the world. But it is increasingly clear that reality is no longer conforming to the model. Many countries that policy makers and aid practitioners persist in calling "transitional" are not in transition to democracy, and of the democratic transitions that are under way, more than a few are not following the model. Sticking with the paradigm beyond its useful life is retarding evolution in the field of democratic assistance and is leading policy makers astray in other ways. It is time to recognize that the transition paradigm has outlived its usefulness and to look for a better lens.

....

CORE ASSUMPTIONS

Five core assumptions define the transition paradigm. The first, which is an umbrella for all the others, is that any country moving *away* from dictatorial rule can be considered a country in transition *toward* democracy. Especially in the first half of the 1990s, when political change accelerated in many regions, numerous policy makers and aid practitioners reflexively labeled any formerly authoritarian country that was attempting some political liberalization as a "transitional country." The set of "transitional countries" swelled dramatically, and nearly 100 countries (approximately 20 in Latin America, 25 in Eastern Europe and the former Soviet Union, 30 in sub-Saharan Africa, 10 in Asia, and 5 in the Middle East) were thrown into the conceptual pot of the transition paradigm. Once so labeled, their political life was automatically analyzed in terms of their movement toward or away from democracy, and they were held up to the implicit expectations of the paradigm, as detailed below. To cite just one especially astonishing example, the U.S. Agency for International Development

(USAID) continues to describe the Democratic Republic of Congo (Kinshasa), a strife-wracked country undergoing a turgid, often opaque, and rarely very democratic process of political change, as a country in "transition to a democratic, free market society."[3]

The second assumption is that democratization tends to unfold in a set sequence of stages. First there occurs the *opening,* a period of democratic ferment and political liberalization in which cracks appear in the ruling dictatorial regime, with the most prominent fault line being that between hardliners and softliners. There follows the *breakthrough*—the collapse of the regime and the rapid emergence of a new, democratic system, with the coming to power of a new government through national elections and the establishment of a democratic institutional structure, often through the promulgation of a new constitution. After the transition comes *consolidation,* a slow but purposeful process in which democratic substance through the reform of state institutions, the regularization of elections, the strengthening of civil society, and the overall habituation of the society to the new democratic "rules of the game."

Democracy activists admit that it is not inevitable that transitional countries will move steadily on this assumed path from opening and breakthrough to consolidation. Transitional countries, they say, can and do go backward or stagnate as well as move forward along the path. Yet even the deviations from the assumed sequence that they are willing to acknowledge are defined in terms of the path itself. The options are all cast in terms of the speed and direction with which countries move on the path, not in terms of movement that does not conform with the path at all. And at least in the peak years of the third wave, many democracy enthusiasts clearly believed that, while the success of the dozens of new transitions was not assured, democratization was in some important sense a natural process, one that was likely to flourish once the initial breakthrough occurred. No small amount of democratic teleology is implicit in the transition paradigm, no matter how much its adherents have denied it.

Related to the idea of a core sequence of democratization is the third assumption—the belief in the determinative importance of elections. Democracy promoters have not been guilty—as critics often charge—of believing that elections equal democracy. For years they have advocated and pursued a much broader range of assistance programs than just elections-focused efforts. Nevertheless, they have tended to hold very high expectations for what the establishment of regular, genuine elections will do for democratization. Not only will elections give new postdictatorial governments democratic legitimacy, they believe, but the elections will serve to broaden and deepen political participation and the democratic accountability of the state to its citizens. In other words, it has been assumed that in attempted transitions to democracy, elections will be not just a foundation stone but a key generator over time of further democratic reforms.

A fourth assumption is that the underlying conditions in transitional countries—their economic level, political history, institutional legacies, ethnic make-up, sociocultural traditions, or other "structural" features—will not be major factors in either the onset or the outcome of the transition process. A remarkable characteristic of the early period of the third wave was that democracy seemed to be breaking out in the most unlikely and unexpected places, whether Mongolia, Albania, or Mauritania. All that seemed to be necessary for democratization was a decision by a country's political elites to move toward democracy and an ability on the part of those elites to fend off the contrary actions of remaining antidemocratic forces.

The dynamism and remarkable scope of the third wave buried old, deterministic, and often culturally noxious assumptions about democracy, such as that only countries with an American-style middle class or a heritage of Protestant individualism could become democratic. For policy makers and aid practitioners this new outlook was a break from the long-standing Cold War mindset that most countries in the developing world were "not ready for democracy," a mindset that dovetailed with U.S. policies of propping up anticommunist dictators around the world. Some of the early works in transitology also reflected the "no preconditions" view of democratization, a shift within the academic literature that had begun in 1970 with Dankwart Rustow's seminal article, "Transitions to Democracy: Toward a Dynamic Model."[4] For both the scholarly and policy communities, the new "no preconditions" outlook was a gratifyingly optimistic, even liberating view that translated easily across borders as the encouraging message that, when it comes to democracy, "anyone can do it."

Fifth, the transition paradigm rests on the assumption that the democratic transitions making up the third wave are being built on coherent, functioning states. The process of democratization is assumed to include some redesign of state institutions—such as the creation of new electoral institutions, parliamentary reform, and judicial reform—but as a modification of already functioning states. As they arrived at their frameworks for understanding democratization, democracy aid practitioners did not give significant attention to the challenge of a society trying to democratize while it is grappling with the reality of building a state from scratch or coping with an existent but largely nonfunctional state. This did not appear to be an issue in Southern Europe or Latin America, the two regions that served as the experiential basis for the formation of the transition paradigm. To the extent that democracy promoters did consider the possibility of state-building as part of the transition process, they assumed that democracy-building and state-building would be mutually reinforcing endeavors or even two sides of the same coin.

INTO THE GRAY ZONE

We turn then from the underlying assumptions of the paradigm to the record of experience. Efforts to assess the progress of the third wave are sometimes rejected as premature. Democracy is not built in a day, democracy activists assert, and it is too early to reach judgments about the results of the dozens of democratic transitions launched in the last two decades. Although it is certainly true that the current political situations of the "transitional countries" are not set in stone, enough time has elapsed to shed significant light on how the transition paradigm is holding up.

Of the nearly 100 countries considered as "transitional" in recent years, only a relatively small number—probably fewer than 20—are clearly en route to becoming successful, well-functioning democracies or at least have made some democratic progress and still enjoy a positive dynamic of democratization. The leaders of the group are found primarily in Central Europe and the Baltic region—Poland, Hungary, the Czech Republic, Estonia, and Slovenia—though there are a few in South America and East Asia, notably Chile, Uruguay, and Taiwan. Those that have made somewhat less progress but appear to be still advancing include Slovakia, Romania, Bulgaria, Mexico, Brazil, Ghana the Philippines, and South Korea.

By far the majority of third-wave countries have not achieved relatively well-functioning democracy or do not seem to be deepening or advancing whatever democratic progress they have made. In a small number of countries, initial political openings have clearly failed and authoritarian regimes have resolidified, as in Uzbekistan, Turkmenistan, Belarus, and Togo. Most of the "transitional countries," however, are neither dictatorial nor clearly headed toward democracy. They have entered a political gray zone. They have some attributes of democratic political life, including at least limited political space for opposition parties and independent civil society, as well as regular elections and democratic constitutions. Yet they suffer from serious democratic deficits, often including poor representation of citizens' interests, low levels of political participation beyond voting, frequent abuse of the law by government officials, elections of uncertain legitimacy, very low levels of public confidence in state institutions, and persistently poor institutional performance by the state.

As the number of countries falling in between outright dictatorship and well-established liberal democracy has swollen, political analysts have proffered an array of "qualified democracy" terms to characterize them, including semi-democracy, formal democracy, electoral democracy, façade democracy, pseudo-democracy, weak democracy, partial democracy, illiberal democracy, and virtual democracy.[5] Some of these terms, such as "façade democracy" and "pseudo-democracy," apply only to a fairly specific subset of gray-zone cases. Other terms, such as "weak democracy" and "partial democracy," are intended to have much broader applicability. Useful though these terms can be, especially when rooted in probing analysis such as O'Donnell's work on "delegative democracy," they share a significant liability: By describing countries in the gray zone as types of democracies, analysts are in effect trying to apply the transition paradigm to the very countries whose political evolution is calling that paradigm into question. Most of the "qualified democracy" terms are used to characterize countries as being stuck somewhere on the assumed democratization sequence, usually at the start of the consolidation phase.

The diversity of political patterns within the gray zone is vast. Many possible subtypes or subcategories could potentially be posited, and much work remains to be done to assess the nature of gray-zone politics. As a first analytic step, two broad political syndromes can be seen to be common in the gray zone. They are not rigidly delineated political-system types but rather political patterns that have become regular and somewhat entrenched. Though they have some characteristics in common, they differ in crucial ways and basically are mutually exclusive.

The first syndrome is feckless pluralism. Countries whose political life is marked by feckless pluralism tend to have significant amounts of political freedom, regular elections, and alternation of power between genuinely different political groupings. Despite these positive features, however, democracy remains shallow and troubled. Political participation, though broad at election time, extends little beyond voting. Political elites from all the major parties or groupings are widely perceived as corrupt, self-interested, and ineffective. The alternation of power seems only to trade the country's problems back and forth from one hapless side to the other. Political elites from all the major parties are widely perceived as corrupt, self-interested, dishonest, and not serious about working for their country. The public is seriously disaffected from politics, and while it may still cling to a belief in the ideal of democracy, it is extremely unhappy about the political life of the country. Overall, politics is

widely seen as a stale, corrupt, elite-dominated domain that delivers little good to the country and commands equally little respect. And the state remains persistently weak. Economic policy is often poorly conceived and executed, and economic performance is frequently bad or even calamitous. Social and political reforms are similarly tenuous, and successive governments are unable to make headway on most of the major problems facing the country, from crime and corruption to health, education, and public welfare generally.

Feckless pluralism is most common in Latin America, a region where most countries entered their attempted democratic transitions with diverse political parties already in place yet also with a deep legacy of persistently poor performance of state institutions. Nicaragua, Ecuador, Guatemala, Panama, Honduras, and Bolivia all fall into this category, as did Venezuela in the decade prior to the election of Hugo Chávez. Argentina and Brazil hover uneasily at its edge. In the postcommunist world, Moldova, Bosnia, Albania, and Ukraine have at least some significant signs of the syndrome, with Romania and Bulgaria teetering on its edge. Nepal is a clear example in Asia; Bangladesh, Mongolia, and Thailand may also qualify. In sub-Saharan Africa, a few states, such as Madagascar, Guinea-Bissau, and Sierra Leone, may be cases of feckless pluralism, through alternation of power remains rare generally in that region.

There are many variations of feckless pluralism. In some cases, the parties that alternate power between them are divided by paralyzing acrimony and devote their time out of power to preventing the other party from accomplishing anything at all, as in Bangladesh. In other cases, the main competing groups end up colluding, formally or informally, rendering the alternation of power unhelpful in a different manner, as happened in Nicaragua in the late 1990s. In some countries afflicted with feckless pluralism, the political competition is between deeply entrenched parties that essentially operate as patronage networks and seem never to renovate themselves, as in Argentina or Nepal. In others, the alternation of power occurs between constantly shifting political groupings, short-lived parties led by charismatic individuals or temporary alliances in search of a political identity, as in

Guatemala or Ukraine. These varied cases nonetheless share a common condition that seems at the root of feckless pluralism—the whole class of political elites, though plural and competitive, are profoundly cut off from the citizenry, rendering political life an ultimately hollow, unproductive exercise.

DOMINANT-POWER POLITICS

The most common other political syndrome in the gray zone is dominant-power politics. Countries with this syndrome have limited but still real political space, some political contestation by opposition groups, and at least most of the basic institutional forms of democracy. Yet one political grouping—whether it is a movement, a party, an extended family, or a single leader—dominates the system in the system such a way that there appears to be little prospect of alternation of power in the foreseeable future.

Unlike in countries beset with feckless pluralism, a key political problem in dominant-power countries is the blurring of the line between the state and the ruling party (or ruling political forces). The state's main assets—that is to say, the state as a source of money, jobs, public information (via state media), and police power—are gradually put in the direct service of the ruling party. Whereas in feckless pluralism judiciaries are often somewhat independent, the judiciary in dominant-power countries is typically cowed, as part of the one-sided grip on power. And while elections in feckless-pluralist countries are often quite free and fair, the typical pattern in dominant-power countries is one of dubious but not outright fraudulent elections in which the ruling group tries to put on a good-enough electoral show to gain the approval of the international community while quietly tilting the electoral playing field far enough in its own favor to ensure victory.

As in feckless-pluralist systems, the citizens of dominant-power systems tend to be disaffected from politics and cut off from significant political participation beyond voting. Since there is no alternation of power, however, they are less apt to evince the "a pox on all your houses" political outlook pervasive in feckless-pluralist systems. Yet those opposition political parties that do exist generally are hard put to gain much public credibility due to their perennial status as outsiders to the main halls of power. Whatever energies and hopes for effective opposition to the regime remain often reside in civil society groups, usually a loose collection of advocacy NGOs and independent media (often funded by Western donors) that skirmish with the government on human rights, the environment, corruption, and other issues of public interest.

The state tends to be as weak and poorly performing in dominant-power countries as in feckless-pluralist countries, though the problem is often a bureaucracy decaying under the stagnancy of de facto one-party rule rather than the disorganized, unstable nature of state management (such as the constant turnover of ministers) typical of feckless pluralism. The long hold on power by one political group usually produces large-scale corruption and crony capitalism. Due to the existence of some political openness in these systems, the leaders do often feel some pressure from the public about corruption and other abuses of state power. They even may periodically declare their intention to root out corruption and strengthen the rule of law. But their deep-seated intolerance for anything more than limited opposition and the basic political configuration over which they preside breed the very problems they publicly commit themselves to tackling.

Dominant-power systems are prevalent in three regions. In sub-Saharan Africa, the widely hailed wave of democratization that washed over the region in the early 1990s has ended up producing many dominant-power systems. In some cases, one-party states liberalized yet ended up permitting only very limited processes of political opening, as in Cameroon, Burkina Faso, Equatorial Guinea, Tanzania, Gabon, Kenya, and Mauritania. In a few cases, old regimes were defeated or collapsed, yet the new regimes have ended up in dominant-party structures, as in Zambia in the 1990s, or the forces previously shunted aside to reclaimed power, as in Congo (Brazzaville).

Dominant-power systems are found in the former Soviet Union as well. Armenia, Azerbaijan, Georgia, Kyrgyzstan, and Kazakhstan fall in this category. The other Central Asian republics and Belarus are better understood as out-and-out authoritarian systems. The liberalization trend that arose in the Middle East in the mid-1980s and has unfolded in fits and starts ever since has moved some countries out of the authoritarian camp into the dominant-power category. These include Morocco, Jordan, Algeria, Egypt, Iran, and Yemen. Dominant-power systems are scarce outside of these three regions. In Asia, Malaysia and Cambodia count as examples. In Latin America, Paraguay may be one case, and Venezuela is likely headed toward becoming a second.

Dominant-power systems vary in their degree of freedom and their political direction. Some have very limited political space and are close to being dictatorships. Others allow much more freedom, albeit still with limits. A few "transitional countries," including the important cases of South Africa and Russia, fall just to the side of this syndrome. They have a fair amount of political freedom and have held competitive elections of some legitimacy (though sharp debate on that issue exists with regard to Russia). Yet they are ruled by political forces that appear to have a long-term hold on power (if one considers the shift from Yeltsin to Putin more as a political transfer than an alternation of power), and it is hard to imagine any of the existing opposition parties coming to power for many years to come. If they maintain real political freedom and open competition for power, they may join the ranks of cases, such as Italy and Japan (prior to the 1990s) and Botswana, of longtime democratic rule by one party. Yet due to the tenuousness of their new democratic institutions, they face the danger of slippage toward the dominant-power syndrome.

As political syndromes, both feckless pluralism and dominant-power politics have some stability. Once in them, countries do not move out of them easily. Feckless pluralism achieves its own dysfunctional equilibrium—the passing of power back and forth between competing elites who are largely isolated from the citizenry but willing to play by widely accepted rules. Dominant-power politics also often achieves a kind of stasis, with the ruling group able to keep political opposition on the ropes while permitting enough political openness to alleviate pressure from the public. They are by no means permanent political configurations; no political configuration lasts forever. Countries can and do move out of them—either from one to the other or out of either toward liberal democracy or dictatorship. For a time in the 1990s, Ukraine seemed stuck in dominant-power politics but may be shifting to something more like feckless pluralism. Senegal was previously a clear case of dominant-power politics but, with the opposition victory in the 2000 elections, may be moving toward either liberal democracy or feckless pluralism.

Although many countries in the gray zone have ended up as examples of either feckless pluralism or dominant-power politics, not all have. A small number of "transitional countries" have moved away from authoritarian rule only in the last several years, and their political trajectory is as yet unclear. Indonesia, Nigeria, Serbia, and Croatia are four prominent examples of this type. Some countries that experienced political openings in the 1980s or 1990s have been so wracked by civil conflict that their political systems are too unstable or incoherent to pin down easily, though they are definitely not on a path of democratization. The Democratic Republic of Congo, Liberia, Sierra Leone, and Somalia all represent this situation.

THE CRASH OF ASSUMPTIONS

Taken together, the political trajectories of most third-wave countries call into serious doubt the transition paradigm. This is apparent if we revisit the major assumptions underlying the paradigm in light of the above analysis.

First, the almost automatic assumption of democracy promoters during the peak years of the third wave that any country moving away from dictatorship was "in transition to democracy" has often been inaccurate and misleading. Some of those countries have hardly democratized at all. Many have taken on a smattering of democratic features but show few signs of democratizing much further and are certainly not following any predictable democratization script. The most common political patterns to date among the "transitional countries"—feckless pluralism and dominant-power politics—include elements of democracy but should be understood as alternative directions, not way stations to liberal democracy. The persistence in official U.S. democracy-promotion circles of using transitional language to characterize countries that in no way conform to any democratization paradigm borders in some cases on the surreal—including not just the case of Congo cited above but many others, such as Moldova ("Moldova's democratic transition continues to progress steadily"), Zambia ("Zambia is . . . moving steadily toward . . . the creation of a viable multiparty democracy"), Cambodia ("policy successes in Cambodia towards democracy and improved governance within the past 18 months are numerous"), and Guinea ("Guinea has made significant strides toward building a democratic society").[6] The continued use of the transition paradigm constitutes a dangerous habit of trying to impose a simplistic and often incorrect conceptual order on an empirical tableau of considerable complexity.

Second, not only is the general label and concept of "transitional country" unhelpful, but the assumed sequence of stages of democratization is defied by the record of experience. Some of the most encouraging cases of democratization in recent years—such as Taiwan, South Korea, and Mexico—did not go through the paradigmatic process of democratic breakthrough followed rapidly by national elections and a new democratic institutional framework. Their political evolutions were defined by an almost opposite phenomenon—extremely gradual, incremental processes of liberalization with an organized political opposition (not softliners in the regime) pushing for change across successive elections and finally winning. And in many of the countries that did go through some version of what appeared to be a democratic breakthrough, the assumed sequence of changes—first settling constitutive issues then working through second-order reforms—has not held. Constitutive issues have reemerged at unpredictable times,

upending what are supposed to be later stages of transition, as in the recent political crises in Ecuador, the Central African Republic, and Chad.

Moreover, the various assumed component processes of consolidation—political party development, civil society strengthening, judicial reform, and media development—almost never conform to the technocratic ideal of rational sequences on which the indicator frameworks and strategic objectives of democracy promoters are built. Instead they are chaotic processes of change that go backwards and sideways as much as forward, and do not do so in any regular manner.

The third assumption of the transition paradigm—the notion that achieving regular, genuine elections will not only confer democratic legitimacy on new governments but continuously deepen political participation and democratic accountability—has often come up short. In many "transitional countries," reasonably regular, genuine elections are held but political participation beyond voting remains shallow and governmental accountability is weak. The wide gulf between political elites and citizens in many of these countries turns out to be rooted in structural conditions, such as the concentration of wealth or certain sociocultural traditions, that elections themselves do not overcome. It is also striking how often electoral competition does little to stimulate the renovation or development of political parties in many gray-zone countries. Such profound pathologies as highly personalistic parties, transient and shifting parties, or stagnant patronage-based politics appear to be able to coexist for sustained periods with at least somewhat legitimate processes of political pluralism and competition.

These disappointments certainly do not mean that elections are pointless in such countries or that the international community should not continue to push for free and fair elections. But greatly reduced expectations are in order as to what elections will accomplish as generators of deep-reaching democratic change. Nepal is a telling example in this regard. Since 1990, Nepal has held many multiparty elections and experienced frequent alternation of power. Yet the Nepalese public remains highly disaffected from the political system and there is little real sense of democratic accountability.

Fourth, ever since "preconditions for democracy" were enthusiastically banished in the heady early days of the third wave, a contrary reality—the fact that various structural conditions clearly weigh heavily in shaping political outcomes—has been working its way back in. Looking at the more successful recent cases of democratization, for example, which tend to be found in Central Europe, the Southern Cone, or East Asia, it is clear that relative economic wealth, as well as past experience with political pluralism, contributes to the chances for democratic success. And looking comparatively within regions, whether in the former communist world or sub-Saharan Africa, it is evident that the specific institutional legacies from predecessor regimes strongly affect the outcomes of attempted transitions.

During the 1990s, a number of scholars began challenging the "no preconditions" line, with analyses of the roles that economic wealth, institutional legacies, social class, and other structural factors play in attempted democratic transitions.[7] Yet it has been hard for the democracy-promotion community to take this work on board. Democracy promoters are strongly wedded to their focus on political processes and institutions. They have been concerned that trying to blend that focus with economic or sociocultural perspectives might lead to the dilution or reduction of democracy assistance. And having set up as organizations with an exclusively political perspective, it is hard for democracy-promotion groups to include other kinds of expertise or approaches.

Fifth, state-building has been a much larger and more problematic issue than originally envisaged in the transition paradigm. Contrary to the early assumptions of democracy-aid practitioners, many third-wave countries have faced fundamental state-building challenges. Approximately 20 countries in the former Soviet Union and former Yugoslavia have had to build national state institutions where none existed before. Throughout much of sub-Saharan Africa, the liberalizing political wave of the 1990s ran squarely into the sobering reality of devastatingly weak states. In many parts of Latin America, the Middle East, and Asia, political change was carried out in the context of stable state structures, but the erratic performance of those states complicated every step.

Where state-building from scratch had to be carried out, the core impulses and interests of powerholders—such as locking in access to power and resources as quickly as possible—ran directly contrary to what democracy-building would have required. In countries with existing but extremely weak states, the democracy-building efforts funded by donors usually neglected the issue of state-building. With their frequent emphasis on diffusing power and weakening the relative power of the executive branch—by strengthening the legislative and judicial branches of government, encouraging decentralization, and building civil society—they were more about the redistribution of state power than about state-building. The programs that democracy promoters have directed at governance have tended to be minor technocratic efforts, such as training ministerial staff or aiding cabinet offices, rather than major efforts at bolstering state capacity.

....

LETTING GO

It is time for the democracy-promotion community to discard the transition paradigm. Analyzing the record of experience in the many countries that democracy activists have been labeling "transitional countries," it is evident that it is no longer appropriate to assume

- that most of these countries are actually in a transition to democracy;

- that countries moving away from authoritarianism tend to follow a three-part process of democratization consisting of opening, breakthrough, and consolidation;

- that the establishment of regular, genuine elections will not only give new governments democratic legitimacy but foster a longer term deepening of democratic participation and accountability;

- that a country's chances for successfully democratizing depend primarily on the political intentions and actions of its political elites without significant influence from underlying economic, social, and institutional conditions and legacies;

- that state-building is a secondary challenge to democracy-building and largely compatible with it.

It is hard to let go of the transitional paradigm, both for the conceptual order and for the hopeful vision it provides. Giving it up constitutes a major break, but not a total one. It does not mean denying that important democratic reforms have occurred in many countries in the past two decades. It does not mean that countries in the gray zone are doomed never to achieve well-functioning liberal democracy. It does not mean that free and fair elections in "transitional countries" are futile or not worth supporting. It does not mean that the United States and other international actors should abandon efforts to promote democracy in the world (if anything, it implies that, given how difficult democratization is, efforts to promote it should be redoubled).

It does mean, however, that democracy promoters should approach their work with some very different assumptions. They should start by assuming that what is often thought of as an uneasy, precarious middle ground between full-fledged democracy and outright dictatorship is actually the most common political condition today of countries in the developing world and the postcommunist world. It is not an exceptional category to be defined only in terms of its not being one thing or the other; it is a state of normality for many societies, for better or worse. The seemingly continual surprise and disappointment that Western political analysts express over the very frequent falling short of democracy in "transitional countries" should be replaced with realistic expectations about the likely patterns of political life in these countries.

Aid practitioners and policy makers looking at politics in a country that has recently moved away from authoritarianism should not start by asking. "How is its democratic transition going?" They should instead formulate a more open-ended query, "What is happening politically?" Insisting on the former approach leads to optimistic assumptions

that often shunt the analysis down a blind alley. To take one example, during the 1990s, Western policy makers habitually analyzed Georgia's post-1991 political evolution as a democratic transition, highlighting the many formal achievements, and holding up a basically positive image of the country. Then suddenly, at the end of the decade, the essential hollowness of Georgia's "democratic transition" became too apparent to ignore, and Georgia is now suddenly talked about as a country in serious risk of state failure or deep sociopolitical crisis.

A whole generation of democracy aid is based on the transition paradigm, above all the typical emphasis on an institutional "checklist" as a basis for creating programs, and the creation of nearly standard portfolios of aid projects consisting of the same diffuse set of efforts all over—some judicial reform, parliamentary strengthening, civil society assistance, media work, political party development, civic education, and electoral programs. Much of the democracy aid based on this paradigm is exhausted. Where the paradigm fits well—in the small number of clearly successful transitions—the aid is not much needed. Where democracy aid is needed most, in many of the gray-zone countries, the paradigm fits poorly.

Democracy promoters need to focus in on the key political patterns of each country in which they intervene, rather than trying to do a little of everything according to a template of ideal institutional forms. Where feckless pluralism reigns, this means giving concentrated attention to two interrelated issues: how to improve the variety and quality of the main political actors in the society and how to begin to bridge the gulf between the citizenry and the formal political system. Much greater attention to political party development should be a major part of the response, with special attention to encouraging new entrants into the political party scene, changing the rules and incentive systems that shape the current party structures, and fostering strong connections between parties and civil society groups (rather than encouraging civil society groups to stay away from partisan politics).

In dominant-power systems, democracy promoters should devote significant attention to the challenge of helping to encourage the growth of alternative centers of power. Merely helping finance the proliferation of nongovernmental organizations is an inadequate approach to this challenge. Again, political party development must be a top agenda item, especially through measures aimed at changing the way political parties are financed. It should include efforts to examine how the over-concentration of economic power (a standard feature of dominant-power systems) can be reduced as well as measures that call attention to and work against the blurring of the line between the ruling party and the state.

In other types of gray-zone countries, democracy promoters will need to settle on other approaches. The message for all gray-zone countries, however, is the same—falling back on a smorgasbord of democracy programs based on the vague assumption that they all contribute to some assumed process of consolidation is not good enough. Democracy aid must proceed from a penetrating analysis of the particular core syndrome that defines the political life of the country in question, and how aid interventions can change that syndrome.

Moving beyond the transition paradigm also means getting serious about bridging the long-standing divide between aid programs directed at democracy-building and those focused on social and economic development. USAID has initiated some work on this topic but has only scratched the surface of what could become a major synthesis of disparate domains in the aid world. One example of a topic that merits the combined attention of economic aid providers and democracy promoters is privatization programs. These programs have major implications for how power is distributed in a society, how ruling political forces can entrench themselves, and how the public participates in major policy decisions. Democracy promoters need to take a serious interest in these reform efforts and learn to make a credible case to economists that they should have a place at the table when such programs are being planned. The same is true for any number of areas of socioeconomic reform that tend to be a major focus of economic aid providers and that have potentially significant effects on the underlying sociopolitical domain,

including pension reform, labor law reform, antitrust policy, banking reform, and tax reform. The onus is on democracy-aid providers to develop a broader conception of democracy work and to show that they have something to contribute on the main stage of the development-assistance world.

These are only provisional ideas. Many other "next generation" challenges remain to be identified. The core point, however, is plain: The transition paradigm was a product of a certain time—the heady early days of the third wave—and that time has now passed. It is necessary for democracy activists to move on to new frameworks, new debates, and perhaps eventually a new paradigm of political change—one suited to the landscape of today, not the lingering hopes of an earlier era.

ENDNOTES

1. Samuel P. Huntington, *The Third Wave: Democratization in the Late Twentieth Century* (Norman: University of Oklahoma Press, 1991).
2. Guillermo O'Donnell and Philippe C. Schmitter, *Transitions from Authoritarian Rule: Tentative Conclusions About Uncertain Democracies* (Baltimore: Johns Hopkins University Press, 1986).
3. "Building Democracy in the Democratic Republic of Congo," *www.usaid.gov/democracy/afr/congo.html*. Here and elsewhere in this article, I cite USAID documents because they are the most readily available practitioners' statements of guidelines and political assessments, but I believe that my analysis applies equally well to most other democracy-promotion organizations in the United States and abroad.
4. See, for example, Giuseppe Di Palma, *To Craft Democracies: An Essay on Democratic Transitions* (Berkeley: University of California Press, 1991). Dankwart Rustow's article "Transitions to Democracy: Toward a Comparative Model," originally appeared in *Comparative Politics* 2 (April 1970), pp. 337–63.
5. David Collier and Steven Levitsky, "Democracy with Adjectives: Conceptual Innovation in Comparative Research," *World Politics* 49 (April 1997), pp. 430–51.
6. These quotes are all taken from the country descriptions in the democracy-building section of the USAID website, *www.usaid.gov/democracy.html*.

7. See, for example, Michael Bratton and Nicolas van de Walle, *Democratic Experiments in Africa: Regime Transitions in Comparative Perspective* (Cambridge: Cambridge University Press, 1997); Valerie Bunce, *Subversive Institutions: The Design and Destruction of Socialism and the State* (Cambridge: Cambridge University Press, 1999); Ruth Collier, *Paths Toward Democracy;* Dietrich Rueschmeyer, Evelyne Huber Stephens, and John D. Stephens, *Capitalist Development and Democracy* (Chicago: Chicago University Press, 1992); Adam Przeworksi, *Democracy and the Market: Political and Economic Reforms in Latin America and Eastern Europe* (Cambridge: Cambridge University Press, 1991); and Adam Przeworksi and Fernando Limongi, "Political Regimes and Economic Growth," *Journal of Economic Perspectives* 7 (Summer 1993), pp. 51–69.

LARRY DIAMOND

26 *Universal Democracy?*

A short while ago, one of the world's most brutal and entrenched dictatorships was swiftly toppled by the military force of the United States and the United Kingdom. The 2003 Iraq war was launched to disarm Saddam Hussein, but for many of its advocates and supporters, the more compelling aim was to bring about regime change. In fact, the goal is not simply "regime change" but a sweeping political transformation in that country—and, it is hoped, in states throughout its neighborhood—towards what has never existed there before: democracy.

This is the most ambitious effort to foster deliberate political change since European colonial rule drew to a close in the early post-World War II era. Can it succeed? Since Iraq lacks virtually all of the classic favorable conditions, to ask whether it can soon become a democracy is to ask, really, whether any country can become a democracy. Which is to ask as well, can *every* country become a democracy?

My answer here is a cautiously optimistic one. The current moment is in many respects without historical precedent. Much is made of the unparalleled gap between the military and economic power of the United States and that of any conceivable combination of competitors or adversaries. But no less unique are these additional facts.

- This breathtaking preponderance of power is held by a liberal democracy.
- The next most powerful global actor is a loose union of countries that are also all liberal democracies.
- The majority of states in the world are already democracies of one sort or another.
- There is no model of governance with any broad normative appeal or legitimacy in the world other than democracy.
- There is growing international legal and moral momentum toward the recognition of democracy as a basic human right of all peoples.
- States and international organizations are intruding on sovereignty in ever more numerous and audacious ways in order to promote democracy and freedom.

In short, the international context has never mattered more to the future of democracy or been more favorable. We are on the cusp of a grand historical tipping point, when a visionary and resourceful strategy could—if it garnered the necessary cooperation and effort *among* the powerful democracies—essentially eliminate authoritarian rule over the next generation or two.

SOURCE: Larry Diamond, "Universal Democracy?," *Policy Review*, no. 119 (June 2003), pp. 3–25. Published by the Hoover Institution, Stanford University. Reprinted by permission of the Hoover Institution.

A QUARTER-CENTURY OF PROGRESS

As Samuel P. Huntington has documented in his seminal work, *The Third Wave: Democratization in the Late Twentieth Century* (University of Oklahoma Press, 1991), a powerful wave of democratic transitions began in April 1974, when the Portuguese dictatorship was overthrown in a military coup. It was far from clear then that Portugal would become a democracy. It had never been one before. It had just been through half a century of quasi-fascist rule. The Spanish dictator Francisco Franco held on to power over the border. Both countries were steeped in a Latin, Catholic culture that was dismissed by many political scientists and commentators as being unsuited to democracy. (That logic was also used to explain the virtual absence of democracy in Latin America at the time.) The Portuguese armed forces movement was split into ideological factions, and the country was plagued for 18 months by coups, counter-coups, and a succession of fragile provisional governments. Yet the triumph of democracy in Portugal was the beginning of a long wave of democratic expansion in the world that continues to this day.

When the third wave of democratization began in 1974, there were only about 40 democracies in the world, and these were mainly in the advanced industrial countries. There were a few other democracies scattered through Africa, Asia, and Latin America—such as India, Sri Lanka, Botswana, Costa Rica, and Venezuela. But military and one-party dictatorships held sway in most of Latin America, Asia, Africa, and the Middle East, while all of Eastern Europe and the Soviet Union were under communist rule.

Since 1974, democracy—a system of government in which the people choose their leaders at regular intervals through free, fair, and competitive elections—has expanded dramatically in the world. The number and percentage of democracies in the world expanded gradually after April 1974, spreading first to Greece and Spain in the mid-1970s.

From 1979 to 1985, the military withdrew in favor of elected civilian governments in about nine Latin American countries. Where military rule was more economically successful, in Chile, the transition was delayed, but it came in 1989, after a heroic effort of peaceful political mobilization.

By then, the third wave of democratization had spread to Asia, first toppling the dictatorship of Ferdinand Marcos in the Philippines in February 1986, then forcing the complete withdrawal of the Korean military in 1987. That same year, martial law was lifted in Taiwan and a more gradual transition to democracy began there, not to be completed until the first direct elections for president in 1996. But by 1991, Pakistan, Bangladesh, and Nepal had all become democracies. Also that year, Thailand suffered what I believe will prove to have been its last military coup, followed by its shortest period of military rule.

By 1987, the third wave had spread to the point where about two of every five states in the world were democracies: all of Western Europe, much of Asia, and most of Latin America. But that still left gaping holes in Eastern Europe, Africa, and the Middle East. Democracy was still a regional phenomenon. This changed dramatically with the fall of the Berlin Wall in 1989 and then the collapse of the Soviet Union in 1991. By 1990, most of the states of Eastern Europe—and even poor and isolated Mongolia—held competitive elections and began to institutionalize democracy.

Freed from the prism of the two superpowers' struggle for geopolitical dominance, and reeling from desperate fiscal crises, African countries began to liberate themselves. In February 1990 two seminal events launched a new wave of democratic transitions in Africa. In Benin, a coalition of forces in civil society, organized in a "sovereign national conference," claimed governing authority and launched a transition to democracy. In South Africa, the apartheid regime released Nelson Mandela from prison and launched a process of political dialogue and normalization that gave birth to democracy in 1994. When these two events occurred, there were only three democracies in Africa—the Gambia,

Botswana, and Mauritius. But starting in 1990, Africa experienced a rolling tide of democratic change. Under heavy pressure from international donors as well as their own peoples, most African states by 1997 had at least legalized opposition parties, opened space in civil society, and held multiparty elections. Many of these openings were largely a façade, marred by continued repression and blatant rigging of the vote. But well over a dozen met the minimum conditions of democracy, and in several cases, long-ruling incumbent parties were defeated.

To appreciate the depth and breadth of the third wave of democratization, consider this: In 1974, there were 41 democracies among the existing 150 states. Of the remaining 109 states, 56 (more than half) of them subsequently made a transition to democracy, and of those 56, only Pakistan, Sudan, and Russia are not democracies today. Moreover, 26 states since 1974 have become independent of colonial rule; 15 of these became democracies upon independence and have remained so, and another six have become democratic after some period of authoritarian rule. Of the 19 new postcommunist states, 11 (58 percent) are democracies. Overall, of the 45 new states created since the third wave began, almost three-quarters (71 percent) are democracies, though in the case of the former Soviet Union, some of them (such as Ukraine, Georgia, and Armenia) are only ambiguously democratic.

As democracy spread to Eastern Europe, a few states in the former Soviet Union, and a number in Africa, while extending deeper into Asia and Latin America, it came during the 1990s to be a *global* phenomenon, the predominant form of government, and the only broadly legitimate form of government in the world. Today, about three-fifths of all the world's states (by the count of Freedom House, 121 of 193) are democracies. There are no global rivals to democracy as a broad model of government. Communism is dead. Military rule everywhere lacks appeal and normative justification. One-party states have largely disappeared, for what single party—in this day and age—can credibly claim the wisdom and moral righteousness to rule indefinitely and without criticism or challenge?

Only the vague model of an Islamic state has any moral and ideological appeal as an alternative form of government—and then only for a small portion of the world's societies. Moreover, the only actual example of such an Islamic state is the increasingly corrupt, discredited, and illegitimate Islamic Republic in Iran, whose own people overwhelmingly desire to see it replaced by a more truly democratic form of government.

Clearly, most states can become democratic because most states already are. Moreover, the overwhelming bulk of the states that have become democratic during the third wave have remained so, even in countries lacking virtually all of the supposed "conditions" for democracy. Pre-1990 Africa aside, only four democracies have been overthrown by the military in a conventional coup. Two of those (Turkey and Thailand) returned fairly quickly to democracy, and the other two (Pakistan and the Gambia) have felt compelled at least to institute civilian multiparty elections. Several democracies have been suspended in "self-coups" by elected civilian leaders, while other elected rulers have more subtly strangled democracy. Overall, however, only 14 of the 125 democracies that have existed during the third wave have become authoritarian, and in nine of these, democracy has since been restored.

If democracy can emerge and persist (now so far for a decade) in an extremely poor, landlocked, overwhelmingly Muslim country like Mali—in which the majority of adults are illiterate and live in absolute poverty and the life expectancy is 44 years—then there is no reason in principle why democracy cannot develop in most other very poor countries. In fact, if we examine the 36 countries that the United Nations Development Programme (UNDP) classifies as having "Low Human Development," 11 are democracies today. If we widen our scope to look at the bottom third of states classified by the UNDP, the percentage of democracies rises from nearly a third to 41 percent. About a dozen of these have been democracies for a decade or longer. That there should be so many democracies among the world's least developed countries is a phenomenon at least as noteworthy as the overall predominance of democracy in the world, and one profoundly in defiance of established social science theories. It deserves more attention, and I attempt to give it some below.

....

CONCEPTUALIZING DEMOCRACY

To comprehend the nature and limits of democratic progress in this third wave, it is useful to conceive of democracy in terms of two thresholds. Countries above the first threshold are, as I have suggested, electoral democracies in the minimal sense that their principal positions of political power are filled through regular, free, fair, and competitive (and therefore multiparty) elections. Electoral democracy can exist in countries with significant violations of human rights, massive corruption, and a weak rule of law. But in order for a country to be a democracy, these defects must be sufficiently contained so that, in elections at least, the will of the voters can be reflected in the outcome and, in particular, unpopular incumbents can be booted from office.[1]

Many people have criticized my emphasis on free, fair, meaningful, and competitive elections as the minimal litmus test of democracy. They say that this may not amount to much. What is the point of having such an "electoral" democracy if the rights of women, minorities, and the poor are extensively violated; if those who are elected take turns plundering the national treasury and abusing power, as happened in Pakistan before the October 1999 coup; if elections merely crown a temporary presidential monarch who can use and abuse power without constraint for his term of office (what University of Notre Dame professor Guillermo O'Donnell calls "delegative democracy")? Indeed, in his new book, *The Future of Freedom: Illiberal Democracy at Home and Abroad* (Norton, 2003), Fareed Zakaria questions whether we might not do better with less democracy and more rule of law.

My answer to this is twofold. Normatively, I do not argue that we should rest content with such an illiberal and hollowed-out democracy as our goal. The goal for every country should be a political system that combines democracy on the one hand with freedom, the rule of law, and good government

on the other—in other words, *liberal democracy*. Beyond the electoral arena, liberal democracy encompasses a vigorous rule of law with an independent and nondiscriminatory judiciary; extensive individual freedoms of belief, speech, publication, association, assembly, and so on; strong protections for the rights of ethnic, cultural, religious, and other minorities; a pluralistic civil society, which affords citizens multiple channels outside of the electoral arena through which to participate and express their interests and values; and civilian control of the military.

Empirically, the implication that authoritarian and conflict-ridden states should emphasize the rule of law rather than democracy is viable only as a transitional strategy. In reality, democracy and freedom are closely related in the world. Even if we forget about the wealthy countries of the West—all liberal democracies—and examine only the developing and postcommunist countries, we find that the countries where civil liberties and the rule of law are best respected are democracies, and the human rights (and humanitarian) emergencies are invariably to be found in non-democracies.

Each year Freedom House rates each country from 1 to 7 along two scales, political rights (basically to participate and compete democratically) and civil liberties, with 1 being most free and 7 most repressive. There are only two countries in the world that are not democracies and yet have a civil liberties score below the midpoint on the seven-point scale: Tonga, and Antigua and Barbuda. One can hardly advance a general theory of political development based on these two microstates. To be sure, there are some pretty illiberal democracies in the world, with serious problems of human rights and the rule of law, but the only countries that give their citizens extensive civic freedom and a thorough rule of law are democracies.

....

THE REGIONAL DISTRIBUTION

In one respect, democracy is still not quite a global phenomenon. In every region of the world—except for one—at least a third of the states are democracies. Thirty of the 33 states in Latin America and the Caribbean are democracies, and about half of them are now fairly liberal in terms of their levels of freedom. Two-thirds of the former communist countries, half of the Asian states, and even about two-fifths of the African states are now democracies. Only in the Middle East is democracy virtually absent. In fact, among the 16 Arab countries, there is not a single democracy and, with the exception of Lebanon, there never has been.

The exceptionalism of the Middle East becomes even more striking when we examine trends in freedom. Every region of the world has seen a rather significant improvement in the level of freedom—except for one. Regions that had been strongholds of authoritarianism have seen their average freedom score on the combined seven-point scale improve by at least a point. There is only one region of the world where the average level of freedom has declined, by almost half a point—again, the Middle East.

Some skeptics believe that democracy is largely a Western, Judeo-Christian phenomenon that is not well suited to other regions, cultures, and religious traditions. They have a ready answer for this freedom gap: Islam. I believe this answer is wrong on substantive grounds that I will come to shortly, but it is also questionable empirically. There are 43 countries in the world that pretty clearly have a Muslim majority. The 27 of these outside the Arab world have an average freedom score (5.04) appreciably better than the Arab states (5.81). A quarter (seven) of these 27 non-Arab, Muslim-majority states are democracies. Moreover, as Columbia University's Alfred Stepan has shown, non-Arab Muslim countries have some considerable cumulative experience over the past 30 years with political freedom.[2]

Democracy, then, exists in virtually all types of states. It is significantly present in almost every region of the world. It is present in countries evincing every major religious or philosophical tradition: Christian, Jewish, Hindu, Buddhist, Confucian, and Muslim. It is much more common in developed countries (all of the top 20 countries in human development are liberal democracies), but it is now significantly present among very poor countries as well. It is much more common—and much

more liberal—in small states of under 1 million. But most of the biggest countries—specifically, eight of the 11 countries with populations over 100 million—are democracies.[3] By any category that is meaningful in the world today, there is only one set of countries that is completely undemocratic: the Arab world.

DEMOCRACY AS A UNIVERSAL VALUE?

There is a possible retort to this claim that democracy is present in virtually every major region of the world and thus is nearly a universal phenomenon. One could dismiss this as a fad, or a contemporary concession to international pressure: Democracy may exist today in far reaches of the globe, but only temporarily and superficially. It is not really valued by the people, and it will not last.

What about persistence? Forty years ago Seymour Martin Lipset argued that the richer the country the greater the chance that it would sustain democracy. In a seminal and methodologically sophisticated study, Adam Przeworski and his colleagues found that there was in fact a striking and monotonic relationship between development level and the probability of sustaining democracy. During the period 1950–1990, the poorest democracies had a 12 percent chance of dying in any particular year, or an average life expectancy of eight years. Several third-wave democracies in their lowest income category have now outlived that expected life span, including Benin, Mali, Malawi, Mozambique, and Nepal.[4] Even among the poorest countries, there have been few breakdowns of democracy.

In fact, a strong case has been made that democracy is not an extravagance for the poor, but very nearly a necessity. Amartya Sen won the Nobel Prize for economics in 1998 in part for showing that democracies do not have famines. "People in economic need," he argues, "also need a political voice. Democracy is not a luxury that can await the arrival of general prosperity." Moreover, "there is very little evidence that poor people, given the choice, prefer to reject democracy."[5] He notes the vigor with which Indians defended their freedom and democracy in the 1977 election, tossing from office the prime minister, Indira Gandhi, who had suspended political and civil rights. But there have been countless other instances—from Burma and Bangladesh to Senegal and South Africa—where poor people have mobilized passionately for (and in defense of) democratic change. The fact that they have sometimes, as in Burma, been crushed by sheer force while a timid world watched and protested ineffectually does not negate the overwhelming expression of their sentiment.

Fortunately, we also have more precise evidence from public opinion survey data as to what ordinary people really think. So far, the data show that the understanding and valuing of democracy is widely shared across cultures. Two-thirds of Africans surveyed (by the Afrobarometer poll in 12 mainly poor countries in 2001) associate democracy with civil liberties, popular sovereignty, or electoral choice. About two-thirds of Africans surveyed (69 percent) also say democracy is "always preferable" to authoritarian rule. The same proportion rejects one-party rule, and four in five reject military or one-man rule. Even many who are not satisfied with democracy believe it is the best form of government, and most Africans who live in democracies recognize there are serious institutional problems that must be addressed. Latin Americans—who have had more time than Africans to become disillusioned with how democracy actually performs in their countries—are more ambivalent; but overall, 57 percent still believe democracy is always preferable, and only about 15 percent might prefer an authoritarian regime. In East Asia, according to data from the East Asia Barometer collected in 2001, only a quarter in Taiwan and Korea, about a fifth in Hong Kong and the Philippines, but less than a tenth in Thailand believe that democracy is not really suitable for their country. In all five of these systems, consistently strong majorities (usually upwards of two-thirds) reject authoritarian alternatives to democracy. So do strong majorities (about seven in 10 overall) in the 10 postcommunist countries now negotiating membership in the European Union.

Although much has been made of the "clash of civilizations," especially since September 11, 2001, the Afrobarometer survey evidence indicates that "Muslims are as supportive of democracy as non-Muslims." Large majorities of African Muslims as well as non-Muslims support democracy, and any hesitancy in supporting democracy among African Muslims "is due more to deficits of formal education and other attributes of modernization than to religious attachments," as the Afrobarometer's analysts put it. Data from Central Asia and the Middle East point in a similar direction.[6] The Middle Eastern data are somewhat dated (from the 1990s) and severely limited by what could be asked, but in two of the four country contexts (Egypt and Palestine), a majority attached at least some importance to the value of democracy. Weighing the evidence, political scientist Mark Tessler concludes, "Islam appears to have less influence on political attitudes than is frequently suggested." Indeed, "support for democracy is not necessarily lower among those individuals with the strongest Islamic attachments."

These popular orientations among the world's Muslims correspond with the thinking of increasingly outspoken moderate Muslim intellectuals, who are making the case either for a liberal interpretation of Islam or for a broader liberal view that deemphasizes the literal meaning of sacred Islamic texts while stressing the larger compatibility between the overall moral teachings of Islam and the nature of democracy as a system of government based on such principles as accountability, freedom of expression, and the rule of law. Islam is undergoing a kind of reformation now, and there is growing momentum among Muslim religious thinkers for a separation of mosque and state.

Significantly, Arab thinkers, scholars, and civil society activists are themselves challenging the democracy and freedom deficit that pervades the Arab world. The Arab authors of the *Arab Human Development Report*—an extraordinary document published by the UNDP [in 2002]—recognize that the global wave of democratization "has barely reached the Arab states. This freedom deficit undermines human development and is one of the most painful manifestations of lagging political development." It was this same broad team of Arab specialists who wrote these words about the reform imperative.

> There can be no real prospects for reforming the system of governance, or for truly liberating human capabilities, in the absence of comprehensive political representation in effective legislatures based on free, honest, efficient and regular elections. If the people's preferences are to be properly expressed and their interests properly protected, governance must become truly representative and fully accountable.

Amartya Sen argues that the mark of a universal value is not that it has the consent of everyone, but that "people anywhere may have reason to see it as valuable." By this measure, there is growing evidence of all kinds that democracy is becoming a truly universal value.

....

DEMOCRACY DRIVERS

To assess whether vastly more countries—and, someday, potentially *all* countries—can become democratic, we must answer four more questions. First, what has been driving democratization in the third wave? *Why* have so many more countries become democratic during this period? Second, why have so few of these new democracies broken down in the last quarter-century? Third, why do the remaining nondemocracies hold out? Logically, the answers to these questions will then provide essential insights with which to answer the most important question: Can the countries that are not now democratic become so? And how would they do that?

In this essay, I can only sketch the answers to these four questions, beginning with the causes of democratization.

Economic development   As Huntington notes, economic development has been a major driver of democratization in the third wave. However, increases in national wealth bring about pressures for democratization only to the extent that they generate several other intervening effects: rising levels of education; the creation of a complex and diverse middle class that is independent of the state; the development of a more pluralistic, active, and resourceful civil society; and, as a result of all of these changes, the emergence of a more questioning, assertive, pro-democratic political culture.

These broad societal transformations have accompanied economic development in a number of countries in recent decades. South Korea and Taiwan stand as the classic examples of economic growth bringing about diffuse social, economic, and cultural change that then generates diffuse societal pressure for democracy. At a somewhat lower level of economic development, this has also been the story of Thailand, Brazil, Mexico, and South Africa. However, where states have managed successfully to control and co-opt civil society and to manipulate cultural symbols and belief systems in a way that legitimizes semi-authoritarian rule, the internal pressure for democratization has been preempted or deflected. This has been the case with Malaysia and especially Singapore, the richest authoritarian state in the history of the world. Alternatively, some states that look economically developed in terms of their per capita income are much less so when we examine education levels, status of women, civic life, and state–society relations. These are the oil-rich states, whose economic and class structures are grossly distorted by the fact of centralized state control of the oil sector.

Economic development that seeps broadly into the social structure and culture of a society will, in most cases, generate powerful pressures for democratization. The authoritarian rulers capable of managing this process of social and economic change as adeptly as Lee Kuan Yew and his successors in Singapore are few and far between. China's communist leaders think they can duplicate Lee's path, but they are wrong.

Economic performance   The second factor that has driven democratic change during the third wave has also been economic, but in the inverse direction of economic crisis, or poor governance performance in general. To the extent that they make an effort to justify their rule on moral and political grounds, conventional authoritarian regimes do so on the basis of performance achievements and imperatives. They claim that their rule is necessary to clean up corruption, fight subversion, unify the country, and/or generate economic growth. This puts authoritarian regimes in a dilemma. If they fail to deliver on these promises, authoritarian rulers forfeit their moral entitlement to rule. Unlike democracy, which people value intrinsically, these run-of-the-mill dictatorships have no other grounds on which to justify their rule except what they can tangibly deliver. Even if they succeed in overcoming the crises of political instability or insecurity that brought them to power, after some time people may feel they have served their purpose (perhaps at great cost to other values) and should go.

However one frames it, performance-based legitimacy is a delicate and perilous strategy for sustaining authoritarian rule indefinitely. Most authoritarian regimes are, in the long run, damned if they do deliver and damned if they don't. Those that care only about their own survival focus on funneling corrupt payoffs to a narrow support circle of cronies, functionaries, soldiers, and thugs who will repress any opposition. In this way, the regime may survive for some time, as in Iraq, while the country slowly crumbles.

International actions and pressures The most distinctive feature of the third wave has been the sweeping change in the policies, actions, and expectations of the established democracies, particularly the United States, as well as regional and international organizations. Beginning under Jimmy Carter, with his new emphasis on human rights, and then, after a false start, continuing with the new emphasis on democracy promotion under Ronald Reagan, U.S. presidential administrations became active in pressing for democratic change. New U.S. institutions, such as the National Endowment for Democracy, were created to provide practical assistance and encouragement to democratic movements, civic organizations, interest groups, parties, and institutions. By the late 1990s, the United States was spending over half a billion dollars a year to foster and support democratic development abroad. Direct and indirect diplomatic

pressure was exerted. With the end of the Cold War, these pressures widened, and a number of African states that had been pawns on a superpower chessboard were suddenly viewed on their own terms. Many African governments that had been lavishly financed and repeatedly bailed out from their misrule suddenly found themselves in acute fiscal crisis, and thus were forced to reform politically.

It was not just the United States that was pressing for democracy. The European Union became increasingly active and outspoken towards the same ends, particularly in its financial and organizational efforts to promote democracy in postcommunist Europe. The driving wedge of Western Europe's democratizing impact was a simple and unyielding condition that all states seeking entry into the European Union had to manifest, in the words of the European Community at the time, "truly democratic practices and respect for fundamental rights and freedoms." Much European Union technical and political assistance over the past 12 years has gone into helping the candidate states for entry meet these political (and other economic) conditions. First in Southern Europe and now in Central and Eastern Europe as well as Turkey, a regression away from democracy has become unthinkable because of the enormous economic and political costs it would impose through isolation from the community of European states and free trade. When we think about the prospects for democratic expansion in the world, the means by which the political will *for* democracy is generated and entrenched must be borne in mind.

More recently, regional pressure for democracy has begun to take hold in the Americas. In June 1991, the Organization of American States (OAS) adopted the "Santiago Commitment to Democracy," which required immediate consultation if a democracy is overthrown. Concerted action by the OAS and by the U.S. and other member states deterred a planned *autogolpe* in Guatemala in 1993 and a rumored military coup in Paraguay later in the decade. And the OAS effectively monitored transitional or controversial elections in a number of its emerging or transitional democratic states.

In fact, international election observation has become one of the most common means by which international actors—the United Nations, regional organizations, other governments, and NGOs—intrude, often by invitation, on the internal politics of sovereign countries. These kinds of political intrusions are reshaping the very idea of sovereignty, negating the longstanding presumption that states are free to do what they like within their own borders.

Changing international norms and conventions. Finally, then, what has changed during the third wave is the normative weight given to human rights—and to democracy *as* a human right—in international discourse, treaties, law, and collective actions. The world community is increasingly embracing a shared normative expectation that all states seeking international legitimacy should manifestly "govern with the consent of the governed"—in essence, a "right to democratic governance" is seen as a legal entitlement.[7] Already effectively implied by the Universal Declaration of Human Rights and the International Covenant on Civil and Political Rights, this right to democratic governance has been articulated more and more explicitly in the documents of regional organizations and affirmed by the growing number of interventions by those organizations and by the United Nations. In June 2000, 106 states, gathered in the "Toward a Community of Democracies" conference, agreed to "respect and uphold" a detailed list of "core democratic principles and practices"—including individual liberties, the rule of law enforced by an "independent and impartial judiciary," and "the right and civic duties of citizens to choose their representatives through regular, free and fair elections with universal and equal suffrage, open to multiple parties, conducted by secret ballot, monitored by independent electoral authorities, and free of fraud and intimidation."

At a minimum, this evolution has done two things. First, it has lowered the political threshold for intervention, not only for the multilateral actors but for states and NGOs as well. Second, it has emboldened domestic advocates of democracy and human rights. No factor has been more important in driving and sustaining the third wave of democratization than this cluster of international normative and legal trends.

FEWER BREAKDOWNS

Drawing from the causal factors above, we can identify three factors that have provided a strong degree of immunity to democratic breakdown during the third wave. First, some countries became democracies after they had become relatively rich—in fact, richer than any country that has ever suffered a breakdown of democracy. Przeworski and his colleagues found that from 1950 to 1990, no country with a per capita income higher than $6,055 (in 1985 Purchasing Power Parity dollars) had ever suffered a breakdown of democracy. (This was the 1975 per capita income of Argentina, the richest country ever to have suffered a coup against democracy.) The equivalent level of economic development in 2000 dollars is $8,773. Taiwan and Korea became democracies at levels of economic development richer than this and are now much richer than this. Several democracies in Central and Eastern Europe and Latin America are also beyond this level.

The second factor is public opinion and normative change within countries. In many of the democracies that have emerged over the past two decades, citizens are broadly dissatisfied with the performance of the political system and distrustful of many of its institutions (especially parties and politicians). Yet they do not see an alternative to democracy. Even in Brazil, where active support for democracy stood at only 37 percent last year, people do not prefer authoritarian rule (only 15 percent could imagine wanting it). The alternative, rather, is apathy and withdrawal. This is bad for democracy, but not as bad as people actively clamoring for an authoritarian alternative. In the 10 postcommunist candidate states for EU accession, 61 percent are dissatisfied with the way democracy works in their country, according to the Centre for the Study of Public Policy's New Europe Barometer survey. Yet, overall, 72 percent would not approve of its suspension.

Belief in the legitimacy—the moral rightness—of a political system is always a relative judgment. In the past several decades, almost every form of nondemocratic government imaginable has been tried: absolute monarchy, personal dictatorship, military rule, colonial rule, fascism, communism, Ba'athism, the socialist one-party state, other forms of one-party rule, the Islamic Republic, pseudo-democracy, semidemocracy, and numerous other permutations. At an accelerating rate, people have opted for democracy. "As democracy has spread, its adherents have grown, not shrunk," Amartya Sen observes. Whatever their naïve assumptions at the beginning, people are sticking with democracy without illusions. They remember in their lifetime one or more of these other forms of rule, and they do not want to go back.

Of course it is possible that some new form of nondemocratic rule will be conjured up and capture the passions and imagination of some peoples; but at this point, more than a decade after the collapse of communism, there is no sign on the horizon of an antidemocratic ideology that could even begin to generate universal claims. Most likely, where authoritarian rule reasserts itself in the coming years, it will do so apologetically, wrapping itself in the moral purpose of democratic restoration and insisting—as General Pervez Musharraf did when he seized power in Pakistan in 1999—that the suspension of democracy would be temporary. Or elected rulers will gradually whittle down the quality and competitiveness of democratic institutions. Or violent insurgencies will grind down the scope of their actual authority to the point where it is just very difficult to determine whether the country meets the minimal test of democracy.

The third factor suppressing potential reversions to authoritarian rule has been the unfavorable climate for such reversals at the regional and international levels. Most of all in Europe, but in Latin America as well, political and military leaders know that they will pay a high price in terms of economic and political standing within their regions if they reverse democracy. On specific occasions, some such leaders who have been tempted to reverse democracy—in Guatemala, in Paraguay, perhaps in Venezuela, and probably in Turkey—have been deterred from doing so by explicit interventions from neighboring countries and from the United States.

But the international environment is a discordant one. There are conflicting signals and incentives.

If we can create a more coherent and vigorous international environment supporting democracy and democratization, we can more effectively bolster the existing democracies against reversion while inducing more transitions to democracy, both gradual and rapid. That is the overriding challenge of the moment.

HOLDOUTS

Several factors explain the tenacious resistance to the democratic trend on the part of roughly 70 countries. The least common explanation is authoritarian success. This can account for Singapore and Malaysia, and perhaps to some extent China with its recent rapid economic growth. But China remains a lower-middle-income country, and the SARS crisis is only the latest demonstration of the contradictions it confronts trying to sustain its phenomenal growth rates while the political system remains closed, corrupt, and unaccountable. Then there are the oil-rich states—the ones with staggering revenue and relatively small populations—which have been able to maintain authoritarian rule because they have had the wealth to buy off their peoples while lavishly financing structures of internal security and control. Even so, their peoples—in Kuwait, in Qatar, in Bahrain, and now in Saudi Arabia—are restive and want more self-determination. With the exceptions of Singapore, Malaysia, possibly for a while China, and these oil-rich states, there are no dictatorships in the world that survive today because they have brought prosperity to their people.

There are a few other holdout communist states in Asia (Vietnam, Laos, North Korea) and Cuba as well. Here, the insular, repressive logic of communist control persists. However, Vietnam is learning from China's model of economic opening, and what is true for China is true for these states as well. The more they open to the outside world in terms of trade, investment, foreign study, foreign travel, and all the other aspects of globalization, the more their people become exposed to education and global culture, the more the insular, repressive logic will weaken. At some unpredictable point, a regime crisis, an economic downturn, a split within the elite could ignite a transition to democracy. There is of course an alternative strategy to bring about regime change: Isolate them from the world. Make it hard for the regime. Then wait for it to collapse. We have tried this strategy for 40 years in Cuba, and all it has done is impoverish the people and entrench their repressive rulers. Precisely in order to generate the social and economic changes that will finally undermine communist rule in Cuba, we should lift the embargo and promote as much exchange and interaction with that country as possible.

Most dictatorships in the world survive for a simple reason. Their leaders enjoy having unchallenged power as well as having the ability that power confers to accumulate great personal wealth. It is just not possible to look at the evidence from the ground (and from the public opinion surveys) in Africa, Asia, and the Middle East and argue that their peoples don't mind living under dictatorship. Of course, no one could maintain that the majority of people in every country want a fully democratic system or that all peoples understand all the institutions of liberal democracy. But most people do want freedom. Given the choice, they would like to be able to constrain the arbitrary power of government, to replace bad and corrupt leaders, to have a predictable and secure life under some kind of just rule of law.

When one assembles these basic political preferences, it begins to look an awful lot like democracy, even if the word may have different (or unsure) meanings in many places.

There is a lot of work to be done around the world to build the culture of democracy—the understanding of its rules, possibilities, obligations, and limits, the norms of tolerance, civility, participation, and mutual respect. Some of this cultural change happens with economic development, increasing education, and exposure to the global environment. Much of it can and should happen through deliberate programs of civic education and civil society construction. External democracy promotion programs and domestic civil society efforts have made some progress toward these goals. Much more remains to be done.

But the principal obstacle to the expansion of democracy in the world is not the people of the remaining authoritarian states. The problem is the ruling elites who have hijacked the structures of state power and barricaded themselves inside. As long as these rulers can corner a sufficient flow of resources to feed their apparatus of political predation and domination, they can survive.

That is where the international environment enters in. Predatory authoritarian regimes do not generate resources organically from within their own societies very well. Rather, they inhibit domestic investment, innovation, entrepreneurship, and hence economic growth by violating property rights and other individual freedoms. Such arbitrary rule also discourages foreign investment—except in the enclave economy of oil or other natural resource extraction. If predatory regimes do not have natural resources, they fall heavily in need of foreign loans and aid. This makes them vulnerable if the sources of those loans start insisting on responsible government.

For the most part, Arab states are rentier states, deriving their revenues mainly from oil or international aid flows rather than from taxes paid by their own people. But there has been another, entirely unique factor in their authoritarian survival. All of these dictatorships have been able to summon up a grand excuse for the failures and disappointments of their systems. First, it was the allegedly "colonial" existence of the state of Israel. For some it is still that, but now in particular it is the plight of the Palestinians and the Israeli–Palestinian conflict. Over the past several decades, this conflict has generated a heavy fog over Arab politics, diminishing political visibility and transparency. Arab governments have used it relentlessly to legitimate their rule—by stressing the authenticity of their commitment to something larger than themselves—and have relied on it more and more as the older forms of nationalism and pan-Arab solidarity have lost their luster. Much of the energy and emotion of Arab intellectuals and political activists has been drawn away from national political failings into protest over this larger political conflict. The debate about the true failings of Arab development—so eloquently expressed in last year's *Arab Human Development Report*—has been distorted and deflected by this powerful symbolic struggle over Arab identity and dignity.

Until the fog of this struggle is lifted—so that the peoples of the Arab world can see and debate more clearly the real nature of the obstacles to national progress, and so that radical Islamists will be deprived of one of their most emotive instruments for mobilizing political support—genuine and lasting democratization will be unlikely in the region.

....

WHAT IS TO BE DONE?

Lenin had a revolutionary agenda for global dictatorship. Some American leaders, such as Woodrow Wilson and Ronald Reagan, have also had a revolutionary global vision, but a vision of democracy. If the whole world is ever to become democratic, the most powerful democracy cannot be passive or timid (yet neither can it transform the world alone). We must craft a global strategy, asking Lenin's classic question: What is to be done?

First, with respect to the Arab world, we must relentlessly pursue a settlement of the Israeli–Palestinian conflict on the basis of the only broadly viable solution: the permanent coexistence and mutual recognition of two separate states, one an Israel that withdraws from most of its settlements in the West Bank and Gaza, the other an essentially demilitarized Palestine. Only the settlement of this conflict can strip Arab dictatorships of political cover for their abuses and free Arab societies to focus on the real sources of their misery and frustration.

Second, we need to open up the closed societies of the world. I do not propose to shower them with aid—far from it—but we should promote trade, travel, and exchanges of all kinds with countries like Cuba, Vietnam, Burma, and, yes, North Korea. The North Korean dictatorship is a house of cards resting on a tissue of lies. Its people, the most physically and intellectually isolated and totally brutalized of any in the world today, do not have a clue as to how the rest of the world lives. Once they find out, the regime will crumble, or else change very rapidly.

Third, we need a new deal in foreign aid and debt relief. Even after the end of the Cold War, even with the new standards and pressures on dictatorships, the resources to sustain them have largely continued to flow. Part of this has simply been inertia. Part of this has been the utterly perverse structural logic of aid agencies and especially the World Bank, whose officials are given portfolios of money to lend and projects to initiate with the understanding that their careers will suffer if they do not push the money out the door. Part of the reason has been fear that if we lean too heavily on weak, oppressive, rotten states, they will collapse altogether into new humanitarian emergencies. Instead, we dawdle and fund them while they disintegrate more slowly and millions of their people live shorter, nastier, more brutish lives because of abusive governance. Finally, part of the problem has been the conflicting priorities of bilateral donors (including the United States) that still want to maintain friendly client states around the world. Some thought this dualism—a polite word for hypocrisy—would come to an end with the demise of the Cold War. And indeed, it did subside for a time. But with the inception of the new war on terrorism since September 11, the problem of selling short our principles in order to nurture authoritarian clients has been reborn with a vengeance.

A new deal on aid would radically accelerate and institutionalize the tentative trends toward encouraging and expecting good governance in exchange for foreign aid. The Bush administration took an important step forward . . . when it announced the creation of a Millennium Challenge Account, which will award a new $5 billion increment in development assistance (about a 50 percent increase over the current U.S. foreign aid budget) to a select number of low- and lower-middle-income countries that compete for it on the basis of three criteria: ruling justly (including democratically and accountably), investing in people, and promoting economic freedom. Hopefully, countries that qualify will start receiving substantial new sums of aid . . . —if Congress allocates the funds.

This is an important departure—indeed, a conceptual revolution—in foreign aid. But it does not go nearly far enough. First, we still need to question what we are doing with the rest of our foreign aid budget. Much of it goes to countries ruled by corrupt, authoritarian regimes. If that aid is delivered to and through civil society rather than the corrupt state itself, it may do some good. But too much is wasted, and there is too little effort to generate leverage for real political change. The big problem is the other donors: the World Bank, the regional development banks, the Japanese, and many of the European aid agencies.

Democratic change is possible in the world's remaining corrupt dictatorships, but it will require a radical manipulation of the incentives their leaders confront. They must know that the party is over, that they cannot any longer play one powerful donor off against another, or one country promoting its own oil industry over another.

[In January 2003], the U.S. Agency for International Development released a report, *Foreign Aid in the National Interest* (available at www.usaid.gov), recommending a new set of strategies for our development assistance based on rewarding demonstrated performance and getting aid dollars into the hands of people in a given country who can do the most good with the money. These new directions, if adopted, could transform the international context in which dictatorships now maneuver to survive. In addition, a greater proportion of total U.S. foreign assistance should be devoted to political assistance to build democracy and improve the quality of governance. In truly intractable cases, helping to generate the demand for democracy and better governance by strengthening the capacity and reform understanding of independent organizations, interest groups, social movements, mass media, universities, and think tanks in civil society may be the main thing the United States can do to aid development. Whatever progress is made on governance will almost certainly have a positive impact on other sectors. Probably no other dimension of foreign assistance yields so many synergies.

The new strategy moves from the current exhausted approach of conditionality to a selectivity that rewards political freedom and accountability. As much as possible, rewards should be structured to lock into place the institutions and practices of democracy and good governance. As we seek to expand NAFTA into a Free Trade Agreement of the Americas, we should adopt a requirement similar to the European Union, that all members uphold democracy and human rights. In the case of debt relief for highly indebted poor countries, future relief should be granted only to countries that have demonstrated a basic commitment to good governance by allowing a free press and civil society, an independent judiciary, and a serious counter-corruption commission. Even in these cases, the debt should not be relieved in one fell swoop, but should be suspended and retired incrementally (for example, at 10 percent per year), generating ongoing incentives for adhering to good governance.

If the United States and the other major bilateral and multilateral donors were to move together toward such a comprehensive strategy affirming democracy and good governance as the basis of development (and hence development assistance), they would generate very powerful new pressures for democratic reform. Not all authoritarian states would be affected immediately because not all of them depend on these flows of assistance. But the overall global climate would shift emphatically in favor of democratic change, generating potent demonstration effects even on the stand-pat regimes.

Of course, this would still leave open the question of *how* democratic change could be accomplished in countries that have never been democracies before. There is no one formula for getting to democracy or for structuring it institutionally so that it works reasonably well. Different countries need different sequences, strategies, and structures. In some cases, the transition to democracy could and should proceed fairly rapidly, since governance is such a mess and viable democratic forces wait in the wings. In other cases—including many of the Arab states—the transition to democracy will need to proceed more cautiously and incrementally.

Another distinctive feature of the Arab world is that the formal political arena has been closed to all but a relatively narrow circle of establishment parties and interest groups, while the chief alternatives (both above ground and below) to these co-opted forces have been Islamist parties and groups mobilizing a considerable network of affection and support, but with an anti-democratic agenda. The more moderate and pro-democratic groups—both Islamist and secular—have been squeezed between the iron fist of the state and the superior popular organization of illiberal Islam. If they are to be given a fair chance to compete in electoral politics, these moderates will need time to surface, organize, advocate, and campaign. While electoral competition for genuine national power is phased in over a period of years, an interim period of political liberalization must be used to build the independent structures of horizontal accountability—the judiciary, audit agency, counter-corruption commission, human rights commission, ombudsman, and electoral administration—that can ensure free and fair electoral competition and constrain whoever wins election in the new system.

The challenge in postwar Iraq will be unique. There, the state and political system must be thoroughly reconstructed at the same time as we rebuild an economy devastated by three major wars and decades of colossal misrule. The one thing we absolutely must not do is impose a leader or solution of our choosing. Iraqis—both those within the country and those returning from exile—must be given the time and space to meet in local groups, select representatives, and assemble a broad-based transitional government. Then they must begin to take responsibility for administering and rebuilding the country while organizing a smaller and more professional new army, debating and drafting a new constitution, then submitting it to a referendum, forming political parties and civic associations, constructing new independent media, electing new municipal and provincial governments, operating these new governments, and—only some years later—holding national elections for a new constitutional government. During this period of political reconstruction and nation-building, which will require a huge international peacekeeping force if it is to have any chance of success, some international authority will need to provide initial supervision of the process, gradually withdrawing as the Iraqi authority is able to assume

greater and greater responsibility. The sooner that authority is internationalized in some way (in military terms, for example, through NATO), the longer it can stay in Iraq with some internal and international legitimacy.

CAN IT BE DONE?

Even to think of democratizing the entire world is a bold endeavor. Perhaps it is too bold. Certainly the above prescriptions are not without flaws. In the near term, we will probably fall short of the courage, imagination, and nerve truly to transform the global political climate. Part of this challenge is deeply political, even in terms of our own national debate. It is important to realize how the current war has further altered the international climate. Increasingly, the United States is seen as an imperial power, imposing its will largely unilaterally on the rest of the world. That may serve our short-term interests in any one conflict or dispute, but it will not facilitate our deeper, long-term interest in building a world of democracies and good governance. We cannot invade and conquer every dictatorship in the world. In fact, our national appetite for forcible regime change will probably be quickly exhausted in postwar Iraq. Unless we learn to work with and through international partners and institutions while seeking to energize, transform, and democratize global structures, our scope to effect further democratic change in the world will shrink.

Whatever may happen in Iraq, we will face sobering challenges of international terrorism, rotten governance, and big-power division. Our moral and political prestige in the world has suffered . . . even as respect for our sheer military power has increased. If the whole world is to keep moving toward democracy, we must recover the former while preserving the latter. Ironically, we will find that we have much greater leverage to advance the cause of freedom in the world if we build and maintain effective partnerships with the other democracies of the world. We cannot always lead from the battleship or the bully pulpit. Sometimes, we must do so more softly and subtly, as part of a team.

We should also not take the existing democracies for granted. There is a new sobriety even among the democracies that are not performing well. People know the alternatives and do not like them. They still embrace democracy. But will they continue to do so a decade or two hence if a new generation—with no direct experience of the costs and illusions of authoritarian rule—finds itself without education, without jobs, without justice, and pretty much without hope? We can travel only so far on democracy as the least bad system. If it turns out to govern badly for a long period of time, some new alternative will eventually come along.

The fully global triumph of democracy is far from inevitable, yet it has never been more attainable. If we manage to sustain the process of global economic integration and growth while making freedom at least an important priority in our diplomacy, aid, and other international engagements, democracy will continue to expand in the world. History has proven that it is the best form of government. Gradually, more countries will become democratic while fewer revert to dictatorship. If we retain our power, reshape our strategy, and sustain our commitment, eventually—not in the next decade, but certainly by mid-century—every country in the world can be democratic.

ENDNOTES

1. Larry Diamond, "Elections Without Democracy: Thinking About Hybrid Regimes," *Journal of Democracy* (April 2002).

2. See the essay by Alfred Stepan in the *Journal of Democracy* (July 2003).

3. The democracies in this set are Bangladesh, Brazil, India, Indonesia, Japan, Mexico, Nigeria, and the United States. The nondemocracies are China, Pakistan, and Russia.

4. Adam Przeworski, Michael E. Alvarez, Jose Antonio Cheibub, and Fernando Limongi, *Democracy and Development: Political Institutions and Well Being in the World, 1950–1990* (Cambridge University Press, 2000), pp. 92–103.

5. Amartya Sen, "Democracy as a Universal Value," in Larry Diamond and Marc F. Plattner, eds., *The Global Divergence of Democracies* (Johns Hopkins University Press, 2001).

6. "Islam, Democracy, and Public Opinion in Africa," Afrobarometer Briefing Paper No. 3 (September 2002); Richard Rose, "How Muslims View Democracy: Evidence from Central Asia," *Journal of Democracy* (October 2002); Mark Tessler, "Islam and Democracy in the Middle East: The Impact of Religious Orientations on Attitudes Toward Democracy in Four Arab Countries," *Comparative Politics* (April 2002).

7. See Thomas Franck, "The Emerging Right to Democratic Governance," *American Journal of International Law* (January 1992).

CHAPTER EIGHT

AUTHORITARIANISM: OLD AND NEW

Aristotle distinguished between democracy (under law) and both kingship and tyranny, corresponding to a difference between participation of all occupational and social groups in collective judgment and rule by one or a few. Societies with large middle classes, in which property as an instrument of power is widely shared, he held, tend toward balance and stability and are less subject to passion and error. His distinction between democracy and authoritarianism carries over into modern societies as well, but both types of government must adapt to new circumstances. After the French Revolution and the creation of mass armies, politics could no longer be confined to royal palaces or small circles. The people became more active; they had to be mobilized as well as controlled.

Modernization ushered in the era of democratic revolutions, but has been compatible also with the emergence of authoritarian regimes. Science and industry may advance rapidly under authoritarian as well as democratic states. Napoleon Bonaparte was one of the great modernizers of the early 19th century. Under the relatively authoritarian regime of Emperor Wilhelm and his chancellor, Otto Bismarck, Germany easily matched more democratic rivals such as Britain and France in industrial and scientific development. Mussolini and Hitler presided over the modernization of their societies. And one of the key events of the 20th century, the Bolshevik Revolution, led to the creation of a communist system in Russia in a first step, and after World War II to extension of communist rule over a large part of the world's population, supported by frequently powerful communist movements everywhere else. Authoritarian regimes have demonstrated remarkable ability to mobilize popular support in the modern period. Yet, communism underwent a severe crisis and collapsed in the Soviet Union and Eastern Europe in the late 1980s. Can modernization theory offer clues as to why communism first flourished and then foundered in Europe, and why communism has survived in Asia?

The question may also be raised, whether Russia and China are evolving from authoritarianism to democracy, or whether the most powerful countries to have undergone the experience of communism are moving in a different direction: a new form of authoritarianism that is a final destination rather than a transitional stage. The issue is explored by Lilia Shevtsova and Andrew J. Nathan.

ARISTOTLE

27 On Democracy and Tyranny

PREREQUISITES OF DEMOCRACY

We proceed now to inquire what form of government and what manner of life is best for communities in general, not adapting it to that superior virtue which is above the reach of the vulgar, or that education which every advantage of nature and fortune only can furnish, nor to those imaginary plans which may be formed at pleasure; but to that mode of life which the greater part of mankind can attain to, and that government which most cities may establish: for as to those aristocracies which we have now mentioned, they are either too perfect for a state to support, or one so nearly alike to that state we are now going to inquire into, that we shall treat of them both as one.

The opinions which we form upon these subjects must depend upon one common principle: for if what I have said in my treatise on Morals is true, a happy life must arise from an uninterrupted course of virtue; and if virtue consists in a certain medium, the middle life must certainly be the happiest; which medium is attainable by every one. The boundaries of virtue and vice in the state must also necessarily be the same as in a private person; for the form of government is the life of the city. In every city the people are divided into three sorts; the very rich, the very poor, and those who are between them. If this is universally admitted, that

the mean is best, it is evident that even in point of fortune mediocrity is to be preferred; . . .

It is also the genius of a city to be composed as much as possible of equals; which will be most so when the inhabitants are in the middle state: from whence it follows, that that city must be best framed which is composed of those whom we say are naturally its proper members. It is men of this station also who will be best assured of safety and protection; for they will neither covet what belongs to others, as the poor do; nor will others covet what is theirs, as the poor do what belongs to the rich; and thus, without plotting against any one, or having any one plot against them, they will live free from danger: for which reason Phocylides wisely wishes for the middle state, as being most productive of happiness. It is plain, then, that the most perfect political community must be amongst those who are in the middle rank, and those states are best instituted wherein these are a larger and more respectable part, if possible, than both the other; or, if that cannot be, at least than either of them separate; so that being thrown into the balance it may prevent either scale from preponderating.

. . . The middle state is therefore best, as being least liable to those seditions and insurrections which disturb the community; and for the same reason extensive governments are least liable to these inconveniences; for there those in a middle state are very numerous, whereas in small ones it is easy to pass to the two extremes, so as hardly to have any in a medium remaining, but the one half rich, the other poor: and from the same principle it is that democracies are more firmly established and of longer continuance than oligarchies; but even in those when there is a want of a proper number of men of middling fortune, the poor extend their

SOURCE: Aristotle, "On Democracy and Tyranny," in *A Treatise on Government*, trans. William Ellis (London: George Routledge and Sons, 1888). Abridged by the Editor. Aristotle taught from 335 to 323 B.C. His writings are drawn from notes taken by his students.

power too far, abuses arise, and the government is soon at an end.

Other particulars we will consider separately; but it seems proper to prove, that the supreme power ought to be lodged with the many, rather than with those of the better sort, who are few; and also to explain what doubts (and probably just ones) may arise: now, though not one individual of the many may himself be fit for the supreme power, yet when these many are joined together, it does not follow but they may be better qualified for it than those; and this not separately, but as a collective body; as the public suppers exceed those which are given at one person's private expense: for, as they are many, each person brings in his share of virtue and wisdom; and thus, coming together, they are like one man made up of a multitude, with many feet, many hands, and many intelligences: thus is it with respect to the manners and understandings of the multitude taken together; for which reason the public are the best judges of music and poetry; for some understand one part, some another, and all collectively the whole. . . .

. . . For the multitude when they are collected together have all of them sufficient understanding for these purposes, and, mixing among those of higher rank, are serviceable to the city, as some things, which alone are improper for food, when mixed with others make the whole more wholesome than a few of them would be.

* * *

Since in every art and science the end aimed at is always good, so particularly in this, which is the most excellent of all, the founding of civil society, the good wherein aimed at is justice; for it is this which is for the benefit of all. Now, it is the common opinion, that justice is a certain equality; and in this point all the philosophers are agreed when they treat of morals: for they say what is just, and to whom; and that equals ought to receive equal: but we should know how we are to determine what things are equal and what unequal; and in this there is some difficulty, which calls for the philosophy of the politician. Some persons will probably say, that the employments of the state ought to be given according to every particular excellence of each citizen, if there is

no other difference between them and the rest of the community, but they are in every respect else alike: for justice attributes different things to persons differing from each other in their character, according to their respective merits. . . .

Now the first thing which presents itself to our consideration is this, whether it is best to be governed by a good man, or by good laws? Those who prefer a kingly government think that laws can only speak a general language, but cannot adapt themselves to particular circumstances; for which reason it is absurd in any science to follow written rule; and even in Egypt the physician was allowed to alter the mode of cure which the law prescribed to him, after the fourth day; but if he did it sooner it was at his own peril: from whence it is evident, on the very same account, that a government of written laws is not the best; and yet general reasoning is necessary to all those who are to govern, and it will be much more perfect in those who are entirely free from passions than in those to whom they are natural. But now this is a quality which laws possess; while the other is natural to the human soul. But some one will say in answer to this, that man will be a better judge of particulars. It will be necessary, then, for a king to be a lawgiver, and that his laws should be published, but that those should have no authority which are absurd, as those which are not, should. But whether is it better for the community that those things which cannot possibly come under the cognizance of the law either at all or properly should be under the government of every worthy citizen, as the present method is, when the public community, in their general assemblies, act as judges and counsellors, where all their determinations are upon particular cases. For one individual, be he who he will, will be found, upon comparison, inferior to a whole people taken collectively: but this is what a city is, as a public entertainment is better than one man's portion: for this reason the multitude judge of many things better than any one single person. They are also less liable to corruption from their numbers, as water is from its quantity: besides, the judgment of an individual must necessarily be perverted if he is overcome by anger or any other passion; but it would be hard indeed if the whole community should be misled by anger. Moreover, let the people be free, and they will do nothing but in conformity to the law, except only in those cases which the law cannot speak to. But though what I am going to propose may not easily be met with, yet if the majority of the state should happen to be good men, should they prefer one uncorrupt governor or many equally good, is it not evident that they should choose the many? But there may be divisions among these which cannot happen when there is but one. In answer to this it may be replied that all their souls will be as much animated with virtue as this one man's.

. . . As for an absolute monarchy as it is called, that is to say, when the whole state is wholly subject to the will of one person, namely the king, it seems to many that it is unnatural that one man should have the entire rule over his fellow-citizens when the state consists of equals: for nature requires that the same right and the same rank should necessarily take place amongst all those who are equal by nature: for as it would be hurtful to the body for those who are of different constitutions to observe the same regimen, either of diet or clothing, so is it with respect to the honors of the state as hurtful, that those who are equal in merit should be unequal in rank; for which reason it is as much a man's duty to submit to command as to assume it, and this also by rotation; for this is law, for order is law; and it is more proper that law should govern than any one of the citizens: upon the same principle, if it is advantageous to place the supreme power in some particular persons, they should be appointed to be only guardians, and the servants of the laws, for the supreme power must be placed somewhere; but they say, that it is unjust that where all are equal one person should continually enjoy it. But it seems unlikely that man should be able to adjust that which the law cannot determine; it may be replied, that the law having laid down the best rules possible, leaves the adjustment and application of particulars to the discretion of the magistrate; besides, it allows anything to be altered which experience proves may be better established. Moreover, he who would place the supreme power in mind, would place it in God and the laws; but he who entrusts man with it, gives it to a wild beast, for such his appetites sometimes make him; for passion influences those who

are in power, even the very best of men: for which reason law is reason without desire.

TYRANNY

It now remains to treat of a tyranny . . . In the beginning of this work we inquired into the nature of kingly government, and entered into a particular examination of what was most properly called so, and whether it was advantageous to a state or not, and what it should be, and how established; and we divided a tyranny into two pieces when we were upon this subject, because there is something analogous between this and a kingly government, for they are both of them established by law; for among some of the barbarians they elect a monarch with absolute power, and formerly among the Greeks there were some such, whom they called aesumnetes. Now these differ from each other; for some possess only kingly power regulated by law, and rule those who voluntarily submit to their government; others rule despotically according to their own will. There is a third species of tyranny, most properly so called, which is the very opposite to kingly power; for this is the government of one who rules over his equals and superiors without being accountable for his conduct, and whose object is his own advantage, and not the advantage of those he governs; for which reason he rules by compulsion, for no freemen will ever willingly submit to such a government. These are the different species of tyrannies, their principles, and their causes.

. . . Tyrannies are preserved two ways most opposite to each other, one of which is when the power is delegated from one to the other, and in this manner many tyrants govern in their states. Report says that Periander founded many of these. There are also many of them to be met with amongst the Persians. What has been already mentioned is as conducive as anything can be to preserve a tyranny; namely, to keep down those who are of an aspiring disposition, to take off those who will not submit, to allow no public meals, no clubs, no education, nothing at all, but to guard against everything that gives rise to high spirits or mutual confidence; nor to suffer the learned meetings of those who are at leisure to hold conversation with each other; and to endeavor by every means possible to keep all the people strangers to each other; for knowledge increases mutual confidence; and to oblige all strangers to appear in public, and to live near the city–gate, that all their actions may be sufficiently seen; for those who are kept like slaves seldom entertain any noble thoughts: in short, to imitate everything which the Persians and barbarians do, for they all contribute to support slavery; and to endeavor to know what every one who is under their power does and says; and for this purpose to employ spies. . . .

. . . A tyrant also should endeavor to engage his subjects in a war, that they may have employment and continually depend upon their general. A king is preserved by his friends, but a tyrant is of all persons the man who can place no confidence in friends, as every one has it in his desire and these chiefly in their power to destroy him. . . .

These and such–like are the supports of a tyranny, for it comprehends whatsoever is wicked. But all these things may be comprehended in three divisions, for there are three objects which a tyranny has in view; one of which is, that the citizens should be of poor abject dispositions; for such men never propose to conspire against any one. The second is, that they should have no confidence in each other; for while they have not this, the tyrant is safe enough from destruction. For which reason they are always at enmity with those of merit, as hurtful to their government; not only as they scorn to be governed despotically, but also because they can rely upon each other's fidelity, and others can rely upon theirs, and because they will not inform against their associates, nor any one else. The third is, that they shall be totally without the means of doing anything; for no one undertakes what is impossible for him to perform: so that without power a tyranny can never be destroyed.

ANDREW C. JANOS

28 What Was Communism?

[The author's discussion of theories concerning the fall of Communism is omitted—ED.]

. . . BACKGROUND TO REVOLUTION

Few historians would disagree with the proposition that the central fact in the history of modern Russia was the country's relative backwardness and its progressive economic marginalization by the successful

SOURCE: Andrew C. Janos, "What Was Communism: A Retrospective in Comparative Analysis," *Communist and Post-Communist Studies*, vol. 29, no. 1 (March 1996): 1–25. Copyright 1996 The Regents of the University of California. Reprinted by permission of the editor, *Communist and Post-Communist Studies*. Article, footnotes, and references abridged by Bernard E. Brown.

industrial revolutions of the West. The recurrent crises that plagued the country from the middle of the 19th century onward can certainly be easily explained by this fact. With its inadequate economic base, the Russian state found it increasingly difficult to interact effectively with more advanced states in international affairs. More specifically, the relative costs of the effective functioning of the state required the extraction of ever larger revenues from a relatively stationary economic base. And if such extractions created a growing sense of absolute deprivation among the peasantry, the rising industrial working class, while its wages were advancing compared to the peasantry, suffered a deep sense of relative deprivation by measuring its condition, via a radical intelligentsia, against the much higher living standards of the West. Not surprisingly, therefore, much of the political discourse in the country around the turn of the past century revolved around the issue of economic backwardness and its possible remedies. The Tsarist governments had experimented with a variety of developmental measures ever since the 1860s, without actually transforming Russia into a modern developmental state by abandoning the traditional principle of divine right. In contrast, their populist opponents, whose movement had grown out of the Slavophile movement, took an anti-developmental stance, hoping to save Russia from the "agonies" of modern industrialism. The socialists in turn first favored an autocratic state in the hope that by modernizing society from above it would create conditions for the rise of a democratic and socialist state. However, after fiercely fighting the populists on this issue, in 1903 the socialists experienced their historical split, and while the Mensheviks bet on a bourgeois democratic state as the likely motor force of industrial development, the Bolsheviks became advocates of a political revolution independent from the stage of socio-economic development.

As is well known, the theoretical underpinnings of the Bolshevik position developed in the course of a prolonged political debate. There were powerful arguments against the Bolshevik position, and they could be expressed within the categories of classical Marxist theory. Specifically, as Plekhanov, Martov, and others close to Menshevism could argue, the exigencies of primary accumulation and industrial development would force socialists to antagonize their popular constituency and to end up presiding over "a political monstrosity, such as the ancient Chinese or Peruvian empires."[1] It is true testimonial to the theoretical acumen of Trotsky and Lenin that they were able to find an appropriate counter-argument, and one that was equally well-grounded in the Marxist frame of reference. According to them, the capitalist world economy was a single, interdependent system that like a chain would break if and when one of its links was exceedingly weak. Russia, with its overburdened state, apathetic peasants, and rebellious workers, was such a weak link in the system, which made it an ideal, and inevitable, choice for beginning the grand historical project of revolutionizing the world . . . To put this formula another way, the Bolsheviks rejected the idea of an internal design for reform and development for an externally oriented strategy of reconstructing the existing world order by means of revolutionary violence.

THE LENINIST STATE

However, the idea of a world revolution, which was to become the fundamental purpose of the Leninist state, was not to come about mechanically by the sheer force of example. This, the Bolsheviks agreed, would be nothing but "petty bourgeois Blanquism" and *putschism* worthy of their populist opponents but not of themselves. The Bolshevik version of world revolution, formulated by Trotsky and Lenin, required an operational plan of fomenting insurrections among the proletariat of the most advanced European societies. Once these insurrections succeeded, the Bolsheviks believed, the center of revolution might shift westward, and Russian socialists might even surrender their leading role to more experienced comrades. It was also believed that such victory in the capitalist metropole would lead to a more equitable distribution of global resources, thus salvaging Russia from the burdens of forced draft accumulation for industrial development.

The operational principles of the political formula were institutionalized in the shape of the Comintern set up in Moscow, but run largely by foreign communists in tandem with, yet in organizational separation from, the Soviet state. The activities of the Comintern have been well recorded (Fischer, 1930; Borkenau, 1962; James, 1993). They included the sponsoring of insurrections in Hungary, Finland, Estonia, Bavaria, Hamburg, and Bulgaria, mutinies in the French navy, and waves of strikes in England and the United States. The existence of the Comintern was thus real and not symbolic, so much so that around its activities there emerged a genuine "transfer culture"[2] of the Leninist period. The elements of this "culture of insurrectionism" are well-known to historians of Leninism. They include an exuberant anarchism, and iconoclastic anti-traditionalism manifest in the artistic modernism of the 1920s in poetry, music, theater, and film-making, in Mme. Kollontai's panegyrics to "free love" and feminism, in denunciations of the traditional family, and in fostering an atmosphere of universalism within which ethnic cultures could flourish at the expense of the culture of the Russian majority (Kollontai, 1963).

Rebellion abroad, however, was only one side of the coin, for its counterpart at home was an autocratic state in which the exercise of freedoms was restricted to those in agreement with the political formula of the regime. This new autocracy, described meticulously by historians (Schapiro, 1965), was to be a temporary phenomenon, until the victory of the revolution abroad. But the Bolsheviks also had arguments that went beyond the Jacobin *cri de coeur* about a revolution endangered, or the higher purpose taking precedence over the principle of rule by majority, for they were aided by the scientific presumptions of Marxism that provided them with a methodology to discern historically correct political positions. It was by reaching out for the scientific argument that the party became the modern counterpart of a traditional priesthood, and that its ideology became the functional equivalent of the doctrine of divine right. For the first time in modern history a movement of the radical left could claim to have the key to absolute wisdom in overriding the principles of popular government.

One should hasten to add that this was not the conventional authoritarianism or traditional autocracy known from the annals of history. This authoritarianism was that of a revolutionary state, because its fundamental purpose was cast in chiliastic–salvationist terms that endowed it "with transcendental significance" and infused it "with all the mystery and majesty of a final eschatological drama" (Cohn, 1961, p. 308). The essence of this chiliasm is the idea of terrestrial perfection in harmony. In the case of Marxism, this chiliasm, articulated in the Communist Manifesto, refers to a condition in which humanity would not only be free from material deprivation, but also from the boredom and frustrations generated by the division of labor and the production process. So described, as a form of social organization socialism would not only be better than any other known form of society, but would be free from conflict, and as such represent a "terminal stage" in history. The tenets of this creed, enunciated by Marx and Engels, were fully embraced

by the leaders of the Bolsheviks. This proposition may strain the credulity of a skeptical posterity, but only a true believer could spend, as did Lenin, the pre-revolutionary months in drafting a vast essay on the withering away of the state, or, like Trotsky, make "red paradise" a standard phrase of his vocabulary and embellish on Marx by proclaiming that under socialism the intelligence of the average person would soar to that of a Michelangelo, Marx, or Aristotle.

The validity of the proposition about the true believer is corroborated by the fact that this chiliasm provided the logic for the political structure of the Leninist state. In the first place, this logic called for charismatic imagery. Where the task is extraordinary, the leader and his following are bound to see themselves as a "special breed of men . . . cut out of a particular stuff,"[3] and attribute to themselves extraordinary qualities. The logic of charismatic salvationism, in turn, is the logic of total devotion (rather than of mechanical obedience), in the name of which the cadre can supersede the narrow mandates of law and even the broader mandates of traditional morality. They can demand sacrifices of themselves and impose it on others with total disregard to cost: where paradise is the reward, the price in human life and suffering is too easily paid. Last but not least, the logic of charisma itself is the logic of perfectionism. Charismatics do not make mistakes. Thus when mistakes occur, they will be attributed not to statistical probability, but to treason or to the infiltration of the organization by enemies.

These operational principles were perhaps most conspicuous in the operation of the Leninist judicial system. Revolutionary tribunals were constantly exhorted not to be guided by the dead letter of the law but by revolutionary conscience and instincts. "Don't tell me," Lenin's chief prosecutor is quoted as saying, "that our criminal courts ought to act exclusively on the basis of written norm. We live in the process of revolution. A tribunal is not the kind of court in which fine points of jurisprudence and clever stratagems are to be restored."[4] In this system of "revolutionary justice" the "proof of guilt [was] relative and approximate" (Solzhenitsyn, 1974, p. 101). An interrogator or judge was to base his conclusions on "intellect, party sensitivity, and moral character" (Solzhenitsyn, 1974, p. 101). But these same principles also applied to the operational code of the rising party apparat and administrative system. As in any large-scale organization geared toward a multiplicity of complex tasks, the performance of administrative and political functions was subject to certain rules and routinization. But these rules served only as guidelines of limited relevance, for unlike the ideal typical bureaucrat, the communist functionary was called upon to make critical judgments, above all the judgment whether a given case should be handled "by the book" or in terms of political expediency expressed in an always changing party line. The cadre who was seen to "cling slavishly" to the book, and refused to make critical political judgments, was as liable to be purged from the organization. While its quantities would vary over time, qualitatively, culturally, and "in spirit" the Leninist system was as terroristic as its successor.

Although time and again attempts have been made both inside and outside the Soviet Union to draw clear dividing lines between Leninism and Stalinism, the above elements of Leninist authority have been well documented by the historiography of the early period. What has been less often, if ever, realized by the historians of the period is the duality of Leninist political culture, and the tension between the political culture of charismatic salvationism and the exuberant anarchism of the political culture of insurrectionism. In the terms of Chalmers A. Johnson, this was a conflict between the "goal culture" and the "transfer culture" of the early Bolshevik regime, between the logic of total and single-minded devotion and the intuitive irreverence of rebels ready to storm the bastions of traditionalism, capitalism, and philistinism. Lenin, deadly serious and obsessed with discipline, was definitely on one side of the cultural divide. But weakened by illness after 1922, he did little more than grumble occasionally about Kollontai's antics and her exuberant advocacy of sexual license and artistic anarchism. A synthesis of the two cultures was impossible, and in time one was to perish.

FROM LENIN TO STALIN

Troublesome as these cultural tensions were, even before Lenin's death in 1924 other issues came to the fore to act as the propellants of political change. Between 1919 and 1923 the operational principles of Leninism–Trotskyism were put into effect via the Comintern but failed to produce the anticipated overthrow of governments of advanced capitalist states. Thus as capitalism and "bourgeois democracy" were consolidating themselves, twenty years after 1903 the Bolsheviks had again to raise the old question of "what is to be done?" The answer would emerge from several years of acrimonious debate (1922–1927) in which the competition for Lenin's mantle became intertwined with three competing political visions for the Soviet state.

The first of these visions was Trotsky's permanent revolution, although it seems that his personal commitment to the idea was faltering after 1924. The second formula, associated with the name of Nikolai Bukharin, emerged from the chaotic experiments of the NEP period and amounted to nothing less than the abandonment of the very idea of world revolution in favor of socialist development. The gist of this design was a project of capital accumulation via the still existing private sector of small enterprise in Soviet agriculture, and a developmental state that would extract surplus by means of taxation and convert it into investment in light industrial enterprise. The intermediate purpose of this strategy was to raise the standard of living of the Soviet working class progressively and above the standards prevailing in the advanced capitalist countries. In the long run, Bukharin argued, the economic success of the design would create its own international demonstration effect that, by the force of example, would persuade the working classes of the superiority of socialism and lead to the progressive liquidation of capitalism in the advanced countries of the world. Had Bukharin had his way, and had it been successful, one could envision a flow of refugees from West to East, and sweeping majorities for the communist parties in England, France, and the United States.

For the majority of the Bolsheviks, however, such a vision has little attraction and many faults in its logic and fundamental premises. On purely doctrinal grounds, there were legitimate objections to a design that, even if only temporarily, would have altered the internal terms of trade in favor of the peasantry and against the urban population, an almost inevitable concomitant of a policy that would have freed markets at a time of substantial shortages in comestibles and other primary products. But objections could be raised also on grounds of purely historical experience, since Russian politicians and economists were fully cognizant of the difficulties involved in developmental strategies and of the experience of the previous century during which few if any of the peripheral economies managed to improve their relative position toward the economically better placed core economies of the world. Yet what gave Bukharin's design the *coup de grâce* in this debate was political and not economic realism—the quite reasonable assumption that while Soviet society would enrich itself peacefully, it might leave itself vulnerable to political aggression in the highly ruthless game of great power politics. It was from this assumption that Stalin proceeded to develop his own political position that eventually won the debate.

Like that of Bukharin, Stalin's vision pivoted around the notion of industrialization. But this design rested on the notions of the rapid and enforced mobilization of economic resources and their investment in heavy industries that would be able to sustain a powerful military establishment with both defensive and offensive capabilities. We need not dwell here on the details of a design that included the forceful collectivization of agriculture, the introduction of draconian labor discipline, and forced labor to enhance the planners' economic flexibility. Suffice it to say that the process bore little resemblance to its counterpart either in Bukharin's design or in the western historical experience on which much of the sociology of modern industrialism is based. What we dealt with in Russia was not only industrialization by, but also for, and almost exclusively for, the state, a process in which the economy became a "mere commissariat" of a militarized society (Spencer, 1972, p. 154) totally subordinated to collective goals and purposes, including the purpose of promoting socialism on a world scale. True, the purposes of Stalin's position were carefully obfuscated for public consumption at home and abroad by appropriating Bukharin's slogan of "building socialism in one country." But the truth of the matter, revealed by Stalin's subsequent actions, was that socialism was first built "in one country, but then in another, and then in yet another" (Faeges, 1994, Part II, Ch. 2). Much like the rulers of Prussia, from the Grand Elector to Wilhelm I, Stalin built for himself an eastern base of power that he was expanding westward in several drives that took him ever closer to the heartland of industrial capitalism. Thus in his first major geopolitical thrust in 1939–1940 he moved against Finland, Poland, Bessarabia, and the Baltic states. In the process, in 1939 he allied himself with Hitler's Germany. In the autumn of 1940, through Molotov, Stalin pressed the Germans for further concessions in Southeastern Europe and Turkey (Shirer, 1941, pp. 565–566, 1967, pp. 1049, 1053–1061), a gambit that most likely convinced Hitler to betray his momentary ally. After the war, another westward thrust yielded the seven countries of East Central Europe and the East Elbian regions of the former German Reich. This was accompanied by maneuverings to move in the direction of the Dardanelles, and was followed by a new geopolitical design to expand into West Europe, indicated in part by the inclusion of Italy and France into the new Cominform and, more directly, by materials that are currently emerging from Soviet archives (Aga-Rossi and Zaslavsky, 1994). This concerted thrust toward the heartlands of capitalism, so much within the spirit of German military, economic, and geopolitical thinkers who affected Bolshevik operational principles, was halted only in the post-Stalin years, and mainly because of the rise of new military technologies and of a credible commitment to use them in the defense of Europe by the United States. While detractors of Stalin hold that he betrayed both the revolution and the ideals of classical Marxism, a strong argument can be made that Stalin merely adapted the Leninist idea of world revolution to new, unforeseen, circumstances, and rather than abandoning the classical tenets of Marxism, he merely made them compatible with new operational principles. Put differently, it may be said that he put these classical principles through the filter of the étatism that now came to occupy a pivotal position in his system of thinking. Using the metaphor of the filter, we then can say that whatever element of classical Marxism was congruous with the idea of maintaining a strong state was kept in, and that whatever seemed to undermine the authority of an all-powerful state, was ruthlessly eliminated. For example, on the one hand, the public ownership of the means of production enhanced the flexibility of the state in mobilizing and allocating resources, so any vestige of private property was eliminated and state socialism was born. Likewise, public education, the spread of literacy, and improvements in the system of health services meshed with the étatist design: Any militarized society, from Prussia onward, needs healthy and literate recruits and workers in the armament industries. These priorities of early socialism therefore became the keystones of Stalinist social policy and perennial proof of its progressiveness to sympathetic outside observers. The same holds true for the celebration of certain aspects of high culture—the cultivation of classical novels, opera, and ballet—which would serve as functional substitutes for scarce material goods and as means to identify Stalinist society as a representative of a superior civilization. On the other hand, those elements of the Marxist (and enlightenment) tradition that were seen to undermine the authority of an all-powerful state—abortion, easy divorce, feminism, sexual license, assaults on the integrity of the traditional family, experimental and modernist art, and the egalitarianism of the 1920s, now denounced as a form of left-wing infantilism—were filtered out of the definition of state socialism.

Out of this Stalinist filter there emerged a new political culture, the political culture of étatism, more in harmony with the chiliastic–salvationism that Stalin inherited from Lenin than with the libertinism and anarchism of the 1920s. Indeed, that culture of irreverence vanished—some of its practitioners were killed, others driven into exile or suicide—and was replaced by a strange mixture of socialist philistinism *(meshchanstvo)* and Prussian military discipline. Military officers were now given back their insignia, including golden braids for generals, together with their manservants. In civilian lives managers now had cars and chauffeurs, and functionaries gradually shed their workman's tunics for dark suits and neckties. In social relations, the emphasis now was on the respectability of rank. . . .

To be sure, in spite of the offhanded dismissals of "egalitarian gamesmanship" *(uravnilovka)*, an element of tension among ranks inevitably crept into this militarized society, and Stalin attempted to resolve it, not altogether without success, by routinizing and theatricalizing the purge. In this scheme of affairs terror was not only an instrument of intimidation, it also became proof for the existence of a rough-and-ready system of social justice that set Stalinism apart from its Tsarist predecessor. Both of these regimes exacted respect for rank. But under the Tsar, the high and the mighty were born in their rank and died in it, whereas in the new order even the mightiest official could fall overnight from the top to the bottomless pit of concentration camps, or to a fate even worse. The purge was thus an integral part of Soviet socialism. It was the price that Stalin paid for militarizing it. Indeed, when the purge was at last eliminated by his successors, rank became entrenched, and hence more resented by the population, by staunch allies, and by fellow travelers. It is well to remember that all told it was not Stalinist terror but Brezhnevite entrenchment that turned Mao against the Soviet Union and was responsible for the rise of the "new left."

Needless to say, the shift from Leninism to Stalinism was not merely a matter of symbolism, but a matter of restructuring certain aspects of public authority. Much of this change, though, was a matter of quantity rather than of quality. Thus Leninist rule in the 1920s was authoritarian by any standard, and its charismatic-salvationist elements represented an implicit rejection of self-imposed restraint or of firm boundary lines between civil society and the state. Thus the new purge, like the old, was inflicted for violating the spirit, and not the letter, of the law. But as the scope of social mobilization increased, so did the scope of the purge and the boundaries of public authority. The petty terror of Leninism became the mass terror of Stalinism, and its totalitarian claims became totalitarian practices as the state penetrated increasingly large areas of what was left of civil society, eliminated autonomous organizations, and, in the standard phrase of the literature on totalitarianism, penetrated "every nook and cranny" of the physical environment. Where tens of thousands had perished in the 1920s, in the 1930s and thereafter the victims would be counted in the millions.

THE POST-STALIN PERIOD

For at least three decades, the changes triggered by Stalin's death and the balance between political continuity and change represented pivotal issues around which the now emerging subdiscipline of comparative politics was built. In examining this balance, the vast majority of the scholarly community agreed that the Soviet, and Soviet-type, political systems retained their authoritarian character. That is, popular, and even party rank-and-file, participation in politics remained devoid of meaningful institutional forms, and popular inputs into policy making were carefully filtered through the councils of the top echelons of a leadership whose members were selected by co-optation from above, rather than by delegation from below. It was also clear that, as a corollary to the above, the process of co-optation and the mode of decision making continued to be legitimated by a historical project, though it was less clear whether this project, "the building of socialism," was to be interpreted to apply globally, or locally, to the societies of the Soviet Bloc. In retrospect, it seems that only a few observers of the Soviet scene recognized the critical, external dimensions of the Brezhnevite project, perhaps none of them more clearly than Seweryn Bialer who recognized that the "future expansion of Soviet rule and that of communism" (Bialer, 1986, p. 191)[5] and the "continuation of the historical trend toward the inevitable victory of socialism over capitalism" (Bialer, 1986, p. 6) were not only rhetorical devices, but genuinely shared objectives that shaped both the structure and the exercise of

public authority. Accordingly, Bialer writes, public policy was "dictated not by the invisible hand of the market but by the very visible hand of the state" (Bialer, 1986, p. 7) and produced a pattern of "development" that was substantially different from patterns familiar from the history of western industrialism. "The rise of labor productivity, innovations, and the diffusion of technology, that is to say, intensive development which has been crucial to the West . . . has been definitely of secondary importance in expanding the command economy" (Bialer, 1986, p. 7). Throughout the Brezhnev years the top priority of public policy thus was to supply the military with the necessary resources. Just as in Spencer's 19th century characterization of a "military society," the "production and distribution of consumer goods [had to] make do with leftovers" (Bialer, 1986, p. 7).

What changed, however, were the operational principles used to attain these universalistic, supraregional objectives: Under the reign of Stalin the logic of nuclear war and of the principle of mutually assured destruction penetrated Soviet strategic thinking only slowly, but they became fully appreciated by the great dictator's successors. While Soviet leaders continued to insist on "burying" capitalism and on surpassing the West both economically and politically, they adapted their geopolitical design to the realities of the nuclear age. This meant a significant shift away from Europe as an immediate target and towards the Third World, and a shift from the doctrine of hitting the heartland in a *coup de main* (a doctrine that Lenin and his successors had learned from Clausewitz and other Prussian military thinkers) to a new doctrine of "nibbling around the peripheries," expressed in a seemingly conflicting commitment to strategic arms limitation and to the support of wars of national liberation and other forms of anti-imperialist struggle likely to take place outside the core regions of the capitalist world system. This last obligation was not undertaken lightly and as a matter of rhetoric, but was lent credence by the support that the Soviet Bloc gave to North Vietnam, Cuba, Angola, Ethiopia, Nicaragua, the rebels of El Salvador, Yemen, for a while Somalia, and to non-Marxist "national progressives" across the world. There were no doubt extensive debates, yet unknown to the external world, about where and how this support should be used. In 1962 Khrushchev attempted to gain geopolitical advantage in the Third World by injecting nuclear weapons into the political game, a maneuver that may have given him tactical advantage (by extorting a tacit recognition of the Cuban communist regime by the United States), but also led to his eventual ouster as a "hare-brained schemer" two years later, and to a return to the use of more conventional military aid in the struggle for supremacy in the non-western world.

A second, and perhaps more dramatic, set of changes in Soviet politics has been well recognized by Sovietology and has served as the mainstay of theories of political change in communist societies throughout the latter part of the Cold War period. These changes took place in the realm of political culture and belief. They were not the result of a rational calculation of costs and benefits, but of a slow and probably painful process of learning that most likely began under Stalin's reign, but could not be articulated before his death. While Stalin may well have been insulated from the outside world and remained engrossed in his chiliastic phantasies behind the Kremlin walls, as Djilas' experiences with him seem to suggest (Djilas, 1962, p. 103), his lieutenants and the lower echelons of his party apparat had to encounter and endure some of the hard realities of Soviet life and the intractabilities of human nature and social existence. Carefully, hiding their experiences behind fulsome praise for the salvationist design, these apparatchiki, hardened in the trenches of economic mobilization and rural class struggle, began to resign themselves to human folly, and the inevitable imperfections of any social mechanism. When Stalin died, this new "pragmatism" quickly bubbled up to the surface, and resulted in what diverse observers in the West described as the "deradicalization" (Tucker, 1970, pp. 172–214) or "rationalization" (Brzezinski, 1967, pp. 53–64) of Soviet ideology. Less convincingly at times, there was also talk of the "de-ideologization" of the Soviet regime. However, the fact is that ideology, the fundamental purpose of "building socialism" or of "full communism," remained crucial to the legitimacy of the

Soviet regime, except that some of the key terms—including socialism and communism—had acquired new meanings. Thus communist (or Soviet-style socialist) society was still regarded as the best conceivable form of social organization, one in which, according to one Soviet academician, the educational system, health care, recreation, transportation, and housing would be better than in any other society in the history of humanity. But despite all the things that this form of collective existence might provide, it still would not have that quality of perfection that would bring the forces of history to a sharp halt. Neither society, nor international affairs, would in the new Soviet mind conform to the utopian vision of Marx and Engels that Lenin, Trotsky, and Stalin proclaimed to be in sight. . . .

To quote Nikita Khrushchev on the subject,

Will there be criminals in Communist society? I personally, as a Communist, cannot vouch that there will not be any. A crime is a deviation from the generally recognized standards of behavior in society, frequently caused by mental disorders. Can there be any diseases, any mental disorders in Communist society? Evidently there can be (Goldhagen, 1963, p. 629)

Post-Stalin political authority, and the political culture surrounding it, reflect this new, "incrementalist" view of social engineering (Hough, 1972, p. 29). By the standards of this culture, the leader is no longer required to perform miracles or superhuman deeds, hence he is no longer under subtle pressure to vest himself in the garb of scientific omniscience or charismatic heroism. Indeed, rather than cultivating the imagery of miracle men and scientific geniuses, the post-Stalin leaders of the Soviet Union, and most of their counterparts in eastern Europe, attempted to establish the legitimacy of self and party on skills in the more mundane arts of administration and management. Among them, Khrushchev delighted in dispensing practical advice as to the milking of cows, the transport of coal, or the proper use of chemical fertilizers. Brezhnev, and later Andropov and Chernenko, were properly described as "clerks"[6] who prided themselves on their attention to petty, bureaucratic detail. . . .

This political culture and imagery of leadership does not in and by itself generate a legal–rational form of political expectations nor a stable, truly bureaucratic, environment, but leaders whose legitimacy derives from the "incremental" and mundane will find it very difficult to exact total commitments from their subordinates, or to blithely disregard rules and regulations that have been issued to ensure the efficient functioning of the political system. In this kind of political culture leaders can penalize subordinates and citizens for violating the letter but not the spirit of the law. Rules and regulations may be broken in the name of terrestrial salvation, but hardly in the name of incremental improvements in the quality of life, whether inside or outside one's own country. It was thus that subjectivism was replaced by "socialist legality" (Lipson, 1962), an operational principle that expressed the desirability of stable expectations and predictability in the system, though in the Soviet–East European case without also providing appropriate procedural safeguards, which made the bureaucratic label less than fully descriptive of Soviet Bloc reality in the post-Stalin years (Pakulski, 1986, pp. 3–4).

Indeed, these changes in the political culture of Soviet communism were accompanied by surprisingly few institutional reforms. The edifices of the Soviet, and—with the Yugoslav exception—East European states, remained much the same as they had been crafted in the earlier, Stalin period. But in its substance, Soviet (and East European) political life had undergone significant change. Once the political culture of chiliastic–salvationism devolved into incrementalism, terror also ceased to be the mainstay of regimes. With the new rhetorical commitment to rules, and even in the absence of strict proceduralism, it became easier for citizens and subordinates to engage in "crypto-politics," the wresting of personal or group advantages by bickering about the meaning of commands, by feigned compliance with them, or by the implicit threat to subvert the leaders' will by mere footdragging and lack of enthusiasm. These means of crypto-politicking and the presence of a feeble legalism were certainly sufficient for the political class of managers and apparat people to extract a degree of immunity, particularly immunity in their pursuit of social reward and privilege. Unlike the days of Stalin there was, whether in legal or extra-legal ways, a steady flow of benefits from the population at large to the political elite, adding domestic social inequalities to the sources of dissatisfaction created by the vision of the material superiority of the capitalist world. It was in this manner that, long before its demise, the Soviet state and its clients acquired third, rather than second, world characteristics, even though their status in the international arena was still enhanced by their military capabilities. As to the state, its totalitarian forms remained unchanged. But behind the totalitarian facade, the effective scope of political authority began to shrink, as people began to reclaim a small private domain in which they could breathe and speak more freely in the circle of friends and family. . . .

ENTER GORBACHEV—EXIT COMMUNISM

In the mid-1980s it was not uncommon for the critics of the Brezhnev decades—most prominent among them Gorbachev—to characterize the previous epoch of Soviet history as one of stagnation and decay. This judgment was one-sided, indeed unjust, for it was between 1965 and 1985 that the Soviet Union had turned from being a regional to a global superpower by acquiring, next to the largest ground army in the world, a "blue-water" navy, an impressive space program and, last but not least, nuclear parity with the United States. By virtue of these accomplishments, the Soviet Union acquired the capacity to project its power into every corner of the globe and to exert its influence on any continent, including those of the western hemisphere.

But while these impressive gains brought power and prestige to the commonwealth of socialist states, both the Soviet and the East European economies continued to lag behind the West. Indeed, by many calculations, they not only lagged, but continued to fall farther and farther behind the core societies of the modern industrial world. . . . The economic system was not designed to produce long-term popular welfare, but short-term coercive potential and military prowess. In its own terms, as it had been copied from the German model of military mobilization during World War I, the system functioned very well in that it was capable not only of sustaining a given level of military power, but of increasing it at a steady rate of 4 percent per annum (Bialer, 1986, p. 46), though not without placing ever larger pressures on the Soviet standard of living and on its ability to acquire a capacity for long-term efficiency in its civilian sector.

In retrospect, Soviet military spending in this period is estimated to have been 20–25 percent of Soviet GNP. Apart from the shortages created by military spending in the narrow sense, Soviet standards of living suffered from expenditures associated with the militarized, or reconstructionist, geopolitical posture taken by the Soviet Union in world affairs. After the first ten or fifteen years of the existence of the Bloc, the Soviet Union reversed its earlier exploitative policies toward eastern Europe and began to subsidize these satellite economies, and especially the economies of the Warsaw Pact countries (minus recalcitrant Romania).[7] After 1960, these expenses were compounded by the outflow of aid, and then subsidy, to Cuba, Vietnam, Nicaragua, Ethiopia, Mozambique, and Angola, as well as to friendly, but "non-socialist," regimes across the world from South America to the Middle East.

In the last analysis, the "resource squeeze" on the Soviet Union was relative. It was a function of the fact that all these military and imperial expenditures were undertaken from a peripheral economic position in geopolitical competition with the most developed industrial countries of the world. Not only was the American GNP two and a half times that of the Soviet, but it had allies in and outside NATO that included Germany, France, Britain, Canada, and Japan. The gap between the GNP's of the NATO and Warsaw Pact nations was about 3:1, and while not all of these countries spent the same proportions for military purposes as the United States, some of them, including Germany and Japan, lavishly subsidized American military

spending by indirect means, such as by purchasing vast quantities of American debt for financing American military preparedness. While the U.S. had Japan and Germany for allies, the Soviet Union had Poland, Hungary, Angola, and Mozambique, to mention but a few for obvious contrast.

Nor did the Soviet Union compete in a static environment. At times, this environment seemed to favor its position, as in the years after 1945 when victory in war gave it considerable momentum, or in the 1960s and 1970s when the West seemed to be divided and the U.S. bogged down in an unpopular war. By the late 1970s, however, the U.S. was shaking off the trauma of a lost war and had begun to respond actively to hostile external stimuli by increasing its own military expenditures. This new round in the armament race coincided with a growing restlessness on the Soviet empire's European periphery.

All this raised serious dilemmas for the Soviet political elite. They now had a series of options, none of them without substantial risks. They could take up the challenge of a new armament race by further diminishing the standard of living of populations at home and in East Europe, thereby raising the risk of popular unrest and of a return to massive terror to pre-empt it or to put it down. Alternatively, they could have acted in 1979 as Hitler had done in 1939 and used their momentary military superiority in some project that would have given them decisive geopolitical advantages in the heartlands of capitalism. This, of course, would have been a high risk option, much riskier than even Hitler's gamble 40 years before. The only other viable alternative was to abandon the Soviet geopolitical design, and with it the political formula and structure of the political system as it had evolved since the days of Lenin.

While a large number of Soviet political actors and observers apparently shared this assessment of options, an aging and ailing leadership was incapable of making a choice among these stark alternatives. Instead, and in likely response to the logic of an anomalous situation in which ever increasing military expenditures yielded ever diminishing returns, they embarked on the Afghani project, a step that allowed them to flex military muscle and engage in self-deception about their willingness to escalate their anti-imperialist strategies. The disastrous consequences of this step are well-known, and by taking it they escalated the crisis rather than alleviating it. The two interim leaders who followed Brezhnev between 1982 and 1985 thus faced still more agonizing dilemmas than their predecessor. It was into this milieu that Mikhail Gorbachev entered in April, 1985, ready to cut the Gordian knot of Soviet politics.

It is not the purpose of this article to review the trials and tribulations of the Gorbachev years. Suffice it to say that, while at the beginning Gorbachev himself might have been satisfied merely to "inject technological dynamism into the Soviet economy" (Schweizer, 1994, p. 247), in time the problems facing his country unfolded in all their painful detail, and he began to urge his subordinates to turn their attention to the nation's domestic development and to reevaluate foreign policy in order "to create the best possible external conditions for reform."[8] More concise and clear-cut formulations were to follow. By 1987 he was ready to accept the "expression of the legitimate interests of all countries" in world politics (Gorbachev, 1987, p. 122), words that translated into the acceptance of the status quo in global politics. Still more explicitly, Gorbachev began to speak of abandoning the "international class struggle" in favor of "international competition," a formula that amounted to nothing less than the abandonment of the old militarized posture of external reconstruction that had sustained Soviet politics from Lenin to Andropov and Chernenko. These elements of a "new thinking" were coupled with an expressed desire for the return of Russia to a "common home" it shared with West Europe. With these words Soviet policy had come full circle. Lenin, too, wanted such a common home, and wanted to liberate Europe so that the more advanced countries could aid Russia to emerge from its condition of backwardness. Now Gorbachev was ready to accept the reality of capitalism in the hope of accomplishing the same objective.

We should remember, though, that while Gorbachev was ready to cross the threshold between global reconstruction and internal development, or, in Herbert Spencer's words, from "militancy" to "industrialism," he was not quite ready to cross the one between democratic and authoritarian politics. Instead, his constitutional maneuverings, and the Duma he created, point to a desire to create a softer authoritarianism, an authoritarianism with a democratic facade to reassure the West while maintaining some capability to mobilize and to accomplish the painful task of dismantling a militarized economic regime. This regime would permit a freer flow of information for the benefit of both emerging markets and the government without full accountability to a fickle public in times of anticipated stress. Such a delicate balance between the two has sustained political regimes in many of the developing countries of the periphery, most recently in the "newly industrialized" countries of the Pacific Rim, but none of these have had to contend with the stresses of multinationality and the liquidation of empire while re-entering a competitive world economy. The Soviet Union did have to contend with these, and Gorbachev's attempt at simulated democracy collapsed under their weight.

CONCLUSION

From this brief review of the 70 years of Soviet communism, there emerge a number of critical differences among communist regimes that, at the same time, can serve as the basis of a broader typology for purposes of macro–political comparisons. The most important of these are the distinctions between developmental and reconstructionist regimes. Within the former, we have been able to distinguish between reformist (neo-liberal) and radical types. Within the latter we encountered salvationist and incrementalist, and insurrectionist vs. étatist, visions and operational principles. These elements of the political formula then tie directly into the political culture—or what should be treated as political culture—with its teleological (goal-oriented) and instrumental (transfer-oriented) elements. These in turn can be linked to variations in the structure, exercise, and scope of public authority. The political history of East

Europe meanwhile allows us to point to communist variants of the developmental states, both radical and reformist, long ignored as such because of rhetorical and institutional facades carefully designed to conceal their real purposes and the distinctions between them and the Soviet state.

For the student of Russia, the model of externally oriented, reconstructionist politics is significant not only as a category for dealing with the Soviet past, but also as a tool for engaging in intellectual discourse about the country's future prospects. Today, much of the scholarly discourse on the subject revolves around the prospects for democracy and development. On the whole, these writings are pessimistic about outcomes, an attitude that most frequently leads to a prediction of chaos and internal conflict that would lead to a diminished capacity for Russia to act in international affairs. Such a prognosis ignores a whole array of options available to political actors in peripheral states, especially in states of substantial size, population, and resources. One of the options that logically presents itself is that of creating a reconstructionist state with a militarized political culture and structure of authority. The validity of this proposition is sadly apparent in contemporary Russia where the opposition to a developmental regime consists largely of characters like Aleksandr Rutskoi and Aleksandr Lebed, and of political parties like the misleadingly named Liberal Democratic Party of Vladimir Zhirinovsky, or the Great Power Party, the program of which is well captured by its name. Although often described as movements of irrationality and cultural despair, these movements are not devoid of an ability to interrelate political ends and means. Those who think otherwise must stop to ponder which scenario is more utopian: Zhirinovsky's vision of Russian soldiers washing their boots in the Indian Ocean (or plundering a prosperous Germany), or the Yeltsin–Gaidar vision of a democratic and capitalist Russia successfully closing the economic gap between itself and the West or the countries of the Pacific Rim and raising the Russian living standard progressively to the level that would satisfy the population's psychological and material needs. In significant ways, this was the dilemma of Germany between the 1890s and the 1930s, though from a position much more advantageous than that of Russia today. True, the prevalence of nuclear arms may moderate the propensity to take major risks for those who care for the fate of their fellow citizens, but then it may also encourage those who do not yet see the enormous potential of the destructive power that can be used in reckless attempts to extort advantages from more prosperous areas.

A similar case may be made for China, a communist regime that survived its European counterparts without shedding its original label. To be sure, the changes that this vast country has experienced over the past two decades have been dramatic and may be best described as a transition from a militantly reconstructionist to a reformist developmental regime. More significantly, the experiment has worked beyond the hopes and dreams of its architects. As of today, China is the prime example of successful economic development in a previously revolutionary regime. But the economic accomplishments have exacted a heavy political price: In 1989 China experienced a major upheaval and as the country lurches toward another change in leadership, its rulers may take another look at the costs and benefits of following the capitalist road. American observers of the Chinese scene can already discern rumblings within the power structure which might presage a major policy debate between developmentalists and reconstructionists (Manni, 1995). If Russia's current dilemmas remind one of Germany in defeat, and the rise of Hitler in the interwar period, China's are more reminiscent of an earlier period. Like Germany in the years between 1870 and 1890, China in the last two decades has experienced spectacular growth, which, by conventional reasoning, should make it a saturated power satisfied with its regional influence and the profits of trade. Yet China's saturation, much like German "saturation" of the last century, may be more obvious to outsiders than to insiders because, as in the case of Germany, the price of economic progress has been political turmoil. Moreover, and not unlike Germany of the past, China faces an inhospitable and increasingly competitive international environment in which the economically advanced nations still have disproportionate influence in setting the terms of exchange. Much like Germany in the distant past, China's leaders today will weigh the advantages and perils of different strategies, and may conclude that a militarized society would yield higher benefits to them at a lower cost and risks. They may, of course, conclude otherwise. But the shell of communist institutions, traditions, and political culture would make a militarist regression just as easy for the Chinese as the reorientation of German society in the context of Prussian traditions and Wilhelminian leadership.

It was more than a hundred years ago that Herbert Spencer wrote his classic statement on militancy and industrialism (Spencer, 1972). Looking at Germany and England he understood full well that these represented alternative models for national (class, or individual) aggrandizement with costs and benefits that rational political actors will weigh. As to the future, Spencer seemed ambivalent, but voiced the faint hope that one day industrialism would prevail, and that an interdependent trading system would emerge worldwide in which the use of force would be an anomaly. A century and two World Wars later, American social science revived this Spencerian hope in countless studies of modernization, industrial societies, and economic development. Today, once again, we are less confident about a new era of order and peace. We now believe that militarism assimilated into a larger revolutionary design is a subject that needs to be studied some more. In the most general terms this essay has been an attempt to respond to this need.

NOTES

1. This quote from Plekhanov appears in Medvedev (1972, p. 359). See Also Wittfogel (1957, pp. 391–395).
2. The terms "transfer" and "goal" culture have been borrowed from Johnson (1970, pp. 7–8). Johnson's own reference is to Wallace (1961, p.148). The terms indicate norms and symbolic expressions related to the fundamental purpose and operational design respectively of a revolutionary system.
3. From Stalin's "Oath to Lenin," in Deutscher (1960, p. 270).
4. From Public Prosecutor Krylenko's *Za pyat let* [in five years], quoted in Solzhenitsyn (1974, p. 308).
5. For others with similar views see Pipes (1990), Feher *et al.* (1983, p. 21), and Odom (1976).
6. Zbigniew Brzezinski quoted in Hough (1972, p. 26).
7. Marrese and Vanous (1983). These authors have their critics, but none of them seems to doubt that Soviet resources were strained by a combination of military spending and geopolitical outlays. See, for example, Desai (1987).
8. Gorbachev, as quoted in Oberdorfer (1991, p. 162).

REFERENCES

Aga-Rossi, Elena and Zaslavsky, Victor (1994) "L'URSS, il PCI e l'Italia: 1944–1948," *Storia Contemporanea*, 6, pp. 929–982.

Arendt, Hannah (1951) *Origins of Totalitarianism*, New York: Harcourt Brace.

Bell, Daniel (1958) "Ten Theories in Search of Reality: the Prediction of Soviet Behavior in the Social Sciences," *World Politics*, 10, pp. 327–365.

Bialer, Seweryn (1986) *The Soviet Paradox*, New York: Alfred Knopf.

Black, Cyril (1966) *The Dynamics of Modernization: A Study in Comparative History*, New York: Harper and Row.

Borkenau, Franz (1962) *World Communism: a History of the Communist International*, Ann Arbor: University of Michigan Press.

Brzezinski, Zbigniew (1960) *The Soviet Bloc*, Cambridge, MA: Harvard University Press.

Brzezinski, Zbigniew (1967) *Ideology and Power in Soviet Politics*, 2nd ed., New York: Praeger.

Carr, E. H. (1970) *A History of Soviet Russia*, Vol. 2. Baltimore, MD: Penguin.

Cohen, Stephen (1975) *Bukharin and the Bolshevik Revolution*, New York: Random House.

Cohn, Norman (1961) *The Pursuit of the Millennium*, New York: Harper and Row.

Colton, Timothy (1984) "The Impact of the Military on Soviet Society," in Erik Hoffman and Robbin Laird (eds.) *The Soviet Polity in the Modern Era*, Hawthorne, NY: Aldine, pp. 393–412.

Desai, Padma (1987) *The Soviet Economy: Problems and Prospects*, Oxford, England: Basil Blackwell.

Deutscher, Isaac (1960) *Stalin: A Political Biography*, New York: Vintage.

Deutscher, Isaac (1984) "Socialism in One Country," in Tariq Ali (ed.) *The Stalinist Legacy: Its Impact on Twentieth–Century World Politics*, Middlesex, England: Penguin Books, pp. 95–105.

Djilas, Milovan (1962) *Conversations with Stalin*, New York: Harcourt, Brace and World.

Faeges, Russel (1994) *Global Visions, Local Realities: Internationalism, Nationality and Soviet Politics*, MS.

Fedorenko, Sergei (1991) "Roots and Origins of the Protracted Soviet Crisis," in Paul Holman *et al.* (eds.) *The Soviet Union After Perestroika: Change and Continuity*, Washington, DC: Brassey's.

Feher, Ferenc, Heller, Agnes, and Markus, György (1983) *Dictatorship over Needs*, Oxford: Basil Blackwell.

Fischer, Louis (1930) *The Soviets in World Affairs*, New York/London: J. Cape and H. Smith.

Goldhagen, Erich (1963) "The Glorious Future: Realities and Chimeras," in Abraham Brumberg (ed.) *Russia under Khrushchev*, New York: Praeger.

Gorbachev, Mikhail (1987) *Perestroika*, New York: Harper and Row.

Hough, Jerry (1969) *The Soviet Prefects: the Local Party Organs in Industrial Decision–Making*, Cambridge, MA: Harvard University Press.

Hough, Jerry (1972) "The Soviet System: Petrification or Pluralism?" *Problems of Communism*, 21.

James, C. L. R. (1993) *World Revolution, 1917–1936: the Rise and Fall of the Communist International*, Atlantic Highlands, NJ: Humanities Press.

Johnson, Chalmers (1970) "Comparing Communist Nations," in C. Johnson (ed.) *Change in Communist Systems*, Stanford, CA: Stanford University Press.

Kautsky, John (1970) *The Political Consequences of Modernization*, New York: John Wiley and Sons.

Kollontai, Alexandra (1963) "The New Woman," transl. Theodore Denno, and "Communism and the Family," in Thornton Anderson (ed.) *Masters of Russian Marxism*, New York: Appleton-Century, pp. 173–179.

Kubalkova, Vendulka and Cruickshank, Albert (1989) *Thinking New About Soviet New Thinking*, Berkeley, CA: Institute of International Studies, University of California.

Lenin, V. I. (1970) "Imperialism, the Highest Stage of Capitalism," in *Selected Works*, Moscow: Progress, pp. 667–768.

Lipson, Leon (1963) "Socialist Legality: the Road Uphill," in Abraham Brumberg (ed.) *Russia Under Khrushchev*, New York: Praeger, pp. 434–469.

Manni, Jim (1995) "U.S. Strategists Fear China Will Become a Threat," *San Francisco Chronicle (Los Angeles Times)*. May 7, p. A6.

Marrese, Michael and Vanous, Jan (1983) *Soviet Subsidization of Trade in Eastern Europe*, Berkeley, CA: Institute of International Studies, University of California.

Medvedev, Roy (1972) *Let History Judge*, New York: Knopf.

Moore, Barrington (1965) *Soviet Politics—the Dilemma of Power*, 2nd ed., New York: Harper.

Mosca, Gaetano (1939) *The Ruling Class*, transl. Hannah Kohn, Arthur Livingston (ed.), New York: McGraw Hill.

Oberdorfer, Don (1991) *The Turn*, New York: Poseidon

Odom, William (1976) "The Militarization of Soviet Society," *Problems of Communism*, 25, pp. 34–51.

Pakulski, Jan (1986) "Bureaucracy and the Soviet System," *Studies in Comparative Communism*, 19 (1).

Pipes, Richard (1990) *The Russian Revolution*, New York: Alfred Knopf.

Schapiro, Leonard (1965) *The Origin of Communist Aristocracy*, New York: Praeger.

Schweizer, Peter (1994) *Victory*, New York: Atlantic Monthly Press.

Shirer, William (1941) *Berlin Diary*, New York: Knopf.

Shirer, William (1967) *The Rise and Fall of the Third Reich*, Fawcett (ed.), New York: Fawcett World.

Solzhenitsyn, Aleksandr (1974) *The Gulag Archipelago*, Vol. 1, New York: Harper and Row.

Spencer, Herbert (1972) "Militancy and Industrialism," in J. D. Y. Peel (ed.) *Herbert Spencer on Evolution*, Chicago, IL: Chicago University Press, pp. 149–166.

Stalin, I. V. (1972) "The Foundations of Leninism," in Bruce Franklin, *The Essential Stalin*, New York: Doubleday, pp. 89–186.

Trotsky, Leon (1969) *Permanent Revolution and Results and Prospects* (1906), transl. John Wright and Brian Price, New York: Merit.

Trotsky, Leon (1970) *The Revolution Betrayed* (1937), transl. Max Eastman, 5th ed., New York: Merit.

Tucker, Robert (1970) *The Marxian Revolutionary Idea*, New York: Norton.

Tucker, Robert (ed.) (1975) *The Lenin Anthology*, New York/London: W. W. Norton and Co.

Ulam, Adam (1965) *The Bolsheviks*, New York: Macmillan.

Venturi, Franco (1966) *Roots of Revolution*, transl. Francis Haskell, New York: Grosset and Dunlap.

Wallace, Anthony (1961) *Culture and Personality*, New York: Random House.

Wittfogel, Karl (1957) *Oriental Despotism: A Comparative Study of Total Power*, New Haven, CT: Yale University Press.

Yarmolinski, Avrahm (1962) *Road to Revolution*, New York: Collier, pp. 168–185.

LILIA SHEVTSOVA

29 The Limits of Bureaucratic Authoritarianism

After communism's collapse and more than a decade of sweeping changes that saw the Soviet Union dissolve, the state monopoly over the means of production end, and a polity founded on elections begin, Russia is returning to traditional ways, albeit in a new post-Soviet key. In a "normal" transitional society, the third election after the onset of political opening is supposed to testify to the consolidation of the democratic process. In Russia, late 2003 to early 2004 witnessed not the third but the *fourth* such round of elections, yet what has emerged from them is not a consolidated democracy, but rather a remodeled form of authoritarianism. After more than a dozen years of attempted reforms, in other words, Russia under President Vladimir Putin is returning to the very relationship between authority and society that it so painfully and fitfully struggled to shed throughout the 1990s.

Putin is the handpicked successor of Boris Yeltsin, who held the Russian presidency from 1991 to 1999. Yeltsin's ambiguous political and economic legacy contained potential for expanded competition in politics and the marketplace, but also for backsliding toward authoritarian politics and the use of power to choke off economic competition. Yeltsin himself seemed a genuinely torn figure, poised uneasily between his roots in the old Soviet era and a desire—often acted upon—to break with them by supporting such things as press freedom, open public debate, and political pluralism. Putin, though a younger and (at least outwardly) more "modern" figure, suffers no such ambivalence. Instead, he has decisively turned his back on the liberal side of Yeltsin's legacy and opted for a made-over authoritarianism.

What factors lie behind democracy's setback in

Russia? Could anything have stopped it from backsliding? To answer these questions, one should begin by noting that Russian politics in the 1990s suffered from intrinsic instability born of mutually exclusive principles. On the one hand, the predominant Russian view of authority continued to see it as something that needs to remain always undivided and personified in a single ruler. On the other hand, with older forms of legitimation (such as dynastic succession or Marxist ideology) having become obsolete, democratic elections became "the only game in town." One might sum up the situation as "monocracy on the basis of mass consent." As one might expect given its inner tension, this system had a restless quality that combined strategic conservatism with tactical innovation. Power was seeking to remain essentially self-replicating and independent of society, yet in service of this "conservative" goal it was also seeking newer and better means of staking a claim to popular legitimacy and democratic consent.

The 1990s also saw democracy's stock drop as economic ills and institutional weakness stirred longings for "a strong hand at the tiller." Old and thoroughly undemocratic cultural archetypes, both Czarist and Soviet, began to rise in prominence. The political and intellectual classes shunned change more intensely than did society at large, and indulged in fresh attempts to prove that liberal institutions and methods of governance are somehow unsuited to Russia's unique circumstances and character. With Yeltsin in declining health, meanwhile, his "clan" was looking for someone with ties to the "power" ministries (interior, defense, state security) to help guarantee its interests. During Yeltsin's last months in office, the shakiness of the arrangement through which he wielded power became evident. In particular, the simultaneous efforts of oligarchic and populist forces to exploit Russia's underdeveloped democratic institutions fed the (almost certainly exaggerated) impression that only an even stronger executive branch could keep

SOURCE: Lilia Shevtsova, "The Limits of Bureaucratic Authoritarianism," *Journal of Democracy,* vol. 15, no. 3 (July 2004), pp. 67–77. © National Endowment for Democracy and The Johns Hopkins University Press. Reprinted with permission of The Johns Hopkins University Press. Abridged by the Editor.

the state from collapsing altogether. Incursions by Chechen separatists into Dagestan, as well as mysterious apartment-building explosions in Moscow and Volgodonsk, also affected the public mood, as did the example set by Yeltsin himself when he seemingly sought to short-circuit democratic political competition by resigning four months ahead of the March 2000 presidential election so that Putin could run as the incumbent. Thus did a number of structural, situational, and sociocultural factors set the conditions for the authoritarian option that Putin has now spent years reinforcing, extending, and elaborating.

A NEW MODEL OF AUTHORITARIANISM

The 2003–2004 parliamentary and presidential elections have formalized Putin's new-model authoritarianism. Gone is Yeltsin's mix-and-match ambivalence, with its elements of pre-Soviet and Soviet-style personalism as well as its respect for pluralism and elementary democratic practices. Putin, like Yeltsin, wants authority to remain concentrated in the presidency, but rejects Yeltsin's somewhat chaotic governing style in favor of a more systematic approach that rests on the state bureaucracy and especially the power ministries. Yeltsin's regime survived at the expense of decentralization of power. Putin is a recentralizer. Yeltsin rotated personnel constantly. Putin prizes stability among the cadres. Yeltsin was suspicious of the secret services and power ministries. Putin has made them pillars of his regime. Many of the liberal technocrats whom Yeltsin employed remain in the echelons of power, but now in largely auxiliary roles. Yeltsin relied on a presidential "family" or "clan" to make his personal power effective. Putin rejects that approach, but the tendency of personified power to resort to "shadow" mechanisms will constantly re-create the basis for nepotism, whether in a strict biological or a looser political sense, and for the emergence of new incarnations of patrimonial politics. Putin's de facto rejection of pluralism, finally, means that there are even

fewer intermediary levels or institutions between the president and society at large. In this sense, Putin has intensified the personalized nature of the system that he inherited from Yeltsin. To sum up, the younger man has heightened the autocratic features of the Russian system of power that comes down from Byzantine and Czarist days via the Soviets and then Yeltsin, while scrapping Yeltsin's tolerance for pluralism and favoring routinization over Yeltsinian haphazardness.

So far, most efforts to describe this state of affairs have fallen back on the vocabulary of "democracy with adjectives." This manner of speaking compares "immature" with "mature" democracies and qualifies the former as "managed" or "electoral" democracies. These attempts ignore important peculiarities of the Russian case (including the differences between Yeltsin and Putin) and seem concerned with salvaging the classic transition paradigm with its deterministic faith that any country which is moving away from totalitarianism must therefore be moving toward democracy. Can Russia be defined as an electoral democracy if the powers that be, more than a decade after communism's collapse, can never lose an election, and if, moreover, guaranteed victory at the polls is a key feature of their regime? Can Russia be even an "electoral" democracy if elections do nothing but legitimize the personalization of power? Life in Russia is freer today than it was in Czarist or Soviet days and Russian politics even has some democratic elements now. But those elements do not yet a democracy make.

Paradoxically enough, when applied to Russia the transition paradigm becomes a source of pessimism—its proponents tend to conclude that what looks to Russian democrats like rank authoritarianism is in fact a "minimalist" form of democracy normal for Russia. Such attempts at explanation could be dismissed as a mere mental game called "classify the hybrid," were it not that attempts to evaluate Russian reality through the prism of "democracy with adjectives" can lead to oversimplified and even dangerously wrong practical conclusions. If what Russia has is a type of democracy, then one may be tempted to assume that all it needs is reform around the edges, or even a hands-off, "wait-and-see" approach that expects "immature" democracy to turn naturally into full-fledged democracy, like fruit ripening on a tree. But what if this assumption is mistaken? What if the system that has emerged in Russia, far from being about to blossom into democracy, is in fact not even capable of beginning to reform itself? What if the one thing most necessary is a rebuilding of the whole from the ground up?

Without getting deeply into definitional debates, we can say that Russia remains in what Larry Diamond calls a political "twilight zone." The situation is still in flux, moreover, which means that various observers may be correct about various aspects of it at various times, which can be useful for those who advocate this or that specific approach, even if a comprehensive classification of this complex hybrid eludes them. I prefer to call Yeltsin's regime an "electoral autocracy," for this allows us to note things that other definitions miss, namely its national and historical context (including its ties to Russia's long autocratic tradition) and its ability to both accept and reject a certain method of succession.

If you call Yeltsin's regime a democracy, however qualified or unripe, then everything that has followed it must appear deviant and unexpected. If you call Yeltsin's regime by its rightful name as an electoral autocracy, then Putin's authoritarianism seems much less anomalous and far more predictable. Putin has retooled Yeltsin's somewhat mercurial brand of electoral autocracy into a more sober and systematic bureaucratic-authoritarian regime. I use this expression, drawn from scholarship on modernizing autocracies in Latin America, to underline a possible cross-regional historical comparison. The term is accurate as applied to Putin's Russia, which features both authoritarianism (in the sense of personified power) and a heavy reliance on bureaucratic structures and methods that are crowding out much of what might otherwise be the realm of political activity.

While scholars seek definitions, Russia's new political reality takes shape. At the start of Putin's second term, the personalistic aspect is predominant, but no one can rule out a rise in bureaucratic influence or even a bureaucratic challenge to Putin

at some point. How might this happen? There are indications that Putin sees himself as a kind of cautiously reformist autocrat. He appears to be pro-Western or at least pragmatic in many of his views, and it may turn out that he will work to defend and promote reforms—including democratic reforms—rather than shore up his regime's bureaucratic structures and foundation. Sensing in such changes a threat to its dominance, the bureaucracy may prove a source of tacit opposition to Putin and a rival to his power.

Even now, Putin's brand of authoritarianism is arguably working to boost not his personal authority, but rather the power of the bureaucratic groups and institutions that act in his name. One cannot avoid the impression that, early in his second term, Putin has already lost an important cabinet-reorganization fight to the bureaucrats. If the president wants to push reform and innovation, he may be able to do so only by appealing directly to the people, effectively bypassing his own bureaucratic base. But one must wonder how far he can hope to go with such a strategy of Bonapartism in the service of modernization.

Compared to Yeltsin's regime, which was torn by internal conflicts and was losing ground with society at large, Putin's Kremlin projects the air of a steady, well-oiled machine. It contains no rival power centers, and is united around the highly popular president. But there is a sense in which such appearances may be deceptive, for nothing is solidly institutionalized. A consolidated democratic regime is supposed to have "rules of the game"—the constitution, other major laws and institutions—that cannot be easily changed. Such is not the case in Vladimir Putin's Russia. The president has changed the constitution and laws (including electoral and political-parties legislation) to give himself and the Kremlin more control. Any future president will likely be able to make similarly sweeping changes more or less at will. The "rules of the game," then, are actually far more fluid than fixed. There remains, moreover, a deep-seated tendency toward political opacity: All too often decisions are made through behind-the-scenes maneuvering and informal methods rather than transparent processes. Can any regime count as consolidated when it depends so heavily on informal means of making decisions? While the current regime certainly looks solid and is free of any acute conflict or crisis, the basis of this putative stability may be far from firm. Much indeed hinges on Putin himself. In the minds of both the political class and society at large, basic questions about Russia's national course remain unresolved: How and how far should privatization be carried out? What role should the state play in economic matters? Should Russia integrate itself into Western structures such as the World Trade Organization? What are the functions and limits of political opposition? In other words, there is no common vision or ideology uniting Russians. Instead, Putin holds them together, aided greatly by the lack of a sense that there are any alternatives, by fears of upsetting the status quo, and by an unwillingness to think seriously about the future.

To put it crudely but not altogether wrongly, Russia's stability is premised on the high price of oil and the high personal popularity of Vladimir Putin. But what if either or both of these numbers begins to dip? The Putin regime's "informal" aspects might give it considerable resilience, but is that the same as a guarantee of real stability? . . .

THE IMPOTENCE OF ABSOLUTE POWER

. . . Putin's most intractable problem is structural. No matter how much personal authority he gathers, he cannot fully subordinate the whole structure of power to his will alone. The power ministries and the bureaucratic machinery that form the sinews of his rule have already begun to push their own agendas. Sizeable swaths of society, with instincts honed by centuries of autocracy, have withdrawn into the informal economy and other "twilight zones" beyond the reach of state authority.

Even if Putin did not have to cope with these internal tensions and could securely consolidate his rule, he could not aspire to a role like those played by Augusto Pinochet in Chile or Park Chung Hee in South Korea. During the twentieth century, authoritarian strongmen could drag agrarian societies into the industrial epoch. Russia today faces complex postindustrial challenges that it can meet only by reforming the traditional state and focusing on ways to give more scope and freer rein to the inner resources and creativity of society and the individual. Sooner or later the Kremlin will have to face the fact that a tradition of overweening centralized authority is more of a hindrance than a help when it comes to achieving fuller modernization. Competition and innovation, not preservation of the status quo at all costs, must become Russia's watchwords. Putin's version of Russian absolutism can prop itself up for the time being, but in the end history will reveal it as a hurdle on the path to a renewed Russia whose government is the legal and institutionalized exponent of its people's will rather than a toy for whatever crew happens to hold the keys to the Kremlin.

Putin was right to try to find a way out of Yeltsin's oligarchic capitalism. Where he went wrong was in his choice to pump up the bureaucrats to take on the oligarchs, rather than choose the harder but truer path of leaving behind the old Russian game of personified, centralized power in order to give civil society and democratic capitalism room to grow. Could he have taken this second path? Few outside influences urged him to.

Certainly there was no serious pressure for fundamental reform from society at large, the ruling class, or an international community that has now come to value stability over democracy in Russian affairs. Russia has liberal democrats, but their influence is marginal. Putin might have used his great popularity and lack of organized electoral opposition to push for a basic transformation of the "Russian system of power," but even then he would have been tempting fate and putting himself in danger of breaking his own political neck. Given all this, it is little wonder that he chose the less inspiring but seemingly safer path.

Today, the emergence of a full-fledged bureaucratic-authoritarian regime in postcommunist Russia has limited both liberal democracy's prospects and Putin's own freedom of action. Ironically, the existence of a real political spectrum with leftists, rightists, and centrists would actually give the president and his men more room to maneuver than they currently have. Perhaps dimly realizing this—and sensing that pliable "liberals" and "democrats" are good to have around for appearance's sake—some of the brighter lights on the Kremlin team may try to create a liberal-democratic movement and with it the semblance of a "normal" political spectrum. But expecting such a puppet opposition to be a force for real reform may be like keeping a paper tiger in one's home in hopes that its painted snarl will help one feel the thrill of the jungle.

Russia's future depends on whether liberals and democrats can gain traction at the grassroots level and emerge as a real alternative to the current powers. The events of 2004 do not offer much promise that anything like this is about to happen. If anything, a stagnant period of post-Soviet "neo-Brezhnevism" seems to be Russia's near-term fate. After Brezhnev eventually came Gorbachev and *perestroika*. Is a similar turn of the wheel in store? Perhaps Putin's solid-looking new order will fall victim to the sources of instability that we outlined above. Before such instability becomes manifest, however, we may have to witness more power grabs by the president and his apparat as the inertial logic of personified rule and bureaucratic authoritarianism drives them willy-nilly to seek total control. . . .

In a regime based on personalized power, the new ruler will always be tempted to seek distinction and legitimacy through attacks on the previous ruler. Russia still needs to grasp the simple truth that power based on institutions and a system of checks and balances is much stabler and safer. Liberal-democratic constitutionalism frees leaders from the need to expunge their predecessors or fear their successors, makes power struggles nonlethal, and gives losers the hope that they can always return to complete another day. Unlike a liberal-democratic leader, the ruler in Russia's system of personified power needs to make a political desert and call it peace. But a political landscape reduced to howling wilderness is an ideal haunt for the spirit of negation that may one day appear with sudden and surprising force.

The crueler and more obdurate a regime of personified power becomes, the more likely it will be to end in violence rather than orderly transition. Vladimir Putin just might have had a chance to run the table and change the game in Russia, shifting its logic of power and succession away from authoritarianism of either a personal or a bureaucratic stripe and toward at least the basics of liberal constitutionalism. But he chose not to take this chance, and one day he will have to face the consequences that flow from the logic of the Russian system of power.

ANDREW J. NATHAN

30 Authoritarian Resilience

After the Tiananmen crisis in June, 1989, many observers thought that the rule of the Chinese Communist Party (CCP) would collapse. Instead, the regime brought inflation under control, restarted economic growth, expanded foreign

SOURCE: Andrew J. Nathan, "Authoritarian Resilience," *Journal of Democracy*, vol. 14, no. 1 (January 2003), pp. 6–17. © National Endowment for Democracy and The Johns Hopkins University Press. Reprinted with permission of The Johns Hopkins University Press. Abridged by the Editor.

trade, and increased its absorption of foreign direct investment. It restored normal relations with the G-7 countries that had imposed sanctions, resumed the exchange of summits with the United States, presided over the retrocession of Hong Kong to Chinese sovereignty, and won the right to hold the 2008 Olympics in Beijing. It arrested or exiled political dissidents, crushed the fledgling China Democratic Party, and seems to have largely suppressed the Falun Gong spiritual movement.

Many China specialists and democracy theorists—myself among them—expected the regime to fall to democratization's "third wave."[1] Instead, the regime has reconsolidated itself.[2] Regime theory holds that authoritarian systems are inherently fragile because of weak legitimacy, over-reliance on coercion, overcentralization of decision making, and the predominance of personal power over institutional norms. This particular authoritarian system, however, has proven resilient.

The causes of its resilience are complex. But many of them can be summed up in the concept of institutionalization—understood either in the currently fashionable sense of behavior that is constrained by formal and informal rules, or in the older sense summarized by Samuel P. Huntington as consisting of the adaptability, complexity, autonomy, and coherence of state organizations.[3] This article focuses on four aspects of the CCP regime's institutionalization: (1) the increasingly norm-bound nature of its succession politics; (2) the increase in meritocratic as opposed to factional considerations in the promotion of political elites; (3) the differentiation and functional specialization of institutions within the regime; and (4) the establishment of institutions for political participation and appeal that strengthen the CCP's legitimacy among the public at large. While these developments do not guarantee that the regime will be able to solve all the challenges that it faces, they do caution against too-hasty arguments that it cannot adapt and survive.

....

NORM-BOUND SUCCESSION POLITICS

As this article is published, the Chinese regime is in the middle of a historic demonstration of institutional stability: its peaceful, orderly transition from the so-called third generation of leadership, headed by Jiang Zemin, to the fourth, headed by Hu Jintao. Few authoritarian regimes—be they communist, fascist, corporatist, or personalist—have managed to conduct orderly, peaceful, timely, and stable successions. Instead, the moment of transfer has almost always been a moment of crisis—breaking out ahead of or behind the nominal schedule, involving purges or arrests, factionalism, sometimes violence, and opening the door to the chaotic intrusion into the political process of the masses or the military. China's current succession displays attributes of institutionalization unusual in the history of authoritarianism and unprecedented in the history of the PRC [Peoples Republic of China]. It is the most orderly, peaceful, deliberate, and rule-bound succession in the history of modern China outside of the recent institutionalization of electoral democracy in Taiwan.[4] . . .

It takes some historical perspective to appreciate this outcome for the achievement that it is. During the Mao years, Party congresses and National People's Congresses seldom met, and when they did it was rarely on schedule. There have never before been effective terms of office or age limits for persons holding the rank of "central leader"; Mao and Deng each exercised supreme authority until the end of his life. Nor has there ever been an orderly assumption of office by a designated successor: Mao purged Liu Shaoqi, the president of the PRC, by having Red Guards seize him and put him in prison, where he died. Mao's officially designated successor, Lin Biao, allegedly tried to seize power from Mao, was discovered, and died in a plane crash while fleeing. Mao appointed Hua Guofeng as his successor simply by stating that Hua was his choice. Hua was removed from office at Deng Xiaoping's behest before Hua's term of office was over. Deng removed from power both of his own chosen successors, Hu Yaobang and Zhao Ziyang. Deng and the other elders overrode the Politburo in 1989 to impose Jiang Zemin as successor to the Party leadership. . . .

Never before in PRC history has there been a succession whose arrangements were fixed this far in advance, remained so stable to the end, and whose results so unambiguously transferred power from one generation of leaders to another. It is not that factions no longer exist, but that their powers are now in a state of mutual balance and that they have all learned a thing or two from the PRC's history. Political factions today have neither the power nor, perhaps more importantly, the will to upset rules that have been painfully arrived at. The absence of anyone with supreme power to upset these rules helps make them self-reinforcing.

....

MERITOCRACY MODIFIES FACTIONALISM

Factional considerations played a role in the succession process. But they were constrained by a twenty-year process of meritocratic winnowing that limited the list of candidates who could be considered in the final jockeying for position. Certainly, except for the period of the Cultural Revolution (1966–76), there have always been both meritocratic and factional elements in promotions within the Chinese party-state. But until now, even at the most meritocratic times, the major criteria for promotion at the top were the ability to shift with changing political lines and personal loyalty to the top leader—first Mao Zedong, then Deng Xiaoping. While those among the new leading group are ideologically alert and politically savvy, and have mostly allied themselves with one senior leader or another, they rose to the top predominantly because of administrative skill, technical knowledge, educational background, and Party, rather than personal loyalty.

The start of this process was Deng Xiaoping's 1980 instruction to senior Party leaders to undertake a "four-way transformation" *(sihua)* of the cadre corps by finding and promoting cadres around the age of 40 who were "revolutionary, younger, more educated, and more technically specialized" *(geminghua, nianqinghua, zhishihua, zhuanyehua)*. . . .

The product of this less factionalized, more regularized process is a competent leadership group that has high morale; that is politically balanced in representing different factions in the Party; that lacks one or two dominant figures, and is thus structurally constrained to make decisions collectively; and that is probably as collegial as any political leadership can be, because all the members came to the top through the same process, which they all view as having been broadly fair.

Whether this event sets the template for future successions remains uncertain, but the chances of that happening are increased insofar as the current succession entrenches—as it does—rules that have elite support (for example, the age-70 rule), historical depth (the rules governing the meritocratic promotion system), and structural reinforcement from the informal political structure of balanced factional power.

....

INSTITUTIONAL DIFFERENTIATION WITHIN THE REGIME

At the high point of political reform in 1987, Zhao Ziyang proposed the "separation of Party and government" and the "separation of Party and enterprise." With Zhao's fall from power in 1989, these ideas were abandoned. Yet in the intervening 14 years, much of what he proposed has happened by evolution, as the separation of responsibilities and spheres of authority—which Max Weber saw as definitive characteristics of the modern state—has gradually increased. What belongs to a given agency to handle is usually handled by that agency not only without interference, but with a growing sense that interference would be illegitimate.

One group of specialists, located in the Party Center, manages ideology, mobilization, and propaganda. . . . Provincial-level governors and Party secretaries have an increasingly wide scope to set local policy in such areas as education, health, welfare, the environment, foreign investment, and economic development. Many large state enterprises have now been removed from state ownership or placed under joint state-private ownership. Enterprise-management decisions are made on predominantly economic rather than political bases. State Council members, provincial-level officials, and enterprise managers are selected increasingly for their policy-relevant expertise. And economic policy makers at all levels suffer less and less frequently from intervention by the ideology-and-mobilization specialists.

The NPC [National People's Congress] has become progressively more autonomous, initiating legislation and actively reviewing and altering the proposals for legislation presented to it. The police and courts remain highly politicized, but in the case of the courts, at least, a norm of judicial independence has been declared (in the 1994 Judges' Law and elsewhere) and judges are applying it more often in economic and criminal cases that are not sensitive enough to draw interference from Party authorities.

The military is still a "Party army," but it has also become smaller, more technically competent, and more professional. The officers being promoted to the CMC [Central Military Commission] in the current succession are, as a group, distinguished more for their professional accomplishments and less for their political loyalties than was the case with previous CMC cohorts. Calls have come, apparently from the younger members of the officer corps, to make the army a nonpartisan national force without the obligation to defend a particular ruling party. And although the incoming leader, Hu Jintao, has rejected these calls, the fact that they were voiced at all is a sign of a growing professional ethos within military ranks.

All Chinese media are owned (at least formally, and for the most part actually) by Party and state agencies. But the media have become more commercialized and therefore less politicized. A handful of important outlets remain under variously direct control by the Party's propaganda department—for instance, *People's Daily*, the New China News Agency, China Central Television, provincial-level Party newspapers, the army newspaper, and so on. But to some extent, these media—and even more so, other newspapers, magazines, and radio or television stations around the country—fight for market share by covering movie and pop stars, sports, and scandals. In the political domain, they often push the envelope of what the regime considers off-limits by investigating stories about local corruption and abuses of power.

To be sure, the Chinese regime is still a party-state, in which the Party penetrates all other institutions and makes policy for all realms of action. And it is still a centralized, unitary system in which power at lower levels derives from grants by the center. But neither the top leader nor the central Party organs interfere as much in the work of other agencies as was the case under Mao and (less so) Deng. Ideological considerations have only marginal, if any, influence on most policy decisions. And staff members are promoted increasingly on the basis of their professional expertise in a relevant area.

All of this is partly to say, as has often been said before, that the regime is pragmatic. But behind the attitude of pragmatism lie increased institutional complexity, autonomy, and coherence—attributes that according to Huntington's theory should equip the regime to adapt more successfully to the challenges it faces.

INPUT INSTITUTIONS AND POLITICAL LEGITIMACY

One of the puzzles of the post-Tiananmen period has been the regime's apparent ability to rehabilitate its legitimacy (defined as the public's belief that the regime is lawful and should be obeyed) from the low point of 1989, when vast, nationwide pro-democracy demonstrations revealed the disaffection of a large segment of the urban population.

General theories of authoritarian regimes, along with empirical impressions of the current situation in China, might lead one to expect that the regime would now be decidedly low on legitimacy: Although authoritarian regimes often enjoy high legitimacy when they come to power, that legitimacy usually deteriorates for want of democratic procedures to cultivate ongoing consent. In the case of contemporary China, the regime's ideology is bankrupt. The transition from a socialist to a quasi-market economy has created a great deal of social unrest. And the regime relies heavily on coercion to repress political and religious dissent.

Direct evidence about attitudes, however, shows the contrary. In a 1993 nationwide random-sample survey conducted by Tianjian Shi, 94.1 percent of respondents agreed or strongly agreed with the statement that, "We should trust and obey the government, for in the last analysis it serves our interests." A 2002 survey by Shi found high percentages of respondents who answered similarly regarding both the central and local governments.[5] There is much other evidence from both quantitative and qualitative studies to suggest that expressions of dissatisfaction, including widely reported worker and peasant demonstrations, are usually directed at lower-level authorities, while the regime as a whole continues to enjoy high levels of acceptance.

A number of explanations can be offered for this pattern. Among them:

- Most people's living standards have risen during two decades of economic growth.

- The Party has coopted elites by offering Party membership to able persons from all walks of life and by granting the informal protection of property rights to private entrepreneurs. This new direction in Party policy has been given ideological grounding in Jiang Zemin's theory of the "Three Represents," which says that the Party should represent advanced productive forces, advanced culture, and the basic interests of all the Chinese working people—that is, that it should stand for the middle classes as much as or more than the workers and peasants.

- The Chinese display relatively high interpersonal trust, an attitude that precedes and fosters regime legitimacy.

- The Chinese population favors stability and fears political disorder. By pointing to the example of postcommunist chaos in Russia, the CCP has persuaded most Chinese, including intellectuals—from whom criticism might be particularly expected—that political reform is dangerous to their welfare.

- Thanks to the success of political repression, there is no organized alternative to the regime.

- Coercive repression—in 1989 and after—may itself have generated legitimacy by persuading the public that the regime's grip on power is unshakeable. Effective repression may generate

only resigned obedience at first, but to maintain cognitive consonance, citizens who have no choice but to obey a regime may come to evaluate its performance and responsiveness (themselves components of legitimacy) relatively highly. In seeking psychological coherence, citizens may convince themselves that their acceptance of the regime is voluntary—precisely because of, not despite, the fact that they have no alternative.

All these explanations may have value. Here, though, I would like to develop another explanation, more directly related to this essay's theme of institutionalization: The regime has developed a series of input institutions (that is, institutions that people can use to appraise the state of their concerns) that allow Chinese to believe that they have some influence on policy decisions and personnel choices at the local level.

The most thorough account of these institutions is Tianjian Shi's *Political Participation in Beijing,* which, although researched before 1989, describes institutions that are still in place. According to Shi, Chinese participate at the local and work-unit levels in a variety of ways. These include voting, assisting candidates in local-level elections, and lobbying unit leaders. Participation is frequent, and activism is correlated with a sense of political efficacy (defined as an individual's belief that he or she is capable of having some effect on the political system). Shi's argument is supported by the work of Melanie Manion, who has shown that in localities with competitive village elections, leaders' policy positions are closer to those of their constituents than in village with noncompetitive voting.[6]

In addition to the institutions discussed by Shi and Manion, there are at least four other sets of input institutions that may help to create regime legitimacy at the mass level.

- The Administrative Litigation Act of 1989 allows citizens to sue government agencies for alleged violations of government policy. According to Minxin Pei, the number of suits stood in 1999 at 98,600. The success rate (determined by court victories plus favorable settlements) has ranged from 27 percent to around 40 percent. In at least one province, government financial support is now offered through a legal aid program to enable poor citizens to take advantage of the program.[7]

• Party and government agencies maintain offices for citizen complaints—letters-and-visits departments *(xinfangju)*—which can be delivered in person or by letter. Little research has been done on this process, but the offices are common and their ability to deal with individual citizen complaints may be considerable.

• As people's congresses at all levels have grown more independent—along with people's political consultative conferences, United Front structures that meet at each level just prior to the meeting of the people's congress—they have become an increasingly important channel by which citizen complaints may be aired through representatives.

• As the mass media have become more independent and market-driven, so too have they increasingly positioned themselves as tribunes of the people, exposing complaints against wrong-doing by local-level officials.

These channels of demand- and complaint-making have two common features. One is that they encourage individual rather than group-based inputs, the latter of which are viewed as threatening by the regime. The other is that they focus complaints against specific local-level agencies or officials, diffusing possible aggression against the Chinese party-state generally. Accordingly, they enable citizens to pursue grievances without creating the potential to threaten the regime as a whole.

AN AUTHORITARIAN TRANSITION?

Despite the institutionalization of orderly succession processes, meritocratic promotions, bureaucratic differentiation, and channels of mass participation and appeal, the regime still faces massive challenges to its survival. This essay does not attempt to predict whether the regime will surmount them. What we can say on available evidence is that the regime is not supine, weak, or bereft of policy options. In contrast with the Soviet and Eastern European ruling groups in the late 1980s and early 1990s, the new Chinese leaders do not feel that they are at the end of history. The policy-statement excerpts contained in their investigation reports show that these leaders think they can solve China's problems. They intend to fight corruption; reform the state-owned enterprises; ameliorate the lot of the peasants; improve the environment; comply with World Trade Organization rules while using transitional privileges to ease China's entry into full compliance; suppress political opposition; meet the challenge of U.S. containment; and, above all, stay in power and direct China's modernization. The argument that democratization, freedom, and human rights would lead to a truer kind of stability—as convincing as it may be to the democrats of the world—holds no appeal for these men.

The theoretical implications of China's authoritarian resilience are complex. For the last half-century, scholars have debated whether totalitarian regimes can adapt to modernity. The implications of the Chinese case for this discussion are two: First, in order to adapt and survive, the regime has had to do many of the things predicted by Talcott Parsons and those who elaborated his theory: The regime has had to (1) abandon utopian ideology and charismatic styles of leadership; (2) empower a technocratic elite; (3) introduce bureaucratic regularization, complexity, and specialization; and (4) reduce control over private speech and action. Second, contrary to the Parsonian prediction, these adaptations have not led to regime change. In Richard Lowenthal's terms, the regime has moved "from utopia to development."[8] But the Party has been able to do all these things without triggering a transition to democracy.

Although such a transition might still lie somewhere in the future, the experience of the past two decades suggests that it is not inevitable. Under conditions that elsewhere have led to democratic transition, China has made a transition instead from totalitarianism to a classic authoritarian regime, and one that appears increasingly stable.

Of course, neither society-centered nor actor-centered theories of democratic transition predict any particular outcome to be inevitable in any particular time frame. The Chinese case may, accordingly, merely reinforce the lesson that the outcome depends on politicians and their will to power. Alternatively, it may end up reminding us that democratic transition can take a long time. But it may also suggest a more disturbing possibility: that authoritarianism is a viable regime form even under conditions of advanced modernization and integration with the global economy.

ENDNOTES

1. As an example, see the multi-author symposium on Chinese democracy in *Journal of Democracy 9* (January 1998).
2. In other words, to adapt a concept from democratic consolidation theory, the CCP has once again made itself the only game in town and is in the process of carrying out a successful transfer of power.
3. Samuel P. Huntington, *Political Order in Changing Societies* (New Haven: Yale University Press, 1968), pp. 12–24.
4. The factual base for this discussion is contained in Andrew J. Nathan and Bruce Gilley, *China's New Rulers: The Secret Files* (New York: New York Review Books, 2002), and is summarized in two articles in the *New York Review of Books*, 26 September and 10 October 2002. These publications are in turn based on Zong Hairen, *Disidai* (The Fourth Generation) (Carle Place, N.Y.: Mirror Books, 2002). Zong Hairen's account of the new generation of Chinese leaders is based on material contained in internal investigation reports on candidates for the new Politburo compiled by the Chinese Communist Party's Organization Department.
5. The 1993 survey was conducted for the project on "Political Culture and Political Participation in Mainland China, Taiwan, and Hong Kong." The 2002 survey was conducted for the project on "East Asia Barometer: Comparative Survey of Democratization and Value Changes." Data courtesy of Tianjian Shi.
6. Tianjian Shi, *Political Participation in Beijing* (Cambridge: Harvard University Press, 1997); Melanie Manion, "The Electoral Connection in the Chinese Countryside," *American Political Science Review* 90 (December 1996), pp. 736–48.
7. Minxin Pei, "Citizens v. Mandarins: Administrative Litigation in China," *China Quarterly* (December 1997), pp. 832–62, and personal communication. On legal aid, see *Disidai*, ch. 7; the province is Guangdong.
8. Talcott Parsons, *The Social System* (New York: Free Press, 1951), pp. 525–35; Richard Lowenthal, "Development vs. Utopia in Communist Policy," in Chalmers Johnson, ed., *Change in Communist Systems* (Stanford: Stanford University Press, 1970), pp. 33–116.

CHAPTER NINE

THE CHALLENGE OF ISLAMISM

On September 11, 2001, a radical Islamic group launched deadly attacks against economic and military icons of American power. No hostile foreign nation or group had conducted a military strike against the United States mainland in almost two centuries. This act of war was followed by a declaration of war, and the promise of more to come. 9/11 for most Americans was a turning point in history, comparable to the onset of the Cold War and the collapse of the Soviet Union. As with all great crises, it led to a burst of creative thinking of particular importance in the field of comparative politics. "When a man knows he is to be hanged in a fortnight," said Dr. Samuel Johnson, "it concentrates his mind wonderfully."

Who are the radical Islamists, where do they come from, why did they lash out at the most powerful nation in the world? The first call went to area specialists, who know intimately and in depth the countries from which radical Islamist leaders come (notably Saudi Arabia, Egypt, and Pakistan), and the country against which an American military counterattack would begin (Afghanistan). Then larger questions were posed about the Greater Middle East, the varieties of beliefs and groups in the Islamic world, and the specific nature of Islamic fundamentalism. Confrontation between Islam and the West has a long history, and may be seen as an integral part of the global process of modernization. We are led back to a reconsideration of classic theories dealt with earlier. Are the perspectives of thinkers such as Emile Durkheim and Max Weber relevant? Do they help us understand the orientation of radical Islamists, including those who have settled, been educated, and prospered in the West? To what extent have Western policies created Islamic hostility? What are the prospects of an evolution of Islam toward democracy and the rule of law?

As is evident in the following essays by Lisa Wedeen, Walter Laqueur, and Fareed Zakaria, analysis of the challenge of Islamism reflects a diversity of approaches concerning modernization, legitimacy, violence, ideology, democracy, social justice—in short, all aspects of comparative politics.

LISA WEDEEN

31 Beyond the Crusades

From literary studies to rational choice theory, issues broadly construed as "cultural" have inspired academic debates, fostered interdisciplinary exchanges, and prompted battles over the methods, evidence, and objectives of scholarly research. In political science (the discipline in which I was trained) the concept of culture used to be associated primarily with the literature on political culture that emerged in the context of postwar political sociology, with its concerns for policy initiatives designed to reproduce the conditions of Western democratization abroad (Somers, 1995, 114). Derived from Max Weber's classic analysis of the "elective affinity" between the Protestant ethic and the rise of capitalism in the West, these studies attempted to demonstrate how cultural attitudes and beliefs either constrained or promoted "progress". Conceived in terms of an alleged set of residual values and norms—what the anthropologist Sherry Ortner (1997, 8–9) has aptly characterized as a "deeply sedimented essence attaching to, or inhering in particular groups"—this notion of culture was prominent in the sociology of Talcott Parsons, in modernization theory, and in the American cultural anthropology of Franz Boas, Margaret Mead, and Ruth Benedict, as well as in the behaviorist revolution of the 1950s and 1960s. Yet despite the seemingly dated quality of such formulations, the seductiveness of cultural essentialism persists.[1] Samuel Huntington's 1993 article "The Clash of Civilizations?" and his subsequent book *The Clash of Civilizations and the Remaking of World Order* (1996) represent a particularly influential and polemical recent example of this kind of political culturalism: Civilizations each have a primordial cultural identity, so that the "major differences in political and economic development among civilizations are clearly rooted in their different cultures."

The "fault lines between civilizations will be the battle lines of the future," Huntington predicted, and the two civilizations that are of particular importance in this narrative of battles and futures are Islam and the West (Huntington, 1993, 22; 1996, 20, 28, 29).

This understanding of culture as a specific group's primordial values or traits is untenable empirically, and yet current scholarly and popular depictions of "Islam" often reproduce such claims and their attendant problems: First, the sedimented essences version of "civilization" or "culture" ignores the specific historical processes and particular power relations that have given rise to the recent phenomenon of radical religious expression. Second, the clash of civilization's story and narratives similar to it ride roughshod over the diversity of views and the experiences of contention among Muslims. Communities of argument arise over what makes a Muslim a Muslim, what Islam means, and what, if any, its political role should be. Third, an essentialist analysis neglects the terrains of solidarity and fluidity that exist between Muslims and non-Muslims, the ways in which political communities of various sorts have depended on the cross-fertilization of ideas and practices. This short essay is devoted to elaborating each of these three points.

PART ONE: HISTORY AND POWER

First, to take into account historical processes would mean to identify the recent and global dimensions of radical religious expression. "Fundamentalism," as radical religious expression is sometimes termed, is not exclusive to Islam. Nor does it have its roots in age-old traditions. Current Islamicist movements are part of a global phenomenon that originates in the late 1970s, and they share with other contemporary movements two key similarities: (a) they resuscitate, invent, or construct an essentialist

SOURCE: Lisa Wedeen, "Beyond the Crusades," *Items and Issues,* vol. 4, no. 2–3 (Summer 2003), pp. 1–6. Published by the Social Science Research Council. Reprinted by permission of the SSRC. Footnotes and bibliography abridged by the Editor.

understanding of political identity based, at least in part, on ascription; (b) although they have important antecedents, they have emerged as a potent contemporary political force at the same time that international market pressures weakened the economic sovereignty of states and undermined their roles as guarantors of citizens' welfare.

The story may by now be a familiar one: In the 1970s, states began withdrawing economically, privatizing property, reducing or eliminating subsidies, deregulating prices, and ceasing to provide services to which people had become accustomed, felt entitled—and needed. As the state has retreated economically in the Middle East, Islamicist movements have tended to fill in the gaps, providing goods and services states do not proffer. Egypt was one of the first Middle Eastern countries to initiate liberalization measures in 1973. Although such measures could be deemed successful during the oil boom years, they were disastrous in the bust period of the mid-1980s. Liberalization measures introduced Egyptians to a number of imported goods and luxury items at the same time that oil revenues and privatization policies generated a new, American-oriented "parvenu" class. This new class enjoyed a lifestyle that stimulated widespread resentment among the urban poor and middle classes. Liberalization programs created markets, but they also enhanced perceptions of corruption, widened income disparities, and fostered considerable economic suffering. Liberalization also removed safety nets that guaranteed people some security. Rising unemployment, decreases in subsidies, housing problems, and population explosions all contributed to the glaring gap between rich and poor. Strikes grew more common in the 1980s, food riots were "a frequent worry" among government officials, and middle and lower class citizens reported economic anxieties.

The undermining of the state as the vehicle of economic development also subverted its role as the carrier of abstract communal solidarities, and it was in this context, often termed "globalization," that politicized religious movements started being mobilized on the basis of a complex blend of ascriptive and behavioral identifications. What is common to most of these movements is that they express anxieties about corroded values and the loss of communal attachments. They register the "moral panic" (Comaroff and Comaroff, 1999; 5) of citizens longing for a state or community capable of protecting and providing for them.

In the Middle Eastern context, Islamicist movements have captured this popular discontent, in part by delivering concrete economic benefits to constituents. They have devised disciplined, effective, skillful organizations for channeling resources and providing goods and services. Some offer housing, books, and health care no longer (or never) provided by the state. Islamicist movements also organize affective attachments in the wake of the failure of Arab states to deliver on Arab nationalist promises.

The appeal of Islamicist groups, then, can be historically situated in the changing relations of global capital (and the concomitant shift from nationalist abstractions to religious ones). Invoking a cultural essentialist argument is also, as the political scientist Chalmers Johnson notes, "a way of evading responsibility for the 'blowback' that US imperial projects have generated" (Johnson, *The Nation,* October 15, 2001). Possible sources of "blowback" include the widely shared views that the United States serves as a proxy for Israel, is responsible for the decade of sanctions against Iraqis, shores up corrupt dictators, stations troops in Saudi Arabia specifically, and upholds double standards between official commitments to democracy and equality, on the one hand, and actual political activities, on the other. Current global economic arrangements are also implicated in beliefs about U.S. imperial projects; they are understood as bringing wealth to the United States and its perceived institutional surrogates, the IMF and World Bank, while making many parts of the world more miserable and destitute.

The fact that economically incapacitated states in the region encourage expressions of popular discontent in forms that deflect attention away from domestic leaders' incompetence may also explain the elective affinity between state discourses and some aspects of Islamicist movements. The available idioms through which experiences of common belonging to a people become institutionalized in the post-Fordist, post-colonial world are confined to what the state will tolerate and what the Islamicists have won. Thus demonstrations of Muslim piety combine with consensual understandings of anti-American and pro-Palestinian solidarities in officials' speeches and in mass demonstrations. Islamicism has become a coherent anti-imperialist doctrine and a way of re-establishing community. It offers visions of an equitable, just, socially responsible way of life, much as the failed, discredited Arab nationalist regimes of the 1950s and 60s did.

To some extent the success of the Islamicist movements also has to be attributed to the state's elimination of leftist opposition by means of incarceration, torture, and cooptation. In Egypt, for example, the regimes of Nasir and Sadat worked actively to demobilize the working class. Sadat found tactical allies among the Muslim Brotherhood and among the newly growing radical Islamic movements in universities. He released imprisoned Muslim Brothers in 1972–73, and encouraged them to attack leftists, whom he regarded as his major political adversary. In Yemen, unification between North and South was followed by the Northern ruling party's consistent assault on its Southern Socialist partners. In 1992–93, there were approximately 150–160 assassination attempts against members of the Yemeni Socialist Party (YSP)—most of them carried out by self-identified radical Islamicists who were encouraged financially and politically by the regime.

Viewing the emergence and appeal of Islamicist movements historically thus compels us to come to terms with the post-Fordist economic world in which the state's economic sovereignty has been undermined globally with consequences for the forms of solidarity and expressions of community currently politicizing citizens in a number of places. A historical account also requires us to recognize the absence of alternative visions of community and authority, as leaders failed to deliver both on their pan-Arab promises and to produce effective state-centered projects for development. With the disintegration of the Soviet Union and the global decline of Soviet ideology as an alternative paradigm to liberal capitalism, Islamicism provides a critical vision of the world and a sense of hope for some people. Islamicist positions on social justice, based on mechanisms of redistribution such as the Islamic *zakat* taxes, avoid the radical land reform projects of old; they also tend to respect the concept of private property and encourage profit as an appropriate outcome for entrepreneurial activity. Islamicists can thus appeal to the middle classes and to the urban poor, even though the credibility of Islamicist solutions to economic problems has been undermined by the failure of some Islamicist firms to deliver on their financial promises.[2]

PART TWO: CONTENTION AMONG MUSLIMS

Despite the success of Islamicists in providing adversarial idioms and resonant political critiques, the struggle among nominally Muslim citizens and Islamicist adherents is as pronounced as the solidarities an Islamicist adversarial politics has fostered. Being "Muslim" might signify a set of religious beliefs, an ascriptive attachment, a "cultural" identification, a state classification, a set of recognizable activities, or none of the above. There are those who see a separation of mosque and state as fundamental, and those who advocate their conjuncture. There are those who think the *shari`a* should be *the* source of legislation, those who view it as *a* source, and those who wish it were irrelevant to contemporary law. There are countries where the `ulama or religious elite is independent of the state, places where mosque sermons are controlled by the state, and places where the `ulama is coterminous with the state. There are, in short, vigorous communities of argument and plural varieties of social and political practice. This plurality makes any invocation of a single political doctrine of Islam empirically untenable and theoretically meaningless. We have to keep this sense of variety and plurality in mind when thinking about political patterns and the terrains of solidarity that might animate future political life.[3]

PART THREE: TERRAINS OF SOLIDARITY

THE MODERNITY OF STATES, THE RULE OF LAW, AND HUMAN RIGHTS

Rather than discussing reified categories such as Islam and democracy in general, we should talk, as the theorist Gudrun Krämer encourages us to do, about "Muslims living and theorizing under specific historical circumstances" (Krämer, 1997, 72).

This may seem obvious, but it is often hard to do, in part because many Muslim authors represent their "views as 'the position of Islam'" (Krämer, 1997, 72).

In addition, some Islamicists may end up adopting the strategic option of democracy because leaders calculate that it is in their interest to do so. Such rational calculations explain how the theologically-minded Belgian Catholic movement, for example, despite members' theocratic inclinations and their lack of commitment to democracy, ended up supporting democratic institutions (Kalyvas, 1998). In other words, a discussion of ideas, values or shared political commitments may exaggerate the importance of particular ways of thinking while underestimating the salience of common strategic interests and trade-offs—the familiar practices of calculating costs and benefits, which many political leaders who share the same vocation (but perhaps not the same values) *do* when making decisions.

Keeping these points in mind, let me suggest three shared understandings that might constitute a terrain of solidarity between Islamicists and liberals (I claim membership in neither group): First, conservative `ulama and moderate Muslim Brothers (in Egypt, Jordan, Tunisia, and Yemen) hold ideas that are fundamentally *modern* (Krämer, 1997, 74; see also Chakrabarty, 2000). Implementing the *sharià* according to these theorists, means building a state whose common bureaucratic institutions are designed to provide goods and services in return for citizens' allegiance and obedience. Humans, endowed by God with reason, have the ability to interpret correctly the purposes of the *sharià* and therefore to define the precise contours and functional tasks state institutions will assume. In this light, the adoption of democratic practices or categories may be "acceptable, recommended, or even mandatory," as long as these do not contravene Islamic principles (Krämer, 1997, 75).

Second, then, is the admissibility of *democratic norms and procedures* in the process of constructing institutions. A fundamental concern of many contemporary Muslims is the need to check the arbitrary powers of leaders and institute the rule of law, and strict application of the *sharià* is seen by many as a way of forefending against tyranny while ensuring procedural justice. Whatever problems one might see

in this proposition, criticisms of despotism and corruption animate the works of both radical and reform-minded Islamicists (as well as those of secularists). Identifying tyranny as a key spiritual and political problem on the grounds that it treats men as gods when there is only one God provides the justification for rendering dictators and those who work for them apostates.[4] Although some groups still advocate the restoration of a "caliphate," many groups, including the Muslim Brothers, use the term in ways analogous to a modern president who is entrusted to execute God's law as a fallible human agent and an accountable political representative of the Muslim community. Thus many Muslim authors claim that the ideal Islamic state is a *dawla madaniyya* (a civil state) rather than a theocracy ruled by the `ulama or an authoritarian state ruled by the military. In Yemen, moderate Islamicists also stress the importance of a *shura* whose actual duties look less like the Prophet Muhammad's version of a consultative body and more like a Western Parliament. Many authors in Yemen and elsewhere accept the importance of a separation of powers in which the executive, the legislature, and the judiciary keep each other in check.

Third, moderate, pragmatic Islamicists and many self-identified Muslim authors also express concerns about *protecting human rights* (although there are also lively debates on the extent to which the importation of allegedly Western understandings of human rights contradict the *shari`a* and/or are used opportunistically by Western NGOs, journalists, and governments to justify intervention).[5] Especially in their role as oppositional political figures, moderate Islamicists have demanded the safeguarding of individual rights and civil liberties from government intrusion, and the human right to live free from repression and torture.

CONCLUSIONS

The vast majority of people in the Middle East probably never ceased to consider themselves Muslim, even at the apogee of secular nationalist movements. But before the 1970s, most Muslims did not seem to identify primarily as Muslims, or rather, that identity did not override other forms of *political* identification. Disillusionment with the performance of states in the 1970s and the creation of parvenu classes that exemplified the ostentatious excesses of the "haves" in contrast to the impoverishment of the "have nots" generated widespread discontent. This discontent was exacerbated with the debt crisis of the 1980s, the decline in the price of oil, and the IMF-imposed restructuring projects that limited state expenditures. At a time when the distributive capabilities of states were undermined and leaders were increasingly perceived to be venal and corrupt, the popularity of Islamicist movements rose considerably. The messages—calls for social equity, political transparency and accountability, and moral piety—were resonant, critical alternatives that gave many a sense of belonging to a common political project with anonymous but like-minded others. It may be difficult to establish a direct causal relationship between economic suffering and political Islamicist movements, but we might acknowledge that fundamentalisms are "intimately connected with material conditions and disaffection" without arguing that such conditions fully explain "the appeal of fundamentalist ideas" (Euben, 1999, 89).

To focus on the economic incentives, discursive content, and political-affective impulses that have underpinned Islamicist projects is not to suggest that there is a single, unified political doctrine of Islam. Islamicists differ from non-Islamicists and from one another. There are pragmatically minded Muslim Brotherhood adherents and radically minded, militantly inclined Islamicists. There are secularists and pious practitioners. Reifying "Islam" not only denies the empirical world of plurality and diversity, it also proves politically dangerous, by making "Islam" into an object rather than a set of polyvalent activities whose practitioners have divergent visions, fantasies, understandings, and interests.

Moreover, the moderate, pragmatic Islamicists have come to articulate recognizable aspects of a modern state and a democratic politics: government accountability, the rule of law, political participation, the separation of powers, and the protection of human rights. As Gudrun Krämer points out, despite these explicit commitments, Muslim Brothers are not, strictly speaking, liberals,

if "liberalism" also means "religious indifference" (Krämer, 1997, 80). But their moral vocabularies, expressions of entitlement, and political practices share important characteristics with liberal formulations of democratic institution building.

Thinking about shared terrains between Islamicists and non-Islamicists and between Muslims and non-Muslims does not mean riding roughshod over important disagreements, nor does it require "fudging" consensus where consensus does not reside. If democrats are to take their own commitments to democratic political life seriously, then they (we) have to embrace the variety and agonistic, contentious politics that allows for differences to thrive.

Focusing exclusively on Islamicists, moreover, does a disservice to other groups and individuals in the Middle East whose ideals may be less resonant with current public opinions, but whose practices forge the conditions of possibility through which future political life may also get created.

Finally and more generally, by ignoring historical processes and specific relations of political power, the treatment of culture (especially in political science) has downplayed the heterogeneous ways people experience the social order within and among groups, while exaggerating the commonality, constancy, and permanence of intra-group beliefs and values. As a result, cultural essentialist explanations of political outcomes such as ethnic or religious violence tend to naturalize categories of groupness, rather than exploring the conditions under which such experiences of groupness come to seem natural when they do.

ENDNOTES

1. This introduction is derived from Lisa Wedeen. "Conceptualizing Culture: Possibilities for Political Science," *American Political Science Review*, vol. 96, no. 4 (December 2002). The article deals in part, with the persistence of the political culture school (see, for example, Putnam, Leonard and Nanetti, *Making Democracy Work: Civic Traditions in Modern Italy* (1993) and the importation of aspects of cultural essentialism into certain rational choice analyses.

2. See, for example, Gilles Kepel's description (2002) of the banking crash in Egypt in the late 1980s, pp. 279–281.

3. Recognizing the fact of diversity does not mean avoiding generalizations, but it may help identify the kinds of generalizations that can plausibly be made.

4. Critiques of dictatorship among Islamicists also use vocabulary that does not carry religious connotations, such as despotism (*istibdad*) and oppression (*zulm*).

5. The status of women, the rights of gay people and of non-Muslim minorities, and the freedom of academic research remain fraught topics. In Yemen, the right of private individuals to retaliate against a crime or to settle accounts privately (*qisas*) is also a particularly charged issue.

REFERENCES

Al-Naqeeb, Khaldoun Hasan. 1991. *Society and State in the Gulf and Arab Peninsula: A Different Perspective.* New York: Routledge.

Beinin, Joel and Joe Stork (eds.). 1997. *Political Islam: Essays from Middle East Report.* Berkeley and Los Angeles: University of California Press.

Chakrabarty Dipesh. 2000. *Provincializing Europe: Postcolonial Thought and Historical Difference.* Princeton: Princeton University Press.

Chaudhry, Kiren Aziz. 1997. *The Price of Wealth: Economics and Institutions in the Middle East.* Ithaca: Cornell University Press.

Comaroff, Jean and John L. Comaroff. May 1999. "Occult economies and the violence of abstraction: Notes from the South African postcolony." *American Ethnologist.*

Euben, Roxanne L. 1999. *Enemy in the Mirror: Islamic Fundamentalism and the Limits of Modern Rationalism, A Work of Comparative Political Theory.* Princeton: Princeton University Press.

Henry, Clement M. and Robert Springborg. 2001. *Globalization and the Politics of Development in the Middle East.* Cambridge: Cambridge University Press.

Huntington, Samuel P. Summer 1993. "The Clash of Civilizations?" *Foreign Affairs,* pp. 22–49.

Huntington, Samuel P. 1996. *The Clash of Civilizations and the Remaking of World Order.* New York: Simon and Schuster.

Johnson, Chalmers. October 15, 2001. "Blowback." *The Nation.*

Kalyvas, Stathis N. June 1998. "Democracy and Religious Politics: Evidence from Belgium." *Comparative Political Studies,* 31: 3, pp. 292–320.

Kepel, Gilles. 2002. *Jihad: The Trail of Political Islam.* Cambridge, MA: The Belknap Press of Harvard University Press.

Krämer, Gudrun. 1997. "Islamist Notions of Democracy." In *Political Islam: Essays from Middle East Report,* edited by Joel Beinin and Joe Stork. Berkeley and Los Angeles: University of California Press.

Ortner, Sherry B. Summer 1997. "Introduction." *Representations, 69.* pp. 1–13.

Sadowski, Yahya 1987. "Egypt's Islamist Movement: A New Political and Economic Force." *Middle East Insight,* pp. 37–45.

Somers, Margaret R. 1995. "What's Political or Cultural about Political Culture and the Public Sphere? Toward an Historical Sociology of Concept Formation." *Sociological Theory,* 13: 2, pp. 113–144.

Waterbury, John. 1983. *The Egypt of Nasser and Sadat: The Political Economy of Two Regimes.* Princeton: Princeton University Press.

Wedeen, Lisa. December 2002. "Conceptualizing Culture: Possibilities for Political Science." *American Political Science Review,* 96: 4, pp. 713–728.

Wickham, Carrie Rosefsky. 2002. *Mobilizing Islam.* New York: Columbia University Press.

Yamani, Mai. 2002. *Changed Identities: Challenge of the New Generation.* Washington, D.C.: The Brookings Institution.

WALTER LAQUEUR

32   The Terrorism to Come

Terrorism has become over a number of years the topic of ceaseless comment, debate, controversy, and search for roots and motives, and it figures on top of the national and international agenda. It is also at present one of the most highly emotionally charged topics of public debate, though quite why this should be the case is not entirely clear, because the overwhelming majority of participants do not sympathize with terrorism.

Confusion prevails, but confusion alone does not explain the emotions. There is always confusion when a new international phenomenon appears on the scene. This was the case, for instance, when communism first appeared (it was thought to be aiming largely at the nationalization of women and the burning of priests) and also fascism. But terrorism is not an unprecedented phenomenon; it is as old as the hills.

Thirty years ago, when the terrorism debate got underway, it was widely asserted that terrorism was basically a left-wing revolutionary movement caused by oppression and exploitation. Hence the conclusion: Find a political and social solution, remedy the underlying evil—no oppression, no terrorism. The argument about the left-wing character of terrorism is no longer frequently heard, but the belief in a fatal link between poverty and violence has persisted. Whenever a major terrorist attack has taken place, one has heard appeals from high and low to provide credits and loans, to deal at long last with the deeper, true causes of terrorism, the roots rather than the symptoms and outward manifestations. And these roots are believed to be poverty, unemployment, backwardness, and inequality.

It is not too difficult to examine whether there is such a correlation between poverty and terrorism, and all the investigations have shown that this is not

the case. The experts have maintained for a long time that poverty does not cause terrorism and prosperity does not cure it. In the world's 50 poorest countries there is little or no terrorism. A study by scholars Alan Krueger and Jitka Maleckova reached the conclusion that the terrorists are not poor people and do not come from poor societies. A Harvard economist has shown that economic growth is closely related to a society's ability to manage conflicts. More recently, a study of India has demonstrated that terrorism in the subcontinent has occurred in the most prosperous (Punjab) and most egalitarian (Kashmir, with a poverty ratio of 3.5 compared with the national average of 26 percent) regions and that, on the other hand, the poorest regions such as North Bihar have been free of terrorism. In the Arab countries (such as Egypt and Saudi Arabia, but also in North Africa), the terrorists originated not in the poorest and most neglected districts but hailed from places with concentrations of radical preachers. The backwardness, if any, was intellectual and cultural—not economic and social.

These findings, however, have had little impact on public opinion (or on many politicians), and it is not difficult to see why. There is the general feeling that poverty and backwardness with all their concomitants are bad—and that there is an urgent need to do much more about these problems. Hence the inclination to couple the two issues and the belief that if the (comparatively) wealthy Western nations would contribute much more to the development and welfare of the less fortunate, in cooperation with their governments, this would be in a long-term perspective the best, perhaps the only, effective way to solve the terrorist problem.

Reducing poverty in the Third World is a moral as well as a political and economic imperative, but to expect from it a decisive change in the foreseeable future as far as terrorism is concerned is unrealistic, to say the least. It ignores both the causes of backwardness and poverty and the motives for terrorism.

SOURCE: Walter Laqueur, "The Terrorism to Come," *Policy Review*, no. 126 (August–September 2004), pp. 48–64. Published by the Hoover Institution, Stanford University. Reprinted by permission of the Hoover Institution. Article abridged by the Editor.

Poverty combined with youth unemployment does create a social and psychological climate in which Islamism and various populist and religious sects flourish, which in turn provide some of the footfolk for violent groups in internal conflicts. According to some projections, the number of young unemployed in the Arab world and North Africa could reach 50 million in two decades. Such a situation will not be conducive to political stability; it will increase the demographic pressure on Europe, since according to polls a majority of these young people want to emigrate. Politically, the populist discontent will be directed against the rulers—Islamist in Iran, moderate in countries such as Egypt, Jordan, or Morocco. But how to help the failed economies of the Middle East and North Africa? What are the reasons for backwardness and stagnation in this part of the world? The countries that have made economic progress—such as China and India, Korea and Taiwan, Malaysia and Turkey—did so without massive foreign help.

All this points to a deep malaise and impending danger, but not to a direct link between the economic situation and international terrorism. There is of course a negative link: Terrorists will not hesitate to bring about a further aggravation in the situation; they certainly did great harm to the tourist industries in Bali and Egypt, in Palestine, Jordan, and Morocco. One of the main targets of terrorism in Iraq was the oil industry. It is no longer a secret that the carriers of international terrorism operating in Europe and America hail not from the poor, downtrodden, and unemployed but are usually of middle-class origin.

....

THE LOCAL ELEMENT

The link between terrorism and nationalist, ethnic, religious, and tribal conflict is far more tangible. These instances of terrorism are many and need not be enumerated in detail. Solving these conflicts would probably bring about a certain reduction in the incidence of terrorism. But the conflicts are many, and if some of them have been defused in recent years, other, new ones have emerged. Nor are the issues usually clear-cut or the bones of contention easy to define—let alone to solve.

If the issue at stake is a certain territory or the demand for autonomy, a compromise through negotiations might be achieved. But it ought to be recalled that al Qaeda was founded and September 11 occurred not because of a territorial dispute or the feeling of national oppression but because of a religious commandment—jihad and the establishment of *shari'ah*. Terrorist attacks in Central Asia and Morocco, in Saudi Arabia, Algeria, and partly in Iraq were directed against fellow Muslims, not against infidels. Appeasement may work in individual cases, but terrorist groups with global ambitions cannot be appeased by territorial concessions. . . .

. . . [T]here should be no illusions with regard to the wider effect of a peaceful solution of one conflict or another. To give but one obvious example: Peace (or at least the absence of war) between Israel and the Palestinians would be a blessing for those concerned. It may be necessary to impose a solution since the chances of making any progress in this direction are nil but for some outside intervention. However, the assumption that a solution of a local conflict (even one of great symbolic importance) would have a dramatic effect in other parts of the world is unfounded. Osama bin Laden did not go to war because of Gaza and Nablus; he did not send his warriors to fight in Palestine. Even the disappearance of the "Zionist entity" would not have a significant impact on his supporters, except perhaps to provide encouragement for further action.

Such a warning against illusions is called for because there is a great deal of wishful thinking and naïveté in this respect—a belief in quick fixes and miracle solutions: If only there would be peace between Israelis and Palestinians, all the other conflicts would become manageable. But the problems are as much in Europe, Asia, and Africa as in the Middle East; there is a great deal of free-floating aggression which could (and probably would) easily turn in other directions once one conflict has been defused. . . .

How to explain the fact that in an inordinate number of instances where there has been a great deal of explosive material, there has been no terrorism?

The gypsies of Europe certainly had many grievances and the Dalets (untouchables) of India and other Asian countries even more. But there has been no terrorism on their part—just as the Chechens have been up in arms but not the Tartars of Russia, the Basque but not the Catalans of Spain. The list could easily be lengthened.

Accident may play a role (the absence or presence of a militant leadership), but there could also be a cultural-psychological predisposition. How to explain that out of 100 militants believing with equal intensity in the justice of their cause, only a very few will actually engage in terrorist actions? And out of this small minority even fewer will be willing to sacrifice their lives as suicide bombers? Imponderable factors might be involved: indoctrination but also psychological motives. Neither economic nor political analysis will be of much help in gaining an understanding, and it may not be sheer accident that there has been great reluctance to explore this political-intellectual minefield. . . .

. . . Where and when are terrorist attacks most likely to occur? They will not necessarily be directed against the greatest and most dangerous enemy as perceived by the terrorist gurus. Much depends on where terrorists are strong and believe the enemy to be weak. That terrorist attacks are likely to continue in the Middle East goes without saying; other main danger zones are Central Asia and, above all, Pakistan.

The founders of Pakistan were secular politicians. The religious establishment and in particular the extremists among the Indian Muslims had opposed the emergence of the state. But once Pakistan came into being, they began to try with considerable success to dominate it. Their alternative educational system, the many thousand madrassas, became the breeding ground for jihad fighters. Ayub Khan, the first military ruler, tried to break their stranglehold but failed. Subsequent rulers, military and civilian, have not even tried. It is more than doubtful whether Pervez Musharraf will have any success in limiting their power. The tens of thousands of graduates they annually produce formed the backbone of the Taliban. Their leaders will find employment for them at home and in Central Asia, even if there is a descalation in tensions with India over Kashmir. Their most radical

leaders aim at the destruction of India. Given Pakistan's internal weakness this may appear more than a little fanciful, but their destructive power is still considerable, and they can count on certain sympathies in the army and the intelligence service. A failed Pakistan with nuclear weapons at its disposal would be a major nightmare. Still, Pakistani terrorism—like Palestinian and Middle Eastern in general—remains territorial, likely to be limited to the subcontinent and Central Asia.

BATTLEFIELD EUROPE

Europe is probably the most vulnerable battlefield. To carry out operations in Europe and America, talents are needed that are not normally found among those who have no direct personal experience of life in the West. The Pakistani diaspora has not been very active in the terrorist field, except for a few militants in the United Kingdom.

Western Europe has become over a number of years the main base of terrorist support groups. This process has been facilitated by the growth of Muslim communities, the growing tensions with the native population, and the relative freedom with which radicals could organize in certain mosques and cultural organizations. Indoctrination was provided by militants who came to these countries as religious dignitaries. This freedom of action was considerably greater than that enjoyed in the Arab and Muslim world; not a few terrorists convicted of capital crimes in countries such as Egypt, Jordan, Morocco, and Algeria were given political asylum in Europe. True, there were some arrests and closer controls after September 11, but given the legal and political restrictions under which the European security services were laboring, effective counteraction was still exceedingly difficult.

West European governments have been frequently criticized for not having done enough to integrate Muslim newcomers into their societies, but cultural and social integration was certainly not what the newcomers wanted. They wanted to preserve their religious and ethnic identity and their way of life, and they resented intervention by secular authorities. In its great majority, the first generation of immigrants wanted to live in peace and quiet and to make a living for their families. But today they no longer have much control over their offspring.

This is a common phenomenon all over the world: the radicalization of the second generation of immigrants. This generation has been superficially acculturated (speaking fluently the language of the host country) yet at the same time feels resentment and hostility more acutely. It is not necessarily the power of the fundamentalist message (the young are not the most pious believers when it comes to carrying out all the religious commandments) which inspires many of the younger radical activists or sympathizers. It is the feeling of deep resentment because, unlike immigrants from other parts of the world, they could not successfully compete in the educational field, nor quite often make it at the work place. Feelings of being excluded, sexual repression (a taboo subject in this context), and other factors led to free-floating aggression and crime directed against the authorities and their neighbors.

As a result, non-Muslims began to feel threatened in streets they could once walk without fear. They came to regard the new immigrants as antisocial elements who wanted to change the traditional character of their homeland and their way of life, and consequently tensions continued to increase. Pressure on European governments is growing from all sides, right and left, to stop immigration and to restore law and order.

This, in briefest outline, is the milieu in which Islamist terrorism and terrorist support groups in Western Europe developed. There is little reason to assume that this trend will fundamentally change in the near future. On the contrary, the more the young generation of immigrants asserts itself, the more violence occurs in the streets, and the more terrorist attacks take place, the greater the anti-Muslim resentment on the part of the rest of the population. The rapid demographic growth of the Muslim communities further strengthens the impression among the old residents that they are swamped and deprived of their rights in their own homeland, not even entitled to speak the truth about the prevailing situation (such as, for instance, to reveal the statistics of prison inmates with Muslim backgrounds). Hence the vio-lent reaction in even the most liberal European countries such as the Netherlands, Belgium, and Denmark. The fear of the veil turns into the fear that in the foreseeable future they too, having become a minority, will be compelled to conform to the commandments of another religion and culture.

True, the number of extremists is still very small. Among British Muslims, for instance, only 13 percent have expressed sympathy and support for terrorist attacks. But this still amounts to several hundred thousands, far more than needed for staging a terrorist campaign. The figure is suspect in any case because not all of those sharing radical views will openly express them to strangers, for reasons that hardly need be elaborated. Lastly, such a minority will not feel isolated in their own community as long as the majority remains silent—which has been the case in France and most other European countries.

The prospects for terrorism based on a substantial Islamist periphery could hardly appear to be more promising, but there are certain circumstances that make the picture appear somewhat less threatening. The tensions are not equally strong in all countries. They are less palpably felt in Germany and Britain than in France and the Netherlands. Muslims in Germany are predominantly of Turkish origin and have (always with some exceptions) shown less inclination to take violent action than communities mainly composed of Arab and North African immigrants.

If acculturation and integration has been a failure in the short run, prospects are less hopeless in a longer perspective. The temptations of Western civilization are corrosive; young Muslims cannot be kept in a hermetically sealed ghetto (even though a strong attempt is made). They are disgusted and repelled by alcohol, loose morals, general decadence, and all the other wickedness of the society facing them, but they are at the same time fascinated and attracted by them. This is bound to affect their activist fervor, and they will be exposed not only to the negative aspects of the world surrounding them but also its values. Other religions had to face these temptations over the ages and by and large have been fighting a losing battle.

It is often forgotten that only a relatively short period passed from the primitive beginnings of

Islam in the Arabian desert to the splendor and luxury (and learning and poetry) of Harun al Rashid's Baghdad—from the austerity of the Koran to the not-so-austere Arabian Nights. The pulse of contemporary history is beating much faster, but is it beating fast enough? For it is a race against time. The advent of megaterrorism and the access to weapons of mass destruction is dangerous enough, but coupled with fanaticism it generates scenarios too unpleasant even to contemplate.

ENDURING ASYMMETRY

There can be no final victory in the fight against terrorism, for terrorism (rather than full-scale war) is the contemporary manifestation of conflict, and conflict will not disappear from earth as far as one can look ahead and human nature has not undergone a basic change. But it will be in our power to make life for terrorists and potential terrorists much more difficult. . . .

Terrorism does not accept laws and rules, whereas governments are bound by them; this, in briefest outline, is asymmetric warfare. If governments were to behave in a similar way, not feeling bound by existing rules and laws such as those against the killing of prisoners, this would be bitterly denounced. When the late Syrian President Hafez Assad faced an insurgency (and an attempted assassination) on the part of the Muslim Brotherhood in the city of Hama in 1980, his soldiers massacred some 20,000 inhabitants. This put an end to all ideas of terrorism and guerilla warfare.

Such behavior on the part of democratic governments would be denounced as barbaric, a relapse into the practices of long-gone pre-civilized days. But if governments accept the principle of asymmetric warfare they will be severely, possibly fatally, handicapped. They cannot accept that terrorists are protected by the Geneva Conventions, which would mean, among other things, that they should be paid a salary while in captivity. Should they be regarded like the pirates of a bygone age as *hostes generis humani*, enemies of humankind, and be treated according to the principle of *à un corsaire,*

un corsaire et demi—"to catch a thief, it takes a thief," to quote one of Karl Marx's favorite sayings?

The problem will not arise if the terrorist group is small and not very dangerous. In this case normal legal procedures will be sufficient to deal with the problem (but even this is not quite certain once weapons of mass destruction become more readily accessible). Nor will the issue of shedding legal restraint arise if the issues at stake are of marginal importance, if in other words no core interests of the governments involved are concerned. If, on the other hand, the very survival of a society is at stake, it is most unlikely that governments will be impeded in their defense by laws and norms belonging to a bygone (and more humane) age. . . .

Terrorists want total war—not in the sense that they will (or could) mobilize unlimited resources; in this respect their possibilities are limited. But they want their attacks to be unfettered by laws, norms, regulations, and conventions. In the terrorist conception of warfare there is no room for the Red Cross.

LOVE OR RESPECT?

The why-do-they-hate-us question is raised in this context, along with the question of what could be done about it—that is, the use of soft power in combating terrorism. Disturbing figures have been published about the low (and decreasing) popularity of America in foreign parts. Yet it is too often forgotten that international relations is not a popularity contest and that big and powerful countries have always been feared, resented, and envied; in short, they have not been loved. This has been the case since the days of the Assyrians and the Roman Empire. Neither the Ottoman nor the Spanish Empire, the Chinese, the Russian, nor the Japanese was ever popular. British sports were emulated in the colonies and French culture impressed the local elites in North Africa and Indochina, but this did not lead to political support, let alone identification with the rulers. Had there been public opinion polls in the days of Alexander the Great (let alone Ghengis Khan), the results, one suspects, would have been quite negative.

Big powers have been respected and feared but not loved for good reasons—even if benevolent, tactful, and on their best behavior, they were threatening simply because of their very existence. Smaller nations could not feel comfortable, especially if they were located close to them. This was the case even in times when there was more than one big power (which allowed for the possibility of playing one against the other). It is all the more so at a time when only one superpower is left and the perceived threat looms even larger.

There is no known way for a big power to reduce this feeling on the part of other, smaller countries—short of committing suicide or, at the very least, by somehow becoming weaker and less threatening. A moderate and intelligent policy on the part of the great power, concessions, and good deeds may mitigate somewhat the perceived threat, but it cannot remove it, because potentially the big power remains dangerous. It could always change its policy and become nasty, arrogant, and aggressive. These are the unfortunate facts of international life.

Soft power is important but has its limitations. Joseph S. Nye has described it as based on culture and political ideas, as influenced by the seductiveness of democracy, human rights, and individual opportunity. This is a powerful argument, and it is true that Washington has seldom used all its opportunities, the public diplomacy budget being about one-quarter of one percentage point of the defense budget. But the question is always to be asked: Who is to be influenced by our values and ideas? They could be quite effective in Europe, less so in a country like Russia, and not at all among the radical Islamists who abhor democracy (for all sovereignty rests with Allah rather than the people), who believe that human rights and tolerance are imperialist inventions, and who want to have nothing to do with deeper Western values which are not those of the Koran as they interpret it. . . .

Big powers will never be loved, but in the terrorist context it is essential that they should be respected. As bin Laden's declarations prior to September 11 show, it was lack of respect for America that made him launch his attacks; he felt certain that the risk he was running was small, for the United States was a paper tiger, lacking both the will and the capability to

strike back. After all, the Americans ran from Beirut in the 1980s and from Mogadishu in 1993 after only a few attacks, and there was every reason to believe that they would do so again.

....

RESPONSE IN PROPORTION TO THREAT

. . . It could well be that, as far as the recent past is concerned, the danger of terrorism has been overstated. In the two world wars, more people were sometimes killed and more material damage caused in a few hours than through all the terrorist attacks in a recent year. True, our societies have since become more vulnerable and also far more sensitive regarding the loss of life, but the real issue at stake is not the attacks of the past few years but the coming dangers. Megaterrorism has not yet arrived; even 9/11 was a stage in between old-fashioned terrorism and the shape of things to come: the use of weapons of mass destruction. . . .

For the first time in human history very small groups have, or will have, the potential to cause immense destruction. In a situation such as the present one there is always the danger of focusing entirely on the situation at hand—radical nationalist or religious groups with whom political solutions may be found. There is a danger of concentrating on Islamism and forgetting that the problem is a far wider one. Political solutions to deal with their grievances may sometimes be possible, but frequently they are not. Today's terrorists, in their majority, are not diplomats eager to negotiate or to find compromises. And even if some of them would be satisfied with less than total victory and the annihilation of the enemy, there will always be a more radical group eager to continue the struggle.

This was always the case, but in the past it mattered little: If some Irish radicals wanted to continue the struggle against the British in 1921–22, even after the mainstream rebels had signed a treaty with the British government which gave them a free state, they were quickly defeated. Today even small groups matter a great deal precisely because of their enormous potential destructive power, their relative independence, the fact that they are not rational actors, and the possibility that their motivation may not be political in the first place.

Perhaps the scenario is too pessimistic; perhaps the weapons of mass destruction, for whatever reason, will never be used. But it would be the first time in human history that such arms, once invented, had not been used. In the last resort, the problem is, of course, the human condition.

In 1932, when Einstein attempted to induce Freud to support pacifism, Freud replied that there was no likelihood of suppressing humanity's aggressive tendencies. If there was any reason for hope, it was that people would turn away on rational grounds—that war had become too destructive, that there was no scope anymore in war for acts of heroism according to the old ideals.

Freud was partly correct: War (at least between great powers) has become far less likely for rational reasons. But his argument does not apply to terrorism motivated mainly not by political or economic interests, based not just on aggression, but also on fanaticism with an admixture of madness.

Terrorism, therefore, will continue—not perhaps with the same intensity at all times, and some parts of the globe may be spared altogether. But there can be no victory, only an uphill struggle, at times successful, at others not.

FAREED ZAKARIA

33   Islam, Democracy, and Constitutional Liberalism

. . . The Arab world today is trapped between autocratic states and illiberal societies, neither of them fertile ground for liberal democracy. The dangerous dynamic between these two forces has produced a political climate filled with religious extremism and violence. As the state becomes more repressive, opposition within society grows more pernicious, goading the state into further repression. It is the reverse of the historical process in the Western world, where liberalism produced democracy and democracy fueled liberalism. The Arab path has instead produced dictatorship, which has bred terrorism. But terrorism is only the most noted manifestation of this dysfunction, social stagnation, and intellectual bankruptcy.

The Middle East today stands in stark contrast to the rest of the world, where freedom and democracy have been gaining ground over the past two decades. In its 2002 survey, Freedom House finds that 75 percent of the world's countries are currently "free" or "partly free." Only 28 percent of the Middle Eastern countries could be so described, a percentage that has fallen during the last twenty years. By comparison, more than 60 percent of African countries today are classified as free or partly free.

Since September 11, the political dysfunctions of the Arab world have suddenly presented themselves on the West's doorstep. In the back of everyone's mind—and in the front of many—is the question why. Why is this region the political basket case of the world? Why is it the great holdout, the straggler in the march of modern societies?

ISLAM'S WIDE WORLD

Bin Laden has an answer. For him the problem with Arab regimes is that they are insufficiently Islamic. Only by returning to Islam, he tells his followers, will Muslims achieve justice. Democracy, for bin Laden, is a Western invention. Its emphasis on freedom and tolerance produces social decay and licentiousness. Bin Laden and those like him seek the overthrow of the regimes of the Arab world—perhaps of the whole Muslim world—and their replacement by polities founded on strict Islamic

SOURCE: Fareed Zakaria, "Islam, Democracy, and Constitutional Liberalism," *Political Science Quarterly,* vol. 119, no. 1 (Spring 2004), pp. 1–20. Reprinted by permission of the *Political Science Quarterly*. Article and footnotes abridged by the Editor.

principles, ruled by Islamic law (*sharia*) and based on the early Caliphate (the seventh-century Islamic kingdom of Arabia). Their more recent role model was the Taliban regime in Afghanistan.

There are those in the West who agree with bin Laden that Islam is the key to understanding the Middle East's turmoil. Preachers such as Pat Robertson and Jerry Falwell and writers such as Paul Johnson and William Lind have made the case that Islam is a religion of repression and backwardness. More serious scholars have argued—far more insightfully—that the problem is more complex: For fundamentalist Muslims, Islam is considered a template for all life, including politics. But classical Islam, developed in the seventh and eighth centuries, contains few of the ideas that we associate with democracy today. Elie Kedourie, an eminent student of Arab politics, wrote, "The idea of representation, of elections, of popular suffrage, of political institutions being regulated by laws laid down by a parliamentary assembly, of these laws being guarded and upheld by an independent judiciary, the ideas of the secularity of state . . . all these are profoundly alien to the Muslim political tradition."[1]

Certainly the Koranic model of leadership is authoritarian. The Muslim holy book is bursting with examples of the just king, the pious ruler, the wise arbiter. But the Bible has its authoritarian tendencies as well. The kings of the Old Testament were hardly democrats. The biblical Solomon, held up as the wisest man of all, was, after all, an absolute monarch. The Bible also contains passages that seem to justify slavery and the subjugation of women. The truth is that little is to be gained by searching in the Koran for clues to Islam's true nature. The Koran is a vast book, filled with poetry and contradictions—much like the Bible and the Torah. All three books praise kings, as do most religious texts. As for mixing spiritual and temporal authority, Catholic popes combined religious and political power for centuries in a way that no Muslim ruler has ever been able to achieve. Judaism has had much less involvement with political power because, until Israel's founding, Jews were a minority everywhere in the modern world. Yet, the word "theocracy" was coined by Josephus to describe the political views of ancient Jews.[2] The founding religious texts of all faiths were, for the most part, written in another age, one filled with monarchs, feudalism, war, and insecurity. They bear the stamp of their times.

Still, Western scholars of the nineteenth and early twentieth centuries often argued that Islam encourages authoritarianism. This assertion was probably influenced by their view of the Ottoman Empire, a community of several hundred million Muslims laboring docilely under the sultan in distant Constantinople, singing hosannas to him before Friday prayers. But most of the world at the time was quite similar in its deference to political authority. In Russia, the czar was considered almost a god. In Japan, the emperor was a god. On the whole, Asian empires were more despotic than Western ones, but Islamic rule was no more autocratic than were Chinese, Japanese, or Russian versions.

Indeed, if any intrinsic aspect of Islam is worth noting, it is not its devotion to authority, but the opposite: Islam has an antiauthoritarian streak that is evident in every Muslim land today. It originates, probably, in several *hadith*—sayings of the Prophet Mohammed—in which obedience to the ruler is incumbent on the Muslim only so far as the ruler's commands are in keeping with God's law.[3] If the ruler asks you to violate the faith, all bets are off. ("If he is ordered to do a sinful act, a Muslim should neither listen to [his leader] nor should he obey his orders.[4]") Religions are vague, of course. This means that they are easy to follow—you can interpret their prescriptions as you like. But it also means that it is easy to slip up—there is always some injunction you are violating. But Islam has no religious establishment—no popes or bishops—that can declare by fiat which is the correct interpretation. As a result, the decision to oppose the state on the grounds that it is insufficiently Islamic can be exercised by anyone who wishes to do so. This much Islam shares with Protestantism. Just as a Protestant with just a little training—Jerry Falwell, Pat Robertson—can declare himself a religious leader, so also can any Muslim opine on issues of faith. In a religion without an official clergy, bin Laden has as much—or as little—authority to issue *fatwas* (religious orders) as does a Pakistani taxi driver in New York City. The problem, in other words, is the absence of religious authority in Islam, not its dominance.

Consider the source of the current chaos in Arab lands. In Egypt, Saudi Arabia, Algeria, and elsewhere, Islamist[5] groups wage bloody campaigns against states that they accuse of betraying Islam. Bin Laden and his deputy, the Egyptian Ayman Zawahiri, both laymen, began their careers by fighting their own governments because of policies they deemed un-Islamic (for Zawahiri, it was Egyptian president Anwar Sadat's 1978 peace treaty with Israel; for bin Laden, it was King Fahd's decision to allow American troops on Saudi soil in 1991). In his 1996 declaration of jihad, bin Laden declared that the Saudi government had left the fold of Islam, and so it was permissible to take up arms against it: "The regime betrayed the *ummah* (community of believers) and joined the *kufr* (unbelievers), assisting and helping them against the Muslims." Bin Laden called for rebellion against rulers, and many responded to his call. The rulers of the Middle East probably wish that Muslims were more submissive toward authority.

There is also the question of timing: If Islam is the problem, then why is this conflict taking place now? Why did Islamic fundamentalism take off only after the 1979 Iranian revolution? Islam and the West have coexisted for fourteen centuries. There have been periods of war but many more periods of peace. Many scholars have pointed out that, until the 1940s, minorities, and particularly Jews, were persecuted less under Muslim rule than under any other majority religion. That is why the Middle East was for centuries home to many minorities. It is commonly noted that a million Jews left or were expelled from Arab countries after the creation of Israel in 1948. No one asks why so many were living in Arab countries in the first place.

The trouble with thundering declarations about "Islam's nature" is that Islam, like any religion, is not what books make it but what people make it. Forget the rantings of the fundamentalists, who are a minority. Most Muslims' daily lives do not confirm the idea of a faith that is intrinsically anti-Western or anti-modern. The most populous Muslim country in the world, Indonesia, has had secular government since its independence in 1949, with a religious opposition that is tiny (although now growing). As for Islam's compatibility with capitalism, Indonesia was until recently the World Bank's model Third World country, having liberalized its economy and grown at 7 percent a year for almost three decades. It has now embraced democracy (still a fragile experiment) and has elected a woman as its president. After Indonesia, the three largest Muslim populations in the world are in Pakistan, Bangladesh, and India (India's Muslims number more than 120 million). Not only have these countries had much experience with democracy, all three have elected women as prime ministers, and they did so well before most Western countries. So although some aspects of Islam are incompatible with women's rights, the reality on the ground is sometimes quite different. And South Asia is not an anomaly with regard to Islamic women. In Afghanistan, before its twenty-year descent into chaos and tyranny, 40 percent of all doctors were women and Kabul was one of the most liberated cities for women in all of Asia. Although bin Laden may have embraced the Taliban's version of Islam, most Afghans did not—as was confirmed by the sight of men in post-Taliban Kabul and Mazar-e-Sharif lining up to watch movies, listen to music, dance, shave, and fly kites.

The real problem lies not in the Muslim world but in the Middle East. When you get to this region, you see in lurid color all the dysfunctions that people conjure up when they think of Islam today. In Iran,[6] Egypt, Syria, Iraq, the West Bank, the Gaza Strip, and the Persian Gulf states, dictatorships pose in various stripes and liberal democracy appears far from reach. The allure of Islamic fundamentalism seems strong, whether spoken of urgently behind closed doors or declared in fiery sermons in mosques. This is the land of flag burners, fiery mullahs, and suicide bombers. America went to war in Afghanistan, but not a single Afghan was linked to any terrorist attack against Americans. Afghanistan was the campground from which an Arab army was battling America.

The Arab world is an important part of the world of Islam—its heartland. But it is only one part and, in numerical terms, a small one. Of the 1.2 billion Muslims in the world, only 260 million live in Arabia. People in the West often use the term "Islamic," "Middle Eastern," and "Arab" interchangeably. But they do not mean the same thing.

THE ARAB MIND

Today, characterizations of "the Oriental" have about them the whiff of illegitimacy, reminders of the days when ideas such as phrenology passed for science. (And if "Orientals" are to include the Chinese and the Indians—as they did then—then what to make of the stunning success of these groups at science, math, and other such manifestations of rationality?) But things have moved from one extreme to the other. Those who have resorted to such cultural stereotypes, the "Orientalists," have been succeeded by a new generation of politically correct scholars who will not dare to ask why it is that Arab countries seem to be stuck in a social and political milieu very different from that of the rest of the world. Nor is there any self-criticism in this world. Most Arab writers are more concerned with defending their national honor against the pronouncements of dead Orientalists than with trying to understand the predicament of the Arab world.

The reality is impossible to deny. Of the twenty-two members of the Arab League, not one is an electoral democracy, whereas 63 percent of all the counties in the world are. And although some—Jordan, Morocco—have, in some senses, liberal authoritarian regimes, most do not. The region's recent history is bleak. Its last five decades are littered with examples of Arab crowds hailing one dictator after another as a savior. Gamal Abdel Nasser in Egypt, Mu'ammer Qaddafi in Libya, and Saddam Hussein in Iraq all have been the recipients of the heartfelt adulation of the Arab masses.

The few Arab scholars who venture into the cultural field point out that Arab social structure is deeply authoritarian. The Egyptian-born scholar Bahgat Korany writes that "Arab political discourse [is] littered with descriptions of the enlightened dictator, the heroic leader, the exceptional Za'im, the revered head of family."[7] The Lebanese scholar Halim Barakat suggests that the same patriarchal relations and values that prevail in the Arab family seem also to prevail at work, at school, and in religious, political, and social organizations. In all of these, a father figure rules over others, monopolizing authority, expecting strict obedience, and showing little tolerance of dissent. Projecting a paternal image, those in positions of responsibility (as rulers, leaders, teachers, employers, or supervisors) securely occupy the top of the pyramid of authority. Once in this position, the patriarch cannot be dethroned except by someone who is equally patriarchal.[8]

THE FAILURE OF POLITICS

It is difficult to conjure up the excitement in the world in the late 1950s as Nasser consolidated power in Egypt. For decades Arabs had been ruled by colonial governors and decadent kings. Now they were achieving their dreams of independence, and Nasser was their new savior, a modern man for the postwar era. He had been born under British rule, in Alexandria, a cosmopolitan city that was more Mediterranean than Arab. His formative years had been spent in the army, the most Westernized segment of Egyptian society. With his tailored suits and fashionable dark glasses, he cut a daring figure on the world stage. "The Lion of Egypt" spoke for all the Arab world.

Nasser believed that Arab politics needed to be fired by ideas such as self-determination, socialism, and Arab unity. These were modern notions; they were also Western ones. Like many Third World leaders of the time, Nasser was a devoted reader of the British *New Statesman*. His "national charter" of 1962 reads as if it had been written by left-wing intellectuals in Paris or London. Even his most passionately pursued goal, pan-Arabism, was European inspired. It was a version of the nationalism that had united first Italy and then Germany in 1870—the idea that those who spoke one language should be one nation.

Before wealth fattened the Gulf states into golden geese, Egypt was the leader of the Middle East. Thus, Nasser's vision became the region's. Every regime, from the Baathists and generals in Syria and Iraq to the conservative monarchies of the Gulf, spoke in similar terms and tones. They were not simply aping Nasser. The Arab world desperately wanted to become modern, and it saw modernity in an embrace of Western ideas, even if it went hand in hand with a defiance of Western power.

The colonial era of the late nineteenth and early twentieth centuries raised hopes of British friendship that were to be disappointed, but still Arab elites remained fascinated with the West. Future kings and generals attended Victoria College in Alexandria, learning the speech and manners of British gentlemen. Many then went to Oxford, Cambridge, or Sandhurst—a tradition that is still maintained by Jordan's royal family, although now they go to American schools. After World War I, a new liberal age flickered briefly in the Arab world, as ideas about opening politics and society gained currency in places like Egypt, Lebanon, Iraq, and Syria. But the liberal critics of kings and aristocrats were swept away along with those old regimes. A more modern, coarser ideology of military republicanism, state socialism, and Arab nationalism came into vogue. These ideas, however, were still basically Western; the Baathists and Nasserites all wore suits and wanted to modernize their countries.

The new politics and policies of the Arab world went nowhere. For all their energy Arab regimes chose bad ideas and implemented them in worse ways. Socialism produced bureaucracy and stagnation. Rather than adjusting to the failures of central planning, the economies never really moved on. Instead of moving toward democracy, the republics calcified into dictatorships. Third World "non-alignment" became pro-Soviet propaganda. Arab unity cracked and crumbled as countries discovered their own national interests and opportunities. An Arab "Cold War" developed between the countries led by pro-Western kings (the Gulf states, Jordan) and those ruled by revolutionary generals (Syria, Iraq). Worst of all, Israel dealt the Arabs a series of humiliating defeats on the battlefield. Their swift, stunning defeat in 1967 was in some ways the turning point, revealing that behind the rhetoric and bombast lay societies that were failing. When Saddam invaded Kuwait in 1990, he destroyed the last remnants of the pan-Arab idea.

By the late 1980s, while the rest of the world was watching old regimes from Moscow to Prague to Seoul to Johannesburg crack, the Arabs were stuck with their corrupt dictators and aging kings. Regimes that might have seemed promising in the 1960s were now exposed as tired kleptocracies,

deeply unpopular and thoroughly illegitimate. In an almost unthinkable reversal of a global pattern, almost every Arab country today is less free than it was forty years ago. There are few places in the world about which one can say that.

THE FAILURE OF ECONOMICS

At almost every meeting or seminar on terrorism organized by think tanks and universities since September 11, 2001, whenever someone wanted to sound thoughtful and serious, he would say in measured tones, "We must fight not just terrorism but also the roots of terrorism." This platitude has been invariably followed by a suggestion for a new Marshall Plan to eradicate poverty in the Muslim world. Who can be opposed to eradicating poverty? But the problem with this diagnosis is that it overlooks an inconvenient fact: the al-Qaeda terrorist network is not made up of the poor and dispossessed.

This is obviously true at the top; bin Laden was born into a family worth more than $5 billion. But it is also true of many of his key associates, such as his deputy, Zawahiri, a former surgeon in Cairo who came from the highest ranks of Egyptian society. His father was a distinguished professor at Cairo University, his grandfather the chief imam of Al Azhar (the most important center of mainstream Islam in the Arab world), and his uncle the first secretary general of the Arab League. Mohammed Atta, the pilot of the first plane to hit the World Trade Center, came from a modern and moderate—Egyptian family. His father was a lawyer. He had two sisters, a professor and a doctor. Atta himself studied in Hamburg, as had several of the other terrorists. Even the lower-level al-Qaeda recruits appear to have been educated, middle-class men. In this sense, John Walker Lindh, the California kid who dropped out of American life and tuned into the Taliban, was not that different from many of his fellow fundamentalists. In fact, with his high school diploma against their engineering degrees, one could say that he was distinctly undereducated by comparison.

In fact, the breeding grounds of terror have been places that have seen the greatest influx of wealth over the last thirty years. Of the nineteen hijackers, fifteen were from Saudi Arabia, the world's largest petroleum exporter. It is unlikely that poverty was at the heart of their anger. Even Egypt—the other great feeder country for al Qaeda—is not really a poor country by international standards. Its per capita income, $3,690, places it in the middle rank of nations, and it has been growing at a decent 5 percent for the last decade. That may not be enough when you take population growth into account—its population growth has been about 3 percent—but many countries around the world are doing far worse. Yet, they have not spawned hordes of men who are willing to drive planes into Manhattan skyscrapers. If poverty were the source of terror, the recruits should have come from sub-Saharan Africa or South Asia, not the Middle East.

There is, however, a powerful economic dimension to the crisis in the Arab world. The problem is wealth, not poverty. Regimes that get rich through natural resources tend never to develop, modernize, or gain legitimacy. The Arab world is the poster child for this theory of trust-fund states. And this is true not only for the big oil producers. Consider Egypt, which is a small but significant exporter of oil and gas. It also earns $2 billion a year in transit fees paid by ships crossing the Suez Canal, and gets another $2.2 billion a year in aid from the United States. In addition, it gets large sums in remittances—money sent home—from Egyptians who work in the Gulf states. All told, it gets a hefty percentage of its GDP from unearned income. Or consider Jordan, a progressive state that is liberalizing; it gets $1 billion a year in aid from the United States. Although that may seem to be a small figure, keep in mind that Jordan's GDP is only $17 billion. Almost 6 percent of its annual income is foreign aid from one country.

Easy money means little economic or political modernization. The unearned income relieves the government of the need to tax its people—and in return provide something to them in the form of accountability, transparency, even representation. History shows that a government's need to tax its people forces it to become more responsive and representative of its people. Middle Eastern regimes ask little of their people and, in return, give little to

them. An other bad effect of natural-resource-derived wealth is that it makes the government rich enough to become repressive. There is always money enough for the police and the army. Saudi Arabia, for example, spends 13 percent of its GDP on the military, as does Oman. Kuwait spends around 8 percent. Various estimates of Iraqi military spending before the Gulf War have put its military spending at somewhere between 25 and 40 percent of annual GDP, an unusually high rate no doubt sustained, in part, by the Iran-Iraq War, but also by the massive internal intelligence network maintained by Saddam Hussein and his Baath Party.

For years, many in the oil-rich states argued that their enormous wealth would bring modernization. They pointed to the impressive appetites of Saudis and Kuwaitis for things Western, from McDonald's hamburgers to Rolex watches to Cadillac limousines. But importing Western goods is easy; importing the inner stuffing of modern society—a free market, political parties, accountability, the rule of law—is difficult and even dangerous for the ruling elites. The Gulf states, for example, have gotten a bastardized version of modernization, with the goods and even the workers imported from abroad. Little of their modernness is homegrown; if the oil evaporated tomorrow, these states would have little to show for decades of wealth except, perhaps, an overdeveloped capacity for leisure.

....

FEAR OF WESTERNIZATION

There is a sense of pride and fall at the heart of the Arab problem. It makes economic advance impossible and political progress fraught with difficulty. America thinks of modernity as all good—and it has been almost all good for America. But for the Arab world, modernity has been one failure after another. Each path followed—socialism, secularism, nationalism—has turned into a dead end. People often wonder why the Arab countries will not try secularism. In fact, for most of the last century, most of them did. Now Arabs associate the failure of their governments with the failure of secularism and of the Western path. The Arab world is disillusioned with the West when it should be disillusioned with its own leaders.

The new, accelerated globalization that flourished in the 1990s has hit the Arab world in a strange way. Its societies are open enough to be disrupted by modernity, but not so open that they can ride the wave. Arabs see the television shows, eat the fast foods, and drink the sodas, but they do not see genuine liberalization in their societies, with ordinary opportunities and dynamism—just the same elites controlling things. Globalization in the Arab world is the critic's caricature of globalization, a slew of Western products and billboards with little else. For the elites in Arab societies, it means more things to buy. But for some of them, it is also an unsettling phenomenon that threatens their comfortable base of power.

This mixture of fascination and repulsion with the West—with modernity—has utterly disoriented the Arab world. Young men, often better educated than their parents, leave their traditional villages to find work. They arrive in the noisy, crowded cities of Cairo, Beirut, or Damascus, or go to work in the oil states. (Almost 10 percent of Egypt's working population has worked in the Gulf states at some point.) In their new world, they see great disparities in wealth and the disorienting effects of modernity; most unsettlingly, they see women, unveiled and in public places, taking buses, eating in cafes, and working alongside them. They come face to face with the contradictions of modern life, seeking the wealth of the new world but the tradition and certainty of the old.

....

THE RISE OF RELIGION

Nasser was a reasonably devout Muslim, but he had no interest in mixing religion with politics, which struck him as moving backward. This became painfully apparent to the small Islamic parties that supported Nasser's rise to power. The most important one, the Muslim Brotherhood, began opposing him vigorously, often violently, by the early 1950s. Nasser cracked down on it ferociously, imprisoning more than a thousand of its leaders and executing six

of them in 1954. One of those jailed was Sayyid Qutb, a frail man with a fiery pen, who wrote a book in prison called *Signposts on the Road,* which in some ways marked the beginning of modern political Islam or what is often called Islamic fundamentalism.

In his book, Qutb condemned Nasser as an impious Muslim and his regime as un-Islamic. Indeed, he went on, almost every modern Arab regime was similarly flawed. Qutb envisioned a better, more virtuous polity based on strict Islamic principles, a core goal of orthodox Muslims since the 1880s. As the regimes of the Middle East grew more distant, oppressive, and hollow in the decades following Nasser, fundamentalism's appeal grew. It flourished because the Muslim Brotherhood and organizations like it at least tried to give people a sense of meaning and purpose in a changing world, something no leader in the Middle East tried to do. In his seminal work, *The Arab Predicament,* which best explains the fracture of Arab political culture, Fouad Ajami explains, "The fundamentalist call has resonance because it invited men to participate . . . [in] contrast to a political culture that reduces citizens to spectators and asks them to leave things to their rulers. At a time when the future is uncertain, it connects them to a tradition that reduces bewilderment." Fundamentalism gave Arabs who were dissatisfied with their lot a powerful language of opposition.

On that score, Islam had little competition. The Arab world is a political desert with no real political parties, no free press, and few pathways for dissent. As a result, the mosque became the place to discuss politics. As the only place that cannot be banned in Muslim societies, it is where all the hate and opposition toward the regimes collected and grew. The language of opposition became, in these lands, the language of religion. This combination of religion and politics has proven to be combustible. Religion, at least the religion of the Abrahamic traditions (Judaism, Christianity, and Islam), stresses moral absolutes. But politics is all about compromise. The result has been a ruthless, winner-take-all attitude toward political life.

Islamic fundamentalism got a tremendous boost in 1979 when Ayatollah Ruhollah Khomeini toppled the staunchly pro-American shah of Iran.

The Iranian Revolution demonstrated that a powerful ruler could be taken on by groups within the society. It also revealed how, in a developing society, even seemingly benign forces of progress—for example, education—can add to the turmoil. Until the 1970s most Muslims in the Middle East were illiterate and lived in villages and towns. They practiced a kind of village Islam that had adapted itself to local cultures and to normal human desires. Pluralistic and tolerant, these villages often worshipped saints, went to shrines, sang religious hymns, and cherished art—all technically disallowed in Islam. By the 1970s, however, these societies were being urbanized. People had begun moving out of the villages to search for jobs in towns and cities. Their religious experience was no longer rooted in a specific place with local customs and traditions. At the same time, they were learning to read, and they discovered that a new Islam was being preached by a new generation of writers, preachers, and teachers. This was an abstract faith not rooted in historical experience but literal and puritanical—the Islam of the high church as opposed to the Islam of the street fair.

In Iran, Ayatollah Khomeini used a powerful technology—the audiocassette. Even when he was exiled in Paris in the 1970s, his sermons were distributed throughout Iran and became the vehicle of opposition to the shah's repressive regime. But they also taught people a new, angry, austere Islam in which the West is evil, America is the "Great Satan," and the unbeliever is to be fought. Khomeini was not alone in using the language of Islam as a political tool. Intellectuals, disillusioned by the half-baked or overly rapid modernization that was throwing their world into turmoil, were writing books against "Westoxification" and calling the modern Iranian man—half Western, half Eastern—"rootless." Fashionable intellectuals, often writing from the comfort of London or Paris, would criticize American secularism and consumerism and endorse an Islamic alternative. As theories like these spread across the Arab world, they appealed not to the poorest of the poor, for whom Westernization was magical, since it meant food and medicine; rather, they appealed to the educated hordes entering the cities of the Middle East or seeking education and

jobs in the West. They were disoriented and ready to be taught that their disorientation would be solved by recourse to a new, true Islam.

In the Sunni world, the rise of Islamic fundamentalism was shaped and quickened by the fact that Islam is a highly egalitarian religion. This for most of its history has proved an empowering call for people who felt powerless. But it also means that no Muslim really has the authority to question whether someone is a "proper Muslim." In the Middle Ages, there was an informal understanding that a trained scholarly-clerical community, the *ulama,* had the authority to pronounce on such matters. But fundamentalist thinkers, from Pakistani Maulana Maududi and Qutb to their followers, have muscled in on that territory. They loudly and continuously pronounce judgment as to whether people are "good Muslims." In effect, they excommunicate those whose Islam does not match their own. This process has terrified the Muslim world. Leaders dare not take on the rising tide of Islamists. Intellectual and social elites, widely discredited by their slavish support of the official government line, are also scared to speak out against a genuinely free-thinking clergy. As a result, moderate Muslims are loath to criticize or debunk the fanaticism of the fundamentalists. Some worry, like the moderates in Northern Ireland, about their safety if they speak their mind. Even as venerated a figure as Naguib Mahfouz was stabbed in Egypt for his mildly critical comments about the Islamists.

Nowhere is this more true than in the moderate monarchies of the Persian Gulf, particularly Saudi Arabia. The Saudi regime has played a dangerous game: It has tried to deflect attention away from its spotty economic and political record by allowing free reign to its most extreme clerics, hoping to gain legitimacy by association. Saudi Arabia's educational system is run by medieval-minded religious bureaucrats. Over the past three decades, the Saudis—mostly through private trusts—have funded religious schools (*madrasas*) and centers that spread Wahhabism (a rigid, desert variant of Islam that is the template for most Islamic fundamentalists) around the world. In the past thirty years, Saudi-funded *madrasas* have churned out tens of thousands of half-educated, fanatical Muslims who view the modern world and non-Muslims with great suspicion. America in this world-view is almost always uniquely evil.

This exported fundamentalism has infected not just other Arab societies but countries outside the Arab world. It often carries with it a distinctly parochial Arab political program. Thus, Indonesian Muslims, who twenty years ago did not know where Palestine was, are today militant in their support of its cause. The Arab influence extends even into the realm of architecture. In its buildings, the Islamic world has always mixed Arab influences with local ones—Hindu, Javan, Russian. But local cultures are now being ignored in places such as Indonesia and Malaysia because they are seen as insufficiently Islamic (meaning Arab).

Pakistan has had a particularly bad experience with exported fundamentalism. During the eleven-year reign of General Zia ul-Haq (1977–1988), the dictator decided that he needed allies, since he had squashed political dissent and opposition parties. He found them in the local fundamentalists, who became his political allies. With the aid of Saudi financiers and functionaries, he set up scores of *madrasas* throughout the country. The Afghan war attracted religious zealots, eager to fight godless communism. These "jihadis" came mostly from Arabia. Without Saudi money and men, the Taliban would not have existed, nor would Pakistan have become the hotbed of fundamentalism that it is today. Zia's embrace of Islam brought him a kind of legitimacy, but it has eroded the social fabric of Pakistan. The country is now full of armed radicals, who first supported the Taliban, then joined in the struggle in Kashmir, and are now trying to undermine the secular regime of General Pervez Musharraf. They have infected the legal and political system with medieval ideas of blasphemy, the subordinate role of women, and the evils of modern banking.

Pakistan is not alone. A similar process has been at work in countries as diverse as Yemen, Indonesia, and the Philippines. During the 1980s and 1990s, a kind of competition emerged between Iran and Saudi Arabia, the two most religious states in the Middle East, to see who would be the greater religious power in the Islamic World. As a result, what

were once small, extreme strains of Islam, limited to parts of the Middle East, have taken root around the world—in the globalization of radical Islam.

THE ROAD TO DEMOCRACY

For the most part, the task of reform in the Middle East must fall to the peoples of the region. No one can make democracy, liberalism, or secularism take root in these societies without their own search, efforts, and achievements. But the Western world in general, and the United States in particular, can help enormously. The United States is the dominant power in the Middle East; every country views its relations with Washington as the most critical tie they have. Oil, strategic ties, and the unique U.S. relationship with Israel ensure American involvement. Washington will continue to aid the Egyptian regime, protect the Saudi monarchy, and broker negotiations between Israel and the Palestinians. The question really is, should it not ask for something in return? By not pushing these regimes, the United States would be making a conscious decision to let things stay as they are—to opt for stability. This is a worthwhile goal, except that the current situation in the Middle East is highly unstable. Even if viewed from a strategic perspective, it is in America's immediate security interests to try to make the regimes of the Middle East less prone to breeding fanatical and terrorist opposition movements.

As a start, the West must recognize that it does not seek democracy in the Middle East—at least not yet. We seek first constitutional liberalism, which is very different. Clarifying our immediate goals will actually make them more easily attainable. The regimes in the Middle East will be delighted to learn that we will not try to force them to hold elections tomorrow. They will be less pleased to know that we will continually press them on a whole array of other issues. The Saudi monarchy must do more to end its governmental and nongovernmental support for extreme Islam, which is now the kingdom's second largest export to the rest of the world. If this offends advocates of pure free speech, so be it. It must rein in its religious and educational leaders and force them to stop flirting with fanaticism. In Egypt, we must ask President Mubarak to insist that the state-owned press drop its anti-American and anti-Semitic rants and begin opening itself up to other voices in the country. Some of these voices will be worse than those we hear now, but some will be better. Most important, people in these countries will begin to speak about what truly concerns them—not only the status of Jerusalem or American policies in the Gulf, but also the regimes they live under and the politics they confront.

Israel has become the great excuse for much of the Arab world, the way for regimes to deflect attention from their own failures. Other countries have foreign policy disagreements with one another—think of China and Japan—but they do not have the sometimes poisonous quality of the Israeli-Arab divide. Israel's occupation of the West Bank and Gaza Strip has turned into the great cause of the Arab world. But even if fomented by cynical Arab rulers, this cause is now a reality that cannot be ignored. There is a new Arab street in the Middle East, built on Al-Jazeera and Internet chat sites. And the talk is all about the plight of the Palestinians. If unaddressed, this issue will only grow in importance, infecting America's relations with the entire Muslim world and ensuring permanent insecurity for Israel. The United States should maintain its unyielding support for the security of Israel. But it should also do what is in the best interest of itself, Israel, and the Palestinians, which is to press hard to broker a settlement that provides Israel and the Palestinians a viable state. Peace between the Israelis and Palestinians will not solve the problem of Arab dysfunction, but it would ease some of the tensions between the Arab world and the West.

The more lasting solution is economic and political reform. Economic reforms must come first, for they are fundamental. Even though the problems facing the Middle East are not purely economic, their solution may lie in economics. Moving toward capitalism, as we have seen, is the surest path to creating a limited, accountable state and a genuine middle class. And just as in Spain, Portugal, Chile, Taiwan, South Korea, and Mexico, economic reform means the beginnings of a genuine rule of law (capitalism needs contracts), openness to the world,

access to information, and, perhaps most important, the development of a business class. If you talk with Arab businessmen and women, they want the old system to change. They have a stake in openness, in rules, and in stability. They want their societies to modernize and move forward rather than stay trapped in factionalism and war. Instead of the romance of ideology, they seek the reality of material progress. In the Middle East today, there are too many people consumed by political dreams and too few interested in practical plans.

There is a dominant business class in the Middle East, but it owes its position to oil or to connections to the ruling families.[9] Its wealth is that of feudalism, not capitalism, and its political effects remain feudal as well. A genuinely entrepreneurial business class would be the single most important force for change in the Middle East, pulling along all others in its wake. If culture matters, this is one place it would help. Arab culture for thousands of years has been full of traders, merchants, and businessmen. The bazaar is probably the oldest institution in the Middle East. And Islam has been historically highly receptive to business—Mohammed himself was a businessman. Ultimately, the battle for reform is one that Middle Easterners will have to fight, which is why there needs to be some group within these societies that advocates and benefits from economic and political reform.

This is not as fantastic an idea as it might sound. Already stirrings of genuine economic activity can be seen in parts of the Middle East. Jordan has become a member of the World Trade Organization (WTO), signed a free-trade pact with the United States, privatized key industries, and even encouraged cross-border business ventures with Israel. Saudi Arabia is seeking WTO membership. Egypt has made some small progress on the road to reform. Among the oil-rich countries, Bahrain and the United Arab Emirates are trying to wean themselves of their dependence on oil. Dubai, part of the United Arab Emirates, has already gotten oil down to merely 8 percent of its GDP and has publicly announced its intention of becoming a trading and banking center—the "Singapore of the Middle East." (It would do well to emulate Singapore's tolerance of its ethnic and religious minorities.)

Even Saudi Arabia recognizes that its oil economy can provide only one job for every three of its young men coming into the work force. In Algeria, President Abdelaziz Bouteflika desperately wants foreign investment to repair his tattered economy.

If we could choose one place to press hardest to reform, it should be Egypt. Although Jordan has a more progressive ruler, and Saudi Arabia is more critical because of its oil, Egypt is the intellectual soul of the Arab world. If Egypt were to progress economically and politically, it would demonstrate more powerfully than any essay or speech that Islam is compatible with modernity, and that Arabs can thrive in today's world. In East Asia, Japan's economic success proved a powerful example that others in the region looked to and followed. The Middle East needs one such homegrown success story.

There is another possible candidate for the role: Iraq. Before it became a playpen for Saddam's megalomania, Iraq was one of the most advanced, literate, and secular countries in the region. It has oil, but more importantly, it has water. Iraq is the land of one of the oldest river-valley civilizations in the world. Its capital, Baghdad, is home to one of the wonders of the ancient world, the Hanging Gardens of Babylon, and has been an important city for thousands of years. Iraq in the 1950s was a country with a highly developed civil society, with engineers, doctors, and architects, many of whom were women. Now that Saddam has been dislodged, the United States must engage in a serious long-term project of nation building, because Iraq could well become the first major Arab country to combine Arab culture with economic dynamism, religious tolerance, liberal politics, and a modern outlook on the world. And success is infectious.

THE IMPORTANCE OF CONSTITUTIONALISM

Spreading democracy is tough. But that does not mean that the West—in particular the United States—should stop trying to assist the forces of liberal democracy. Nor does it imply accepting blindly authoritarian regimes as the least bad alternative. It does, however, suggest the need for a certain sophistication. The haste to press countries into elections over the last decade has been, in many cases, counterproductive. In countries such as Bosnia, which went to the polls within a year of the Dayton peace accords, elections only made more powerful precisely the kinds of ugly ethnic forces that have made it more difficult to build genuine liberal democracy there. The ethnic thugs stayed in power and kept the courts packed and the police well fed. The old system has stayed in place, delaying real change for years, perhaps decades. In East Timor and Afghanistan, a longer period of state-building has proved useful. In general, a five-year period of transition, political reform, and institutional development should precede national multiparty elections. In a country with strong regional, ethnic, or religious divisions—like Iraq—this is crucial. It ensures that elections are held after civic institutions, courts, political parties, and the economy have all begun to function. As with everything in life, timing matters.

Although it is easy to impose elections on a country, it is more difficult to push constitutional liberalism on a society. The process of genuine liberalization and democratization, in which an election is only one step, is gradual and long term. Recognizing this, governments and nongovernmental organizations are increasingly promoting an array of measures designed to bolster constitutional liberalism in developing countries. The National Endowment for Democracy promotes free markets, independent labor movements, and political parties. The U.S. Agency for International Development funds independent judiciaries. In the end, however, elections trump everything. If a country holds elections, Washington and the world will tolerate a great deal from the resulting government, as they did with Russia's Boris Yeltsin, Kyrgystan's Askar Akayev, and Argentina's Carlos Menem. In an age of images and symbols, elections are easy to capture on film. But how to do you televise the rule of law? Yet, there is life after elections, especially for the people who live there.

Conversely, the absence of free and fair elections should be viewed as one flaw, not the definition of tyranny. Elections are an important virtue of governance, but they are not the only virtue. It is more important that governments be judged by yardsticks related to constitutional liberalism. Economic, civil, and religious liberties are at the core of human autonomy and dignity. If a government with limited democracy steadily expands these freedoms, it should not be branded a dictatorship. Despite the limited political choice they offer, countries such as Singapore, Malaysia, Jordan, and Morocco provide a better environment for the life, liberty, and happiness of citizens than do the dictatorships in Iraq and Libya or the illiberal democracies of Venezuela, Russia, or Ghana. And the pressures of global capitalism can push the process of liberalization forward, as they have in China. Markets and morals can work together.

The most difficult task economically is reforming the trust-fund states. It has proved nearly impossible to wean them of their easy money. In 2002, the World Bank began experimenting with a potentially pathbreaking model in the central African country of Chad. Chad has major oil fields, but foreign companies were wary of major investments to extract and transport the oil because of the country's history of political instability. The World Bank agreed to step in, bless the project, and loan the government money to partner with a multinational consortium—led by ExxonMobil—to get the oil flowing. But it also put in place certain conditions. Chad's parliament had to pass a law guaranteeing that 80 percent of the oil revenues would be spent on health, education, and rural infrastructure, 5 percent would be spent on locals near the oil fields, and 10 percent would be put into an escrow account for future generations. That leaves the government 5 percent to spend as it wishes. To ensure that the system works in practice as well as in theory, the bank required that all oil revenues be deposited in an offshore account that is managed by an independent oversight committee (made up of some of Chad's leading citizens). It is too soon to tell if this model works, but if it does, it could be copied elsewhere. Even in countries that do not need the World Bank's help, it could have a demonstration effect. The Chad model provides a method by which natural-resource revenues can become a blessing for countries rather than the curse they currently are.

Finally, we need to revive constitutionalism. One effect of the overemphasis of pure democracy is that little effort is given to creating imaginative constitutions for transitional countries. Constitutionalism, as it was understood by its greatest eighteenth-century exponents, such as Montesquieu and Madison, is a complicated system of checks and balances designed to prevent the accumulation of power and the abuse of office. This is accomplished not by simply writing up a list of rights but by constructing a system in which government will not violate those rights. Various groups must be included and empowered because, as Madison explained, "ambition must be made to counteract ambition."

Constitutions were also meant to tame the passions of the public, creating not simply democratic but also deliberative government. The South African constitution is an example of an unusually crafted, somewhat undemocratic structure. It secures power for minorities, both those regionally based, such as the Zulus, and those that are dispersed, such as the whites. In doing so it has increased that country's chances of success as a democracy, despite its poverty and harrowing social catastrophes.

Unfortunately, the rich variety of unelected bodies, indirect voting, federal arrangements, and checks and balances that characterized so many of the formal and informal constitutions of Europe are now regarded with suspicion. What could be called the Weimar syndrome—named after Germany's beautifully constructed constitution, which nevertheless failed to avert fascism—has made people regard constitutions as simply paperwork that cannot make much difference (as if any political system in Germany would have easily weathered military defeat, social revolution, the Great Depression, and hyperinflation). Procedures that inhibit direct democracy are seen as inauthentic, muzzling the voice of the people. Today, around the world, we see variations on the same majoritarian theme. But the trouble with these winner-take-all systems is that, in most democratizing countries, the winner really does take all.

Of course, cultures vary, and different societies will require different frameworks of government. This is a plea not for the wholesale adoption of any one model of government but rather for a more variegated conception of liberal democracy, one that emphasizes both words in that phrase. Genuine democracy is a fragile system that balances not just these two but other forces—what Tocqueville called "intermediate associations"—to create, in the end, a majestic clockwork. Understanding this system requires an intellectual task of recovering the constitutional liberal tradition, central to Western experience and to the development of good government throughout the world.

This recovery will be incomplete if we limit it in our minds to what is happening in faraway countries that are troubled and poor and utterly different from the prosperous, democratic West. Democracy is a work in progress, abroad as well as at home. The tension between democracy and liberalism is one that flourished in the West's own past. In a very different form, it still exists and is growing in the Western world. It is most widely prevalent in one country in particular: the United States of America.

ENDNOTES

1. Elie Kedourie, *Democracy and Arab Political Culture* (Washington, DC: Washington Institute for Near East Studies, 1992), p. 5.

2. Bernard Lewis, *What Went Wrong: Western Impact and Middle Eastern Response* (Oxford: Oxford University Press, 2002), p. 97.

3. The *hadith* are often more important than the Koran because they tell Muslims how to implement the sometimes general Koranic injunctions. For example, the Koran commands Muslims to pray, but it does not tell them how to pray; this is found in the *hadith*. (There are, of course, many *hadith,* many of dubious authenticity, and sometimes they contradict each other.)

4. *Sahih Muslim,* book 20, *hadith* 4533.

5. "Islamist" refers to people, like bin Laden, who want to use Islam as a political ideology, setting up an Islamic state that follows Islamic law strictly. I use this term interchangeably with the more commonly used "Islamic fundamentalist," although many scholars prefer the former.

6. I often lump Iran together with Arab countries. It is technically not one of them; Iranians speak Farsi, not Arabic. But Iran's Islamic Revolution of 1979 gave an enormous fillip to the broader fundamentalist movement and, for now, has dulled the age-old divide between the two largest sects of Islam, Sunni (mostly Arabs) and Shia (mostly Iranians).

7. Bahgat Korany, "Arab Democratization: A Poor Cousin?" *PS: Political Science and Politics,* vol. 27, no. 3 (September 1994), p. 511.

8. Halim Barakat, *The Arab World: Society, Culture, and State* (Berkeley: University of California Press, 1993), p. 23.

9. There are some exceptions to this rule in Gulf states such as Dubai, Bahrain, and even Saudi Arabia.

PART THREE

Political Dynamics, Decisions, and Efficacy

The pursuit of power—the capacity to command the actions of others—by individuals and groups is a universal phenomenon. Individuals and groups are organized through specialized associations representing their interests; they also promulgate or associate themselves with ideological orientations. By *political dynamics* we mean the interplay of social groups, organized interests, and ideologies that generally takes place through political parties and institutions in order to shape public policy.

The process whereby groups compete for positions and advantage takes place in all political systems, and hence it can be studied functionally and comparatively. Citizens press their demands and claims mainly through "interest" or "pressure" groups; others use the parties or administration. Comparative analysis can be conducted by studying the diverse patterns of interest articulation. Interest groups can be considered in terms of their size, membership, leadership, organization, relations with political parties, and means used to mobilize public opinion, gain access to the state, and influence decisions. Group analysis has the merit of bringing the student directly into the heart of the political process—social conflict and its resolution. By studying the "interest group universe" in a given political system, we gain a good insight into the distribution of power in that society.

One of the striking features of industrialized societies is the development and proliferation of specialized groups. In a modern society they represent every conceivable social, economic, religious, and professional interest. The largest and most powerful groups speaking on behalf of the major social classes are the business, labor, and agricultural organizations. Every modern political system must provide these associations or interest groups with the opportunity to gain access to the policy makers and make known their proposals or demands.

Reconciliation of the demands of interest groups and, broadly speaking, of social forces, is perhaps the most serious single challenge confronting any political system. We are not referring here to the demands, say, of trade unions and management for a minimum wage fixed at a particular level, though this kind of conflict is quite intense. We refer rather to the attitude of social groups toward the political process itself, the acceptance of the "rules of the game" by all the players. For example, there is a complex network of specialized associations in both Great Britain and France. In both countries we find powerful trade unions, business groups, churches, and associations of farmers, veterans, teachers, and so on. Some French groups are more powerful than their opposite numbers in Britain (for example, farmers, small merchants, lay Catholics) and vice versa (British trade unions and business groups are more highly organized than their counterparts in France).

Yet the basic attitudes of the groups were significantly different in the past. In spite of their political rivalry, expressed through support of the Labor and Conservative parties, the trade unions and business groups in Britain accepted a commitment to parliamentary institutions. With a few exceptions (such as Irish nationalists), they were willing to work within the existing system in order to realize their goals and did not turn against it when they lost. The habits of compromise were solidly established in British society; the actors abided by fundamental rules embodied in the constitutional system.

In France, however, the same economic or social interests were not in agreement on the values of the state or on political procedures to be used in the resolution of group conflicts. The labor and business groups were fundamentally hostile to each other. The most powerful trade union in France, the General Confederation of Labor, was led by Communists; that is, the industrial proletariat in France expressed its demands through a party that rejected the system. Important elements of the business community not only distrusted the workers, but wished to introduce a "strong" state to deal with them. In addition, the parliamentary system was held in low repute by other important interests, and political debates and meetings were marked by verbal and physical violence. In practice the disaffected groups were generally unable to overthrow the system and accepted it provisionally. Compromise was difficult to achieve and broke down altogether during political crises. There was a distinct tendency to change the rules of the game (usually by promulgating a new constitution) whenever the balance shifted and one constellation of groups or forces gained the upper hand.

Important changes took place in the French political system in the 1970s and 1980s. With the rise of a strong Socialist party, the balance of power within the Left shifted away from the Communist party, which saw its popular vote reduced from over 25 percent after the Liberation, to about 18 to 20 percent in the 1960s, rapidly descending to less than 10 percent after the election of Socialist François Mitterrand to the presidency in 1981. Working class support for the Communist-led trade union, the General Confederation of Labor, also fell off dramatically, from 50 percent of the votes in elections to enterprise committees in the 1960s to about half that in the 1980s. In addition, the Communist party itself underwent a transformation, roundly criticizing the Soviet model (termed "authoritarian socialism") and proclaiming its commitment to democracy. Nonetheless, the Communist party continues to consider itself a Leninist organization; it defines democracy in a way compatible with Leninism, rejects capitalism in principle, and still enjoys the confidence of perhaps 5 percent of the electorate. On the first ballot in the presidential election of April 2002, the two Trotskyite candidates together received about 10 percent of the vote, and the Communist candidate almost 4 percent. The candidate of the extreme Right-wing National Front, Jean-Marie Le Pen, rejects many underlying features of parliamentary democracy. He won almost 17 percent of the vote, putting him ahead of the Socialist candidate and in the runoff. The hostility of almost one-third of the electorate to mainstream institutions and values makes the style of politics in France more complicated than in most other modern democracies. Thus, one of the most important questions to pose about a political system is the attitude of the principal organized groups toward each other and toward the system itself.

INTERESTS

There are two basic models for viewing the relationship between the state and interest groups in democracies: pluralist and corporatist. Each model, in turn, has versions reflecting the unique traditions and circumstances of individual nations.

In the pluralist model, interests (such as trade unions, business groups, professional associations, or churches) are autonomous and free to act. They make demands through publicity, electoral pressure, and direct or indirect action on the state. Their aim is to maximize their own interests at the expense of others, but in most cases they are prepared to accommodate others and compromise. The state and its agencies respond to the constant demands of interest groups, and the public good is considered the sum total of particular interests. Critics on the Left believe that moneyed interests enjoy a clear advantage over more popular groups, particularly consumers. For critics on the Right, pluralism too often leads to stalemate, when competing interests are evenly matched. Political institutions, including parties, are unable to create a synthesis among competing and conflicting interests. The state becomes a captive of an interest universe that it cannot transcend.

In the interwar period an authoritarian version of corporatism was installed in fascist regimes such as Italy, Germany, Spain and Portugal, and in France under Vichy. Corporatism was intended to be a rejection of and improvement upon pluralist democracy. Groups were organized under the aegis of the state, and took the place of parliaments elected through competitive parties and universal suffrage. It was assumed that clashes among interests were prejudicial to the public good. It was therefore necessary to secure cooperation among interests (and classes) under the overall direction and control of the state. Interest groups did not enjoy autonomy; their relations with other groups were structured and supervised by public agencies. They were not free to pressure the state, nor to communicate among themselves in order to make compromises or strike bargains. They functioned as part of the state structure, not as free agents acting upon the state.

In communist systems the means of production and virtually all economic activity were run by the state and its agencies. Interest groups had no independent resources, no freedom to take their case to the public, and no autonomy. The political elite dominated the interest universe and infused it with its own purpose and imperatives; how effectively depended on a number of factors: the strength of the single political party, the appeal of the official ideology, the tenacity of past political culture, and the level and degree of economic modernization.

Although European fascism disappeared in the wake of World War II, some elements of the corporatist model were kept and adapted to democratic circumstances. The major economic groups, especially trade unions and business associations, are involved along with the state in negotiations concerning a range of problems, including all aspects of labor-management relations (wages, hours, conditions of labor, and benefits). Legitimacy is thus conferred upon the groups and the agreements reached by them. Specific powers are also delegated to interests, for example, to fix prices, organize production in various sectors of the economy, and assume responsibility for social and welfare services. The "neo-corporatist" model seems to be appropriate in particular in Austria, Germany, and Sweden, with some aspects of the model applicable also to France.

Pluralist and neo-corporatist models do not exist in a "pure" or ideal form. In most democracies the pluralist model has been qualified by corporatist practices whereby interest groups and professional associations work closely with state agencies in the making and carrying out of public policy. In no case has any democracy, despite the prevalence of corporatist procedures, ever replaced freely elected parliaments as the makers of major policy decisions. The balance between pluralism and corporatism in modern democracies reflects orientations concerning the proper balance between the market and the state. Reliance on the market translates into more power and autonomy for interest groups. Analysis of the interest group universe is a fruitful way of dealing with otherwise elusive questions of political culture, consensus, and performance.

POLITICAL PARTIES

Max Weber's definition of party places the subject in broad social and historical perspective. The term political party, he suggested,

> will be employed to designate an associative type of social relationship, membership in which rests on formally free recruitment. The end to which its activity is devoted is to secure power within a corporate group for its leaders in order to attain ideal or material advantages for its active members. These advantages may consist in the realization of certain objective policies or the attainment of personal advantages or both.[1]

As Weber uses the term, a "party" can exist in any corporate group—unions, fraternal orders, churches, university faculties, and corporations. It can be oriented toward personal interest or toward broad policy. Political victory in party terms means that its adherents, in assuming direction of the state, can realize party proposals. Political parties thus are complex social institutions holding together those who have a common program and those who strive for power and personal advantage. They are specialized associations that become more complex, organized, and bureaucratic as a society approaches the "modern" type.

The political party is the most important single link between groups, the people, and the government in a democracy. Through the party, leadership is able to reach out into the masses for support and new sources of strength, while the masses in turn are able to focus criticism and make demands upon it. The party, if backed by a majority of the electorate, coordinates the multifarious functions of the government in order to achieve coherently stated aims. A minority party gives like-minded individuals and groups an opportunity to rally their forces, develop a program, and prepare for the day when power might be wielded or at least shared. Competitive political parties are a fundamental feature of all modern democracies.

In many of the new democracies created after World War II parties received special recognition in their constitutions. Parties were specifically mentioned as necessary to the functioning of democracy by the German Basic Law, and the constitutions of Italy, the Fifth French Republic, Spain, Portugal, and Greece. In some cases, an attempt was made in the constitution to draw a line between democratic and non-democratic parties. The German Basic Law states bluntly (Article 21.2) that parties seeking to "impair or abolish the free democratic basic order or to endanger the existence of the Federal Republic of Germany, shall be unconstitutional." In 1951 the federal government, with the approval of the Constitutional Court, banned a neo-Nazi party and the Communist party. In practice, it is difficult to outlaw political movements in a democracy. The neo-Nazi and Communist parties in Germany simply took new names. But all democracies discriminate, through electoral laws and political practice, against those parties that reject the system.

The existence of extremist movements is a reminder that parties are not and in the past were not considered always constructive agencies of progress. Parties were not even studied systematically until the modern period, when they were fully developed. John Stuart Mill's treatise *On Representative Government,* written in 1861, contained an extensive plea for proportional representation but no treatment of parties. Most students of political parties at the turn of the century were concerned with the shortcomings and deficiencies of political parties: bossism, manipulation of voters, and corruption. James Bryce, M. I. Ostrogorski, and Robert Michels fully documented the growth of mass political parties with complex structures in the United States, Britain, and Germany. They assumed that democracy somehow involves meaningful participation by the masses in the making of important decisions. They agreed that parties were controlled by a handful of politicians and leaders. Democracy therefore becomes less and less feasible as parties become more and more complex.[2]

The widespread view of parties as destructive of democracy gave way only gradually to the growing consensus that parties are indispensable to the operation of democratic institutions. American political scientists were especially affected by the New Deal, which seemed to demonstrate the potential utility of political parties in mobilizing public support for a program of social reform. Also, the hostile reaction to the Nazi regime included searching appraisal of the one-party system. In defense of Western democracy against the challenge of fascism and communism, it was discerned that democracy was bound up somehow with the existence of at least two parties. The previously despised parties were elevated to positions of great prestige by political philosophers and researchers.

The role of parties in the democratic process was emphasized by such writers as A. D. Lindsay, R. M. MacIver, C. J. Friedrich, Joseph Schumpeter, and Walter Lippmann, to name but a few.[3] They argued that a distinctive element of democracy, as contrasted with fascism and communism, was the existence of an opposition. But it is not sufficient to grant an abstract right of opposition to individuals. To be effective, opposition must be enabled to organize—that is, to form a party. In the absence of parties, there would be no check upon the egoistic impulses of the rulers. Also, the masses can participate effectively in government only through the agency of parties. Thus, parties organize the "chaotic public will," educate the private citizens to public responsibility, connect government with public opinion, and select the political leadership. In answer to Michels's criticism of oligarchy, it has been argued that even oligarchical parties may serve democratic purposes—provided that there is free competition among the parties.[4] Maurice Duverger spoke for most political scientists when he concluded, shortly after World War II, that "liberty and the party system coincide."[5]

Criticism of parties flares up regularly, especially in countries where large social groups have not been fully integrated into the political system, as evidenced by massive support for antiparliamentary parties. Nor does a competitive party system appear appropriate in societies where the overwhelming majority of the people is illiterate and therefore not in a position to make informed judgments among candidates and programs. Different kinds of questions about both parties and democracy are raised: how the elite is recruited, what role is played by the party in mobilizing the masses and breaking up the traditional society, what kind of values are held by the educated elite, and so on. The trend in interpreting the democratic nature of parties in developing nations is to assess their role in the transition from traditional to more modern forms of social organization. Mass participation in politics is one of the social conditions of democratic government. In some cases the party asserts a monopoly of power in order to create a modern society with the support, even if without the understanding, of the peasantry. In other cases, the party seeks to preserve the power of a traditional group. Dominant parties may seek to crush opposition or may tolerate criticism and respect an independent judiciary. Theory concerning the role of parties in a democracy is thus being modified in the light of the experience of developing nations.

In an authoritarian system the overriding task of the party is to mobilize the masses. This is a major trend also in developing nations, where a small, educated elite is determined to bring about modernization. Even in parliamentary democracies parties must be able to generate widespread popular support for the policies of the executive, or else the regime is in serious trouble. Totalitarian parties in particular secure the adherence of masses of people by offering them an opportunity to gratify social impulses, but democratic parties likewise engage in some of the same activities. Most studies of totalitarian parties have emphasized the role of the party as an instrument of the leadership, whereas most studies of democratic parties stress the role of the party in limiting leadership and permitting popular participation in the decision-making process. Yet, all parties may be viewed and compared in both ways.

Thus, groups organize, present their claims to the parties, and are in turn courted by party leaders. Decision makers are themselves members of parties and are dependent upon the support of groups for maintenance in office. The delicate process of compromise must take place somewhere within the political system. Is it within the single party, or the major party of a two-party system, or a parliamentary assembly? How can we account for similarities and differences?

CLASSIFICATION OF PARTY SYSTEMS

Classification is a first step in comparison of party systems because it enables the observer to select for analysis the like elements of various political systems. One such classification is based on the means employed in appealing to the electorate and organizing opinion. Some commentators distinguish between parties of interest and parties of principle, or parties of personalities and parties of program, "broker" parties and "missionary" parties. American parties would thus be considered examples of interest appeal and personalities, whereas British and continental parties would be programmatic. Yet this classification does not fully explain modern trends. American parties reflect ideological orientations, and continental parties represent interests and may be led by forceful personalities.

A more useful scheme of classification is in terms of degree of centralization and discipline. Robert Michels, in his *Political Parties,* argued that the dominance of the leadership characterizes *all* mass parties, including those whose ideology is militantly democratic. Michels raised a significant problem of democratic theory. Democracy obviously involves some kind of control over the rulers by the people. Every democracy is run by political parties. But who runs the parties? To what extent can the leaders be controlled by those who hold subordinate positions in the organization?

Democratic parties vary greatly as regards the relative power of local units, members, national agencies, and leaders. American parties, for instance, are federations of state political organizations. There is no formal chain of command. National leadership results from coalitions among local party leaders, though national committees recently have gained power through their superior ability to raise money. British parties, on the other hand, are national organizations with local branches. In both the Conservative and Labor parties decision making is vested in the leaders. Parties in parliamentary democracies run the gamut from the British model to the American. The two large parties of the Federal Republic of Germany are structurally similar to the British parties. Leadership in both the Social Democratic party and the Christian Democratic Union is concentrated at the national level and personalized. On the other hand, conservative and moderate parties in multiparty systems have relatively few active members and are run mainly by parliamentarians.

In all parties, then, there is a sharp distinction between the leadership and the followers, and the latter are rarely in a position to shape or control policy. But parties are complex organizations and cannot be reduced merely to structures. Leaders within a party are engaged in constant competition with each other; they also must reach out to the electorate and try to gain support for programs and policies. Party leaders must deal with government officials (legislators and ministers), who usually claim a large measure of independence; and they must negotiate also with highly organized groups linked to the party, such as trade unions and business associations, whose leaders cannot easily be manipulated. The degree of centralization and discipline within parties largely determines the "style" of the political process—that is, the level of the political system at which compromises are made, the degree of cohesion of parliamentary groups, and the nature of electoral appeals.

Perhaps the most popular classification of party systems is in terms of the number of parties in the field. In his influential book, *Political Parties,* Maurice Duverger points out that the one-party, two-party, and multiparty systems tend to correspond to the major types of contemporary regimes. Thus, dictatorships are characterized by the single party, and democracies by either a two- or multiparty system. The two-party system is frequently held up as a model form, permitting the majority to govern and the minority to criticize. Multiparty systems are usually considered less stable but offer the voter a greater choice of alternatives.

However, this classification has come under attack. One-party systems, as we have seen, may serve as transitional forms, making possible the creation of a more democratic regime at a later time. Two-party systems are not as simple or stable as might appear on the surface. In the United Kingdom, a classic example of the two-party system, up to one-fourth of the electorate since 1979 has supported minor parties (mainly liberals or social democrats, and Welsh, Scottish, and Irish nationalists). Even though the two major parties have dominated Parliament, their leaders have had to adjust programs and appeals accordingly. And multiparty systems may be more coherent and stable than generally assumed. French political scientists have called attention to the agreements (electoral alliances and cabinet coalitions) between parties of the same political family, which provide a measure of coherence. In run-off elections under the Third and Fifth Republics the French voter has virtually been presented with a choice between only two (rarely three) serious candidates. Similarly, students of Scandinavia have pointed out that these multiparty systems are capable of sustaining dynamic and stable governments. The parties form coalitions in the same way that wings of a major party in Britain or the United States come to agreement on a common policy or leader. It may be more fruitful to view party systems in terms of the nature of the national consensus—that is, whether or not the major parties (within either a two- or multiparty system) and in turn the major social groups on which they are based share the same attitudes toward basic values and goals and the means by which they are to be attained.

THE CRISES OF MODERNIZATION

Party systems may also be appraised in the context of the general process of modernization. As a traditional society breaks up and takes on the characteristics of "modernity," it goes through a series of political crises. The first is a crisis of *legitimacy*. Values sanctioning rule by a traditional monarchy or aristocracy are called into question and are eventually replaced by values such as parliamentary democracy or nationalism that are more consonant with mass participation in the political system. This goes hand-in-hand with a crisis of *participation*. New social groups, in particular an industrial middle class and a working class, make their appearance and demand entry into the political system. In mature industrial societies there is a continuing crisis of *conflict management*. The political system is confronted by the need to facilitate economic growth, reconcile the claims of powerful social groups for a greater share of wealth and power, and ensure the continued adherence of these groups to the system itself.

Political parties have gone through stages of development that correspond to the successive crises of legitimacy, participation, and conflict management. Parties throughout Europe in the early part of the nineteenth century were primarily concerned with new principles of legitimacy and the representation of fairly narrow interests. With the extension of suffrage in the course of the nineteenth century the parties created mass organizations outside of parliament. Mass parties, like the German Social Democrat, British Liberal, and, later, Labor parties, sought to defend the interests of the new middle and working classes and to mobilize popular support for their policies. At this stage the parties tended to reflect sharp ideological orientations. The "parties of participation" had to make adjustments in order to cope with the demands of late industrialization, when problems became more complex and less susceptible to ideological solutions. They became more concerned with the management of conflict and tensions when in power, and more pragmatic in their appeals to the electorate.

One of the most noticeable trends affecting parties at present is the development of plebiscitary government. Its main trait is the bypassing or the diminution of the powers of all representative bodies in favor of personalized leadership stemming from direct popular support in periodic elections. In France under the Gaullist constitution, the President, as the political leader and head of the executive, now derives his powers from direct election. This is also the case for the American president and the British cabinet under the leadership of the prime minister, who is head of the majority party. The political parties select and nominate a leader who then appeals directly to the public. Although the parties may set broad policy guidelines, the personal appeal of leaders and their ability to secure widespread support may be the decisive factor for victory or defeat at the polls.

In France, plebiscitary government has an old and venerable lineage that goes back to Bonapartism. In all countries it is a reflection of profound social changes that have led to an increasingly homogeneous body politic. Under these altered circumstances the parties can no longer sell their ideological or policy programs. Large national formations vie for support on the basis of broadly similar appeals to consumer interests. As a result, identification with the party becomes weaker, or, to put it another way, the personality of a leader becomes more important. Correspondingly, the ratio of party members to voters, for the whole community and for each party, goes down, while there are growing numbers of independents or "floaters."

In authoritarian systems the ruling party excludes competition and uses the election as a well-controlled plebiscitary instrument. In presidential systems nonparty people may, without any prior screening or testing, avail themselves of the plebiscitary character of the election. Even in Britain and other parliamentary democracies the struggle for leadership of the party, and certainly the general election itself, is greatly influenced by the personal qualities of the contending leaders. The logic of plebiscitary government applies to both Western democracies and authoritarian systems. The intermediary organs—including the parties and representative assemblies—are weakened, and power is concentrated in the political executive. A continuing problem in all modern political systems is to create institutions that might counterbalance the tremendous political and decision-making powers of plebiscitary leaders.

······························

CONSTITUTIONS

The general organization and structure of authority is in essence a "constitution." Whether written or unwritten a constitution expresses the "fundamental agreement" of the political society on how it will be governed. It usually defines the scope of governmental authority, the way in which decisions are made, and the manner in which decision makers are selected and held accountable. It both creates and limits power. The legacy of the Middle Ages was to define rights that limit arbitrary power and narrow the scope of the state's authority. With the beginning of the nineteenth century most political systems began to establish responsibility of the governors to the through representative assemblies and periodic elections.

A system in which a constitution is widely accepted may be referred to as *consensual;* that is, the people in it agree on how they will resolve their differences. They do not "bicker about fundamentals." Political systems may well be classified, therefore, in terms of this criterion. In some systems the agreement on fundamentals is not widely shared or intensely felt—they have a *low degree of consensus or legitimacy.* In others, there is no such agreement—they are *highly divided or transitional systems.* In still others, the agreement is overtly manufactured through the control of the media of communication by a small group of political leaders—this is the case in authoritarian systems. But authoritarianism is not in itself evidence of low consensus, for in some cases leadership may bring about a high degree of unity and perhaps popular support.

The distinction between consensual and highly divided systems may be illustrated by the cases of Great Britain and France. In both countries the feudal scheme was disrupted, the traditional monarchy was severely restricted or overthrown, and parliamentary democracy was introduced. The British monarch during the seventeenth century proved to be less adaptable than the French. The loss of its prerogatives was registered in the Declaration and Bill of Rights of 1689. That is, by the end of the seventeenth century parliamentary sovereignty was enunciated as the basic principle of the British constitution. Political conflict did not disappear, and the monarch continued to exert great influence upon ministers and Parliament. With the extension of suffrage in the nineteenth century, the political base of the House of Commons was transformed. Its legitimacy now derived from the people, whose will was expressed and shaped by mass political parties. These new forces accepted the venerable principle of parliamentary sovereignty and the practice of parliamentary government.

The new interests and classes created by the Industrial Revolution thus found a ready-made instrument for the resolution of their conflicts. Slowly the system absorbed, or rather integrated, the new groups, notably the industrial middle class and the workers. But in so doing the political institutions were themselves greatly modified. The country was governed not by an independent and narrowly based House of Commons, but rather by disciplined parties, the cabinet, and the civil service. The need for strong leadership and the increasing importance of the personality of the leader strengthened the position of the prime minister; on the other hand, the growing complexity of administration made it difficult for the cabinet to function as a collective agency. The trend in the modern era has been toward the concentration of power in the prime minister, who dominates the cabinet much as the cabinet previously dominated Parliament.

In France and other countries of the continent, a different situation prevailed. Parliaments in these countries knew an uneasy and eventful life, becoming the source of unresolved opposition to the powers of the king or the nobility. The French representative assemblies were not allowed to meet for over a century and a half. When finally they met in 1789, they set aside the powers of the king and ushered in a period of turmoil. A democratic constitution was accepted only by a part of the population. The nineteenth century was a period of conflict and struggle in which sometimes democracy and sometimes monarchy or personal government (Bonapartism) triumphed. The working classes found it impossible to accommodate themselves to one or the other form and developed a utopian or revolutionary outlook. Thus by the end of the nineteenth century there was no widespread agreement in France about any constitution; sizable fractions of the population had not been integrated into the system; and people remained divided not only about interests and aspirations but also on how they should resolve their conflicts. The French found it difficult to "agree on how they were to disagree."

Throughout the nineteenth and twentieth centuries, constitutional instability was also the rule in most other European countries where sharp incompatibilities and ideological divisions were very much in evidence. The threat of revolutionary uprising by the underprivileged groups that had never been fully integrated into the system was ever present. The Bolshevik Revolution of 1917 gave sharpness and meaning to their demands. The Nazi system in Germany and, to a lesser degree, the fascist system in Italy, gave hope to the wealthier groups, to the military, to some of the conservative elements of the Church, and to the many lower-middle-class groups that a "strong" government based on one-party rule could provide stability and unity. Both the Bolshevik and Fascist movements imperiled democratic constitutionalism and provided their followers with an armed vision that undermined the tolerance and agreement on which democracy rests.

All West European political systems, including those that went through periods of authoritarianism and instability (notably major powers such as France, Germany, Italy, and Spain), and Japan, are now stable democracies with roughly similar levels of prosperity, literacy, and education, compared to the rest of the world. Nonetheless, the paths followed by these countries to democracy and modernity make each political system distinctive. Even when past regimes were repudiated (for example, monarchy and fascism in France, fascism in Germany and Italy, most recently communism in Russia), patterns of behavior and sometimes parts of institutional structures persist. French political life is still affected by the tradition of state centralization dating from the old regime and personal rule combined with rationalization of society and economic advance under the Bonapartes; similarly, German political life still shows traces of the bureaucratic and elitist traditions of nineteenth-century Prussia. The receptivity of electorates to extremist parties today reflects favorable memories by some groups of past experience with authoritarianism and revolution. Deep cleavages in the past have a disconcerting way of resurfacing in times of crisis. As democracies confront the challenges of late modernization (amply documented in the readings in this volume), whether or not their governments in the past rested upon a large consensus becomes a critical factor in the making of effective policy.

GOVERNMENTAL INSTITUTIONS

The decision-making functions of all political societies have been divided traditionally into three separate types: the executive, the legislative, and the judicial. However, this threefold division is not a realistic guide to the exercise of political power. In some systems the legislature assumed the totality of decision-making power, with the executive simply executing the will of the lawmakers and the judiciary applying and interpreting the law in case of litigation. In other instances, a precarious balance between the executive and the legislature was established, with the executive slowly assuming increased powers and independence of action. In other systems—notably those with a federal organization of power—the judiciary emerged as a genuinely independent organ with wide latitude to interpret the constitution and in so doing to limit the powers of the legislature and the executive.

The nineteenth century was the period of legislative supremacy in most of the Western constitutional democracies. Walter Bagehot, writing in the latter part to the century, pointed out that the Parliament nominated the members of the executive, passed laws, prepared and voted the budget, supervised the cabinet, and finally aired grievances and ventilated issues, thus helping to mold and shape public opinion. It was primarily a body of people who represented the upper and middle classes of the community, who fundamentally agreed about the policies to be pursued, and who embodied the complacency and stability of the Victorian period. They usually debated broad political problems—educational reform, extension of the franchise, the rights of associations and individuals, and international treaties. Controversy was resolved in compromise that could be spelled out in general parliamentary enactments. This was also the case in some other systems in which parliamentary democracy developed—Sweden, Holland, Norway, and Denmark. In the United States the pendulum swung between "presidential" government, especially in times of crisis, and "congressional" government.

On the continent representative assemblies were often regarded as the instruments of popular rule against the privileged groups. They claimed on behalf of the people the totality of political power, and they relegated the executive to the role of an agent. This was notably the case of France, where the legislative assemblies reduced the cabinet to a subservient role.

Outside of Western Europe, North America, and the British Dominions, representative government in the nineteenth century was virtually unknown. In Eastern Europe and Latin America, constitutions and parliamentary institutions were provided on paper, but the practice belied the constitutional forms. Most of these systems were oligarchies in which political power, irrespective of the forms, was in the hands of the landowners, the military, or the Church. Others were traditional societies, in which political rule was hereditary. They had not experienced the conflicts and modernization, associated with the French Revolution and industrialization, that led to progressive political emancipation of the masses in Europe. Their political systems were encrusted in tradition and immemorial custom.

With the beginning of the twentieth century, an important change in the organization and functioning of democratic institutions can be discerned. The internal balance of power between the three organs—executive, legislative, and judicial—began to shift in favor of the executive. This trend reflects profound modifications in the social and political structures of modern societies.

Representative institutions operated well when the pressure upon them to make decisions was light. The free-market system provided an automatic mechanism of decision-making. Matters of wages, hours of work, employment, social security, education, technological improvement, investment, and economic development were largely outside of the province of the state. The increasing complexity of the industrial society called, however, for regulation of economic activity. The need for state intervention grew, leading to an immense expansion of the state bureaucracy. Today roughly 40 percent of the gross national product in a modern democracy is appropriated by the state in order to pay for administrative expenses as well as to redistribute national income. In the 1970s a conservative movement (led by Margaret Thatcher in the United Kingdom, Ronald Reagan in the United States) sought to reduce the role of the state; it succeeded in bringing down the rate of expansion of bureaucracy, not in actually reducing its size.

Running a complex economy, and deciding how to divide responsibility between the state and civil society (including the market), demands special knowledge and skill. Legislatures proved singularly unfit to perform these tasks. The legislature was cumbersome; its members had neither technical knowledge, nor expertise, nor time. Slowly the burden of decision making shifted to the political executive and the civil service.

Political reasons also accounted for this shift. Most significant were the extension of suffrage and the growth of large national parties. The two phenomena are historically associated. Elections increasingly became confrontations between two or more parties appealing to a mass electorate on specific issues or on a general program for action. Thus the legislature was bypassed, for victory at the polls meant that the leadership of the majority party would form a government to carry out its pledges. Wherever party discipline was strong, therefore, popular elections were equivalent to the selection of the "government," i.e., the executive.

Political and technical trends reinforced each other, and during the interwar years the executive assumed more and more powers. Representative assemblies have lost virtually all of the functions attributed to them by Walter Bagehot in the nineteenth century. The vast majority of legislative projects emanate from the executive; the preparation of the budget has become an executive function in which the cabinet, in association with the top civil service or independent executive bodies, drafts the specifications involving public expenditures and revenue. Parliament has even virtually lost the power to nominate the cabinet. Finally, the very scope of lawmaking has changed. Special laws or regulations are needed that can best be made by those in touch with the problems of developed societies—that is to say, by the executive departments and the civil service. Thus the legislature has fallen into the habit of drafting general laws in which regulatory powers are generously delegated to the executive. For all practical purposes such delegation is so broad as to invest the executive and civil service with virtual lawmaking powers.

In modern political systems, then, leadership has shifted to the executive. Legislatures continue to play a role in focusing public attention on policy problems, and sometimes in investigating corruption and abuses of power. But the executive has taken the initiative as regards general lawmaking, foreign and defense policy, and direction of the economy. Assumption of these responsibilities and the concentration of these functions in the executive branch have led to a proliferation of new agencies and bureaus. The political executive has become "bureaucratized." It initiates policy, coordinates policy decisions, and is responsible for their implementation and execution. Institutions corresponding to these three phases of the policy-making process have developed within the executive.

In both presidential and parliamentary systems, a small group of political leaders is in charge of overall policy initiation and formulation. They are the president (or the prime minister) and his or her immediate advisers. To assist the top leaders in the formulation of policy there are a number of "adjunct" administrative staff organizations. They draft policy papers on economic planning, foreign policy, defense, and the budget. In the United States, the Office of Management and the Budget, the National Security Council, and the Council of Economic Advisers perform important deliberative and policy-initiation functions. In Britain and France, cabinet and presidential committees are responsible for similar activities. Thus deliberation is institutionalized at the executive level.

Policy proposals put forward by various executive agencies must then be coordinated. Suggestions and countersuggestions are thrashed out in the cabinet, or in small ministerial committees made up of top civil servants, the chiefs of staff, and the personal advisers to the president or prime minister. Reconciliation of conflicting proposals may require the ultimate personal intervention of the president or prime minister. The interdependence of military, economic, and foreign policy has called increasingly for such interdepartmental coordination.

Finally, it is necessary to implement decisions. This is the task of the vast majority of civil servants—to inspect, repair, perform, and check. They do what the employees of any large corporation do—they perform on the basis of orders and regulations decided by their superiors.

THE BUREAUCRACY

It is one of the characteristics of industrial societies, irrespective of their form of government, to develop a civil service recruited on the basis of specific technical requirements. "Bureaucratic administration means fundamentally the exercise of control on the basis of knowledge," observed Max Weber. It is above all a rational organization characterized by: (1) a clearly defined sphere of competence subject to impersonal rules; (2) a hierarchy that determines in an orderly fashion relations of superiors and subordinates; (3) a regular system of appointments and promotions based on free contract; (4) recruitment on the basis of skills, knowledge, or technical training; and (5) fixed salaries.

The Prussian civil service was an early example of a professional service with clear-cut demarcation of spheres of competence, rigid rules of recruitment, and allocation of posts on the basis of skills. It reflected the high degree of military organization and centralization of that country.

In Great Britain professionalization was introduced officially in 1853 by the Northcote-Trevelyan Report on the "Organization of the Permanent Civil Service," which opened the civil service to talent through competitive examinations. Until then civil service appointments were made on political considerations and were, by and large, restricted to the nobility. The civil service was divided into three "classes," each corresponding to a distinct function: (1) the administrative class, which is the highest policy-making group within the departments; (2) the executive class, whose main task is the execution of policies; and (3) the clerical or manipulative class, whose work is primarily clerical and manual. A recent reform introduced a single-tier system in order to encourage greater mobility and flexibility, but the old distinctions have persisted in practice.

In France it was only after the Liberation in 1944 that drastic reforms—inspired in large measure by the organization of the civil service in Britain—were made. First, a general entrance examination was established for all candidates: previously, each department did its own recruiting. The examination stresses law, political science, economics, and social sciences in general. Second, the civil service was broadly divided into two classes: (1) civil administrators (approximating the British administrative class) and (2) "secretaries of administration" (corresponding to the executive class). Third, the *Ecole Nationale d'Administration* was founded to serve as the training school for all prospective civil administrators. Students are considered public officials from the moment they enter, they receive a stipend, and after successful completion of their studies and the passing of the final examinations they are assigned to an executive department. Throughout their training, which is jointly offered by civil servants and academicians, an effort is made to depart from the formalistic and legalistic approach so typical of the past and to create a self-reliant and imaginative civil servant.

The American civil service has also been "professionalized," beginning with the Pendleton Act of 1883. Recruitment is by competitive examinations, but the emphasis tends to be on specialized knowledge rather than a broad, liberal education. There is no clear-cut division between an administrative and an executive class in terms of rigidly separate educational requirements and examinations, though of course those who occupy the highest "general classes" within the hierarchy in effect perform the policy-making function. The American civil service thus is not as homogeneous as its European counterparts. American top-level administrators are graduates of universities all over the nation and are drawn from a wider range of social classes. There is also considerable movement of individuals between the civil service and private life (business, universities, and law practice, for example), not common in Europe. The undoubted advantage of the European system is the creation of a corps of administrators who have demonstrated brilliance in academic studies during their youth and who have shared common experiences; the result is a remarkable *esprit de corps*. In the United States, on the other hand, it is easier to invigorate the administrative establishment by providing new recruits from private life, and also to make use of talented individuals who may not have distinguished themselves in universities.

Traditionally "bureaucracy" has been viewed as an instrument of enforcement and execution of the law. Impartial and neutral—at least in theory—it was also remote, incarnating the authority and majesty of the state. It emphasized legality rather than equity, application of rules rather than innovation, continuity rather than change. The civil servant (or "mandarin" as called by the French) remained aloof from everyday affairs, saw more files than citizens, and made decisions of a quasi-judicial character.

But in some respects modern bureaucracy has departed from the Weberian model of a legal-rational organization. The increase in sheer numbers and the expansion of functions produced profound changes. The civil servant became ubiquitous and, as a result, less aloof and remote from the society that was governed. By taking on new responsibilities, bureaucrats were transformed from guardians of the law into quasi-legislators. Their powers became increasingly political and had immediate consequences for those affected by their decisions and for the whole society. The bureaucrats' world was expanded, and they began to view their constituency not as a host of individual plaintiffs who sought redress in accordance with the law, but as groups and interests pressing for decisions affecting the very nature of social relations. They found themselves confronted with conflicts among interests that called for political analysis and choice among alternatives. While still clinging to the tradition of statism and neutrality, the bureaucrat and the bureaucracy as a whole became integral parts of the policy-making process.

The civil servants' mentality inevitably changed when they entered the realm of direct action in the world of commerce and industry. The skills required to set regulations for, let us say, credit, are different from those needed to apply laws in individual cases. The people responsible for the use of atomic energy to produce electricity, for construction of new cities, for settlement of labor disputes, or for maintenance of full employment no longer resemble their nineteenth-century counterparts. The requisites of bureaucratic decision making are knowledge, expertise, originality, inventiveness, and an ability to gain cooperation and support from the interests involved. Civil servants who participate in the drafting of an economic plan must not only know their own jobs, but must be in touch with the interest groups that are affected by the plan.

Consultation between organized interests and the civil service has become general. The old bureaucracy based on "imperative coordination" has become a "consultative" bureaucracy making decisions that affect the whole society, thoroughly permeated by the interests it serves. Interest groups in the past have attempted to colonize, influence, or neutralize the bureaucracy, and they usually tried to maintain anonymity while doing so. Now the dialogue is open, the anonymity has been shed, and decisions engage the responsibility of the civil servants who make them. The bureaucracy thus takes on some of the characteristics of political parites in seeking close ties with specific interests (like business or labor) and broad popular support from all consumers and citizens. The "mandarin" has become a manager and a politician, and the spokepersons of interest groups and executives of private corporations are directly involved in the decision-making process. A "new corporatism" seems to be emerging in all modern political systems.

The executive has thus become in all contemporary industrialized societies a huge bureaucracy in which millions of people work and perform thousands of interrelated tasks. A small group of people are ultimately responsible for the policies made and the manner in which they are implemented. They alone have to confront the public in periodic elections and give an account of their activities. They have to answer questions raised in the representative assemblies and reply to criticism. They have the burden of political responsibility—and this applies to authoritarian and democratic systems alike, though the forms of enforcement may differ.

But political responsibility, even when enforced through periodic elections and accountability to legislative assemblies, is not enough. The magnitude and the complexity of modern government are so great that no legislature (not even through its committees) can take full cognizance of them. Legislative control has often proven inadequate for effective supervision of the operations of nationalized industries, the performance of regulatory agencies, and many other technical decisions.

A crucial problem facing all democratic systems today is to devise other forms and techniques of executive accountability. One possibility is the development of a sense of "internal responsibility" within the civil service itself. This can be inculcated by education and the development of strict rules of performance and rules of accountability of subordinate to superior. Another technique often suggested is the creation of specialized legislative committees to deal with specific areas of executive activity—nationalized industries, delegated legislation, defense, and the budget. A third one is the establishment of advisory bodies in which the major interests affected by policy decisions may participate. One recent innovation has been the creation of an Ombudsman (Grievance Person) in Scandinavian countries to hear appeals by citizens who have complaints against the state. A number of countries, including Britain, France, Germany, and Italy, have experimented with "mediators" (the term usually used) between citizens and the administration, but they have so far played only a modest role. None of the above techniques appear to be fully successful, and the truth of the matter is that they cannot be. The notion of "political responsibility" appears to be increasingly anachronistic in an era of massive technological development. The leaders of any modern society—democratic or authoritarian—confront the challenge of implementing common aspirations. Success or failure depends mainly upon the technical competence and skill of the political leadership.

The growth of the executive and its assumption of policy-making functions, the tremendous expansion of public services coupled with the ineffectiveness of political controls over the bureaucracy, pose serious threats to individual freedom. A highly complex bureaucratized apparatus geared to performance is potentially an ever-present danger to the individual, even when it claims to serve his or her interests. To the old "reason of state" may be added a new, perhaps even more dangerous "reason of service." Managerialism or *technocratie,* as the French call it, may finish by exalting efficiency, skill, and organization over criticism, freedom, and individualism. It may encourage conformity rather than eccentricity, unity rather than pluralism, action rather than thought, and discipline rather than freedom.

The rise of the large bureaucratized state as well as the example of totalitarianism have aroused widespread concern for the protection of individual rights and freedoms. In some post-Second World War constitutions, higher courts were given power to scrutinize legislative acts and see to it that the legislative and executive branches remained within the confines of the constitution. In West Germany, Italy, Austria, France, Spain, and Portugal, constitutional courts were established for this purpose. In both Britain and the United States administrative courts have been created to try cases involving litigation between the state and individuals. "Administrative law," long misunderstood by American and British observers of the French scene, has developed slowly as a guarantee of the rights of individuals in their dealings with the administrative and regulatory agencies of the state.

Other safeguards have also been sought. Federalism, for instance, has as a major purpose internal limitation upon the omnicompetence of the state. Even in unitary states like Britain and France, efforts have been made to revitalize local governments in order to stimulate experimentation and avert uniformity and rigidity of centralized control.

Judicial review, administrative law, and federalism are undeniably valuable counterweights to concentrated power at the center, but they have not been sufficient to bring bureaucracy under effective political or legal control. How to protect citizens by enforcing responsibility of those who govern complex societies remains a major political problem.

EFFECTIVENESS AND PERFORMANCE

All social groups have goals or purposes in terms of which their discipline is justified. The effectiveness of the organization— be it church, trade union, corporation, or state—must be appraised in relation to its success in achieving stated goals. An army, for example, has well-defined goals: the application of superior firepower at a given point or, more broadly, defense of the country. An army is disciplined—command and obedience relations are established in unequivocal fashion, and criticism of its code is severely limited. It is an organization geared to performance, so that an order by a single chief moves masses of men and equipment. The efficiency of the "army model" accounts for widespread admiration of autocratic and authoritarian political systems and constantly feeds the antidemocratic schools of thought. Lenin fashioned his theory of the Communist party after the army model, calling for rigorous discipline and total commitment of its members. Many of the symbols of fascist and other authoritarian parties are borrowed from the military. Order, discipline, and unquestioning obedience are equated with performance and effectiveness.

The army is a single or limited-purpose organization. Politics, on the other hand, entails regulation and control of a society that contains many organizations, each striving to attain unique and frequently divergent goals. The family, school, church, corporation, and university are concerned with such distinctly different activities as reproduction of the species, rearing of the young, education, religion, industrial production, and the acquisition of scientific knowledge. The state is not only a relationship of command and obedience; it also involves conciliation and supports. Complex societies are participant societies. The "army model" is relevant only to the coercive aspect of a political system.

As Karl Deutsch suggests in his *Nerves of Government,*[6] a political system may be viewed as complex sets of messages with a communication system that has been learned and internalized by all members of the society. A structured and learned communication system makes the government a sensitive instrument for the satisfaction of demands and interests of the citizens, and it also makes the citizens receptive to the needs and directives of the government. The government and citizens are mutually supportive.

The "communications model" is useful in analyzing performance. It suggests that obedience to commands is learned and willed; that the government is constantly listening to the messages that come from all social groups and individuals; that so long as official directives are generally consonant with demands and expectations they are likely to be obeyed—indeed, obedience is taken for granted; and that if such a pattern of relations is established over a period of time the relationship between government and citizens will become intimate and positive, characterized by marked interdependence and mutual trust. The capabilities of the government to act are immense because it can count on popular support. It can mobilize the citizenry for common purposes.

But what are these common purposes? In terms of what criteria is the effectiveness of a political system to be appraised? Every political society sets for itself varying goals, both specific (such as the creation of the infrastructure of a modern economy) and broad (the realization of values like equality or freedom). Comparison of political systems in terms of performance is difficult: What is considered success in one society may be failure in another, for their goals or values may be entirely different. There are, however, some generally accepted ends to which all political systems are committed—the survival of their societies in a hostile world; the maintenance of order; and the resolution of conflicting demands and the allocation of goods in a manner that provides maximum satisfaction for all. The system must be able to maintain itself as it adjusts to constantly changing environmental factors. It must resolve problems as they arise and provide mechanisms for settling them.

A consensual democratic system derives its strength from the open communication between state and society. It contains a responsive mechanism that permits the articulation of interests and demands on the part of the governed, gears its decisions to those demands, and, by so doing, elicits supports that can again be converted into a resource for the achievement of common ends. Emerging conflicts engage the attention of government and citizens so that the way is paved for their resolution. Broad participation in the system and the open nature of communications guarantee acceptance of policy and help legitimize the state. A consensual system does not hesitate to arm the citizens, to draft them into the army, and to decree stringent measures calling for individual restraints in order to safeguard collective ends.

But consensus is never universal in complex societies. The very openness of communications in democratic regimes permits dissident elements ample opportunity to clash with each other and with the government. Indeed, dissidence may be so widespread that no majority can form, and the ability of the political system to formulate public policy is reduced. Authoritarian regimes do not enjoy the advantages of an open communication system between leaders and the people. Because the citizens do not have the right to express their criticism, it is difficult for those in power to understand the nature of popular expectations and to assess the effectiveness of policy. There is always a danger of solving political problems by violence, which includes popular uprisings as well as repression by the state. But some dictatorships have demonstrated a remarkable ability to mobilize popular energies and resources and to promulgate effective policy. This requires exceptional dynamism and perspicacity on the part of the leaders, who in effect give the people what they want without going through the bother of inquiring beforehand or afterward. The citizens may be reasonably content, even if they have no opportunity to criticize, under conditions of full employment and material progress, and especially if the regime succeeds in embodying nationalistic sentiment. Military victory is also a good way of arousing popular enthusiasm for any regime, democratic or authoritarian. Popular support for authoritarian regimes is most likely in countries that have been governed previously by ineffective parliamentary democracies. It is noteworthy that the most important dictatorships in modern Europe—bolshevism in Russia, fascism in Italy, and nazism in Germany—all replaced nonconsensual and ineffective democracies.

ENDNOTES

1. See Max Weber, *The Theory of Social and Economic Organization,* London: Oxford University Press, 1947, pp. 407–412.
2. See James Bryce's preface to M. Ostrogorski, *Democracy and the Organization of Political Parties,* New York: Macmillan, 1902, and Robert Michels, reprinted below.
3. See A. D. Lindsay, *The Modern Democratic State,* New York, 1947; R. M. MacIver, *The Web of Government,* New York, 1947; Carl J. Friedrich, *Constitutional Government and Democracy,* Boston, 1946; Joseph Schumpeter, *Capitalism, Socialism and Democracy,* New York, 1947; and Walter Lippmann, *Public Opinion,* New York, 1945.
4. See the argument in R. T. McKenzie, *British Political Parties,* London, 1955.
5. M. Duverger, *Les partis politiques,* Paris: Armand Colin, 1954, p. 465.
6. Karl Deutsch, *Nerves of Government,* rev. ed., New York: Free Press, 1966.

CHAPTER TEN

POLITICAL PARTIES

Much of the literature on political parties deals with organization and structure, or the relationship between militants and their leaders. The position of members within parties is analogous to that of the people within a democratic state. In neither case can the masses directly control the organization that acts in their name. All large groups, including political parties, are run by a band of interested persons united by a common set of beliefs or desire for power, or both. Political parties are especially susceptible to oligarchic tendencies. If a party is decentralized and undisciplined, no machinery exists to be used by the membership in order to make their control effective. In well-organized parties elaborate provision is made for consultation of the rank-and-file in party congresses and conventions. But the party leadership, when united, can dominate proceedings. The rank-and-file may play an important role only when mobilized by rival leaders. The classic discussion of oligarchy is in Robert Michels, *Political Parties,* excerpted below. Can Michels's "iron law of oligarchy" be falsified? Can the student find any party or large group in which a mass membership takes the initiative and dispenses with leaders? Or can oligarchs be controlled only within a larger system of checks and balances, including the right of other parties (even if oligarchic) to oppose or govern?

Gunther and Diamond present a comprehensive classification of parties based on three criteria: organization, program, and long-term strategy, leading them to distinguish fifteen different "species" of parties. They point out that their models of parties are *ideal types*, in the sense used by Max Weber, enabling us to understand a complex reality. Real parties do not conform fully to all features of any model. But conceptualizing parties on the basis of the model permits us to see differences between parties and understand their evolution from one type to another. Readers will wish to test the utility of the model with reference to political parties in individual party systems, for example the major parties in the United States as compared to parties in any other advanced democracy.

For the authors, the purpose of a classification is to facilitate the formulation and testing of hypotheses leading to explanatory theory. What kind of hypotheses are suggested by this classification? How can the evolution of parties and party systems be related to crises in the modernizing process: legitimacy (replacement of traditional by more rational institutions), participation (mobilization and organization of social classes produced by industrialization), and tension-management (need for effective policy, especially in post-industrial societies)? Is it possible to identify stages in the evolution of parties?

Seymour Martin Lipset contends that the European Left has become "Americanized," and Piero Ignazi believes that left libertarian/Green and extreme Right-wing parties are diverging outcomes of post-industrial (or post-materialist) societies. Does the classification and perspective offered by Gunther and Diamond help us better understand the phenomena described by Lipset and Ignazi?

ROBERT MICHELS

34   The Iron Law of Oligarchy

DEMOCRACY AND ARISTOCRACY

In modern party life aristocracy gladly presents itself in democratic guise while the substance of democracy is permeated with aristocratic elements. On the one side we have aristocracy in a democratic form, and on the other democracy with an aristocratic content.

The democratic external form which characterizes the life of political parties may readily veil from superficial observers the tendency toward aristocracy, or rather toward oligarchy, which is inherent in all party organization. If we wish to obtain light upon this tendency, the best field of observation is offered by the intimate structure of the democratic parties, and, among these, of the socialist and revolutionary labor party. In the conservative parties, except during elections, the tendency to oligarchy manifests itself with that spontaneous vigor and clearness which corresponds with the essentially oligarchical character of these parties. But the parties which are subversive in their aims exhibit the like phenomena no less markedly. The study of the oligarchical manifestations in party life is most valuable

SOURCE: Robert Michels, *Political Parties: a Sociological Study of the Oligarchic Tendencies of Modern Democracy*, New York: Dover Publications, 1959. First published in Germany in 1912, and in the United States in 1915.

and most decisive in its results when undertaken in relation to the revolutionary parties, for the reason that these parties, in respect of origin and of program, represent the negation of any such tendency, and have actually come into existence out of opposition thereto. Thus the appearance of oligarchical phenomena in the very bosom of the revolutionary parties is conclusive proof of the existence of immanent oligarchical tendencies in every kind of human organization which strives for the attainment of definite ends. . . .

THE NEED FOR ORGANIZATION

Democracy is inconceivable without organization. A few words will suffice to demonstrate this proposition.

A class which unfurls in face of society the banner of certain definite claims, and which aspires to be the realization of a complex of ideal aims deriving from the economic functions which that class fulfills, needs an organization. Be the claims economic or be they political, organization appears the only means for the creation of a collective will. Organization, based as it is upon the principle of least effort, that is to say, upon the greatest possible economy of energy, is the weapon of the weak in their struggle with the strong.

The chances of success in any struggle will depend upon the degree to which this struggle is carried out upon a basis of solidarity between individuals whose interests are identical. In objecting, therefore, to the theories of the individualist anarchists that nothing could please the employers better than the dispersion and disaggregation of the forces of the workers, the socialists, the most fanatical of all the partisans of the idea of organization, enunciate an argument which harmonizes well with the results of scientific study of the nature of parties.

We live in a time in which the idea of cooperation has become so firmly established that even millionaires perceive the necessity of common action. It is easy to understand, then, that organization has become a vital principle in the working class, for in default of it their success is *a priori* impossible. The refusal of the worker to participate in the collective life of his class cannot fail to entail disastrous consequences. In respect of culture and of economic, physical, and physiological conditions, the proletarian is the weakest element of our society. In fact, the isolated member of the working classes is defenseless in the hands of those who are economically stronger. It is only by combination to form a structural aggregate that the proletarians can acquire the faculty of political resistance and attain to a social dignity. The importance and the influence of the working class are directly proportional to its numerical strength. But for the representation of that numerical strength organization and coordination are indispensable. The principle of organization is an absolutely essential condition for the political struggle of the masses.

Yet the politically necessary principle of organization, while it overcomes that disorganization of forces which would be favorable to the adversary, brings other dangers in its train. We escape Scylla only to dash ourselves on Charybdis. Organization is, in fact, the source from which the conservative currents flow over the plain of democracy, occasioning there disastrous floods and rendering the plain unrecognizable. . . .

Is it impossible for a democratic party to practice a democratic policy, for a revolutionary party to pursue a revolutionary policy? Must we say that not *socialism* alone, but even a socialistic *policy*, is utopian?

Within certain narrow limits, the democratic party, even when subjected to oligarchical control, can doubtless act upon the state in the democratic sense. The old political caste of society, and above all the "state" itself, are forced to undertake the revaluation of a considerable number of values—a revaluation both ideal and practical. The importance attributed to the masses increases, even when the leaders are demagogues. The legislature and the executive become accustomed to yield, not only to claims proceeding from above, but also to those proceeding from below. This may give rise, in practice, to great inconveniences, such as we recognize in the recent history of all the states under a parliamentary regime; in theory, however, this new order of things signifies an incalculable progress in respect of public rights, which thus come to conform better with the principles of social justice. This evolution will, however, be arrested from the moment when the governing classes succeed in attracting within the governmental orbit their enemies of the extreme left, in order to convert them into collaborators. Political organization leads to power. But power is always conservative. In any case, the influence exercised upon the governmental machine by an energetic opposition party is necessarily slow, is subject to frequent interruptions, and is always restricted by the nature of oligarchy. . . .

As the organization increases in size, the struggle for great principles becomes impossible. It may be noticed that in the democratic parties of today the great conflicts of view are fought out to an ever-diminishing extent in the field of ideas and with the weapons of pure theory, that they therefore degenerate more and more into personal struggles and invectives, to be settled finally upon considerations of a purely superficial character. The efforts made to cover internal dissensions with a pious veil are the inevitable outcome of organization based upon bureaucratic principles, for, since the chief aim of such an organization is to enroll the greatest possible number of members, every struggle on behalf of ideas within the limits of the organization is necessarily regarded as an obstacle to the realization of its ends, an obstacle, therefore, which must be avoided in every possible way. This tendency is reinforced by the parliamentary character of the political party. "Party organization" signifies the aspiration for the greatest number of members. "Parliamentarism" signifies the aspiration for the greatest number of votes. The principal fields of party activity are electoral agitation and direct agitation to secure new members. What, in fact, is the modern political party? It is the methodical organization of the electoral masses. The socialist party, as a political aggregate endeavoring simultaneously to recruit members and to recruit votes, finds here its vital interests, for every decline in membership and every loss in voting strength diminishes its political prestige. Consequently great respect must be paid, not only to new members, but also to possible adherents, to those who in Germany are termed *mitläufer,* in Italy *simpatizzanti,* in Holland *geestverwanten,* and in England *sympathizers.* To avoid alarming these individuals, who are still outside the ideal worlds of socialism or democracy, the pursuit of a policy based on strict principle is shunned, while the consideration is ignored whether the numerical increase of the organization thus effected is not likely to be gained at the expense of its quality. . . .

THE IRON LAW OF OLIGARCHY

The party, regarded as an entity, as a piece of mechanism, is not necessarily identifiable with the totality of its members, and still less so with the class to which these belong. The party is created as a means to secure an end. Having, however, become an end in itself, endowed with aims and interests of its own, it undergoes detachment from the teleological point of view, from the class which it represents. In a party, it is far from obvious that the interests of the masses which have combined to form the party will coincide with the interests of the bureaucracy in which the party becomes personified. The interests of the body of employees are always conservative, and in a given political situation these interests may dictate a defensive and even a reactionary policy when the interests of the working class demand a bold and aggressive policy; in other cases, although these are very rare, the roles may be reversed. By a universally applicable social law, every organ of the collectivity, brought into existence through the need for the division of labor, creates for itself, as soon as it becomes consolidated, interests peculiar to itself. The existence of these special interests involves a necessary conflict with the interests of the collectivity. Nay, more, social strata fulfilling peculiar functions tend to become isolated, to produce organs fitted for the defense of their own peculiar interests. In the long run they tend to undergo transformation into distinct classes.

The sociological phenomena whose general characteristics have been discussed in this chapter and in preceding ones offer numerous vulnerable points to the scientific opponents of democracy. These phenomena would seem to prove beyond dispute that society cannot exist without a "dominant" or "political" class, and that the ruling class, while its elements are subject to a frequent partial renewal, nevertheless constitutes the only factor of sufficiently durable efficacy in the history of human development. According to this view, the government, or, if the phrase be preferred, the state, cannot be anything other than the organization of a minority. It is the aim of this minority to impose upon the rest of society a "legal order," which is the outcome of the exigencies of dominion and of the exploitation of the mass of helots effected by the ruling minority, and can never be truly representative of the majority. The majority is thus permanently incapable of self-government. Even when the discontent of the masses culminates in a successful attempt to deprive the bourgeoisie of power, this is after all, so Mosca contends, effected only in appearance always and necessarily there springs from the masses a new organized minority which raises itself to the rank of a governing class. Thus the majority of human beings, in a condition of eternal tutelage, are predestined by tragic necessity to submit to the dominion of a small minority, and must be content to constitute the pedestal of an oligarchy. . . .

Thus the social revolution would not effect any real modification of the internal structure of the mass. The socialists might conquer, but not socialism, which would perish in the moment of its adherents' triumph. We are tempted to speak of this process as a tragicomedy in which the masses are content to devote all their energies to effecting a change of masters. All that is left for the workers is the honor "de participer an recrutement governmental."[1] The result seems a poor one, especially if we take into account the psychological fact that even the purest of idealists who attains to power for a few years is unable to escape the corruption which the exercise of power carries in its train. In France, in work-class circles, the phrase is current, *homme élu, homme foutu.*[2] The social revolution, like the political revolution, is equivalent to an operation by which, as the Italian proverb expresses it. "Si cambia il maestro di capella, ma la musica è sempre quella"[3]. . . .

History seems to teach us that no popular movement, however energetic and vigorous, is capable of producing profound and permanent changes in the social organism of the civilized world. The preponderant elements of the movement, the men who lead and nourish it, end by undergoing a gradual detachment from the masses, and are attracted within the orbit of the "political class." They perhaps contribute to this class a certain number of "new ideas," but they also endow it with more creative energy and enhanced practical intelligence, thus providing for the ruling class an ever-renewed youth. The "political class" (continuing to employ Mosca's convenient phrase) has unquestionably an extreme fine sense of its possibilities and its means of defense. It displays a remarkable force of attraction and a vigorous capacity for absorption which rarely fail to exercise an influence even upon the most embittered and uncompromising of its adversaries. From the historical point of view, the anti-romanticists are perfectly right when they sum up their scepticism in such caustic phraseology as this: "Qu'est ce qu'une révolution? Des gens qui se tirent des coups de fusil dans une rue: cela casse beaucoup de carreaux; il n'y a guère que les vitriers qui y trouvent du profit. Le vent emporte la fumée". . . .[4] Or we may say, as the song runs in *Madame Angot:* "Ce n'est pas la peine de changer de gouvernement!"[5] In France, the classic land of social theories and experiments, such pessimism has struck the deepest roots.

FINAL CONSIDERATIONS

We are led to conclude that the principal cause of oligarchy in the democratic parties is to be found in the technical indispensability of leadership.

The process which has begun in consequence of the differentiation of functions in the party is completed by a complex of qualities which the leaders acquire through their detachment from the mass. At the outset, leaders arise *spontaneously;* their functions are *accessory* and *gratuitous.* Soon, however, they become *professional* leaders, and in this second stage of development they are *stable* and *irremovable.*

It follows that the explanation of the oligarchical phenomenon which thus results is partly *psychological;* oligarchy derives, that is to say, from the psychical transformations which the leading personalities in the parties undergo in the course of their lives. But also, and still more, oligarchy depends upon what we may term the *psychology of organization* itself, that is to say, upon the tactical and technical necessities which result from the consolidation of every disciplined political aggregate. Reduced to its most concise expression, the fundamental sociological law of political parties (the term "political" being here used in its most comprehensive significance) may be formulated in the following terms: "It is organization which gives birth to the dominion of the elected over the electors, of the mandatories over the mandators, of the delegates over the delegators. Who says organization, says oligarchy."

Every party organization represents an oligarchical power grounded upon a democratic basis. We find everywhere electors and elected. Also we find everywhere that the power of the elected leaders over the electing masses is almost unlimited. The oligarchical structure of the building suffocates the basic democratic principle. That which *is* oppresses *that which ought to be.* For the masses, this essential difference between the reality and the ideal remains a mystery. Socialists often cherish a sincere belief that a new *élite* of politicians will keep faith better than did the old. The notion of the representation of popular interests, a notion to which the great majority of democrats, and especially the working-class masses of the German-speaking lands, cleave with so much tenacity and confidence, is an illusion engendered by a false illumination, is an effect of mirage. In one of the most delightful pages of his analysis of Modern Day Quixotism, Alphonse Daudet shows us how the "brav' commandant" Bravida, who has never quitted Tarascon, gradually comes to persuade himself, influenced by the burning southern sun, that he has been to Shanghai and has had all kinds of heroic adventures.[6] Similarly the modern proletariat, enduringly influenced by glib-tongued persons intellectually superior to the mass, ends by believing that by flocking to the poll and entrusting its social and economic cause to a delegate, its direct participation in power will be assured.

The formation of oligarchies within the various forms of democracy is the outcome of organic necessity, and consequently affects every organization, be it socialist or even anarchist. . . . In every form of social life relationships of dominion and of dependence are created by Nature herself. The supremacy of the leaders in the democratic and revolutionary parties has to be taken into account in every historic situation present and to come, even though only a few and exceptional minds will be fully conscious of its existence. The mass will never rule except *in abstracto*. Consequently the question we have to discuss is not whether ideal democracy is realizable, but rather to what point and in what degree democracy is desirable, possible, and realizable at a given moment. . . .

The objective immaturity of the mass is not a mere transitory phenomenon which will disappear with the progress of democratization *au lendemain du socialisme*. On the contrary, it derives from the very nature of the mass as mass, for this, even when organized, suffers from an incurable incompetence for the solution of the diverse problems which present themselves for solution—because the mass *per se* is amorphous, and therefore needs division of labor, specialization, and guidance. "L'espèce humaine veut être gouvernée; elle le sera. J'ai honte de mon espèce," wrote Proudhon from his prison in 1850.[7] Man as individual is by nature predestined to be guided, and to be guided all the more in proportion as the functions of life undergo division and subdivision. To an enormously greater degree is guidance necessary for the social group. . . .

The writer does not wish to deny that every revolutionary working-class movement, and every movement sincerely inspired by the democratic spirit may have a certain value as contributing to the enfeeblement of oligarchic tendencies. The peasant in the fable, when on his deathbed, tells his sons that a treasure is buried in the field. After the old man's death the sons dig everywhere in order to discover the treasure. They do not find it. But their indefatigable labor improves the soil and secures for them a comparative well-being. The treasure in the fable may well symbolize democracy. Democracy is a treasure which no one will ever discover by deliberate search. But in continuing our search, in laboring indefatigably to discover the indiscoverable, we shall perform a work which will have fertile results in the democratic sense. We have seen, indeed, that within the bosom of the democratic working-class party are born the very tendencies to counteract which that party came into existence. Thanks to the diversity and to the unequal worth of the elements of the party, these tendencies often give rise to manifestations which border on tyranny. We have seen that the replacement of the traditional legitimism of the powers-that-be by the brutal plebiscitary rule of Bonapartist parvenus does not furnish these tendencies with any moral or aesthetic superiority. Historical evolution mocks all the prophylactic measures that have been adopted for the prevention of oligarchy. If laws are passed to control the dominion of the leaders, it is the laws which gradually weaken, and not the leaders. . . .

In view of the perennial incompetence of the masses, we have to recognize the existence of two regulative principles—

1. The *ideological* tendency of democracy toward criticism and control;
2. The *effective* counter-tendency of democracy toward the creation of parties ever more complex and ever more differentiated—parties, that is to say, which are increasingly based upon the competence of the few.

To the idealist, the analysis of the forms of contemporary democracy cannot fail to be a source of bitter deceptions and profound discouragement.

Those alone, perhaps, are in a position to pass a fair judgement upon democracy who, without lapsing into dilettantist sentimentalism, recognize that all scientific and human ideals have relative values. If we wish to estimate the value of democracy, we must do so in comparison with its converse, pure aristocracy. The defects inherent in democracy are obvious. It is none the less true that as a form of social life we must choose democracy as the least of evils. The ideal government would doubtless be that of an aristocracy of persons at once morally good and technically efficient. But where shall we discover such an aristocracy? We may find it sometimes, though very rarely, as the outcome of deliberate selection; but we shall never find it where the hereditary principle remains in operation. Thus monarchy in its pristine purity must be considered as imperfection incarnate, as the most incurable of ills; from the moral point of view it is inferior even to the most revolting of demagogic dictatorships, for the corrupt organism of the latter at least contains a healthy principle upon whose working we may continue to base hopes of social [recovery]. It may be said, therefore, that the more humanity comes to recognize the advantages which democracy, however imperfect, presents over aristocracy, even at its best, the less likely is it that a recognition of the defects of democracy will provoke a return to aristocracy. Apart from certain formal differences and from the qualities which can be acquired only by good education and inheritance (qualities in which aristocracy will always have the advantage over democracy —qualities which democracy either neglects altogether, or, attempting to imitate them, falsifies them to the point of caricature), the defects of democracy will be found to inhere in its inability to get rid of its aristocratic scoriæ. On the other hand, nothing but a serene and frank examination of the oligarchical dangers of democracy will enable us to minimize these dangers, even though they can never be entirely avoided.

The democratic currents of history resemble successive waves. They break ever on the same shoal. They are ever renewed. This enduring spectacle is simultaneously encouraging and depressing. When democracies have gained a certain stage of development, they undergo a gradual transformation, adopting the aristocratic spirit, and in many cases also the aristocratic forms, against which at the outset they struggled so fiercely. Now new accusers arise to denounce the traitors; after an era of glorious combats and of inglorious power, they end by fusing with the old dominant class; whereupon once more they are in their turn attacked by fresh opponents who appeal to the name of democracy. It is probable that this cruel game will continue without end.

ENDNOTES

1. "The honor of being recruited in the government."
2. "A man elected is a man lost."
3. "There is a new conductor but the music is the same."
4. "What is revolution? People who fire on each other in the street; that breaks a lot of windows; only the glaziers profit. The wind carries away the smoke."
5. "It is not worth the bother to change governments!"
6. Alphonse Daudet, Tartarin de Tarascon, Paris: Marpon et Flammarion, 1880, p. 40.
7. The human species wants to be governed; it will be. I am ashamed of my species.

RICHARD GUNTHER and LARRY DIAMOND

35   Species of Political Parties

For nearly a century, political scientists have developed typologies and models of political parties in an effort to capture the essential features of the partisan organizations that were the objects of their analysis. The end result is that the literature today is rich with various categories of party types, some of which have acquired the status of "classics" and have been used by scholars for decades (e.g. Duverger, 1954; Kirchheimer, 1966; Neumann, 1956). We believe, however, that the existing models of political parties do not adequately capture the full range of variation in party types found in the world today, and that the various typologies of parties, based on a wide variety of definitional criteria, have not been conducive to cumulative theory-building. This article, therefore, is an attempt to re-evaluate the prevailing typologies of political parties, retaining widely used concepts and terminology wherever possible, consolidating and clarifying party models in some cases, and defining new party types in others. . . .

Our typology of parties is based upon three criteria. The first of these involves the nature of the *formal organization* of the party. Some parties are organizationally thin, while others develop large mass-membership bases with allied or ancillary institutions engaged in distinct but related spheres of social life; some rely on particularistic networks of personal interaction or exchange, while others are open and universalistic in membership and appeal; and some rely heavily, if not exclusively, on modern techniques of mass communication and ignore the development of primary, face-to-face channels of communication or secondary associations. The second classificatory criterion involves the nature of the party's *programmatic* commitments. Accordingly, some parties derive programmatic stands

from well-articulated ideologies rooted in political philosophies, religious beliefs or nationalistic sentiments; others are either pragmatic or have no well-defined ideological or programmatic commitments; still others are committed to advance the interests of a particular ethnic, religious or socio-economic group, or geographically defined constituency, in contrast to those that are heterogeneous if not promiscuously eclectic in their electoral appeals to groups in society. The third criterion involves the strategy and behavioural norms of the party, specifically, whether the party is *tolerant and pluralistic* or *proto-hegemonic* in its objectives and behavioural style: Some parties are fully committed to democratic rules-of-the-game, are tolerant and respectful towards their opponents, and are pluralistic in their views of polity and society; others are semi-loyal to democratic norms and institutions, or are explicitly anti-system, favouring the replacement of the existing pluralistic democracy with a regime that would be more uniformly committed to the achievement of their programmatic objectives.

In our more detailed discussion of parties that are characteristic of each party model, we also deal with two other dimensions of party life that are significant and have been extensively dealt with in the existing literature on parties. One of these is sociological, i.e. the nature of the clientele towards which the party pitches its appeals, and whose interests it purports to defend or advance. The second involves the internal dynamics of party decision making, particularly the nature and degree of prominence of the party's leader, ranging from a dominant charismatic figure, at one extreme, to more collective forms of party leadership, at the other. We hypothesize that party types (defined by the *organizational, programmatic* and *strategic* criteria listed above) are often associated with particular social clienteles and/or leadership patterns, but not in a deterministic manner, and certainly not to the extent that these sociological and leadership dimensions are built into the definition of the party type.

SOURCE: Richard Gunther and Larry Diamond, "Species of Political Parties: A New Typology," in *Party Politics,* Vol. 9, No. 2 (March 2003), pp. 167–168, 171–193. Copyright 2003 Sage Publications Ltd. Reprinted by permission of Sage Publications. Article and footnotes abridged by the Editor.

It is important to note that the models of political parties that we describe below are *ideal types,* in the strictest Weberian sense of that term. As such, they are heuristically useful insofar as they give easily understandable labels that will help the reader more easily comprehend otherwise complex, multi-dimensional concepts. Moreover, they facilitate analysis insofar as they serve as baselines for comparisons involving real-world cases, or as extreme end-points of evolutionary processes that might never be fully attained. As with all ideal types, however, one should not expect that real-world political parties fully conform to all of the criteria that define each party model; similarly, some parties may include elements of more than one ideal type. Perhaps most importantly, individual parties may evolve over time, such that they may have most closely approximated one party type in an earlier period, but shift in the direction of a different type later on.

....

TYPES OF POLITICAL PARTIES

On the basis of these three criteria, we identify 15 different "species" of party that we believe better capture the basic essence of political parties around the world, and during various historical eras, than do most of the established party typologies. We also recognize, however, a negative trade-off that is implicit in this approach: the obvious lack of parsimony may confuse the reader or make it difficult to appreciate the most crucial differences among these numerous party types. We therefore privilege one of our three classificatory dimensions—the types of party organization. Borrowing an analogy from biology, we regard the type of party organization as defining as a *genus* which, in turn, encompasses several *species* of political party. These genera are *elite-based parties, mass-based parties, ethnicity-based parties, electoralist parties* and *movement parties.* These can be seen in Figure 1, which displays these party types in a two-dimensional array with "organizationally thin" parties towards the left and "organizationally thick" parties towards the right side of the diagram, and with party types that emerged in

earlier historical periods towards the top of the diagram, and more recent entrants on the scene appearing towards the bottom.

The correlation between the degree of organizational thinness/thickness of the party and the temporal dimension is not accidental. A political party comes into existence within a specific social and technological context that may evolve over time, and this "founding context" can leave a lasting imprint on the basic nature of the party's organization for decades to come. Parties are channels of intermediation between political elites and voters, and a particular organizational type ability to mobilize voters effectively is highly contingent upon that context. As we argue, in the nineteenth century in most Western (especially Southern) European countries and well into the twentieth century in most Latin American countries, "politically unmobilized" peasants, many of whom were illiterate and lived in isolated rural areas, made up a sizeable segment of the electorate. Within these sectors of society, traditional elites, or "local notables," exercised considerable influence. Hence, organizationally thin elite-based parties emerged. A few decades later, urbanization, industrialization, the political mobilization of the working class and the expansion of suffrage required the development of different kinds of parties. The electoral mobilization of these newly enfranchised voters was most effectively performed by parties with large mass-membership bases and an extensive organizational infrastructure. By the final four decades of the twentieth century, however, the advent of television had made it possible for political elites to communicate with voters directly, and massive party organizations appeared to be relatively less effective as the principal vehicle for electoral mobilization. At the same time, secularization and decreases in trade-union membership in several countries shrank many of the allied secondary associations upon which the classic mass-based party had so heavily relied. In short, one could advance an argument that the social/technological context within which parties function has a direct bearing on the effectiveness of different types of partisan organizations, and the dominant features of this context will systematically evolve over time. This helps to explain both the emergence of the

• **FIGURE 1** •

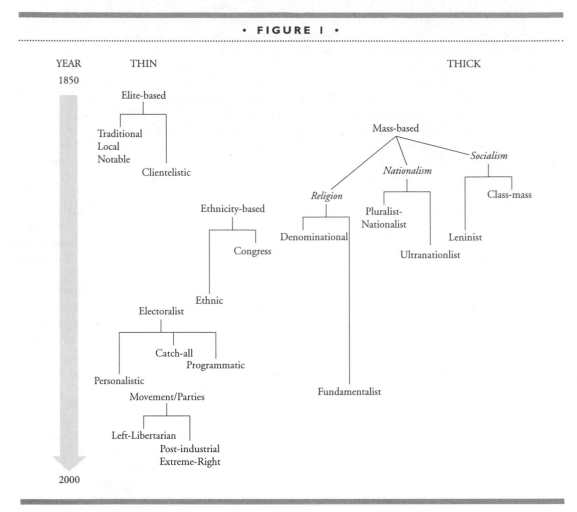

Extent of organization

mass-based party and the decline of elite-based parties in the early twentieth century, as well as the subsequent displacement of mass-based parties by organizationally thinner parties as the dominant organizational type towards the end of that century. It also fits well with empirical studies showing that membership in political parties has been declining in most established democracies in recent years.

This general relationship between the historical dimension and the appearance of different types of party organization does not imply, however, that we are asserting or implying that any one type of party was, is, or will be dominant within any particular

period of time. Instead, we are impressed with the persistence and diversity of party types that exist today, even when many of the social or cultural circumstances that originally gave birth to them have long since disappeared. Neither do we assert that one party type is likely to follow a predictable trajectory, evolving into another type. This is for two reasons. First, once a party has become institutionalized in accord with a particular organizational type, the basic nature of the party's organizational structure may be "frozen" and therefore become resistant to pressures for change. Thus, parties founded when local notables were politically powerful (such as the Japanese Liberal

Democratic Party) may remain under the domination of elite factions well past the time when a majority of voters ceased to deferential to notable elites; similarly, parties may retain sizeable mass-membership bases and institutionalized ties to secondary associations even after the party has adopted a predominantly catch-all electoral strategy and internal decision-making style (e.g. the German SPD under Gerhard Schröder or British Labour under Tony Blair). Secondly, while the social/technological context may evolve systematically over time (accounting for general trends in recent decades from organizational thickness to parties in which less well-developed organizational bases have been observed), the relationship between social or technological change and the programmatic or strategic motivations of party leaders is much more tenuous or non-existent. We shall present a more extensive discussion of this indeterminacy at the end of this article.

With regard to the individual species that make up these broader general, it should be noted that, whenever possible, the names we have chosen for each party type were derived from the existing literature: This is true of Kirchheimer's Class-mass, Denominational and Catch-all parties, as well as Kitschelt's Left-libertarian, Ignazi's Post-industrial Extreme-right movement/parties and the Programmatic party of Wolinetz. In other instances, we either gave a name to a party type that was implicit in a large body of literature (such as the Traditional Local Notable and Clientelistic parties), or we renamed and more fully developed the party model, such as the Leninist party (which Duverger referred to as the "devotee" party), the Ethnic party (the "particularistic sociocultural party," in Kitschelt's terminology), and the Personalistic party (called the "non-partisan party" by Ignazi). In one prominent case, we found that a commonly used party-type label really referred to a particular genus of party: Panebianco's "electoral-professional party" roughly corresponds to our genus of Electoralist parties, within which we delineate three more specific "species" or party types. Finally, there were some party labels that simply did not fit within this typological scheme (such as the cartel party), and there were some types of party (the Religious Fundamentalist, Ethnicity-based and Nationalist

parties) for which no clear conceptual definition had previously appeared in the literature.

ELITE PARTIES

"Elite-based" parties are those whose principal organizational structures are minimal and based upon established elites and related interpersonal networks within a specific geographic area. Deference to the authority of these elites is a feature shared by the two species of parties that fall within this "genus." Whatever national-level party structure exists is based upon an alliance among locally based elites. In programmatic terms, these parties are not ideological. At the lowest level within the party (i.e. the linkage between voters and the local candidate) the principal electoral commitment involves the distribution of particularistic benefits to residents of a geographically defined constituency or to "clients" at the bottom of a patron—client hierarchy. Such parties do not have ambitions of hegemony, and are tolerant and collaborative towards one another within a parliamentary (but not necessarily democratic) regime.

Historically, the first party type to emerge was what we call the *traditional local notable* party. This early-to-mid-nineteenth century development emerged at a time of sharply limited suffrage in semi-democratic regimes. Given that the right to vote and hold office was restricted in most of these countries to males owning substantial property, this competitive game was limited to the upper socio-economic strata. And given that election to office required appeals to a small number of enfranchised voters, campaigns did not require an extensive organizational effort. Local notables could often count on their traditionally-based prestige or personal relationships with their few and socially homogeneous constituents to secure office. Central party bureaucracies did not exist, and national-level "party" organizations consisted of relatively loose alliances or cliques linking elected members of parliament on the basis of shared interests or bonds of mutual respect. The parliamentary factions that dominated the British House of Commons in the first half of the nineteenth century, French conservative parties in the nineteenth and first half of the twentieth century, and several conservative parties in Brazil today are examples of this variety of elite party. Expansion of suffrage and socio-economic modernization (which entailed the political mobilization of formerly excluded sectors of society) progressively limited the electoral effectiveness of such poorly institutionalized and resource-poor parties, while urbanization made the predominantly rural traditional notables increasingly irrelevant to most voters.

The *clientelistic party* began to emerge just as the traditional local notable party was subjected to challenges from newly enfranchised segments of the electorate within societies undergoing industrialization and urbanization. Indeed, it is reasonable to hypothesize that the emergence of the clientelistic party was a direct response by local elites to the challenges posed by the political mobilization of formerly "subject" populations: as traditional deference to local elites began to break down, electoral mobilization relied increasingly on an exchange of favours or overt coercion. The clientelistic party, as we shall define it, is a confederation of notables (either traditional or of the newly emerging liberal-professional or economic elite), each with his own geographically, functionally or personalistically based support; organized internally as particularistic factions. Such a party typically has a weak organization and places little or no stress on programme or ideology. Its principal function is to coordinate the individual campaign efforts of notables, usually indirectly or loosely, for the purpose of securing power at the national level. Their campaign activities, in turn, are based on hierarchical chains or interpersonal relationships of a quasi-feudal variety, in which relatively durable patterns of loyalty are linked with the exchange of services and obligations.

While all clientelistic parties are characterized by particularistic factional organization, in their heyday in the late nineteenth and early twentieth centuries—in Southern Europe, Latin America and North American big-city machines and southern rural politics—the exchange of personalistic favours also served as a principal tool for electoral mobilization at the mass level. Such relationships are most common in rural, premodern societies: Under conditions of geographical isolation from a domi-

nant centre of government, coupled with low levels of functional literacy and poorly developed transportation and communications media, a localized patron–client relationship can be mutually beneficial to both the patron and the client.[1] In the United States, this variety of politics focused on immigrant populations that lacked political resources, and even some basic skils (such as command of the English language) or personal connections necessary to thrive economically. As socio-economic modernization proceeds—as shrinking rural populations become increasingly literate, exposed to mass communications media, and "mobilized" politically (or as immigrant populations in the United States learned English, became educated and assimilated into American society)—the utility of the patron to the citizen declines, and the patron's attempts to influence voting decisions are increasingly resisted. Under these circumstances, more coercive forms of patron–client exchanges tended to emerge, often involving the threat to withhold economic benefits from the client unless his/her political support is pledged, or overt vote-buying displaces the exchange of favours. Over the long run, however, socio-economic modernization and the increasing "cognitive mobilization" of the mass public greatly reduce the utility of clientelism as a vehicle for electoral mobilization.

Once institutionalized and embedded within the structure of political parties, however, these patron–client relationships may take on a life of their own, independent of the socio-economic conditions that had given rise to them originally. In both Italy and Japan, whose post-war party systems were established in less modernized societies (particularly in the south of Italy and rural parts of Japan), clientelism was embedded into the very structure of the dominant parties (the Christian Democratic Party and the Liberal Democratic Party, respectively). Once established, these factional networks became the principal bases of elite recruitment within the governing parties of both party systems, and were perpetuated well beyond the time when the socio-economic conditions that had given birth to them had largely disappeared. While these organizations survived for decades, it is interesting to note that the clientelistic exchanges on which they were based may contain the seeds of their own eventual destruction. Particularism and the distribution of rewards based upon faction membership easily evolve into overt corruption. Not surprisingly, clientelistic parties in both of these systems ultimately suffered serious—and in the case of the Italian parties, fatal—electoral setbacks as part of a popular reaction against corruption scandals. (The same has happened more recently in Thailand and the Philippines although some parties in each of these countries retain features of the clientelistic model.) Since social change had made these kinds of exchanges increasingly repugnant to ever larger numbers of voters, when high-level scandals were exposed, a series of defections from the once dominant governing parties drastically undermined their organizational unity and strength.

....

MASS-BASED PARTIES

The second genus of party has deep roots in the literature, as well as in the nineteenth and early twentieth century history of Europe. The quintessential "externally created party," the mass-based party, emerged as a manifestation of the political mobilization of the working class in many European polities.[2] Organizationally, it is characterized by a large base of dues-paying members who remain active in party affairs even during periods between elections. In an effort to disseminate the party's ideology and establish an active membership base, the party seeks to penetrate into a number of spheres of social life. Affiliated trade union, religious and other social organizations serve not only as political allies (helping to mobilize supporters at election time), but for the projection of the programmatic objectives of the party from the electoral-parliamentary arena into a variety of spheres of social life. Extensive arrays of supportive organizations are established, including party newspapers and recreational clubs, and networks of local party branches are established nationwide. These organizational networks not only serve as a framework for mobilization at election time, but also provide side benefits for party members, such as opportunities for fraternization and recreation.

Two types of distinctions further divide this genus into six different species of party. The first involves the basic thrust of the party's programmatic commitments, ideology, and/or unifying belief system. Most commonly, these have involved varying types of commitment to (1) socialism, (2) nationalism or (3) religion. The second dimension involves the extent to which each of these is either tolerant and pluralistic, on the one hand, or is committed to securing a hegemonic position within the political system and imposing its radical programmatic commitments on society. Pluralist parties assume that they will always be functioning within a democratic system; they therefore accept its institutions and rules of the game. Proto-hegemonic parties, in contrast, strive over the long term towards the replacement of the existing pluralist society and democratic system with one that is better suited for the achievement of their radical transformative objectives. Accordingly, they accept existing institutions and rule only insofar as they are expedient and cannot be replaced over the short run, and their behaviour is, at best, semi-loyal.

Pluralist mass-based parties seek to win elections as the principal avenue towards achieving their programmatic objectives, and their vote-mobilizational strategy relies heavily on the development and activation of a mass-membership base. Party militants perform a variety of tasks, ranging from proselytizing to distribution of printed propaganda to escorting voters to the polls. The party's allied secondary organizations (trade unions, religious groups and/or fraternal organizations) urge their members to support the party, and if the party has succeeded in establishing its own communications media, its newspaper and/or radio and television broadcasts are flooded with partisan messages. Recruitment of militants to the party is open, although some re-socialization of new party members is required.

Proto-hegemonic mass-based parties, by contrast, place greater emphasis on discipline, constant active commitment and loyalty on the part of party members for the conduct of political conflict in both electoral and extra-parliamentary arenas. Thus, recruitment of members is highly selective, indoctrination is intensive, and acceptance of the ideology and short-term party line is demanded of all members. In some instances (particularly when the proto-hegemonic party exists clandestinely), a secret, conspiratorial cell structure is adopted, in contrast to the open "branch" organization that characterizes pluralist mass-based parties. In the aggregate, the distinction between pluralist and proto-hegemonic mass-based parties comes close to Duverger's differentiation between branch-based mass parties and cell-based "devotee" parties (1954: 63–71), as well as Neumann's (1956) separation of parties of "social integration" from parties of "total integration."

Parties with socialist ideological commitments have taken the form of either democratic socialist (or social-democratic) "class-mass" parties, or have adopted the proto-hegemonic stance of the "Leninist" party. In the typical *class-mass party* (to use Kirchheimer's [1966] terminology), the centre of power and authority in the party is located in the executive committee of its secretariat, although formally the ultimate source of legitimate authority is the full party congress. In addition, the parliamentary leadership of the party occasionally challenges the party secretariat for control of the programmatic agenda and the nomination of candidates. Invariably, the open, tolerant stance of these parties has made possible considerable intra-party conflict, particularly between pragmatists whose primary concern is electoral victory and ideologues who place much higher value on "constituency representation" and ideological consistency with a more orthodox reading of the party's ideology (see Michels, 1915). In some cases, this may give rise to a split of the party into two separate organizations (such as the former Partito Socialista Democratico Italiano and Partito Socialista Italiano of Italy's "first republic"). Much more commonly, this has culminated in the gradual conversion of more maximalist socialist parties into more moderate and pragmatic parties.

Class-mass parties establish bases within their class constituency through groups organized both geographically (the local "branch") and functionally (trade unions). While they seek to proselytize prospective members or voters, indoctrination and the demand for ideological conformity are minimal.

While social integration through the activities of party and trade union allies is a significant objective, the party is primarily concerned with winning elections and taking part in the formation of governments. Recruitment of members is quite open, and the larger the party's mass base, the better, given the party's primary concern with securing electoral majorities and its traditional reliance on electoral mobilization through the activities of members. The social-democratic parties of Germany, Sweden and Chile are good examples of this party type.

Leninist parties (as we define them, based on a class ideology and proto-hegemonic) have as their objective the overthrow of the existing political system and the implementation of revolutionary change in society. Given that their revolutionary goals are likely to be vigorously opposed if not repressed by their opponents, the party adopts a closed structure based on the semi-secret cell (rather than the open branch, which characterizes pluralist class-mass parties). Membership is highly selective, and the party demands strict loyalty and obedience on the part of members. Ideological indoctrination of party members is intense and uncompromising, and the party penetrates into key sectors of society (especially trade unions and the intellectual middle class in Western countries, and the peasantry in Asia) in an effort to secure tactical allies over the short term and converts over the long term. Decision making within the party is highly centralized and authoritarian, even if "democratic centralism" often allows for open debate prior to the taking of an official stand. The party sees itself as the "vanguard" of the proletariat, and even though the party portrays itself as representing the working class, it performs an explicitly directive and top-down role of leading the class that it represents and defining its interests. While the initial stand of the prototypical Leninist parties—those belonging to the Comintern—was to reject "bourgeois" representative institutions and parliaments, most communist parties participated as anti-system or semi-loyal contenders in electoral politics in Western democracies. The ultimate objective of the party is the seizure of power, by force if necessary. In Western democracies, parties that were originally Leninist have either undergone gradual transformations—generally in the direction of becoming pluralist class-mass parties—or schisms, separating moderate, democratic parties (such as the Italian Partito Democratico della Sinistra, now Democratici della Sinistra) from more orthodox rump parties (such as Rifondazione Comunista).

If the party succeeds in coming to power, as it did in Central and Eastern Europe and parts of Asia, it modifies its self-defined role and its behaviour towards other social and political groups. It sees itself as nothing less than the "organized expression of the will of society." In the former Soviet Union, "it is the expression 'of the interests of the entire nation:' for the Chinese it represents 'the interests of the people'". As such, it establishes hegemonic control over the political and economic system, abolishing or taking over established secondary organizations, and using virtually all organized social groups as arenas for the social integration of individuals into the new society which it hopes to create. The party will direct the activities of the state and preside over the recruitment of governing elites.

While the classic Leninist parties were those belonging to the Comintern and embracing Lenin's 21 Points (which differentiated communist parties from other Marxist parties), some non-communist parties (such as the Kuomintang prior to Taiwan's democratization in the late 1980s and 1990s) conformed to many of these organizational and operational characteristics.

Pluralist nationalist parties, such as the Basque Partido Nacionalista Vasco and, until the late 1990s, the Taiwanese Democratic Progressive Party, have taken on a variety of forms. Most of these involve mass-membership bases, extensive party organizations, and collaboration with ancillary secondary groups usually including cultural organizations and sometimes trade unions. The electoral clientele of these parties will be those individuals who subjectively define themselves as belonging to a distinct national group. While most commonly these national identities will revolve around some objective social characteristic (especially involving language and culture), the boundaries of the electoral clientele will be quite malleable. Indeed, one of the key functions of nationalist parties is not only

to convince citizens to cast ballots for the party, but also to use the party's election campaign and its affiliated secondary organizations to foster and intensify their identification with the national group and its aspirations. Moreover, those aspirations, by definition, involve a demand for some level of territorial self-governance, ranging from autonomy within a multinational state to outright independence or the redrawing of international boundaries in response to an irredentist claim. Accordingly, even though these parties may be moderate in their policy preferences concerning economic, religious and most other issues on the left–right continuum, they may assume a semi-loyal or anti-system stand regarding issues of territorial governance. Internally, moreover, there will often be tension between those demanding a more militant stance in defence of the group's nationalist demands and those stressing cooperation with other parties in forming government coalitions and pressing for the enactment of incrementally beneficial legislation.

Ultranationalist parties are proto-hegemonic in their aspirations. They advance an ideology that exalts the nation or race above the individual, detests minorities and openly admires the use of force by a strong, quasi-military party often relying upon a uniformed party militia. In some respects, they may share many organizational and behavioural characteristics with Leninist parties, especially the highly selective recruitment process, intensive indoctrination of members, strict internal discipline, the overriding objective of seizing power through force if necessary and anti-system or semi-loyal participation in parliament. Also like Leninist parties, if they come to power they seek hegemonic domination of polity and society through repression or cooptation of existing secondary organizations, coupled with a broad penetration into society in an effort to resocialize all persons to actively support the regime. They differ from Leninist parties not only with regard to the content of their ideologies, but also insofar as these ideologies are less precisely stated and subject to reinterpretation by a charismatic national leader.[3] In addition, the national leader will be the ultimate source of power and authority, and the party's bureaucracy will be supportive if not servile. Hitler's Nazi party and Mussolini's fascists are good examples of such parties, with the Croatian Democratic Union (HDZ) under Franjo Tudjman and the Russian National Unity party of Aleksandr Barkashov as more recent manifestations of this party type. The striking frequency with which a charismatic leader dominates in this type of party suggests there is something about the social/historical circumstances giving rise to ultranationalist and fascist parties, and something about the personalities drawn to such parties (Adorno et al., 1950) that generate intense and submissive devotion to an exceptional, all-powerful leader.

A third programmatic basis for mass-based parties is religion. Again, two different variants can identified. The first is pluralist, democratic and tolerant. While the origins of the *denominational mass-party* (again, using Kirchheimer's [1966] terminology) can be traced back to the late nineteenth century, this type of party reached its maximum ascendancy in the aftermath of World War II. Examples of denominational parties include numerous Christian democratic parties in Western Europe that have played important political roles, particularly since World War II (in Italy, Germany, Belgium, The Netherlands and elsewhere), as well as, more recently, Christian Democracy in Poland (ZChM). They share many of the organizational characteristics of the mass-based party, including the existence of a large base of dues-paying members, hierarchically structured party organizations linking the national and local levels, party newspapers and broadcasting outlets, allied secondary organizations (generally religious, but, in some instances, trade unions). Nonetheless, they differ in one important respect from parties based on secular ideologies: Since the basis of the party's programmes is a set of religious beliefs that are determined by a combination of tradition and interpretation by clerics and/or a religious institution outside of the party itself, the party is not fully in control of its core ideological precepts whenever they are directly linked to religious values (such as those relating to abortion, divorce, sexual preference or some manifestations of artistic expression). This can lead to intraparty tensions whenever party leaders choose to modify the party's electoral appeals or programmatic commitments in such a manner as to conflict with those values. The Italian Christian Democratic party, for example, experienced serious internal tensions in dealing with legalization of divorce, which was stoutly opposed by the Catholic church hierarchy. Insofar as religious beliefs may be subject to varying interpretations, considerable heterogeneity may exist within denominational-mass parties that can periodically give rise to such conflicts.

The final mass-based party is the proto-hegemonic religious party, or religious *fundamentalist* party. The principal difference between this and the denominational-mass party is that the fundamentalist party seeks to reorganize state and society around a strict reading of religious doctrinal principles, while denominational-mass parties are pluralist and incremental in their agenda. For fundamentalist parties, there is little or no room for conflicting interpretations of the religious norms and scriptures that serve as the basis of the party's programme and of laws which it seeks to impose on all of society. The authority of religious leaders to interpret that text and translate it into politically and socially relevant terms is unequivocally acknowledged. In this theocratic party model, there is no separation between religion and the state, and religious norms are imposed on all citizens within the polity, irrespective of their own personal religious beliefs. Given the far-reaching objectives of these parties (which may verge on the totalitarian), the organizational development of these parties and the scope of their activities are extensive. Member involvement and identification is substantial and even intense, and ancillary organizations establish a presence at the local level throughout society. Given the religious fundamentalist nature of these parties and their strict reading of religious texts, authority relations within the party are hierarchical, undemocratic and even absolutist, and members are disciplined and devoted. Religious fundamentalist parties mobilize support not only by invoking religious doctrine and identity, and by proposing policies derived from those principles, but also through selective incentives; they often perform a wide range of social welfare functions which aid in recruiting and solidifying the loyalty of members.

This web of organized activities and services encapsulates members within a distinct subculture. Although these are not class-based parties, they disproportionately attract support from the poor and down-trodden and the marginalized middle class, among whom denunciations of injustice and corruption have a particular resonance. Algeria's Islamic Salvation Front is one example of this kind of organization, with Turkey's now-banned Welfare Party sharing some of these characteristics.

....

ETHNICITY-BASED PARTIES

Parties based on ethnicity typically lack the extensive and elaborate organization of mass-based parties. What most distinguishes them, however, are their political and electoral logics. Unlike most mass-based parties, they do not advance a programme (whether incremental or transformative) for all of society. Their goals and strategies are narrower: to promote the interests of a particular ethnic group, or coalition of groups. And unlike nationalist parties, their programmatic objectives do not typically include secession or a high level of decision-making and administrative autonomy from the existing state. Instead , they are content to use existing state structures to channel benefits towards their particularistically defined electoral clientele.

The purely *ethnic party* seeks only to mobilize the votes of its own ethnic group. Classic historical examples are the Northern People's Congress and the Action Group of Nigeria's First Republic, and, more recently, South Africa's Inkatha Freedom Party, the Turkish minority party (DPS, Movement of Rights and Freedoms) in Bulgaria, the Democratic Union of Hungarians in Romania and the (Sikh) Akali Dal in India's Punjab state. Although it may run candidates in other geographic constituencies, or raise larger national or even ideological issues, these only thinly and half-heartedly mask its true ethnic (or regional) purpose. As Kitschelt (2001) argues, the defining feature of ethnic parties (which he refers to as "particularistic sociocultural parties") is that they limit

their appeal to a particular sectional constituency, and "explicitly seek to draw boundaries" between ethnic "friends" and "foes." The principal goal of the ethnic party is not any universalistic programme or platform, but rather to secure material, cultural and political benefits (and protections) for the ethnic group in its competition with other groups. As such, ethnic parties have an extremely low level of ideological or programmatic commitment and coherence. Neither do they typically have a very developed organizational structure or formal membership base. Lacking any functional interests or ideological agenda, the ethnic party tends to mobilize pre-existing clientelistic relations, and as such its structure and internal authority relations resemble the clientelistic party. Given the fact that ethnic parties mobilize powerfully emotive symbolic issues of identity and even cultural survival, they are prone to be dominated by, and even organized around, a single charismatic leader (such as the NPC'S Ahmadu Bello, the Action Group's Obafemi Awolowo and Inkatha's Mangosuthu Buthelezi). The electoral logic of the ethnic party is to harden and mobilize its ethnic base with exclusive and often polarizing appeals to ethnic group opportunity and threat. Unlike virtually all other political parties (including nationalistic parties), electoral mobilization is not intended to attract additional sectors of society to support the party[4] whose interests are perceived as intrinsically in conflict with those of other ethnic groups. Thus, even more than the religious fundamentalist party, the potential electoral clientele of the party is strictly defined and limited by ethnicity, although within that definitional category cross-class electoral appeals may lead to the adoption of eclectic programmatic objectives. Because ethnic parties are, by definition, unable to expand significantly beyond their ethnic electoral base, they are unable to pursue hegemony, unless they attain a demographic majority or quash democracy. Through electoral fraud and rigging of the census, Nigeria's NPC sought to do both, and thereby to achieve ethnoregional domination during the First Republic. The pursuit of such domination by an ethnic party can lead to violent conflict, and was indeed a contributing factor to the Nigerian civil war.

A *congress party* is a coalition, alliance or federation of ethnic parties or political machines, although it may take the form of a single, unified party structure. Hence, at the local level it may share some organizational features and programmatic commitments with the ethnic party (such as the distribution of benefits through a vast array of patron–client networks), but within the national political system it behaves dramatically differently. Its electoral appeal is to national unity and integration rather than division, to ethnic sharing and coexistence rather than domination and threat. Where a consociational system tries to share power and resources among, and assure the mutual security of, each group within a coalition government formed *after* the election, a congress party constructs the coalitional guarantees in advance, within the broad tent of its party organization. If the tent it builds is broad enough, it can become a dominant party, like the archetype of this model, the Congress Party during India's first two decades of independence; less democratic examples of the congress party are the Kenya African National Union under Jomo Kenyatta and the Barisan Nasional (National Front coalition) of Malaysia. If the coverage of the multi-ethnic tent is incomplete, the congress party may merely be the first among equals, as with the National Party of Nigeria during the Second Republic (1979–83) or Nigeria's current ruling party, the People's Democratic Party. In either case, the congress party allocates party posts and government offices, and distributes patronage and other benefits in accord with proportional or other quasi-consociational formulas. Its social base is broad and heterogeneous, and the party's goal is to make it as inclusive as possible. However, its very breadth renders it vulnerable to fracture along ethnic or regional lines.

ELECTORALIST PARTIES

There are three party types in the broader genus of "electoralist parties," the fundamental characteristics of which are similar to those upon which Panebianco (1988) developed his concept of the "electoral-professional party".[5] Parties belonging to this genus are organizationally thin, maintaining a relatively skeletal existence (the offices and staffs supporting their parliamentary groups notwithstanding). At election time, however, these parties spring into action to perform what is unequivocally their primary function, the conduct of the campaign. They utilize "modern" campaign techniques (stressing television and the mass-communications media over the mobilization of party members and affiliated organizations), and they rely heavily on professionals who can skilfully carry out such campaigns. The personal attractiveness of the party's candidates is an important criterion for nomination at the expense of other considerations, such as length of service to, or formal organizational position within, the party. We resist the temptation to regard electoralist parties as of one type, however, because they differ in some important respects that significantly affect their behaviour and, in turn, the quality of democracy. Accordingly, we set forth three different ideal types of parties that fall within this genus. These three party types all share the organizational characteristics described above, but they differ with regard to our other two defining dimensions: Two of them lack strong ideological or programmatic commitments, while one does seek to advance a distinct set of programmes; and two of them are decidedly pluralistic, while the third may or may not have hegemonic ambitions.

The first of these is the *catch-all party*. This pluralistic and tolerant ideal type is primarily distinguished by the party's shallow organization, superficial and vague ideology, and overwhelmingly electoral orientation, as well as by the prominent leadership and electoral roles of the party's top-ranked national-level candidates. The overriding (if not sole) purpose of catch-all parties is to maximize votes, win elections and govern. To do so, they seek to aggregate as wide a variety of social interests as possible. In societies where the distribution of public opinion (on a left–right continuum) is unimodal and centrist, catch-all parties will seek to maximize votes by positioning themselves toward the centre of the spectrum, appearing moderate in their policy preferences and behaviour. In an effort to expand their electoral appeal to a wide variety of groups, their policy orientations are eclectic and shift with the public mood. Lacking an explicit ideology, catch-all parties tend to emphasize the attractive personal attributes of their candidates, and nominations are largely determined by the electoral resources of the candidates rather than by such organizational criteria as years of experience in, or service to, the party, or position within key factions within the party. The Democratic Party of the United States, Labour under Tony Blair, the Hungarian Democratic Forum and Spain's Socialist party (PSOE) and Partido Popular are clear examples of this party type, and Taiwan's Kuomintang is completing its extremely long-term transformation from a quasi-Leninist to a catch-all party. Korea's principal parties manifest many features of the catch-all party but remain heavily regional in their electoral bases and identities, giving them some of the flavour of ethnic parties.

It should be noted that our conceptualization of the catch-all party departs from the classic party type described by Kirchheimer (1966) in some important respects. The first is based on the observation that Kirchheimer does not describe a stable ideal type; his vision of the catch-all party is one that is evolving away from an earlier type of party, and therefore is defined more by what it is not than by what it is. Specifically, Kirchheimer's definition lists several ways in which the catch-all party departs from the previously dominant mass-integration model of party,[6] and is therefore still within the long-term evolutionary trajectory of such parties. Our ideal type is a purer distillation of defining features that do not presuppose that the party has "ideological baggage," a "*classe gardée*" or a sizeable membership base. This has the result of shedding from our conceptualization a number of secondary consequences that we do not regard as necessary components of the model. Obviously basing his analysis on the experience of centralized West European socialist parties, Kirchheimer posited, for example, that, as the importance of party militants as vote mobilizers declines, control over the party and its nomination of candidates would increasingly fall into the hands of dominant national-level party leaders. The experience of American catch-all parties clearly indicates that this is not an essential component of the model: Indeed, the

increase in television-dominated, issue- or personally-oriented campaigns and the shifting or weakening of party alliances with the social groups serving as their traditional electoral clienteles has gone hand-in-hand with the spread of primary elections as the principal form of candidate nomination and the commensurate decline of party bosses. By relaxing the organizational determinism inherent in Kirchheimer's model and eliminating this redundant feature, its applicability to a broader array of real-world cases is strengthened, and some other typologies in the comparative parties literature can be more easily subsumed within this species of party.

Like the catch-all party, the *programmatic party* is a modern-day, pluralist/tolerant, thinly organized political party whose main function is the conduct of election campaigns, and those campaigns often seek to capitalize on the personal attractiveness of its candidates. However, the programmatic party is closer to the classic model of a mass-based, ideological party in three respects. First, it has much more of a distinct, consistent and coherent programmatic or ideological agenda than does the ideal-type catch-all party, and it clearly incorporates those ideological or programmatic appeals in its electoral campaigns and its legislative and government agenda. If it operates within a majoritarian electoral system, as in Britain, the United States or Mexico (e.g. the Conservatives under Margaret Thatcher, the Republicans since 1980 and the Partido de Acción Nacional), it must still broadly aggregate interests, but its issue appeals are less diffuse, vague and eclectic than those of the catch-all party. Thus, second, it seeks to win control of government (or a place in it) precisely through this sharper definition of a party platform or vision. Third, while its organization and social base may, in a majoritarian system, resemble that of the catch-all party, in a highly proportional system, such as Israel's, the programmatic party has a narrower, more clearly defined social base, and possibly some firmer linkages to like-minded organizations in civil society. In this case its electoral strategy is to mobilize its core constituency rather than to enlarge it through interest aggregation. Other examples of programmatic parties include the Civic Democratic Party (ODS) of

Vaclav Klaus, the Communist Party of Bohemia and Moravia (KSCM) and the Czech Social Democratic Party (CSSD) in the Czech Republic, the Democratic Union in Poland, and the Hungarian Socialist Party (MSzP), the Civic Democratic Party-Young Democrats (Fidesz, formerly the Alliance of Young Democrats) in Hungary, and the Democratic Progressive Party (DPP) in Taiwan.

The most purely electoralist party is what we call the *personalistic* party (called the "non-partisan party" by Ignazi [1996: 552]), as its *only* rationale is to provide a vehicle for the leader to win an election and exercise power. It is not derived from the traditional structure of local notable elites, but, rather, is an organization constructed or converted by an incumbent or aspiring national leader exclusively to advance his or her national political ambitions. Its electoral appeal is not based on any programme or ideology, but rather on the personal charisma of the leader/candidate, who is portrayed as indispensable to the resolution of the country's problems or crisis. While it may make use of clientelistic networks and/or broadly distribute particularistic benefits to party supporters, its organization is weak, shallow and opportunistic. Indeed, it may be so temporary that, even in the service of an incumbent president, such as Alberto Fujimori in Peru, it may change its name and structure with every election. Numerous other twentieth-century examples abound, including Silvio Berlusconi's Forza Italia, the Congress-I rump which defected from the rest of the Congress Party in support of Indira Gandhi, the Pakistan People's Party that Benazir Bhutto inherited from her father (hence, with deeper roots than some personalistic parties), and the hastily established electoral vehicles created to support the electoral aspirations of Hugo Chávez Frias in Venezuela, Fernando Collor de Mello in Brazil and Joseph Estrada in the Philippines. A recent classic example is the Thai Rak Thai Party of the Thai business tycoon Thaksin Shinawatra, whose personality and vast personal fortune gained his party an unprecedented absolute majority of parliament even though it was formed only a few months before the November 2000 elections. Most of these parties are or were pluralist and tolerant in their behavioural styles, but this is not invariably true, as the proto-

hegemonic behaviour of Peru's Fujimori and Venezuela's Chávez clearly reveal.

....

MOVEMENT PARTIES

Finally, there is a type of partisan organization that straddles the conceptual space between "party" and "movement". The prominent examples of the German Greens and the Austrian Freedom Party, however, make it clear that these types of organizations must be included in this comprehensive typology since they regularly field candidates, have been successful in electing members of parliament and, in Germany in 1999, in forming part of a coalition government at the national level and in several Länder. The most prominent examples of movement parties in Western Europe today are of two types: *left-libertarian parties and post-industrial extreme right parties.* However, this genus of party types should be regarded as "open-ended," since its fluid organizational characteristics may be manifested in a wide variety of ways in other parts of the world or over the course of history. It is particularly appropriate for newly emerging parties prior to their institutionalization (such as Labour in Britain at the beginning of the twentieth century and the French Gaullists prior to 1958).

Herbert Kitschelt presents the most detailed analysis of the "left-libertarian" variety of the movement party. These he contrasts with "conventional parties" in Western Europe, which are principally oriented towards winning government power through elected office; have a professional staff of party functionaries and an extensive party organization; represent economic interest groups (labour or business); and are mainly concerned with economic distributive issues (Kitschelt, 1989: 62). Instead, "left-libertarian" parties are quintessentially "post-materialist" in their attitudinal orientation and behaviour. They reject the paramount status of economic issues and are characterized by "a negative consensus that the predominance of markets and bureaucracies must be rolled back in favor of social solidarity relations and participatory institutions" (Kitschelt, 1989: 64). Indeed, since there is no consensus in support of a single comprehensive ideology or set of programmatic preferences, this "negative consensus" functions as the very lowest common denominator shared by an otherwise heterogeneous clientele, and the party's agenda revolves around a multiplicity of issues not limited to a single arena. There are no barriers to membership in the group, which is open to all who wish to participate, making the social base and attitudinal orientation of activists even more diverse. The strong commitment to direct participation leads to the weakness (even rejection) of centralized organization and leadership, and a sometimes chaotic "assembly" organizational style (as best illustrated by the water-balloon attack on Foreign Minister Joshka Fischer at the 1999 congress of the German Greens). Organizationally, the movement party is based on "loose networks of grass-roots support with little formal structure, hierarchy and central control" (Kitschelt, 1989: 66). Finally, the left-libertarian movement party stresses "constituency representation" over the logic of electoral competition, making it a sometimes unpragmatic and unreliable coalition partner.

Piero Ignazi (1996) presents a succinct overview of the *post-industrial extreme right* party, which he regards as a different kind of reaction against the conditions of post-industrial society. As he points out, where the left-libertarians place greatest emphasis on self-affirmation, informality and libertarianism in their reaction against modern society and state institutions, supporters of the extreme right have been driven by their atomization and alienation to search for more order, tradition, identity and security, at the same time as they attack the state for its intervention in the economy and for its social welfare policies (Ignazi, 1996: 557). Like their fascist predecessors, they embrace the "leadership principle" and do not question the directives of the party's paramount leader (e.g. the Front National's Le Pen or the Freedom Party's Haider). However, they differ from fascists (who supported a strong, disciplined and militant party as a weapon to be used against their enemies, especially socialist and communist parties), in that they are hostile to "party" and "the establishment" more generally. Instead, xenophobic, racist hostility toward migrants is a highly salient line of conflict. In addition, where fascists favoured the construction of a strong state, neo-

conservative anti-state rhetoric and attacks on the social welfare state permeates the speeches and programme proposals of party leaders and candidates.[7]

....

FIFTEEN IDEAL-TYPE "SPECIES" OF PARTIES AND THEORY-BUILDING

The typology developed here is certainly less parsimonious than the two-, three- or four-category frameworks that have dominated the comparative literature on political parties to date. Scholars who prefer styles of theory-building based upon deduction from a simpler set of one-dimensional criteria may not welcome this contribution on the grounds that its complexity and multidimensionality may hinder theory-building. We respectfully disagree. We believe that social science theories that purport to explain human behaviour or institutional performance must accurately reflect real-world conditions. As stated earlier, we have found most of the previously dominant typologies lacking insofar as they were based upon the historical experience of Western Europe from the nineteenth through mid-twentieth centuries. Accordingly, they do not adequately reflect the much more diverse reality of political parties in other parts of the world: As we have suggested, the deep ethnic cleavages that divide many societies in Africa and Asia have no counterpart in the much more ethnically, linguistically, religiously and culturally homogeneous context of Western Europe. Hence, in order for a typology of parties to be useful for broad, cross-regional comparative analysis it must allow for the emergence of distinct types in greatly different kinds of social contexts, such as the ethnic, congress and religious-fundamentalist parties described above.

Similarly, it cannot be assumed that typologies based on characteristics of West European parties in the late nineteenth or early twentieth centuries will be valid for all time even within that single region. The socio-economic context and communication technologies continue to evolve, and these have important implications for the structure, resources, objectives and behavioural styles of political parties.

Accordingly, a dichotomous division of cadre-versus-mass parties, or parties of individual representation versus parties of social or total integration may have accurately reflected the reality of Western Europe throughout the first half of the twentieth century However, by the second half of that century it had become clear that these classic party models were increasingly incapable of capturing the diversity of party types present within established democracies. Kirchheimer's (1966) catch-all model certainly helped to address this shortcoming by identifying ways in which many parties were tending to deviate from the mass-based party model. Over the following decades, however, the catch-all label was being used to describe an excessively wide variety of parties whose electoral strategies and programmatic commitments differed substantially. Accordingly, we found it necessary to break down that classic but "overaggregated" party type into three different kinds of electoralist party.

Hypothesis-testing and theory-building are facilitated by ideal types that capture all of the defining elements of a concept, but at the same time do not "overaggregate" by including elements that do not conceptually or empirically belong together. As Peter Mair (1989) has pointed out, for example, the catch-all party model as elaborated by Kirchheimer (1966) includes both an ideological and an organizational component: The down-grading of a party's ideological commitment is integrally linked to the "thinning" of the party's organizational structure and an increased emphasis (both electorally and organizationally) on the party's national-level leadership. With Wolinetz (1991), we believe that it is necessary to separate the ideological and organizational dimensions (as we have in elaborating our catch-all, programmatic and personalistic party models) both in order to reflect reality more accurately and to facilitate analysis of the causes of party change.

We regard this as desirable because the evolution of parties or the emergence of new types of parties may be the product of several fundamentally distinct causal processes, not all of which would move the transformation of the party in the same direction, and not all of which are unilinear in their evolutionary implications. With regard to the organizational dimension of the classic catch-all party, Kirchheimer's prediction (actually, lament) regard-

ing the general decline of mass parties and their replacement by or evolution into what we have called electoralist parties has certainly come true. Numerous empirical studies have documented a decline in party membership and the loosening or rupture of ties linking parties to communications media and secondary associations in most West European countries, as well as the emergence of organizationally thin parties in the new democracies of the former Soviet Bloc. Indeed, since Kirchheimer was writing at a time that predated the emergence of television as by far the dominant medium of campaign communication throughout the world, he actually understated the extent to which electoral politics would be personalized and freed of dependence on a mass base of party militants.

But Kirchheimer's prediction that these organizational changes would be accompanied by a progressive downgrading of parties' ideological commitments has not come true, at least not in countries like the United States and Britain. Some electoralist parties, such as the British Conservatives under Margaret Thatcher and the U.S. Republicans at the national level[8] since 1980, have adopted a much more intense ideological commitment and confrontational style, at the same time as they have mastered "the new campaign politics." Others, such as the Dutch Socialists, have gone full cycle over the past three decades, sharply shifting towards a more radical leftist posture in the late 1960s, then returning to the political center two decades later. Thus, it is necessary to separate the organizational from the ideological/programmatic dimensions both in order to describe accurately these diverging evolutionary tendencies and to try to account for them.

Thus, we have broken down overaggregated party models into leaner and more theoretically modest types in order to facilitate future analyses of the separate impacts of distinct causal processes which may be moving parties in different directions simultaneously. To be sure, much of the variation in party organizational forms and campaign modalities may be explained largely by long-term processes of socio-economic development (altering the society within which campaigns will be conducted) and by technological advances. Technological change, for example, and especially the emergence of television as the dominant medium of political communication in nearly all democracies (and, more recently, the Internet as a new form of "narrow casting") has opened up more direct channels of party-elite access to voters, making older and less efficient vehicles for voter mobilization based on door-to-door campaigning by party militants unnecessary. But while these socio-economic and technological developments may create circumstances favourable to the development and progressive dominance of organizationally thin parties, they cannot predict precisely what kind of party is likely to emerge, let alone become a dominant model. Elite decisions to pursue different strategies of voter mobilization or different goals altogether (e.g. constituency representation instead of vote maximization) can lead to the adoption of a much more sharply defined ideological or programmatic stand. These latter decisions may be influenced by, but are not simply determined by, socio-economic or technological factors,[9] and thus cannot be assumed to evolve in a unilinear fashion.

Party ideologies, philosophies of representation and, to some extent, organizational styles may be affected by other societal trends that may have little to do with socio-economic or technological change. Rather than evolving in a unilinear manner, the defining characteristics of some partisan political subcultures appear to emerge, instead, through a dialectical process *in reaction against* certain features of the status quo. Indeed, one could hypothesize a chain of reactive changes in party ideologies whose temporal origins can be traced back to the earliest period covered in our survey of political parties, with the emergence of elite-based parties of individual representation in the early nineteenth century in Western Europe. These tended to be either traditionalist conservative or liberal in their ideological orientations. Traditionalist conservative parties defended various aspects of the *ancien regime* that were threatened by political and socio-economic change, while classical liberalism emerged as a reaction against that old order. Since the traditional, predemocratic social and political order in Western Europe was characterized by mercantilism, monarchy, aristocratic privilege and established state regions, it was not surprising that classical liberalism would stress free-market capitalism, individualism and religious freedom or anticleri-

calism. In the second half of the nineteenth century it was free-market capitalism that defined the status quo, with social polarization between the economically privileged and working classes fuelling the emergence of socialist parties, stressing class solidarity and economic equality. In turn, by the early twentieth century, conflict between free-market capitalism and socialist alternatives largely defined the parameters of institutionalized political conflict, leading to the articulation of a corporatist "third way" as an alternative. This advanced a view of society upon which both denominational parties and ultranationalist parties (twentieth-century West European examples of which were rooted in an integral organic corporatist vision of society) could be based. And by the late twentieth-century, widespread affluence, Keynesian interventionism and a large social welfare state defined a status quo against which both left-libertarian and post-industrial extreme right parties would react.[10] Accordingly, we can see that the defining features of important political ideologies emerged not as the product of unilinear evolutionary processes—such as long-term, continuous processes of socio-economic modernization—but through a discontinuous reactive process that was driven by political and social elites. While this dialectical interpretation of the emergence of ideologies and parties is speculative, it represents the kind of hypothesis that can be empirically tested using a more fine-grained differentiation among political parties, such as we have proposed.

Political parties have not emerged or evolved in a continuous, unilinear manner, and neither have they converged on a single model of party. Instead, we believe that changes in the organizational forms, electoral strategies, programmatic objectives and ideological orientations of parties are the products of multiple causal processes—some of them related to broader, long-term processes of social or technological change, others involving the less predictable innovative behaviour of political and social elites. If this is true, then it would be a mistake to rely on an excessively restricted number of party types. This would lead scholars to attempt to cram new parties into inappropriate models, or to abort the theory-building process by concluding in frustration that existing theories and models simply do not fit with established party types. Accordingly, we believe that the typology presented here—less parsimonious but more fully reflective of the real variation in party types around the world—should facilitate the testing of numerous hypotheses about the origins, functions and evolutionary trajectories of political parties in widely varying social, political, technological and cultural contexts.

ENDNOTES

1. As a party official in a socio-economically lagging, rural part of Spain described it: "The citizen who is worried about resolving problems with the doctor or the school . . . , or the problem of an unjust accusation before the courts, or of delinquency in paying his taxes to the state, etc., . . . has recourse to an intermediary . . . who can intercede on his behalf, but in exchange for pledging his very conscience and his vote" (Gunther et al., 1986: 84–85).

2. It should be noted that some peasant parties shared many characteristics with the working-class mass party, including many organizational features and similar historical origins. We are restricting our attention here to the more widespread working-class variant of the mass-based party, which provides a fuller manifestation of the various characteristics of this model.

3. As Mussolini once described his fellow fascists: "We allow ourselves the luxury of being aristocrats and democrats; conservatives and progressives; reactionaries and revolutionaries; legitimists and illegitimists; according to conditions of time, place and circumstance" (quoted in Schmidt, 1939: 97).

4. This is the key factor which separates the ethnic party from nationalist parties. The latter seek to expand their electoral base by convincing ever larger numbers of citizens that they should identify with the national group and its mission, and often define the "nation" in a flexible manner that facilitates this objective. The ethnic party takes the demographically defined boundaries of the group as "given," and seeks to represent its interests exclusively.

5. Panebianco (1988: 264) summarized the dominant characteristics of electoral-professional parties as (1) a central role of professionals with expertise in electoral mobilization; (2) weak vertical ties to social groups and broader appeals to the "opinion electorate"; (3) the pre-eminence of public representatives and personalized leadership; (4) financing through interest groups and public funds (as contrasted with past reliance on members' dues); and (5) an emphasis on issues and leadership.

6. In Kirchheimer's classic formulation (1966: 190), the defining features of the catch-all party include a "drastic reduction of the party's ideological baggage . . . [a f]urther strengthening of top leadership groups, whose actions and omissions are now judged from the viewpoint of their contribution to the efficiency of the entire social system rather than identification with the goals of their particular organization . . . [d]owngrading of the role of the individual party member, a role considered a historical relic which may obscure the newly built-up catch-all party image . . . [d]eemphasis of the *classe gardée,* specific social-class or denominationally clientele, in favor of recruiting voters among the population at large . . . [and s]ecuring access to a variety of interest groups." It should be noted that all of these defining characteristics pertain to ways in which the catch-all party departs from the former mass-integration model of party.

7. One is tempted to speculate that this fundamental difference is the product of differences in the social and political status quo that the party is reacting against. In the 1920s, the state was "thin," and the principal threat to the social order came from militant parties of the Marxist left. In the 1930s, the depression made the call for a more activist state a reasonable response to widespread unemployment and poverty. By the 1980s and 1990s, however, the social welfare state had been fully developed in most West European countries (especially Austria and France, where these extreme right parties have had greatest political impact), so attack on the interventionist state represented the obvious "reaction" in this dialectical process of ideology formation. In addition, the decline of militant Marxism and the mass-based class party, coupled with massive migration into many West European countries from Third World and post-soviet countries effectively created a new minority to be detested by these xenophobic parties.

8. It is exceedingly difficult to categorize American parties according to a single party type, since parties in the U.S. are really confederations of state parties (see Beck, 1997) which may vary quite considerably (some approximating the catch-all or programmatic models, while others may still include strong clientelistic elements). Thus, at the same time as the Republican Party in Congress has become increasingly programmatic, many state governors and their supportive parties have remained centrist and pragmatic practitioners of catch-all politics.

9. Increased affluence and the growth of a sizeable middle class, for example, may undercut the credibility and attractiveness of ideologies or programmes calling for radical socio-economic change.

10. For an excellent overview of the emergence of European political parties in conjunction with these ideological trends, see von Beyme (1985: 29–158). von Beyme's classification scheme bears some resemblance to ours, it is based primarily on the ideological or programmatic orientations of parties (see Ware, 1996: 21–49). Accordingly, it overlooks some of the organizational features and behavioural characteristics that we regard as of considerable importance.

REFERENCES

Adorno, T. W., Else Frenkel-Brunswik, Daniel J. Levinson and R. Nevitt Sanford (1950) *The Authoritarian Personality.* New York: Harper.

Barnes, Samuel H. (1967) *Party Democracy: Politics in an Italian Socialist Federation.* New Haven, CT: Yale University Press.

Beck, Paul Allen (1997) *Party Politics in America,* 8th ed. New York: Longman.

Betz, Hans-Georg and Stefan Immerfall (eds) (1998) *The New Politics of the Right: Neo-Populist Parties and Movements in Established Democracies.* New York: St. Martin's Press.

Beyme, Klaus von (1985) *Political Parties in Western Democracies.* Aldershot: Gower.

Chambers, William Nisbet and Walter Dean Burnham (1967) *The American Party Systems: Stages of Political Development.* Oxford and New York: Oxford University Press.

Dalton, Russell J. and Martin P. Wattenberg (2000) *Parties Without Partisans: Political Change in Advanced Industrial Democracies.* Oxford: Oxford University Press.

Diamond, Larry and Richard Gunther (eds) (2001) *Political Parties and Democracy.* Baltimore and London: John Hopkins University Press.

Duverger, Maurice (1954) *Political Parties.* London: Methuen.

Eldersveld, Samuel (1964) *Political Parties: A Behavioral Analysis.* Chicago, IL: Rand-McNally.

Epstein, Leon D. (1967) *Political Parties in Western Democracies.* New York: Praeger.

Fogarty, Michael Patrick (1957) *Christian Democracy in Western Europe, 1820–1953.* Notre Dame, IN: University of Notre Dame Press.

Gosnell, Harold Foote (1939) *Machine Politics: Chicago Style.* Chicago IL: University of Chicago Press.

Gunther, Richard, José Ramón Montero and Juan J. Linz (eds) (2002) *Political Parties: Old Concepts and New Challenges.* Oxford: Oxford University Press.

Gunther, Richard and Anthony Mughan (eds) (2000) *Democracy and the Media: A Comparative Perspective.* Cambridge and New York: Cambridge University Press.

Huntington, Samuel P. and Joan M. Nelson (1976) *No Easy Choice: Political Participation in Developing Countries.* Cambridge, MA: Harvard University Press.

Ignazi, Piero (1996) "The Crisis of Parties and the Rise of New Political Parties," *Party Politics* 2: 549–66.

Katz, Richard S. and Peter Mair (eds) (1994) *How Parties Organize: Change and Adaptation in Party Organization in Western Democracies.* London and Thousand Oaks: Sage.

Katz, Richard S. and Peter Mair (1995) "Changing Models of Party Organization and Party Democracy," *Party Politics* 1:5–28.

King, Anthony (1969) "Political Parties in Western Democracies: Some Sceptical Reflections," *Polity* 2: 111–41.

Kirchheimer, Otto (1966) "The Transformation of the Western European Party Systems," in Joseph LaPalombara and Myron Weiner (eds) *Political Parties and Political Development.* Princeton, NJ: Princeton University Press.

Kitschelt, Herbert (1989) *The Logics of Party Formation.* Ithaca, NY: Cornell University Press.

Kitschelt, Herbert (1994) *The Transformation of European Social Democracy.* Cambridge and New York: Cambridge University Press.

Kitschelt, Herbert (2001) "Divergent Paths of Postcommunist Democracies," in Larry Diamond and Richard Gunther (eds) *Political Parties and Democracy.* Baltimore, MD: Johns Hopkins University Press.

Koole, Ruud (1996) "Cadre, Catch-all or Cartel? A Comment on the Notion of the Cartel Party," *Party Politics* 2: 507–23.

LaPalombara, Joseph and Myron Weiner (1966) "The Origin and Development of Political Parties," in Joseph LaPalombara and Myron Weiner (eds) *Political Parties and Political Development.* Princeton, NJ: Princeton University Press.

Linz, Juan J. (1978) *The Breakdown of Democratic Regimes: Crisis, Breakdown and Reequilibration.* Baltimore and London: Johns Hopkins University Press.

Mair, Peter (1989) "Continuity, Change and the Vulnerability of Party," *West European Politics* 12: 169–87.

Mair, Peter and Ingrid van Biezen (2001) "Party Membership in Twenty European Democracies, 1980–2000," *Party Politics* 7: 5–21.

Michels, Robert (1915) *Political Parties: A Sociological Study of the Oligarchical Tendencies of Modern Democracy.* New York: Hearst's International Library.

Neumann, Sigmund (1956) "Towards a Comparative Study of the Political Parties," in Sigmund Neumann (ed.) *Modern Political Parties.* Chicago, IL: University of Chicago Press.

Panebianco, Angelo (1988) *Political Parties: Organization and Power.* Cambridge and New York: Cambridge University Press.

Schmidt, Carl T. (1939) *The Corporate State in Action.* London: Victor Gollanz.

Schurmann, Franz (1966) *Ideology and Organization in Communist China.* Berkeley, CA: University of California Press.

Wolinetz, Steven (1991) "Party System Change: The Catch-all Thesis Revisited," *West European Politics* 14: 113–128.

Wolinetz, Steven (2002) "Beyond the Catch-all Party: Approaches to the Study of Parties and Party Organization," in Richard Gunther, José Ramón Montero and Juan J. Linz (eds) *Political Parties: Old Concepts and New Challenges.* Oxford: Oxford University Press.

SEYMOUR MARTIN LIPSET

36 The Americanization of the European Left

In a book published in 1998, a distinguished sociologist asserted. "No one any longer has any alternatives to capitalism—the arguments that remain concern how far and in what ways capitalism should be governed and regulated." What makes these words especially noteworthy is that the man who wrote them, Anthony Giddens, was also widely known as the intellectual guru to British prime minister and Labour Party leader Tony Blair. By embracing "The Third Way" (the title of Gidden's book), explicitly understood as a middle path that avoided both the anticapitalism of the left and the conservatism of the right, Blair helped bring to an end a century-long period in which the European left had been dominated by socialists. By so doing, he and his counterparts on the continent have also furthered the process of making political party divisions in Europe resemble more closely those of the United States, where socialism never gained a serious foothold.

Socialist theorists from the late nineteenth century on have been bedeviled by the question of why

SOURCE: Seymour Martin Lipset, "The Americanization of the European Left," *Journal of Democracy,* vol. 12, no. 2 (April 2001), pp. 74–87. © National Endowment for Democracy and The Johns Hopkins University Press. Reprinted with permission of The Johns Hopkins University Press. Footnotes abridged by the Editor.

the United States, alone among industrial societies, has lacked a significant socialist movement or labor party. Friedrich Engels tried to answer it in the last decade of his life. In 1906, the German sociologist Werner Sombart published a major book on this theme, *Why Is There No Socialism in the United States?* That same year, the Fabian H.G. Wells also addressed the question in *The Future in America.* Both Lenin and Trotsky were deeply concerned with the phenomenon, for it questioned the inner logic of Marxist historical materialism, as expressed by Marx himself in *Das Kapital,* where he stated that "the country that is more developed [economically] shows to the less developed the image of their future."[1] From the last quarter of the nineteenth century on, the United States has been that country.

Given Marx's dictum, leading pre–World War I Marxists believed that the most industrialized capitalist country would lead the world into socialism. This position became entrenched in Marxism. While still an orthodox Marxist (before he became the most influential revisionist of Marxist ideas), Edward Bernstein noted, "We see modern socialism enter and take root in the United States in direct relation to the spreading of capitalism and the appearance of a modern proletariat." In 1902, Karl Kautsky, considered the German Social Democratic Party's leading theoretician, wrote that "America shows us our future, in so far as one country can reveal it at all to another." He elaborated this view in 1910, anticipating that the "overdue sharpening of class conflict" would develop "more strongly" in America than anywhere else. August Bebel, the political leader of the German Social Democrats, stated unequivocally in 1907, "Americans will be the first to usher in a Socialist republic."[2] This belief—at a time when the German party was already a mass movement with many elected members of the Reichstag, while the American Socialist Party had secured less than 2 percent of the vote—was based on the fact that the United States was far ahead of Germany in industrial development.

The continued inability of socialists to create a viable movement in the United States was a major embarrassment to Marxist theorists who assumed that the "superstructure" of a society, which encompasses political behavior, is a function of the underlying economic and technological systems. Max Beer, whose 50-year career in international socialism included participation in the Austrian, German, and British parties, and who worked for the Socialist International, described the anxiety voiced in private discussions by European Marxist leaders regarding the weakness of socialism in America. They knew that it was a "living contradiction of . . . Marxian theory" and that is raised questions about the validity of Marxism itself.[3]

In a 1939 publication intended for a popular American audience, Leon Trotsky reprinted the sentence from *Das Kapital* quoted above, only to dismiss it with the comment, "under no circumstances can this . . . be taken literally."[4] Trotsky, of course, knew his Marxism and was well aware that the theory demanded that the United States should have been the first on the path to socialism. His comment suggests that the contradiction was much on his mind. His effort to dismiss it as a figurative statement indicates that he had no answer to the conundrum it posed.

Yet in spite of the sorry record of organized socialism in America, it may be argued that, in a sense, Karl Marx was right in saying that the most developed country "shows to the less developed the image of their future." American political culture—as it actually developed, not as Marxists hoped it

would—reflects the logic of an economically and technologically advanced society. The never-feudal United States has been the prototypical bourgeois society. As Max Weber understood, the United States could become the world's most productive economy precisely because its culture thoroughly encompassed capitalist values. The ideal-typical capitalist man was an American—Benjamin Franklin. For Weber, "the spirit of capitalism" was best expressed in the Pennsylvanian's writings.[5]

The argument that American nonsocialist politics would prove to be the model for the European left was presented in full flower in 1940 by Lewis Corey (Louis Fraina), an early leader of the American Communist Party, in a series of articles in the Lovestoneite organ *Workers Age*. Corey's insight is summarized by Harvey Klehr as follows:

> Rather than being an exception, America was actually the model for capitalist countries. Only the positions in the race had been changed; European socialists could see in America the image of their own unhappy future. Far from being a unique or even only slightly different case, America was the prototype for capitalism. In a curious reversal of roles, it was now the European socialists who could look across the ocean to see the future of their own movement. American development was not different than Europe's; it was merely at a more advanced stage.[6]

CHANGING SOCIETIES, CHANGING POLITICS

As Corey anticipated, the left in the other Western democracies has become increasingly like the American nonsocialist left. To a greater or lesser degree, all major parties of the left now reject statist economies and accept competitive markets as the way to achieve economic growth and raise standards of living. Social-democratic and labor parties are now socially and ideologically pluralistic. The Socialist International has effectively been recast into a new grouping of progressive parties, dubbed the "third way," in which the Democratic Party represents the United States.

This change in the character of the European parties reflects a transformation of economic and class structures that has made them resemble those of the United States. The emphasis on fixed, explicitly hierarchical social classes derived from a feudal and monarchical past has declined greatly. The growth in the European economies, together with the consequent increase in consumption goods and a more equitable allocation of education, has greatly reduced the differences in style of life, including accents and dress, among social classes. The distribution of income and occupational skills has changed from the pyramidal shape that characterized the late nineteenth and early twentieth centuries to one that resembles a diamond, bulging in the middle.

Political parties on the left now seek to appeal more to the growing middle strata than to industrial workers and the impoverished, who constitute a declining proportion of the population. In the United States—the prototype of industrialized societies—the proportion of those employed in non-manual pursuits increased from 43 percent in 1960 to 58 at the end of the century, while the proportion of the workers employed in manufacturing fell from 26 to 16 percent. The corresponding dropoff for the United Kingdom was from 36 percent to 19 percent; for Sweden, from 32 percent to 19 percent; for the Netherlands, from 30 percent to 19 percent; and for Australia, from 26 percent to 13.5 percent. The declines have been less dramatic but still pronounced for France (28 to 20 percent) and Germany (34 to 29 percent).

America has always placed a lesser emphasis on class awareness and organization than European societies; in any case, these have been declining on both sides of the Atlantic. Union membership, the predominant base of parties on the left, has fallen in proportional terms in four-fifths of the 92 countries surveyed by the International Labor Organization. Between 1985 and 1995, union membership rates declined by 21 percent in the United States. As of 2000, only 13.5 percent of employed American workers—and less than 10 percent of those in private employment—are members of trade unions. These declines have been even

greater in France and Britain (37 and 28 percent, respectively), while Germany fell off by 18 percent.[7] The European and Australasian social-democratic parties, like the Democrats in the United States, have become more socially heterogeneous in membership and support. The correlations between class and voting, which are lower in the United States than elsewhere in the industrialized world, have been falling in most developed nations in recent decades as the distribution of economic classes and consumption levels have changed.

Some of the underlying forces giving rise to these developments have been specified by a number of neo-Marxist social scientists in discussing the emergence of "postindustrial society," "postmaterialism," and the "scientific-technological revolution." Daniel Bell, a lifelong social democrat, has been the central figure in conceptualizing these changes in the West. Radovon Richta and his associates in the Czechoslovak Academy of Sciences projected similar developments in Eastern Europe and the Soviet Union.[8]

The consequent changes in class and political relations within industrially developed societies, much like the shifts in left-wing politics in the United States and Europe, may be analyzed within the framework of an "apolitical" Marxism—that is, by accepting the proposition that technological advances and the distribution of economic classes determine the political and cultural "superstructures," but without assuming that socialism will succeed capitalism. Many of the trends anticipated by Marx—the growth of factories, a steady increase in the industrial proletariat, a decline in self-employment—have ended. The proportion of people employed in tertiary technological and service occupations has been increasing rapidly. The number of university graduates and students in higher education has grown sharply. Alain Touraine, a leading French sociologist and leftist intellectual, suggests that the basis of power has changed as a result of these developments: "If property was the criterion of membership in the former dominant class, the new dominant class is defined by knowledge and a certain level of education."[9]

Neo-Marxists and technological determinists have stressed the extent to which theoretical and scientific knowledge has become the principal source of social and economic change, altering social structures, values, and mores in ways that have given considerable prestige and power to scientific and technological elites. The emerging strata of postindustrialism—whose roots are in the university, the scientific and technological worlds, the industries spawned by computers, the public sector, and the professions—have developed their own distinctive values.

Ronald Inglehart, the most important empirical analyst of postindustrialism, points out that "postmaterialist" value changes and the decline of class conflict are also functions of the growing climate of affluence in the last half-century. The generations that came of age during the second half of the twentieth century hold different values than their predecessors, who were reared in an atmosphere of economic scarcity and experienced severe economic depressions. Survey data gathered by Inglehart over the past quarter-century have shown clear generational effects and links to the massive growth in educational attainments that have made the expansion in high-tech and scientific pursuits possible.[10]

These developments have profoundly affected the political scene in industrially advanced societies. With the growth of market power in the economic arena, postindustrial politics has been marked by a decline in ideological conflict over the role of the state. The citizenry, now better-educated, has become increasingly concerned with noneconomic or social issues—the environment, health, the quality of education, the culture, greater equality for women and minorities, the extension of democratization and freedom at home and abroad, and (last, but far from least) questions of personal morality, particularly as they affect family matters and sexual behavior. In some polities, including France and Germany, environmental reformers have taken the lead in creating new Green parties, generally allied in coalition with the new social democrats.

Just as the United States has set a model for less statist, more market-oriented polities, more recently it has been in the forefront of the postmaterialist "new politics," which has traveled, so to speak, from Berkeley and Madison to Paris and Berlin. The French political analyst Jean-François Revel, writing

in the early 1970s, noted that the newer forms of movement protest, whether in Europe or elsewhere, are "imitations of the American prototype."[11]

Many political analysts, while recognizing major reformulations by the left within their own countries, do not realize the extent to which these changes reflect developments that are common throughout the economically advanced democracies. To point out the magnitude and congruence of these events, I will summarize the ways in which left-wing politics in country after country has taken an "American" path. This, of course, does not mean that parties and ideologies are the same cross-nationally. There are important variations reflecting diverse historical backgrounds, the varying nature of political cleavages, and the structural and demographic patterns underlying them. Yet the similarities among the polities are considerable. As Tony Blair has stressed, "it's a perfectly healthy thing if we realize there are common developments the whole world over."[12]

THE NEW SOCIAL DEMOCRATS

Following a meeting of European social-democratic leaders with Bill Clinton in New York on 24 September 1998, Tony Blair proclaimed their new "third way" doctrine.

> In the economy, our approach is neither laissez faire nor one of state interference. The government's role is to promote macroeconomic stability; develop tax and welfare policies that encourage independence, not dependence; to equip people for work by improving education and infrastructure; and to promote enterprise. We are proud to be supported by the business leaders as well as trade unions. . . . In welfare and employment policy, the Third Way means reforming welfare to make it a pathway into work where possible. It promotes fair standards at work while making work pay by reducing the taxes and penalties that discourage work and the creation of jobs.[13]

The 1997 British election, won overwhelmingly by the Labour Party after it had rejected its historic emphasis on public ownership, put an end to a century of socialist efforts to reduce the degree of private ownership or to eliminate it altogether. Tony Blair deliberately stressed his agreement with the free-market, smaller-government policies of Bill Clinton. Even before Clinton, Blair proclaimed that the era of big government was over and promised to govern from the center. Blair reformulated his party's image as "New Labour," a nonsocialist party that is not committed to working with the trade unions. He emphasized that he wants unions to cooperate "with management to make sure British industry is competitive." Peter Mendelson, then the ideologist of the Blairites, proudly asserted that Labour is now "a market capitalist party."[14]

Even more notable was Blair's advice to labor organizations in a 1994 article in the *New Statesman* that "it is in the unions' best interest not to be associated with one political party." Blair argued that unions "should be able to thrive with any change of government or no change in government"—this from the leader of a party largely founded by trade unions and subsidized by them for all of its history. During the 1997 campaign, the Labour Party released a special manifesto aimed at business promising that a Blair government would retain the "main elements" of Margaret Thatcher's restrictions on unions and would resist unreasonable economic demands. Blair noted in an interview that his administration would "leave British [labor] law the most restrictive on trade unionism in the Western world."[15]

The Labour Party's manifesto proclaimed, "Tax and spend is being replaced by save and invest." Its general election platform not only stated that "healthy profits are an essential motor of a dynamic market economy" but also emphasized that the goal of low inflation requires that wage gains be held down. It is not surprising that Baroness Thatcher, at the start of the 1997 campaign, said, "Britain will be safe in the hands of Mr. Blair." Speaking to a meeting of the Socialist International, Blair returned the compliment, saying, "There were certain things the 1980s got right—an emphasis on enterprise, more flexible labour markets." One of his first actions after taking office was to shift the power to control monetary policy and interest rates from the Treasury to the Bank of England. Another, taken after his first meeting with Bill Clinton on 31 May 1997, was to launch welfare reform designed to reduce the numbers on the dole by pressing single mothers to take paying jobs. At this meeting, Clinton and Blair asserted that the "progressive parties of today are the parties of fiscal responsibility and prudence."

The same pattern is evident the world over. During the 1980s, the Labor governments of Australia and New Zealand cut income taxes, pursued economic deregulation, and privatized various industries. The Australian Labor party reached an "accord" with trade unions that resulted in reducing real wages by at least 1 percent in each of the eight years the Prime Minister Robert Hawke headed the government. The story is similar in New Zealand, where the Labour Party during 1984–90 ended "the tradition of taxation according to ability to pay," dismantled the welfare state, and privatized many state enterprises. According to a report in a social-democratic magazine, Prime Minister David Lange argued that "social democrats must accept the existence of economic inequality because it is the engine which drives the economy."

The same pattern holds for the parties of the left outside the English-speaking world. The Swedish Social Democrats reversed their previous wage-growth, high–income-tax, and strong–welfare-state orientations and undertook several privatization measures as well. The late American socialist leader, Michael Harrington, reported critically that Prime Minister Olof Palme's government increased employment by reducing the real income of those with a job.[16]

In Spain, three-term Socialist prime minister Felipe González converted his party—Marxist in its initial post-Franco phase—into a supporter of privatization, the free market, and NATO. He once noted, in a near-Churchillian formulation, that a competitive free-market economy is marked by greed, corruption, and the exploitation of the weak by the strong, but "capitalism is the least-bad economic system in existence." *The Economist* described his economic policies as having made his government "look somewhat to the right of Mrs. Thatcher's."

The oldest major Marxist party in the world, the Social Democrats of Germany (SPD), rejected Marxism at their Bad Godesberg conference in 1959. American political scientist Russell Dalton later commented on their program: "Karl Marx would have been surprised to . . . learn that free economic competition was one of the essential conditions of a social democratic economic policy." Speaking in 1976, Social Democratic Chancellor Helmut Schmidt argued that the interests of the workers required expanding profits, noting that "the profits of enterprises today are the investments of tomorrow, and the investments of tomorrow are the employment of the day after." The SPD's 1990 program noted in classical liberal fashion that within a "democratically established setting, the market and competition are indispensable." In 1995, Rudolph Scharping, then the SPD candidate for chancellor and currently minister of defense, emphasized that his party's historic assumptions had proven wrong, stating, "We Social Democrats created an overly regulated, overly bureaucratic, and overly professionalized welfare state."[17]

The chancellor elected in 1998, Gerhard Schröder, continues in this tradition. He sees the SPD not as part of the left but as occupying a "New Middle," a place where, as John Vinocur puts it, "words like 'risk,' 'entrepreneurial spirit,' and 'flexible labor markets' coincide with expressions of allegiance to social justice and fair income distribution." Schröder has promised to improve the German economy and reduce its high unemployment rate by lowering its "prohibitive labor costs" and "providing incentive for new capital investment." He notes that the SPD is "breaking with . . . statist social democratic attitudes. . . . [W]e've understood that the omnipotent and interventionist state doesn't have its place in the current circumstances."[18]

In his inaugural speech after being inducted as chancellor on 10 November 1998, Schröder stressed continuity with the outgoing Christian Democratic government of Helmut Kohl, saying, "We do not want to do everything differently, but many things better." To help reduce unemployment, he has cut corporate taxes from the maximum rate of 47 percent under Kohl to 35 percent, and has called for business and unions to cooperate in a formal "alliance for jobs." He also proposes to foster private pension schemes, to encourage personal responsibility, and to concentrate state subsidies and spending on the "truly needy," while, in the words of the *Financial Times,* linking "fiscal policy with supply side measures, including deregulation and the opening of markets."

In the past, socialist parties created extensive welfare states that required a steadily increasing proportion of GDP (in some cases, more than half) to go to the government. Today, however, these same parties recognize that they simply cannot compete in the world market unless they reduce government expenditures. Their electoral situation forces them to try to appeal to middle-class and affluent skilled workers and high-tech employees. Hence, like Blair, Clinton, and Schröder, they seek to lower taxes, reduce welfare entitlements, and balance their budgets, but also to press for postmaterialist reforms aimed at cleaning up the natural, social, and economic environment. Even Sweden, the prototypical social-democratic polity, sped up its efforts to strengthen its economy by privatizing an additional 25 enterprises in 1999. Finland and Denmark have pursued similar policies under social-democratic leadership.

The only exceptions to the move away from state intervention among socialist parties have occurred in Norway and, to some extent, in France, both of which still favor extensive welfare policies (though not, it should be noted, nationalization of industry). Norway can retain a belief in "old-fashioned socialism" because of its abundant oil resources, which pay for its welfare state. The French left operates within a society in which *dirigisme,* the idea of a strong directing state, has been as much a part of the national culture as antistatism has been in America. Both the right and left in France have approved of a powerful state, an emphasis that goes back to the Empire, the Revolution, and the monarchy. Journalist Roger Cohen has noted that "the Gaullist attachment to the state and rejection of market reform encouraged the Socialists to keep further to the left, to distinguish themselves." As Ezra Suleiman, an academic authority on French politics, emphasizes, "The right can't let go of the state, so the left stays left."[19] Thus it is not surprising that the

Socialists campaigned and won in 1997 promising a massive program of government-sponsored job creation and the protection of the welfare state from budget cuts.

Yet in an interview with *Le Nouvel Observateur,* socialist prime minister Lionel Jospin sounded like other European socialists in saying he favors a move away from "statism," with more decentralization and increased individual initiative. He has praised the extensive privatization measures carried through by François Mitterrand during his 14 years as president. Jospin has also spoken of the need for France to emulate the American economy. In 1998, he criticized leftist disdain for the level of U.S. job growth, saying, "Contrary to what we have claimed and indeed believed, the jobs being created in the United States are not only, or even mainly, low-paid, dead-end jobs, but skilled ones in the service and high-tech industries." According to *The Economist,* Jospin has stressed that the French "could learn much about America's economic dynamism, the vitality of its research and innovation, its competitive spirit and capacity for renewal."[20]

Curiously, the model late-1990s country, frequently cited as such by European social democrats and others, is the Netherlands, with an unemployment rate of 6.5 percent in 1997 (far below the major Continental economies), and a growth rate higher than in Britain, France, or Germany. The Dutch, under a government headed by former union leader Wim Kok of the Labor Party, have kept down "wages, inflation and interest rates, and . . . [eased] the rules of hiring and firing and for opening new businesses." Unemployment benefits have been cut, while the rules for sick and disability pay have been tightened. Thomas Friedman of the *New York Times* described the policy as "U.S. style downsizing, privatizing, and loosening up of labor rules."[21]

In a "social pact" negotiated between the unions, then led by Kok, and the employers, labor agreed to limit wage increases to 2 percent a year. Whether due to these policies or not, the subsequent near-full-employment economy has led to an increase in income inequality, much as in the United States and other industrialized countries. In high-tech economies, the better-educated and highly skilled are much more in demand than industrial workers and the less skilled, and thus they are relatively much better paid.

Far from a politically "backward" United States following the lead of a more "progressive" Europe, the Old World left is now becoming more like the American left, as Lewis Corey had anticipated. Hence one may indeed say that, in political terms, the United States has shown Europe the image of its future. As European countries reached new heights of affluence and mass consumption, they began, as Antonio Gramsci had anticipated, to resemble the United States, with societies that are less stratified, less status-bound, and much better educated. Consequently their less privileged strata are much less class-conscious than before. Today, Europe's now-nonsocialist "progressive" parties seek, as Adam Przeworski notes, to make capitalism more humane and more efficient. As François Mitterrand's former advisor Regis Debray put it, the objective of European socialist leaders is "to carry out the politics of the Right, but more intelligently and in a more rational manner."[22]

OLD TERMS, NEW DEFINITIONS

None of this is meant to suggest that the political divisions of modern democracy, conceptualized since the French Revolution on a spectrum between left and right, have disappeared. Democrats and Republicans, or Social Democrats and Conservatives, still provide choices on the ballot, although their ideological bearings and internal factions are changing.

Cleavages linked to social stratification are no longer the main correlates of a party's position on the left or right of the political spectrum. Issues revolving around morality, abortion, "family values," civil rights, gender equality, multiculturalism, immigration, crime and punishment, foreign policy, and supranational communities push individuals and groups in directions that are independent of their socioeconomic position. Yet most of these matters can be related to social ideology, which in turn correlates with religion and education.

The meanings of the terms "left" and "right" are changing. As we have seen, the parties of the left, although still identifying themselves as social democratic or socialist, have largely reconstituted themselves as liberals in the American sense of the word, emphasizing postmaterialist themes like environmentalism, equality for women and gays, minority rights, and cultural freedoms. The right has moved, in varying degrees, toward classical liberalism or libertarianism. The left stresses group equality and economic security; the right, equality of opportunity and the weakening of state power. Logically, the right should also support personal freedom, along the lines favored by nineteenth-century liberals, but the political alliances between economic conservatives and religious traditionalists have fostered cultural conservatism on issues relating to sex, the family, and style of life. Given the complex variations in the political cleavage structure, it is difficult today to specify a consistent pattern that differentiates left from right. For example, some advisers to . . . U.S. president George W. Bush have suggested that his outlook is "communitarian," a label previously associated with some advisers to Bill Clinton.

No major tendency, left or right, retains a belief in a utopia, a solution to all major problems through dramatically reconstructing society and polity. These post–Cold War conditions bode well for democratic stability and for international peace. It has become a truism that democracies do not wage war against each other, and most of the world is now democratic. While extremist movements and parties exist, all of them are relatively weak, at least in the West. The strongest are Jörg Haider's Freedom Party in Austria, with 27 percent of the vote, and Jean-Marie Le Pen's National Front in France, which is supported by 15 percent of the electorate. No other is close to these levels. There are no charismatic leaders, and little political enthusiasm. Youth, who Aristotle noted "have exalted notions . . . [and who] would rather do noble things than useful ones," are necessarily frustrated.

Will this situation change? Of course it will; economies, and consequently societies, never remain in a steady state. The inner dynamics of market systems produce reverses in the business cycle that can threaten democratic stability. The Japanese collapse has replaced the Japanese miracle. France's move to the left in 1997 and Le Pen's support on the right were facilitated not only by the country's statist values but also by an unemployment rate of 12 percent. Demographic factors threaten to undermine the financial underpinnings of social security and health systems. The rise of new major players in the international arena, such as China, can and will result in new trade disequilibriums. But all these prospects and more are for the future.

For now, the end of the Cold War seemingly has given America and its ideology an almost total victory. The United States is now the *only* superpower. Its economy is the most productive. The major recent movements for egalitarian social change and for improving the quality of life—feminism, environmentalism, civil rights for minorities, gay rights—all diffused from America, much as the democratic revolutions of the nineteenth century had. The developed world has been more successful than ever in satisfying the consumption desires of its people, manual workers and intellectual strata alike.

All this should make for more conservative and smug societies. Yet the standards by which Western countries now judge themselves are derived from the French, American, and Marxist revolutionary creeds. These proclaim that "all men are created equal" and share the goal of "life, liberty and the pursuit of happiness." Yet all polities, even the classically liberal ones, must fail to live up fully to the inherently utopian objectives of libertarianism and egalitarianism. Americans still lean more to the libertarian side, Europeans to the egalitarian. Both tendencies favor freedom for all and strong juridical restraints on state power. Americans prefer a meritocratic, libertarian society with an effective but weak government. They will not attain these objectives in any absolute sense, but they will keep trying. It may be noted that socialists from Marx and Engels to Antonio Gramsci, Anthony Crosland, and Michael Harrington all have acknowledged that the United States came closer socially (though obviously not economically) to their ideological goal of a classless society with a weak state than any other system they knew in their lifetimes. Leon Samson, a left-wing American Marxist, concluded in the early 1930s that American radicals could not sell socialism to a people who believed they already lived in a society that operationally, though obviously not terminologically, was committed to socialist objectives.

America still has an ideological vision with which to motivate its young. Europeans are increasingly committed to a similar social vision, derived in large measure from the French Revolution and social democracy. Both accept the competitive market as the means to increase productivity, thereby diminishing differences in consumption styles linked to class. Both are enlarging the scope of higher education, with a consequent enhancement of access into elite ranks. Emphasis on status differences in Europe is declining. Economic inequality, of course, is still great, and even increasing during periods of technological innovation such as the present, because new skills are in much greater demand than old ones. But since patterns of deference and social class inferiority are declining, while access to information is widening with the spread of the Internet, power is becoming more dispersed.

These profound social and economic changes will continue to reshape the nature of party cleavages in the coming decades, no doubt in ways that cannot now be fully anticipated. Yet just as the era of big government, according to Tony Blair and Bill Clinton, is now over, so the recent evolution of parties on the left heralds an end to class as the dominant cleavage structuring party politics. Parties in advanced industrial democracies will continue to sort themselves along a left-right spectrum, but "left" and "right" will never again be defined by the contest between socialism and capitalism. With the end of that grand ideological competition, the differences between parties have narrowed and become more fluid. Today, most parties lean toward the center on economic issues, while party systems float in search of a new grand line of cleavage. The social bases for that new defining cleavage may not emerge any time soon.

ENDNOTES

1. Karl Marx and Friedrich Engels, "Unpublished Letters of Karl Marx and Friedrich Engels to Americans," in *Science and Society* 2 (1938), p. 368; H.G. Wells, *The Future in America* (New York:

Harper and Brothers, 1906); Karl Marx, *Capital*, vol. 1 (Moscow: Foreign Languages Publishing House, 1958), pp. 8–9. For Lenin's writings, see Harvey Klehr, "Leninist Theory in Search of America," *Polity* 9 (1976), pp. 81–96.

2. Cited in R. Laurence Moore, *European Socialists and the American Promised Land* (New York: Oxford University Press, 1970), pp. 70, 58, 102, and 77, respectively.

3. Max Beer, *Fifty Years of International Socialism* (London: George Allen and Unwin, 1935), pp. 109–10.

4. Leon Trotsky, *The Living Thoughts of Karl Marx* (New York: Longmans, Green, 1939), pp. 38–39.

5. Max Weber, *The Protestant Ethic and the Spirit of Capitalism* (New York: Charles Scribners and Sons, 1958), pp. 64–65.

6. Harvey Klehr, "The Theory of American Exceptionalism," Ph.D. diss., Department of History, University of North Carolina–Chapel Hill, 130. The full discussion of Fraina-Corey is on pp. 126–30.

7. "ILO Highlights Global Challenges to Trade Unions," *ILO News,* 4 November 1997.

8. Daniel Bell, *The Coming of Post-Industrial Society* (New York: Basic Books, 1978); Radovon Richta, et al., *Civilizations at the Crossroads* (White Plains, N.Y.: International Arts and Sciences Press, 1969).

9. Alain Touraine, *The Post-Industrial Society: Tomorrow's Social History* (New York: Random House, 1971).

10. Ronald Inglehart, "The Silent Revolution in Europe: Intergenerational Change in Post-Industrial Societies," *American Political Science Review* 65 (December 1971), pp. 991–1017. See also Ronald Inglehart, *Modernization and Postmodernization* (Princeton, N.J. Princeton University Press, 1997).

11. Jean-François Revel, *Without Marx or Jesus* (Garden City, N.Y.: Doubleday, 1971), pp. 6–7.

12. John F. Harris and Fred Barbash, "Blair Savors Colleague Clinton's Arm on His Shoulder," *Washington Post,* 30 May 1997, pp. A27–28.

13. Tony Blair, "Third Way, Better Way," *Washington Post,* 27 September 1998, p. C7.

14. George Will, "Last Rite for Socialism," *Washington Post,* 21 December 1997, p. C7.

15. Tony Blair, "No Favours," *New Statesman and Society,* 28 November 1994, p. 33; Madaline Druhan, "Union Reforms Stay, Labour Leader Says," *Globe and Mail* (Toronto), 1 April 1997.

16. Michael Harrington, *The Next Left: The History of a Future* (New York: Holt, 1987). pp. 130–31.

17. Rudolf Scharping, "Freedom, Solidarity, Individual Responsibility: Reflections on the Relationship Between Politics, Money and Morality," *The Responsive Community* 6 (Fall 1996), p. 53.
18. John Vinocur, "Downsizing German Politics," *Foreign Affairs* 77 (September–October 1998), pp. 11–12.
19. Roger Cohen, "France's Old Soldier Fades Away," *New York Times,* 8 June 1997, p. E5.
20. "Jospin Discovers America," *The Economist,* 27 June 1998, p. 50.
21. Thomas L. Friedman, "The Real G-7's," *New York Times,* 19 June 1997, p. A35.
22. Adam Przeworski, *Capitalism and Social Democracy* (Cambridge: Cambridge University Press, 1985), p. 206; Regis Debray, "What's Left of the Left?" *New Perspectives Quarterly* 7 (Spring 1990), p. 27.

PIERO IGNAZI

37   The Rise of New Political Parties

[The author's discussion of the "party decline" thesis has been omitted—ED.]

. . . What is the current meaning of the decline or crisis of party? First, in terms of organization, the loss of strength and appeal is empirically verifiable by membership size, number and strength of party identifiers and level of volatility. However, none of these measures are substantively satisfactory because (a) in the case of membership, the information is superficial, rough and sometimes unreliable, while what is needed (in accordance with Janda's suggestion) is a multidimensional index of organizational strength; and (b) in the case of the other two indicators, they do not refer to the party organization as they measure different properties. Moreover, it is doubtful that parties are facing a decline in their organizational strength. Second, in terms of functions, it is less doubtful that parties are confronted with rising difficulties in performing their traditional functions. The challenge addresses mainly their channelling performance—the capacity to voice the popular will—both for structural reasons (party structure is no longer satisfactory for mobilized citizens) and for agenda-setting (some crucial issues are not dealt with by traditional parties, or by parties at all).

Taking for granted that the crisis of party is mainly related to the unfulfilment of functions traditionally performed by parties—in particular the expressive one—what outcome has this impasse produced?

PARTY DECLINE AND NEW SOCIAL MOVEMENTS

The safety valve to the supposed gloomy trend of party decline has been identified by many analysts in the new parties which arose in the 1980s, the left-libertarian or the ecologists (see Dalton, 1988, 1991 for a synthetic overview on the point). In a way, the new parties have performed the function of diversifying the genus to strengthen the species. The role of the new parties is relevant not only because they transfused fresh blood into the party system, providing new channels of expression *always in the party realm,* and therefore pushing aside the attack of nonpartisan organizations, but because they offered a new role to the members. Leaving aside, for a moment, the aspect of issues, New Politics parties emerged to respond to a need for more participation and for a different way of making politics. Dissatisfaction with the "traditional" internal mechanisms of the mass parties, with their bureaucratization, with the unresponsiveness of their leaders, with the insignificant role of individual members, with the absence of a sense of community, all pushed a portion of active, young, well-educated citizens to

SOURCE: Piero Ignazi, "The Crisis of Parties and the Rise of New Political Parties," *Party Politics,* vol. 2, no. 4 (1996), pp. 549–565. Copyright 1996 by Sage Publications Ltd. Reprinted by permission of Sage Publications Ltd. and the author. Article, footnotes, and references abridged by the Editor.

look for a different *locus* for expressing their wills. The demand for more instruments, more channels and more means of participating by a citizenry animated by the civic virtue of democratically influencing the decision-making process is at the basis of the development of these new parties.

In reality, not all the "traditional" means of participation have been proved and considered useful by the activists and, cycle after cycle, some have activated different, unconventional forms of participation. In the early-mid-1970s, the number of people who were inclined to use unconventional and even non-legal acts comprised more than one-third of the population. The availability of such a protest potential set the condition for the later development of new social movements. The crucial point, then, is to ascertain whether the protest concerned the means, i.e. *parties,* or the ends, i.e. *the democratic system as such.*

The puzzle has not been disentangled by the literature but the prevailing view points to a widespread acceptance of the democratic system even by the new social movements and the left-libertarian parties. The failure to secure their demands and the dissatisfaction/inefficacy of the classical means of expression have "forced" them to by-pass the traditional parties. The New Politics parties demanded, together with libertarian and equalitarian issues, more efficacy and/or more effectiveness of the system, not a radical change of the "rules of the game." The protest pointed to more democracy, freedom and means of expression, and to less order, hierarchy and authority. They argued for a new form of democracy, not for something different from democracy. Therefore, with the exclusion of those protestors influenced by Marxist-Leninist ideology (or by a surrogate of it), which by definition wanted to overcome democracy, the social movements' leaders aimed mainly at a better functioning of democracy, with an emphasis on direct democracy.

Coming back to the question of the role of party membership, it is not the decline in party strength that paved the way for new parties, but the decline in the *role* of party members. The perceived lack of internal democracy (once again since the imperial SPD [German Social Democratic Party]),[1] the frustration with the feeling of insignificance in the complex, rigid, "bureaucratic" structure, the weakening of collective and symbolic incentives, linked to the declining of ideological competition and to the waning of clear-cut identities, the ritualist emphasis on member recruitment by the dominant coalition; all are factors shifting involvements from party to social movements and to a different type of party. Following this line of reasoning the crisis of party is due to a certain type of organization, which combines the vices of both the mass party (bureaucratization, rigidity, etc.) and the catch-all party (absence of collective benefits, looseness of identity, feeling of insignificance, etc.). This mixed organizational profile could be also described in terms of power relations: The asymmetric balance of power between leaders and rank and file tends to be more and more skewed against the members. Only when the balance of power is reversed in favour of individual members does the party gain new attractiveness. But this does not apply to the traditional parties (except for some symbolic involvement).

Mobilized citizens—vividly described by Dalton (1988)—could therefore satisfy their desires for participation by by-passing the party and directing their involvement towards social movements and/or new political organizations. Both the latter, at the very beginning, form "an equality area" (Pizzorno, 1969)—a setting where everybody feels equal and participation is highly stimulated and rewarding. The new ecologist parties, defined as "the parliamentary arm of the New Politics movement" (Dalton, 1991: 55), present, *in their originary model* (Panebianco, 1988), an internal structure characterized by involvement of the rank and file, open access to party meetings, no office accumulation, strong control of the elected and turnover in office (see Kitschelt, 1989; Pogunkte, 1989, 1993). They have an "open and decentralised political structure . . . and represent a new style of partisan politics" (Dalton, 1991: 55–56). This connotation derives from their "originary model," while the process of institutionalization has (inevitably) imposed some restraints on those traits.

The crisis of parties and the development of new social movements and left-libertarian/green parties are related: The latter grow out of the defaults of the former. Issues and means of actions ("*actions repertoire*") have had such an impact on the European party system that parties have tried—unsuccessfully—to accommodate themselves both to a more open and "democratic" internal structuring and to a more responsive (i.e. postmaterialist) agenda. Old parties decline because of their incapacity to adapt to the modified environment and new ones arise, thanks to their different organizational profile (and more successful agenda). This argument has been partially rejected by those arguing that "the conflict between parties and social movements has been exaggerated" and "if there has been a decline in partisanship, the rise of the new agenda is an unlikely candidate for causing that trend" (Reiter, 1993: 102).[2] Moreover, the hypothesis that the new type of party has, in a way, counterbalanced the crisis of traditional parties has to face two more questions. First, the decline of all major parties cannot be counterbalanced by new *small* parties, which have little impact in national elections, except in Belgium, where the Greens reached and maintained 10 percent of the votes; if a new cleavage dimension is appearing, a more dramatic effect should be shown. Second, and more important, the decline of parties for the unfulfillment of the channelling function is based on the premise that a demand for participation is spreading around the western countries. But this is not the case. The limited interest in politics (Commission of the European Communities, 1994) indicates that the opposite is true. And finally, other parties which did not care at all for a more participatory internal structure also emerged in the 1980s: the extreme right parties.

THE DIVERGING OUTCOMES OF POSTINDUSTRIAL SOCIETY

All the analysts of new movements and value change state that the structural changes in western countries are the *primum mobile* for the rise of the New Politics parties. Inglehart, for one, bases his seminal work on value change on clearly stated structural factors: The post-war socio-economic transformations—prosperity *thus* (internal) security—have allowed different value priorities. These new attitudes have then been taken on by newcomers in the political arena, the New Politics parties. However, if this is true, why, at the same time and in the same societies (that is, given the same conditions) does a different kind of party, on the other side of the political spectrum, develop? Why have postindustrial societies generated or revived, in the 1980s, totally diverging parties, such as the extreme right ones? (Ignazi, 1992). Apparently, the same factors that have explained the rise of new social movements and left-libertarian parties—structural changes in the society—have led to very different outcomes. The extreme right parties are in fact the (unaccounted) outcome of the same process. The structural explanation per se does not account for the variation in the effects of socio-economic changes. Only if one considers a non-structural element, values, does the different path becomes clear. What makes the difference is thus the value system.

The question should be reformulated as an investigation of the reason why a certain value system seemed to be the necessary outcome of postindustrialism. Expressed differently, socialization in an environment of "material saturation and security" plus unprecedented higher education, exposure to mass media and mobility—Inglehart's "socialization hypothesis" (1985: 103)—*should have* produced a new value priority which goes under the postmaterial label. A line of explanation comes from the advocates of the postindustrial society who underlined that "the decline of the imprint of the machine and of its rhythms on the character of work," implied by the growth of the service sector, and the loss of the centrality of "labour conflicts as the crucial and potentially destructive conflict" (Bell, 1973: 160ff) would have broken traditional attitudes and behaviours, leaving to the individual as unforeseeable freedom of choice.[3] Self-affirmation in a period of affluence and faith in a better future nurtured the youth revolution of the late 1960s. The modernization critique of that period, which inveighed against "fundamental aspects of modern life such as commercialization, industrialization, political centralization, bureaucratization and democratization, cultural rationalization and pluralization" (Brand, 1990: 28), was imbued with optimism. The *Zeitgeist* which prevailed in the late 1960s and early 1970s favoured the affirmation of the postmaterial agenda but contained in itself also some elements of anti-modernism which emerged when the economic cycle slowed down.

The same structural transformations could produce a different, rather opposite outcome, partially forecast by the theoreticians of the mass society. They argued that the by-product of mass society was the destruction of the bonds of family, kinship and (small) community. The loss of social and affective roots would have produced insecurity and anomie which, in turn, would have favoured authoritarian attitudes.

In sum, the reaction to the postindustrial society, depending on which cultural mood prevailed, has two opposite outcomes: more self-affirmation on one side (New Politics) but also more atomization/alienation on the other (authoritarian neoconservatism). The representatives of New Politics seek more auto-direction, informality and libertarianism; their right-wing counterparts search for more order, tradition, identity and security/reassurance.

The rise of the extreme right in the 1980s represents another answer to the postindustrial society. These parties were capable of mobilizing resources (citizenry unsupportive of the system, alienated from politics, attentive to non-politicized issues such as immigration, morality and national pride) by political entrepreneurs who exploited a favourable structure of opportunity at the political level (system polarization and radicalization) and at the cultural level (the rise of a neoconservative movement in the intellectual elite with its impact on the mass level beliefs).

This outcome has been unperceived because, on one side the *Zeitgeist* favoured, at first, a postmaterialist value change, and, on the other, *no manifest mobilization of the right-wing tendency emerged.* Those who wanted to answer differently from the pacifists, civil rights militants, feminists, ecologists, and so on to the postindustrial society kept silent until a political entrepreneur came to mobilize their support. But even so, their political style is different: While the New Politics parties advocate more participation and more citizen involvement, and were quite visible in the streets, extreme right parties neither supported

not exhibited anything similar. Their *"action repertoire"* is not ascertainable because no social movement grew in that political space, with a few exceptions (the USA is the most relevant) in some phases. The most visible presence of such tendencies was given by the violent, fascist-like manifestations of small chapels of militants, recently reinforced by the "skin-head" or "nazi-skin" aggression against immigrants all over Europe. These acts, however, involve a very small number of persons and they are not an expression of something like a social movement.

It could be argued, then, that for a long time a right-wing value system was already defined but it was invisible, it did not manifest itself, it did not act; rather, it was "silent."

WHY THE EXTREME RIGHT PARTIES?

General societal trends have shaken the role and the centrality of parties, and these changes have fostered the development of new parties. Let us analyse more closely the opportunity structures which favoured the rise of one corner of the novelty, the extreme right parties in the 1980s. Two main levels of analysis can be distinguished: The first, more specific, regards the cultural-political setting; the second, more general, refers to the "crisis of legitimacy" in western society.

Starting from the latter level, it could be stated that left-libertarian parties themselves profited from this crisis (or rather from the perception of such a crisis). But their answer, consciously or not, propitiated the recovery of the system. They overcame the defaults of democracy both at the system and the intra-party level by offering, in the first stages, a "different" type of party organization and a higher participatory involvement. On the other hand, extreme right parties do not support the system, either with unconventional participation or direct action, or by expressing confidence; their anti-system connotation pushes them to delegitimize the fundamentals of democracy. Therefore, while a crisis of legitimacy (emphasized well beyond its reality) had fostered both offspring of the malaise, a deepening of such crises would fuel the anti-system parties rather than the "reformist" ones. This is why the crisis of legitimacy is more relevant for the fate of the extreme right.

On the cultural-political level the crucial factor concerns the development of a new, right-wing cultural mood—neoconservatism. At the elite-intellectual level, neoconservatism emerged as a reaction against the post-war consensus on the Keynesian political economy of the "collectivist age" and the costs of the welfare system. In order to overcome the overloading burden of state provision, neoconservatism advocated the revival of laissez-faire, free market, individual enterpreneurship, privatization of the public sector and cuts in the welfare system. This new set of attitudes towards the economic sphere was accompanied by the revitalization of traditional values (order, hierarchy, patriotism, family, authority, morality), partly redefined in response to the post-materialist agenda. The neoconservatism offered a non-materialist answer to the New Politics: It opposed the postmaterialists not in the name of more "material security" but on the same ground. This set of attitudes was adopted by many "conservative" parties, such as, at different times, the French Gaullists and the UDF (Union for French Democracy—Centrist), the British Tories and the German CDU–CSU (Christian Democratic Union and its Bavarian affiliate, Christian Social Union). Such a conservative shift, therefore, favoured a radicalization of the political conflict. The agenda of the "conservative" parties became, in the early 1980s, quite radical—compared to the preceding decades—and, even if in certain cases it was abandoned when those parties came back to power (as in the German and French cases), they nevertheless paved the way to new and/or newly formulated issues. But when the "conservative" parties abandoned the more radical stands on certain issues (such as aggressive nationalism, social Darwinism, xenophobia, authoritarian and hierarchic social relations, law and order provisions, more traditionalism), new actors came to maintain and even radicalize them.

Therefore, the new extreme right parties which emerged in the 1980s could profit from the circulation of ideas that were previously kept out of the political realm: the "boundaries of politics" enlarged, including a set of issues that was never treated except by the neofascist parties (and even so with substantial differences). These themes, however, could never have gained room if, on the one hand, the party system was not under a polarizing tendency. The radicalization of the conservative parties and the simultaneous emergence, on the other side of the political spectrum, of the left-libertarian parties and, in some cases, of the radicalization of the traditional leftist parties, enlarged the political space in many western countries in the early 1980s. More or less in the same period, as soon as the "conservative" parties returned to power their agenda became more consensual; this change opened the way to hardline parties which had no problem at all in overpromising and in presenting very radical stances. Therefore, even after the deradicalization of "conservative parties" the system did not shrink again after its previous enlargement because the space at the extreme right was occupied.

A new cultural mood (neoconservatism), the emergence/politicization of new, salient issues, and a dynamic of radicalization and system polarization, all set the conditions for extreme right parties to emerge. However, in order to mobilize the electorate, a political entrepreneur had to appear. While for the New Politics parties this role has been played by a collective actor—the new social movements—on the extreme-right side a single leader was the catalyst of the success. Le Pen in France, Haider in Austria, Dillen in Flemish Belgium, Janmaat in the Netherlands and Schönhuber (to a lesser extent) in Germany (plus Glistrup in Denmark, Lange and Hagen in Norway and Karlsson and Watchmeister in Sweden) were gifted political leaders who emerged suddenly as national figures and attracted consent for their outspoken language. Consequently some have used the term "right-wing populism" (Pfahl-Traughber, 1993; Betz, 1994). In most cases, extreme right parties' internal organization reflects a caesaristic profile; *Führerprinzip* (leadership principle) and mobilization rather than participation are the distinctive features. The French case is exemplary: Le Pen is the uncontested chairman and has the right to select the other party leaders. The Italian case is somewhat different: The former MSI (Italian social movement—neofascist) now AN (Alleanza Nazionale, National Alliance), was an established party which exhibited a formal democratic internal structure; however, its recent success is closely linked to the image of the leader as well.

Up to now we have defined extreme right parties as new parties, but the extreme right is an old presence in European political systems. While the New Politics really is novel in the partisan constellation, the extreme right dates back to historic fascism (leaving aside the counter-revolutionary tradition of de Maistre and de Bonald). However, the post-war presence of neofascist parties was limited to the Italian MSI, always present in parliament since 1948 with around 5 percent of votes (until the last election when it reached an unprecedented 13.5 percent) and to the German NDP (National Democratic Party) for a couple of years in the late 1960s, until it failed to enter the Bundestag in the 1969 election. All the other parties were small groups without any relevance in their respective party systems. On the other hand, the parties that emerged (or became significant) in the 1980s—the French Front National, the German Republikaner, the Austrian FPÖ (Austrian Freedom Party—which shifted from liberal-conservatism to right-extremism), the Belgian Vlaams Blok and Front National and the smaller Dutch Cetrumpartij (plus the special Scandinavian cases, Danish and Norwegian Progress parties and Swedish New Democracy)[4]—are quite different from the traditional neofascist parties.

This group of parties is alien to fascist imprint. They are the by-product of the conflicts of the postindustrial society where material interests are no longer central and bourgeoisie and working class are neither so neatly defined nor so radically confronted. The post-war economic and cultural transformations have blurred class identification and loosened the traditional loyalties linked to precise social groups. While fascism represented the highest point of a conflict over interests at the moment of mass mobilization—and the present neofascists are the nostalgic remnants of that conflict, the new extreme right parties emerge when a conflict over value allocation reaches its maturity. Following the Offe (1985) model of conflict and alliance in postindustrial societies, we can argue that sectors of the traditional working class and of the poorly educated middle class now face the new middle class

in a conflict which has at its core values, rather than material interests. The conflict over the distribution of resources is more and more overcome by that over value allocation.

The established parties have tried to give an answer to the modified structure of conflict but, inevitably, new actors respond better than old ones to new challenges. In fact, the extreme right parties developed most recently offer an answer to demands and needs that have arisen under postindustrialism and not been satisfied by traditional parties. The defence of the national community from foreigners—hence racism and xenophobia—responds to the identity crisis produced by atomization. Moreover, the claim for more law and order, the search for a "charismatic" leader, the seeking of harmony and security, the irritation towards representation mechanisms and procedures: All express a desire for an authoritative guide in a society where self-achievement and individualism have disrupted the protective network of traditional social bonds. And, finally, the recall of rigid moral standards is the counterpart of postmaterialist libertarianism.

All this does not flow into a corporative architecture of society, or into a "new order," but rather into a mix, often magnificent and fallacious, of private initiative and social protection (but limited to the native), of modernizing inputs and traditional reminiscences. In sum, the newly born parties are not old, disguised neofascist parties. Nevertheless, their value system is conceived to undermine system legitimacy; therefore, they can be labelled *postindustrial extreme right parties*.

....

CONCLUDING REMARKS

The crisis of party has been interpreted as the crisis of a certain type of party. Following Katz and Mair's (1995) hypothesis, the interpenetration between party and state has reduced the former to a brokerage function; therefore, the function of representation has been shrunk. The alternative to this fate was traced in the New Politics party which reaffirmed the importance of channelling, adopting organizational changes that should have assured a different, more rewarding role to the member (and the citizenry in general).

However, an unexpected alternative, which emerged with a certain time-lag compared to the Green parties, has been produced by the same postindustrial setting. "The new protesters of the right," as Katz and Mair (1995: 25) say, "see themselves as representing a challenge to the cartel party, a challenge which may well be fuelled by the actions of the cartel parties themselves, and which, in the longer term, may therefore help to legitimate their protest." The two authors conclude that these protest parties "do not represent a challenge to party; their protest, after all is organized by party" (1995: 24). This is true but, if we identify the "protest party" with the extreme right, their ideology is profoundly hostile to party per se; their cultural references bring a genetic code which considers the party a "faction," a dividing tool. To accept a party means to accept pluralism; but the cultural heritage and belief of extreme right parties, either imbued with fascism or with less defined sets of values, are essentially monist. In this view, the party is just a transient means to the seizure of power. The deepening of the crisis of party might therefore foster the more coherent anti-party parties, i.e. the extreme right ones.

The same societal changes have produced both left-libertarian parties and extreme right parties. The extreme right parties born in the 1980s denied any clear reference to fascism and any linkage with the traditional neofascist parties: They attained a certain success because, instead of reviving the fascist mythology, either they represented issues that were not treated by the traditional parties or they offered a different, more radical answer to old issues. A new type of an old political family thus entered the European party system: the postindustrial extreme right party. The answer to postmaterialism has taken an unforeseen direction.

ENDNOTES

1. Michels was right writing at the end of his book that: "The cruel play between the incurable idealism of the young and the incurable seeking of power of the old will never end. New waves will again and again crash against this same rock" (Michels, 1966: 533; my translation).
2. Reiter (1993: 100) adds that "the distinction to join or identify with a party and the incentive to participate in or sympathize with a movement may have

been overdrawn . . . the difference between the traditional political agenda and that of the newer movements may have been similarly overstated, for many elements of the newer agenda fit into the traditional political agenda with little adjustment."
3. The same Daniel Bell, however, recognized that self-realization without a morally authoritative guide would have led to social decay and individual loss of identity.
4. The question of the inclusion of the Scandinavian parties in the extreme right political family is still open. Some indicators—extreme location on the left-right continuum, typical extreme right set of attitudes (xenophobia, law and order, social Drawinism), anti-politics sentiment—suggest their belonging to the extreme right. But it is questionable if they are really anti-system parties (see Andersen and Bjørklund, 1992; Harmel and Gibson, 1995).

REFERENCES

Andersen, Jørgen, G. and Tor Bjørklund, 1990, "Structural Changes and New Cleavages: The Progress Parties in Denmark and Norway," *Acta Sociologica* 33: 195–217.

Bardi, Luciano, 1992, "The Empirical Study of Party Membership Change," paper presented at the ECPR Joint Session of Workshops, Limerick.

Bell, Daniel, 1973, *The Coming of Postindustrial Societies.* New York: Basic Books.

Betz, Hans-George, 1994, *Radical Right-wing Populism in Western Europe.* New York: St Martin's Press.

Blondel, Jean, 1991, "Are Ministries 'Representative' or 'Manager,' 'Amateur' or 'Specialist'? Similarities and Differences across Western Europe," in Hans Dieter Klingemann, Richard Stöss and Bernard Wessel (eds.) *Politische Klasse un politische Institutionen.* Opladen: Westdeutscher Verlag, 187–207.

Brand, Karl W., 1990, "Cyclical Aspects of New Social Movements: Waves of Cultural Criticism and Mobilization Cycles of New Middle-class Radicalism," in Russell Dalton and Manfred Kuechler (eds.) *Challenging the Political Order.* Cambridge: Polity Press, 23–42.

Commission of the European Communities, 1994, *Eurobarometer Trend Variables 1974–1994.* Brussels: Commission of the European Communities.

Daalder, Hans, 1992, "A Crisis of Party?", *Scandinavian Political Studies* 15, 269–88.

Dalton, Russell J, 1988, *Citizens Politics in Western Democracies.* Chatham, NY: Chatham House.

Dalton, Russell J., 1991, "Responsiveness of Parties and Party Systems to the New Politics," in Hans-Dieter Klingemann, Richard Stöss and Bernard Wessel (eds.) *Politische Klasse un politische Institutionen.* Opladen: Westdeutscher Verlag, 39–56.

Dalton, Russell, Scott Flanagan and Lewis Beck, eds., 1984, *Electoral Change in Advanced Industrial Democracies.* Princeton, NJ: Princeton University Press.

Harmel, Robert and Rachel Gibson, 1995, "Right-Libertarian Parties and the 'New Values': A Re-examination," *Scandinavian Political Studies* 18, 97–118.

Ignazi, Piero, 1992, "The Silent Counter-revolution: Hypotheses on the Emergence of Extreme Right-wing Parties," *European Journal of Political Research* 22, 3–34.

Ignazi, Piero, 1993, "Istituzioni politiche e partiti liberali nell'Europa occidentale," in D. da Empoli (ed.) *Le Vie della Libertà: Il liberalismo come teoria e come politica negli anni novanta.* Rome: Fondazione Luigi Einaudi, 108–12.

Ignazi, Piero, 1994a, *L'estrema destra in Europa.* Bologna: Il Mulino.

Ignazi, Piero, 1994b, "The Extreme Right in Europe: A Survey," paper presented at the XVI IPSA World Congress, Berlin.

Ignazi, Piero, 1994c, *Postfascisti? Dal Movimento sociale ad Alleanza nazionale.* Bologna: Il Mulino.

Ignazi, Piero, 1996, "The Intellectual Basis of Right-wing Anti-Partysm," *European Journal of Political Research* 29, 279–96.

Inglehart, Ronald, 1985, "New Perspectives on Value Change," *Comparative Political Studies* 17, 485–532.

Inglehart, Ronald, 1990, *Culture Shift.* Princeton, NJ: Princeton University Press.

Janda, Kenneth, 1983, "Cross-National Measures of Party Organizations and Organizational Theory," *European Journal of Political Research* 11, 319–32.

Katz, Richard, 1986, "Party Governments: A Rationalistic Conception," in Frank G. Castles and Rudolf Wildemann (eds.) *The Future of Party Government,* vol. I. Berlin: De Gruyter.

Katz, Richard and Peter Mair, eds., 1992, *Party Organization 1960—1990: A Data Handbook.* London: Sage.

Katz, Richard and Peter Mair, 1995, "Changing Models of Party Organization and Party Democracy: The Emergence of the Cartel Party," *Party Politics,* 1, 5–28.

Kitschelt, Herbert, 1989, *The Logics of Party Formation.* Ithaca, NY: Cornell University Press.

Koole, Ruud, 1994, "The Vulnerability of the Modern Cadre Party in the Netherlands," in Richard Katz and Peter Mair (eds.) *How Parties Organize.* London: Sage, 278–303.

Lawson, Kay and Peter Merkl, 1988, "Alternative Organizations: Environmental, Supplementary, Communitarian and Antiauthoritarian," in Kay Lawson and Peter H. Merkl (eds.) *When Parties Fail.* Princeton, NJ: Princeton University Press, 3–12.

Mair, Peter, 1984, "Party Politics in Contemporary Europe: A Challenge to Party," *West European Politics* 7, 170–83.

Mair, Peter, 1989, "Continuity, Change and the Vulnerability of Party," *West European Politics* 12, 169–86.

Mair, Peter, 1994, "Party Organizations: From Civil Society to the State," in Richard Katz and Peter Mair (eds.) *How Parties Organize.* London: Sage, 1–22.

Mair, Peter, 1995, "Political Parties, Popular Legitimacy and Public Privilege," *West European Politics* 18, 40–57.

Michels, Roberto, 1966, *Sociologia del partito politico.* Bologna: Il Mulino.

Offe, Klaus, 1985, "Challenging the Boundaries of Institutional Politics: Social Movements since the 1960s," in Charles S. Maier (ed.) *Changing Boundaries of the Political.* Cambridge: Cambridge University Press, 63–107.

Offerlé, Michel, 1991, *Les parties politiques.* Paris: PUF.

Panebianco, Angelo, 1988, *Political Parties: Organization and Power.* Cambridge: Cambridge University Press.

Pfahl-Traughber, Armin, 1993, "Rechtpopulistische Parteien in Westeuropa," in Eckhard Jesse (ed.) *Politischer Extremismus in Deutschland und Europa.* Munich: Bayerische Landzentrale für Politische Bildungsarbeit, 39–56.

Pizzorno, Alessandro, 1969, "Elementi di uno schema teorico con riferimento ai partiti politici," in Giordano Sivini (ed.) *Partiti e partecipazione politica in Italia.* Milano: Giuffré, 3–40.

Poguntke, Thomas, 1989, "The 'New Politics Dimension' in European Green Parties," in Ferdinand Müller-Rommel (ed.) *New Politics in Western Europe: The Rise and Success of Green Parties and Alternative Lists.* Boulder, CO: Westview, 175–93.

Poguntke, Thomas, 1993, *Alternative Politics.* Edinburgh: Edinburgh University Press.

Reiter, Howard L., 1993, "The Rise of the 'New Agenda' and the Decline of Partisanship," *West European Politics* 16, 89–104.

Schlesinger, Joseph A., 1984, "On the Theory of Party Organization," *Journal of Politics* 46, 369–400.

Selle, Per and Lars Svåsand, 1991, "Membership in Party Organization and the Problem of Decline of Parties," *Comparative Political Studies* 23, 459–77.

CHAPTER ELEVEN

DO INSTITUTIONS MATTER?

Few would deny that underlying social forces and economic interests are important and often dominant factors in explaining political outcomes. Yet states and political leaders do or can make a difference. New constitutions changed the direction of political evolution in the United States in 1787, and in France in 1958; and charismatic figures like Bonaparte, Lincoln, Lenin, Hitler, Stalin and De Gaulle helped transform their societies.

Political institutions matter, argue James C. March and Johan P. Olsen. An institutional perspective emphasizes regularities of behavior and the effects of structures on political life, in contrast to an interpretation of politics based on actors making rational choices among conflicting interests. Whether institutions matter is a problem posed inescapably when countries confront the necessity of drafting a constitution. The breakup of the Soviet empire and collapse of communist rule throughout East Europe led to a spate of constitutional conventions. Developing countries emerging from the turmoil of decolonization, ethnic conflict, or civil war also must endow themselves with basic institutions. Even the advanced democracies of Europe in 2002 convened a "Convention on the Future of Europe" under the presidency of Giscard d'Estaing to draft a new "constitutional treaty" for the European Union. Arend Lijphart synthesizes a massive literature on constitutional design, particularly in divided societies, which he contends is based on a strong scholarly consensus and solid empirical evidence. Is Lijphart's argument in favor of parliamentary over presidential government, and proportional representation over plurality voting, support by the examination of the nature of political institutions in the essay by March and Olsen? Would you agree that Lijphart's recommendations should form a starting point for deliberations by framers of constitutions today?

Whether institutions matter is a question of special interest to students of the judiciary. What are the consequences of according to a supreme or constitutional court the power to strike down legislative and executive acts? Does judicial review weaken democracy by constraining popular majorities, or does it strengthen democracy by guarding against authoritarian impulses? The issue has been confronted in every nation emerging from fascist rule after World War II (notably Germany, Italy, and Japan) or from authoritarianism

(Spain, Portugal, and France after Vichy), in all nations making the transition from communism to democracy following the collapse of the Soviet Union, and in many developing nations. The issue is examined by Nathan J. Brown, with particular reference to the experience of the Arab world.

....

JAMES MARCH and JOHAN OLSEN

38   Institutional Perspectives

Political science as a field is defined less by a set of theoretical concepts than by an empirical focus on concrete political institutions and processes. Legislatures, bureaucracies, legal systems, political parties, mass media, and all the other institutions of contemporary politics are objects of study. Although political scientists occasionally examine other institutions, such as business firms, churches, or armies, and use various forms of political analysis to interpret them, the discipline persistently retreats from attempts to generate distinctive theoretical tools and returns to concerns about identifiable political institutions.

Historically, theoretical political science has been more an interweaving of metaphors than a theoretically coherent discipline or even an arena for competition among alternative metaphors. It has combined the traditions of Aristotle and Tocqueville with those of Hobbes and Bentham and grafted onto those roots various elements of the wisdom of Freud, Marx, Durkheim, Adam Smith, and Darwin. In recent years, this pragmatic approach to ideas has been expressed most conspicuously in efforts to reconcile an exchange conception of politics drawn particularly from ideas of social contracts, the utilitarians, and modern microeconomics with an institutional conception that builds on jurisprudence, sociological and psychological conceptions of identity, and modern organization theory.

SOURCE: James March and Johan Olsen, "Institutional Perspectives on Political Institutions," *Governance*, vol. 9, no. 3 (July 1996), pp. 247–264. © Blackwell Publishing Ltd. Reprinted by permission of Blackwell Publishing Ltd. Footnotes and references abridged by the Editor.

This article is in that tradition of political science. We examine some basic assumptions about the nature of political institutions, the ways in which the practices and rules that comprise institutions are established, sustained, and transformed, and the ways in which those practices and rules are converted into political behavior through the mediation of interpretation and capability. Without denying the elements of exchange in politics and the many ways in which politics aggregates exogenous individual preferences and responds to exogenous distributions of resources and capabilities, we discuss an institutional approach to political life—one that emphasizes the endogenous nature and social construction of political institutions, identities, accounts, and capabilities.

....

TELLING STORIES ABOUT POLITICS

The stories of politics are stories attached to real political events in real political institutions. Why did the Weimar Republic fail? How do we account for the historical divergence of the political institutions of Canada and the United States? What explains post-communist political developments in Hungary? The stories about such events and institutions constructed within political science are organized around a few themes of how political institutions work. Politics is organized by (and helps to organize) theses stories of history.

There are two conventional stories of democratic politics. The first story sees politics as a market for trades in which individual and group interests are pursued by rational actors. It emphasizes the negotiation of coalitions and "voluntary" exchanges. The second story is an institutional one. It characterizes politics in a more integrative fashion, emphasizing the creation of identities and institutions as well as their structuring effects on political life.

POLITICS AS ARRANGING EXCHANGES

Politics can be seen aggregating individual preferences into collective actions by some procedures of bargaining, negotiation, coalition formation, and exchange. In such a view, individual actors have prior desires (preferences, interests) which they use to determine the attractiveness of expected consequences. Collective actions depends on the negotiation of bargains and side-payments among potential trading partners. Exchange stories of politics and governance have roots in the doctrines of social contract theory which arose in the seventeenth century. The political community is seen as atomistic. Society is constituted of individuals for the fulfillment of individual ends. Individuals have rights but no obligations or bonds, except those created through consent and contracts based on calculated advantage.

The ability of any particular actor to realize his or her desires in such a system of exchange depends on what the desires are, what exchangeable resources that actor possesses, and what political rights he or she has. Wants that are consistent with the wants of others are more easily satisfied than wants that compete with others. The greater the exchangeable resources (initial endowments) and the more rights to political voice, the stronger the trading position. One version of the exchange story emphasizes the pareto-optimal qualities of exchange and gains from trade—the achievements of outcomes that make at least some people better off and no one worse off than before the exchanges. A second version of the exchange story emphasizes the coercive qualities of exchange when initial endowments are unequal, the way in which "voluntary exchange" results in one group of actors imposing its will on other groups.

POLITICS AS CREATING AND SUSTAINING INSTITUTIONS

An alternative story emphasizes the role of institutions. The exchange vision of human nature as static and universal and unaffected by politics is replaced by a view of the political actor as flexible, varied, malleable, culture-dependent, and socially constructed. Intentional, calculative action is embedded in rules and institutions that are constituted, sustained and interpreted in a political system. The core notion is that life is organized by sets of shared meanings and practices that come to be taken as given for a long time. Political actors act and organize themselves in accordance with rules and practices which are socially constructed, publicly known, anticipated and accepted. Actions of individuals and collectivities occur within these shared meanings and practices, which can be called institutions and identities.

In the institutional story, people act, think, feel, and organize themselves on the basis of exemplary or authoritative (and sometimes competing or conflicting) rules derived from socially constructed identities, belongings, and roles. Institutions organize hopes, dreams, and fears as well as purposeful actions. Institutionalized rules proscribe or prescribe emotions and expression of emotions. Sentiments of love, loyalty, devotion, respect, friendship, as well as hate, anger, fear, envy, and guilt are made appropriate to particular identities in particular situations.

Institutions constitute and legitimize political actors and provide them with consistent behavioral rules, conceptions of reality, standards of assessment, affective ties, and endowments, and thereby with a capacity for purposeful action. Along the way, political institutions create rules regulating the possession and use of political rights and resources. Even the conception of an autonomous agent with a particularistic way of feeling, acting, and expression is an acquired identity, a socialized understanding of self and others.

Action is taken on the basis of a logic of appropriateness associated with roles, routines, rights, obligations, standard operating procedures, and practices. The perspective is more behavioral than moral but it echoes an Aristotelian judgment: "As man is the best of all animals when he has reached his full development, so he is the worst of all when divorced from law and morals."

....

INSTITUTIONAL PERSPECTIVES

The word "institutional" has come to mean rather different things to different authors. The institutional alternatives to voluntary exchange stories about politics with which we are concerned here are infused with two basic themes.

1. A theme that pictures political action as driven less by anticipation of its uncertain consequences and preferences for them than by a logic of appropriateness reflected in a structure of rules and conceptions of identities;

2. A theme that pictures political change as matching institutions, behaviors, and contexts in ways that take time and have multiple, path-dependent equilibria, thus as being susceptible to timely interventions to affect the meander of history and to deliberate efforts to improve institutional adaptiveness.

INSTITUTIONAL CONCEPTIONS OF POLITICAL ACTION

Institutional theories supplement exchange theories of political action in two primary ways: First, they emphasize the role of institutions in defining the terms of rational exchange. Rational action depends on subjective perceptions of alternatives, their consequences, and their evaluations. Pictures of reality and feelings about it are constructed within social and political institutions. Second, without denying the reality of calculations and anticipations of consequences, institutional conceptions see such calculations and anticipations as occurring within a broader framework of rules, roles, and identities. Indeed, at the limit, self-interested calculation can be seen as simply one of many systems of rules that may be socially legitimized under certain circumstances.

Institutional Bases of Rational Exchange

In exchange theories, political action (decision making, resource allocation) is a result of bargains negotiated among individual actors pursuing individual interests. The theories presume that individuals pursue their interests by considering alternative bargains in terms of their anticipated consequences for individual preferences and choosing those combinations of bargains that serve their preferences best. Political actors are imagined to be endowed with preferences or interests that are consistent, stable, and exogenous to the political system. They act on the basis of incomplete and possibly biased information. In short, exchange theories of politics are special cases of rational actor theories of human behavior.

Institutional theories focus on the behavioral and social bases of information and preferences in a theory of rational choice. They picture preferences as inconsistent, changing, and at least partly endogenous, formed within political institutions. Interests and cleavages are seen as created by institutional arrangements and maintained by institutional processes of socialization and co-optation. Institutional theories similarly emphasize the ways in which institutions shape the definition of alternatives and influence the perception and construction of the reality within which action takes place. Institutional capabilities and structures affect the flow of information, the kinds of search undertaken, and the interpretations made of the results.

Awareness of the limits of rationality and of the embedding of rationality in an institutional context had led to a considerable restructuring of theories of rational exchange, including political theories based on an exchange perspective. This restructuring has come to picture rational exchange as framed by and dependent on political norms, identities, and institutions. Insofar as political actors act by making choices, they act within definitions of alternatives, consequences, preferences (interests), and strategic options that are strongly affected by the institutional context in which the actors find themselves. Exploring the ways in which institutions affect the definition of alternatives, consequences, and preferences, the cleavages that produce conflict, and the enforcement of bargains have become major activities within modern choice theory.

Rules and Identities

Institutional conceptions of action, however, differ from rational models in a more fundamental way. Most people in politics and political institutions follow rules most of the time if they can. The uncertainties they face are less uncertainties about consequences and preferences than they are uncertainties about the demands of identity. Actions are expressions of what is exemplary, natural, or acceptable behavior according to the (internalized) purposes, codes of rights and duties, practices, methods, and techniques of the constituent group and of the self. As a result, the institutional axiomatics for political action begin not with subjective consequences and preferences but with rules, identities, and roles.

Political institutions matter. Institutionalized identities create individuals: citizens, officials, engineers, doctors, spouses. Rule-following can be viewed as contractual—an implicit agreement to act appropriately in return for being treated appropriately. Such a contractual view has led game theorists and some legal theorists to interpret norms and institutions as meta-game agreements, but the term "contract" is potentially misleading. The terms are often unclear enough to be better called a "pact" than a "contract" and socialization into rules and their appropriateness is ordinarily not a case of willful entering into an explicit contract.

Within an institutional framework, "choice" if it can be called that, is based more on a logic of appropriateness than on the logic of consequence that underlies conceptions of rational action. Institutionalized rules, duties, rights, and roles define acts as appropriate (normal, natural, right, good) or inappropriate (uncharacteristic, unnatural, wrong, bad). The impact of rules of appropriateness and standard operating procedures in routine situations is well known. But the logic of appropriateness is by no means limited to repetitive, routine worlds. It is also characteristic of human action in ill-defined, novel situation. Civil unrest, demands for comprehensive redistribution of political power and welfare, as well as political revolutions and major reforms often follow from identity-driven conceptions of appropriateness more than conscious calculations of costs and benefits. Appropriateness has overtones of morality, but it is in this context primarily a cognitive, or perhaps teleological, concept. Rules of action are derived from reasoning about the nature of the self. People act from understandings of the nature of things, form self-conceptions of society, and from images of proper behavior. Identities define the nature of things and are implemented by a cognitive process of interpretation.

Neither the definition of an identity nor its achievement is necessarily trivial. Fulfilling an identity through following appropriate rules involves matching a changing (and often ambiguous) set of contingent rules to a changing (and often ambiguous) set of situations. As a result, institutional approaches to behavior make a distinction between a rule and its behavioral realization in a particular instance. Identities and rules assure neither consistency not simplicity. The elements of openness in their interpretation mean that while institutions structure politics, they ordinarily do not determine political behavior precisely. The processes through which rules are translated into actual behavior through constructive interpretation and available resources have to be specified.

As they try to understand history and self, and as they try to improve the often confusing, uncertain, and ambiguous world they live in, individuals and collectivities interpret what rules and identities exist, which ones are relevant, and what different rules and identities demand in specific situations or spheres of behavior. Individuals may have a difficult time resolving conflicts among contending imperatives of appropriateness, among alternative concepts of the self. They may not know what to do. They may also know what to do but not have the capabilities to do it. They are limited by the complexities of the demands upon them and by the distribution and regulation of resources, competencies, and organizing capacities— that is, by the capability for acting appropriately.

Processes of constructive interpretation, criticism, and justification of rules and identities are processes familiar to the intellectual traditions of the law. Such processes are highly relevant for the ambiguities of identities, rules, and factual situations. They give specific content in specific situations both to such heroic identities as patriot or statesman and to such everyday identities as those of an accountant, police officer, or citizen.

Identities, Interests, and the Common Good

Some of the more celebrated differences between exchange theories of politics and institutional theories concern the concept of the "common good," the idea that individuals might, under some circumstances, act not in the name of individual or group interest but in the name of the good of the community. Exchange traditions downplay the significance or meaning of virtue in the values of the citizenry and doubt the relevance of social investment in citizenship. The assumption is that interests cannot (and should not) be eliminated or influenced. The object is to provide a neutral arena for voluntary exchange among them. If leaders wish to control the outcomes of this self-seeking behavior, they do so by designing incentives that induce self-interested individuals to act in desired ways as much as possible. Political norms are seen as negotiated constraints on fundamental processes of self-serving rationality rather than constitutive. From this perspective, a community of virtuous citizens is Gemeinschaftschwermerei—a romantic dream (Yack 1985). The fantasy in some democratic thought that modern society can be held together by, and that conflicts can be resolved through, references to either a moral consensus or a shared conception of the common good is deemed to be wrong as a description and pernicious as an objective.[1]

In virtually all institutional theories of politics, on the other hand, humans (through their institutions) are seen as able to share a common life and identity, and to have concern for others. Either what is good for one individual is the same as what is good for other members of the community, or actions are supposed to be governed by what is best for the community as a whole. Although the idea of a common good is plagued by the difficulty of defining what is meant by the term and by the opportunities for exploitation of individual gullibility that lie in an uncritical embrace of hopes for community values, many institutional theorists criticize presumptions of individual self-interested behavior that are standard in the rational tradition.

Indeed, the civic basis of identities is often intrinsic to the concept of a person, citizen, or public official. Giving priority to private interests and preferences is not merely a corruption of the political process but also a corruption of the soul and a fall from grace. Social identities are the building blocks of the self. Anyone incapable of achieving an identity based on constitutive attachments—if such a person could be imagined—should not be described as a free and rational agent, but as a being without character or moral depth, a non-person.

This folding of communitarian values into institutional theories of politics is almost universal in modern discussions of political democracy, and it leads to a tendency to confuse two related but distinct notions. The first notion is the idea that political democracy requires a sense of community. Exactly what constitutes a sense of community varies a bit from one communitarian author to another, but a common element is the idea that individuals might (and should) have empathy for the feelings and desires of others and under some circumstances might (and should) subordinate their own individual or group interests to the collective good of the community.

The second notion is the idea that democracy is built upon visions of civic identity and a framework of rule-based action—what we have called a logic of appropriateness. Embedded in this notion are ideas about the obligations of citizenship and office, the commitment to fulfill an identity without regard to its consequences for personal or group preferences or interests. The self becomes central to personhood, and civic identity becomes central to the self.

The two notions share some common presumptions, but they have quite different perspectives about the fundamental basis for democratic action. The communitarian ideal of shared preferences, including a preference for the common good, presumes that individual action is based on individual values and preferences. The model is one of individual, consequential, preference-based action. Strategies for achieving democracy emphasize constructing acceptable preferences.

On the other hand, the civic identity ideal presumes, that action is rule-based, that it involves matching the obligations of an identity to a situation. Pursuit of the common good is not so much a personal value as a constitutive part of democratic political identities and the construction of a meaningful person. The community is created by its rules, not by its intentions. Strategies for achieving democracy emphasize molding rules and identities and socializing individuals into them.

The distinctions are worth maintaining. When they are confounded, there is a tendency to see the problems of modern polities as lying primarily in the value premises of individual preference-based action rather than in a structure of political rules, institutions, and identities. In fact, many of the greatest dangers to the democratic policy come not from particularistic individual self-seeking but from deep, group-based identities that are inconsistent with democracy, for example, strong feelings of religious, class, and national identities. And efforts to build a personal set of communitarian values enhancing concern for the common good will be of little use—even if successful—if anti-democratic action stems primarily not from preferences and their associated values but from commitments to identities that are inconsistent with democratic institutions.

INSTITUTIONAL CONCEPTIONS OF POLITICAL CHANGE

Exchange theories of political change are largely theories of the adjustment of political bargains to exogenous changes in interests, rights, and resources. When values change, political coalitions change. For example, when attitudes with respect to the role of women in society shift, so also do political parties. When resources are redistributed, political coalitions change. For example, when the age composition of society shifts in the direction of older citizens, so also do political programs. The presumption is that political bargains adjust quickly and in a necessary way to exogenous changes.

In contrast to political accounts drawn from an exchange tradition, which are organized primarily around stories of how resources and interests shape the outcomes of politics, students of political institutions are generally less confident of the efficiency of history in matching political outcomes to exogenous pressures. They see the match between an environment of interests and resources on the one hand

and political institutions on the other as less automatic, less continuous, and less precise. They see a world of historical possibilities that includes multiple stable equilibria. They see the pressures of survival as sporadic rather than constant, crude rather than precise. They see institutions and identities as having lives and deaths of their own, sometimes enduring in the face of apparent inconsistency with their environments, sometimes collapsing without obvious external cause.

The Nature of History

Although their many different manifestations allow numerous variations on theories of history, institutional and exchange conceptions of politics tend to be divided by a grand debate in historical interpretation. On one side in that debate is the idea that politics follows a course dictated uniquely by exogenous factors. From such a perspective, history is efficient in the sense that it matches political institutions and outcomes to environments uniquely and relatively quickly. This side of the debate is typical of exchange theories and theories of rational choice.

Some version of an efficient history assumption also underlies traditional comparative statics as applied to political institutions. Why do political institutions differ from one country to another? It is because the social and economic environments of the countries differ. How does one explain specific differences in institutions? It is by pointing to specific differences in their environments. As long as history is efficient in the sense of driving institutions to a unique equilibrium quickly, variations in institutional structures can be predicted without identifying the underlying processes of change.

On the other side of the debate is the idea typical of institutional theories that history follows a less determinate, more endogenous course. They generally presume that the conditions under which political development is driven quickly to a unique outcome in which the match between a political system and the political environment has some properties of unique survival advantage seem relatively restricted. There is no guarantee that the development of identities and institutions will instantaneously or uniquely reflect functional imperatives or demands for change. Political institutions and identities develop in a world of multiple viable possibilities. Moreover, the paths they follow seem determined in part by internal dynamics only loosely connected to changes in their environments.

Even in an exogenous environment, there are lags in matching an environment, multiple equilibria, path dependencies, and interconnected networks of diffusion. In addition, environments are rarely exogenous. Environments adapt to institutions at the same time as institutions adapt to environments. Institutions and their linkages coevolve. They are intertwined in ecologies of competition, cooperations, and other forms of interaction. And institutions are nested, so that some adapting institutions (e.g., bureaus) are integral parts of other adapting institutions (e.g., ministries).

The complications tend to convert history into a meander. There are irreversible branches, involving experimentation, political alliances, communication contacts, and fortuitous opportunities. The direction taken at any particular branch sometimes seems almost chance-like, yet it is likely to be decisive in its effect on subsequent history. Institutional histories require an understanding of both the origins of an institution and the paths by which it has developed.

The path of development is produced by a comprehensible process, but because of its indeterminate meander the realized course of institutional development is difficult to predict very far in advance. Wars, conquests, and occupation are significant in changing the political maps of the world. "Timely interventions" at historical junctions may make a difference. This ability to create change, however, does not guarantee either that any arbitrary change can be made at any time or that changes will turn out to be consistent with prior intentions. Institutions may be established to serve the interests of a specific group, but the long run results may be quite deleterious to the same interests.

In general, neither competitive pressure nor current conditions uniquely determines institutional options or outcomes. Institutional development depends not only on satisfying current environmental and political conditions but also on an institution's origin and history. Political technologies and practices are stabilized by positive local feedback leading to the endurance of institutions, competency traps, and misplaced specialization. The adaptation of identities and institutions to an external environment is shaped and constrained by internal dynamics by which identities and institutions modify themselves endogenously.

Autonomous Institutional Development

Politics is not simply a matter of negotiating coalitions of interests within given constraints of rights, rules, preferences, and resources. Politics extends to shaping those constraints, to constructing accounts of politics, history, and self that are not only bases for instrumental action but also central concerns of life.

Autonomous Identities Identities are responsive to external forces. Religious movements, great social and economic transformations, war, conquest, and migration all leave their marks. But political identities, such as those of the citizen or the public official, also evolve endogenously within a political process that includes conflict, public discourse, civic education, and socialization. Politics develops values and identities. In the context of political life, citizens struggle to understand "who they are, where they come from historically, what they stand for, and what is to be done about the perils and possibilities that lie ahead of them as a people" (Wolin 1989, 14).

In the course of that struggle, individuals come to define identities such as that of the democratic citizen and public official and to mold those identities to a specific set of historical and political experiences and conditions. Clearly, there are limits. It has been argued that there are eradicable and irreconcilable differences among cultures, making some immigrants "unassimilable." For instance, the processes that used to turn foreigners into Frenchmen are faltering. Nevertheless, the self is not so much a premise of politics as it is one of its primary creations.

Autonomous Institutions The story of institutional change is a story of many failed experiments. At every level of adaptation—at the level of interpretations, rules, institutional forms, and specific institutions—changes usually lead to increased vulnerability. Nevertheless, in the struggle to survive, institutions transform themselves. Changes may be discontinuous, contested, and problematic. They may represent "punctuated equilibrium" (Krasner 1984) and "critical junctions" (Collier and Collier 1991), and be linked to "performance crises" (March and Olsen 1989) which stimulate departures from established routines and practices. Many important institutional changes have been associated with the rare cataclysms and metamorphoses at breaking points in history where considerable resources are mobilized and one definition of appropriateness replaces another.

However, change also occurs through mundane processes of interpretation, reasoning, education, imitation, and adaptation. Institutions create elements of temporary and imperfect order and historical continuity. They give rules communicable meaning so they can be diffused and passed on to new generations. Indeed, institutions are usually associated with routinization and repetition, persistence and predictability, rather than with political change and flexibility, agency, creativity, and discretion. Surviving institutions seem to stabilize their norms, rules, and meanings so that procedures and forms adopted at birth have surprising durability.

The processes of securing stability, however, introduce two important sources of change. First, the same institutional stability that provides advantage (and may even be essential to survival in the short run) can easily become a source of vulnerability. Institutional competence and reliability become a barrier to change, thus a likely precursor of long run obsolescence. Second, communicable meaning is subject to reinterpretation. Institutions change as individuals learn the culture (or fail to), forget (parts of) it, revolt against it, modify it, or reinterpret it. The resulting drifts in meaning lead to changes that explore alternative political paths and create the divergences of politics.

The Pursuit of Intelligence

The logic of consequence and the logic of appropriateness are equally logics of thoughtfulness, and the cognitive demands for each are substantial. In the case of a logic of consequence, there are requirements for knowledge about the future and for consistency and clarity in preferences. In the case of a logic of appropriateness, there are requirements for knowledge about the situation and for consistency and clarity in identities. Under appropriate circumstances action based on either logic can lead to achieving outcomes that are judged to be attractive or contribute (over some time horizon) to survival advantage. However, neither rational exchange nor rule-following (and the learning and selection of rules that lies behind it) is assured of being intelligent. The intelligence of each depends on the ways in which their imperatives are interpreted and on the extent to which capabilities for meeting them exist.

IMPLICATIONS FOR A RESEARCH AGENDA

Institutional perspectives on political institutions and politics provide a set of ideas for thinking about research that is different from ideas drawn from an exchange perspective. Emphasis on modeling the bargaining of exchanges among self-interested individuals within constraints of prior preferences, resources, and rights is replaced by a broader conception that includes attention to the constraints, indeed places them at the center of attention.

Such a framework invites research on the ways in which a political order of rights, rules, and institutions is constructed and maintained through active education and socialization of citizens and officials; on the ways individual and collective capabilities for action evolve endogenously through the allocation of resources and capabilities; on the ways conceptions of identity are developed and shared; on the construction of meaning, including an understanding of history and self, through political and social experience; and on histories in which institutions, behaviors, and contexts are matched in ways that take time and have multiple, path-dependent equilibria.

Within such a conception, research might focus particularly on four grand factors in political development.

First, politics depends on the *identities* of citizens and communities in the political environment. Preferences, expectations, beliefs, identities, and interests are not exogenous to political history. They are created and changed within that history. Political actors act on the basis of identities that are themselves shaped by political institutions and processes. When they act in ways that support a democratic system, they do so because they have come to see such action as part of their own identities.

Second, politics depends on the distribution of *capabilities* for appropriate political action among citizens, groups, and institutions. Acting appropriately to fulfill an identity requires not only the will to do so but also the ability. Those capabilities are not just imposed on a political system or the individuals in it but are distributed and developed within the system as well. It is possible to study the ways individuals and institutions garner the rights, authorities, resources, competencies, and organizing capacities necessary to do what is expected of them and the processes by which they achieve or fail to achieve the fruits of those capabilities.

Third, politics depends on *accounts* of political events and responsibility for them, interpretations of political history. Accounts form the basis for defining situations within which identities are relevant. Meanings and histories are socially constructed. Political myths are developed and transmitted. Accountability is established. It is possible to study the processes by which a current situation is defined or history is understood and by which political events and possibilities are interpreted, as well as the possibilities for transmission, retention, and retrieval of the lessons of history.

Fourth, politics depends on the ways in which a political system *adapts* to changing demands and changing environments. Such adaptiveness involves a balance between exploring new possibilities and exploiting existing capabilities, a balance that is easily upset by dynamics leading to excessive experimentation or excessive stability. Studies of the ways in which political systems reinterpret the meaning of stable identities and institutions and the circumstances and manner in which they are transformed are essential to a comprehension of political continuity and change.

ENDNOTES

1. Both Habermas and Rawls suggest that we have to avoid models which overburden citizens ethically by assuming a political community united by a comprehensive substantive doctrine. At the same time, both seem to suggest that citizens may share some aims and ends which do not make up a comprehensive doctrine, as well as basic rules for regulating their political co-existence in the face of persistent disagreements and different ways of life (Habermas 1992; 1994; Rawls 1993).

REFERENCES

Apter, D.A. 1991. Institutionalism Reconsidered. *International Social Science Journal* 8, 463–481.

Berman, H.J. 1983. *Law and Revolution. The Formation of the Western Legal Tradition.* Cambridge MA: Harvard University Press.

Broderick, A. 1970. *The French Institutionalists.* Cambridge MA: Harvard University Press.

Chapman, J.W. and W.A. Galston, eds. 1992. *Virtue.* Nomos XXXIV. New York: New York University Press.

Coleman, J.S. 1966. The Possibility of a Social Welfare Function. *American Economic Review* 56, 1105–1122.

———. 1986. *Individual Interests and Collective Action.* Cambridge: Cambridge University Press.

Downs, A. 1967. *Inside Bureaucracy.* Boston: Little, Brown.

Dworkin, R. 1986. *Law's Empire.* Cambridge MA: Cambridge University Press.

Eisenstadt, S. and S. Rokkan, eds. *1973. Building States and Nations* (I, II). Beverly Hills: Sage.

Elster, J. 1989a. *The Cement of Society.* Cambridge MA: Cambridge University Press.

——— 1989b. Demokratiets verdigrunnlag og verdikonflikter. In *Vitenskap og politikk,* ed. J,. Elster. Oslo: Universitetsforlaget.

——— and R. Slagstad, eds. *Constitutionalism and Democracy.* Oslo: Norwegian University Press.

Furubotn, E.G. and R. Richter, eds. 1984. The new institutional economic. A symposium. Special Issue: *Zeitschrift für die gesamte Staatswissenschaft* 149 (1).

——— and ———, eds. 1993. The new institutional economics. Recent progress; expanding frontiers. Special Issue, *Zeitschrift für die gesamte Staatswissenschaft* 149 (1).

Grafstein, R. 1992. *Institutional Realism.* New Haven: Yale University Press.

Greber, E.R and J.E. Jackson. 1993. Endogenous Preferences and the Study of Institutions. *American Political Sceince Review* 87, 639–656.

Habermas, J. 1992. *Faktizität und Geltung: Beiträge zur Diskurstheorie des rechts und des demokratischen Rechtsstaats.* Frankfurt am Main: Suhrkamp.

——. 1994. Three Normative Modes of Democracy (manuscript).

Hannan, M.T. and J. Freeman. 1989. *Organizational Ecology.* Cambridge MA: Harvard University Press.

Hechter, M., K-D Opp and R. Wippler. 1990. *Social Institutions. Their Emergence, Maintenance and Effects.* New York: deGruyter.

Kitcher, P. 1985. *Vaulting Ambition.* Cambridge MA: MIT Press.

Krasner, S.D. 1988. Sovereignty: An institutional perspective. *Comparative Political Studies* 21, 66–94.

Mansbridge, J.J., ed. 1990. *Beyond Self-Interest.* Chicago: University of Chicago Press.

March, J.G. and J.P. Olsen. 1984. The New Institutionalism: Organizational Factors in Political Life. *American Political Science Review* 78, 734–749.

—— and ——. 1989. *Rediscovering Institutions.* New York: Free Press.

—— and ——. 1994. Institutional Perspectives on Governance. *In Systemrationalität und Partialinteversse,* eds. H.U. Derlien, U. Gerhardt and F. W. Scharpf. Baden-Baden: Nomos.

—— and —— 1995. *Democratic Governance.* New York: Free Press.

Moe, T.M. 1990. Political Institutions: The Neglected Side of the Story. *Journal of Law, Economics, and Organizations* 6, 213–266.

North, D.C. 1981. *Structure and Change in Economic History.* New York: Norton.

——. 1990. *Institutions, Institutional Change and Economic Performance.* Cambridge: Cambridge University Press.

Orren, K. and S. Skowronek. 1994. Beyond the Iconography of Order: Notes for a "New Institutionalism." In *The Dynamics of American Politics,* eds. L.C. Dodd and C. Jillson. Boulder: Westview Press.

Rawls, J. 1993. *Political Liberalism.* New York: Columbia University Press.

Sandel, M.J. 1982. *Liberalism and the Limits of Justice.* Cambridge: Cambridge University Press.

——. 1984. The Procedural Republic and the Unencumbered Self. *Political Theory* 12, 81–96.

Searing. D.D. 1991. Roles, Rules and Rationality in the New Institutionalism. *American Political Science Review* 85, 1239–1260.

Selznick, P. 1949. *TVA and the Grass Roots.* Berkely: University of California Press.

——. 1992. *The Moral Commonwealth.* Berkeley: University of California Press.

Sened, I. 1991. Contemporary Theory of Institutions in Perspective. *Journal of Theoretical Politics* 3, 379–402.

Shepsle, K.A. 1989. Studying Institutions. Some Lessons from the Rational Choice Approach. *Journal of Theoretical Politics* 1, 131–147.

——. 1990. *Perspectives on Positive Economy.* Cambridge: Cambridge University Press.

Skowronek, S. 1982. *Building a New American State.* Cambridge: Cambridge University Press.

Steinmo, S., K. Thelen and F. Longstreeth, eds. 1992. *Structuring Politics. Historical Institutionalism in Comparative Analysis.* Cambridge: Cambridge University Press.

Thomas, G.M. et al. 1987. *Institutional Structure. Constituting State, Society, and the Individual.* Beverly Hills CA: Sage.

Weaver, R.K. and B.A. Rockman, eds. 1993. *Do Institutions Matter?* Washington DC: Brookings.

Wildavsky, A. 1987. Choosing Preferences by Constructing Institutions: A Cultural Theory of Preference Formation. *American Political Science* Review 81, 3–22.

Wolin, S.S. 1989. *The Presence of the Past. Essays on the State and the Constitution.* Baltimore: The Johns Hopkins University Press.

Yack, B. 1985. Concept of Political Community in Aristotle's Philosophy. *The Review of Politics* 47, 92-112.

....

AREND LIJPHART

39 Constitutional Design for Divided Societies

Over the past half-century, democratic constitutional design has undergone a sea change. After the Second World War, newly independent countries tended simply to copy the basic constitutional rules of their former colonial masters, without seriously considering alternatives. Today, constitution writers choose more deliberately among a wide array of constitutional models, with various advantages and disadvantages. While at first glance this appears to be a beneficial development, it has actually been a mixed blessing: Since they now have to deal with more alternatives than they can readily handle, constitution writers risk making ill-advised decisions. In my opinion, scholarly experts can be more helpful to constitution writers by formulating specific recommendations and guidelines than by overwhelming those who must make the decision with a barrage of possibilities and options.

This essay presents a set of such recommendations, focusing in particular on the constitutional needs of countries with deep ethnic and other cleavages. In such deeply divided societies the interests and demands of communal groups can be accommodated only by the establishment of power sharing, and my recommendations will indicate as precisely as possible which particular power-sharing rules and institutions are optimal and why. (Such rules and institutions may be useful in less intense forms in many other societies as well.)

Most experts on divided societies and constitutional engineering broadly agree that deep societal divisions pose a grave problem for democracy, and that it is therefore generally more difficult to establish and maintain democratic government in divided than in homogeneous countries. The experts also agree that the problem of ethnic and

other deep divisions is greater in countries that are not yet democratic or fully democratic than in well-established democracies, and that such divisions present a major obstacle to democratization in the twenty-first century. On these two points, scholarly agreement appears to be universal.

A third point of broad, if not absolute, agreement is that the successful establishment of democratic government in divided societies requires two key elements: power sharing and group autonomy. Power sharing denotes the participation of representatives of all significant communal groups in political decision making, especially at the executive level; group autonomy means that these groups have authority to run their own internal affairs, especially in the areas of education and culture. These two characteristics are the primary attributes of the kind of democratic system that is often referred to as power-sharing democracy or, to use a technical political-science term, "consociational" democracy.[1] A host of scholars have analyzed the central role of these two features and are sympathetic to their adoption by divided societies. But agreement extends far beyond the consociational school. A good example is Ted Robert Gurr, who in *Minorities at Risk: A Global View of Ethnopolitical Conflicts* clearly does not take his inspiration from consociational theory (in fact, he barely mentions it), but based on massive empirical analysis reaches the conclusion that the interests and demands of communal groups can usually be accommodated "by some combination of the policies and institutions of *autonomy* and *power sharing.*"[2]

The consensus on the importance of power sharing has recently been exemplified by commentators' reactions to the creation of the Governing Council in Iraq: The Council has been criticized on a variety of grounds, but no one has questioned its broadly representative composition. The strength of the power-sharing model has also been confirmed by its frequent practical applications. Long before scholars began analyzing the phenomenon of

SOURCE: Arend Lijphart, "Constitutional Design for Divided Societies," *Journal of Democracy*, vol. 15, no. 2 (April 2004), pp. 97–109. © National Endowment for Democracy and The Johns Hopkins University Press. Reprinted with permission of The Johns Hopkins University Press. Footnotes abridged by the Editor.

power-sharing democracy in the 1960s, politicians and constitution writers had designed power-sharing solutions for the problems of their divided societies (for example, in Austria, Canada, Colombia, Cyprus, India, Lebanon, Malaysia, the Netherlands, and Switzerland). Political scientists merely discovered what political practitioners had repeatedly—and independently of both academic experts and one another—invented years earlier.

CRITICS OF POWER SHARING

The power-sharing model has received a great deal of criticism since it became a topic of scholarly discourse three decades ago. Some critics have argued that power-sharing democracy is not ideally democratic or effective; others have focused on methodological and measurement issues.[3] But it is important to note that very few critics have presented serious alternatives to the power-sharing model. One exception can be found in the early critique by Brian Barry, who in the case of Northern Ireland recommended "cooperation without cooptation"—straightforward majority rule in which both majority and minority would simply promise to behave moderately.[4] Barry's proposal would have meant that Northern Ireland's Protestant majority, however moderate, would be in power permanently, and that the Catholic minority would always play the role of the "loyal" opposition. Applied to the case of the Iraqi Governing Council, Barry's alternative to power sharing would call for a Council composed mainly or exclusively of moderate members of the Shi'ite majority, with the excluded Sunnis and Kurds in opposition. This is a primitive solution to ethnic tensions and extremism, and it is naïve to expect minorities condemned to permanent opposition to remain loyal, moderate, and constructive. Barry's suggestion therefore cannot be—and, in practice, has not been—a serious alternative to power sharing.

The only other approach that has attracted considerable attention in Donald L. Horowitz's proposal to design various electoral mechanisms (especially the use of the "alternative vote" or

"instant runoff") that would encourage the election of moderate representatives.[5] It resembles Barry's proposal in that it aims for moderation rather than broad representation in the legislature and the executive, except that Horowitz tries to devise a method to induce the moderation that Barry simply hopes for. If applied to the Iraqi Governing Council, Horowitz's model would generate a body consisting mainly of members of the Shi'ite majority, with the proviso that most of these representatives would be chosen in such a way that they would be sympathetic to the interests of the Sunni and Kurdish minorities. It is hard to imagine that, in the long run, the two minorities would be satisfied with this kind of moderate Shi'ite representation, instead of representation by members of their own communities. And it is equally hard to imagine the Kurdish and Sunni members of a broadly representative constituent assembly would ever agree to a constitution that would set up such a system. . . .

The main point that is relevant here is that it has found almost no support from either academic experts or constitution writers. Its sole, and only partial, practical application to legislative elections in an ethnically divided society was the short-lived and ill-fated Fijian constitutional system, which tried to combine the alternative vote with power-sharing; it was adopted in 1999 and collapsed in 2000. With all due respect to the originality of his ideas and the enthusiasm with which he has defended them, Horowitz's arguments do not seem to have sparked a great deal of assent or emulation.

"ONE SIZE FITS ALL"?

In sum, power sharing has proven to be the only democratic model that appears to have much chance of being adopted in divided societies, which in turn makes it unhelpful to ask constitution writers to contemplate alternatives to it. More than enough potential confusion and distraction are already inherent in the consideration of the many alternatives *within* power sharing. Contrary to Horowitz's claim that power-sharing democracy is a crude "one size fits all" model,[6] the power-sharing systems adopted prior to 1960 (cited earlier), as well as more recent cases (such as Belgium, Bosnia, Czechoslovakia, Northern Ireland, and South Africa), show enormous variation. For example, broad representation in the executive has been achieved by a constitutional requirement that it be composed of equal numbers of the two major ethnolinguistic groups (Belgium); by granting all parties with a minimum of 5 percent of the legislative seats the right to be represented in the cabinet (South Africa, 1994–99); by the equal representation of the two main parties in the cabinet and an alternation between the two parties in the presidency (Colombia, 1958–64); and by permanently earmarking the presidency for one group and the prime ministership for another (Lebanon).

All of these options are not equally advantageous, however, and do not work equally well in practice, because the relative success of a power-sharing system is contingent upon the specific mechanisms devised to yield the broad representation that constitutes its core. In fact, the biggest failures of power-sharing systems, as in Cyprus in 1963 and Lebanon in 1975, must be attributed not to the lack of sufficient power sharing but to constitution writers' choice of unsatisfactory rules and institutions.

These failures highlight the way in which scholarly experts can help constitution writers by developing recommendations regarding power-sharing rules and institutions. In this sense, Horowitz's "one size fits all" charge should serve as an inspiration to try to specify the optimal form of power sharing. While the power-sharing model should be adapted according to the particular features of the country at hand, it is not true that *everything* depends on these individuals characteristics. In the following sections I outline nine areas of constitutional choice and provide my recommendations in each area. These constitute a "one size" power-sharing model that offers the best fit for most divided societies regardless of their individual circumstances and characteristics.

1. The legislative electoral system The most important choice facing constitution writers is that of a legislative electoral system, for which the three broad categories are proportional representation (PR), majoritarian systems, and intermediate systems. For divided societies, ensuring the election of a broadly representative legislature should be the crucial consideration, and PR is undoubtedly the optimal way of doing so.

Within the category of majoritarian systems, a good case could be made for Horowitz's alternative-vote proposal, which I agree is superior to both the plurality method and the two-ballot majority runoff.[7] Nevertheless, there is a scholarly consensus against majoritarian systems in divided societies. As Larry Diamond explains,

> If any generalization about institutional design is sustainable . . . it is that majoritarian systems are ill-advised for countries with deep ethnic, regional, religious, or other emotional and polarizing divisions. Where cleavage groups are sharply defined and group identities (and intergroup insecurities and suspicions) deeply felt, the overriding imperative is to avoid broad and indefinite exclusion from power of any significant group.[8]

The intermediate category can be subdivided further into semi-proportional systems, "mixed" systems, and finally, majoritarian systems that offer guaranteed representation to particular minorities. Semi-proportional systems—like the cumulative and limited vote (which have been primarily used at the state and local levels in the United States) and the single nontransferable vote (used in Japan until 1993)[9]—may be able to yield minority representation, but never as accurately and consistently as PR. Unlike these rare semi-proportional systems, mixed systems have become quite popular since the early 1990s.[10] In some of the mixed systems (such as Germany's and New Zealand's) the PR component overrides the plurality component, and these should therefore be regarded not as mixed but as PR systems. To the extent that the PR component is not, or is only partly, compensatory (as in Japan, Hungary, and Italy), the results will necessarily be less than fully proportional—and minority representation less accurate and secure. Plurality combined with guaranteed representation for specified minorities (as in India and Lebanon) necessarily entails the potentially invidious determination of which groups are entitled to guaranteed representation and which are not. In contrast, the beauty of PR is that in addition to producing proportionality and minority representation, it treats all groups—ethnic, racial, religious or even noncommunal groups—in a completely equal and evenhanded fashion. Why deviate from full PR at all?

2. Guidelines within PR Once the choice is narrowed down to PR, constitution writers need to settle on a particular type within that system. PR is still a very broad category, which spans a vast spectrum of complex possibilities and alternatives. How can the options be narrowed further? I recommend that highest priority be given to the selection of a PR system that is simple to understand and operate—a criterion that is especially important for new democracies. From that simplicity criterion, several desiderata can be derived: a high, but not necessarily perfect, degree of proportionality; multimember districts that are not too large, in order to avoid creating too much distance between voters and their representatives; list PR, in which parties present lists of candidates to the voters, instead of the rarely used single transferable vote, in which voters have to rank order individual candidates; and closed or almost closed lists, in which voters mainly choose parties instead of individual candidates within the list. List PR with closed lists can encourage the formation and maintenance of strong and cohesive political parties.

One attractive model along these lines is the list-PR system used in Denmark, which has 17 districts that elect an average of eight representatives each from partly open lists. The district are small enough for minority parties with more than 8 percent of the vote to stand a good chance of being elected. In addition to the 135 representatives elected in these districts, there are 40 national compensatory seats that are apportioned to parties (with a minimum of 2 percent of the national vote) in a way that aims to maximize overall national proportionality. The Danish model is advantageous for divided societies, because the compensatory seats plus the low 2 percent threshold give small minorities that are not geographically concentrated a reasonable chance to be represented in the national legislature. While I favor the idea of maximizing proportionality, however, this system does to some extent detract from the goal of keeping the electoral system as simple and transparent as possible. Moreover, national compensatory seats obviously make little sense in those divided societies where nationwide parties have not yet developed.

3. Parliamentary or presidential government The next important decision facing constitution writers is whether to set up a parliamentary, presidential, or semi-presidential form of government. In countries with deep ethnic and other cleavages, the choice should be based on the different systems' relative potential for power sharing in the executive. As the cabinet in a parliamentary system is a collegial decision-making body—as opposed to the presidential one-person executive with a purely advisory cabinet—it offers the optimal setting for forming a broad power-sharing executive. A second advantage of parliamentary systems is that there is no need for presidential elections, which are necessarily majoritarian in nature. As Juan Linz states in his well-known critique of presidential government, "perhaps the most important implication of presidentialism is that it introduces a strong element of zero-sum game into democratic politics with rules that tend toward a 'winner-take-all' outcome."[11] Presidential election campaigns also encourage the politics of personality and overshadow the politics of competing parties and party programs. In representative democracy, parties provide the vital link between voters and the government, and in divided societies they are crucial in voicing the interests of communal groups. Seymour Martin Lipset has recently emphasized this point again by calling political parties "indispensable" in democracies and by recalling E.E. Schattschneider's famous pronouncement that "modern democracy is unthinkable save in terms of parties."[12]

Two further problems of presidentialism emphasized by Linz are frequent executive-legislative stalemates and the rigidity of presidential terms of office. Stalemates are likely to occur because president and legislature can both claim the democratic legitimacy of being popularly elected, but the president and the majority of the legislature may belong to different parties or may have divergent preferences even if they belong to the same party. The rigidity inherent in presidentialism is that presidents are elected for fixed periods that often cannot be extended because of term limits, and that cannot easily be shortened even if the president proves to be incompetent, becomes seriously ill, or is beset by scandals of various kinds. Parliamentary systems, with their provisions for votes of confidence, snap elections, and so on, do not suffer from this problem.

Semi-presidential systems represent only a slight improvement over pure presidentialism. Although there can be considerable power sharing among president, prime minister, and cabinet, the zero-sum nature of presidential elections remains. Semi-presidential systems actually make it possible for the president to be even more powerful than in most pure presidential systems. In France, the best-known example of semi-presidentialism, the president usually exercises predominant power; the 1962–74 and 1981–86 periods have even been called "hyperpresidential" phases.[13] The stalemate problem is partly solved in semi-presidential systems by making it possible for the system to shift from a mainly presidential to a mainly parliamentary mode if the president loses the support of his party or governing coalition in the legislature. In the Latin American presidential democracies, constitutional reformers have often advocated semi-presidential instead of parliamentary government, but only for reasons of convenience: A change to parliamentarism seems too big a step in countries with strong presidentialist traditions. While such traditional and sentimental constraints may have to be taken into account in constitutional negotiations, parliamentary government should be the general guideline for constitution writers in divided societies.

There is a strong scholarly consensus in favor of parliamentary government. In the extensive literature on this subject, the relatively few critics have questioned only parts of the pro-parliamentary consensus. Pointing to the case of U.S. presidentialism, for instance, they have noted that the stalemate problem has not been as serious as Linz and others have alleged—without, however, challenging the validity of the other charges against presidential government.

4. Power sharing in the executive The collegial cabinets in parliamentary systems facilitate the formation of power-sharing executives, but they do not by themselves guarantee that power sharing will be instituted. Belgium and South Africa exemplify the two principal methods of doing so. In Belgium, the constitution stipulates that the cabinet must comprise equal numbers of Dutch-speakers and French-speakers. The disadvantage of this approach is that it requires specifying the groups entitled to a share in power, and hence the same discriminatory choices inherent in electoral systems with guaranteed representation for particular minorities. In South Africa there was so much disagreement and controversy about racial and ethnic classifications that these could not be used as a basis for arranging executive power sharing in the 1994 interim constitution. Instead, power sharing was mandated in terms of political parties: Any party, ethnic or not, with a minimum of 5 percent of the seats in parliament was granted the right to participate in the cabinet on a proportional basis.[14] For similar situations in other countries, the South African solution provides an attractive model. But when there are no fundamental disagreements about specifying the ethnic groups entitled to a share of cabinet power, the Belgian model has two important advantages. First, it allows for power sharing without mandating a grand coalition of all significant parties and therefore without eliminating significant partisan opposition in parliament. Second, it allows for slight deviation from strictly proportional power sharing by giving some overrepresentation to the smaller groups, which may be desirable in countries where an ethnic majority faces one or more ethnic minority groups.

5. Cabinet stability Constitution writers may worry about one potential problem of parliamentary systems: The fact that cabinets depend on majority support in parliament and can be dismissed by parliamentary votes of no-confidence may lead to cabinet instability—and, as a result, regime instability. The weight of this problem should not be overestimated; the vast majority of stable democracies have parliamentary rather than presidential or semi-presidential forms of government.[15] Moreover, the position of cabinets vis-à-vis legislatures can be strengthened by constitutional provisions designed to this effect. One such provision is the constructive vote of no confidence, adopted in the 1949 constitution of West Germany, which stipulates that the prime minister (chancellor) can be dismissed by parliament only if a new prime minister is elected simultaneously. This eliminates the risk of a cabinet being voted out of office by a "negative" legislative majority that is unable to form an alternative cabinet. Spain and Papua New Guinea have adopted similar requirements for a constructive vote of no confidence. The disadvantage of this provision is that it may create an executive that cannot be dismissed by parliament but does not have a parliamentary majority to pass its legislative program—the same kind of stalemate that plagues presidential systems. A suggested solution to this potential problem was included in the 1958 constitution of the French Fifth Republic in the form of a provision that the cabinet has the right to make its legislative proposals matters of confidence, and these proposals are adopted automatically unless an absolute majority of the legislature votes to dismiss the cabinet. No constitution has yet tried to combine the German and French rules, but such a combination could undoubtedly give strong protection to cabinets and their legislative effectiveness—without depriving the parliamentary majority of its fundamental right to dismiss the cabinet and replace it with a new one in which parliament has greater confidence.

6. Selecting the head of state

In parliamentary systems, the prime minister usually serves only as head of government, while a constitutional monarch or a mainly ceremonial president occupies the position of head of state. Assuming that no monarch is available, constitution writers need to decide how the president should be chosen. My advice is two-fold: to make sure that the presidency will be a primarily ceremonial office with very limited political power, and not to elect the president by popular vote. Popular election provides democratic legitimacy and, especially in combination with more than minimal powers specified in the constitution, can tempt presidents to become active political participants—potentially transforming the

parliamentary system into a semi-presidential one. The preferable alternative is election by parliament.

A particularly attractive model was the constitutional amendment proposed as part of changing the Australian parliamentary system from a monarchy to a republic, which specified that the new president would be appointed on the joint nomination of the prime minister and the leader of the opposition, and confirmed by a two-thirds majority of a joint session of the two houses of parliament. The idea behind the two-thirds rule was to encourage the selection of a president who would be nonpartisan and nonpolitical. (Australian voters defeated the entire proposal in a 1999 referendum mainly because a majority of the pro-republicans strongly—and unwisely—preferred the popular election of the president.) In my opinion, the best solution is the South African system of not having a separate head of state at all: There the president is in fact mainly a prime minister, subject to parliamentary confidence, who simultaneously serves as head of state.

7. Federalism and decentralization

For divided societies with geographically concentrated communal groups, a federal system is undoubtedly an excellent way to provide autonomy for these groups. My specific recommendation regards the second (federal) legislative chamber that is usually provided for in federal systems. This is often a politically powerful chamber in which less populous units of the federation are overrepresented (consider, for example, the United States Senate, which gives two seats to tiny Wyoming as well as gigantic California). For parliamentary systems, two legislative chambers with equal, or substantially equal, powers and different compositions is not a workable arrangement: It makes too difficult the forming of cabinets that have the confidence of both chambers, as the 1975 Australian constitutional crisis showed. The opposition-controlled Senate refused to pass the budget in an attempt to force the cabinet's resignation, although the cabinet continued to have the solid backing of the House of Representatives. Moreover, a high degree of smaller-unit overrepresentation in the federal chamber violates the democratic principle of "one person, one vote." In this respect, the German and Indian federal models are more attractive than the American, Swiss, and Australian ones.

Generally, it is advisable that the federation be relatively decentralized and that its component units (states or provinces) be relatively small—both to increase the prospects that each unit will be relatively homogeneous and to avoid dominance by large states on the federal level. Beyond this, a great many decisions need to be made regarding details that will vary from country to country (such as exactly where the state boundaries should be drawn). Experts have no clear advice to offer on how much decentralization is desirable within the federation, and there is no consensus among them as to whether the American, Canadian, Indian, Australian, German, Swiss, or Austrian model is most worthy of being emulated.

8. Nonterritorial autonomy   In divided societies where the communal groups are not geographically concentrated, autonomy can also be arranged on a nonterritorial basis. Where there are significant religious divisions, for example, the different religious groups are often intent on maintaining control of their own schools. A solution that has worked well in India, Belgium, and the Netherlands is to provide educational autonomy by giving equal state financial support to all schools, public and private, as long as basic educational standards are met. While this goes against the principle of separating church and state, it allows for the state to be completely neutral in matters of education.

9. Power sharing beyond the cabinet and parliament   In divided societies, broad representation of all communal groups is essential not only in cabinets and parliaments, but also in the civil service, judiciary, police, and military. This aim can be achieved by instituting ethnic or religious quotas, but these do not necessarily have to be rigid. For example, instead of mandating that a particular group be given exactly 20 percent representation, a more flexible rule could specify a target of 15 to 25 percent. I have found, however, that such quotas are often unnecessary; it is sufficient to have an explicit constitutional provision in favor of the general objective of broad representation and to rely on the power-sharing cabinet and the proportionally constituted parliament for the practical implementation of this goal.

OTHER ISSUES

As far as several other potentially contentious issues are concerned, my advice would be to start out with the modal patterns found in the world's established democracies, such as a two-thirds majority requirement for amending the constitution (with possibly a higher threshold for amending minority rights and autonomy), a size of the lower house of the legislature that is approximately the cube root of the country's population size (which means that a country with about 25 million inhabitants, such as Iraq, "should" have a lower house of about 140 representatives), and legislative terms of four years.

While approval by referendum can provide the necessary democratic legitimacy for a newly drafted constitution, I recommend a constitutional provision to limit the number of referenda. One main form of referendum entails the right to draft legislation and constitutional amendments by popular initiative and to force a direct popular vote on such propositions. This is a blunt majoritarian instrument that may well be used against minorities. On the other hand, the Swiss example has shown that a referendum called by a small minority of voters to challenge a law passed by the majority of the elected representatives may have the desirable effect of boosting power sharing. Even if the effort fails, it forces the majority to pay the cost of a referendum campaign; hence the potential calling of a referendum by a minority is a strong stimulus for the majority to be heedful of minority views. Nevertheless, my recommendation is for extreme caution with regard to referenda, and the fact that frequent referenda occur in only three democracies—the United States, Switzerland, and, especially since about 1980, Italy—underscores this guideline.

Constitution writers will have to resolve many other issues that I have not mentioned, and on which I do not have specific recommendations: for example, the protection of civil rights, whether to set up a special constitutional court, and how to make a constitutional or supreme court a forceful protector of the constitution and of civil rights without making it too interventionist and intrusive. And as constitution writers face the difficult and time-consuming task of resolving these issues, it is all the more important that experts not burden or distract them with lengthy discussions on the relative advantages and disadvantages of flawed alternatives like presidentialism and non-PR systems.

I am not arguing that constitution writers should adopt all my recommendations without *any* examination of various alternatives. I recognize that the interests and agendas of particular parties and politicians may make them consider other alternatives, that a country's history and traditions will influence those who must draft its basic law, and that professional advice is almost always—and very wisely—sought from more than one constitutional expert. Even so, I would contend that my recommendations are not merely based on my own preferences, but on a strong scholarly consensus and solid empirical evidence, and that at the very least they should form a starting point in constitutional negotiations.

ENDNOTES

1. The secondary characteristics are proportionality, especially in legislative elections (in order to ensure a broadly representative legislature—similar to the aim of effecting a broadly constituted executive) and a minority veto on the most vital issues that affect the rights and autonomy of minorities.

2. Ted Robert Gurr, *Minorities at Risk: A Global View of Ethnopolitical Conflicts* (Washington, D.C.: U.S. Institute of Peace Press, 1993), p. 292, italics added.

3. I have responded to these criticisms at length elsewhere. See especially Lijphart, "The Wave of Power-Sharing Democracy," in Andrew Reynolds, ed., *The Architecture of Democracy: Constitutional Design, Conflict Management, and Democracy* (Oxford: Oxford University Press, 2002), pp. 40–47; and Lijphart, *Power-Sharing in South Africa*, pp. 83–117.

4. Brian Barry, "The Consociational Model and Its Dangers," *European Journal of Political Research* 3 (December 1975), p. 406.

5. Donald L. Horowitz, *A Democratic South Africa? Constitutional Engineering in a Divided Society* (Berkeley, Calif.: University of California Press, 1991), pp. 188–203; and "Electoral Systems: A Primer for Decision Makers," *Journal of Democracy* 14 (October 2003), pp. 122–23. In alternative-vote systems, voters are asked to rank order the candidates. If a candidate receives an absolute majority of first preferences, he or she is elected; if not, the weakest candidate is eliminated, and the ballots are redistributed according to second preferences. This process continues until one of the candidates receives a majority of the votes.

6. Donald. L. Horowitz, "Constitutional Design: Proposals versus Processes," in Andrew Reynolds, ed., *The Architecture of Democracy*, p. 25.

7. In contrast with plurality, the alternative vote (instant runoff) ensures that the winning candidate has been elected by a majority of the voters, and it does so more accurately than the majority-runoff method and without the need for two rounds of voting.

8. Larry Diamond, *Developing Democracy: Toward Consolidation* (Baltimore: Johns Hopkins University Press, 1999), p. 104.

9. All three of these systems use multi-member election districts. The cumulative vote resembles multi-member district plurality in which each voter has as many votes as there are seats in a district, but, unlike plurality, the voter is allowed to cumulate his or her vote on one or a few of the candidates. In limited-vote systems, voters have fewer votes than the number of district seats. The single nontransferable vote is a special case of the limited vote in which the number of votes cast by each voter is reduced to one.

10. See Matthew Soberg Shugart and Martin P. Wattenberg, eds., *Mixed-Member Electoral Systems: The Best of Both Worlds?* (Oxford: Oxford University Press, 2001).

11. Juan J. Linz, "Presidential or Parliamentary Democracy: Does It Make a Difference?" in Juan J. Linz and Arturo Valenzuela, eds., *The Failure of Presidential Democracy* (Baltimore: Johns Hopkins University Press, 1994), p. 18.

12. Seymour Martin Lipset, "The Indispensability of Political Parties," *Journal of Democracy* 11 (January 2000), pp. 48–55; E.E. Schattschneider, *Party Government* (New York: Rinehart, 1942), p. 1.

13. John T.S. Keeler and Martin A. Schain, "Institutions, Political Poker, and Regime Evolution in France," in Kurt von Mettenheim, ed., *Presidential Institutions and Democratic Politics: Comparing Regional and National*

Contexts (Baltimore: Johns Hopkins University Press, 1997), pp. 95–97. Horowitz favors a president elected by the alternative vote or a similar vote-pooling method, but in other respects his president does not differ from presidents in pure presidential systems; see his *A Democratic South Africa?*, pp. 205–14.

14. The 1998 Good Friday Agreement provides for a similar power-sharing executive for Northern Ireland.

15. In my comparative study of the world's stable democracies, defined as countries that were continuously democratic from 1977 to 1996 (and had populations greater than 250,000), 30 of the 36 stable democracies had parliamentary systems. See Lijphart, *Patterns of Democracy: Government Forms and Performance in Thirty-Six Countries* (New Haven: Yale University Press, 1999).

....

NATHAN J. BROWN

40   *Judicial Review*

In recent years, the global spread of democracy has been accompanied by far less noticed, but even more pervasive political change: the acceptance of judicial review and the establishment of specialized constitutional courts. Judicial review has become nearly ubiquitous in emerging democracies and is increasingly viewed as a prerequisite of healthy democratic development. The democratic acceptance of judicial review has been both imperceptible and widespread, but this should not obscure an underlying puzzle. How did the least democratic branch of government—the judiciary—come to be seen as the necessary guardian of democratic values? Historically, democrats had regarded judicial review with some suspicion. Examining how and why this perception has changed helps us understand the necessity for judicial review as well as its limitations.

Not only is the democratic acceptance of judicial review a historical and ideological puzzle, it also poses an immensely important practical challenge for emerging democracies. How can judicial review operate effectively in societies where democratic institutions and practices are still embryonic? In establishing constitutional courts as one of the first steps in the construction of a new democratic system, countries in transition have typically copied institutions that have functioned well in established democracies. But such models might be inappropriate for transitional countries where constitutional courts are asked to function in far less auspicious circumstances. A more useful, if unusual, parallel may be drawn with the Arab world, where constitutional courts have a history of operating in nondemocratic settings. Understanding the operation and limits of constitutional courts in the Arab world sheds unexpected light on the development of judicial review in transitional countries.

Judicial review developed initially as a byproduct of constitutionalism. Under a constitutional system, public authorities, even those elected by the people, must operate within the limits defined by constitutional law. While constitutionalism is now widely viewed as intimately related to democracy, this has not always been the case. Constraining democratic governments by law was once seen as denying the majority its wishes. In the past, many a constitutionalist regarded popular majorities with suspicion, fearful that they might violate fundamental rights and principles for ephemeral or self-interested reasons. Many a democrat, on the other hand, regarded constitutionalism as an attempt to contain the popular will with dry legalism and outdated documents. Democratic suspicion of constitutionalism once extended to judicial review, as the latter was often seen as a way of allowing judges, rather than the people's elected representatives, to interpret constitutional texts.

It should not be at all surprising, therefore, that judicial review initially emerged in the United States, the first country to attempt to contain

SOURCE: Nathan J. Brown, "Judicial Review and the Arab World," *Journal of Democracy*, vol. 9, no. 4 (October 1998), pp. 85–99. © The National Endowment for Democracy and The Johns Hopkins University Press. Reprinted by permission of The Johns Hopkins University Press. Article abridged by the Editor.

democratic practices within constitutional limits. American constitutionalism sought to allow democracy to operate while curbing its excesses; judicial review came to be seen as a vital corrective to unlimited democracy. Yet even as other countries followed the American example of adopting a written constitution, most rejected judicial review. European democracies, in particular, tended to take a hostile view of judicial review because it threatened to restrict the authority of popularly elected legislatures. If a constitution emanated from the sovereign will of a people, then the people's representatives, sitting in parliament, were assumed to be the best interpreters of that will. In France, constitutional supervision originally emerged as a function of the legislature and not of the judiciary, as prerevolutionary judicial activism had led most French democrats to view the judiciary as a potential bastion of privilege and reaction. In other European countries, such as Sweden and Norway, the parliament played a major, often preponderant, role in constitutional supervision. In most democracies, judicial review came to be seen as a limitation on the sovereignty of the people. Communist states later adopted the same view.

Democratic suspicions of judicial review were well-founded, for it had indeed often been instituted in order to restrict popular majorities, as represented in parliaments. Instead of emerging as a result of judicial initiative or customary practice, judicial review was advocated in Sweden in response to universal male suffrage and parliamentary supremacy.[1] In France, the Council of State, an advisory and judicial body, asserted the right to review administrative acts during the Vichy regime.[2] When a fuller form of judicial review emerged in France under the Fifth Republic (by making the Constitutional Council a quasi-judicial rather than parliamentary institution, albeit with restricted access), the purpose was to keep a check on the parliament and augment presidentialism.[3] Even in the United States, the birthplace of judicial review, the practice was widely perceived in the first half of the twentieth century as operating to protect privilege and frustrate popular desires.

In the early twentieth century, a few democrats began to rethink their opposition to judicial review.

In Austria, a constitutional court was introduced in 1920 as part of a new democratic constitution. This limited experiment lasted barely a decade before the court was brought under executive control and eventually abandoned under fascist rule.[4]

....

AFTER TOTALITARIANISM

Fascism put an end to the Austrian experiment but actually shocked most democrats into setting aside their doubts about judicial review. In fact, the Austrian constitutional court remains, directly or indirectly, the model emulated most often in the rest of the world. By the middle of the twentieth century, the experience of fascism and communism had led most Europeans to forget whatever tension might exist between constitutionalism and democracy. Gradually but consciously, judicial review was instituted to secure rather than restrict democratic gains. European democrats did not allow judicial review to be exercised by ordinary judges but instead created special bodies explicitly charged with constitutional interpretation.

The half-century since the Second World War has seen a tremendous expansion in the construction of such specialized constitutional courts. In many cases, they have come into being to serve as an antidote to previous nonconstitutional and nondemocratic rule. Rather than being viewed as a possible bulwark against popular majorities, judicial review has come to be seen as one of a set of tools to prevent future bouts of authoritarianism.

This view lies behind the two major waves of judicial review that have swept the world over the past 50 years. In the first wave, immediately after the Second World War, the defeated and occupied Axis powers of Germany, Italy, and Japan all adopted judicial review, while Austria revived it. In all these cases, the defense of individual liberties probably stood as the most immediate reason for the adoption of judicial review; such a defense was seen as necessary to prevent the reemergence of fascist and authoritarian government. Constitutionalism seemed to shift from a method of limiting democracy's excesses to a method of protecting it. The tyranny of the executive branch and not that of the majority became the principal concern. The second wave of judicial review began in the 1980s on the eve of the collapse of the Eastern bloc and the Soviet Union.

. . . With the collapse of communism constitutional courts came to be seen as linchpins in the struggle to protect democratic procedures, individual liberties, and civil society. In 1989, Hungary instituted an independent constitutional court that has since emerged as the boldest judicial actor in the former Soviet bloc (and perhaps in the world). Russia formed a constitutional committee in 1991 and a full constitutional court after the failed coup attempt in August of that year. After playing a leading role in precipitating (but also in attempting to mediate) the 1993 crisis between President Boris Yeltsin and the Russian parliament, the constitutional court was brought to heel, but not eliminated. In 1991 and 1992, Czechoslovakia, Bulgaria, and Romania all established constitutional courts; Albania and some of the states that broke away from Yugoslavia did the same. The breakdown of communist rule in Poland diminished the possibility that the Polish parliament would exercise its right to overturn court rulings.[5] Throughout Eastern Europe, constitutional courts sometimes came into being sooner than new constitutions; efforts during transitions focused on improving and enforcing the old constitution before writing a new one. Constitutional courts were instrumental in these efforts to bring to life constitutional rights and procedures that had existed only on paper in the communist era.[6]

There is thus a strong dilemma, even an irony, in the new conception of the role of judicial review. In its earlier incarnation, judicial review was generally perceived as a tool to defend constitutionalism against ephemeral or tyrannical majorities. Now, judicial review is increasingly seen as necessary to constrain *all* government action, not just that of popularly elected legislatures. The new adversary is untrammeled executive authority that may claim to act in the name of the people but that often has little credibility in doing so. Judges are not to restrain the base or momentary passions of the people but the abuses of governments acting on their own. An Austrian constitutional court judge analyzing the transitional countries goes so far as to say, "It is

mainly up to the judges of the constitutional courts to safeguard human rights and democracy."[7]

With eyes on the past as much as on the future, the architects of constitutionalism in these countries have seen constitutional courts and judicial review as a way of preventing authoritarianism and executive domination. This logic was followed in South Africa, where the tension between majority rule and protection of the status of the white minority took a very old form: The African National Congress demanded a strong constitutional court despite vehement opposition from several quarters, including the Afrikaner right. In other words, judicial review was valued more by the majority about to assume power than by the minority facing a diminution of its power.

Thus those who work to construct constitutional courts are attempting to defend democracy with institutions that are designed to restrain it. How well will this work? The question is particularly acute in transitional countries, where constitutional judiciaries are asked to help establish democracy, not simply to defend it at the margins. Constitutional courts must operate in uncertain settings where many authoritarian structures, practices, and doctrines persist. Can such courts be relied upon to deter officials from overstepping their authority? Can the courts deter presidents from acting only to maintain their position? Can they be counted on to stop officials from flouting devices designed to ensure accountability? These types of questions, which transitional countries are beginning to grapple with, arose much earlier in the Arab world. To understand the role of constitutional courts in undemocratic settings and to explore their possible role in transitional countries, it makes sense to examine the Arab world's experiences with constitutionalism.

....

CONSTITUTIONAL COURTS IN THE ARAB WORLD

Judicial review, generally in the form of specialized constitutional courts, is a surprisingly common feature among Arab states. A commitment to judicial review has emerged in Algeria, Bahrain, Egypt, Iraq, Jordan, Kuwait, Lebanon, Libya, Morocco, Somalia,

Sudan, Syria, Tunisia, the United Arab Emirates, and Yemen. Only a handful of countries (Qatar, Oman, and Saudi Arabia) have refrained completely from involving the judiciary in constitutional matters. Interestingly, Arab courts have, on occasion, been assertive: While judicial review has most often been established by clear constitutional mandate rather than by a judicial decision, courts in Egypt, Tunisia, and Jordan have joined their counterparts in the United States and Israel in asserting a right to judicial review despite the absence of explicit constitutional authorization. These decisions are notable, through they remain exceptional. For the most part, judicial review in the Arab world is exercised by specialized constitutional courts created in part by explicit constitutional provisions.

Despite the widespread acceptance of judicial review in the Arab world, only a few of the bodies charged with the task are viewed as effective defenders of constitutionalism. Beginning in the late 1970s, limited political liberalization in parts of the Arab world brought possibilities for bolder uses of judicial review and stronger structures capable of exercising it. Constitutional bodies in Egypt and Lebanon have forced modifications of electoral laws, while in Egypt and Jordan the executive's authority to issue emergency legislation has been seriously challenged. Efforts to build bold constitutional judiciaries have recently increased. The Palestinian Legislative Council has passed a basic law (yet to be approved by Yasir Arafat) designed to foster the rule of law by way of an independent judiciary and constitutional court. The Egyptian Supreme Constitutional Court has struck the most aggressive pose, issuing decisions that lessened restriction on political parties, circumscribed executive authority over taxation, and removed restrictions on freedom of the press. The Court has twice forced the dissolution of parliament and new elections by finding an electoral law unconstitutional.

The record of the Egyptian Supreme Constitutional Court, coupled with the seemingly growing potential for judicial boldness in a few other cases, has led some to see constitutional judiciaries as strong actors in the struggle to establish constitutionalism and democracy in the Arab world. Yet the obstacles to using constitutional courts and judicial review to achieve such goals are formidable. . .

TRANSITIONAL COUNTRIES AND THE ARAB EXPERIENCE

By adopting judicial review, transitional countries are attempting to use a tool designed to restrict democracy in order to protect it. They are trying to institute simultaneously the rule of law and the rule of the people in an environment where neither principle operated effectively in the past.

When the constitutional courts of transitional countries are examined in light of the Arab experience, it becomes clear that they may emerge as strong actors only so long as democracy and political pluralism also operate smoothly. Most courts have been designed in a way that will make them strong—perhaps too strong—only under favorable conditions.

First, with regard to *appointment procedures,* most transitional countries have borrowed mechanisms aimed at ensuring the accountability of judges in stable democracies, rather than insulating judges in authoritarian systems. Far more attention has been focused on preventing the removal of judges than on the process of appointing them in the first place. In general, appointments are made either exclusively by parliament or are shared between the president and the parliament. The record in the Arab world shows that such mechanisms will secure judicial independence only after political pluralism has been established. The Arab experience also suggests one possible remedy—allowing not simply judges but the judiciary as a whole to become independent, exercising authority even over its own appointment and promotion. Other mechanisms are also available to render the executive and legislative role less direct and thus increase the strength of the court, for example, nomination by the judiciary, reliance on academics, or appointment by a president who does not serve as head of government. Most transitional countries have eschewed these options. With judges' terms often running less than a decade, courts could be remade in fairly short order. As long as a pluralist political order prevails, the constitutional courts may become independent and quite strong, but should authoritarianism return, their independence would quickly disappear.

Second, with respect to *procedures for bringing cases,* most constitutional bodies in transitional countries lean toward abstract (though not always prior) review. As the Arab experience indicates, this means that as long as the executive dominates the legislature, constitutional challenges on serious issues are unlikely to be made. Allowing individuals to resort to the court through a concrete case (an approach adopted by several East European states[8]) may not help much, for it requires that the court of original jurisdiction pass the case on to the constitutional court. The effect is to make constitutional litigation dependent on the independence of other judges and their acceptance of the work of the constitutional court. Based on the Arab experience, this will not always be forthcoming. Indeed, the problem may have already developed in Hungary, though the constitutional court there—arguably the most powerful in the world—has more than enough tools to deal with recalcitrant lower courts.[9] The second solution is to allow decentralized judicial review. This expands the number of judicial actors allowed to review the constitutionality of executive and legislative acts, but at the cost of weakened judicial authority. In the civil-law tradition that prevails in most countries outside the Anglo-American legal world, a court ruling has comparatively little value as precedent. Thus an individual who convinces a court that a specific statute or administrative action is unconstitutional will have only won the case at hand. The law or regulation remains in force; only if every court rules in a similar manner will the law be robbed of its effect.

The Hungarians have devised a radical solution: All individuals are allowed by statute to bring abstract cases directly to the Constitutional Court. This allows them to resort directly to that court without being referred by a court of original jurisdiction. Not surprisingly, this has resulted in a very busy and active Constitutional Court.

Third, with regard to *constitutional text,* many transitional countries use language that is at least as restrictive as that used by their Arab counterparts. Arab constitutions call for legislation to guarantee or organize freedoms; most constitutions in the former Soviet bloc do the same. The Hungarian Constitution, for instance, guarantees

such freedoms and calls for legislation passed by a super-majority to govern the matter. There remains ambiguity on the leeway for parliamentary action—ambiguity which the parliament and the Constitutional Court will have to work out in practice. (Even most matters related to the functioning of the Hungarian Constitutional Court itself are left to legislation.) Slovakia's Constitution guarantees an impressive catalog of freedoms, but allows some—including freedom of religion and expression—to be limited "if such a measure is unavoidable in a democratic society to protect public order, health, morality, or the rights and liberties of others" (Article 24). By allowing such restrictive legislation, and by failing to define who may determine if such legislation is "unavoidable," the drafters have made it possible for a future parliament to justify a wide range of limitations on basic freedoms.

By requiring or encouraging such legislation on basic freedoms, the constitutional document risks inviting the parliament to regard rights as subject to definition and restriction. This increases the possibility that the basic freedoms defined by constitutions will need a robust and liberal court to defend them. This problem has not gone unnoticed. Indeed, the Egyptian Supreme Constitutional Court has already begun to develop approaches designed to buttress shaky constitutional rights. The Hungarian court has introduced its own principle that "the essential content of a constitutional right cannot be limited by law."[10] A similar principle was incorporated into the Polish Constitution of 1997. It remains to be seen how much political will constitutional courts will show in applying such principles.

This brings us to the fourth condition, involving *judicial culture* and dominant strands of jurisprudence. It is not yet clear what direction the new constitutional courts will take, nor is it clear what constitutional architects and others can do (beyond fostering judicial independence) to guarantee that a strong constitutional vision will develop. Nevertheless, some signs indicate that, in certain countries, constitutional architects have succeeded in creating the bold defenders of constitutionalism that they had sought. In 1992, for instance, the Hungarian court ruled against a law suspending the statute of limitations for crimes committed under communist rule. In South Africa, the country's new Constitutional Court lost no time in overturning the country's death penalty, despite the absence of an explicit constitutional text on the issue. In Russia, the new Constitutional Court immediately (and perhaps fatally) involved itself in some of the most sensitive issues in the country, and thus found itself an active participant, rather than a removed constitutional guardian, in the 1993 struggle between President Boris Yeltsin and the parliament. Accused by Yeltsin of placing the country in danger of civil war, the court had its work suspended and some members lost their seats. Clearly, at least some of the new courts do not shy away from transforming indeterminate constitutional language into real restrictions on the executive and legislature.

The courts are aided in this task by a notable internationalization of constitutional jurisprudence. It has become routine for constitutional judiciaries to rely not only on their own jurisprudence but also that of their most prestigious counterparts in other countries. In striking down the death penalty, for instance, the South African court gave extensive attention to the findings of foreign courts. And the most prestigious courts are often the most activist ones. Thus American, German, and Indian constitutional decisions have been cited outside of their own countries. In striking down Egypt's electoral law, its Supreme Constitutional Court based its decision less on previous Egyptian constitutional thinking than on the U.S. Supreme Court's ruling in *Baker v. Carr*. Egyptian jurisprudence, in turn, is influential throughout the Arab world. Thus constitutional judges seem to have been emboldened by the findings of their colleagues abroad, augmenting a global trend of more activist constitutional jurisprudence.

···

CONSTITUTIONALISM VS. DEMOCRACY

This brings us to the final irony of the increased democratic reliance on judicial review and specialized constitutional courts. Most of the constitutional documents of transitional countries are based on little awareness of the historic tension between constitutionalism and democracy. Most of the newly designed constitutional courts are part of a strategy to ensure the creation of a new democratic and liberal political order. If that new order does come into being, however, the constitutional courts may soon be resented for their undemocratic features. That is, if government really comes to reflect the will of the majority, activist courts will soon come to restrict that will. The analysis presented here suggests that so long as a pluralist political order operates, most of the new constitutional courts will be strong ones and may thus be resistant to popular influence. If the transitional countries are successful in establishing democracies, they may find that they have succeeded too well in building strong courts. (Some Hungarians may currently be coming to precisely that conclusion.)

If, however, the new political orders do not emerge in the manner hoped for by democratic activists, the new courts may not be the bulwarks of constitutionalism desired. The experience of the Arab world shows that constitutional courts can move in constitutionalist directions even in an authoritarian context—if certain conditions are met. Yet several of those conditions have not been met in constructing the most recent wave of new constitutional courts. Therefore, it should come as no surprise if many fail when put to the test. Indeed, the legal—and even constitutional—basis exists in most transitional countries to create a docile constitutional judiciary.

In the literature on constitutionalism, Thomas Jefferson is frequently cited for his call for constitutional flexibility: Each new generation needs to redefine its constitutional order. At times, the constitution-writing of past generations needs to be disregarded; "the dead," after all, "have no rights."[11] Today's new constitutional courts may become structures that take away the rights of the living without even conferring them on the dead; they may wind up restricting popular majorities in democratic orders and serving autocrats in autocratic ones.

NOTES

1. See Nils Stjernquist, "Judicial Review and the Rule of Law: Comparing the United States and Sweden," *Policy Studies Journal* 19 (Fall 1990), pp. 106–15.

2. See Mauro Cappelletti, *Judicial Review in the Contemporary World* (Indianapolis: Bobbs-Merrill, 1971), pp. 17–18.

3. Alec Stone, "The Birth and Development of Abstract Review: Constitutional Courts and Policymaking in Western Europe," *Policy Studies Journal* 19 (Fall 1990), p. 84.

4. Hans Kelsen, "Judicial Review of Legislation: A Comparative Study of the Austrian and the American Constitution," *Journal of Politics* 4 (May 1942), p. 183.

5. As it happens, this parliamentary prerogative was removed in the 1997 Constitutions.

6. There are many surveys of constitutional courts in Eastern Europe; one of the earliest is still one of the best: Georg Brunner, "Development of a Constitutional Judiciary in Eastern Europe," *Review of Central and Eastern European Law* 18 (1992), pp. 535–53.

7. Rudolf Machacek, *Austrian Contributions to the Rule of Law: The Constitutional Court, the Administrative Court, European Perspectives* (Kehl, Germany: N.P. Engel, 1994, p. 75.

8. Brunner, "Development of a Constitutional Judiciary," p. 546. Brunner lists Poland, Hungary, Romania, and Czechoslovakia. The Slovak Republic, when it broke off from the Czech Republic, followed the same course.

9. See László Sólyom, "The Hungarian Constitutional Court and Social Change," *Yale Journal of International Law* 19 (Winter 1994), p. 226.

10. On the Egyptian court, see Nathan Brown, *The Rule of Law in the Arab World* (Cambridge: Cambridge University Press, 1997), ch. 4. On Hungary, see Sólyom, "Hungarian Constitutional Court," p. 228.

11. See, for instance, Cass Sunstein, "Constitutions and Democracies," in Jon Elster and Rune Slagstad, eds., *Constitutionalism and Democracy* (Cambridge: Cambridge University Press, 1998), p. 327.

CHAPTER TWELVE

POLITICAL PERFORMANCE

Any analysis of political institutions must include an appraisal of their effectiveness in achieving larger goals. Do they enable a society to survive in a hostile world, promote the general welfare, offer opportunities for individual development, and create a sense of social purpose? The connection between political process, political substance (or policies), and social outcomes is examined in the essay by Joel D. Abernach and Bert A. Rockman. They emphasize the importance of evaluating government by the consequences of policies, in turn affected by its distinctive structures and processes. The challenge in studying governance, they suggest, is to demonstrate that assumptions about linkage (among processes, policies, and outcomes) are grounded in reality.

One central issue in all political systems is where to draw the line between public and private sectors. In mixed economies the balance swings back and forth between state and markets, responding to electoral judgments of constant experimentation. The collapse of communism in Europe brought into discredit the model of a command economy. At the same time the welfare state, one of the great achievements of social democracy, was accused by critics of fostering a "culture of dependency." In the 1980s a shift took place in public opinion and policy throughout much of the world away from decisions made by the state and in favor of decisions made by the private sector. It became increasingly difficult for states to coordinate, much less directly manage, complex economies; state enterprises tended to be sluggish, less able than their private competitors to perform efficiently. The new watchwords were decentralization and flexibility in order to satisfy consumer demands and innovate. However, markets need to be regulated and private associations must be made somehow accountable. The state decides on the dividing line between public and private sectors and retains power to make strategic policy. For Herbert Simon, organization is a means of human cooperation, and is essential in public and private sectors alike. Graham Wilson likewise takes note of the strong points of both state and market, as each seeks to adapt to the challenges of globalization. Nonetheless, he concludes that there has been a significant change in "the state of the state" in the past several decades.

Another challenge confronting all governments is to provide incentives for economic growth and at the same time reduce or legitimate social disparities. The issue of equality both among and within nations is explored in the essay by Robert A. Dahl. Which countries are most successful in achieving equality along with prosperity, and why?

....

JOEL D. ABERBACH and BERT A. ROCKMAN

41   Governance and Outcomes

At the beginning of a recent essay, Anthony King and Giles Alston make reference to two murals by Lorenzetti covering opposite walls in the old city hall of Siena (King and Alston 1991). One of the murals depicts good government and its consequences. The other depicts bad government and its consequences. As King and Alston put it, Lorenzetti's murals obviously imply some connection between political process and political substance. As the question— really the two questions—posed in the title of this article suggests, it is precisely this connection that we intend to explore.

The connection (or lack thereof) is a subject of enormous breadth. We should begin with the last link in a complex chain and work back from there. This last link is the connection between political substance (public policy) and social outcomes. Efforts to address public policy problems effectively can be torn asunder by uncontrollable events. The 1990 budget summit in the United States, for example, produced a set of outcomes designed to increase revenues and to control discretionary spending. The outcomes achieved through the budget agreement certainly did not relieve the budget problem fully, but it made a good start. The first year of the budget deal, which was estimated to save $100 billion, however, was soon overwhelmed by events, namely the continued drain on the U.S. treasury caused by the bailout of failed thrift

institutions and by the lingering recession. The bailout greatly influenced expenditures, while the recession especially affected revenues. The lesson is that policies frequently can be overtaken by events, no matter how good the policies may be.

In spite of Lorenzetti's depiction of the benefits of good government, then, it is unlikely that good government alone (whatever it is) can create the Elysian fields he depicted. Bad government, of course, can create a hell—Hitler's Germany and Ceausescu's Romania serve among all too numerous 20th-century examples. Unfortunately, we rarely can define good and bad government in an *a priori* fashion. We know each mostly by its consequences. And, despite the horrible consequences of both the Nazi government and the Ceausescu Communist government, each also was regarded by some at a point in its being as having been "successful" in at least one dimension. The Nazi government dramatically decreased unemployment, for example, through its combination of military mobilization and vast public works projects. The Ceausescu government rid Romania of the burdens of international debt by essentially requiring its citizens to live at an abysmal standard even for a Communist government. Even demonic government, then, may leave a small residue of ambiguity. After all, the successor government in Romania has one silver lining in dealing with an otherwise bleak situation: It has no one to pay off.

The Lorenzetti murals make an assumption common to the way that citizens often think of government; that government can be evaluated only by the consequences that seem to derive from it whether or not these actually are attributable to the processes of governing.

SOURCE: Joel D. Aberbach and Bert A. Rockman, "Does Governance Matter, and If So, How? Process, Performance, and Outcomes," *Governance,* vol. 5, no. 2 (April 1992), pp. 135–153. © Blackwell Publishing Ltd. Reprinted by permission of Blackwell Publishing Ltd. Footnotes and references abridged by the Editor.

Political scientists, however, would likely examine the hypothesized linkages between process, performance, and outcomes by posing some key analytic distinctions and requiring some necessary definitions. Some of the key analytic distinctions are represented below.

DISTINCTIONS

1. *Exogenous vs. Endogenous Effects.* Unless one thinks that the institutions and processes of government fully determine outcomes, there is no doubt that events and conditions outside of the arrangements of government influence the fate of a government's citizens. Probably, what lies outside of the "tool box" of government is more important than what is in it. This does not make governmental processes unimportant, just as the immutable condition of mortality does not lessen the value of the physician's craft. It does, however, place it in perspective.

2. *Macro vs. Micro Level Effects and Influences.* Richard Rose nicely demonstrates the relative stability of macroeconomic indicators in Britain under Conservative and Labor governments (Rose 1984). New hands on the steering wheel do not by themselves permit U-turns in direction. Steering government (if that indeed is even meaningful and nonpresumptuous language) does not mean that the past and its constraints on the present are easily swept away. Nor do new hands on the steering wheel mean that the obvious can be disregarded, i.e., the forces of markets (hence, such matters as the worthiness of one's currency and the costs of borrowing), the allocation of resources (Egypt has a lot of sand and a small amount of oil while Saudi Arabia has a lot of sand and a lot of oil), and so on.

   All things considered, it is more likely that a government that is governing well can monitor the overhead costs on its contracts or the flow of funds for its projects than that it can successfully shape the national economy (which these days, of course, is greatly affected by economic forces beyond the direct jurisdiction of national authorities). The more expansive the set of problems a government seeks to deal with, however, the more likely its actions are affected, if not overwhelmed, by exogenous influences.

3. *Design and Chance.* No system design is flawless. Thus, engineers build in redundancies when safety is an issue, whether these involve the functioning of aircraft or nuclear power plants. Similarly, in his classic article, Martin Landau argued the utility of the engineering analogy of redundancy for the organization of government (Landau 1969). Redundancy, however, is a better system for the control of ill-effects or dangers than for the design of efficiency. Nevertheless, it is certainly true that we have learned important things about organizational design. But it is equally true that these point in no single direction as a remedy for all problems. Moreover, as Machiavelli once noted, and as Herbert Kaufman more recently has shown (1985), chance plays a large role in determining successful outcomes. Quite possibly, we may need to revise our expectation about the relative effects of design and random error. The Scottish poet, Robert Burns, may have had it right when he wrote, "The best laid plans of mice and men oft go astray." We need then to consider how organizational design can influence process and how it, in turn, can influence outcome. But we would be wise to realize that the science of social and political design lags far behind the science of physical design.

4. *Structures vs. People.* The objective of organizations is to compensate for the deficiencies in people. Organizations, for example, are presumed to keep better records than individuals and are thus presumed to have better memories than individuals because they have definable routines for the collection and storage of information. Whether this actually is true or not is, of course, an empirical matter. But it is a presumption.

   An important question, however, is whether organizations actually can perform this compensatory function or whether good individuals will overcome virtually any system. Clearly poor structures (as yet undefinable) impede good people (equally undefinable as yet) and may over time diminish the quality of people who operate within them. Oppositely, good structures (still undefined) probably will not work if manned by inept individuals.

Obviously, structures and people should be synergistic, not an "or" but an "and." This construction is, however, merely a heartwarming platitude. Organizations typically do not have a single mission, and when broken into their constituent elements, none can optimize their own function and expect the larger system of which they are a part to survive. This is patently true whether we are speaking of a set of units, each seeking to optimize its function within a governmental department, or a set of governmental departments seeking to optimize its function within the government as a whole. The analogy equally applies to business firms or to non-profit institutions. It is a fact of organization life that all constituent elements of an organization whatever the level of aggregation cannot simultaneously optimize their functions and missions without bankrupting the larger system of which they are part. Hence, organizational leaders who are deeply committed to the performance of their mission may be dysfunctional to the larger organization and ultimately to their own organizational unit.

Clearly, however, we would not think well of organizational leaders who were not committed to the achievement of their organizational mission. It is a characteristic of successful organizational leaders that they are individuals who have enough commitment to drive achievement and enough acuity and political sensitivity to operate within a context of diverse preferences and organizational coalitions. Having said that, we have, unfortunately, little to go on that is particularly tangible. The problem in linking organizational structures with individuals is that theories of organizations are contingent on goals and missions as well as on contexts and environments, and so are theories of individual leadership. We are faced, then,

with having to decide what values we want to have more of and which ones we are willing to settle for less of to get the proper mix of organizational possibilities and individual talents and skills.

In this regard, though, as Herbert Simon long since pointed out, operative organizational goals do not inhere in an organization but are instead continuously given meaning by dominant governing coalitions within an organization (Simon 1964). Although the goals of dominant coalitions undoubtedly do vary, actors at the top of the organizational grid are likely to want to arrive at an organizational equilibrium that generates slack resources and allocates them to the top (and thereby maximizes discretion at that level). In short, financial equilibrium is of greater concern at the top of an organization while goal achievement is more likely to drive its parts. Hence, meshing people and organizations is no simple task because few persons are for all seasons, and because it is easier to design organizational controls (and proliferate red tape) than to facilitate through organizational structure the accomplishment of mission.

DEFINITIONS

Having introduced some critical distinctions needed to think through the logic of the links between process, performance, and output, it is necessary also to note some conceptual problems of a definitional nature. Again, let us begin at the end of the chain.

1. *Outcomes.* What is a desirable social outcome? This is a question that moral philosophers, welfare economists, and political theorists obviously have devoted their efforts to answering, but unfortunately without success as yet (or perhaps "without total success"). Pareto optimality—the bettering of one person's welfare without the diminution of another's—comes as close as any criterion to wide acceptance. By virtue of this criterion, Pareto optimality virtually precludes redistribution.

Thus, those seeking to apply the criterion of Pareto optimality must assume either that the status quo is essentially just, or that, as John Rawls (1973) has argued, existing inequalities can be justified only by the compensating benefits of increased efficiency.

This is not an appropriate place for an extended discussion of how we might do what others more adept than us have been unable to do, i.e., define a general social welfare function, but rather merely to point out just how mind-boggling this task truly is. The fact that we frequently disagree on just what the preferred outcome should be is, after all, what gives rise to politics. Under democratic rule, political organizations (especially parties) then further structure these divisions of opinion organizationally, sociologically, and historically. Under less civil circumstances, the disagreements give rise to violence and war.

Clearly, one of the most important value conflicts was illuminated by the late Arthur Okun (1975) as that between efficiency and equity. Without efficiency, the pie diminishes and the distributive struggle is over smaller and smaller slices until these eventually become scraps. The demise of most communist regimes and the teetering status of the remaining ones testify to their inability to deal with the efficiency problem. Alternatively, systems organized solely around the efficient accumulation of wealth without regard to its distributive consequences are likely to foster resentment, social disintegration, and, in extreme cases, revolution.

In short, we have no agreed upon definition of what is a desirable social equilibrium. If we did, we would no doubt have the end of politics (and probably also of social ideas). Yet, we have no end of ideas as to what "good government" should be and what it should produce, i.e., a state of affairs that maximizes our own individual preferences.

2. *Performance.* What do "good governments" do, and, by implication at least, what do they do differently from bad governments? S. E. Finer (1980) stipulates three principles of democratic governance: (1) representativeness, (2) stability, and (3) futurity.

How well can governments represent and through what means should they represent are questions that extend back to Hobbes, Locke, Rousseau, Burke and John Stuart Mill. Indeed, what does representation mean? Is there representation for a collective goods function (the Hobbesian vestment of state authority to deter us from killing one another)? Is there representation for classes or groups of persons (Lenin's vanguard party, the representation of states in the U.S. Senate or the German Bundesrat)? Is there unbiased representation for individual preferences (a welfare economist's unobtainable utopia as one of them, Kenneth Arrow (1952), showed four decades ago)? And, is there representation for those who cannot represent themselves (future generations)?

How do votes translate into seats and political power? Can majority governments be formed with a minority of the votes? How is proportional representation aggregated in forming governments? Is one frequent consequence tying legislative seats closely to the proportionality of the vote that of giving pivotal power to parties that get only marginal shares of the vote? When we separate authority, as in the United States, do we also, through electoral outcomes that produce divided majorities, separate our preferences? If so, through what mechanism can they be aggregated, if at all?

Representativeness is a criterion of governmental performance. Yet, it also has a determining effect on the capability of government to perform in other repects.[1] For example, forms of representation that lead to more powerful policy-deciding and management capabilities (those that produce majority party governments) exacerbate resentment and inefficacy on the part of the minority. Lacking points of political pressure and responsiveness, policy losers, as in France, frequently apply pressure in the streets or on the highways—by blocking them (Wilsford 1989).

Stability is not as such a democratic value, of course, but it is a value related to the judicious and prudential behavior of governments. Bureaucracy is the ballast of the democratic state—so much so, that it is often feared as an undemocratic element. The concern of democrats is that the bureaucracy will continue to do what it has been doing and is comfortable with doing regardless of the preferences of the newly elected or the mandates they claim. The positive side of stability clearly lies in the affirmation of the values of experience and continuity in policymaking. Stability, in this positive sense, provides a certain degree of slack for planning longer-term policy responses. Beyond the potentially undemocratic character of superstable policy and program commitments enforced and supported by the bureaucracy, the ambivalence of the value of stability can be seen also in its potential transformation into deadlock. Here, political structure assumes importance because the likelihood of deadlock for system level policymaking increases with the multiplication of veto points in the government.

The futurity principle is the third element of governmental performance suggested by Finer. The notion of providing for the well-being of society into the future is viewed by some as the most important criterion of the performance of government. Those who desire to strengthen the authority of government and limit the number of veto points that governmental action might be subject to are especially concerned with bolstering the capability of government to meet difficult challenges that have high short-term costs. Unfortunately, bolstering governmental authority by no means guarantees that government will behave in the prescribed manner. Even more fundamental, though, is that we often disagree on the means by which government can stimulate responses to long-range problems even if it were inclined to do so. Do we, for example, advance the prospect of adequate energy supplies through programs of governmental intervention in stimulating alternative energy sources, encouraging conservation of fuel, and taxing its use? Or do we advance that prospect by allowing the market to equilibrate demand and supply, thus using price mechanisms to induce conservation and to provide incentives for developing alternative energy sources?

How might government be attuned to the collective good and to the long-term viability of the society it governs? Skepticism is rampant as to whether the governors have these concerns, or at least whether they have them intensely enough so that they are willing to give priority to long-term societal needs when they are confronted with strong constituency pressures to respond to immediate concerns. But assuming these long-term needs are the principal concerns on which the governors act, could we agree on what courses of action follow from them? The answer, we are confident, is no

3. *Process.* Institutional and organizational structures set the likely range of processes, but institutional and organizational rules and norms define processes in more precise form. Essentially, processes in democratic systems tend to be organized around three principles: (1) majoritarianism, (2) conflicting interests, and (3) collaborating interests.

Majoritarian systems deter the proliferation of veto points and thus make it easier to act. But if there is fairly regular alternation of parties, there may be little policy stability. Majoritarianism also operates on exclusivity. It is difficult to register an effective dissent until the next election. Majoritarian principles, however, are action facilitating ones.

The principle of controlling authority through checkmating is at the core of the system of conflicting interests. This principle is most clearly embraced in the American separation-of-powers system which, in turn, reflects the Madisonian idea of "countering ambition with ambition." The principle of conflicting interests, then, is designed to do exactly the opposite of majoritarianism, i.e., increase access for participation, hinder governmental action, and cement policy stability by making it difficult to mobilize sufficient support to reverse policies already enacted (Vogel 1986). The control of conflicting interests is largely based on a structural design that includes separation of powers, concurrent majorities, bicameralism, federalism, and other features meant to hinder the facile exercise of authority. The structural features may or may not facilitate protection of minorities (Dahl 1956), but they do proliferate veto points and widen access to authority.

Normative behavior, on the other hand, is crucial to any system of collaborating interests, though some structural features inhibit collaborative behavior while others allow latitude for such behavior. The norm of collaborating interests is associated with corporatism. Collaboration is most likely to occur under conditions of single-party dominance and political stability, where the dominant party also has social outreach needs. It can best achieve them through arrangements that trade off some sectoral autonomy for broader governmental support. The condition of single party dominance, however, does not determine the presence of collaborative or consensual arrangements; norms about inclusion and the role of government in problem-solving are crucial in facilitating this form of behavior (Olsen 1983). However, the likelihood of these norms emerging under systems organized around the idea of conflicting interests and, especially, under majority party systems is low because the incentives for long-term mutual accommodations are minimal.

One set of processes, then, emphasizes the unabashed rights of the majority to set the course of society; a second set emphasizes the value of clashing interests in limiting the opportunities of tyrannical control; and a third emphasizes the inclusionary principle and the value of consensus. Which is best? That question might in turn be preceded by the question of which is most possible. If Mancur Olson is correct, a system of collaborating interests is feasible only where there is a social surplus that can be used to pay off the collaborating interests (Olson 1986).

PROCESS AND PERFORMANCE FROM THE WORM'S EYE VIEW

If there is one thing that can be gleaned from our comments so far, it is that the bird's eye view is perhaps less helpful than the worm's eye view in linking governmental process and performance. The bird's encompassing view takes in too much scenery. The impact of exogenous factors can be vast, and the uncertainties of what we are looking for are monumental. This is not to say that the quality of government looked at in a macrocosmic way does not influence the outcomes; it is to say that its effects are rarely unidirectional and that there is much betwixt governance and outcomes. Of course, there certainly

is some evidence that how government is organized affects its prospective capabilities in both managing policies and managing politics.[2] But, as we earlier noted, the more our attention is drawn to the macro level, the more the qualities of governance become overwhelmed by exogenous influences such as the nature of the problems that governments face and the political conditions under which they operate. We can, indeed must, include qualities of leadership as an element of governance, but there is no singular definition of leadership (Rockman 1984, 175–219). There also is some reason to believe that the emergence of leadership is fundamentally idiosyncratic and unpredictable.

We need to train our attention more narrowly if we are to discern the connection between governance and performance, and especially how we might improve the latter by manipulating the former. We may need to look at matters as the worm might. How can we at least improve the performance of government at the margin?

PERFORMANCE CRITERIA

WHAT CAN GOVERNMENT DO BETTER?

No doubt, any discussion of government can list a lengthy set of criteria for evaluating its performance. Four considerations seem to us of special importance, although we readily admit to some arbitrariness in focusing on them. The four that we stipulate are

1. *the quality of decision making,*
2. *the knowledge capability of government,*
3. *the capacity to mediate between government and interests, and*
4. *implementation capabilities.*

The quality of decision making refers to whether critical information was absorbed and assimilated, whether it was encouraged, and whether the system of decision making allowed alternatives to be discussed freely and without the limiting effects of strong *a priori* biases.

The knowledge capability of government refers to what it is that governments know, the mechanisms that exist for information to reach decision makers, and the quality of the information being conveyed.

The mediating capacity of government refers to the relations between the government or any of its empowered bodies (administrative agencies, for example) and affected interests when an existing equilibrium is disturbed.

The implementing capability of government refers to the learning ability of government in the process of implementing policy, and the extent to which the learning can be put to effective use. Ironically, the easier any act of implementation appears to be, the less learning is likely to be absorbed from it. Central control can impose a heavy handed will, but whether it can implement complexity effectively is a different matter.

ORGANIZATIONS AND PEOPLE

Both organizational and leadership factors are relevant to these four considerations. Within a moderate range, these performance criteria are value free from the standpoint of substantive policy preference. Our concerns are at the level of process, and, in this regard, they are surely (and intentionally) value laden. It is likely that our views of an effective governing process will not appeal to those with messianic or utopian inclinations. A good process, as we think of it, is apt to be inhospitable to doctrinaire ideologues. No system other than one of authoritarian command is likely to be compatible with the goals of the passionately committed. We assume, however, that a good process should work well for governors with different policy preferences so long as the way these preferences are held does not preclude openness to alternatives. Yet no system, however constructed, can substitute for irreconcilable differences within a society and, particularly, within its leadership class. Furthermore, as we noted earlier, no system can be immunized from manipulation when the governors have a powerful will either to overcome previously imposed constraints or to respond to strong constituency signals.[3]

The quality of governance, then, is hardly all structure and organization. The leadership of the governing strata is vital as well. But it seems that the quality of leadership is not particularly predictable from the way in which leaders are recruited. The fact is that recruitment, selection processes, and background characteristics provide few specific insights about leaders *qua* leaders. The arrow from recruitment and background to leadership behavior and skills is remarkably indeterminate. Consequently, we have even less theoretical clarity about leadership behavior than we have about organization and structure.

In spite of these complications, one important stream of public administration thinking, dating back to at least five decades ago, suggests that high quality, professionally socialized civil servants inculcated in a democratic political culture could be counted on to make government work if the civil servants were given a long leash (Friedrich 1940). In other words, people count, and the quality of the civil service corresponds to the discretion available to them to be creative.

Alternatively, a different tradition emphasizes the formal roots of accountability and control.[4] The way to make the management of the state either democratic or proficient (and sometimes both) is to impose formal mechanisms of control and accountability. The mechanisms would require omni-present supervision by administrative or political means.

The debate as to whether the primary explanation for governmental performance is to be found in organizations and structures or in people continues to rage. We can hardly settle that issue here. There is, though, little doubt that scholars of public administration are often advocates of the professional civil service and are, thus, fond of placing discretion in the hands of civil servants because they presume that good things will follow from doing so. These "good things" are thought to be the natural consequence of decisions and choices made by an elite (civil servants) more likely than politicians to be chosen on the basis of merit. Due to their selection on the basis of merit, civil servants are regarded as more likely to make meritorious choices than are politicians. At the same time that their advocates desire discretion for civil servants, they also want to distance them from political risks of the sort that politicians are often subject to. It's a nice job if one can get it. But these days it is rarely available.

We cannot solve the "organizations versus people" problem other than to recognize the importance of each, and their interdependence. Structures that serve to diminish risks are not likely to acquire risk-takers. Structures that reduce complex tasks to menial ones are not likely to be attractive to creative people. Organizations that mainly focus on control are likely to suppress entrepreneurial people. Alternatively, organizations that grant latitude may attract creative entrepreneurs. They also may attract people tempted by power and its various corrupting forms. Ultimately, organizational forms are statements of human nature. Do we think that people perform best when unconstrained or more constrained? There is no definitive answer to that imposing question because, as we have noted, structuring organizations for one type of function is likely to weaken them for others, and recruiting people of certain dispositions and under certain settings is unlikely to make them equally equipped to handle all things.

In view of this seeming paradox and the limits of both organizational design and personal qualities, are there ways in which we can improve governmental performance according to the four criteria we set forth? The answer is, we think so. It is necessary, however, to be aware of the inherently ambivalent nature of "solutions" since these readily become the source of tomorrow's problems. If we compare the task of governmental reform to that of gardening, we have few perennials to plant. Tending to the garden is a constant task, for we can expect few things to sprout up automatically. The task of governmental reform is anything but mechanistic or final; it is, instead, always a set of iterative adjustments. The process of adjustment must recognize the fallibility of formulas (such as budget balancing algorithms) and the dangers of adhering to singular values.

....

PERFORMANCE, VALUES, AND CRITERIA OF EFFECTIVENESS

We have emphasized the functions of decision making, mediation, implementation, and the role of knowledge that needs to permeate all of these functions. We asked earlier how can we improve decision making in government, the knowledge capability of government, the mediating capacity of government, and government's implementing capability? These functions, we should point out, are interdependent. Knowledge is crucial to decision making, to mediation, and to implementation. Moreover, the character of decision making affects implementation. Since decision makers and implementors typically are different people, prospect of translating the two processes may be a function of the quality of mediation. Decision-making processes that depend upon papering over differences provide few clear signals for implementation from the top down. Rather, as Braybrooke and Lindblom (1963) noted in advancing the idea of a process of "disjointed incrementalism," goals are discovered through the process of decision making (which Braybrooke and Lindblom see as a continuous function that includes implementation rather than as a discrete and separate category of activity).

Not only, then, are these functions interdependent, we also suggest that efforts to improve each tend to reflect a value conflict between one set of values that emphasizes innovation, change, bias-free knowledge, and action facilitation and another set that emphasizes the role of policy communities, of experiential knowledge, the importance of participating in repeated games, and the value of second sober thoughts. Some years ago, along with our colleague, Robert Putnam, we noted that politicians tended to be attracted to many of the values of the first set whereas civil servants tended to be more partial to values represented in the second set (Aberbach, Putnam and Rockman 1981).

Much decision-making literature wrestles with the question of how information can be brought to bear on decision making in ways that permit as free a flow of ideas as possible. Irving Janis (1982), for example, worries about the desire of individuals to please superior authority in small group situations, leading decision making to conform with prevailing premises. Alexander George (1972; 1980) worries about information distortion in organizations and about the capacity of key advisers with strong policy agendas to position themselves to block or distort the advice of others. Michael Cohen (1981;

1984) suggests that parallel search processes may work better than ones meeting at a central point in that they are less likely to be affected by biases.

One of the key value conflicts here, therefore, is whether it is desirable to move decision-making processes past the point of shared premises—those, for example, likely to be held by a policy community. If we think that is important, then clearly a competitive process of decision making that is seeded with diverse perspectives is called for. Alternatively, shared premises are often vital to both mediation and implementation on the grounds that the more sharing of premises there is, the more likely it is that there will be common understandings throughout the system, enabling mediation and implementation to proceed accordingly. Both systems use information, but value it in different ways. Brainstorming and crisis decision making often benefit from the direct clash of ideas. Decision making that has to anticipate more durable (programmatic) outcomes and complex coordination processes might fare better under a system in which the decision makers must live with the consequences of their decisions. Under these circumstances, there is likely to be more emphasis in decision making on the role of policy communities, including civil servants, as repeated participants in a durably structured game. Working from shared premises may be more conducive to dealing effectively with problems that have long-time horizons than it is to dealing with crisis situations. Knowledge capability is important either way, but that capability is defined differently in each case.

A major distinction often cited between European and American civil servants is that the Europeans are neck deep in mediating between the government and external interests whereas the Americans leave this role more often in the hands of appointed political executives (Polsby 1981; Aberbach and Rockman 1990). The political appointees naturally are likely to carry out their mediation efforts in a more biased manner than civil servants might. When administrative or program adjustments take place, civil servants, on the other hand, are likely to take a more expansive view about the composition of program constituents. Political appointees will have as their foremost

concern handling the problems of their party's constituents. Civil servants are more likely, though, to have detailed knowledge about programs and what an adjustment in them is likely to mean to program clienteles. In brief, when civil servants play the role of mediation, they are more likely to be part of a policy community with shared premises than is the case when outside political appointees perform this function. Indeed, during the years of the Reagan administration in the United States (perhaps an anomalous presidential administration), appointed officials were frequently selected on grounds that they decidedly were not members of existing policy communities.

The extent to which mediation is valued depends on how much partisanship and policy innovation are also valued. Obviously, marginally adjusting the status quo or sustaining it nurtures existing policy communities. Concerns for assuring the support of affected interests constrain, but also can nurture, policy innovation. But partisan policy innovation generally needs to create new policy communities as the Roosevelt New Deal administration did or destroy existing ones as the Reagan administration tried to. Partisan policy innovation designed to destroy existing networks requires virtually no policy mediation at all.

Just as knowledge is a vital element in decision making as well as in mediation and implementation, mediation also is a critical element in effective implementation. Developing understandings and trust between the administrative agencies and program constituencies is crucial to learning on the part of both the agencies and the constituencies and, therefore, is likely to lead to a smoother process of implementation. Such "cozy" settings, though, have been vigorously criticized, particularly in the United States, as a kind of private government, as interest group domination, and as a form of mutual protection from freshets of policy innovation. These connections between agencies and interests exist also in European administration where fewer eyebrows are raised about them because the myth of the electoral mandate may actually be less powerful than in the Unites States.

The very nature of a policy innovation influences our perception of how it can be implemented.

If a policy innovation uproots everything in its path, then implementation is of no concern—at least in a form that assumes the existing policy networks might be carried on. On the other hand, if an innovation is perceived as carrying with it consequences for implementation and if there will be continuity in policy participants despite changes in programmatic means, then much attention has to be given to developing understandings of what the effects of change will be and what bargains might be reached to soften the disruptive effects of change.

To recapitulate the argument, we find that the criteria of effective governance are interrelated, at least as long as we assume that they all are important. We also conclude that two sets of distinct values are important in considering each of these criteria. One set emphasizes innovation, change, and action facilitation. The other emphasizes continuity, shared premises, and incremental behavior. Knowledge, as we treat it here, comes in two forms. Externally based knowledge frequently breaks through biases in existing premises, but there also is the knowledge of shared experiences and premises. Neither is more valid than the other. Each is helpful. But they serve different functions. The front end of policymaking (decision making as it is commonly referred to) seems to be most positively affected by values of the first sort and by the role of external indicators and suppliers of knowledge. This, however, depends to some extent on the time frame of the policy and the premises of its continuance. The shorter the time frame, the more valuable unbiased information that breaks through preexisting premises can be. The longer the time frame of the policy, the more valuable it is that information be within the shared premises of the existing players because the processes of mediation and implementation virtually require that. This, of course, means that the consequences of decision making have important effects on mediation and implementation. On the whole, unless there is a profound desire to clear-cut existing networks and remake the policy world, continuity and experience are necessary. Policy communities mitigate against radical change, but unless there are policy communities, government is apt to experience radical oscillations in policy and program.

There is no single formula to make government perform better. We need, though, to be aware that performance has many aspects, and that these aspects are interrelated. Changes in one almost always affect the others.

STRUCTURES, ORGANIZATION, PERFORMANCE, AND OUTCOMES: THE NEXT STEP

Why should we be interested in the structures and processes of government? Other than pure curiosity, we study them because we believe that they are important in some direct or indirect way in producing such valued ends as legitimacy, citizen consent, and quality of governmental output. If the structures, organization, and internal processes of government matter little for such ends, then they are mere ornaments.

However, the relationship between governmental structures and processes on the one hand and legitimacy or performance on the other is difficult to establish. To take one example, levels of economic development, regardless of state structures or organization, are major determinants of what the state does and how well it does it.[5] And governmental output and external political processes such as elections may determine legitimacy, with little regard to governmental structures or organization.

Confining our interest here to the administrative side of government, it is not likely that most citizens care much about how civil service systems are structured or even how government organizations are structured. Citizens probably care a great deal about the location of government offices and agents (access to service) and about due process when they must deal with government, but that is likely to be the major extent of their concerns. If this is so, then, other things being equal, almost any administrative system that does not overly offend citizens or neglect their interests is likely to be looked upon as legitimate, unless citizens are constantly told that the system is the source of profligacy, unresponsiveness, and other evils.

What is apparently key for citizens is outcomes. If the economy is robust, for example, citizens tend to support the presidential incumbent's party in the U.S. They do not ask whether civil servants have had a role in policymaking or whether organizational structure *a* is more or less efficient than organizational structure *b*. Politicians may well try to deflect citizen anger by blaming government structures and organization, but that is a matter we shall put aside for the moment.

So, we come to the question, how, if at all, do government structures and processes influence outcomes? Researches on government structures and organization implicitly assume that some linkage exists. For example, it is usually assumed that the quality of decision making is related to the quality of outputs. We presumably care whether government decision processes are structured so that accurate information is available or alternatives discussed because we assume that these factors are linked to better outcomes. We care about the role of senior civil servants in policy development because we assume that civil servants carry with them a reserve of knowledge and experience that contributes to effective outcomes (or, at least, helps to restrain impulses to do ineffective or harmful things). And we care about government structures because we think that some institutional arrangements are more efficient than others: they save money, produce better outcomes (or at least affect outcomes).

Much of this is plausible, but it is very hard to demonstrate. An important challenge for those of us who study governance is to demonstrate that our assumptions are grounded in reality.

ENDNOTES

1. For example, R. Kent Weaver and Bert A. Rockman (1993) note that electoral laws and systems of representation tend to be powerful institutional mediators of a variety of governmental capabilities.
2. Weaver and Rockman's volume, *Do Institutions Matter?* (1993), examines, through a set of comparative case studies, the performance of governments with different institutions. Institutions do affect performance capabilities, but rarely unequivocally, and they do so only in interaction with exogenous political circumstances.
3. In the U.S. the demise of the Gramm-Rudman budget law setting deadlines for deficit reduction testifies to the ability of the governors to skirt around

their own legally imposed constraints when doing otherwise is unpalatable, i.e., cutting spending and raising taxes in amounts large enough to have met the Gramm-Rudman requirements.

According to Eric Uslaner (1989), the imposition of constituency preferences, rather than the organization of Congress, was responsible for the incoherence of American energy policy in the decades of the 1970s and 1980s.

4. See Herman Finer's article (1941) written in response to Friedrich's essay (1940). Note that both the Madisonian tradition of conflicting principals and the Weberian tradition of unity of command are both principles or organizational control and accountability, if very different. Neither assumes that people are the answer. Each assumes the system is the solution.
5. Putnam et al. (1983; 1988) argue that structures and institutions are important within a constrained range of economic development levels.

REFERENCES

Aberbach, Joel D., Robert D. Putnam and Bert A. Rockman. 1981. *Bureaucrats and Politicians in Western Democracies.* Cambridge: Harvard University Press.

Aberbach, Joel D. and Bert A. Rockman. 1990. What Has Happened to the U.S. Senior Civil Service? *The Brookings Review* 8, 35–41.

Arrow, Kenneth J. 1952. *Social Choice and Individual Values.* New York: Wiley.

Braybrooke, David E. and Charles E. Lindblom. 1963. *A Strategy of Decision.* New York: Free Press of Glencoe.

Cohen, Michael D. 1981. The Power of Parallel Thinking. *Journal of Economic Behavior and Organization* 1, 285–306.

———. 1984. Conflict and Complexity: Goal Diversity and Organizational Search Effectiveness. *American Political Science Review* 78, 435–451.

Dahl, Robert A. 1956. *Preface to Democratic Theory.* Chicago: University of Chicago Press.

Finer, Herman. 1941. Administrative Responsibility in Democratic Government. *Public Administration Review* 1, 335–350.

Finer, S. E. 1980. Princes, Parliaments, and the Public Service. *Parliamentary Affairs* 33, 353–372.

Friedrich, Carl J. 1940. Public Policy and the Nature of Administrative Responsibility. *Public Policy* 1, 3–24.

George, Alexander L. 1972. The Case for Multiple Advocacy in Making Foreign Policy. *American Political Science Review* 66, 751–785.

——. 1980. *Presidential Decisionmaking in Foreign Policy: The Effective Use of Information and Advice.* Boulder Co: Westview.

Janis, Irving J. 1982. *Groupthink: Psychological Studies of Policy Decisions and Fiascoes.* Boston: Houghton Mifflin.

Kaufman, Herbert. 1985. *Time, Chance, and Organizations: Natural Selection in a Perilous Environment.* Chatham NJ: Chatham House.

King, Anthony and Giles Alston. 1991. Good Government and the Politics of High Exposure. In *The Bush Presidency: First Appraisals,* eds. Colin Campbell, S. J. and Bert A. Rockman. Chatham NJ: Chatham House.

Landau, Martin. 1969. Redundancy, Rationality, and the Problem of Duplication and Overlap. *Public Administration Review* 29, 346–358.

Okun, Arthur S. 1975. *Efficiency and Equality: The Big Trade-Off.* Washington DC: The Brookings Institution.

Olsen, Johan P. 1983. *Organized Democracy: Political Institutions in a Welfare State—The Case of Norway.* Bergen: Universitetsforlaget.

——. 1991. Modernization Programs in Perspective. *Governance* 4, 125–149.

Olson, Mancur. 1986. A Theory of the Incentives Facing Organizations: NeoCorporatism and the Hegemonic State. *International Political Science Review* 7, 165–189.

Polsby, Nelson. 1981. Some Landmarks in Modern Presidential-Congressional Relations. In *Both Ends of Pennsylvania Avenue,* ed. Anthony King. Washington DC: American Enterprise Institute.

Putnam, Robert, D., Robert Leonardi, Raffaella Nanetti and Franco Pavoncello. 1983. Explaining Institutional Success: The Case of Italian Regional, Government. *American Political Science Review* 77, 55–74.

Putnam, Robert D. with Robert Leonardi and Raffaella Y. Nanetti. 1988. Institutional Performance and Political Culture: Some Puzzles about the Power of the Past. *Governance* 1, 221–242.

Rawls, John. 1973. *A Theory of Justice.* Cambridge: Harvard University Press.

Rockman, Bert A. 1984. *The Leadership Question: The Presidency in the American System.* New York: Praeger.

Rose, Richard. 1984. *Do Parties Make a Difference?* Chatham NJ: Chatham House.

Simon, Herbert A. 1964. On the Concept of Organizational Goal. *Administrative Science Quarterly* 9, 1–22.

Uslaner, Eric. M. 1989. *Shale Barrel Politics: Energy and Legislative Leadership.* Stanford: Stanford University Press.

Vogel, David. 1986. *National Styles of Regulation: Environmental Policy in Great Britain and the United States.* Ithaca: Cornell University Press.

Weaver, R. Kent and Bert A. Rockman, eds. 1993. *Do Institutions Matter? Government Capabilities in the United States and Abroad.* Washington DC: The Brookings Institution.

Wilsford, David. 1989. Tactical Advantages Versus Administrative Heterogeneity: The Strengths and Limits of the French State. In *The Elusive State: International and Comparative Perspectives,* ed. James A. Caporaso. Newbury Park CA: Sage Publications.

··

HERBERT SIMON

42 Organizations and Markets

. . . Why, in a modern society, do we have markets, and why do we have organizations, and what determines the boundary between these two mechanisms for social organization? These questions go to the heart of the roles of our diverse political and administrative institutions, pubic and private, in contemporary society.

··

MARKETS AS COORDINATING MECHANISMS

If we were to take an extreme libertarian view, both markets and organizations would be unnecessary. For the libertarian, human beings are Leibnitzian

SOURCE: Herbert Simon, "Public Administration in Today's World of Organizations and Markets," *PS, Political Science and Politics,* vol. 33, no. 4 (December 2000), pp. 749–756. © American Political Science Association. Reprinted with the permission of Cambridge University Press. Article abridged by the Editor.

monads: hard, elastic little particles that bounce off each other without any other interaction, certainly without either responding to or influencing each others' values. Libertarians can hold to their faith only on the absurd assumption that my exercise of freedom never affects your ability to exercise yours. Quite the opposite: The freedoms and the fates of all six billion of us who occupy this globe are inextricably interwoven.

Markets and organizations allow human beings to do together, through interchange of information and the ensuing coordination of activity, things they could not do independently. Coordination simply means organizing activity in such a way as to handle the problems that arise because the behavior of each participant depends in some ways on the behaviors of the others. I hardly need explain why such dependence is often valuable; if you absent-mindedly drive in the right instead of the left lane while visiting Britain, you will find out all too soon.

Organizations, some quite large, especially armies, have been with us since the earliest historic times and earlier. Perhaps for that reason, we take them for granted, and they excite in us less wonder than do markets, which developed somewhat later, first locally, then over increasingly long distances. The most peculiar characteristic of markets, Adam Smith's "invisible hand," is their ability to secure coordination without obvious central planning, and without a common interest among their members, for each buyer and seller is supposed to be pursuing independently his or her own private interest.

But this invisibility of mutual dependence is deceptive. The usefulness of markets depends on a shared knowledge of the prices and the characteristics of goods that are being traded, and absence of serious third-person effects (so-called "externalities") that are not reflected in prices, and sufficient stability of products and manufacturing practices so that both sellers and buyers can plan their activities rationally and make rational decisions to sell and buy at the prices at which the markets equilibrate. They also depend critically on the safety of transit routes. The effects upon buyers and sellers of agricultural products of prolonged drought, or the effects of closing a strategic strait in a major trade route between India and Europe provide vivid examples of the fragility of markets in the face of various forms of uncertainty, and the social and human distress that can be caused by their malfunctioning. . . .

In summary, markets are, indeed, remarkable coordinating mechanisms in the parsimony of their requirements for information. But they are far less parsimonious than they appear at first blush, for they require a high degree of economic stability and a low level of externalities in order to operate. Moreover, in important classes of market transactions, much product information must flow in the negotiation of the exchange and the subsequent manufacturing process. Adam Smith's invisible hand is often highly visible. Consequently, when the qualifying conditions for stability of markets are not met, as, for example, in wartime, we see a rapid movement toward centralized planning as the preferred coordinating mechanism for many activities.

FROM A MARKET ECONOMY TO AN ORGANIZATIONAL ECONOMY

We are so accustomed to hearing our society described as a market economy that we are often surprised to observe that, since the time of Adam Smith, markets have steadily declined, and business (and governmental) organizations have steadily grown as the principal coordinators of economic activity. In Adam Smith's time, almost the only economic organizations beyond scale of individual families were agricultural estates directly managed by their owners or through stewards, and relatively small shops owned by guild masters. The putting-out system was a market system, not an organizational system, though one with a special coordinating role for the capitalist who contracted for the successive stages of manufacture of the products—from flax to yarn to cloth to a peasant's blouse. The contractor did not operate as an employer managing a factory.

Adam Smith took a dim view of large organizations where management became separated from the direct oversight of the owner. Looking around for examples of such organizations, he found mainly universities like Oxford and Cambridge, which he described as inept, inefficient, and corrupt. (One could claim that Smith anticipated our golden parachutes for salaried executives. Perhaps he was forewarned by the not-infrequent peculations by stewards of the estates of the gentry and aristocracy.)

But in spite of Smith's skepticism, organizations have grown until the vast bulk of our economy's activity takes place within the walls of individual large business corporations, not in markets. This growth had already begun to root itself, in the coal mining, iron, ceramics, and textile industries, at the time that Smith was writing his great work, and entered into land and sea transportation a generation or two later. (He foreshadowed it just a bit in his tale of the efficiency of specialization in the manufacture of pins.) It was triggered in large measure by technological advance, especially the invention of the steam engine and its applications as a centralized power source for a factory or mine and, later, for a ship or train.[1]

Today, in consequence of these developments, we do not live in a market economy, but in an organization economy, or at most, in an organization/market economy, with a predominance of organizational over market activity. It is ironic that one of the first industries to move toward this new kind of organizational society was transportation, where the railroads enabled an enormous rise of market exchanges over long distances, with correspondingly large factories to produce the goods that were exchanged. Electronics is now completing the comparable transformation of communication.

Now, before going on to my next topic, I must issue one caveat. Current developments in electronics, notably the development of the World Wide Web and e-markets, and the enhanced abilities of organizations to manage geographically dispersed activities, provide new opportunities of unknown magnitude for coordination at a distance. Today, we have very little experience with these new developments, both their current forms and their potential. Hence, there is as yet little basis for judging whether markets or organizations will be best able to make use of the new opportunities and whether, as a consequence, we will see a continuation or acceleration of the current trend towards concentration of productive activity within organizations, or will see that trend slowed or even reversed in favor of markets.

HOW ORGANIZATIONS COORDINATE

To understand this growth in organizations, business and governmental, we must understand organizations' ability to coordinate complex activities efficiently, and at far higher levels than markets can attain. As organization theory has long taught us, coordination is not a good but a necessity. Coordination is costly and imperfect, and we wish to introduce no more of it than the structure and intricacy of our goals calls for.

Stated a little more positively, organization design focuses on balancing the gains from coordination against its costs. The first step in designing an effective organization is to determine what kinds of interdependencies in its activities will benefit from coordination, and then to minimize the amount of coordination required by partitioning activities in such a way that a much lower rate of interaction, on a more leisurely time scale, is required between subunits at any level than is required within each subunit. This is the familiar division of work. The same issues of balance between the benefits and costs of coordination that guide organizational design also play a major role in defining the boundaries between organizations and markets, which are defined by the decisions of when to make things or perform services within the organization and when to buy them from outside vendors.

In any case, the basic reality of the division of work is that high rates of rapid communication are required among people who perform activities that are highly interdependent, much less frequent communication is required among those carrying out activities that are independent, and this distinction should be clearly reflected in organization structure. Systems whose structure reflects these properties are referred to as "nearly decomposable." And a formal mathematical theory exists today that describes them and makes important predictions, as we shall see, about their behavior.

It is the organizational identification of members, more than any other of their characteristics, that gives organizations their remarkable power to secure coordinated behavior of large numbers of people to accomplish organizational goals, thereby playing a major role during the past two centuries in the rise of modern organizations and in their successful competition with traditional market mechanisms.[2] Identification has received too little attention in our research on organizations.

Organizational identification does not depend on profit motives; it can work within governmental and university organizations as powerfully as within profit-making businesses. Such studies as have been made (not as numerous as one would like) show that, on average, profit-making and governmental organizations that produce the same products, both operating in markets, attain about the same levels of efficiency—the profit motive appears to give no visible competitive edge to private business. So the increasing tendency in recent decades for government agencies to contract out many of their activities evidently is not driven by considerations of efficiency—or, if it is, there is little solid empirical evidence for this preference.

What are the implications of this picture for the role of organizations, and especially governmental organizations, in our society?

ORGANIZATIONAL INNOVATION AND ADAPTATION TO CHANGE

. . . [W]e might read the history of the past 200 years of industrializing societies as showing that, with the growing advantage that large organizations secured from advanced technology, and our increased skills in designing large organizations that achieve high levels of coordination which maintain a reasonable approximation to near decomposability of their components, we have enlarged greatly the area within which organizations are more effective than markets. This conclusion applies to governmental as well as to business organizations, for both have followed similar paths in the development of their designs.

SOCIAL IMPLICATIONS

Let me turn now from these rather abstract and high-level pictures of social systems and the course of their development and ask why it matters. I will focus on two issues: first, the distribution of power in modern society, and, second, the distribution of the social product. I'm afraid that the picture my crystal ball displays is still abstract, but it does refer to matters that are of very practical concern to all of us, individually and collectively.

THE DISTRIBUTION OF POWER

Lord Acton said it very well, and I don't think I can say it better: "Power tends to corrupt, and absolute power corrupts absolutely."

A central problem in democratic institutions at all times and in all places has been and is to create a broad distribution of power, and to keep that distribution in stable equilibrium. A basic tenet of democratic theory, well supported by historical and other evidence, is that self interest is such a strong motive that no fraction of members of a society can be safely entrusted with the freedom and welfare of others who do not participate in the decision-making processes.

During the twentieth century, two massive experiments were carried out, as well as numerous smaller ones, to determine whether major changes in political and economic institutions could produce the "new person" and the new institutions required to realize basic human goals within a highly centralized system of power. It is now widely agreed that the new institutions didn't work well and, especially, that the "new person" didn't appear. The personal motives that emerged in Soviet Russia and in Maoist China appeared to be no less selfish or more virtuous than the motives of people in other parts of the world— in fact, they were discouragingly familiar.

Among neoclassical economists, the outcome of these experiments was widely interpreted as a clear vindication of markets being the bulwark of freedom and productivity. The years since the dissolution of the Soviet Union and the complex developments in an industrializing China have shown that matters are not so simple. As to Russia, it has become painfully clear that the introduction of markets without the coincident introduction of socially enforced rules of the game for their operation and the simultaneous creation of viable and effectively managed organizations cannot create a productive economic system. Nor has a stable equilibrium of diffused power been established in Russia. In China, there remain substantial deficiencies in the social enforcement of market rules and, at the same time, continuing governmental interference with normal market operations, as well as equally evident deficiencies in organizational skills and steadfast resistance to the decentralization of power.

Nothing that we have seen in these two histories challenges the thesis that diffusion of power requires, in addition to markets, a multiplicity of effective organizations to perform a society's productive and service tasks. In fact, it can well be argued that the most important role markets play in a modern society is to diffuse power by holding organizations, through competition, to the tasks of providing efficiently the things demanded in the markets, thus preventing them from using their resources as power bases for extending their social influence and control by direct influence upon government. A multiplicity of organizations competing vigorously in markets is a strong protection against diversion of resources (by either for-profit or not-for-profit organizations) to political objectives.

By the same token, diffusion of power calls for governmental organizations that maintain a reasonable balance between the effectiveness that large business organizations can sometimes provide and an avoidance of concentration of power in a few places. The many experiments with privatization of services that had previously, for good or indifferent reasons, been supplied by public agencies, are beginning now to show us that switching to the market/business-organization system is not a sovereign remedy for all administrative ills.

To illustrate what I have in mind, I need merely mention the complex mixture of gains and losses that deregulation of the air transportation industry has brought to its customers (in spite of rosy reports of fare savings). The same can be said of deregulation and privatization of energy

distribution, education, and communications, all of which are faced today with perplexing economic and organizational problems. I could add other examples, notably the prison industry, which has not become a magical cure for criminal tendencies as a result of experiments in privatization.

Nor can we say that we have solved all of the organizational problems posed by public goods and by such externalities as those associated with preservation of the environment. Experience has indicated that a wide range of essential services can be provided better by government than by any private business arrangement thus far invented, or, as in the case of basic research, will be undersupplied because of public goods aspects, if left to competitive markets.

We do not need to reinvent government. Governmental organizations are needed, as they have always been needed, to enforce the rules of the game (including the rules of market contracting), to facilitate coordination of private organizations, and to perform services that are unlikely to be performed effectively by the private sector. The legal institutions must be vigorous and independent enough to curb corruptions of the rules of the game by bribery and other illegal activities. And the rules of the game themselves (e.g., rules for political campaign contributions) must themselves not enable influence buying.[3] In performing these functions, government agencies themselves, of course, become centers of power that help balance the power exerted by the private sector in its own interests.

DISTRIBUTION OF THE SOCIAL PRODUCT: LEVELS OF EMPLOYMENT AND PRODUCTION

There is little consensus in economics today about how to maintain high levels of employment and production, even though, at the moment, we are enjoying these conditions; many economists, when asked why, look toward Heaven and sigh. Among those of my friends and acquaintances who are macroeconomists or specialists on money, I find only one point of general agreement (and even here there is dissent from diehard believers in the gold standard). Most agree that money is neither a solid substance, nor a liquid, nor a gas; it is simply a state of mind. More precisely, money's value is a collection of states of mind of all the people who use it. These states of mind, as history shows, can change in a short time from utmost confidence in a currency to utmost skepticism, and vice versa. On the role of government spending and monetary policy in determining the level of activity, "expert" opinions range from the laissez-faire of rational expectations to Keynesianism and beyond.

Having identified this important topic and the disarray of expert views about it, there is only one thing about it that I can say with confidence: Maintaining economic equilibrium cannot be left to the invisible hand of the market, it requires governmental attention. What economists call Say's Law guarantees that the economy can be in equilibrium at any level of activity from 100% employment of workers and capital to zero percent. At both of these levels, and all between, the income from selling goods will just balance the costs of producing them plus the profits of owners. So production produces total incomes that are just sufficient to purchase the marketed product. When markets are not at full employment equilibrium, as they often aren't, neoclassical theory does not explain why, nor what to do about it.

DISTRIBUTION OF THE SOCIAL PRODUCT: FAIRNESS

Just as competitive markets cannot, by themselves, guarantee an adequate distribution of power in a society or full employment, so they do not guarantee that markets will distribute income and wealth in a way that will satisfy our notions of fairness. "Fairness" is, of course, not a question of fact, but of values. What is fair cannot be settled by our science. Hence, I will limit myself to showing the consequences of a particular definition of fairness that has wide currency in our society today: that it is fair that people receive and be allowed to retain what they earn. I am not advocating your adoption of this definition, I'm simply using it to illustrate complexities of the design of social systems that take the question of fairness into account.

Let me pose a simple question. Consider the income that you or your family now earn as members of American society (which most of you are) and compare it with the income that you would expect to earn if you were equally hardworking members of Chinese or Indian society, or the society of any other Third World nation. I expect that for most of you, the difference between the two incomes is one or more orders of magnitude, at least 10 to 1 and perhaps even more than 100 to 1.

Now, I would like you to consider the causes for the gap between the 10 and the 1 or the 100 and the 1. How much of it do you wish to attribute to your superior energy, motivation, and application of effort as compared with your Third World counterparts? And how much do you wish to attribute to your good luck or good judgment in being born in, or joining, the highly productive and democratic American society?

If we are very generous with ourselves, I suppose we might claim that we "earned" as much as one fifth of it. The rest is the patrimony associated with being a member of an enormously productive social system, which has accumulated a vast store of physical capital, and an even larger store of intellectual capital—including knowledge, skills, and organizational know-how held by all of us—so that interaction with our equally talented fellow citizens rubs off on us both much of this knowledge and this generous allotment of unearned income.

Again, I have no specific proposal for allocating the "unearned" income of an affluent society. That, of course, is one of the important things we will be voting on in November. Clearly, the allocation of income in a society is a matter of values to be decided by political processes.

What I wish to emphasize is simply that public attitudes about the fair allocation of income are necessarily and justifiably a major factor in determining the scope and nature of public organizations in the society. There is no way in which the proper allocation of the social product can be left solely to the market in a private-organization/market/public-organization society, or solely to considerations of productive efficiency. Society is demonstrably not a collection of Leibnitzian monads. Much more flows between the members of a society, in the form of exchange of information and cooperation, than the simple interchange of momentum by impact. Market equilibria that are Pareto efficient will often be inferior to other equilibria, Pareto efficient or not, when criteria of fairness are applied.

....

CONCLUSION

It is not too fanciful to think of writing a history of human civilization in terms of progress in the means of human cooperation, that is, of organization. In that history, hierarchical and nearly decomposable systems would play a central role. Almost from the beginning, the division of work into component tasks and the assembly of the components into a hierarchy were discovered to be powerful means for achieving efficient coordination of effort. In a later period, markets entered as a means of coordinating certain kinds of transactions that required very limited communication, and therefore can take place over long distances. Then, long before the Christian era, nation-states and empires emerged that show there is almost no upper limit to the sizes to which organizations can aspire.

The system, after more than a millennium and a half, entered a new stage when the social store of knowledge and innovation in technologies begin to accelerate, with markets again at first playing a central role in enabling these developments. Gradually, increases in the demands for, and in the advantages of, more coordination in economic activity, together with the accumulation of skills of organizing, brought into existence ever-larger corporations that begin to emulate in size the administrative organizations of the nation-states—and we were launched into our modern world.

Both private and public organizations have played essential roles in these modern developments, complementing each others' functions, learning from each other, and, at the same time, competing for power to steer and manage the systems that have emerged. That process has not reached its end, and political science and economics must continue their mutual education, with each discipline learning from the other.

The education must be symmetric. Its goal is not to convert political science into a theory of the "public choices" of a mythical, utility-maximizing "economic person." Its goal is to understand how human behavior molds and is molded by the complex structures it employs to secure the coordination needed to accomplish most of its goals, and how this can be accomplished while preserving the wide dispersion of power that is consistent with democratic institutions.

ENDNOTES

1. For an excellent classical account of the sequence of events, see Hammond and Hammond (1926).
2. It also, regrettably, causes human beings identified with particular groups to commit terrible atrocities against human beings in other groups that are viewed as competitive or threatening, but that is another story.
3. I have no particularly novel ideas to propose for accomplishing these goals, still very imperfectly realized in our society. Whenever simple solutions are proposed for problems of social organization, we must be careful to test them against these goals.

REFERENCES

Alt, James E., Margaret Levi, and Elinor Ostrom, eds. 1999. *Competition and Cooperation: Conversations with Nobelists about Economics and Political Science.* New York: Russell Sage Foundation.

Gaus, John M., and Loen O. Wolcott. 1940. *Public Administration and the United States Department of Agriculture.* Chicago: Public Administration Service.

Hammond, J. L., and Barbara Hammond. 1926. *The Rise of Modern Industry.* New York: Harcourt Brace.

Simon, Herbert A., D. W. Smithburg, and A. V. Thompson. 1950. *Public Administration.* New York: Knopf. [Reprinted in 1991 by Transaction Publishers: New Brunswick, NJ].

Smith, Adam. [1937] 1978. *The Wealth of Nations.* 5th ed. New York: Modern Library.

GRAHAM WILSON

43   In a State?

Revolutions are successful when their leaders have passed from the scene but the changes they have made are accepted by all, including their opponents. By this standard, although leaders such as Thatcher and Reagan of the campaign against the "big state" which occurred in the 1980s have passed from the scene, their revolution has indeed triumphed. The successors to the leaders of the right-wing revolution, such as Blair and Clinton, have acknowledged that, in the words of the latter, "The era of big government is over." The Center-Left regained power in Britain and the United States only after it had made clear its willingness to accept the accomplishments of the Right, including sharply reduced direct taxation (especially on upper-income groups), privatization of government-owned industry and housing, and an end to the upward trend in public expenditure as a percentage of gross national product. No model of political economy challenged the intellectual hegemony the Right had achieved. The collapse of the Soviet Union discredited all forms of socialism, not just Leninism, and the continuing economic difficulties of Japan throughout the 1990s discredited the "state-led" models of political economy that had so impressed commentators previously. Such alternatives as were proposed to the Right's agenda of shrinking the state and liberating markets were really not so very different. The "Polder Model" of the Netherlands, which attracted some favorable attention in the late 1990s, was really based on a claim that labor markets could be liberalized and welfare payments reduced through consensual neocorporatist discussion rather than the politics of confrontation that Thatcherism had entailed. Nations such as France and Germany that failed to adopt the Right's agenda were generally regarded not as champions of an alternative model but as victims of *immobilisme,*

SOURCE: Graham Wilson, "In a State?," *Governance,* vol. 13, no. 2 (April 2000), pp. 235–242. © Blackwell Publishing Ltd. Reprinted by permission of Blackwell Publishing Ltd.

nations that could not make the hard necessary decisions and thereby were condemned to pay a high price in terms of uncompetitiveness and high unemployment.

The rhetoric of revolutionaries should never be confused, however, with analysis of the consequences of their revolution. The consequences of revolutions are often less dramatic than revolutionaries and their enemies claim. We should be wary of claims by the "revolutionaries" of the Right that shrinking the state resulted in a significant reduction by historical standards of the reach of the state in economic and social life even in those countries in which their power was greatest. Of course, their task was daunting. To the extent that politicians such as Thatcher were, as she claimed in her famous Brugges speech in 1985, intent on rolling back the frontiers of the state, they were struggling against modern states that had become unprecedentedly ambitious in terms of the variety of their goals and activities. The model of the Keynesian welfare state that shaped policy thinking in all advanced democracies—including the United States—by the early 1970s attempted to achieve goals that previous generations would have thought beyond the reach of the state. A far from exhaustive list of these goals includes the eradication of poverty, health care for all, the transformation of racial and gender relations, the achievement of high levels of educational achievement (as opposed to basic competence) by large sectors of the population, increased rates of economic growth, and unprecedentedly high levels of consumer and environmental protection.

I do not wish to suggest than any or all of the goals were undesirable or excessive. It is worth noting, however, how high were expectations of the state by historical standards in the 1970s on the eve of the accession of Thatcher and Reagan even in countries regarded as having "small states." Consider the changes that have occurred in the lifetime of an elderly citizen of the United States, a land still regarded as having "small government" by international standards. When our elderly citizen was born, before World War I, governments of all kinds spent less than 10 percent of national income; today, governments of all kinds spend about one third of national income and control day-to-day life to a greater degree than this figure suggests through an elaborate network of tax allowances and regulations. Indeed, the costs and impact of the unusually comprehensive and intrusive regulatory regime of the United States may do much to discredit claims that the state is significantly smaller in the United States than in OECD nations is general. The American state (in its social science sense) was seen as having major responsibilities in almost every aspect of daily life ranging from the workings of the economy to the sexual behavior of adults as well as children. Even outside the leading welfare states of northern Europe, in short, almost everyone associated the state with a range of responsibilities that would have been regarded earlier in this century as far beyond the reach of the state.

It is hard to recall how modest were the goals and capacities of states early in this century. We should recall that prior to Word War I, most states did not control their own economics because they were on the gold standard, had no controls over the movement of capital, and, most striking by modern standards, had no control over immigration or emigration, in most cases not even requiring travelers to carry passports. Phileas Fogg could set out from the Reform Club in London to travel around the world in eighty days equipped with gold coins and without a passport; a British tourist in the 1960s not only needed a passport but was subjected to limits (fortunately since abolished) on how much he or she could spend overseas. In contrast, huge capital investment flowed from nineteenth-century London to finance developments not only in the British Empire but in the United States, Argentina, and Chile as well; the notion that governments should attempt to control these flows would have seemed odd. As critics of the concept of globalization like to point out, foreign trade as a percentage of GNP has only recently *regained* the levels it was at in many nations, including the United States, prior to 1914. It is perhaps suggestive that, for the economic historian, it is the period of national economies, from about 1930 to about 1973, that appears exceptional.

It the state was shrunk in the 1980s, therefore, it was shrunk having been stretched unprecedentedly far in the previous era. Part of the feeling that there has been a crisis of state authority results not from the actual shrinkage of the state but from the end of the era in which national boundaries and those who exercised within them had become more important economically, culturally, socially, and emotionally than ever before. Our familiar images of the extensive state reflect not an enduring historical pattern but a very specific era in which economies were unusually domestically oriented and in which states were able to expand their policy ambitions. If states have reduced the range of their policy ambitions and are more constrained by international factors, it is, to an important degree, a case of "back to the past." Two questions present themselves. First, Why did the period of expanding the reach of the state come to an end? Second, Did the Right really shrink the state?

THE RHETORICAL REACTION AGAINST THE STATE

There were a number of factors that produced the rhetorical reaction against the state. First, the end of the long period of economic growth that began in the late 1940s, known in France as the *trente glorieuses*, ended the ability of states to fund their expansion through economic growth. In the early years of the Johnson administration, some administration economists worried about the ability of government to keep spending the extra revenue that economic growth would generate. There were no such worries in the 1970s. Second, inflation which characterized the period produced "bracket creep" through which many modest wage earners found themselves paying higher and higher tax rates, producing in turn taxpayer revolts from Denmark to California. In their early days, welfare states were often presented as systems financed by the wealthy and supporting the needy. By the 1970s many working-class taxpayers felt they were paying too much to support too many possibly undeserving recipients of welfare benefits—particularly if the beneficiaries were "different"—Turks in Germany, West Indians in Britain, Arabs in France, African Americans in the United States. Third, experience seemed to suggest that many of the new endeavors of the state were failures. Keynesian economic policies in practice arguably accentuated economic fluctuations rather than reduced them, even when as in Britain the institutional setting for Keynesianism seemed most propitious. The new art or science of policy analysis seemed to document failure after failure, often accompanied by significant unintended and perverse consequences in policy area after policy area. For thirty years after the Great Depression there had been an intellectual climate in which confidence in the capacity of the state to ameliorate economic and social problems flourished. From the early 1970s onward that faith diminished. This intellectual sea change was illustrated most clearly in economics where confidence in government intervention to stabilize the economy and promote growth was replaced by the monetarists' creed that it was better to have a fixed, stable increase in the money supply with little opportunity for government to interfere. Fourth, politicians and senior bureaucrats came to fear that they could not in practice carry the amount of responsibility that the range of the state's current responsibilities and popular expectations, often encouraged by politicians at election time, imposed on them. The very influential "overload" literature of the 1970s argued that states were caught in a trap; the expectations of their citizens of what the state should deliver were constantly increasing; the capacity of the state to deliver was diminishing (Crozier, Huntington, and Watanuki 1975; King 1996).

Although not originally stressed by overload theorists, globalization came to be seen as a major part of the reduction in the capacity of the nation-state. The arguments about the consequences of globalization are familiar. The ease of movement of goods and particularly capital around the world eroded the capacity of states to impose taxes or regulations on corporations, thereby tilting the postwar balance of power between capital, labor, and the state heavily in favor of capital. States foolish enough to follow policies unwelcome to capital would experience a severe loss of investment, triggering financial crises in the short term and economic decline in the long. These arguments are so common that they need little elaboration and, indeed, have now been subjected to considerable criticism. As noted above, the importance of trade in GNPs of all advanced democracies, even the United States, has increased tremendously but has returned only to levels common early in this century. Capital does move around the world much more easily than in the past, but financial crises in Mexico and Asia may have made the dangers of moving capital more apparent; in any case, differences in interest rates around the world and the fact that most investment is still financed from domestic sources suggest that capital is still not as mobile as we supposed. Evidence of a "race to the bottom" in which states reduce levels of social protection and regulation in order to attract investment is slight. Indeed, Vogel has argued that, on the contrary, standards tend to rise internationally to the highest level of protection, rather than sink to the worst (Vogel 1995). Yet while revisionism has its place and value, it is hard to resist the conclusion that something has indeed changed in the balance between state and market, compared with the recent past when capital was much more attached, partly through government controls, to its native country. Levels of international trade may have been as high early in this century as today, but it is probable that it was a different type of international trade, based more on comparative advantage than today's competitive trade in which different economies vie to be the dominant source of, for example, automobiles. In all events, the popularity of the idea of globalization may in itself have accomplished a shift in the balance of power between state and capital. So long as many people think that globalization reduces the power of the state, politicians and bureaucrats are less likely to assert its power. Thus, whether the idea is true or false, talk of globalization does indeed reduce the power of the state.

One further development called into question the status of a number of states, including some of the world's oldest. The rise of nationalist separatist movements in Canada (Quebec), Britain (Northern

Ireland, Scotland, and Wales), Belgium (both Flanders and Wallonia), Spain (the Basque lands and Catalonia), Italy (the Northern League), and France (Corsica and, to some extent, Brittany) threatened nation-states from below just as their authority was challenged from above by globalization. Indeed, this movement fed off economic integration. An independent Quebec within NAFTA or an independent Scotland within the European Union (EU) would pay a much smaller price for independence than would have been the case in the recent past. Arguments that "you can't afford to leave" were less convincing given the fact that NAFTA, the EU, and, on a global scale, the World Trade Organization would provide newly independent states with continuing free access to their old markets. The recently almost unimaginable possibility of an old state such as Britain disintegrating made the idea of the nation-state itself seem what it is, namely, historically contingent. Nation-states were the exception rather than the rule during the lifetimes of composers such as Mozart who still constitute the bedrock of our musical tradition; at the end of the twentieth century, nation-states seemed challenged from both above and below.

BUT HAS THE STATE SHRUNK?

It is one thing to say that faith in the state and its power diminished. It is another thing to show that the state actually shrank.

We should notice at the outset that in some respects the "project" (to use the fashionable term) of the Right often involved *strengthening,* not weakening, the state. In Britain, for example, privatizing government-owned industries and ending policies such as price and income controls which could be implemented only with the help of major economic interest groups increased the autonomy of the government of the state. Monetarism is, as Johnson has noted, an approach to economic policy that depends far less than did the policies it displaced on the collaboration of powerful societal interests; monetary policy is simply made and imposed by an

instrument of the state, namely, the central bank (Johnson 1998). The description of Thatcherism as the quest for a stronger because smaller state reminds us that there is no correspondence between the size of the state measured by its budget or the size of its bureaucracy and its strength; Italy's government spends a high proportion of GNP and has a large bureaucracy because the Italian state is weak, not because it is strong. Thatcher's policies often required extensive use of state power, such as the deployment of large numbers of police during the miners' strikes, to defeat groups opposed to them. More generally, the conservative policy mood which has been so widespread has also strengthened one of the core competencies of the state, namely, repression. The vast upsurge in the prison population of the United States, for example, is not a sign of a reduced role for the state. To take another traditional role of the state, defense, the right-wing revolutions in both the United States and Britain produced significantly increased expenditures on the military and the police. In the United States increased military expenditures made a significant contribution to budget deficits, which were a familiar part of American government.

The most important factor preventing the shrinking of the state, however, has been the enduring popularity of the most comprehensive and therefore most expensive parts of the welfare state, those programs that have a large middle- and professional-class clientele. It was on the rock of these programs that the ring-wing revolutions broke. Again, Britain and the United States, countries in which the Right revolution ran strongest, serve to make the point. In Britain, Thatcher, far from privatizing the National Health Service, was forced by its popularity to insist that it was "safe in our hands" and to boast in election campaigns of how she had raised spending on it significantly in real terms. In the United States, only the probably false claim that the Social Security (old age pension) system faces bankruptcy has allowed debate on the future of this immensely popular program. The poor might lose benefits which account for a tiny proportion of the national budget; the middle and professional classes successfully cling to theirs. As these are the really expensive programs, extended periods of right-wing rule have not shrunk significantly the size of the American or British states in terms of the proportion of GNP they control. There is in fact no simple answer as to whether or not the share of GNP in OECD countries has shrunk or not. Some of the states at the high end of the distribution (such as the Netherlands) have indeed cut back; more modest spenders such as Britain have seen little overall reduction in the share of GNP claimed by government, and Japan has seen a significant increase.

Even privatization has not resulted in an unqualified shrinking of the state. In Britain, for example, a leading proponent of privatization which continues even under a Labour government, the privatization of previously state-owned industries was followed by the creation of an extensive network of regulatory agencies with inelegant titles (OFFGAS, OFFELECTRIC, et cetera) to protect consumers. Such agencies are familiar to Americans but were new to British government, made necessary by the practice of placing what are still mostly "natural monopolies" in the hands of private investors. The creations of these regulatory agencies added an important component to state capacity.

As the travails of formerly communist countries building capitalist systems remind us, one of the most important roles of the state has been to structure social action. Markets, for example, are not naturally occurring phenomena but are created by legislation and regulations. Changes in legislation and regulations change the balance of advantage in these markets between different types of enterprise and between workers, employers, and consumers. This structuring activity of the state may have been particularly important for right-wing reformers. In the both Britain and the United States, for example, significant changes in labor law contributed powerfully to the decline of the labor unions.

This structuring role of the state is in a sense the underpinning of globalization. No doubt there are aspects of globalization that are beyond the control of states; the internet and the popularity of McDonald's with Europeans spring to mind. In economic life, however, globalization did not just happen but was the result of concerted activity by states, generally led by the United States. Governments created the General Agreement on Tariffs and Trade which through successive rounds of negotiations lowered industrial tariffs to negligible levels; it was governments that created the World Trade Organization now preoccupied largely with eliminating non-tariff barriers to trade. Similarly, the creation of a more global capital market—and the process is far from complete—depended on state action eliminating capital controls, foreign exchange restrictions, and other such barriers to the free movement of capital. Although globalization has been seen as destroying the capacity of the state, it is states through their ability to structure economic action that have created the globalized world economy.

....

STILL IN A STATE?

Historians will probably conclude that the movement to shrink the state in the late twentieth century was stronger in rhetoric than in reality. Citizens continued to look to the state for a variety of services and responsibilities that would have astounded their great-grandparents. Politicians and bureaucrats continued to use the powers of the state to tax, coerce, imprison, regulate, and subsidize with vigor. In the OECD as a whole, the proportion of GNPs claimed by governments remained much the same in 1999 as in 1979. Had nothing changed?

I suggest that there had indeed been a significant shift in the state of the state. Rhetoric matters in politics, particularly, as in this case, when it is reinforced with institutional changes. The frequently reiterated claims that the era of big government was over, that government could not solve every problem, and that globalization had reduced the capacity of national government to act did indeed produce a significant change from the decades following the Great Depression in which faith in the capacity of the state to solve problems was so high. More to the advantage than disadvantage of politicians, this reduction in expectations, resting on the belief that numerous social and economic problems were outside the control of government, was reinforced by a number of institutional reforms that tended in the same direction. The contracting out of government services, privatizations, the creation of semi-autonomous executive agencies to administer existing programs, and the handing over of economic policy to central banks all diminished the range of important issues that were subject to political decision making. Privatization ended British politicians' responsibility to attempt to make the trains run on time. Monetarism transferred responsibility for avoiding inflation and unemployment from the president and Congress to Alan Greenspan and the similarly unelected European Central Bank. Moves in government toward the creation of semi-autonomous agencies (as in New Zealand and Great Britain) ended the theoretical responsibility of elected politicians for the day-to-day working of the government machine. Even globalization could be presented as the ultimate excuse for why governments could not deliver the services demanded of them. The increased preference for markets rather than state reduced the standing of government but also provided it with a marvelous excuse for unwelcome situations, summarized in Thatcher's TINA (There Is No Alternative). In brief, a number of changes in the states reduced the acute exposure of politicians

to democratic accountability for the vast range of problems they had come to endure by the 1970s, and which were described in the overload literature. We have witnessed not the decline of the state but its successful adaptation after the crisis of governance that erupted in the 1970s.

REFERENCES

Crozier, M., S. Huntington, and J. Watanuki. 1975. *The Crisis of Democracy: A Report on the Governability of Democracies to the Trilateral Commission.* New York: New York University Press.

Johnson, P. A. 1998. *The Government of Money: Monetarism in Germany and the United States.* Ithaca, NY: Cornell University Press.

King, A., ed. 1996. *Why is Britain Becoming Harder to Govern?* London: BBC Books.

Vogel, D. 1995. *Trading Up: Consumer and Environmental Protection in Global Economy.* Cambridge: Harvard University Press.

Wilson, G. K. 1998. *Only in America?* Chatham, NJ: Chatham House.

....

ROBERT A. DAHL

44   *Equality versus Inequality*

Human beings are fundamentally equal from a moral point of view. They are not, and never have been, fully equal from a descriptive, factual, or empirical point of view. For some of us equality in its moral meaning is a goal, an aim, an ideal, a hope, an aspiration, an obligation. The goal is never fully attained nor is it likely to be. Egalitarian goals and aspirations confront stubborn human limitations.

SOURCE: Robert A. Dahl, "Equality versus Inequality," *PS, Political Science and Politics,* vol. 29, no. 4 (December 1996), pp. 639, 645–648. © American Political. Science Association Reprinted with the permission of Cambridge University Press. Article abridged by the Editor.

Yet in a few times and places in recorded history, conditions have enabled certain groups of human beings to move closer to some egalitarian goals. History also records that these rare, though limited, triumphs were succeeded by epochs of dreadful and pervasive inequalities. The conditions that made the Athenian democracy and the Roman Republic possible were superseded by conditions that instead fostered hierarchy and despotism.

In the opening pages of *Democracy in America* (1961), Tocqueville described the gradual and inexorable advance of equality of conditions "throughout the whole of Christendom" as "a providential fact . . . [that] . . . possesses all the characteristics of a Divine decree: it is universal, it is durable, it constantly eludes all human interference, and all events as well as all men contribute to its progress." Were he to look back today over the intervening period he would conclude that his youthful vision was not far off the mark. Whether or not the trajectory Tocqueville envisioned will continue through the next century, I cannot say. My aim instead is to describe in very general terms some of the dynamics of equality and inequality, and to assess briefly the play of forces pushing in the two opposing directions in our own time, particularly the forces of democracy and capitalism. . . .

DEMOCRACY, POLYARCHY, AND MARKET CAPITALISM

To avoid misunderstanding, let me say that neither democracy nor market capitalism should be understood as "pure" systems. By market capitalism I mean an economic order in which goods and services are predominantly produced and allocated by more or less competitive firms that are predominantly "privately" owned and strongly influenced by market prices and by the goal of profitability. This loose definition is meant to fit the economic order of most advanced industrial and postindustrial countries in this century.[1]

By a democratic country, I mean one that possesses all the political institutions characteristic of a modern representative government with universal or nearly universal suffrage—what I call polyarchy, or if you like polyarchal democracy. Despite its name, polyarchal democracy is not fully democratic. Just as we would surely agree that polyarchy meets democratic criteria more fully than nineteenth century representative governments based on a restricted suffrage, so we could probably agree that a political system is imaginable that would satisfy ideal democratic criteria better than polyarchal democracy.

Many resources that flow directly or indirectly from one's position in the economic order can be converted into political resources. Consequently, the initial distribution of political resources is highly, though not exclusively, dependent on the economic

order. In our time the economic order prevailing in all democratic countries is market capitalism.

Polyarchal democracy and market-oriented capitalism are closely intertwined. Polyarchal democracy exists only in countries that also possess a market-oriented capitalist economy. If the two systems, political and economic, are in that sense obviously compatible, in another sense they are profoundly incompatible.[2] They exist in a kind of antagonistic symbiosis. Their incompatibilities are revealed at two levels, one the level of theoretical interpretation and justification, the other at the empirical level of historical experience.

I. THEORETICAL INCOMPATIBILITIES[3]

The theoretical vision of democracy focusses on persons as citizens. The standard theoretical interpretation of market capitalism focusses on persons as consumers of goods and services.[4] The citizen exists within a definitely and often narrowly bounded political system—a city-state or in modern times the national-state or country. The state is, or at least once was thought to be, a hard-edged system: Your specific liberties, equalities, and obligations depend on your being inside or outside the system. Producers and consumers exist in an almost unbounded economic system that may in principle cover the globe. The citizen is expected to feel and generally does feel attached to others living within a particular state, to a historically specific, unique aggregation of human beings. The producer/consumer is—in the theoretical imagination, if not in actuality—a supremely rational computer, forever calculating and comparing precise increments of gain and loss at the margin and acting always to maximize net utilities. Loyalty may be an aspect of human beings everywhere but in the standard theoretical perspective of market capitalism it is not characteristic of rational economic actors.

In the democratic vision, opportunities to exercise power over the government of the state ought to be distributed equally among all citizens. In the standard economic interpretation of capitalism, relations of power and authority do not exist.

Their place is entirely taken by exchanges and contracts freely entered into by rational actors. An equality of economic resources, which might help to facilitate political equality, is not necessarily a desirable goal, much less a likely outcome of market decisions.

In the democratic vision, political equality must be maintained by a definite set of legal and constitutional arrangements. In the theoretical vision of economics, a state somehow lays down and enforces rules governing contracts, property, and competition that are necessary to the functioning of markets. But why and whether political leaders will undertake the tasks assigned to them, and whether and how much they will or should alter the distribution of wealth and income resulting from market forces, are questions that, strictly speaking, the standard economic theory is not expected to answer, or can.

In the democratic vision, the freedom achieved by a democratic order is above all the freedom of self-determination in making collective decisions: that is, the self-determination of citizens entitled to participate as political equals in making the laws and rules under which they will live together as citizens. A democratic society would therefore manage to allocate its resources so as to insure political equality and the rights and liberties necessary to the democratic process.

In the standard economic view of a market economy, the freedom achieved by a privately owned, competitive economic order is the primary freedom in the market place—of consumers to choose among goods and services, businessmen to compete in offering commodities and services and acquiring the necessary resources to produce them, or workers to contract with employers in exchange for wages.

Thus are the seeds of discord between democracy and market capitalism scattered by the winds of doctrine. If income and wealth are political resources, and if they are distributed unequally, then how can citizens be political equals? Conversely, if citizens are to be political equals, then will not democracy require something other than a market capitalist economic order—or at the very least a pretty drastic modification of capitalism?

2. INCOMPATIBILITIES IN PRACTICE

If the differing theoretical visions of market capitalism and political equality reveal incompatibilities, so too does historical experience. In practice, market capitalism makes political equality all but impossible to achieve. At the same time, however, polyarchal democracy makes a strictly free-market economy all but impossible to achieve. As a consequence of its link with market-oriented capitalism, polyarchal democracy is less democratic than the democratic vision would prescribe; but as a consequence of its link with polyarchal democracy, modern capitalism is less market-oriented than the theoretical vision would prescribe. The causal arrow runs both ways.

The consequences of market capitalism for democracy might be summarized in a broad generalization: In the twentieth century, the existence of a market-oriented capitalist economy in a country has been favorable to democratization up to the level of polyarchy; but it is unfavorable to democratization beyond the level of polyarchy. Many systemic features of an advanced market economy and society support the development and maintenance of democratic beliefs and practices. These include a stable legal system, considerable decentralization of economic decisions, wide use of information, persuasion, inducements and rewards rather than open coercion to influence the behavior of economic actors, the creation of a middle class, access to fairly reliable information, and so on. In addition, by stimulating economic growth, market capitalism has produced a high level of average personal income in many democratic countries, and as Adam Przeworski (1996) and others have shown high levels of income (GDP per capita) are strongly associated with the stability of democratic systems.

At the same time, however, market-oriented capitalism generates initial inequalities in access to potential political resources, including money, wealth, social standing, status, information, coercive capacities, organizations, means of communication, "connections," and others. Initial inequalities like these are inherent in an economic order based on markets.

Within some limits that are not at all well understood and are subject to intense political controversy, the initial inequalities generated by markets can be modified by government intervention. Economics matters, but politics also matters. And it is a fact that in every democratic country the distribution that would otherwise result from the market is modified to some extent by government intervention.[5] However, the extent of the alteration varies greatly among democratic countries. They differ greatly, for example, in levels of taxation, transfers, and the percentage of GDP going to the government. Here again, politics matters. The extent and direction of the alteration appear to depend, for example, on the relative strength of social democratic parties in government[6] and on public attitudes toward the role of government, which vary significantly among democratic countries.

Public attitudes[7] and the absence of a strong social democratic party and tradition may help to explain why disposable income is distributed more unequally in the United States than in all other economically advanced democratic countries; why, despite widespread resentment of "high" taxes, citizens are least taxed in the United States; why the American government transfers less income to the bottom fifth of its people than almost all the other advanced democratic countries; and in part, perhaps, why inequality in the distribution of both incomes and wealth has been on the increase in this country.[8]

THE PROSPECTS FOR POLITICAL EQUALITY IN COUNTRIES WITH MARKET ECONOMIES

Let me now put all the other factors bearing on political inequality to one side in order to pose an old problem that remains of cardinal importance. How, if at all, can we reduce the obstacles to greater political equality, and thus to the further democratization of polyarchy, that are presented by market-oriented capitalism?

I can pose the question but I cannot hope to answer it here. I can, however, sketch some limits and possibilities in very broad strokes.

One possibility that trails a long lineage behind it is to replace market-oriented capitalism with an economic order that would be more favorable, because of its inherent effects on the distribution of wealth, income, and power, to political equality and democracy. This was the essence of the Jeffersonian ideal of an agrarian democratic republic based on an economy and society of free farmers. Yet that alternative is surely irrelevant to our present condition.

For well over a century, many socialists believed that a nonmarket economy based on some form of collective ownership would provide a solution. The alternative structures that socialists had in mind, however, were often vague at best and, if more fully specified, we were highly contested not only by nonsocialists but by other socialists as well. The system that was often proposed was a centrally directed nonmarket economy based on state owned enterprises. The defects of that solution have become so evident, however, that in all democratic countries today its supporters are scarce on the ground. What is more, its advocates are not all that common, it seems, even in an officially socialist country like China.

No feasible and attractive alternative to a predominantly market economy, whether capitalist or socialist, seems to loom on the horizon. If we take some kind of market economy as pretty much given, what can we say about the prospects for a socialist or collectively owned market economy? In all democratic countries today the advocates of a socialist market economy, in whatever form they conceive it, are a tiny minority of persons who have no significant influence on public policy, or for that matter even on public discussion. If not a dead issue, a socialist market economy can hardly be said to have much visible life.

It is possible, of course, that in the coming century a solution that would unite a market economy with some form of ownership and control more conducive to political equality will be advanced, and will attract sufficient support to bring it about. Although some of us might hope for such a development, it is not, at present, even a speck on the distant horizon.

Finally, we dare not assume that a market economy, no matter what general form it takes, would *by itself* eliminate inequalities in economic resources and thereby eliminate political inequalities deriving primarily from such resources. For any market economy would surely produce significant differences in workers' incomes and wealth arising in different firms and regions; just as in a market-capitalist economic order so in a socialist market economy, or any other market economy, these could be converted into inequalities in political resources.

If that is so, the only feasible alternative, economically and politically, is to make it impossible, or at least far more difficult, for citizens to convert unequal economic resources and positions into unequal political resources. That would require sweeping government policies and actions far more extensive than now exist or are now on the political agenda in any democratic country.

Among the most unlikely candidates for such extensive reforms is the United States. Here, widespread beliefs about capitalism have always collided with widespread beliefs about democracy. The antagonistic symbiosis between market capitalism and polyarchy will surely remain in this country as elsewhere. The American system of market capitalism will continue to be regulated in some significant respects and some not altogether trivial redistributions will take place. As for the American polyarchal democracy, the substantial political inequalities that originate in economic inequalities will without doubt also persist.

If we assume that a predominantly market economy is more desirable than any feasible alternative, then we are obliged to confront a number of hard questions, or perhaps different versions of the same question:

- Can polyarchy be made more democratic? If so, how?

- How *could* we reduce the political inequalities in existing polyarchies that result directly and indirectly from the unequal distribution of resources inevitably created by market economies?

- Even if we could do so, *should we*? Taking various consequences and trade-offs into account can we find solutions that are both feasible and desirable?

- If polyarchy is destined to co-exist with a market economy, how can we best attain both the efficiencies of markets and democratic goals?

- Will the political institutions of polyarchy, which have served democratic ends fairly well in the century now passing, serve equally well in the coming century? Could we not reasonably hope to do much better? Under twenty-first century conditions would democracy be better served by some new institutions, that would complement or perhaps even replace those of polyarchy?

These are formidably difficult questions. Perhaps they deserve a better formulation. Nonetheless, they present a challenge to which political scientists in the twenty-first century will, I hope, respond.

ENDNOTES

1. Thus a more fitting label might be Charles E. Lindblom's "market-oriented private enterprise system." *Politics and Markets, The World's Political-Economic Systems* (New York: Basic Books, 1997), pp. 107ff.

2. Lindblom makes a similar point in his description of "The close but uneasy relation between private enterprise and democracy" in *ibid.*, Part V, pp. 161–233.

3. This section is adapted from the introduction to my *Democracy, Liberty, and Equality* (Oslo: Norwegian University Press, 1986), pp. 8–11.

4. For a powerful critique of the psychological inadequacies and errors of the focus on human beings as consumers in economic theory, see Robert E. Lane, *The Market Experience* (Cambridge: Cambridge University Press, 1991).

5. See "Why All Democratic Countries Have Mixed Economies," in John W. Chapman and Ian Shapiro, eds., *NOMOS XXXV, Democratic Community* (New York: New York University Press, 1993), pp. 259–82.

6. See David Cameron, "Politics, Public Policy, and Distributive Inequality: A Comparative Analysis," in Ian Shapiro and Grant Reeher, *Power, Inequality, and Democratic Politics* (Boulder: Westview Press, 1988), Ch. 12, pp. 219–259.

7. See Jennifer Hochschild, *What's Fair? American Beliefs About Distributive Justice* (Cambridge: Harvard University Press, 1981).

8. See Anthony B. Atkinson, Lee Rainwater, and Timothy M. Smeeding, *Income Distribution in OECD Countries* (Paris: OECD, 1995).

REFERENCES

de Tocqueville, Alexis, 1961. *Democracy in America.* New York: Schocker Books.

Przeworski, Adam, Michael Alvarez, José Antonio Cheibub, and Fernando Limongi.

——. "What Makes Democracies Endure?" *Journal of Democracy* (1996) 7, 40–55.

SELECT BIBLIOGRAPHY

INTRODUCTION: ON COMPARING NATIONS

HOW AND WHY TO COMPARE

Almond, Gabriel A. *A Discipline Divided: Schools and Sects in Political Science.* Newberry Park, CA: Sage, 1990.

Chilcote, Ronald H. *Theories of Comparative Politics: The Search for a Paradigm.* 2nd ed. Boulder, CO: Westview, 1994.

Dogan, Mattei, and Ali Kazancigil, eds. *Comparing Nations: Concepts Strategies, Substance.* Oxford: Blackwell, 1994.

Easton, David. *A Framework for Political Analysis.* Englewood Cliffs, NJ: Prentice-Hall, 1965.

Friedman, Jeffrey, ed. *The Rational Choice Controversy.* New Haven, CT: Yale University Press, 1996.

Green, Donald P., and Ian Shapiro. *Pathologies of Rational Choice Theory.* New Haven: Yale University Press, 1994.

Holmes, Jennifer S., ed. *New Approaches to Comparative Politics: Insights from Political Theory.* Lanham, MD: Lexington Books, 2003.

King, Gary, Robert O. Keohane, and Sidney Verba. *Designing Social Inquiry: Scientific Inquiry in Qualitative Research.* Princeton, NJ: Princeton University Press, 1994.

Kohli, Atul et al. Symposium on "The Role of Theory in Comparative Politics," *World Politics,* vol. 48, no. 1 (October 1995), pp. 1–49.

Kopstein, Jeffrey, and M. Lichbach, eds. *Comparative Politics: Interests, Identities and Institutions in a Changing Global Order.* New York: Cambridge University Press, 2000.

Lichbach, Mark I. *Is Rational Choice Theory All of Social Science?* Ann Arbor: University of Michigan Press, 2003.

—————, **and Alan S. Zuckerman, eds.** *Comparative Politics: Rationality, Culture and Structure.* New York: Cambridge University Press, 1997.

Macridis, Roy C. *The Study of Comparative Government.* New York: Random House, 1955.

Mahoney, James, and D. Rueschemeyer, eds., *Comparative Historical Analysis in the Social Sciences.* New York: Cambridge University Press, 2003.

Mayer, Lawrence. *Redefining Comparative Politics: Promise versus Performance.* Beverly Hills, CA: Sage, 1989.

Rustow, Dankwart, and Kenneth F. Erickson, eds. *Comparative Political Dynamics.* New York: Harper Collins, 1990.

Sartori, Giovanni. *Social Science Concepts.* Newberry Park, CA: Sage, 1985.

Skocpol, Theda, and Margaret Somers. "The Uses of Comparative History in Macrosocial Inquiry," *Comparative Studies in Society and History,* vol. 22 (1980), pp. 174–197.

Stepan, Alfred. *Arguing Comparative Politics.* New York: Oxford University Press, 2001.

Weber, Max. "Politics as a Vocation" and "Science as a Vocation," in *From Max Weber,* eds. H. H. Gerth and C. W. Mills. New York: Oxford University Press, 1958, pp. 77–156.

Wiarda, Howard J. *Introduction to Comparative Politics: Concepts and Processes.* Belmont, CA: Wadsworth, 1993.

————, **ed.** *New Directions in Comparative Politics.* 2nd ed. Boulder, CO: Westview, 1990.

————. "Is Comparative Politics Dead? Rethinking the Field in the Post-Cold War Era." *Third World Quarterly,* vol. 19, no. 5 (1998), pp. 935–949.

PART ONE POLITICAL CHANGE AND THE STATE

MODERNIZATION/GLOBALIZATION

Almond, Gabriel A., and James S. Coleman, eds. *The Politics of Developing Areas.* Princeton, NJ: Princeton University Press, 1960.

Apter, David E. *Rethinking Development: Modernization, Dependency and Postmodern Politics.* Newbury Park, CA: Sage, 1987.

Bell, Daniel. *The Coming of Post-Industrial Society.* New York: Basic Books, 1973.

Binder, Leonard et al. *Crises and Sequences in Political Development.* Princeton, NJ: Princeton University Press, 1971.

Black, Cyril E. *The Dynamics of Modernization: A Study in Comparative History.* New York: Harper & Row, 1966.

————, **ed.** *Comparative Modernization: A Reader.* New York: Free Press, 1976.

Greenfeld, Liah. *The Spirit of Capitalism: Nationalism and Economic Growth.* Cambridge, MA: Harvard University Press, 2001.

Grew, Raymond, ed. *Crises of Political Development in Europe and the United States.* Princeton, NJ: Princeton University Press, 1978.

Hardt, Michael, and Antonio Negri. *Empire.* Cambridge, MA: Harvard University Press, 2000.

Huntington, Samuel P. *Political Order in Changing Societies.* New Haven, CT: Yale University Press, 1972.

Inglehart, Ronald. *Culture Shift in Advanced Industrial Societies.* Princeton, NJ: Princeton University Press, 1990.

————. *Modernization and Postmodernization: Cultural, Economic, and Political Change in 43 Societies.* Princeton, NJ: Princeton University Press, 1997.

————. *Human Values and Social Change: Findings from the Values Surveys.* Leiden and Boston: Brill, 2003.

————, **and Pippa Norris.** *Rising Tide: Gender Equality and Cultural Change.* New York: Cambridge University Press, 2003.

Landes, David S. *The Wealth and Poverty of Nations.* New York: Norton, 1998.

Lipset, Seymour Martin. *The First New Nation: The United States in Historical and Comparative Perspective.* New York: Basic Books, 1963.

Olson, Mancur. *Rise and Decline of Nations: Economic Growth, Stagflation, and Social Rigidities.* New Haven, CT: Yale University Press, 1982.

Rustow, Dankwart A. *A World of Nations: Problems of Political Modernization.* Washington, DC: The Brookings Institution, 1967.

Wallerstein, Immanuel. *World Systems Analysis: An Introduction.* Durham: Duke University Press, 2004.

Weber, Eugen. *Peasants into Frenchmen: The Modernization of Rural France.* Stanford: Stanford University Press, 1976.

Weiner, Myron, and Samuel P. Huntington, eds. *Understanding Political Development: An Analytic Study.* Boston: Little, Brown, 1987.

STATE AND IDENTITY

Anderson, Benedict. *Imagined Communities: Reflections on the Origin and Spread of Nationalism.* London: Verso, 1983.

Bendix, Reinhard. *Nation-Building and Citizenship.* New York: Wiley, 1964.

Breuilly, John. *Nationalism and the State.* 2nd ed. Chicago: University of Chicago Press, 1994.

Connor, Walker. *Ethnonationalism.* Princeton, NJ: Princeton University Press, 1994.

Esman, Milton I. *Ethnic Politics.* Ithaca, NY: Cornell University Press, 1994.

Eisenstadt, S. N., and Stein Rokkan. *Building States and Nations.* Beverly Hills, CA: Sage, 1977.

Evans, Peter, and Theda Skocpol, eds. *Bringing the State Back In.* New York: Cambridge University Press, 1985.

Gellner, Ernest. *Nations and Nationalism.* Ithaca, NY: Cornell University Press, 1983.

Greenfeld, Liah. *Nationalism: Five Roads to Modernity.* Cambridge, MA: Cambridge University Press, 1992.

Gurr, Ted Robert. *Peoples versus States: Minorities at Risk in the New Century.* Washington, DC: United States Institute of Peace, 2000.

Horowitz, Donald L. *Ethnic Groups in Conflict.* Berkeley, CA: University of California Press, 1985.

——————. *The Deadly Ethnic Riot.* Berkeley, CA: University of California Press, 2001.

Huntington, Samuel P. *The Clash of Civilizations and the Remaking of World Order.* New York: Simon & Schuster, 1996.

Migdal, Joel. *Strong Societies and Weak States: State-Society Relations and State Capabilities in the Third World.* Princeton, NJ: Princeton, University Press, 1988.

——————, **A. Kohli, and V. Sue, eds.** *State Power and Social Forces: Domination and Transformation in the Third World.* New York: Cambridge University Press, 1994.

Moynihan, Daniel P. *Pandaemonium: Ethnicity in International Politics.* New York: Oxford University Press, 1993.

Smith, Anthony D. *The Ethnic Origins of Nations.* New York: Blackwell, 1987.

Tilly, Charles, ed. *The Formation of National States in Europe.* Princeton, NJ: Princeton University Press, 1975.

GOVERNING GLOBALIZATION

Cooper, Robert. *The Breaking of Nations: Order and Chaos in the Twenty-First Century.* New York: Atlantic Monthly Press, 2003.

Cowles, Maria G., and D. Dinan. *Developments in the European Union.* New York: Palgrave Macmillan, 2004.

Greven, Michael, and L. W. Pauly, eds. *Democracy Beyond the State? The European Dilemma and the Emerging World Order.* New York: Rowman and Littlefield, 2000.

Kagan, Robert. *Of Paradise and Power: America and Europe in the New World Order.* New York: Alfred A. Knopf, 2003.

Kahler, Miles, and D. A. Lake, eds. *Governance in a Global Economy: Political Authority in Transition.* Princeton, NJ: Princeton University Press, 2003.

Krasner, Stephen. *Sovereignty: Organized Hypocrisy.* Princeton, NJ: Princeton University Press, 1999.

Lentner, Howard H. *Power and Politics in Globalization: The Indispensable State.* New York: Routledge, 2004.

Risse, Thomas, S. C. Ropp, and K. Sikkink, eds. *The Power of Human Rights.* New York: Cambridge University Press, 1999.

Rosenau, James N. *Distant Proximities: Dynamics Beyond Globalization.* Princeton, NJ: Princeton University Press, 2003.

Ruggie, John G. *Constructing the World Polity.* New York: Routledge, 1998.

REVOLUTION AND PROTEST

Ackerman, Peter, J. Duvall, et al. Symposium on "Nonviolent Power in the Twentieth Century." *PS: Political Science and Politics,* vol. 33, no. 2 (June 2000), pp. 147–187.

Apter, David. *Against the State: Politics and Social Protest in Japan.* Cambridge, MA: Harvard University Press, 1984.

Arendt, Hannah. *On Revolution.* New York: Viking Press, 1963.

Brinton, Crane. *The Anatomy of Revolution.* Rev. ed. Englewood Cliffs, NJ: Prentice-Hall, 1952.

Dunn, John. *Modern Revolutions* 2nd ed. New York: Cambridge University Press, 1989.

Goldstone, Jack. *Revolution and Rebellion in the Early Modern World.* Berkeley: University of California Press, 1991.

————, **ed.** *Revolutions of the Late Twentieth Century.* Boulder, CO: Westview Press, 1991.

————, **ed.** *Revolutions: Theoretical, Comparative, and Historical Studies.* 2nd ed. Fort Worth: Harcourt Brace College Publishers, 1994.

Goodwin, Jeff. *No Other Way Out: States and Revolutionary Movements.* New York: Cambridge University Press, 2001.

Gurr, Ted Robert. *Why Men Rebel.* Princeton, NJ: Princeton University Press, 1970.

Johnson, Chalmers. *Revolutionary Change.* 2nd ed. Stanford, CA: Stanford University Press, 1982.

Lipset, Seymour Martin. *Revolution and Counter-Revolution: Change and Persistence in Social Structures.* Rev. ed. New Brunswick, NJ: Transaction, 1988.

Moore, Barrington, Jr. *Social Origins of Dictatorship and Democracy: Lord and Peasant in the Making of the Modern World.* Boston: Beacon Press, 1966.

Skocpol, Theda. *States and Social Revolution.* New York: Cambridge University Press, 1979.

——————. *Social Revolutions in the Modern World.* New York: Cambridge University Press, 1994.

Tarrow, Sidney. *Power in Movement: Social Movements, Collective Action and Politics.* 2ⁿᵈ ed. New York: Cambridge University Press, 1998.

De Tocqueville, Alexis. *The Old Regime and the French Revolution.* Garden City, NY: Anchor, 1955.

PART TWO   PARTTERNS OF LEGITIMACY

....

DEMOCRACIES

Aron, Raymond. *Democracy and Totalitarianism.* New York: Praeger, 1968.

Benjamin, Roger, and Stephen L. Elkin, eds. *The Democratic State.* Lawrence, KA: University Press of Kansas, 1985.

Bobbio, Norberto. *The Future of Democracy: A Defense of the Rules of the Game.* Minneapolis, MN: University of Minnesota Press, 1987.

Crozier, Michel, S. P. Huntington, and J. Watanuki. *The Crisis of Democracy.* New York: New York University Press, 1975.

Dahl, Robert A. *Polyarchy: Participation and Opposition.* New Haven, CT: Yale University Press, 1971.

——————. *Dilemmas of Pluralist Democracy.* New Haven, CT: Yale University Press, 1982.

——————, *Democracy and Its Critics.* New Haven, CT: Yale University Press, 1989.

Dogan, Mattei. *Comparing Pluralist Democracies: Strains on Legitimacy.* Boulder, CO: Westview Press, 1988.

Guttman, Amy, and D. Thompson. *Why Deliberative Democracy?* Princeton, NJ: Princeton University Press, 2004.

Lijphart, Arend. *Democracies: Patterns of Majoritarian and Consensus Government in Twenty-One Countries.* New Haven, CT: Yale University Press, 1984.

MacIver, Robert M. *The Web of Government.* New York: Macmillan, 1947.

Mansbridge, Jane. *Beyond Adversary Democracy.* Chicago: University of Chicago Press, 1983.

Norris, Pippa. *Democratic Phoenix: Reinventing Political Activism.* New York: Cambridge University Press, 2002.

Popper, Karl R. *The Open Society and Its Enemies.* 2 vols. 5ᵗʰ ed. London: Routledge & Kegan Paul, 1945.

Putnam, Robert. *Making Democracy Work: Civil Traditions in Modern Italy.* Princeton, NJ: Princeton University Press, 1993.

Sartori, Giovanni. *Theory of Democracy Revisited.* 2 vols. Chatham, NJ: Chatham House, 1987.

Schumpeter, Joseph A. *Capitalism, Socialism, and Democracy.* 3ʳᵈ ed. New York: Harper & Row, 1950.

Shapiro, Ian. *The State of Democratic Theory.* Princeton, NJ: Princeton University Press, 2003.

Whitehead, Laurence. *Democratization: Theory and Experience.* Oxford: Oxford University Press, 2002.

....

TRANSITION TO DEMOCRACY

Diamond, Larry et al. *Democracy in Developing Countries.* Boulder, CO: Lynne Rienner, 1988.

Di Palma, Giusseppe. *To Craft Democracies: An Essay on Democratic Transitions.* Berkeley, CA: University of California Press, 1990.

Huntington, Samuel P. *The Third Wave: Democratization in the Late Twentieth Century.* Norman, OK: Oklahoma University Press, 1991.

Linz, Juan, and Alfred Stepan, eds. *The Breakdown of Democratic Regimes.* 2 vols. Baltimore: The Johns Hopkins University Press, 1978.

Mainwaring, Scott, G. O'Donnell, and J. S. Venezuela, eds. *Issues in Democratic Consolidation: the New South American Democracies in Comparative Perspective.* Notre Dame, IN: University of Notre Dame Press, 1992.

O'Donnell, Guillermo, P. Schmitter, and L. Whitehead, eds. *Transition from Authoritarian Rule.* 4 vols. Baltimore: The Johns Hopkins University Press, 1986.

AUTHORITARIANISM: OLD AND NEW

Arendt, Hannah. *The Origins of Totalitarianism.* 2nd ed. New York: Harcourt Brace Jovanovich, 1973.

Bermeo, Nancy. *Ordinary People in Extraordinary Times: The Citizenry and the Breakdown of Democracy.* Princeton, NJ: Princeton University Press, 2003.

Bracher, Karl D. *The German Dictatorship: the Origin, Structure and Effects of National Socialism.* New York: Praeger, 1970.

Bunce, Valerie. *Subversive Institutions: The Design and Destruction of Socialism and the State.* New York: Cambridge University Press, 1999.

Colton, Timothy, and Robert Legvold, eds. *After the Soviet Union.* New York: Norton, 1992.

Crawford, Beverly, and Arend Lijphart, eds. *Liberalization and Leninist Legacies.* Berkeley, CA: International and Area Studies, 1997.

Daniels, Robert V. *The End of the Communist Revolution.* New York: Routledge, 1993.

Laqueur, Walter. *The Dream That Failed. Reflections on the Soviet Union.* New York: Oxford University Press, 1994.

McFaul, Michael. *Russia's Unfinished Revolution: Political Change from Gorbachev to Putin.* Ithaca, NY: Cornell University Press, 2001.

————, and K. Stoner-Weiss, eds. *Ten Years Since the Collapse of the Soviet Union: Comparative Lessons and Perspectives.* New York: Cambridge University Press, 2004.

Nathan, Andrew J. *China's Transition.* New York: Columbia University Press, 1997.

————, ed. *The Tiananmen Papers.* New York: Public Affairs, 2001.

Neumann, Franz. *The Democratic and the Authoritarian State.* New York: Free Press, 1957.

Ottaway, Marina S. *Democracy Challenged: the Rise of Semi-Authoritarianism.* Washington, DC: Carnegie Endowment for International Peace, 2003.

White, Stephen. "Rethinking Postcommunist Transition," *Government and Opposition,* vol. 38, no. 4 (Autumn 2003), pp. 417–435.

THE CHALLENGE OF ISLAMISM

Almond, Gabriel, R. S. Appleby, and E. Sivan. *Strong Religion: The Rise of Fundamentalisms Around the World.* Chicago: University of Chicago Press, 2003.

Berman, Sheri. "Islamism, Revolution, and Civil Society." *Perspectives on Politics,* vol. 1, no. 2 (June 2003), pp. 257–272.

Butterworth, Charles, and I. William Zartman, eds. *Between the State and Islam.* New York: Cambridge University Press, 2001.

Huntington, Samuel P. *The Clash of Civilizations and the Remaking of World Order.* New York: Simon & Schuster, 1996.

Kepel, Gilles. *Revenge of God: the Resurgence of Islam, Christianity and Judaism in the Modern World.* University Park, PA: Pennsylvania State University Press, 1994.

————. *Jihad: The Trail of Islam.* Cambridge, MA: Harvard University Press, 2002.

————. *The War for Muslim Minds: Islam and the West.* Cambridge, MA: Harvard University Press, 2004.

Lewis, Bernard. *Islam and the West.* New York: Oxford University Press, 1993.

————. *What Went Wrong? Western Impact and Middle Eastern Response.* New York: Oxford University Press, 2002.

————. *The Crisis of Islam: Holy War and Unholy Terror.* New York: Modern Library, 2003.

Roy, Olivier. *The Failure of Political Islam.* Cambridge, MA: Harvard University Press, 1994.

————. *Globalised Islam: the Search for a New Ummah.* London: Hurst, 2004.

PART THREE POLITICAL DYNAMICS, DECISIONS, AND EFFICACY

POLITICAL PARTIES

Dalton, Russell J., and M. Wattenberg, eds. *Parties Without Partisans: Political Change in Advanced Industrial Democracies.* Oxford: Oxford University Press, 2000.

Diamond, Larry, and Richard Gunther, eds. *Political Parties and Democracy.* Baltimore: John Hopkins University Press, 2001.

Duverger, Maurice. *Political Parties.* 3rd ed. London: Methuen, 1969.

Epstein, Leon. *Political Parties in Western Democracies.* New Brunswick, NJ: Transaction Books, 1980.

Gunther, Richard, J. R. Montero, and Juan J. Linz, eds. *Political Parties: Old Concepts and New Challenges.* Oxford: Oxford University Press, 2002.

Hirschman, Albert O. *Exit, Voice, and Loyalty.* Cambridge, MA: Harvard University Press, 1970.

Katz, Richard S., and Peter Mair, eds. *How Parties Organize: Change and Adaptation in Party Organization in Western Democracies.* London: Sage, 1994.

LaPalombara, Joseph, and Myron Weiner, eds. *Political Parties and Political Development.* Princeton, NJ: Princeton University Press, 1996.

Lawson, Kay, and Peter Merkl, eds. *When Parties Fail.* Princeton, NJ: Princeton University Press, 1988.

Lipset, Seymour Martin. *Political Man: The Social Bases of Politics.* Rev. ed. Baltimore: The Johns Hopkins University Press, 1981.

Panebianco, Angelo. *Political Parties: Organization and Power.* New York: Cambridge University Press, 1988.

Sartori, Giovanni. *Parties and Party Systems.* New York: Cambridge University Press, 1976.

Von Beyme, Klaus. *Political Parties in Western Democracies.* Aldershot: Gower, 1985.

Ware, Alan. *Political Parties and Party Systems.* Oxford: Oxford University Press, 1996.

Webb, Paul et al. *Political Parties in Advanced Industrial Societies.* Oxford: Oxford University Press, 2003.

DO INSTITUTIONS MATTER?

Aberbach, Joel D., R. E. Putnam, and B. A. Rockman. *Bureaucrats and Politicians in Western Democracies.* Cambridge, MA: Harvard University Press, 1981.

Crozier, Michel. *The Bureaucratic Phenomenon.* Chicago: University of Chicago Press, 1964.

LaPalombara, Joseph, ed. *Bureaucracy and Political Development.* Princeton, NJ: Princeton University Press, 1963.

Lijphart, Arend, ed. *Parliamentary versus Presidential Government.* New York: Oxford University Press, 1992.

North, Douglass C. *Institutions, Institutional Change, and Economic Performance.* New York: Cambridge University Press, 1990.

Norton, Philip, ed. *Legislatures.* Oxford: Oxford University Press, 1990.

Peters, B. Guy. *Institutional Theory in Political Science.* London: Printer, 1999.

Reynolds, Andrew, ed. *The Architecture of Democracy: Constitutional Design, Conflict Management, and Democracy.* Oxford: Oxford University Press, 2002. Note especially essays by Lijphart and Horowitz.

Rose, Richard, and Ezra Suleiman, eds. *Presidents and Prime Ministers.* Washington, DC: American Enterprise Institute, 1980.

Shapiro, Ian, and S. Macedo, eds. *NOMOS XLII: Designing Democratic Institutions.* New York: New York University Press, 2000.

Suleiman, Ezra, ed. *Bureaucrats and Policy Making.* New York: Holmes and Meier, 1984.

————, **ed.** *Parliaments and Parliamentarians in Democratic Politics.* New York: Holmes and Meier, 1986.

Weaver, R. Kent, and Bert A. Rockman. *Do Institutions Matter? Government Capabilities in the United States and Abroad.* Washington, DC: The Brookings Institution, 1993.

POLITICAL PERFORMANCE

APSA Task Force Report. "American Democracy in an Age of Rising Inequality," and Special Issue on Equality and Inequality. *Perspectives on Politics,* vol. 2, no. 4 (December 2004), pp. 651–689.

Berman, Sheri. *The Social Democratic Moment: Ideas and Politics in the Making of Interwar Europe.* Cambridge, MA: Harvard University Press, 1998.

Hall, Peter A. *Governing the Economy: the Politics of State Intervention in Britain and France.* New York: Oxford University Press, 1986.

————, **ed.** *The Political Power of Economic Ideas: Keynesianism Across Nations.* Princeton, NJ: Princeton University Press, 1989.

————, **and D. Soskice, eds.** *Varieties of Capitalism: The Institutional Foundations of Comparative Advantage.* Oxford: Oxford University Press, 2001.

Heidenheimer, Arnold J., Hugh Heclo, and Carolyn Teich Adams. *Comparative Public Policy: The Politics of Social Choice in Europe and America.* 3rd ed. New York: St. Martin's Press 1990.

Jackman, Robert W. *Politics and Social Equality: A Comparative Analysis.* New York: Wiley, 1975.

Katzenstein, Peter. *Small States in World Markets: Industrial Policy in Europe.* Ithaca, NY: Cornell University Press, 1985.

Lijphart, Arend. *Patterns of Democracy: Government Forms and Performance in Thirty-Six Countries.* New Haven, CT: Yale University Press, 1999.

Lindlblom, Charles. *Politics and Markets.* New York: Basic Books, 1977.

Pierre, Jon, ed. *Debating Governance.* Oxford: Oxford University Press, 2000.

————, **and B. Guy Peters.** *Governance, Politics and the State.* New York: St. Martin's Press, 2000.

Schmidt, Vivien A. *The Futures of European Capitalism.* New York: Oxford University Press, 2002.

Suleiman, Ezra. *Dismantling Democratic States.* Princeton, NJ: Princeton University Press, 2003.

Wilensky, Harold, *Rich Democracies: Political Economy, Public Policy, and Performance.* Berkeley: University of California Press, 2002.